MIS

Eleventh Edition

Management Information Systems

Hossein Bidgoli, Ph.D.
California State University–Bakersfield

Australia • Brazil • Canada • Mexico • Singapore • United Kingdom • United States

MIS, **Eleventh Edition**
Hossein Bidgoli

SVP, Product: Erin Joyner

VP, Product: Thais Alencar

Product Director: Mark Santee

Product Manager: Natalie Onderdonk

Product Assistant: Ethan Wheel

Learning Designer: Carolyn Mako

Content Manager: Michele Stulga and Marlena Sullivan

Digital Delivery Quality Partner: Jim Vaughey

Developmental Editor: Dan Seiter

VP, Product Marketing: Jason Sakos

Director, Product Marketing: Danaë April

Product Marketing Manager: Mackenzie Paine

IP Analyst: Ann Hoffman

IP Project Manager: Lumina Datamatics

Production Service: Straive

Designer: Erin Griffin

Cover Image Source: gremlin/E+/Getty Images

For product information and technology assistance, contact us at
Cengage Customer & Sales Support, 1-800-354-9706
or support.cengage.com.

For permission to use material from this text or product, submit all requests online at **www.copyright.com**.

Library of Congress Control Number: 2022913850

SE ISBN: 978-0-357-88386-0

LLF ISBN: 978-0-357-95151-4

Cengage
5191 Natorp Boulevard
Mason, OH 45040
USA

Cengage is a leading provider of customized learning solutions. Our employees reside in nearly 40 different countries and serve digital learners in 165 countries around the world. Find your local representative at: **www.cengage.com**.

To learn more about Cengage platforms and services, register or access your online learning solution, or purchase materials for your course, visit **www.cengage.com**.

Notice to the Reader

Publisher does not warrant or guarantee any of the products described herein or perform any independent analysis in connection with any of the product information contained herein. Publisher does not assume, and expressly disclaims, any obligation to obtain and include information other than that provided to it by the manufacturer. The reader is expressly warned to consider and adopt all safety precautions that might be indicated by the activities described herein and to avoid all potential hazards. By following the instructions contained herein, the reader willingly assumes all risks in connection with such instructions. The publisher makes no representations or warranties of any kind, including but not limited to, the warranties of fitness for particular purpose or merchantability, nor are any such representations implied with respect to the material set forth herein, and the publisher takes no responsibility with respect to such material. The publisher shall not be liable for any special, consequential, or exemplary damages resulting, in whole or part, from the readers' use of, or reliance upon, this material.

Printed at CLDPC, USA, 02-24

BIDGOLI

MIS
11th Edition

Brief
Contents

Contents

Part 1
Fundamentals of Information Systems

iv

Module 3
Data and Business Intelligence

Module 4
Personal, Legal, Ethical, and Organizational Issues

Part 2

Data Communication, the Internet, E-Commerce, and Global Information Systems

Module 6

Data Communication: Delivering Information Anywhere and Anytime

Module 7
A Connected World

Module 8
E-Commerce

Module 9
Global Information Systems

Part 3
IS Development, Enterprise Systems, MSS, AI, and Emerging Trends

Module 10
Building Successful Information Systems

Module 11
Enterprise Systems

Module 14
Emerging Trends, Technologies, and Applications

To so many fine memories of my mother, Ashraf,
my father, Mohammad, and
my brother, Mohsen, for their uncompromising belief
in the power of education.
—Hossein Bidgoli

Preface

Through a dozen focus groups of students and faculty, the first edition of *Management Information Systems* was initiated in 2008. After several content reviews, the first edition was published in 2010. With the assistance of the original team under the leadership of Charles McCormick, Jr., a former Senior Acquisition Editor at Cengage, I was able to put together a solid foundation for the textbook that has been evolving ever since.

From the beginning, our textbook had three core emphases in mind: currency, a practical approach, and student engagement. I am grateful for the feedback from students and faculty of more than 1,000 colleges and universities throughout the world that have adopted this textbook and made it so successful.

We are very pleased to present the eleventh edition, which has kept its original core emphases. It has also kept its currency as we continually review leading IS/IT publications as well as the ongoing development of computer and IT companies' current practices and products. As a result, we integrate cutting-edge topics and technology into each new edition.

The book has kept its practical approach as we carefully analyze and review the latest IT/IS applications in businesses and public organizations that have made them competitive, reduced the cost of operations, and improved customer service. This approach has improved student engagement by covering topics that have direct impacts on their personal and professional lives. After reading the textbook, students literally see MIS applications all around them, from schools to grocery stores to their workplaces. We have also introduced projects and assignments that enable students to understand, analyze, create, and evaluate the material and then apply what they learn in the course in their future employment opportunities.

The Approach

Writing a textbook for the first course in Information Systems is a challenging task. Students come to the course with different backgrounds, and some come with little or no background. Writing a textbook in a pure theory format would be uninteresting, and writing it in a purely technical manner could discourage certain students. We have created a textbook with a balanced approach to appeal to both groups and with student engagement in mind.

Management Information Systems, Eleventh Edition, is divided into three parts: Part 1—Fundamentals of Information Systems (Modules 1 through 5), Part 2—Data Communication, the Internet, E-Commerce, and Global Information Systems (Modules 6 through 9), and Part 3—IS Development, Enterprise Systems, MSS, AI, and Emerging Trends (Modules 10 through 14).

Module 1 uses Michael Porter's three strategies (cost leadership, differentiation, and focus) and the Five Forces model to establish a framework and examine how IS/IT-supported businesses operate and compete in the real world. This presentation brings a practical perspective to the textbook and shows students that every tool, technique, and concept they study has practical applications in the real world and prepares them for their future employment.

Each module introduces five to twelve learning objectives and contains in-depth coverage accompanied by charts, tables, exhibits, and information boxes to corroborate the achievement of the objectives. One of the book's unique features is the frequent appearance of information boxes strategically placed throughout each module. These information boxes clearly illustrate how real companies and organizations are using the technologies and applications covered. This presentation connects theory to practice and helps students better understand the material.

Each module ends with several features: an Industry Connection box, a Module Summary, Key Terms, eight Reviews and Discussions questions, six Projects, a Module Quiz consisting of six true/false and multiple-choice questions, and two case studies. These features collectively provide assessment tools and help students to understand the book's material from different angles.

Prerequisites

Familiarity with basic productivity software such as Microsoft Excel and Access is useful. Prior programming experience is not required. Instructors have a lot of options for the hands-on portions of this course. The MindTap platform offers several choices and options for hands-on coverage. Also, the textbook could be bundled with several offerings from the publisher.

Intended Audience

The textbook is written in a comprehensive manner that allows instructors to adopt the materials within a wide range of academic levels. The content, currency, and practical coverage of this textbook are in high demand and are applicable in programs for two-year degrees, four-year degrees, graduate degrees, executive courses, and adult continuing education. The textbook is written in an easily approachable style that starts with the most basic concepts and builds to advanced topics. The modular presentation makes it easy for instructors to adapt the coverage to the level of sophistication that is most appropriate for their students.

New to this Edition

As in previous editions, information on IS/IT statistics, hardware, software, and applications has been updated. When necessary, cases and information boxes have been updated. Specific changes to each module are as follows:

Module 1

- A section on strategic information systems has been added.
- The information boxes on Home Depot and Netflix have been expanded.

Module 2

- Information on NVMe (non-volatile memory express) has been added.
- The information box on Summit has been replaced by new information within the module.

Module 3

- Sections on text-mining analysis and data lakes have been added.
- Case Study 3-2 has been replaced.

Module 4

- A section on cheap fakes, misinformation, and disinformation has been added.
- A section on digital citizenship has been added.
- The Industry Connection feature has been replaced.

Module 5

- Sections on gray-hat hackers and alternatives to passwords have been added.

Module 6

- A table describing selected wireless standards has been added.
- A section on 6G mobile technology has been added.

Module 7

- A section on TikTok has been added.
- The information boxes titled "What Is HTML?" and "Social Media Applications at Walmart" have been expanded.

Module 8

- Sections on conversational commerce, Google Pay, and digital marketing have been added.
- The Home Depot information box has been expanded.

Module 9

- The section discussing the requirements of global information systems has been expanded.
- Table 9.1 has been replaced.

Module 10

- A section on low-code and no-code software has been added.
- Case Study 10-1 has been replaced.
- The information box titled "Preventing IT Project Failures Using Best Practices" has been eliminated. Its core materials have been integrated into section 10-5a, "IT Project Management."

Module 11

- The sections on quick response codes and knowledge management have been expanded.
- The Industry Connection feature has been expanded.
- Case Study 11-1 has been replaced.

- The "Knowledge Management in Action" information box has been replaced with a new information box on BMW.

Module 12

- The information box titled "Decision Support Systems at Family Dollar" has been replaced by an information box on Nestlé.
- The information box titled "GISs for Fighting Disease" has been expanded.

Module 13

- The section on robotics has been expanded and a section on ambient computing has been added.

Module 14

Sections on the following topics have been added:

- Non-fungible tokens (NFTs) and their business applications
- The metaverse and its applications
- Data as a service (DaaS), backup as a service (BaaS), and security as a service (SECaaS)
- Distributed cloud computing
- Blockchain as a service (BaaS)

Also, the sections on edge computing and cryptocurrency have been expanded.

The section on Facebook's Libra system has been eliminated.

Unique Features of the Textbook

Management Information Systems, Eleventh Edition, is the most practical MIS textbook on the market. It includes more than 100 information boxes and cases that illustrate how information systems are being used in real-life applications.

The book offers current IS statistics and current information on hardware, software, and applications.

The book's Facebook, Twitter, and LinkedIn accounts provide daily updates on IS applications, new developments, breaking news, IT jobs, and case examples.

The text discusses business examples and cases about companies and products that students can relate to—Microsoft, Google, YouTube, Facebook, Netflix, Amazon, iPads, iPhones, and many more. Students learn about cutting-edge topics, including cryptocurrencies, blockchain, mobile analytics, data lakes, text mining, 3D/4D printing, the Internet of Things (IoT), virtual reality, augmented reality, the ethics of artificial intelligence, quantum computing, NFTs, and the metaverse.

The book comes with completely redesigned Mind-Tap resources that offer a robust digital learning experience, including updated concept videos, interactive case studies, Use It activities, new Reflection and MIS for Life activities that focus on today's challenges and successes, and coding IDE labs.

The text explains and integrates key concepts, skills, and cases identified by corresponding AACSB standards to ensure that your students master critical information.

The book is designed in a modular fashion. For instructors who need additional hands-on coverage beyond MindTap, the book can be bundled with other Cengage textbooks at a moderate cost. The book is available in various affordable pricing models and is available through the Cengage Unlimited subscription model.

MindTap for MIS 11

MindTap for *Management Information Systems, Eleventh Edition*, is an online learning solution designed to help students master the skills they need to thrive in today's workforce. Research shows employers need critical thinkers, troubleshooters, and creative problem solvers to stay relevant in our fast-paced, technology-driven marketplace. MindTap helps prepare students for that marketplace with relevant assignments and activities that include hands-on practice. Students are guided through assignments that progress from basic knowledge and understanding to more challenging problems. MindTap activities and assignments are tied to validated learning objectives.

Additional Resources for Students and Instructors

Instructor and student resources for this product are available online. Instructor assets include an instructor manual, a solution and answer guide, an educator's guide, PowerPoint® slides, and a test bank powered by Cognero®. Student assets include access to the SAM app and SQL labs. Sign up or sign in at *www.cengage.com* to search for and access this product and its online resources.

For further details about instructor resources, read on.

Instructor Manual

The instructor manual that accompanies this course provides additional instructional materials to assist in class preparation, including suggestions for classroom activities and discussion topics.

Solution and Answer Guide

This guide contains answers to the book's Reviews and Discussions questions, Projects, Module Quiz questions, and case studies.

Cengage Testing Powered by Cognero

Cognero is a flexible online system that allows you to:

- Author, edit, and manage test bank content from multiple Cengage solutions.
- Create multiple test versions in an instant.
- Deliver tests from your LMS, your classroom, or wherever you want.

PowerPoint Presentations

This course comes with Microsoft® PowerPoint slides for each module. These are included as a teaching aid for classroom presentation, to make available to students on the network for module review, or to be printed for classroom distribution. Instructors, please feel at liberty to add your own slides for additional topics you introduce to the class.

SAM App

The SAM app in MindTap allows you to further your students' proficiency in Microsoft Office skills as part of your course. SAM is an interactive online learning environment designed to help students master Microsoft Office and computer concepts essential to academic and career success. Students observe, practice, and apply concepts in a simulated environment and then complete projects live in the application. All Office 365/2021 trainings, exams, and projects are available in this edition's MindTap.

SQL Labs: Essentials for the Real World

This course provides access to a self-contained SQL micro-course that will help enable students to dig deeper into database concepts and MySQL. The coding IDE and self-paced structure of this activity allows students to propel their passions and interest while keeping your class time focused on foundational concepts.

Appendices

There are four appendices online. Appendix A explores the modeling and number-crunching features of Excel, Appendix B presents the graphics and charting features of Excel, Appendix C illustrates data management capabilities of Excel, and Appendix D introduces the basics of Web design using Microsoft Expression Web 4.

About the Author

Hossein Bidgoli, Ph.D., is professor of Management Information Systems at California State University. Dr. Bidgoli helped set up the first PC lab in the United States and served as its initial director. He is the author of 54 textbooks, 27 manuals, and more than 200 technical articles and papers published and presented throughout the world on various aspects of computer applications, information systems and network security, e-commerce, and decision support systems. Dr. Bidgoli also serves as the editor-in-chief of *The Handbook of Technology Management*, *The Handbook of Computer Networks*, *The Handbook of Information Security*, *The Internet Encyclopedia*, and *The Encyclopedia of Information Systems*. *The Encyclopedia of Information Systems* was named one of the Library Journal's Best Reference Sources for 2002. *The Internet Encyclopedia* was a recipient of one of the 2004 PSP Awards (Professional and Scholarly Publishing) by the Association of American Publishers. Dr. Bidgoli was chosen as the 2001–2002 Professor of the Year and the 2015–2016 Researcher of the Year by California State University–Bakersfield.

Acknowledgments

Many professionals are involved in a project of this size. Many thanks go to my students in undergraduate, graduate, and executive seminar series who took MIS classes from me and provided feedback throughout the years. Several of our adopters shared feedback that assisted us to further improve the content through various editions. We are grateful for their assistance.

The following colleagues reviewed the textbook for the eleventh edition and provided insightful feedback. We appreciate their efforts and thank them for their assistance.

- Carlos G. Bodden, Computer Technology Instructor, Fayetteville Technical Community College
- Brent M. Ferns, Sr., Palm Beach State College
- Nicholas Pierce, Virginia Peninsula Community College

I thank my wonderful Cengage team that has provided guidance, support, and assistance throughout the years. Mark Santee, product director, had faith in this project and provided support. Natalie Onderdonk, product manager, was always available, positive, promptly responded to any queries, and provided guidance. Content managers Michele Stulga and Marlena Sullivan provided guidance and flawlessly managed the completion of the project. Dan Seiter, the developmental editor, made sure that every paragraph is as understandable as possible. His thorough review and specific queries made the textbook easy to follow.

Carolyn Mako, our superb learning designer, made sure that learning objectives are stated clearly and that the right assessment tools have been provided in each module. Our weekly Zoom meetings with the team were at times demanding but always insightful and kept the project on schedule. Ethan Wheel, product assistant, managed the communication log and kept everybody informed about the project's progress. Our great marketing manager, Mackenzie Paine, and her team introduced the textbook and its unique features to colleges and universities around the world.

Last, but not least, I want to thank my wonderful wife, Nooshin, and my two lovely children, Mohsen (Alan) and Morvareed (Moury), for being so supportive during this venture. Nooshin did not mind many lost weekends and vacations and was truly supportive. Alan, our son, now CEO of his company, was always available and answered occasional technical questions for Dad. Moury, our daughter, just completed her Ph.D. and participated in several brainstorming sessions about certain topics in the textbook. You two make Mom and Dad proud every day. Also, my two sisters, Azam and Akram, provided moral support throughout my life. To this family, any expression of thanks is insufficient.

Part 1
Fundamentals of Information Systems

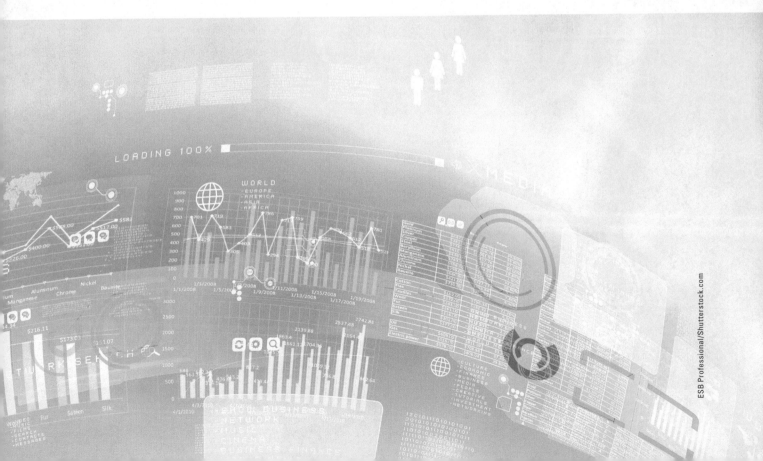

Module

1

Information Systems in Business

Learning Objectives

After studying this module, you should be able to…

1.1 Discuss common applications of computers and information systems.

1.2 Explain the differences between computer literacy and information literacy.

1.3 Define transaction-processing systems.

1.4 Define management information systems.

1.5 Describe the four major components of an information system.

1.6 Define strategic information systems.

1.7 Discuss the differences between data and information.

1.8 Explain the importance and applications of information systems in functional areas of a business.

1.9 Analyze how information technologies are used to gain a competitive advantage.

1.10 Apply the Five Forces Model and strategies for gaining a competitive advantage.

1.11 Review the IT job market.

1.12 Summarize the future outlook of information systems.

iStock.com/ipopba

This module starts with an overview of common uses for computers and information systems, explains the difference between computer literacy and information literacy, and reviews transaction-processing systems as one of the earliest applications of information systems. Next, the module discusses the components of a management information system, including data, databases, processes, and information; explains strategic information systems and their applications; and then delves into how information systems relate to information technologies (IT). This module also covers the roles and applications of information systems and explains the Five Forces Model, which is used to develop strategies for gaining a competitive advantage. Finally, the module reviews the IT job market and touches on the future of information systems.

> Organizations use computers and information systems to reduce costs and gain a competitive advantage in the marketplace.

1-1 Computers and Information Systems in Daily Life

Organizations use computers and information systems to reduce costs and gain a competitive advantage in the marketplace. Throughout this book, you will study many information system applications. For now, you will look at some common applications used in daily life.

Computers and information systems are all around you. As a student, you use computers and office suite software and might take online classes. Computers are often used to grade your exam answers and generate detailed reports comparing the performance of each student in your class. Computers and information systems also calculate grades and grade point averages (GPAs) and can deliver this information to you.

Computers and information systems are commonly used in grocery and retail stores as well. For example, a point-of-sale (POS) system speeds up service by reading the universal product codes (UPCs) on items in your shopping cart (see Exhibit 1.1). This same system also manages store inventory, and some information systems can even reorder stock automatically. Banks, too, use computers and information systems for generating your monthly statement, running automatic teller machines (ATMs), and for many other banking activities.

Many workers are telecommuters who perform their jobs at home, especially during the COVID-19 pandemic, and others often use their mobile devices to conduct business while on the go. The most common mobile device is a smartphone (such as an iPhone, Galaxy, or Pixel). Smartphones are mobile phones with advanced capabilities,

Exhibit 1.1
A point-of-sale system

Taras Vyshnya/Shutterstock.com

much like a mini-PC. They include e-mail and Web-browsing features, and most have a built-in keyboard or an external USB keyboard (see Exhibit 1.2). Tablet computers, such as iPads, are increasingly being used. These tablets come with apps (small programs) for common applications, and they can improve the user's efficiency. The "Smartphones Everywhere and for Everything" box highlights several popular applications of smartphones.

The Internet is used for all kinds of activities, from shopping to learning to working. Search engines and broadband communication bring information to your desktop in seconds. The Internet is also used for social purposes. With social networking sites—such as Facebook, Twitter, LinkedIn, and Foursquare—you can connect with friends, family, and colleagues online and meet people with similar interests and hobbies. Twitter (*www.twitter.com*), for example, is a social networking and short-message service. Users can send and receive brief text updates, called tweets. These posts are displayed on one's profile page, and other users can sign up to have them delivered to their in-boxes. As an example, the author of this

Exhibit 1.2
Examples of smartphones

Scanrail/Shutterstock.com

Smartphones Everywhere and for Everything

⏩ Finance | Technology in Society | Application

With the growing number of apps available for both iPhones and Android phones, individuals and businesses are using their smartphones as a productivity tool and as an intelligent assistant for all sorts of activities. Here are a few popular examples.

Group texting app GroupMe is used for sending a message to a group of employees or customers. The Samsung iPolis app, a video camera security system, is used to remotely watch video that monitors the location of a business or home. Apps are available to pay bills, update a company's Web site, market and advertise a product or service, reach out to customers, and keep in touch with employees from anywhere. Some businesses give out their Google Voice phone number to customers so that they can text an order. Google's calendar is used to coordinate events, and Instagram is used to post photos of new merchandise.[1]

Numerous apps that run on iPhones and iPads can assist small-business owners to run their businesses more efficiently. Smartsheet is a project management tool that helps keep track of employees and the latest status of the projects they are working on. QuickBooks is designed for account management. You can use it to create and send professional invoices and estimates to your clients in a timely manner. Evernote allows note taking for personal or business use in an efficient and effective manner.[2]

Starwood Hotels & Resorts Worldwide, Inc., plans to offer customers a virtual key at two of its hotels in Harlem, New York, and Cupertino, California. Guests can bypass the crowded check-in desk and enter their rooms using their smartphones. Guests receive a message on Starwood's app that will unlock their rooms with a tap or twist of their smartphones, using Bluetooth technology. Marriott International, Inc., also does mobile check-ins at some of its hotels. Loyalty program customers can check in via their smartphones and then go to a separate check-in desk to pick up a key.[3]

Questions and Discussions

1. What are two applications of Smartsheet?
2. What are two advantages of mobile check-ins?

textbook sends daily tweets that consist of links to current articles about information systems applications, new developments, breaking news, IT jobs, and case examples. You can read these tweets on Twitter, Facebook, or LinkedIn.

Organizations also use social networking sites to give customers up-to-date information and how-to support via videos. These sites can reduce organizations' costs by providing an inexpensive medium for targeting a large customer base.

In addition, people use video-sharing sites to watch news, sporting events, and entertainment videos. One of the most popular sites is YouTube (*www.youtube.com*). You can upload and share video clips via Web sites, mobile devices, blogs, and e-mails. Users upload most of the content on YouTube, although media corporations such as CBS, BBC, Sony Music Group, the Sundance Channel, and others also provide content. Anyone can watch videos on YouTube, but you must register to upload videos.

Businesses are increasingly using YouTube to promote their products and services. See the "A New Era of Marketing: YouTube" box, which highlights a few such companies.

A New Era of Marketing: YouTube

➡️ **Finance | Technology in Society | Application | Global**

Companies use newspapers, magazines, TV shows, and search engines to promote their products, services, and brands. YouTube is a popular video-sharing service that can be used as a marketing tool. The videos on YouTube are very well indexed and organized. They are categorized and sorted by "channels." The channels range from film and animation to sports, short movies, and video blogging. Individual YouTube users employ this marketing tool to share videos and stories. One popular application is watching how-to videos for repairing cars, home appliances, and so forth. Corporations can also take advantage of this popular platform. YouTube represents a great opportunity for marketers to reach consumers who are searching for information about a brand or related products and services. The service can also be used as a direct-marketing tool. The following are examples of corporations that are using YouTube to promote their products and services:

Quiksilver—This manufacturer of apparel and accessories, including the Roxy brand, frequently posts new videos of its products, continually renewing its Web presence.

Ford Models—Since 2006, it has uploaded hundreds of videos promoting its brand.

University of Phoenix Online—This site has hundreds of video testimonials, reviews, and documentaries that promote the university's degree programs.

The Home Depot—Free content, including practical knowledge and money-saving tips for home improvements, may be found at this site.

Nike Football—Nike maintains several distinct YouTube channels that cater to specific audiences. Consumers can find what is relevant to their needs without having to sift through a lot of content.[4, 5]

However, there are some challenges in using YouTube as an advertising medium. In 2017, several companies—including Starbucks, Pepsi, AT&T, Verizon, Johnson & Johnson, Volkswagen, and Walmart—pulled YouTube ads after Google's algorithm placed them on uploaded videos that contained racist material and other unpleasant content.[6]

In 2018, YouTube faced obstacles in its effort to restrain fraudulent content, misinformation, and disinformation similar to that on other social media such as Facebook and Google.[7] In 2019, Nestlé, Disney, and several other companies suspended YouTube ads over news of a pedophile network on the site.[8] Alphabet, the parent company of YouTube, has taken steps to fix this problem by involving more people in reviewing videos and developing more sophisticated algorithms to instruct its computers to eliminate this problem.

Questions and Discussions

1. What are two advantages of using YouTube as a marketing tool?
2. What are two challenges of using YouTube as a marketing tool?

Rawpixel.com/Shutterstock.com

So, what do all these examples mean to you? Computers and information technology will help the knowledge workers of the future perform more effectively and productively, no matter what profession they choose. In addition, these workers will be able to connect to the rest of the world to share information, knowledge, videos, ideas, and almost anything else that can be digitized. Throughout this book, these opportunities are explored, as well as the power of computers and information systems.

During the COVID-19 pandemic, computers and information technologies played a major role in nearly all aspects of our daily lives, including contact tracing, real-time monitoring, online shopping, digital and contactless payment systems, remote work, distance learning (Zoom video, Canvas, and Blackboard), telemedicine, online entertainment, 3D printing, robotics, and drone deliveries.

TikTok, a video-based social media platform, has also become very popular, particularly among young adults. All sorts of businesses use it to promote their products and services.

Social Networking and the Vulnerability of Personal Information

▶ Technology in Society | Application | Social and Ethical Issues

The popularity of social networking sites such as Facebook, Twitter, Snapchat, TikTok, and Foursquare is on the rise. As of September 2021, worldwide, there were over 2.89 billion monthly active users (MAU) of Facebook. According to Meta, 3.51 billion people were using at least one of the company's core products (Facebook, WhatsApp, Instagram, or Messenger) each month, and the number is increasing on a daily basis.[9] But so is the potential risk. According to an InfoWorld study, over half of all users of social networks in this country are putting themselves at risk by posting information that could be misused by cybercriminals. Many social networkers post their full birth dates, their home addresses, photos of themselves and their families, and the times when they will be away from home. This information could be used by cybercriminals for malicious purposes. According to the report, 9 percent of the 2,000 people who participated in the study had experienced some kind of computer-related trouble, such as malware infections, scams, identity theft, or harassment. To reduce risk and improve the privacy of your personal information, the study offers several tips:[10]

- Always use the privacy controls offered by social networking sites.
- Use long passwords (12 characters or longer) that mix uppercase and lowercase letters with numbers and symbols.
- Do not post a phone number or a full address.
- Do not post children's names, even in photo tags or captions.
- Do not be specific when posting information about vacations or business trips.

Questions and Discussions

1. What are three examples of popular social networking sites?
2. What are three recommendations for reducing risk and improving the privacy of your personal information when using social media?

As you read, keep in mind that the terms *information systems* and *information technologies* are used interchangeably. Information systems are broader in scope than information technologies, but the two overlap in many areas. Both are used to help organizations be more competitive and to improve their overall efficiency and effectiveness.

Information technologies offer many advantages for improving decision making but involve some challenges, too, such as security and privacy issues. The "Social Networking and the Vulnerability of Personal Information" box describes one of the potential challenges.

1-2 Computer Literacy and Information Literacy

In the 21st century, knowledge workers need two types of knowledge to be competitive in the workplace: computer literacy and information literacy. **Computer literacy** is skill in using productivity software, such as word processors, spreadsheets, database management systems, and presentation software, as well as having a basic knowledge of hardware and software, the Internet, and collaboration tools and technologies. **Information literacy**, on the other hand, is understanding the role of information in generating and using business intelligence. **Business intelligence (BI)** is more than just information. It provides historical, current, and predictive views of business operations and environments and gives organizations a competitive advantage in the marketplace. (BI is discussed in more detail in Module 3.) To summarize, knowledge workers should know the following:

- Internal and external sources of data
- How data is collected
- Why data is collected
- What type of data should be collected
- How data is converted to information and eventually to business intelligence
- How data should be indexed and updated
- How data and information should be used to gain a competitive advantage

> In the 21st century, knowledge workers need two types of knowledge to be competitive in the workplace: computer literacy and information literacy.

1-3 The Beginning: Transaction-Processing Systems

For the past 60 years, **transaction-processing systems (TPSs)** have been applied to structured tasks such as record keeping, simple clerical operations, and inventory control. Payroll, for example, was one of the first applications to be automated. TPSs focus on data collection and processing, and they have provided enormous reductions in costs.

Computers are most beneficial in transaction-processing operations. These operations are repetitive, such as printing numerous checks, or involve enormous volumes of data, such as inventory control in a multinational textile company. When these systems are automated, human involvement is minimal. For example, in an automated payroll system, there is little need for managerial judgment in the task of printing and sending checks, which reduces personnel costs.

Transaction-processing systems have come a long way. For example, the first ATM opened for business in 1969 with some very basic features. Similar to other information technologies, ATMs have gone through major changes and improvements.[11] Later, JPMorgan Chase introduced electronic banking kiosks (EBKs). Using these kiosks, customers can withdraw cash in a variety of denominations ($10, $20, and so on). These machines also allow customers to cash a check and receive exact change.[12] Customers can be identified using biometrics, such as scanning a fingerprint or the iris of an eye.[13]

The cardless ATM is one of the recent technologies deployed by some banks to attract younger customers. An app provided by the bank is used to withdraw cash. The customers set the amount using the app and receive a code on their smartphones that is scanned by the bank's ATM when customers get there. The ATM

Computer literacy is skill in using productivity software, such as word processors, spreadsheets, database management systems, and presentation software, as well as having a basic knowledge of hardware and software, the Internet, and collaboration tools and technologies.

Information literacy is understanding the role of information in generating and using business intelligence.

Business intelligence (BI) provides historical, current, and predictive views of business operations and environments and gives organizations a competitive advantage in the marketplace.

Transaction-processing systems (TPSs) focus on data collection and processing; the major reason for using them is cost reduction.

dispenses the cash and sends a receipt over the phone, or it can be printed at the ATM.[14]

According to the Chicago-based BMO Harris Bank, mobile withdrawal reduces fraud and increases efficiency, as a mobile cash transaction takes 15 seconds compared to 45 seconds for a card-based withdrawal.[15]

Some recent ATM innovations include the ability to make cash withdrawals by tapping smartphones to the ATM, using the technology similar to Apple Pay; allowing withdrawals of up to $3,000 on some ATMs; and allowing customers to make their credit card and mortgage payments at the ATM.[16]

Information Technologies at Domino's Pizza

➤➤ Finance | Technology in Society | Application | Reflective Thinking

In 1960, Domino's Pizza opened its first store. Today, there are nearly 18,000 stores, more than half of them outside the United States. In 2007, Domino's started online and mobile ordering. Today, customers can order online at *www.dominos.com* or they can use apps for the iPhone, Android, or Kindle Fire.[17] This allows them to customize their pizzas with any combination of ingredients, enhancing their sense of participation while also saving Domino's the labor costs associated with phone orders. After placing the order, the customer can track it all the way to when it is sent out for delivery, keeping an eye on an estimated delivery time.

Susan Montgomery/Shutterstock.com

In 2012, Domino's surpassed $1 billion in annual sales through its Web site, proving that electronic sales will continue to play a large role in the company's success.[18]

At Domino's, online ordering seamlessly accomplishes multiple objectives without the customer even taking notice. First, it creates the feeling among customers that they are an active part of the pizza-making process. Second, it results in greater efficiency at the various stores because employees do not have to spend as much time taking orders. They merely need to prepare the orders, which appear in an instant order queue, with all the customers' specifications.

Domino's now has the ability to store online orders in its database. This data can then be used for many purposes, including target marketing and deciding which pizzas to offer in the future. The company is also actively using social media, including Facebook and Twitter, to promote its products and gather customers' opinions.

In 2014, Domino's began allowing customers to order pizza using a voice app called "Dom," powered by Nuance Communications. It enables users of iOS and Android devices to place orders using their voices.

Twitter is now a part of the ordering system at Domino's. As of 2015, U.S. customers can order pizza by tweeting a pizza emoji.[19]

Starting in 2016, customers were able to order Domino's pizza from a Facebook Messenger bot.[20] Also in 2016, Domino's began testing a delivery robot called DRU in New Zealand.[21] And the company also announced plans to beat Amazon and Google to delivery using drones.[22]

In 2017, Domino's tested self-driving pizza delivery in a joint project with Ford using a specially equipped Ford Fusion that comes with both self-driving technology and an oven.[23]

In 2018, Domino's started pizza delivery to more than 150,000 "hot spots" nationwide, allowing customers to order delivery to beaches, sports arenas, parks, and other locations that don't have a residential address.[24] In 2019, Domino's designed an app so that customers can order and receive pizza in their cars,[25, 26] allowing IT to further expand the company's customer reach and its market share.

In 2021, Domino's started a robot car delivery service to select customers in Houston. For those who opt in, their pizzas will arrive in a fully autonomous vehicle made by Nuro.[27]

Questions and Discussions

1. What are two advantages of online ordering in a fast-food chain such as Domino's Pizza?
2. What are four examples of information technology tools being used at Domino's Pizza? What are they used for?

However, there are some security risks associated with using ATMs. ATM skimming is a worldwide problem that costs more than $2 billion a year in fraudulent charges. Skimmers, by using a card the size of a credit card installed inside the ATM or on the top of the machine, are able to record PIN numbers and other financial information of users. This could happen when you swipe your card at the ATM or even at a gas station. Skimmers have been stealing financial information from cards with magnetic strips, as chip-based cards are more difficult to steal from. To protect your financial information while using an ATM, follow these steps:[28]

- Check your bank statements regularly. Usually, if you report fraudulent charges within two days, your bank will reimburse you for anything over $50.

- Watch for signs that the ATM of a gas pump may have been tampered with. This can be done by physically touching the machine or checking on Bluetooth for unusual Wi-Fi networks.

- Cover your PIN number when entering it.

In recent years, it has been reported that some ATMs have fallen victim to a technique used by hackers called *jackpotting*, where machines are forced to spit out cash. Although the number of victims and the amount of money lost are not clear because victims and police often do not disclose details, banking officials should be aware of these criminal activities and guard against them.[29]

ATMs are not as popular as they used to be, given the development of online and mobile banking. An increasing number of banking customers also use dedicated apps from their favorite banks or financial apps and electronic payment systems such as PayPal and Venmo for their financial and banking needs.

1-4 Management Information Systems

A **management information system (MIS)** is an organized integration of hardware and software technologies, data, processes, and human elements designed to produce timely, integrated, relevant, accurate, and useful information for decision-making purposes.

The hardware components of an MIS, which are discussed in more detail in Module 2, include input, output, and memory devices and vary depending on the application and the organization. MIS software, also covered in Module 2, can include commercial programs, software developed in-house, or both. The application or organization determines the type of software used. Processes are usually methods for performing a task in an MIS application. The human element includes users, programmers, systems analysts, and other technical personnel. This book emphasizes users of MISs.

A **management information system (MIS)** is an organized integration of hardware and software technologies, data, processes, and human elements designed to produce timely, integrated, relevant, accurate, and useful information for decision-making purposes.

> If an organization has defined its strategic goals, objectives, and critical success factors, then structuring the data component to define what type of data is collected and in what form is usually easy.

In designing an MIS, the first task is to clearly define the system's objectives. Second, data must be collected and analyzed. Finally, information must be provided in a useful format for decision-making purposes.

Many MIS applications are used in both the private and public sectors. For example, an MIS for inventory control provides data (such as how much of each product is on hand), what items have been ordered, and what items are backordered. Another MIS might forecast sales volume for the next fiscal period. This type of system uses recent historical data and mathematical or statistical models to generate the most accurate forecast, and sales managers can use this information for planning purposes. In the public sector, an MIS for a police department, for example, could provide information such as crime statistics, crime forecasts, and allocation of police units. Management can examine these statistics to spot increases and decreases in crime rates or types of crimes and analyze this data to determine future deployment of law enforcement personnel.

As you will see in this book, many organizations use information systems to gain a competitive advantage. The information box on Domino's Pizza describes one example of this. (*Note*: MISs are often referred to as just *information systems*, and these terms are used interchangeably in this book.)

1-5 Major Components of an Information System

In addition to hardware, software, and human elements, an information system includes four major components, which are discussed in the following sections: data, a database, a process, and information (see Exhibit 1.3).[30]

Exhibit 1.3
Major components of an information system

Data	Database	Process	Information

1-5a Data

The **data** component of an information system is considered the input to the system. The information that users need affects the type of data that is collected and used. Generally, there are two sources of data: external and internal. An information system should collect data from both sources, although organizational objectives and the type of application also determine what sources to use. Internal data includes sales records, personnel records, and so forth. The following list shows some examples of external data sources:

- Customers, competitors, and suppliers
- Government agencies and financial institutions
- Labor and population statistics
- Economic conditions

> **Data** consists of raw facts and is a component of an information system.
>
> A **database** is a collection of all relevant data organized in a series of integrated files.

Typically, data has a time orientation, too. For example, past data is collected for performance reports, and current data is collected for operational reports. In addition, future data is predicted for budgets or cash flow reports. Data can also be collected in different forms, such as aggregated (e.g., subtotals for categories of information) or disaggregated (e.g., itemized lists). An organization might want disaggregated data to analyze sales by product, territory, or salesperson. Aggregated data can be useful for reporting overall performance during a particular sales quarter, for example, but it limits the ability of decision makers to focus on specific factors.

If an organization has defined its strategic goals, objectives, and critical success factors, then structuring the data component to define what type of data is collected and in what form is usually easy. On the other hand, if there are conflicting goals and objectives or the company is not aware of critical success factors, many problems in data collection can occur, which affects an information system's reliability and effectiveness.

1-5b Database

A **database**, the heart of an information system, is a collection of all relevant data organized in a series of integrated files. (You will learn more about databases in Module 3.) A comprehensive database is essential for the success of any information system. To create, organize, and manage databases, a database management system (DBMS) is used, such as Microsoft Access or OpenOffice Base for home or small-office use. In a large organization, a DBMS such as Oracle or Microsoft SQL Server might be used.

Databases are also important for reducing personnel time needed to gather, process, and interpret data manually. With a computerized database and a DBMS, data can be treated as a common resource that is easy to access and use.

Joe Techapanupreeda/Shutterstock.com

1-5c Process

The purpose of an information system's **process** component is generating the most useful type of information for making decisions. This component generally includes transaction-processing reports and models for decision analysis that can be built into the system or accessed from external sources.

An information system can include a wide range of models to support all levels of decision making. Users should be able to query an information system and generate a variety of reports. In addition, an information system should be able to grow with the organization so users can redefine and restructure models and incorporate new information into their analyses.

1-5d Information

Although they might seem the same, data and information are different. Data consists of raw facts and by itself is difficult to use for making decisions. **Information** — the output of an information system—consists of facts that have been analyzed by the process component and are therefore more useful to the MIS user. For example, XYZ Company's total sales last month were $5 million. This number is data because it does not tell you how the company performed. Did it meet the sales goal? Did sales increase or decrease from the previous month? How did the company perform against its top competitors? These questions and more can be answered by the information that an information system provides.

The quality of information is determined by its usefulness to users, and its usefulness determines the success of an information system. Information is useful if it enables decision makers to make the right decision in a timely manner. To be useful, information must have the following qualities:

- Timeliness
- Integration with other data and information
- Consistency and accuracy
- Relevance

If information lacks any of these qualities, the results are incorrect decisions, misallocation of resources, and overlooked windows of opportunity. If the system cannot give users a minimum level of confidence in its reliability, it will not be used, or users might dismiss the reports it generates. Information must provide either a base for users to explore different options or insight into tasks.

Another factor affecting the usefulness of information is the information system's user interface. Because this interface must be flexible and easy to use, most information systems make use of graphical user interfaces (GUIs), with features such as menus and buttons. To be useful, information systems should also produce information in different formats, including graphics (e.g., pie charts and bar graphs), tables, and exception reports, which highlight information that is outside a specified range. Supplying information in a variety of formats increases the likelihood of users understanding and being able to use the information. Note that, in addition to the formal information that an information system generates, users need to be able to make use of informal information—such as rumors, unconfirmed reports, and stories—when solving problems.

The ultimate goal of an information system is to generate business intelligence (BI), described earlier in this module. As you will learn throughout this book, many different tools, techniques, and types of information system technologies are used to generate BI.

1-5e Examples of Information Systems

To better understand the four main components of an information system, take a look at the following two examples.

Example 1 A state university stores all student data in a database. The collected data includes each student's first name, last name, age, gender, major, nationality, and so forth. The process component of the information system performs all sorts of analysis on this data. For example, the university's DBMS has a built-in query capability that can generate the following information:

- How many students are in each major?
- Which major is the fastest growing?
- What is the average age of the student body?
- Among the international students, which country is home to the highest number of students?
- What is the ratio of gender identities in each major?

Many other types of analysis can be done. A forecasting model (part of the process component) could be used to generate the estimated number of students for 2030, for instance. In addition, predictions could be made or improved, based on information this system provides. For example, knowing which major is the fastest growing can help with decisions on hiring faculty and knowing

> The **process** component of an information system generates the most useful type of information for decision making, including transaction-processing reports and models for decision analysis.
>
> **Information** consists of facts that have been analyzed by the process component and is an output of an information system.

the estimated number of students for 2030 can help with planning facilities.

Example 2 Teletech, an international textile company, uses a database to store data on products, suppliers, sales personnel, costs, and so forth. The process component of the information system conducts analysis on the data to provide the following information about the preceding month:

- Which salesperson generated the highest sales?
- Which product generated the highest sales? The lowest sales?
- Which region generated the highest sales?

Again, forecasting models can be used to generate predictions for the next sales period, and these predictions can be broken down by product, region, and salesperson. Based on this information, many decisions could be made, such as allocating the advertising budget to different products and regions.

1-6 Strategic Information Systems

Strategic information systems (SISs) focus on big-picture, long-term goals and objectives and assist an organization or a decision maker to achieve them. SISs support or shape competitive strategies and can be found in all types of organizations around the world. An SIS usually includes the same four components found in an MIS (data, database, process, and information), but the types of data that it collects, its sources of data, and the types of processes and analytics it performs are different. The emphasis is at the strategic level of the organization; SISs are oriented toward the long term, and they can be used to create new market opportunities.

Strategic information systems are used for gaining competitive advantage by assisting an organization in formulating business strategies for entering a new market, offering a new product, eliminating an old product, and improving an existing product. SISs are the key companion to Porter's three strategies and the Five Forces Model, all of which are discussed later in the module. Major functional areas in an organization, such as production, manufacturing, marketing, human resources, and finance, may develop

Strategic information systems (SISs) focus on big-picture, long-term goals and objectives and assist an organization or a decision maker to achieve them.

their own SISs to achieve their long-term goals. An SIS assists an organization to achieve and implement the following strategies:[31]

- Reduce the threats of substitute products or services by supplying products and services that are difficult to duplicate or that are used primarily to aid highly specialized networks of businesses.
- Enhance product differentiation by utilizing big data analytics and marketing tools to promote sales and marketing tactics.
- Improve customer and supplier relationships by rapidly responding to their current and future needs.
- Identify and deploy information technology tools throughout the supply chain to assist an organization to achieve cost leadership in the marketplace. Information technologies can be used to support a variety of strategic objectives, including creation of innovative products and services, coordination with business partners, reduction of costs, and gathering competitive intelligence.

Key characteristics of strategic information systems include:[32]

- They are goal-oriented—they are designed to achieve a specific goal, mostly in the long term.
- They involve top management in development process and use throughout the life cycle of the system.
- They are multidisciplinary and include input from functional areas of a business, including marketing, finance, human resources, and manufacturing.
- They are oriented to the future by creating forecasts that enable decision makers to create plans and choose the most promising strategic options.
- They are dynamic because they constantly analyze the business environment and deliver the right information to the right decision makers at the right time.

1-7 Using Information Systems and Information Technologies

Information systems are designed to collect data, process the collected data, and deliver timely, relevant, and useful information that can be used for making decisions. To achieve this goal, an information system might use many different **information technologies**. For example, organizations often use the Internet as a worldwide network to communicate with one another. Computer networks (wired and wireless), database systems, POS systems, and radio-frequency identification (RFID) tags are just a few examples of information technologies used to support information systems. The "Information Technologies at Home Depot" box gives you an idea of how companies use information technologies to stay competitive.

1-7a The Importance of Information Systems

Information is the second most important resource (after the human element) in any organization. Timely, relevant, and accurate information is a critical tool for enhancing a company's competitive position in the marketplace and managing the four Ms of resources: manpower, machinery, materials, and money.

To manage these resources, different types of information systems have been developed. Although all have the major components shown in Exhibit 1.3, they vary in the kind of data they collect and the analyses they perform. This section discusses some major types of information systems, focusing on the types of data and analysis used in each.

> **Information technologies** support information systems and use the Internet, computer networks, database systems, POS systems, and RFID tags.

Information Technologies at Home Depot

▶▶ Finance | Technology in Society | Application | Reflective Thinking

The Home Depot revolutionized the do-it-yourself home-improvement industry in the United States. Its stores use a POS system both for fast customer service and improved inventory management as well as a wireless network for efficient in-store communication.[33] The Home Depot has a Web site to communicate with customers and increase sales with online orders. It also uses RFID tags to better manage inventory and improve the efficiency of its supply chain network.

The Home Depot maintains a high-speed network connecting its stores throughout North America, and it uses a data-warehousing application to analyze variables affecting its success—customers, competitors, products, and so forth. The information system gives Home Depot a competitive advantage by gathering, analyzing, and using information to better serve customers and plan for customers' needs.[34]

In 2010, Home Depot launched a transition to Fujitsu U-Scan self-checkout software in its U.S. and Canadian retail stores. The software offers retailers the flexibility to quickly make changes to their POS systems and offers savings in labor costs.[35]

Other information technologies used in some Home Depot stores include virtual and augmented reality (discussed in Module 14), mobile checkout, and heat mapping to reduce in-store congestion. This technology assists the store manager to deploy more associates to congested areas within the store.[36]

The Home Depot mobile app is available for nearly all mobile devices and serves as a product locator, similar to a GPS, that helps customers quickly navigate their way through the aisles of a local store and find what they need.

Shoplifting is a major problem for all retailers. Cameras and barcodes have been somewhat helpful. To combat shoplifters to some degree, Home Depot stocks power tools that won't work if they're stolen. The tool only works if it is properly scanned and activated at the register via Bluetooth technology. If a shoplifter managed to smuggle a power drill out of the store without paying, the drill simply wouldn't turn on.[37]

Sergey Yechikov/Shutterstock.com

Questions and Discussions

1. How has information technology enhanced do-it-yourself home improvement at Home Depot?
2. What are four examples of information technology tools being used at Home Depot? How have information technology tools differentiated Home Depot from its competitors?

A personnel information system (PIS) or human resource information system (HRIS) is designed to provide information that helps decision makers in personnel carry out their tasks more effectively. Web technologies have played a major role in improving the efficiency and effectiveness of HR departments. For example, intranets are often used to provide basic HR functions, such as employees checking how much vacation time they have left or looking up how much money they have in their 401(k) plans. Intranets reduce personnel costs and speed up responses to common employee requests. As discussed in Module 7, an intranet is a network within an organization that uses Internet protocols and technologies for collecting, storing, and disseminating useful information that supports business activities such as sales, customer service, human resources, and marketing. The main difference between an intranet and the Internet is that intranets are private and the Internet is public. A PIS/HRIS supports the following decisions, among others:

- Choosing the best job candidate
- Scheduling and assigning employees
- Predicting the organization's future personnel needs
- Providing reports and statistics on employee demographics
- Allocating human and financial resources

The "Human Resource Information Systems in Action" box highlights some real-world applications of an HRIS.

A logistics information system (LIS) is designed to reduce the cost of transporting materials while maintaining safe and reliable delivery. The following are a few examples of decisions supported by an LIS:

- Improving routing and delivery schedules
- Selecting the best modes of transportation
- Improving transportation budgeting
- Improving shipment planning

The information box featuring UPS shows uses of information systems and information technologies, particularly logistics information systems.

A manufacturing information system (MFIS) is used to manage manufacturing resources so companies can reduce manufacturing costs, increase product quality, and make better inventory decisions. MFISs can perform many types of analysis with a high degree of timeliness and accuracy. For example, managers could use an MFIS to assess the effect on final product costs of a 7 percent increase in raw materials or to determine how many assembly-line workers are needed to produce 200 automobiles in the next three weeks. Manufacturing and operations management can also use social media information systems (SMISs, discussed in Module 8) for crowdsourcing. This platform provides a global reach to all sorts of talented people throughout the world for performing certain manufacturing tasks at a moderate cost. Here are some decisions that an MFIS supports:

- Ordering decisions
- Product cost calculations

Human Resource Information Systems in Action

Large organizations have been using HRISs for years by deploying software platforms such as SAP HR software and Oracle PeopleSoft. With cost reduction, ease of use, and the availability of cloud-based HR software or software as a service (SaaS, discussed in Module 14), small and mid-sized organizations can now benefit from HRISs.

Sarnova Inc., a medical products company based in Columbus, Ohio, with over 500 employees, replaced its paper-based system with an HRIS. They used Workforce from ADP for this implementation. The HRIS enables Sarnova to track employees by region, title, and category, among other things. According to Christy Gigandet, senior HR partner at Sarnova, the most beneficial feature of the system is managing the open enrollment for employee benefits. This automation process has saved the company "at least a month in man hours." The system has automated the printing and mailing of employee paperwork and has made it a self-service-driven process.[38]

Workday, UltiPro, Sage HRMS, and SuccessFactors are among the most popular HRIS software applications on the market. They all offer basic HR functions such as time management, payroll, talent management, scheduling, and workforce planning.[39]

Information Technologies at UPS

➤ Finance | Technology in Society | Application | Reflective Thinking | Global

Established in 1907, United Parcel Service (UPS) is now a global company worth $159.83 billion as of October 2021. It uses a sophisticated information system to manage the delivery of more than 14 million packages a day.[40] The company uses several types of networks in its operations—particularly, GPS and wireless networks. Its GPS network includes an algorithm that has helped drivers reduce the number of left turns they have to take, particularly on commercial roads. This, along with a vehicle telemetric system, has reduced the number of accidents and delivery times, thus saving the company over 20 million miles a year.[41, 42]

lightpoet/Shutterstock.com

To better serve customers, UPS has developed UPS Delivery Intercept, a Web-based service that allows customers to intercept and reroute packages before they are delivered, thus avoiding potentially costly mistakes and wasted time and costs. UPS calls the technology behind this service Package Flow Technology; it is also used to map efficient routes for drivers and mark packages for special handling. Kurt Kuehn, senior vice president of worldwide sales and marketing, said, "Innovations like Package Flow Technology and services like UPS Delivery Intercept are key components of UPS's drive to treat each of our millions of customers as if they're our only customer. We're constantly working on new and innovative ways to harness technology to help our customers meet their unique needs."[43]

Questions and Discussions

1. Explain UPS Delivery Intercept. How is this information technology tool being used as a strategic tool at UPS?
2. What are three examples of information technology tools being used at UPS? What are they used for?

- Space utilization
- The bid evaluation process used with vendors and suppliers
- Analysis of price changes and discounts

The goal of a financial information system (FIS) is to provide information to financial executives in a timely manner. Here are some decisions an FIS is used to support:

- Improving budget allocation
- Minimizing capital investment risks
- Monitoring cost trends
- Managing cash flows
- Determining portfolio structures

In addition, marketing information systems (MKISs) are used to improve marketing decisions. An effective MKIS should provide timely, accurate, and integrated information about the marketing mix, or the 4Ps: price,

promotion, place, and product. A growing number of information technology tools are being used in the marketing field and could play a major role in running an effective marketing operation in all types of organizations. One of these technology tools is database marketing, discussed in Module 3. Other marketing technology tools are covered below. These IT tools help organizations with direct marketing and help them grow leads, opportunities, and revenue.[44]

- Business, Web, and mobile analytics (discussed in Module 3) enable an organization to pinpoint the performance of marketing channels, technologies in use, ad campaigns and offers, and everything else that is trackable. Popular tools include Twitter Analytics Tools, Google Analytics, and Adobe Analytics.
- E-mail marketing (discussed in Module 7) enables an organization to be in constant contact with its

customers in an effective and efficient manner. Popular tools include MailChimp (now a part of Intuit Corporation) and Constant Contact.

- Search engine marketing (discussed in Module 7) that includes both paid search ads and search engine optimization (SEO) helps an organization to get top-rank listings of its Web site. Popular tools include Google AdWords, Bing, and Yahoo!

- Digital and Web marketing (discussed in Module 8) enable an organization to effectively promote its products and services in all types of digital platforms.

- Mobile technologies (discussed in Module 6) enable an organization to sell products and services to mobile users, which is important because their number is increasing on a daily basis.

- Marketing automation helps an organization bring all other IT tools together, including analytics, online forms, customer tracking, personalization technology (discussed in Module 11), customer relation management (CRM, discussed in Module 11), and automated alerts to salespeople. Popular tools include HubSpot and Act-On.

Here are some decisions that an MKIS supports:

- Analyzing market share, sales, and sales personnel
- Sales forecasting
- Price and cost analysis of items sold

1-7b Using Information Technologies for a Competitive Advantage

Michael Porter, a professor at Harvard Business School, identified three strategies for successfully competing in the marketplace:[45]

- Overall cost leadership
- Differentiation
- Focus

Information systems can help organizations reduce the cost of products and services and, if designed correctly, can assist with differentiation and focus strategies. Throughout this book, you will see many examples of the cost savings that organizations have achieved with information systems and technologies. For example, Walmart has been using overall cost leadership strategies

> **Information technologies can help bottom-line and top-line strategies.**

successfully (see the upcoming information box).

Information technologies can help bottom-line and top-line strategies. The focus of a bottom-line strategy is improving efficiency by reducing overall costs. A top-line strategy focuses on generating new revenue by offering new products and services to customers or increasing revenue by selling existing products and services to new customers. For example, e-commerce businesses are adapting business models to reduce distribution costs dramatically. A good example is antivirus vendors using the Internet to distribute software. For a subscription fee of around $30, you can download the software and receive updates for a year. Without the Internet for easy, inexpensive distribution, vendors could not afford to offer software at such a low price.

As discussed in Module 11, many organizations use enterprise systems—such as supply chain management (SCM), customer relationship management (CRM), enterprise resource planning (ERP), knowledge management (KM), and collaboration software (discussed in Module 12)—to reduce costs and improve customer service. The goal of these systems is to use information technologies to create the most efficient and effective link between suppliers and consumers. A successful CRM program, for example, helps improve customer service and create a long-term relationship between an organization and its customers.

After overall cost leadership, the second set of strategies are differentiation strategies, in which organizations try to make their products and services different from their competitors'. Apple has been successful with this strategy by designing its computers to look very different

Peshkova/Shutterstock.com

Information Technologies at Walmart

⟫ Finance | Technology in Society | Application | Reflective Thinking

Walmart (*http://walmartstores.com*), the largest retailer in the world, built the Walmart Satellite Network, which is the largest private satellite communication system in the United States. The network links branch stores with the home office in Bentonville, Arkansas, by using two-way voice and data and one-way video communication. In addition to the POS systems used for many years, Walmart uses the following information technologies to gain a competitive advantage:

Vdovichenko Denis/Shutterstock.com

- Telecommunications is used to link stores with the central computer system and then to suppliers' computers. This system creates a seamless connection among all parties.

- Network technologies are used to manage inventory and implement a just-in-time inventory system. As a result, products and services can be offered at the lowest possible prices.

- Walmart uses an extranet, called RetailLink, to communicate with suppliers. Suppliers are able to review product sales records in all stores and track current sales figures and inventory levels.[46] (Extranets are discussed in Module 7.)

- Electronic data interchange (EDI), discussed in Module 11, is used to streamline the order–invoice–payment cycle, reduce paperwork, and improve accuracy.

- Walmart is a major user of RFID technologies, which have improved its supply chain and inventory management systems.

- Since 2017, Walmart has used virtual reality (discussed in Module 14) to help train its employees on topics such as management and customer service. It is estimated that over 150,000 employees go through the program each year.[47]

- In 2017, Walmart introduced robots in over 50 locations. These 2-foot-tall robots perform tasks such as checking stock, finding mislabeled or unlabeled products, and assisting employees to fulfill orders for online customers.[48]

- In 2018, Walmart rolled out mobile checkout in some of its stores using a program called "Me," a significant move toward full in-aisle mobile checkout.[49] The same year, Walmart initiated shopping by text message in some of its stores using a platform called Jetblack. This platform costs members $50 per month to have access to personal shoppers who will offer recommendations when a customer texts. It is also able to send items from other retailers such as Saks, Bluemercury, and Pottery Barn for same-day or next-day delivery, including complimentary gift wrapping and easy returns.[50]

Questions and Discussions

1. What are two advantages of using virtual reality as a training tool at Walmart?
2. Mobile checkout is being used increasingly by companies such as Walmart. What are two advantages of this technology?

from PCs and focusing on its computers' ease of use. As another example, Amazon has differentiated its Web site by using certain information technologies, such as personalization technologies (covered in more detail in Module 11), to recommend products to customers based on their previous purchases. Amazon also uses the one-click system for fast checkout. With this system, customers can enter credit card numbers and addresses once and, in subsequent visits, simply click once to make a purchase without having to enter information again.

With focus strategies, organizations concentrate on a specific market segment to achieve a cost or differentiation advantage. Apple has also used this strategy to target iPhones to consumer users rather than business users. Similarly, Macintosh computers are heavily marketed to creative professionals such as designers, photographers, and writers. As another example, Abercrombie & Fitch targets high-end clothing to low-income customers, such as teenagers and young adults, while Nordstrom targets its high-end clothing to high-income customers. Information technologies could assist these companies in reaching their target market segments more cost-effectively.

Remember that focus and differentiation strategies work only up to a certain point. Customers are often willing to pay more for a unique product or service or one with a specific focus. However, cost still plays a major role. If a product or service becomes too expensive, customers might not be willing to purchase it.

1-7c Porter's Five Forces Model: Understanding the Business Environment

Harvard Business School's Michael Porter created a comprehensive framework called the **Five Forces Model** for analyzing an organization, its position in the marketplace, and how information systems could be used to make the organization more competitive.[51] The five forces, shown in Exhibit 1.4, are:

- Buyer power
- Supplier power
- Threat of substitute products or services
- Threat of new entrants
- Rivalry among existing competitors

Buyer power is high when customers have many choices and low when they have few choices. Typically, organizations try to limit buyers' choices by offering services that make it difficult for customers to switch, which is essentially using a differentiation strategy. For example, Dell Computer was among the first to offer computer customization options to customers, and other computer manufacturers followed suit. Grocery stores, such as Sam's Club, offer club cards that encourage customers to shop by giving them big discounts, an example of overall

Exhibit 1.4
The Five Forces Model

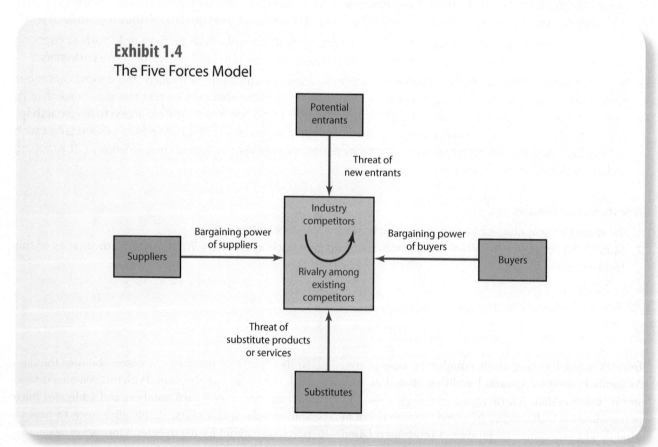

cost leadership strategies. Similarly, airlines and hotels offer free mileage and points when customers use their services. Information systems can make managing these strategies easier and more cost-effective.

Organizations use these strategies to increase customer loyalty, thus combating the threat of new entrants or substitute products. However, certain information technology tools, such as the Internet, have evened the playing field by giving customers more access to all sorts of data, such as the various prices for products and services. This increases buyers' bargaining power and decreases supplier power, which is discussed next.

Supplier power is high when customers have fewer options and low when customers have more options.

Organizations might use information systems to make their products and services cheaper or to offer more services in order to distinguish themselves from competitors (another use of a differentiation strategy). Netflix, for example, uses information technologies to offer products and services, which increases its power in the marketplace. (For examples of how these focus strategies get used, see the information box on Netflix.) Organizations have tools other than information systems and technologies to increase their power. For example, drug companies obtain patents for their products to reduce competition.

The threat of customers choosing substitute products or services is high when many alternatives to an organization's products and services are available. Some

Information Technologies at Netflix

➤ Finance | Technology in Society | Application | Reflective Thinking | Global

Using a wide variety of devices, over 209 million Netflix subscribers in the United States and around the world connect to the company's Web site and watch unlimited movies and TV episodes.[52] The users can also receive DVDs through the mail. The Internet, personalization technologies, and effective inventory management techniques have revolutionized rental entertainment at Netflix. Any user with an Internet connection can go to the Web site and

watch movies and TV episodes streamed and delivered instantly to a user's device. Netflix is currently using Amazon Web Services (AWS), which has provided the company with a high degree of availability and speed.[53]

Using data-mining and collaborative filtering technologies, Netflix's personalization system actively searches information to discover relationships and patterns and make recommendations based on a user's past movie-viewing history and questions that the user answered on the Web site. Based on these techniques, Netflix has created CineMatch, an algorithm that recommends other movies the customer might enjoy.[54]

Netflix uses big data analytics to create content and enhance user experience. It is estimated

Maxxa Satori/Shutterstock.com

that 80 percent of the content streamed on Netflix is influenced by its recommendation system. A good example is the introduction of the popular House of Cards show.[55] Netflix has successfully been using artificial intelligence, data science, and machine learning for personalization of movie recommendations, autogeneration and personalization of thumbnails and artwork, location scouting for movie production (pre-production), movie editing (post-production), and streaming quality.[56]

Questions and Discussions

1. What is the function of CineMatch at Netflix?
2. What are three examples of information technology tools being used at Netflix? What are they used for?

organizations add services—such as Amazon's personalized recommendations—to make their positions in the marketplace more distinctive. Other organizations use fees to discourage customers from switching to a competitor, such as when cell phone companies add charges for switching to another provider before the customer contract term is finished.

The threat of new entrants into the marketplace is low when duplicating a company's product or service is difficult. Organizations often use focus strategies to ensure that this threat remains low. For example, developing a search engine that could compete successfully with Google would be difficult. In addition, organizations use information technologies to increase customer loyalty, as mentioned previously, which reduces the threat of new entrants. For example, banks offer free bill paying to attract customers and keep them from switching to another bank; setting up a bill-paying service at another bank takes time that most customers do not want to spend. Similarly, after customizing their home pages with options offered by sites such as Yahoo! and Google, many users do not want to repeat this process at a new site.

Rivalry among existing competitors is high when many competitors occupy the same marketplace position; it is low when there are few competitors. For example, online brokerage firms operate in a highly competitive environment, so they use information technologies to make their services unique.

The "Digital Innovation in Retail Industry Using Information Technologies" box highlights the role of information technologies in making retail businesses more competitive. A growing number of retailers are using elements of Porter's Five Forces Model.

How should businesses use Porter's three strategies and Five Forces Model? Businesses could use Porter's three strategies in two ways:

1. **Before a new business starts its operation, sometime in the planning phase, the three strategies must be carefully analyzed as they relate to the business**. At this point the business owner(s) should decide which strategy will be emphasized and followed in the business and then act accordingly. If overall cost leadership is the goal, then the business owner must deliver a similar product or service that is cheaper than the competitors' offerings. If differentiation strategy is chosen, then the business owner(s) must deliver a product or service that is different from those in the market and at a competitive price. If the focus strategy is chosen, then the business owner(s) must clearly define the target market

and the audiences that the business will serve. Over 100 information boxes and cases presented throughout this book clearly show how various information technology tools and information systems have helped businesses to reduce the cost of operation. In many cases these technologies have also helped businesses to differentiate themselves by offering better and faster customer service. Information technology and information systems could also help a business to improve focus by identifying customers' needs that are underserved and then acting accordingly.

2. **Existing businesses could also analyze the three strategies and evaluate their position within the market they are serving, and then deploy selected information technology tools and information systems that could improve their market position**. As an example, Walmart acquired Jet.com to improve its position in the e-commerce area and better compete with Amazon. Small and medium-sized businesses use mobile apps and other information technology tools to perform many of their business functions at a moderate cost. The "Smartphones Everywhere and for Everything" box illustrates one example of this deployment.

The Five Forces Model can also be used both by new and existing businesses. If buyer power is high, then the business should deploy information technology to make it difficult for customers to switch. If supplier power is high, then the business should continue to use information technology to maintain this power. This is evident with companies like Apple that constantly improve the features of its iPhone to maintain its market share and possibly increase it. Threat of substitute products or services always exists, and information technology could assist businesses to maintain their market position by continuing R&D, improving customer service, and creating a loyal ecosystem, as Apple has been able to achieve. Similarly, threat of new entrants always exists, and businesses must constantly analyze their market position and deploy information technology to stay competitive. There are many examples of newcomers replacing businesses that used to have a strong market position; consider Netflix as one example, which has replaced Blockbuster, and Best Buy as another example, which has replaced Circuit City. Also, there is always rivalry among existing competitors in all segments of the marketplace. Businesses that stay competitive are those that use all sorts of policies, strategies, and the latest information technology tools. As you will read throughout this book, information technology and information systems play a major role.

Digital Innovation in Retail Industry Using Information Technologies

⟫⟫ Finance | Technology in Society | Application | Reflective Thinking

To reduce costs and minimize the gap between e-commerce and traditional commerce, brick-and-mortar retailers are increasingly using information technologies. This not only improves customer service, but it also sets these retailers apart from the competition. Here are a few examples of information technologies being deployed in the retail business:[57, 58, 59]

UfaBizPhoto/Shutterstock.com

Digital signage or dynamic signage—These are kiosks placed throughout stores with dynamic content update capabilities that provide shoppers with up-to-date information on product offerings and the latest promotional campaigns. They also allow customers to print coupons.

Beacon marketing—Use of Apple's iBeacon or similar technologies allows retailers to deliver in-store targeted marketing to customers' smartphones or other handheld devices.

Interactive touch display—These are virtual sales assistants that help shoppers locate a product in the store through high-definition graphics similar to those that shoppers see online.

Image search—Retailers using Google, TinEye, or other search engines allow shoppers to take a photo or submit a photo to search the retailer's Web site and then buy the item in the store or online.

Digital wallet—This allows customers to store their credit, debit, or loyalty cards, as well as coupons, and redeem them electronically in the store. Digital wallets also allow customers to validate tickets, redeem vouchers, make transactions, and use multiple loyalty services. Customers can also perform mobile checkouts, either at the cash register or with a walking sales associate equipped with a handheld device.

Smart fitting rooms—Wall-mounted tablets inside fitting rooms provide side-by-side comparisons with video of the various looks a customer has with different clothes. Customers can actually try on the clothes or just overlay the clothes on their image without changing clothing.

Questions and Discussions

1. What is beacon marketing? How are businesses using this technology to better serve their customers?
2. What are four examples of information technology tools being used by the retail industry? What are they used for?

1-8 The IT Job Market

During the past decade, the IT job market has been one of the fastest-growing segments in the economy, and it continues to be so. Even during the economic downturn, certain segments of the IT job market—such as Web design, infrastructure, and computer and network security—have shown growth compared to the rest of the job market. Currently, cloud computing–related jobs (discussed in Module 14) are in high demand.[60] Broadly speaking, IT jobs fall into the following categories:

- Operations and help desk
- Programming
- Systems design
- Web design and Web hosting
- Network design and maintenance
- Database design and maintenance
- Robotics and artificial intelligence

The educational backgrounds for an IT position can include an AA, BA, BS, MS, MBA, or Ph.D. in information systems and related fields. The salaries vary based on educational background, experience, and the job's location. They range on average from $89,000 for a programmer to over $240,000 for a chief information security officer.

Popular jobs in the information systems field are described in the following sections.

1-8a CTO/CIO

The top information systems job in a company belongs to either the chief technology officer (CTO) or the chief information officer (CIO). This person oversees long-range planning and keeps an eye on new developments in the field that can affect a company's success. Some organizations also have a chief privacy officer (CPO). This executive position includes responsibility for managing the risks and business impacts of privacy laws and policies.

1-8b Manager of Information Systems Services

This person is responsible for managing all the hardware, software, and personnel within the information systems department.

1-8c Systems Analyst

Systems analysts are responsible for the design and implementation of information systems. In addition to computer knowledge and an information systems background, this position requires a thorough understanding of business systems and functional areas within a business organization.

1-8d Network Administrator

This person oversees a company's internal and external network systems, designing and implementing network systems that deliver correct information to the right decision maker in a timely manner. Providing network security and cybersecurity is part of this position's responsibility.

Due to the increasing number of data breaches and security threats, large organizations have created a relatively new job title called a chief information security officer (CISO). This executive position is responsible for establishing and implementing policies to ensure that information assets and technologies are protected against internal and external threats. The salary of this executive position could be well over $240,000 per year.[61]

1-8e Database Administrator

A database administrator (DBA) is responsible for database design and implementation. Additionally, a database administrator should have knowledge and understanding of data warehouses and data-mining tools.

1-8f Computer Programmer

A computer programmer writes programs or software segments that allow the information system to perform a specific task. There are many computer languages available, and each one requires specific knowledge suitable for a specific application. Because of the popularity of smartphones and mobile devices, many programmers are now developing apps for iOS and Android devices. There is a huge demand for these applications and for the programmers who develop them.

1-8g Webmaster

A webmaster designs and maintains the organization's Web site. Because of the popularity of e-commerce applications, webmasters have been in high demand.

In recent years, new IT-related jobs have been created that also appear to be in high demand.[62, 63] These jobs include:

- Data scientist (see the following paragraph for further explanation of this job title)
- Social media/online-community manager
- Social media architect
- Telework manager or coordinator
- Search engine optimization specialist
- Business architect
- Mobile technology expert
- Enterprise mobile developer
- Cloud architect

Recently, a growing number of companies have been hiring data scientists (DS) in different sectors of the economy: sports, politics, agriculture, technology, and retail. Companies such as Microsoft, Google, Facebook, Bank of America, JPMorgan Chase, and Target are a few examples.[64] So what does a DS do? A DS may perform different tasks in different disciplines. A DS may interact with different users to automate data collection, aggregation, and visualization. Data scientists deploy statistical and mathematical models and certain artificial intelligence technologies. The ultimate goal is to help generate business intelligence (BI) and actionable information for decision making.[65] The following are a few specific tasks that a DS performs:[66]

- Identify the problem that an organization faces.
- Identify and collect data sets and variables.
- Ensure the accuracy and completeness of data sets.
- Apply models and algorithms to data sets.
- Analyze and interpret the results for the decision makers.

The top five qualities of an effective data scientist include:[67]

- Analytical skills and quantitative reasoning.
- Storytelling ability—be able to explain data to nontechnical team members.
- Be a team player—work and interact effectively with team members.
- Be a problem solver.
- Have a sense of curiosity—help the organization find new uses for the collected data.

The background and educational degrees for a DS vary. Generally speaking, some knowledge of mathematics, statistics, and MIS is needed. There are a variety of courses and degree programs that prepare students to become a DS. In 2016, Microsoft launched an online data science degree program with the goal of addressing a shortage of workers with data science skills.[68]

1-9 Outlook for the Future

By examining various factors related to designing, implementing, and using information systems, the following predictions can be made:

- Hardware and software costs will continue to decline, so processing information will be less expensive. These cost savings should make information systems affordable for any organization, regardless of its size and financial status.
- Artificial intelligence and related technologies will continue to improve and expand, which will have an impact on information systems. For example, further development in natural language processing should make information systems easier to use. Also, robots will play a major role in the workforce of the future. According to Gartner, by 2025, one in three jobs will be taken by software or robots.[69]
- The computer literacy of typical information system users will improve, as computer basics are taught more in elementary schools.

Rawpixel.com/Shutterstock.com

- Networking technology will improve, so connecting computers will be easier and sending information from one location to another will be faster. Compatibility issues between networks will become more manageable, and integrating data, voice, and video on the same transmission medium will improve communication quality and information delivery.

- Personal computers and tablets will continue to improve in power and quality, so most information system software will be able to run on them without problems. This trend should make information systems more affordable, easier to maintain, and more appealing to organizations.

- Internet growth will continue, which will put small and large organizations on the same footing, regardless of their financial status. Internet growth will also make e-collaboration easier, despite geographical distances.

- Hackers will become more sophisticated and protecting personal information will become more difficult.

Major computing trends that are already underway and should continue into the future include:[70]

- Ubiquitous computing—Computing devices everywhere with different sizes and power and accessed through multiple formats such as voice, touch, and gesture (discussed in Module 2).

- The Internet of Things (IoT), the Internet of Everything (IoE), Industrial Internet of Things (IIoT), and the Internet of Me (IoM)—Connected devices through the Web that will be used by businesses and individuals for increasing productivity and cost savings (discussed in Module 7).

- 3D and 4D printing—Creating a physical object from a 3D and 4D digital model for individual use and businesses. This could significantly bring down manufacturing costs (discussed in Module 11).

- Pervasive analytics—Building and integrating analytics capabilities into all everyday business activities (discussed in Module 3).

- Context-aware computing—Widespread applications and deployment of devices that know users, their devices, and their locations and serve as intelligent assistants to businesses and individuals (discussed in Module 13).

- Smart machines and devices—Continuous improvements in autonomous cars, trucks, drones, and robots, such as self-driving cars (discussed in Module 13).

- Cloud computing—Growth in cloud computing for multiple applications and multiple users (discussed in Module 14).

- Software-defined applications and infrastructures—The trend toward dynamically assembled infrastructures that are more responsive to user needs and able to deliver results faster, as opposed to predefined infrastructures.

- Security and privacy—The importance of computer and network security and privacy will increase, and more attention will be given to application self-protection (discussed in Modules 4 and 5).[71]

The Industry Connection highlights Microsoft and its products and services.

Industry Connection: Microsoft Corporation[72]

Microsoft, founded in 1975, is the world's largest software company and is involved in all aspects of desktop computing. In recent years, Microsoft has also become a major cloud provider. It is best known for the Disk Operating System (DOS), Windows operating systems, and office software suites such as Office. Here are some of the products and services Microsoft offers:

Windows: The most popular operating system for PCs and PC-compatible computers

Windows 7, Windows 8, Windows 10, and Windows 11: Four widely used OSs for PCs

Windows Server 2010, 2012, 2016, 2019, and 2022: Five widely used server operating systems in network environments

Office: The most widely used office suite; includes Word, Excel, Access, PowerPoint, and Teams

(Continued)

Office 365: An online service, similar to Google Apps for Work, that lets users collaborate on documents, spreadsheets, and e-mail using a combination of subscription desktop software and Web apps; includes Word, Excel, Outlook, PowerPoint, and Teams

Microsoft Edge and Internet Explorer: Popular Web browsers

Expression Web and SharePoint Designer: HTML editors and Web design programs for developing Web pages and other HTML applications

MSN: An Internet portal combining Web services and free Web-based e-mail (Hotmail)

SharePoint Server: A platform for facilitating information sharing, collaboration, and content management

SQL Server 2012, 2014, 2016, 2019, and 2021: Widely used database management systems

Xbox: A video game system

Visual Studio: An integrated development environment (IDE) that can be used to program applications in a number of different languages (such as C++, Java, Visual Basic, and C#); used for console or GUI applications as well as Web applications

Windows Live ID: A single sign-on service for multiple Web sites

Skype: A software application that allows users to communicate using voice, video, and data over the Internet

Teams: Collaboration and communication software used for audio and video conferencing

Surface: A tablet designed to compete with the iPad

Azure: A cloud-computing platform

Module Summary

1-1 Discuss common applications of computers and information systems. These include tasks such as using computers and office suite software to do homework or using computers to grade exam answers and generate detailed reports comparing the performance of each student in a class.

1-2 Explain the differences between computer literacy and information literacy. Computer literacy is skill in using productivity software, such as word processors and spreadsheets. Information literacy is understanding the role of information in generating and using business intelligence.

1-3 Define transaction-processing systems (TPSs). They focus on data collection and processing; the major reason for using them is cost reduction. This may include payroll processing or ATMs in a bank.

1-4 Define management information systems. MISs are an organized integration of hardware and software technologies, data, processes, and human elements designed to produce timely, integrated, relevant, accurate, and useful information for decision-making purposes.

1-5 Describe the four major components of an information system. They include data, a database, a process, and information.

1-6 Define strategic information systems (SISs). They focus on big-picture, long-term goals and objectives and assist an organization or a decision maker to achieve them. SISs support or shape competitive strategies and can be found in all types of organizations around the world.

1-7 Discuss the differences between data and information. Data consists of raw facts and information consists of facts that have been analyzed by the process component and are used for effective decision making.

1-8 Explain the importance and applications of information systems in functional areas of a business. Information is the second most important resource (after the human element) in any organization. Timely, relevant, and accurate information is a critical tool for enhancing a company's competitive position in the marketplace and managing the four Ms of resources: manpower, machinery, materials, and money.

1-9 Analyze how information technologies are used to gain a competitive advantage. They are used to analyze and apply Porter's three strategies and the Five Forces Model for successfully competing in the marketplace.

1-10 Apply the Five Forces Model and strategies for gaining a competitive advantage. The Five Forces Model and strategies can be used both by new businesses and established businesses. If buyer power is high, then the business should deploy information technology to make it difficult for customers to switch. If supplier power is high, then the business should continue to use information technology to maintain this power. The same approach could be applied to the other forces in the model.

1-11 Review the IT job market. Broadly speaking, IT jobs fall into the following categories: operations and help desk, programming, systems design, Web design and Web hosting, network design and maintenance, database design and maintenance, robotics, artificial intelligence, and so forth.

1-12 Summarize the future outlook of information systems. The future outlook examines several different factors that impact design and utilization of information systems, such as cost of hardware and software, artificial intelligence, computer literacy, and information privacy and security.

Key Terms

- Business intelligence (BI)
- Computer literacy
- Data
- Database
- Five Forces Model
- Information

- Information literacy
- Information technologies
- Management information system (MIS)
- Process
- Strategic information systems (SISs)
- Transaction-processing systems (TPSs)

Reviews and Discussions

1. What are four major components of an information system?

2. What are three characteristics of a strategic information system?

3. What are three differences between computer literacy and information literacy?

4. What are two applications of transaction-processing systems?

5. Provide one example of management information systems in the private sector and one in the public sector. What are two differences between MISs and SISs?

6. What are two differences between data and information?

7. Explain three applications of computers and information systems in the daily life of a college student.

8. List three decisions that are supported by an HRIS, FIS, and LIS.

Projects

1. Identify three applications of information systems at the college or the university that you are attending. Write a one-page paper that describes these three applications and provide an example of the type of decisions that are being improved by each application. How are multiple-choice and true-false questions graded?

2. Grocery chains have been using information technologies for several decades. After reading the information presented in this module and other sources, write a one-page paper that describes three such technologies. What are two advantages of a POS system?

3. RFID tags are being increasingly used by companies such as Macy's, Walmart, and Home Depot. Identify an additional company that uses RFIDs and write a one-page paper that describes the company's specific application of RFIDs. What are two differences between an RFID and a UPC system?

4. Apply Michael Porter's three strategies and the Five Forces Model for successfully competing in the marketplace to a new business and to an established business. How might the strategies differ? Identify a business not already mentioned in this module that has successfully implemented each strategy.

5. After reading the information presented in this module and other sources, write a one-page paper that supports the claim that, in the future, hackers will become more sophisticated and that protecting personal information will become more difficult. How should individuals guard against this threat?

6. Banks are promoting online banking to a broad range of customers. After reading the information presented in this module and other sources, write a one-page paper that lists three advantages and three disadvantages of online banking. Why are some customers reluctant to use online banking? What are two examples of popular apps that your own bank uses?

Module Quiz

1. Computer literacy is understanding the role of information in generating and using business intelligence. True or False?

2. Strategic information systems (SISs) focus on big-picture, long-term goals and objectives and assist an organization or a decision maker to achieve them. True or False?

3. Michael Porter's Five Forces Model analyzes an organization, its position in the marketplace, and how information systems could be used to make it more competitive. True or False?

4. All of the following are among the future outlook of information systems except:
   a. Hardware and software costs will continue to decline.
   b. The computer literacy of typical information system users will improve.
   c. Hackers will become more sophisticated.
   d. All of these choices

5. Information technologies are used to gain a competitive advantage by doing all of the following except:
   a. Helping in reducing cost of operations
   b. Delivering timely and accurate information
   c. Replacing all key decision makers in an organization
   d. Providing business intelligence

6. All of the following are among the new IT-related jobs except:
   a. Data scientist
   b. Systems analyst
   c. Social media/online-community manager
   d. Search engine optimization specialist

Case Study 1-1
Using Information Technologies at Federal Express

➤ Finance | Technology in Society | Application | Reflective Thinking | Global

Federal Express (FedEx), founded in 1971, handles an average of 3 million package-tracking requests every day (*http://about.van.fedex.com/*). To stay ahead in a highly competitive industry, the company focuses on customer service by maintaining a comprehensive Web site, FedEx.com, where it assists customers and reduces costs. For example, every request for information that is handled at the Web site rather than by the call center saves an estimated $1.87. FedEx has reported that customer calls have decreased by 83,000 per day since 2000, which saves the company $57.56 million per year. And because each package-tracking request costs FedEx 3 cents, costs have been reduced from more than $1.36 billion to $21.6 million per year by customers using the Web site instead of the call center.

Another technology that improves customer service is Ship Manager, an application installed on customers' sites so users can weigh packages, determine shipping charges, and print shipping labels. Customers can also link their invoicing, billing, accounting, and inventory systems to Ship Manager.[73]

However, FedEx still spends almost $326 million per year on its call center to reduce customers' frustration when the Web site is down or when customers have difficulty using it. The company uses customer relationship management software called Clarify in its call centers to make customer

Denise Kappa/Shutterstock.com

service representatives' jobs easier and more efficient and to speed up response time.[74]

Answer the following questions:

1. Is technology by itself enough to ensure high-quality customer service?
2. What are FedEx's estimated annual savings from using information technology?
3. What are two examples of information technologies used by FedEx? How might these technologies help FedEx maintain a competitive advantage?

Case Study 1-2
Mobile Technology: A Key Player for Future Shopping

➤ Finance | Technology in Society | Application | Reflective Thinking

Faced with strong competition by online stores, retailers are looking for new ways to improve customer service and lower operating costs. They have found mobile technology to be the key for achieving this goal. Scan-as-you-go mobile devices are a logical next step after the self-checkout used by many retailers. Retail experts predict the new mobile-based retail devices could eventually bring about the end of traditional cash register systems. The mobile checkout stations pioneered at Apple stores appear to be the future. The goal is to speed up and improve customer service and to keep consumers in stores and spending.

Ahold USA's Stop & Shop retail stores use a mobile device called Scan It that hangs on the handle of the shopping cart

panuwat phimpha/Shutterstock.com

and allows customers to shop and scan as they go through the aisles. If there is a coupon for an item, the device quickly gives the customer a credit and the total is recalculated. The device is smart enough to alert the customer if there is a coupon for a complementary item, such as coffee creamer if the customer has purchased coffee. Shoppers who use the Scan It device spend about 10 percent more than average.

Clothing retailer Nordstrom is also using mobile devices, which it issues to its sales associates on the floor so they can scan items on the spot and let customers pay without going through the cash registers. Home Depot uses a device called First Phones as an inventory tracker. If an item is out of stock, First Phones quickly notifies the customer whether a nearby store has it, then holds the item for the customer to pick up. Starbucks is using a digital wallet model that allows customers to pay using their smartphones.[75]

Answer the following questions:

1. How will scan-as-you-go mobile devices and digital wallets impact the retail sector?
2. Which of Porter's three strategies are evident in the use of scan-as-you-go mobile devices and digital wallets in these examples?
3. What will be the role of smartphones in the future of shopping?

Module 2

Computers and Their Business Applications

Learning Objectives

After studying this module, you should be able to…

2.1 Define a computer system and its components.

2.2 Discuss the history of computer hardware and software.

2.3 Analyze the impact of the three factors distinguishing the computing power of computers.

2.4 Summarize the three basic computer operations.

2.5 Discuss the types of input, output, and memory devices.

2.6 Explain how computers are classified and their business applications.

2.7 Apply knowledge of two major types of software and their use in a business setting.

2.8 List the five generations of computer languages.

2.9 Define object-oriented programming.

iStock.com/metamorworks

In this module, you will learn about the major components of a computer and what factors distinguish computing power. You will review a brief history of computer hardware and software and learn an overview of computer operations. You will also go into more detail on specific computer components: input, output, and memory devices. You will learn how computers are classified, based on size, speed, and sophistication, and about the two major types of software—system software and application software—the five generations of computer languages, and an overview of object-oriented programming.

> If airplanes had developed as computers have developed, today you would be able to go around the globe in less than 20 minutes for just 50 cents.

2-1 Defining a Computer

If airplanes had developed as computers have developed, today you would be able to go around the globe in less than 20 minutes for just 50 cents. Computers have gone through drastic changes in a short time. For example, a computer that weighed more than 18 tons 60 years ago has been replaced by one that now weighs less than 2 pounds. There has been a trillion-fold increase in computing power and performance in a 60-year span.

As you learned in Module 1, you use computers every day for a multitude of purposes. You even use them indirectly when you use appliances with embedded computers, such as TVs and microwaves. Computers have become so ubiquitous, in fact, that a cashless and checkless society is likely just around the corner. Similarly, computers might eliminate the need for business travel. Even now, the widespread availability of telecommuting technologies and collaboration systems (discussed in Modules 4 and 12) means that knowledge workers seldom need to leave their homes or offices for meetings or other work-related tasks in other locations.

Computers are used in a wide variety of tasks, including report distribution in businesses, rocket guidance control in the NASA space program, and DNA analysis in medical research. This book could not have been published in such a timely manner without the use of computers. The text was typed and revised with word-processing software, and composition software was used to typeset the pages. Printing, warehousing, inventory control, and shipping for the book were accomplished with the help of computers.

So what is a computer? Many definitions are possible, but in this book a **computer** is defined as a machine that accepts data as input, processes data without human intervention by using stored instructions, and outputs information. The instructions, also called a *program*, are

> A **computer** is a machine that accepts data as input, processes data without human intervention by using stored instructions, and outputs information.

(Mclek/Shutterstock.com)

The **central processing unit (CPU)** is the heart of a computer. It is divided into two components: the arithmetic logic unit (ALU) and the control unit.

The **arithmetic logic unit (ALU)** performs arithmetic operations (+, −, *, /) as well as comparison or relational operations (<, >, =); the latter are used to compare numbers.

The **control unit** tells the computer what to do, such as instructing the computer which device to read or send output to.

step-by-step directions for performing a specific task, written in a language the computer can understand. Remember that a computer only processes data (raw facts); it cannot change or correct the data that is entered. If data is erroneous, the information the computer provides is also erroneous. This rule is sometimes called *GIGO*, or garbage in, garbage out.

To write a computer program, first you must know what needs to be done, and then you must plan a method to achieve this goal, including selecting the right language for the task. Many computer languages are available; the language you select depends on the problem being solved and the type of computer you are using. Regardless of the language, a program is also referred to as the *source code*. This source code must be translated into object code—consisting of binary 0s and 1s. *Binary code*—a set of instructions used to control the computer—uses 0s and 1s, which the computer understands as on or off signals. You will learn more about the binary system and computer languages later in this module.

2-1a Components of a Computer System

A computer system consists of hardware and software. Hardware components are physical devices, such as keyboards, monitors, and processing units. The software component consists of programs written in computer languages.

Exhibit 2.1 shows the building blocks of a computer. Input devices, such as keyboards, are used to send data and information to the computer. Output devices, such as monitors and printers, display the output a computer generates.

Main (primary) memory is where computers store data and instructions, similar to a human brain. The **central processing unit (CPU)** is the heart of a computer. It is divided into two components: the **arithmetic logic unit (ALU)** and the **control unit**. The ALU performs arithmetic operations (+, −, *, /) as well as comparison or relational operations (<, >, =); the latter are used to compare numbers. The control unit tells the computer what to do, such as instructing the computer which device to read or send output to.

Some computers have a single processor; other computers, called *multiprocessors*, contain multiple processors. Multiprocessing is the use of two or more CPUs in a single computer system. Generally, a multiprocessor computer performs better than a single-processor computer in the same way that a team would perform better than an individual on a large, time-consuming project. Some computers use a dual-core processor, which is essentially two processors in one, to improve processing power. Dual-core processors are common in new PCs and Apple

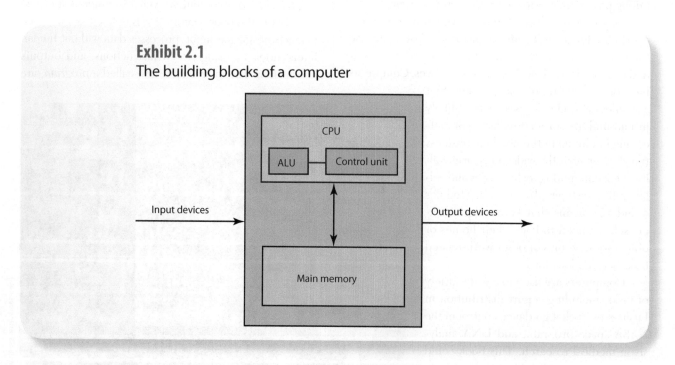

Exhibit 2.1
The building blocks of a computer

CPU

ALU   Control unit

Input devices

Output devices

Main memory

computers. In recent years, multicore processors have been introduced. A quad-core processor contains four cores, a hexa-core processor contains six cores, and an octa-core processor contains eight cores. Simply put, these new chips are making computers faster than their predecessors.

Another component that affects computer performance is a **bus**, which is the link between devices connected to the computer. A bus can be parallel or serial, internal (local) or external. An internal bus enables communication between internal components, such as a video card and memory; an external bus is capable of communicating with external components, such as a USB device.

Other factors that affect computer performance include the processor size and the operating system (OS). Some 32-bit computers still exist, but virtually all new computers have a 64-bit processor. A 32-bit system runs a 32-bit operating system, while a 64-bit system can run either a 32-bit or 64-bit operating system. A 32-bit processor can use 2^{32} bytes (4 GB) of RAM, and in theory, a 64-bit processor can use 2^{64} bytes (16 EB, or exabytes) of RAM. So, a computer with a 64-bit processor can perform calculations with larger numbers and be more efficient with smaller numbers; it also has better overall performance than a 32-bit system. However, to take advantage of this higher performance, you must also have a 64-bit OS.

Exhibit 2.2 shows additional components of a computer system. A **disk drive** is a peripheral device for writing (storing), reading (retrieving), deleting, and modifying data. A **CPU case** (also known as a computer chassis or tower) is the enclosure containing the computer's main components. A **motherboard** is the main circuit board containing connectors for attaching additional cards. In addition, it usually contains the CPU, basic input/output system (BIOS), memory, storage, interfaces, serial and parallel ports, expansion slots, and all the controllers for standard peripheral devices, such as the display monitor, disk drive, and keyboard. A serial port is a communication interface through which information is transferred one bit at a time; a parallel port is an interface between a computer and a printer that enables the computer to transfer multiple bits of information to the printer simultaneously.

2-2 The History of Computer Hardware and Software

Major developments in hardware have taken place over the past 80 years. To make these developments clearer, computers are often categorized into "generations" that mark technological breakthroughs. Beginning in the 1940s, first-generation computers used vacuum tube technology. They were bulky and unreliable, generated excessive heat, and were difficult to program. Second-generation computers used transistors and were faster, more reliable, and easier to program and maintain.

Exhibit 2.2
Components of a computer system

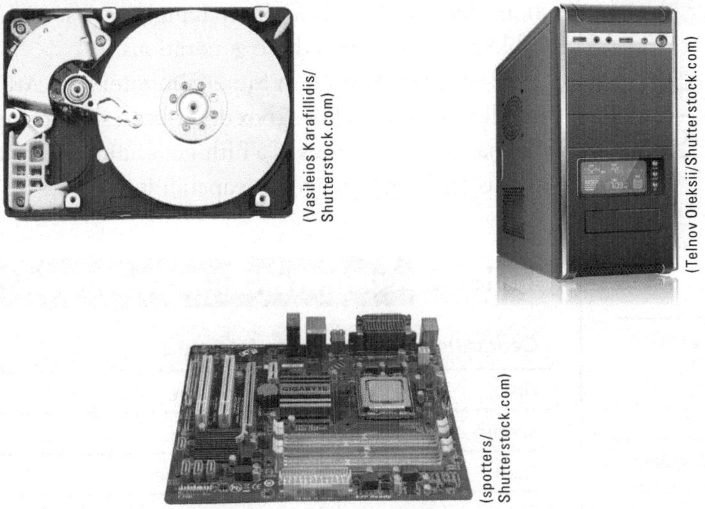

(Vasileios Karafillidis/Shutterstock.com)

(Telnov Oleksii/Shutterstock.com)

(spotters/Shutterstock.com)

A **bus** is a link between devices connected to the computer. It can be parallel or serial, internal (local) or external.

A **disk drive** is a peripheral device for recording, storing, and retrieving information.

A **CPU case** is also known as a computer chassis or tower. It is the enclosure containing the computer's main components.

A **motherboard** is the main circuit board containing connectors for attaching additional boards. It usually contains the CPU, basic input/output system (BIOS), memory, storage, interfaces, serial and parallel ports, expansion slots, and all the controllers for standard peripheral devices, such as the display monitor, disk drive, and keyboard.

Third-generation computers operated on integrated circuits, which enabled computers to be even smaller, faster, more reliable, and more sophisticated. Remote data entry and telecommunications were introduced during this generation. Fourth-generation computers continued several trends that further improved speed and ease of use: miniaturization, very-large-scale integration (VLSI) circuits, widespread use of personal computers, and optical discs (discs written or encoded and read using a laser optical device). The current fifth-generation computers include parallel processing (computers containing hundreds or thousands of CPUs for rapid data processing), gallium arsenide chips that run at higher speeds and consume less power than silicon chips, and optical technologies. Table 2.1 summarizes these hardware generations.

Because silicon cannot emit light and has speed limitations, computer designers have concentrated on technology using gallium arsenide, in which electrons move almost five times faster than silicon. Devices made with this synthetic compound can emit light, withstand higher temperatures, and survive much higher doses of radiation than silicon devices. The major problems with gallium arsenide are difficulties in mass production. This material is softer and more fragile than silicon, so it breaks more easily during slicing and polishing. Because of the high costs and difficulty of production, the military is currently the major user of this technology. However, research continues to eliminate some of its shortcomings.

IBM has already started using carbon nanotubes (CNTs) instead of silicon in its computer chips. CNTs are developed using nanotechnology, which is discussed in Module 14. It is one of the methods that should keep chip sizes shrinking after the current silicon-based technology has reached its limit.[1]

CNTs are relatively new technology and are a few years away from widespread production and adoption. Because of their unique features, such as durability, high security, small size, and energy efficiency, they are prime candidates for transistors and next-generation memory. Recently, a team of materials scientists successfully created a carbon nanotube transistor that's 25,000 times smaller than the width of a human hair. Industries that will benefit from CNTs include the automotive industry, space exploration and communications, industrial applications, and electronics.[2]

IBM has also produced a prototype chip with transistors that are just 7 nanometers wide, or about 1/10,000th the width of a human hair. Models in current use are twice as big as these prototypes.[3]

In May 2021, IBM unveiled the foundation of the world's first 2-nanometer transistor technology. This breakthrough could lead to 45 percent higher performance and 75 percent lower energy use than today's 7 nm processors.[4]

The field of optical technologies involves the applications and properties of light, including its interactions with lasers, fiber optics, telescopes, and so forth. These technologies offer faster processing speed, parallelism (several thousand light beams can pass through an ordinary device), and interconnection; much denser arrays of interconnections are possible because light rays do not affect each other. Optical computing is in its infancy, and more research is needed to produce a full-featured optical computer. Nevertheless, storage devices using this technology are revolutionizing the computer field by enabling massive amounts of data to be stored in very small spaces.

Computer languages and software have also developed through five generations. They are discussed in more detail in the "Computer Languages" section, but Table 2.2 summarizes these generations.

The "IBM Watson: A Supercomputer with Artificial Intelligence Capabilities" box describes a supercomputer that has several features of a fifth-generation computer as well as artificial intelligence capabilities.

Table 2.1 Hardware Generations

Generation	Date	Major Technologies	Example
First	1946–1956	Vacuum tube	ENIAC
Second	1957–1963	Transistors	IBM 7094, 1401
Third	1964–1970	Integrated circuits, remote data entry, telecommunications	IBM 360, 370
Fourth	1971–1992	Miniaturization, VLSI, personal computers, optical discs	Cray XMP, Cray II
Fifth	1993–present	Parallel processing, gallium arsenide chips, optical technologies	IBM System zEnterprise EC12

Table 2.2 Computer Language Trends

Generation	Major Attribute
First	Machine language
Second	Assembly language
Third	High-level language
Fourth	Fourth-generation language
Fifth	Natural language processing (NLP)

IBM Watson: A Supercomputer with Artificial Intelligence Capabilities

➤➤ Finance | Technology in Society | Analytical Thinking | Application

On February 16, 2011, an IBM supercomputer named Watson beat two former champions of the television game show *Jeopardy* and took away the $1 million prize. At first, Watson did poorly on a variety of subjects, from politics to *USA Today's* 2008 price hike. The supercomputer also did not know that Slovenia was the only former Yugoslav republic currently in the European Union. Eventually, though, it pulled ahead, with 18 correct answers compared to Ken Jennings's seven and Brad Rutter's four.

To achieve its victory, Watson needed massive computing power and storage space, including 10 server racks, each with 10 IBM Power 750 servers; it drew on 200 million pages of content stored on 4 terabytes of disk space.[5] Thousands of algorithms and computer programs allowed it to break down human language into pieces so it could search for answers in its massive database. It answered questions without exactly understanding them, but it answered them with a high degree of confidence! Overall, this was a significant improvement in a computer's ability to understand context in human language. IBM believes that the technology behind Watson can be applied to a variety of fields, including medicine. Voice integration is the next step in the development of Watson-related applications.[6, 7]

Watson-powered apps are now available that can serve as a personal shopping assistant and help brick-and-mortar companies to increase their cross-sell and up-sell opportunities.[8]

IBM and Pathway Genomics are developing an app that uses personal history and genetics to evaluate risks and recommend exercises. This app enables an individual to find out what exercises to do, what food to eat, and what medical tests to request from a doctor.[9]

Watson has also been used as a trip-planning service, providing travelers with relevant information so they can better plan their trips.[10]

As another example, H&R Block, an American tax preparation company, is using Watson to improve the client experience and assist in identifying credits and deductions. Watson will be able to find the best outcome for each and every unique tax situation and maximize tax returns. At the same time, it will assist clients to better understand how different filing options can impact their tax returns.[11]

Some of the new features and capabilities of Watson include vision-recognizing images and patients' records,[12] battling cancer with advanced genomics,[13] and managing call centers.[14]

Questions and Discussions

1. For what purpose is H&R Block using Watson?
2. What are two Watson applications in the medical field?

2-3 The Power of Computers

Computers draw their power from three factors that far exceed human capacities: speed, accuracy, and storage and retrieval capabilities. These are discussed in the following sections.

2-3a Speed

Computers process data with amazing speed. They are capable of responding to requests faster than humans can, which improves efficiency. Today's high-speed computers make it possible for knowledge workers to perform tasks much faster than with the slower computers of the past. Typically, computer speed is measured as the number of instructions performed during the following fractions of a second:

- Millisecond: 1/1,000 of a second
- Microsecond: 1/1,000,000 of a second
- Nanosecond: 1/1,000,000,000 of a second
- Picosecond: 1/1,000,000,000,000 of a second

2-3b Accuracy

Unlike humans, computers do not make mistakes. To understand computer accuracy more clearly, take a look at these two numbers:

- 4.00000000000000000000000001
- 4.00000000000000000000000002

To humans, these two numbers are so close that they are usually considered equal. To a computer, however, these two numbers are completely different. This degree of accuracy is critical in many computer applications. On a space mission, for example, computers are essential for calculating reentry times and locations for space shuttles. A small degree of inaccuracy could lead a space shuttle to land in Canada instead of the United States.

2-3c Storage and Retrieval

Storage means saving data in computer memory, and *retrieval* means accessing data from memory. Computers can store vast quantities of data and locate a specific item quickly, which makes knowledge workers more efficient in performing their jobs.

In computers, data is stored in bits. A bit is a single value of 0 or 1, and 8 bits equal 1 byte. A byte is the size of a character. For example, the word *computer* consists of 8 characters or 8 bytes (64 bits). Table 2.3 shows storage measurements.

Every character, number, or symbol on the keyboard is represented as a binary number in computer memory. A binary system consists of 0s and 1s, with a 1 representing "on" and a 0 representing "off," similar to a light switch.

Computers and communication systems use data codes to represent and transfer data between computers and network systems. The most common data code for text files, PC applications, and the Internet is the American Standard Code for Information Interchange (ASCII), developed by the American National Standards Institute. In an ASCII file, each alphabetic, numeric, or special character is represented with a 7-bit binary number (a string of 0s or 1s). Up to 128 (2^7) characters can be defined. There are two additional data codes used by many operating systems: Unicode and Extended ASCII. As of version 13.0, the Unicode standard contains 143,859 characters. Extended ASCII is an 8-bit code that also allows representation of 256 characters.

Before the ASCII format, IBM's Extended Binary Coded Decimal Interchange Code (EBCDIC) was popular.

Table 2.3 Storage Measurements (Approximations)

1 bit	A single value of 0 or 1
8 bits	1 byte or character
2^{10} bytes	1,000 bytes, or 1 kilobyte (KB)
2^{20} bytes	1,000,000 bytes, or 1 megabyte (MB)
2^{30} bytes	1,000,000,000 bytes, or 1 gigabyte (GB)
2^{40} bytes	1,000,000,000,000 bytes, or 1 terabyte (TB)
2^{50} bytes	1,000,000,000,000,000 bytes, or 1 petabyte (PB)
2^{60} bytes	1,000,000,000,000,000,000 bytes, or 1 exabyte (EB)

In an EBCDIC file, each alphabetic, numeric, or special character is represented with an 8-bit binary number.

The "A Supercomputer in Your Pocket" box highlights the power of smartphones that are faster than a supercomputer of a few years ago.

2-4 Computer Operations

Computers can perform three basic tasks: arithmetic operations, logical operations, and storage and retrieval operations. All other tasks are performed using one or a combination of these operations. For example, playing a computer game could require a combination of all three operations. During a game, your computer may perform calculations in order to make a decision (such as whether to move from point A to point B), it may compare two numbers, and it may perform storage and retrieval functions for going forward with the process.

Computers can add, subtract, multiply, divide, and raise numbers to a power (exponentiation), as shown in the following examples:

A + B (addition)	$5 + 7 = 12$
A − B (subtraction)	$5 - 2 = 3$
A * B (multiplication)	$5 * 2 = 10$
A / B (division)	$5 / 2 = 2.5$
A ^ B (exponentiation)	$5\text{^}2 = 25$

Computers can perform comparison operations by comparing two numbers. For example, a computer can compare x to y and determine which number is larger.

Computers can store massive amounts of data in very small spaces and locate a particular item quickly. For example, you can store the text of

> **You can store the text of more than 1 million books in a memory device about the size of your fist.**

A Supercomputer in Your Pocket

➤➤ Finance | Technology in Society | Application

A modern smartphone today has more computing power and memory than all of NASA during its 1969 mission that placed two astronauts on the moon and brought them back safely.[15] The *Apollo 11* astronauts' guidance computer was 2 feet wide, weighed 70 pounds, and had 4 KB of memory. Its cost in today's dollars was about $150,000.[16] The Apple iPhone 13 Pro Max has 6 GB of RAM and the iPhone 13 Mini has 4 GB of RAM. They start at 128 GB of storage capacity and go up to 256 GB, 512 GB, and 1 TB. They are more than 2,000 times faster than the *Apollo 11* computer at a fraction of its cost.

You can use your smartphone to order a latté or perform a sophisticated statistical analysis. You can shop or manage a smart home (a home connected to the Internet) from thousands of miles away. Smartphones serve as the gate to the Internet of Things (IoT), discussed in Module 7, that can connect you to billions of devices. As of September 2021, there were more than 2.79 million apps for Android devices at Google Play.[17] As of August 2021, there were more than 3.74 million apps for iOS devices at App Store. The Apple Watch and Apple TV apps aren't counted as part of the total apps because they have slightly separate App Stores.[18]

When you combine the speed, memory, and ease of use of smartphones with the number, variety, and sophistication of over 6 million apps, many of which are available for free, you can easily see that a supercomputer is in the palm of your hand.

The *Apollo 11* lunar module ascends from the moon in this July 20, 1969, photo.

Everett Historical/Shutterstock.com

Questions and Discussions

1. While there are over 6 million apps, what makes certain apps stand out from the rest?
2. What are three applications of smartphones?

---

more than 1 million books in a memory device about the size of your fist. Later in this module, you will learn about different storage media, such as magnetic disks and tape.

2-5 Input, Output, and Memory Devices

To use a computer and process data, three major components are needed: input, output, and memory devices. These are discussed in the following sections.

2-5a Input Devices

Input devices send data and information to the computer. They are constantly being improved to make data input easier. Examples of input devices include:

- *Keyboard*—This is the most widely used input device. Originally, keyboards were designed to resemble typewriters, but several modifications have been made to improve their

> **Input devices** send data and information to the computer. Examples include a keyboard and mouse.

ease of use. For example, most keyboards include control keys, arrow keys, function keys, and other special keys. In addition, some keyboards, such as the split keyboard, have been developed for better ergonomics. You can perform most computer input tasks with keyboards, but for some tasks a scanner or mouse is faster and more accurate.

- *Mouse*—This pointing device moves the cursor on the screen, allowing fast, precise cursor positioning. With programs that use graphical interfaces, such as Microsoft Windows or macOS, the mouse has become the input device of choice.

- *Touch screen*—This is a combination of input devices, often used when working with menus. Some touch screens rely on light detection to determine which menu item has been selected; others are pressure sensitive. Touch screens are often easier to use than keyboards, but they might not be as accurate because selections can be misread or mistouched. You probably saw touch screens used extensively on television during the 2020 presidential election to quickly show electoral maps and analyze election data in different ways. The "Touchless Computing: The New Paradigm in User System Interface" box discusses touchless computing, which may become popular in the near future.

- *Stylus*—This is a small metal or plastic device that looks like a tiny ink pen but uses pressure instead of ink. It is used to enter commands on a computer screen, mobile device, or graphics tablet.

- *Trackball*—This is kept in a stationary location, but it can be rolled on its axis to control the on-screen cursor. Trackballs occupy less space than a mouse, so they are ideal for notebook computers. However, positioning with a trackball is sometimes less precise than with a mouse.

- *Data tablet*—This consists of a small pad and a pen. Menus are displayed on the tablet, and you make selections with the pen. Data tablets are used most widely in computer-aided design and manufacturing applications.

An **output device** is capable of representing information from a computer. The form of this output might be visual, audio, or digital; examples include printers, display monitors, and plotters.

- *Barcode reader*—This is an optical scanner that uses lasers to read codes in bar form. These devices are fast and accurate and have many applications in inventory, data entry, and tracking systems. They are used mostly with UPC systems in retail stores.

- *Optical character reader (OCR)*—This works on the same principle as a barcode reader but reads text instead. OCRs must be able to recognize many special characters and distinguish between uppercase and lowercase letters, so using one is more difficult than using a barcode reader. Nevertheless, OCRs have been used successfully in many applications and are improving steadily. The U.S. Postal Service uses OCRs to sort mail.

- *Magnetic ink character recognition (MICR) system*—This reads characters printed with magnetic ink and is used primarily by banks for reading the information at the bottom of checks.

- *Optical mark recognition (OMR) system*—This is sometimes called a "mark sensing" system because it reads marks on paper. OMRs are often used to grade multiple-choice and true/false tests.

- *Camera and microphone*—Due to the prevalence of videoconferencing and multimedia applications, two additional devices have gained popularity in recent years: the camera and microphone. A *digital camera* may serve as both an input and output device by having the user take a picture and then send the picture to a computer or another device for display. A *microphone* is used as an input device to input sound to a computer, which will be stored in a digital format. Sound could be added to a multimedia presentation or used for generating music or an advertising piece.

2-5b Output Devices

Many **output devices** are available for both mainframes and personal computers. Output displayed on a screen is called "soft copy." The most common output devices for soft copy are liquid crystal display (LCD), light emitting diode display (LED), and the organic light-emitting diode (OLED) display. OLED screens are brighter, thinner, and consume less power than LCD technology. However, they are more expensive than LCD.

Touchless Computing: The New Paradigm in User System Interface

▶ Finance | Technology in Society | Application

Imagine using your tablet, PC, or Macintosh without needing a mouse, keyboard, or touchpad. You are able to interact with your device without touching it, using only gestures. In fact, touchless computing enables you to control what is on the screen with the movements of your finger. The goal of touchless computing is to provide an environment similar to the real world, in which you are able to manipulate objects using only your fingers.[19]

(Bosca78/iStock Unreleased/Getty Images)

This technology should be particularly useful for social networking sites such as Facebook, in situations where a user wants to navigate through different types of data in multiple settings. A San Francisco-based startup company named Leap Motion has designed a device called the Leap that is the size of a thumb drive. The Leap enables you to control your computer with a high degree of accuracy by waving your hands around. This technology could also radically change our TV interaction. You will be able to navigate through channels and programs without touching the remote or the TV.[20]

Engineers who use this technology will be able to manipulate 3D models on the screen by mere gesture. The *New York Times* has developed a 3D news reader and video reader based on this technology.[21]

Questions and Discussions

1. Which businesses or applications may benefit the most from touchless computing?
2. What are two advantages of touchless computing?

A new type of screen that can fold and roll is being introduced for tablets, wearable devices, and smartphones. These displays are based on OLED technology. Because OLEDs don't have lighted back panels, they are thinner and more power-efficient. Their advantages include increasing device mobility (a user can change the shape of a device), slimness, less weight, and durability.

In February 2019, Samsung introduced the first foldable smartphone, named the Galaxy Fold, for $1,980.[22] It can be used as a tablet or, in smaller form, as a phone. Some of the advantages of a foldable smartphone include its larger screen, multitasking ability, and improved productivity. Some of the disadvantages include its high cost, limited battery life, lack of apps, reliability, hardware complexity, fragility, and heavier weight.[23, 24, 25] This new design may reignite interest in the smartphone market, as the current market is near saturation.

In October 2021, Microsoft released Surface Duo 2, the company's second folding phone, for $1,500. It is a major improvement from the first Surface Duo. It appears that Microsoft has addressed nearly all the problems that users faced in the first version.[26]

The other common type of computer output is "hard copy," for which the most common output device is a printer. Inkjet and laser printers are standard printers used today. Inkjet printers produce characters by projecting onto paper electrically charged droplets of ink that create an image. High-quality inkjet printers use multicolor ink cartridges for near-photo-quality output and are often used to print digital photographs. Inkjet printers are suitable for home users who have limited text and photo printing needs. When selecting a printer, consider cost (initial and maintenance), quality, speed, the space that it occupies, and networking facilities.

Laser printers use laser-based technology that creates electrical charges on a rotating drum to attract toner. The toner is fused to paper using a heat process that creates high-quality output. Laser printers are better suited to larger office environments with high-volume and high-quality printing requirements.

Some organizations use cloud printing instead of having dedicated printers for each workstation or computer. Cloud printing is a service that allows users to print from any device on a network and implement a print-on-demand strategy. Simply put, it connects networked devices such as smartphones, tablets, laptops, and workstations with printer stations. Users can print remotely from their personal devices. The advantages of cloud printing include reduced cost and convenience. Users no longer have to worry about software, drivers, or cables, as cloud printing eliminates compatibility issues. It also helps organizations to achieve their "going green" objectives (discussed in Module 4) by lowering carbon emissions from transportation and reducing the amount of waste generated.[27]

Other output devices include plotters for converting computer output to graphics and voice synthesizers for converting computer output to voice. Voice synthesis has become common. Cash registers at grocery stores use it to repeat item prices. When you call directory assistance, the voice you hear is probably computer generated. Voice output is also being used for marketing. A computer can dial a long list of phone numbers and deliver a message. If a number is busy, the computer makes a note and dials the number again later. Although the value of this method has been questioned, it is constructively used in some political campaigns to deliver messages about voting.

One of the recent applications of converting computer output to voice is utilized by digital assistants such as Apple's Siri, Amazon's Alexa, and Google's Home. As an example, Google's virtual assistant mimics a human voice to book an appointment by phone. These kinds of applications have huge business potential because they can perform many of the tasks performed by a human assistant.[28]

Foldable or rollable screens are the newest use of OLED technology.

iStock.com/Chesky_W

2-5c Memory Devices

Two types of memory are common to any computer: main memory and secondary memory. **Main memory** stores data and information and is usually volatile, meaning its contents are lost when electrical power is turned off. **Secondary memory**, which is nonvolatile, holds data when the computer is off or during the course of a program's operation. It also serves as archival storage. Main memory plays a major role in a computer's performance; to some extent, the more memory a computer has, the faster and more efficient its input/output (I/O) operations are. *Graphics cards*, also called *video adapters*, enhance computer performance, too. High-end graphics cards are important for graphic designers, who need fast rendering of 3D images. Many video games also require high-end graphics cards for the best display.

Main Memory Devices

The most common type of main memory is a semiconductor memory chip made of silicon. A semiconductor memory device can be volatile or nonvolatile. Volatile memory is called **random access memory (RAM)**, although you could think of it as "read-write memory." In other words, data can be read from and written to RAM. Some examples of the type of information stored in RAM include open files, the Clipboard's contents, and running programs.

A special type of RAM, called **cache RAM**, resides on the processor. Because memory access from main RAM storage generally takes several clock cycles (a few nanoseconds), cache RAM stores recently accessed memory, so the processor is not waiting for the memory transfer.

Nonvolatile memory is called **read-only memory (ROM)**; data cannot be written to ROM. The type of data

Main memory stores data and information and is usually volatile; its contents are lost when electrical power is turned off. It plays a major role in a computer's performance.

Secondary memory, which is nonvolatile, holds data when the computer is off or during the course of a program's operation. It also serves as archival storage.

Random access memory (RAM) is volatile memory, in which data can be read from and written to; it is also called read-write memory.

Cache RAM resides on the processor. Because memory access from main RAM storage takes several clock cycles (a few nanoseconds), cache RAM stores recently accessed memory so the processor is not waiting for the memory transfer.

Read-only memory (ROM) is nonvolatile; data cannot be written to ROM.

usually stored in ROM includes BIOS information and the computer system's clock. There are two other types of ROM. *Programmable read-only memory (PROM)* is a type of ROM chip that can be programmed with a special device. However, after it has been programmed, the contents cannot be erased. *Erasable programmable read-only memory (EPROM)* is similar to PROM, but its contents can be erased and reprogrammed.

Secondary Memory Devices

Secondary memory devices are nonvolatile and are used for storing large volumes of data for long periods. As mentioned earlier, they can also hold data when the computer is off or during the course of a program's operation. There are three main types: magnetic disks, magnetic tape, and optical discs. Large enterprises also use storage area networks and network-attached storage (discussed in the next section) for storing massive amounts of data in a network environment.

A **magnetic disk**, made of Mylar or metal, is used for random-access processing. In other words, data can be accessed in any order, regardless of its order on the surface. Magnetic disks are much faster but more expensive than tape devices.

Magnetic tape is made of a plastic material and stores data sequentially. Records can be stored in a block or separately, with a gap between each record or block called the *interrecord gap (IRG)*. Magnetic tape is sometimes used for storing backups, although other media are more common now.

Other secondary memory devices include hard disks, USB flash drives, and memory cards. Hard disks come in a variety of sizes and can be internal or external; their costs have been decreasing steadily. Memory sticks have become popular because of their small size, high storage capacity, and decreasing cost. Flash memory is nonvolatile memory that can be electronically erased and reprogrammed. It is used mostly in memory cards and USB flash drives for storing and transferring data between computers and other devices. Table 2.4 compares the capacity of common storage devices.

Table 2.4	Capacity of Secondary Memory Devices
Device	**Storage Capacity**
Memory stick	2 TB
Hard disk	16 TB
SD Card	1 TB
SSD	100 TB

Another popular type of memory device is the *solid-state drive (SSD)*. With SSDs, similar to a memory stick, there are no moving parts. That is why an SSD-equipped PC will boot much faster than a PC equipped with a hard disk. For example, Samsung sells an SSD for laptops and desktops that offers 8 TB of capacity in a 2.5-inch form factor. Other alternatives include Sabrent Rocket Q, Corsair MP400, and Western Digital Blue.[29]

An alternative to SSD is NVMe. NVMe (non-volatile memory express) is a transfer protocol for accessing data quickly from flash memory storage devices. The difference between SSD and NVMe is that SSD stores data by using integrated circuits, while NVMe is an interface used to access the stored data at a high speed.

A **redundant array of independent disks (RAID)** system is a collection of disk drives used for fault tolerance and improved performance and is typically found in large network systems. Data can be stored in multiple places to improve the system's reliability. In other words, if one disk in the array fails, data is not lost. In some RAID configurations, sequences of data can be read from multiple disks simultaneously, which improves performance.

Cloud storage (discussed in Module 14) has become a popular option for many organizations and individuals in recent years. Used for online storage and backup, it involves multiple virtual servers that are usually hosted by third parties. Examples include Box, Dropbox, One-Drive, and Google Drive. Cloud storage may reduce the demand for some traditional storage devices or even replace some of them.[30]

There are several advantages for using cloud storage compared to traditional storage devices:[31, 32]

- Access to your files anytime, anywhere—This is particularly important for remote workers and those who travel, as a growing percentage of the workforce works remotely at least part of the time.

A **magnetic disk**, made of Mylar or metal, is used for random-access processing. In other words, data can be accessed in any order, regardless of its order on the surface.

Magnetic tape is made of a plastic material and stores data sequentially.

A **redundant array of independent disks (RAID)** system is a collection of disk drives used for fault tolerance and improved performance and is typically found in large network systems.

Used for online storage and backup, **cloud storage** involves multiple virtual servers that are usually hosted by third parties. Customers buy or lease storage space from third parties based on their current or future needs.

- Preventing data loss—Remote backup of your files is always available in the cloud for immediate access.

- Reduced cost—The cloud provides a cheaper alternative to your organization compared to traditional storage devices. With cloud storage, you will save on the purchase of the storage device and on maintenance of servers.

- Improved collaboration—The file syncing of cloud storage ensures that you are always working on the most current version of a file, regardless of which device you are using within or outside of the organization. Also, the live collaboration features available in most cloud storage allows multiple users to access the same file at the same time.

- Improved security—Although some people think that cloud storage may be less secure than traditional storage, you should remember that most providers of cloud storage will have multiple copies of your data for redundancy, often in different geographic locations; therefore, it is highly unlikely that they will lose your data.

- No maintenance—Maintaining servers is a constant job and companies have to employ a large IT staff to manage them, which is a costly proposition.

Cloud storage was a key factor in the timely publication of this book. Communication and collaboration were key, and cloud storage provided these features to the team. Using Box, the publisher created several folders for the different versions of the textbook during the various stages of the publishing process. The author and editors all had immediate access to all these folders. As soon as a file was edited, it was loaded to Box and all the team members were immediately notified that a file had been loaded. Box also kept a complete history of all the work done by different members of the team. This was a timely, error-free process, and at a moderate cost.

Large corporations and enterprises that need a lot of storage space use a server farm or server cluster. This is a collection of hundreds or thousands of computers that require a large amount of power to run and keep cool.

A **storage area network (SAN)** is a dedicated high-speed network consisting of both hardware and software used to connect and manage shared storage devices, such as disk arrays, tape libraries, and optical storage devices.

Network-attached storage (NAS) is essentially a network-connected computer dedicated to providing file-based data storage services to other network devices.

Storage Area Networks and Network-Attached Storage

A **storage area network (SAN)** is a dedicated high-speed network consisting of both hardware and software used to connect and manage shared storage devices, such as disk arrays, tape libraries, and optical storage devices. A SAN makes storage devices available to all servers on a local area network (LAN) or wide area network (WAN). (LANs and WANs are discussed in Module 6.) Because a SAN is a dedicated network, servers can access storage devices more quickly and do not have to use their processing power to connect to these devices. Typically, SANs are used only in large enterprises because of their cost and installation complexity.

SANs speed up data access performance and, despite their cost, are more economical than having storage devices attached to each server. A SAN's capacity can be extended easily, even to hundreds of terabytes.

Network-attached storage (NAS), on the other hand, is essentially a network-connected computer dedicated to providing file-based data storage services to other network devices. Software on the NAS handles features such as data storage, file access, and file and storage management.

When choosing between a SAN and a NAS system, consider the following factors:

- Hybrid solutions (combining a SAN and a NAS) might be available.

- A SAN offers only storage; a NAS system offers both storage and file services.

- NAS is popular for Web servers and e-mail servers because it lowers management costs and helps make the servers more fault-tolerant. It is also becoming a useful solution for providing large amounts of heterogeneous data (text, documents, voice, images, movies, etc.) for consumer applications.

- The biggest issue with NAS is that, as the number of users increases, its performance deteriorates. However, it can be expanded easily by adding more servers or upgrading the CPU.

2-6 Classes of Computers

Usually, computers are classified based on cost, memory, speed, and sophistication. Using these criteria, computers are classified as subnotebooks, notebooks, personal computers, minicomputers, mainframes, or supercomputers.

Supercomputers are the most powerful; they also have the highest storage capabilities and the highest price.

Mainframe computers are usually compatible with the IBM System/360 line introduced in 1965. As mentioned in the Industry Connection feature later in this module, IBM System zEnterprise EC12 is the latest example in this class. Systems that are not based on System/360 are referred to as servers (discussed in the next section) or supercomputers. Supercomputers are more expensive and much bigger and faster than personal computers, minicomputers, and mainframes.

According to a report on the top 500 supercomputers that was published in June 2021, the top 10 supercomputers and the countries that own them include the following:[33]

1. Fugaku (Japan)
2. Summit (United States)
3. Sierra (United States)
4. Sunway TaihuLight (China)
5. Perlmutter (United States)
6. Selene (United States)
7. Tianhe-2A (China)
8. JUWELS Booster Module (Germany)
9. HPC5 (Italy)
10. Frontera (United States)

Applications for computers include anything from doing homework on a subnotebook or notebook computer to launching space shuttles using a supercomputer. Because all computers are steadily increasing in speed and sophistication, delineating different classes of computers is more difficult now. For example, a notebook computer today has more power than a mainframe of the 1970s, and all indications suggest that this trend will continue. The "Popular iPad Business Applications" box highlights some of the business applications available for the iPad.

Popular iPad Business Applications

▶ Finance | Technology in Society | Application

The iPad is a tablet computer designed and developed by Apple. iPad users can browse the Web, read and send e-mail, share photos, watch HD videos, listen to music, play games, read e-books, and much more by using a multitouch user interface. Currently, iPads are used by many business professionals, including the following:[34, 35]

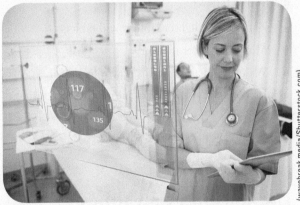

(wavebreak media/Shutterstock.com)

Healthcare workers—To access medical applications and for bedside care

Sales agents and service workers—To perform on-the-road sales presentations and display product information

Insurance agents—To display quotes

Real estate agents—To provide remote, interactive, visual home tours for interested home buyers

Legal professionals—To access legal documents and conduct a LexisNexis search from a car, office, or courtroom

Teachers and students—To access Windows applications and resources

Financial professionals—To access Windows trading applications, dashboards, documents, real-time quotes, Bloomberg Anywhere, and portfolio analysis tools

Corporate campus workers—To access corporate data for collaboration with colleagues while moving from office to office

Remote and mobile workers—To access Windows business applications, desktops, and data while at home and on the road

Questions and Discussions

1. What are three business applications of iPads?
2. How might an industrial worker use an iPad?

In addition to their applications in healthcare, wearable devices are being used in other fields to improve productivity. In the manufacturing field, for example, they are being used to do the following:[36, 37, 38]

- Improve employee safety by providing a hands-free environment to work.
- Improve employee monitoring by helping to keep track of what's going on.
- Provide service support by helping employees to access online tools and resolve issues faster.
- Provide support for plant monitoring by offering warnings when a component fails.
- Provide support for video applications by offering hands-free, real-time video that can be saved and analyzed later.

Experts believe we are entering the era of wearable, ubiquitous computing. See the "Ubiquitous Computing" information box for more on this topic.

Current trends in input/output devices may be summarized as follows:[39]

- Thinner and lighter laptops and tablets
- More and faster memory
- Widespread applications of wireless devices
- Increased applications of interactive computing using gesture, touch, and voice

2-6a Server Platforms: An Overview

A **server** is a computer and all the software for managing network resources and offering services to a network. Many different server platforms are available for performing specific tasks, including the following:

- *Application servers* store computer software, which users can access from their workstations.
- *Database servers* store and manage vast amounts of data for access from users' computers.
- *Disk servers* contain large-capacity hard drives and enable users to store files and applications for later retrieval.
- *Fax servers* contain software and hardware components that enable users to send and receive faxes.
- *File servers* contain large-capacity hard drives for storing and retrieving data files.
- *Mail servers* are configured for sending, receiving, and storing e-mail.
- *Print servers* enable users to send print jobs to network printers.
- *Remote access servers (RAS)* allow off-site users to connect to network resources, such as network file storage, printers, and databases.
- *Web servers* store Web pages for access over the Internet.
- *Authentication servers* verify credentials when a person or another server needs to prove who they are to an application.

Ubiquitous Computing

▶ Finance | Technology in Society | Application

Experts describe the current state of computing—the third wave—as ubiquitous computing or pervasive computing. The first wave was identified by mainframe computers, the second wave by personal computers, and the third wave by small computers embedded into many devices used daily—cellphones, cameras, watches, and so forth. Because people usually carry these devices around, the term "wearable" has been coined to describe them. Wearable computers are also used in medical monitoring systems, and they can be helpful when people need to use computers—to enter text, for example—while standing or walking around. There are many platforms and several players in this market. The following are popular examples:[40]

Google Glass—Displays information in a hands-free format; can communicate with the user and the Web in a natural language

(Koksharov Dmitry/Shutterstock.com)

(Continued)

Fitbit—Tracks physical activity and is designed to help you become more active

A new type of wearable computer with ingestible sensors and implantable chips, now used in Sweden, may soon become common. A tiny microchip about the size of a grain of rice is implanted under the skin. These devices can be used to collect information about what is going on inside a person's body. They can be used for treating chronic illnesses and could assist the medical community in coming up with more suitable drugs faster. At the same time, these devices may create some legal issues. For instance, they could reveal that someone has a particular illness, which could result in higher insurance rates. The devices could also store critical information such as financial information, health data, and access codes. Their advantages include never getting lost, providing easy access to a patient's health data, and allowing users to automatically control many of their devices, including access to building or computer facilities. They are relatively safe; however, security experts caution about privacy and security risks.[41]

Apple Watch is the dominant player in this fast-growing market. The popularity of wearable devices continues to grow. In 2018, United Healthcare announced that it will offer free Apple Watches to customers who meet walking goals—for example, walking 10,000 steps per day. This could help bring the device to more of United Healthcare's 20 million members.[42]

Questions and Discussions

1. What are some medical applications of wearable computers?
2. What are the benefits and risks of wearable computers?

2-7 What Is Software?

Software is all the programs that run a computer system. It can be classified broadly as system software and application software. For example, system software such as Microsoft Windows is the operating system for most PCs. This type of software works in the background and takes care of housekeeping tasks, such as deleting files that are no longer needed. Application software is used to perform specialized tasks. Microsoft Excel, for example, is used for spreadsheet analysis and number-crunching tasks. The "Microsoft Office 365: Making Data and Applications Portable" box highlights Office 365, a Web-based software application.

Microsoft Office 365: Making Data and Applications Portable

▶▶ Finance | Technology in Society | Application

Office 365 was first released in June 2011. A user can choose to pay for an Office 365 subscription on a monthly or annual basis, and several subscription plans are offered for business or home use.

For example, a subscription to Microsoft 365 Business Standard costs $12.50 per user each month. It includes traditional Office tools such as Word, Excel, PowerPoint, Outlook, Publisher (PC only), and Access (PC only). Office 365 also includes 1 TB of OneDrive cloud storage. OneDrive enables users to access their data from anywhere using any device.[43, 44]

Some of the unique features of Office 365 include (1) a fixed monthly fee instead of a one-time purchase of the package, (2) access anytime and anywhere both to Office applications and data, (3) access to the latest version of Office at any time, and (4) communication and collaboration inside and outside of the organization with trusted business partners.[45] Availability of network and Internet access, reliability, bandwidth, security, and privacy issues related to all cloud-based applications (discussed in Module 14) are among the concerns for this platform.[46]

Questions and Discussions

1. How might Office 365 be used in the workplace?
2. What are three concerns or drawbacks while using Office 365?

2-7a Operating System Software

An **operating system (OS)** is a set of programs for controlling and managing computer hardware and software. It provides an interface between a computer and the user and increases computer efficiency by helping users share computer resources and by performing repetitive tasks for users. A typical OS consists of control programs and supervisor programs.

Control programs manage computer hardware and resources by performing the following functions:

- *Job management*—Control and prioritize tasks performed by the CPU.

- *Resource allocation*—Manage computer resources, such as storage and memory. In a network, control programs are also used for tasks such as assigning a print job to a particular printer.

- *Data management*—Control data integrity by generating checksums to verify that data has not been corrupted or changed. When the OS writes data to storage, it generates a value (the checksum) along with the data. The next time this data is retrieved, the checksum is recalculated and compared with the original checksum. If they match, the integrity is intact. If they do not, the data has been corrupted somehow.

- *Communication*—Control the transfer of data among parts of a computer system, such as communication between the CPU and I/O devices.

iOS: The Brain Behind Apple Devices

⇒ Technology in Society | Application

iOS is the operating system that enables all apps to run on an iPhone, iPad, and iPod Touch. It offers major updates to popular apps and several new features, including the 3D Touch app switcher gesture, new emoji characters, additional camera and TV app settings, celebration message effects, and new wallpapers.[47] Major features and components of iOS include the following:

Maps—Provides visual and spoken turn-by-turn navigation and real-time traffic updates

Siri—Provides a voice interface for many ordinary tasks, including information on restaurants, movies, and sports

Facebook integration—Allows direct interaction from your Apple device using voice or typed instructions without leaving your app

AirDrop—Allows you to share photos, videos, and contacts from any app with a Share button

Control Center—Gives you quick access to frequently used apps

Shared photo stream—Allows sharing just the photos you want, with the people you choose

Passbook—Allows you to add passes to Passbook through apps, e-mail, and Web sites from participating airlines, theaters, stores, and more

FaceTime—Allows you to see the person you are talking to on your iPhone or iPad

Phone—Allows you to decline an incoming call, instantly reply with a text message, or set a callback

Mail—Allows you to set up a VIP list so you will never miss an important message from important people in your list

Safari—In addition to navigation, now allows you to save Web pages as well as links

Accessibility—Makes it easier to use Apple devices for people with vision, hearing, learning, and mobility disabilities

Camera with Panorama—Allows you to shoot up to 240 degrees horizontally as well as vertically

Questions and Discussions

1. How is iOS unique from Android?
2. What is the function of AirDrop?

The supervisor program, also known as the kernel, is responsible for controlling all other programs in the OS, such as compilers, interpreters, assemblers, and utilities for performing special tasks.

In addition to single-tasking and multitasking OSs, time-shared OSs allow several users to use computer resources simultaneously. OSs are also available in a variety of platforms for both mainframes and personal computers. Microsoft Windows, macOS, and Linux are examples of personal computer OSs; mainframe OSs include UNIX and OpenVMS as well as some versions of Linux.

Two new operating systems for smartphones and other handheld devices have attracted much attention in recent years: iOS and Android. The iOS product and its various versions run on iPad, iPhone, and iPod Touch. (See the "iOS: The Brain Behind Apple Devices" box.) The Android operating system by Google runs on non-Apple smartphones and handheld devices, such as HTC Inspire, Samsung Galaxy, and LG Thrill.

2-7b Application Software

A personal computer can perform a variety of tasks by using **application software**, which can be commercial software or software developed in-house. In-house software is usually more expensive than commercial software but is more customized and often fits users' needs better. For almost any task you can imagine, a software package is available. The following sections give you an overview of common categories of commercial application software for personal computers. In addition to these, many other categories of software are available, such as information management software, Web-authoring software, and photo and graphics software.

Word-Processing Software

You are probably most familiar with word-processing software, which is used to generate documents. Typically, this includes editing features, such as deleting, inserting, and copying text. Advanced word-processing software often includes sophisticated graphics and data management features. Word-processing software saves time, particularly for repetitive tasks, such as sending the same letter to hundreds of customers. Most word-processing software offers spell checkers and grammar checkers. Some popular word-processing programs are Microsoft Word, Corel WordPerfect, and OpenOffice.

Spreadsheet Software

A *spreadsheet* is a table of rows and columns, and spreadsheet software is capable of performing numerous tasks with the information in a spreadsheet. You can even prepare a budget and perform a "what-if" analysis on the data. For example, you could calculate the effect on other budget items of reducing your income by 10 percent, or you could see the effect of a 2 percent reduction in your mortgage interest rate. Common spreadsheet software includes Microsoft Excel, Apple Numbers, and Google Sheets.

> **Application software** can be commercial software or software developed in-house; it is used to perform a variety of tasks on a personal computer.

Database Software

Database software is designed to perform operations such as creating, deleting, modifying, searching, sorting, and joining data. A database is essentially a collection of tables consisting of rows and columns. Database software makes accessing and working with data faster and more efficient. For example, manually searching a database that contains thousands of records would be almost impossible. With database software, users can search information quickly and even tailor searches to meet specific criteria, such as finding all Accounting students younger than the age of 20 who have GPAs higher than 3.6. You will learn more about databases in Module 3. Popular database software for personal computers includes Microsoft Access, Ninox, and OpenOffice Base.

High-end database software used in large enterprises includes Oracle, IBM DB2, and Microsoft SQL Server.

Presentation Software

Presentation software is used to create and deliver slide shows. Microsoft PowerPoint is the most commonly used presentation software; other examples include Google Slides and Canva. You can include many types of content in slide shows, such as bulleted and numbered lists, charts, and graphs. You can also embed graphics as well as sound and movie clips.

Presentation software also offers several options for running slide shows, such as altering the time interval between slides. In addition, you can usually convert presentations into other formats, including Web pages and photo albums with music and narration. Another option in some presentation software is capturing the contents of the computer screen and then combining several screen captures into a video for demonstrating a process, which can be useful in educational settings or employee training seminars, for example.

Graphics Software

Graphics software is designed to present data in a graphical format, such as line graphs and pie charts. These formats are useful for illustrating trends and patterns in data and for showing correlations. Graphics are created with integrated packages, such as Excel, Apple Numbers, and Google Sheets, or with dedicated graphics packages, such as Adobe Photoshop and Adobe Illustrator. Exhibit 2.3 shows the types of graphs you can create in Microsoft Excel.

Desktop Publishing Software

Desktop publishing software is used to produce professional-quality documents without expensive hardware and software. This software works on a "what-you-see-is-what-you-get" (WYSIWYG, pronounced "wizzy-wig") concept, so the high-quality screen display gives you a good idea of what you will see in the printed output. Desktop publishing software is used for creating newsletters, brochures, training manuals, transparencies, posters, and even books. Many desktop publishing packages are available; three popular ones are Xara Page & Layout Designer, Adobe InDesign, and Microsoft Office Publisher.

Financial Planning and Accounting Software

Financial planning software, which is more powerful than spreadsheet software, is capable of performing many types of analysis on large amounts of data. These analyses include present value, future value, rate of return, cash flow, depreciation, retirement planning, and budgeting. A widely used financial planning package is Intuit Quicken. Using this package, you can plan and analyze all kinds of financial scenarios. For example, you can calculate how much your $2,000 IRA will be worth at 5 percent interest in 30 years or you can determine how to save $150,000 in 18 years toward your child's college education using a fixed interest rate.

In addition to spreadsheet software, dedicated accounting software is available for performing many sophisticated accounting tasks, such as general ledgers,

Exhibit 2.3
Types of graphs in Microsoft Excel

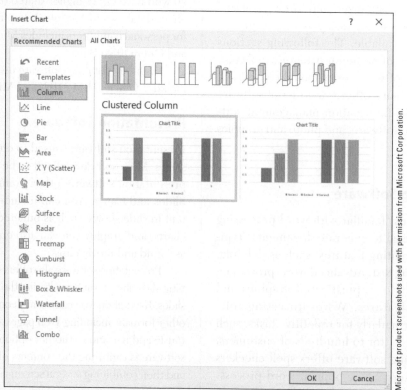

Microsoft product screenshots used with permission from Microsoft Corporation.

accounts receivable, accounts payable, payroll, balance sheets, and income statements. Some popular accounting software packages include Quickbooks, Xero, and Zoho Books.

Project Management Software

A project, such as designing a Web site or setting up an order entry system, consists of a set of related tasks. The goal of project management software is to help project managers keep time and budget under control by solving scheduling problems, planning and setting goals, and highlighting potential bottlenecks. You can use such software to study the cost, time, and resource impact of schedule changes. There are several project management software packages on the market, including ClickUp, monday.com, and Smartsheet.

Computer-Aided Design Software

Computer-aided design (CAD) software is used for drafting and design and has replaced traditional tools, such as T-squares, triangles, paper, and pencils. It is used extensively in architecture and engineering firms, but because of major price reductions and increases in PC power, small companies and home users can now afford this software. Widely used CAD software includes AutoCAD, TinkerCAD, and FreeCAD.

iStock.com/gorodenkoff

CAD software allows architects and engineers to create 3D visualizations of homes and other structures.

2-8 Computer Languages

As mentioned earlier, computer languages have developed through four generations, and the fifth generation is currently being developed. The first generation of computer languages, **machine language**, consists of a series of 0s and 1s representing data or instructions. Machine language depends on the machine, so code written for one type of computer does not work on another type of computer. Writing a machine-language program is time-consuming and painstaking.

Assembly language, the second generation of computer languages, is a higher-level language than machine language but is also machine dependent. It uses a series of short codes, or mnemonics, to represent data or instructions. For example, ADD and SUBTRACT are typical commands in assembly language. Writing programs in assembly language is easier than in machine language.

Third-generation computer languages are machine independent and are called **high-level languages**. Three of the most widely used languages are C++, Python, and JavaScript. These languages are used mostly for Web development and Internet applications. High-level languages are more like English, so they are easier to learn and code. In addition, they are self-documenting, meaning that you can usually understand the programs without needing additional documentation.

Fourth-generation languages (4GLs) are the easiest computer languages to use. The commands are powerful and easy to learn, even for people with little computer training. Sometimes, 4GLs are called non-procedural languages, which means you do not need to follow a rigorous command syntax to use them. Instead, 4GLs use macro codes that can take the place of several lines of programming. For example, in a 4GL you might issue the PLOT command, a macro code that takes the place of 100 or more lines of

Machine language, the first generation of computer languages, consists of a series of 0s and 1s representing data or instructions. It is dependent on the machine, so code written for one type of computer does not work on another type of computer.

Assembly language, the second generation of computer languages, is a higher-level language than machine language but is also machine dependent. It uses a series of short codes, or mnemonics, to represent data or instructions.

High-level languages are machine independent and part of the third generation of computer languages. Many languages are available, and each is designed for a specific purpose.

Fourth-generation languages (4GLs) use macro codes that can take the place of several lines of programming. The commands are powerful and easy to learn, even for people with little computer training.

high-level programming code. One simple command does the job for you. SQL (Structured Query Language), which is discussed in Module 3, is an example of a 4GL.

Fifth-generation languages (5GLs) use some artificial intelligence technologies (discussed in Module 13), such as knowledge-based systems, natural language processing (NLP), visual programming, and a graphical approach to programming. Codes are automatically generated and designed to make the computer solve a given problem without a programmer or with minimum programming effort. These languages are designed to facilitate natural conversations between you and the computer. Imagine that you could ask your computer, "What product generated the most sales last year?" Your computer, equipped with a voice synthesizer, could respond, "Product X." Dragon NaturallySpeaking Solutions is an example of NLP. Research continues in this field because of the promising results so far. Programming languages used for Internet programming and Web development include ActiveX, C++, Java, JavaScript, Perl, Python, PHP, Visual Basic, and Extensible Stylesheet Language (XSL). The most important Web development languages are Hypertext Markup Language (HTML) and eXtensible Markup Language (XML). Both languages are markup languages, not full-featured programming languages.

The 10 best and most popular programming languages in 2021 included (1) Python, (2) Java, (3) JavaScript, (4) C#, (5) PHP, (6) C/C++, (7) R, (8) Typescript, (9) Swift, and (10) Objective-C.[48]

2-9 Object-Oriented Programming: A Quick Overview

Most popular programming languages in use today, such as Java, Ruby, Swift, C#, and Visual Basic, are based on a methodology called **object-oriented programming (OOP)**. This methodology is further discussed in Module 3 under "Object-Oriented Databases." It is increasingly being used for software and application development. An OOP language is organized around a system of objects that represent the real world, as opposed to a series of computational steps used in traditional languages. Simplicity and adaptability are among the key features of OOP.

Two important parts of an OOP language are objects and classes. An **object** is an item that contains both data and the procedures that read and manipulate it. Examples include a person, an event, or a transaction. A **class** defines the format of the object and the action that it performs. For example, an automobile is an example of a class that may include several different makes and models. Consider BMW as a make and the 3, 4, 5, 6, and 7 series as a model.

Abstraction, inheritance, polymorphism, and encapsulation are four key principles of OOP. *Abstraction* is used to handle complexity by hiding unnecessary details from the user. This principle looks at a problem from a higher level and then gets into detail in later stages of code development. *Inheritance* enables new objects to take on the properties of existing objects. This feature reduces application development time by using existing code. *Polymorphism* is the ability to process objects differently depending on their data type or class. As an example, this technique enables a programmer to define different shapes such as circles, rectangles, and triangles from a base class shape. *Encapsulation* means grouping related items into a single unit. This helps programmers handle more complex types of data, such as images and graphs. Each OOP language is tailored to a specific OS and programming environment. For example, Swift is mostly used for programming environment and apps development for macOS and iOS; C#, developed by Microsoft, is mostly used for Windows apps and Windows programming environment; and Java is used for cross-platform development.

Exhibit 2.4
Key principles of object-oriented programming

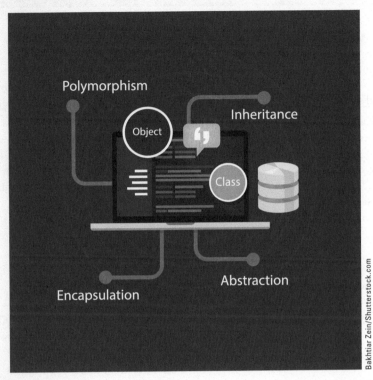

Bakhtiar Zein/Shutterstock.com

Exhibit 2.4 highlights the key principles of OOP. Major advantages of OOP are the following:

- Modularity—Code is written for specific and self-contained modules. This makes it easier to write code, modify it, and troubleshoot it. New features can easily be added as new modules without any impact on existing modules.

- Reuse of code for other purposes—Code written for one object can be easily modified by maintaining the major parts and applying them to another object.

- Effective problem solving—OOP languages allow the programmer to break down a program into small problems that a programmer can solve one module or one object at a time.

The upcoming Industry Connection highlights IBM and its most popular product areas.

Industry Connection: International Business Machines (IBM)[49]

IBM, one of the largest technology companies in the world, is active in almost every aspect of computing, including hardware, software, services, and collaboration tools such as groupware and e-collaboration. IBM has also been a leader in developing mainframe computers; its latest mainframe is the IBM System zEnterprise EC12. IBM's most popular product areas include the following:

Software: IBM offers software suites for all types of computers. Lotus, for example, includes features for e-mail, calendaring, and collaborative applications as well as business productivity software, much like Microsoft Office does. Tivoli, another software suite, has many features for asset and security management, backup and restore procedures, and optimization of storage systems and data management. IBM also offers several different types of software for business analytics.

Storage: IBM's storage devices include disk and tape systems, storage area networks, network-attached storage, hard disks, and microdrives. A microdrive is a 1-inch hard disk designed to fit in a CompactFlash Type II slot.

Servers: IBM offers a variety of servers, including UNIX and Linux servers, Intel-based servers, AMD-based servers, and more.

IBM is also active in e-commerce software, hardware, and security services, such as encryption technologies, firewalls, antivirus solutions, and cloud computing. In addition, IBM develops cognitive systems such as IBM Watson.

Module Summary

2-1   Define a computer system and its components. A computer is a machine that accepts data as input, processes data without human intervention by using stored instructions, and outputs information. A computer system consists of hardware and software.

2-2   Discuss the history of computer hardware and software. Computer hardware has gone through five generations: vacuum tube, transistors, integrated circuits, miniaturization, and parallel processing. Computer software has gone through five generations as well: machine language, assembly language, high-level language, fourth-generation language, and natural language processing.

2-3   Analyze the impact of the three factors distinguishing the computing power of computers. Computers draw their power from three factors that far exceed human capacities: speed, accuracy, and storage and retrieval capabilities.

2-4   Summarize the three basic computer operations. Computers can perform three basic tasks: arithmetic operations, logical operations, and storage and retrieval operations. All other tasks are performed using one or a combination of these operations.

2-5   Discuss the types of input, output, and memory devices. To use a computer and process data, three major components are needed: input (keyboard), output (printer), and memory devices (main memory and secondary memory).

2-6   Explain how computers are classified and their business applications. Usually, computers are classified based on cost, amount of memory, speed, and sophistication. Using these criteria, computers are classified as subnotebooks, notebooks, personal computers, minicomputers, mainframes, or supercomputers.

2-7   Apply knowledge of two major types of software and their use in a business setting. The two types can be classified broadly as system software and application software. For example, Microsoft Windows is the OS for most PCs and is system software. Application software is used to perform specialized tasks. Microsoft Excel, for example, is used for spreadsheet analyses and number-crunching tasks and is an example of application software.

2-8   List the five generations of computer languages. These are machine language, assembly language, high-level language, fourth-generation language, and natural language processing.

2-9   Define object-oriented programming. An object-oriented programming (OOP) language is organized around a system of objects that represent the real world, as opposed to a series of computational steps used in traditional languages. Simplicity and adaptability are among the key features of OOP. Two main parts of an OOP language include objects and classes.

Key Terms

- Application software
- Arithmetic logic unit (ALU)
- Assembly language
- Bus
- Cache RAM
- Central processing unit (CPU)
- Class
- Cloud storage
- Computer
- Control unit

- CPU case
- Disk drive
- Fifth-generation languages (5GLs)
- Fourth-generation languages (4GLs)
- High-level languages
- Input devices
- Machine language
- Magnetic disk
- Magnetic tape
- Main memory

- Motherboard
- Network-attached storage (NAS)
- Object
- Object-oriented programming (OOP)
- Operating system (OS)
- Output devices

- Random access memory (RAM)
- Read-only memory (ROM)
- Redundant array of independent disks (RAID)
- Secondary memory
- Server
- Storage area network (SAN)

Reviews and Discussions

1. Define a computer and its main components.
2. What are the five generations of computer hardware?
3. Computers derive their power from three factors. What are these three factors?
4. What are three basic computer operations?
5. List two examples apiece of input, output, and memory devices.
6. What are four classes of computers?
7. What is the difference between application software and system software?
8. What are four key principles of OOP?

Projects

1. A local law firm needs your advice. It currently has 20 PCs being used by its attorneys and staff, and it is debating whether to use Google Apps for Work or Office 365 as its productivity tools. Write a two-page paper that summarizes your recommendation. What are two advantages and two disadvantages of each choice? Which alternative is less expensive? What are two advantages of Office 365 over traditional Office?

2. Object-oriented programming (OOP) is increasingly being used for application and software development. After reading the information presented in this module and other sources, write a one-page paper that describes three advantages of OOP methodology. Reuse of code for other purposes is among the advantages of OOP. Explain how this is achieved. Also list four programming languages that are based on this methodology.

3. A classmate of yours is not sure whether to buy a PC or a tablet. Your classmate needs the device for schoolwork (mostly Microsoft Office), for Web access, and as an e-reader. After reading the information presented in this module and other sources, write a one-page paper that summarizes your recommendation to this fellow student. Also mention two choices that you consider as top of the line for each alternative.

4. IBM Watson has created a lot of excitement in the computing field. After reading the information presented in this module and other sources, write a one-page paper that summarizes three commercial applications of this platform. What are two advantages of using Watson compared to using humans in the medical field? What are two disadvantages? How can Watson be used as a trip-planning service?

5. Android and iOS are two major operating systems for smartphones and other mobile devices. After reading the information presented in this module and other sources, write a two-page paper that summarizes the key features of each OS. What are two advantages and two disadvantages of each? Which OS has a bigger market share and why?

6. Dragon NaturallySpeaking Solutions is an example of an NLP. After reading the information presented in this module and other sources, write a two-page paper that describes five commercial applications for this platform. Which businesses will benefit the most from this platform? What are two other products that compete with this software?

Module Quiz

1. Application software can be commercial software or software developed in-house; it is used to perform a variety of tasks on a personal computer. True or False?

2. Machine language is the first generation of computer languages and consists of a series of 0s and 1s representing data or instructions. True or False?

3. The arithmetic logic unit (ALU) performs only arithmetic operations. True or False?

4. Choose the wrong answer:
   a. The first generation of computers is identified by vacuum tubes.
   b. The second generation of computers is identified by transistors.
   c. The third generation of computers is identified by miniaturization.
   d. The fourth generation of computers is identified by VLSI, personal computers, and optical discs.

5. All of the following are among the advantages of object-oriented programming except:
   a. Modularity
   b. Reuse of code for other purposes
   c. Effective problem solving
   d. All of these choices

6. Choose the wrong answer:
   a. The first generation of computer languages is machine language.
   b. The second generation of computer languages is assembly language.
   c. The third generation of computer languages is high-level language.
   d. The fourth generation of computer languages is natural language processing.

Case Study 2-1
Become Your Own Banker and Financial Advisor
➤➤ Finance | Technology in Society | Application

Using one of the many financial apps (most of them are free) that are available for your tablet or smartphone these days, you can become your own banker. In fact, trips to the bank or even to an ATM could soon become a thing of the past. The new apps let you do all the functions that you could do on a bank's Web site, and more. For example, to deposit a check into your banking account, you can simply take a photograph of the front and back of the check, after which the app will ask you for the amount you want to deposit. Then you type the account number and press "OK" to complete the deposit. With the Mint app (mint.com) from Intuit, you can perform all sorts of analytics on your account. For example, you can establish a budget and keep track of expenses in various categories, such as food, gas, and groceries. Another app that offers similar services is HelloWallet (hellowallet.com).

Still other apps help you track and report work-related travel expenses. An example is an iPhone app called Quick-Shot. It allows you to take photos of your receipts, and the photos are automatically stored in an account on Dropbox, an Internet file-storage service.[50] Banks, brokerage firms, and other financial institutions have developed their own apps that simplify their customers' financial interactions with the institutions.

(Bloomicon/Shutterstock.com)

In addition, computers and robots are increasingly playing a role in the areas of finance and banking—for example, high-frequency trading in which bots account for up to 80 percent of the daily volume on the stock market and can buy and sell stocks in microseconds. Another growing application is the rise of the "robo-advisor." This is a method to automate the asset allocation of investments using a computer algorithm. When it comes to investing, a typical investor has three choices: do-it-yourself, a robo-advisor, or a financial advisor. Which option to choose depends on several factors such as the cost of the investment, age of the investor, amount of investment, risk tolerance, and knowledge of investing. According to research, using a robo-advisor is certainly a viable choice. The three largest robo-advisors by assets under management are Vanguard, Schwab Intelligent Portfolios, and Betterment. Some are fully automated, and some are run in human-assisted mode.[51]

Answer the following questions:

1. What are some examples of analytics that can be done using financial apps?
2. How are these new financial apps changing the banking industry? Are the new tools primarily coming from new entrants or longstanding companies?
3. What is a robo-advisor? Which factors should an investor consider before selecting an investing option?

Case Study 2-2
iPads: New Productivity Tools for Service Workers
➤➤ **Finance | Technology in Society | Application**

Cornell University's utilities department serves over 30,000 people in the campus community in Ithaca, New York. In the past, when there was an outage related to power, water, or steam (used for heating), the utility manager was contacted by phone to look into the problem and come up with a course of action to fix it. This usually caused some delays, as a manager might be off campus or busy with other things.

Those phone calls are still being made in some cases, but most utility personnel are now able to use their iPads to log on to the system and diagnose the problem—and even fix it remotely. They can also use their iPhones to log on to the system. The university issues iPads to all mechanics and technicians for the same reason.

The equipment used by Cornell University's utilities department comes from GE and has an iOS app for drilling down into the utility management system and analyzing the available data. The utility personnel have access to a Web app for analyses that are not suitable for the iOS app.

The Web app allows personnel to control the equipment and see more detailed information, such as the percentage of valves that are open.

The utility personnel can use the Web app to remotely control the utility management system from their browsers. Access is given through a virtual private network (discussed in Module 5) to increase the security of the system and to provide additional authentication. According to the university, the iPad provides easy access to key information anywhere and at any time.[52]

Answer the following questions:

1. What impact does this new technology have on outage reporting and response time?
2. What are the two apps that are being used by the utilities department?
3. How could this technology approach be used in other settings?

Module 3

Data and Business Intelligence

Learning Objectives

After studying this module, you should be able to…

3.1 Define a *database* and a *database management system*.

3.2 Explain logical database design and the relational database model.

3.3 Define the five components of a database management system.

3.4 Summarize three recent trends in database design and use.

3.5 Analyze the four major components and functions of a data warehouse and their use for business.

3.6 Describe the functions of a data mart.

3.7 Compare and contrast data lakes with data warehouses.

3.8 Describe the role of business analytics in the decision-making process.

3.9 Examine the advantages and challenges of big data and predictive analytics for a business.

3.10 Explain database marketing and its business applications.

3.11 Explain key features of Tableau and Power BI as two popular business intelligence and visualization platforms.

This module gives you an overview of databases and database management systems and their importance in information systems. You will learn about the types of data in a database, methods for accessing files, and physical and logical views of information. You will also review the most common data model, the relational model, and the major components of a database management system. This module also discusses recent trends in database use, including data-driven Web sites, distributed databases, and object-oriented databases. Next, the module provides an overview of data warehouses, data marts, and data lakes and their roles in generating business intelligence, then reviews business analytics and its role in gaining a competitive advantage. The module concludes with an overview of big data and its growing business applications and explains database marketing and its business applications.

> **In a database system, all files are integrated, meaning information can be linked.**

3-1 Databases

A **database** is a collection of related data that is stored in a central location or in multiple locations. You can think of it as being similar to a filing cabinet, in which data is organized and stored in drawers and file folders. As you can imagine, however, retrieving data from a database is much faster.

Although a database can consist of only a single file, it is usually a group of files. A university database, for example, might have files for students, staff, faculty, and courses. In a database, a file is a group of related records, and a record is a group of related fields. This structure is called a **data hierarchy**, as shown in Exhibit 3.1. In the university database example, fields consist of Social Security number, student name, and address. All the fields storing information for Mary Smith, for instance, constitute a record, and all three records in Exhibit 3.1 make up the student file.

In a database system, all files are integrated, meaning information can be linked. For example, you can retrieve the names of all students enrolled in Professor Thomas's MIS 480 course from the courses file or look up Professor Thomas's record to find out other courses he is teaching in a particular semester.

A database is a critical component of information systems because any type of analysis that is done is based on data available in the database. To make using databases more efficient, a **database management system (DBMS)** is used. A DBMS is software for creating, storing, maintaining, and accessing database files. Its major components are discussed in the "Components of a DBMS" section later in this module. If you are familiar with Microsoft Office software, you know that you use Word to create a document and Excel to create a spreadsheet. You can also use Access to create and modify a database, although it does not have as many features as other DBMSs.

For now, take a look at Exhibit 3.2, which shows how users, the DBMS, and the database interact. The user issues a request, and the DBMS searches the database and returns the information to the user.

In the past, data was stored in a series of

> A **database** is a collection of related data that is stored in a central location or in multiple locations.
>
> A **data hierarchy** is the structure and organization of data, which involves fields, records, and files.
>
> A **database management system (DBMS)** is software for creating, storing, maintaining, and accessing database files. A DBMS makes using databases more efficient.

Exhibit 3.1
Data hierarchy

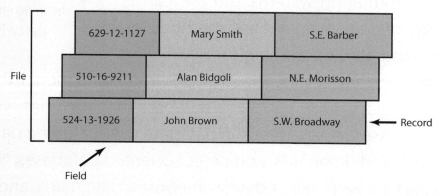

files that were called "flat files" because they were not arranged in a hierarchy, and there was no relationship among these files. The problem with this flat file organization was that the same data could be stored in more than one file, creating data redundancy. For example, in a customer database, a customer's name might be stored in more than one table. This duplication takes up unnecessary storage space and can make retrieving data inefficient. Updating a flat file system can be time-consuming and inefficient. Data might not be updated in all files consistently, resulting in conflicting reports generated from these files.

In summary, a database has the following advantages over a flat file system:

- More information can be generated from the same data.
- Complex requests can be handled more easily.
- Data redundancy is eliminated or minimized.
- Programs and data are independent, so more than one program can use the same data.
- Data management is improved.
- A variety of relationships among data can be easily maintained.
- More sophisticated security measures can be used.
- Storage space is reduced.

3-1a Types of Data in a Database

As you learned in Module 1, to generate business intelligence (BI), the database component of an information system needs access to two types of data: internal and external. Internal data is collected from within an organization and can include transaction records, sales records, personnel records, and so forth. An organization might use internal data on customers' past purchases to generate BI about future buying patterns, for example. Internal data is usually stored in the organization's internal databases and can be used by functional information systems.

Collecting and using external data can be more challenging. External data comes from a variety of sources and is often stored in a data warehouse (discussed later in the module).

Exhibit 3.2
Interaction between the user, DBMS, and database

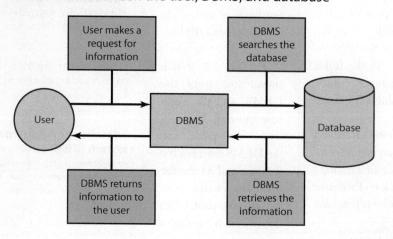

BI in Action: Law Enforcement

➤ Finance | Technology in Society | Application | Social and Ethical Issues

Business intelligence (BI) is used in law enforcement as well as in the business world. In Richmond, Virginia, data entered into the police department's information system includes crime reports from the past five years, records of 911 phone calls, details about weather patterns, and information about special events. The system generates BI reports that help pinpoint crime patterns and are useful for personnel deployment, among other purposes. The system has increased public safety, reduced 911 calls, and helped management make better use of Richmond's 750 officers.

(iStock.com/avid_creative)

Recently, the department refined its reports by separating violent crimes into robberies, rapes, and homicides to help them discover patterns for certain types of crime. For example, the department discovered that Hispanic workers were often robbed on paydays. By entering workers' paydays into the system and looking at robbery patterns, law enforcement officers were able to identify days and locations on which incidents were likely to occur. Moving additional officers into targeted areas on paydays has reduced the number of robberies.[1]

Questions and Discussions

1. What are the applications of the BI reports at the Richmond, Virginia, police department?
2. How might the BI reports impact how the department leverages resources and influences outcomes?

The following are examples of sources for external data:

- Competitors, customers, and suppliers
- Distribution networks
- Economic indicators (e.g., the consumer price index)
- Government regulations
- Labor and population statistics
- Tax records

In the "Data Warehouses" section later in this module, you will learn how information from external data sources is used to conduct analyses and generate reports for BI. The information box "BI in Action: Law Enforcement" discusses how BI is used in other fields—in this case, law enforcement.

3-1b Methods for Accessing Files

In a database, files are accessed by using a sequential, random, or indexed sequential method. In a **sequential access file structure**, records in files are organized and processed in numerical or sequential order, typically the order in which they were entered. Records are organized based on what is known as a "primary key," discussed later in this module, such as Social Security numbers or account numbers. For example, to access record number 10, records 1 through 9 must be read first. This type of access method is effective when a large number of records are processed less frequently, perhaps on a quarterly or yearly basis. Because access speed usually is not critical, these records are typically stored on magnetic tape. Normally, a sequential file structure is used for backup and archive files because they rarely need updating.

In a **random access file structure**, records can be accessed in any order, regardless of their

In a **sequential access file structure**, records in files are organized and processed in numerical or sequential order, typically the order in which they were entered.

In a **random access file structure**, records can be accessed in any order, regardless of their physical locations in storage media. This method of access is fast and very effective when a small number of records needs to be processed daily or weekly.

With the **indexed sequential access method (ISAM)**, records can be accessed sequentially or randomly, depending on the number being accessed. For a small number, random access is used, and for a large number, sequential access is used.

The **physical view** involves how data is stored on and retrieved from storage media, such as hard disks or magnetic tapes.

The **logical view** involves how information appears to users and how it can be organized and retrieved.

A **data model** determines how data is created, represented, organized, and maintained. It usually contains a data structure, operations, and integrity rules.

In a **hierarchical model**, the relationships between records form a treelike structure (hierarchy). Records are called *nodes*, and relationships between records are called *branches*. The node at the top is called the *root*, and every other node (called a *child*) has a *parent*. Nodes with the same parents are called *twins* or *siblings*.

physical locations in storage media. This method of access is fast and very effective when a small number of records needs to be processed daily or weekly. To achieve this speed, records are often stored on magnetic disks. Disks are random access devices, whereas tapes are sequential access devices.

With the **indexed sequential access method (ISAM)**, records can be accessed sequentially or randomly, depending on the number being accessed. For a small number, random access is used, and for a large number, sequential access is used. This file structure is similar to a book index that lists page numbers where you can find certain topics. The advantage of this method is that both types of access can be used, depending on the situation and the user's needs.[2]

ISAM, as the name suggests, uses an index structure and has two parts: the indexed value and a pointer to the disk location of the record matching the indexed value. Retrieving a record requires at least two disk accesses: once for the index structure and once for the actual record. Because every record needs to be indexed, if the file contains a huge number of records, the index is also quite large. Therefore, an index is more useful when the number of records is small. Access speed with this method is fast, so it is recommended when records must be accessed frequently. This advice, however, was more applicable when processors were slow and memory and storage were expensive. Given the speed and low storage costs of today's computers, the number of records might not be as important, meaning more records could be accessed and processed with this method.

3-2 Logical Database Design

Before designing a database, you need to know the two ways information is viewed in a database. The **physical view** involves how data is stored on and retrieved from storage media, such as hard disks or magnetic tapes. For each database, there is only one physical view of data. The **logical view** involves how information appears to users and how it can be organized and retrieved. There can be more than one logical view of data, depending on the user. For example, marketing executives might want to see data organized by top-selling products in a specific region; the finance officer might need to see data organized by cost of raw materials for each product.

The first step in database design is defining a **data model**, which determines how data is created, represented, organized, and maintained. A data model usually includes these three components:

- *Data structure*—Describes how data is organized and the relationship among records
- *Operations*—Describe methods, calculations, and so forth that can be performed on data, such as updating and querying data
- *Integrity rules*—Define the boundaries of a database, such as maximum and minimum values allowed for a field, constraints (limits on what type of data can be stored in a field), and access methods

Many data models are used. The most common, the relational model, is described in the next section, and you learn about the object-oriented model later in the module, in the "Object-Oriented Databases" section. Two other common data models are hierarchical and network, although they are not used as much now.

In a **hierarchical model**, as shown in Exhibit 3.3, the relationships among records form a treelike structure (hierarchy). Records are called *nodes*, and relationships among records are called *branches*. The node at the top is called the *root*, and every other node (called a *child*) has a *parent*. Nodes with the same parents are called *twins* or *siblings*. In Exhibit 3.3, the root node is a supplier, which provides three product lines, each considered a sibling of the other two. Each product line has categories of products, and each category has specific products. (The categories and specific products are also siblings of each other.) For example, Supplier A supplies three product lines: soap, shampoo, and toothpaste. The toothpaste product line has two categories (P6 and P7): whitening and cavity-fighting toothpaste. The P7 category has three specific cavity-fighting products: S, T, and U.

Exhibit 3.3
A hierarchical model

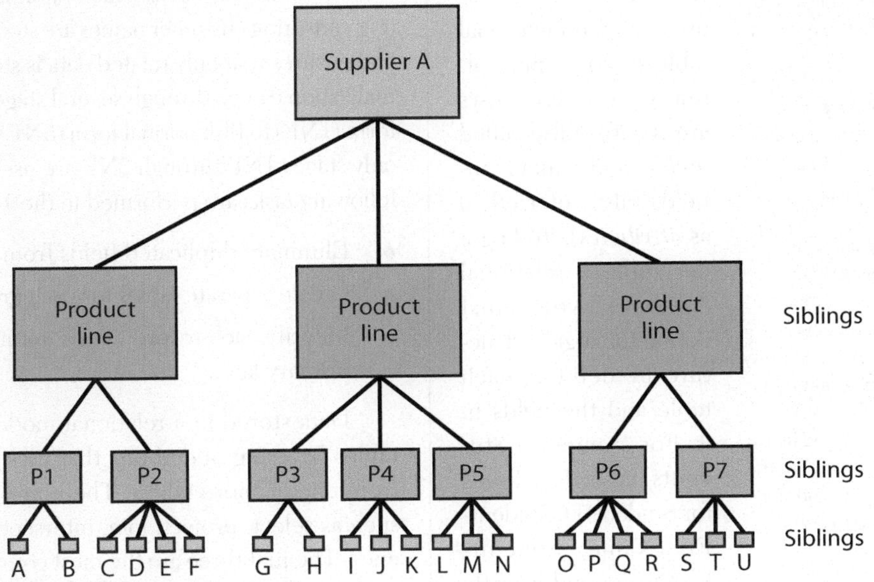

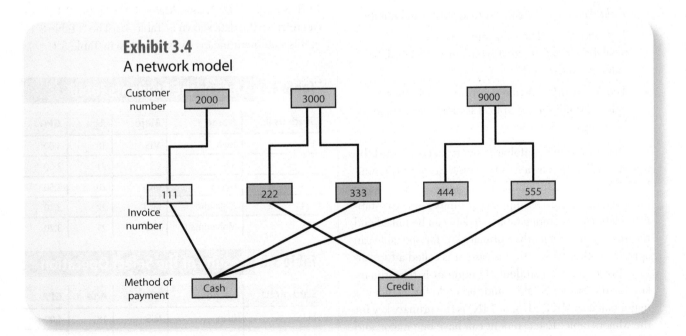

The **network model** is similar to the hierarchical model, but records are organized differently, as shown in Exhibit 3.4. This example links an invoice number, customer number, and method of payment. For example, invoice 111 belongs to customer 2000, who paid with cash. Unlike the hierarchical model, each record in the network model can have multiple parent and child records. For example, in Exhibit 3.4, a customer can have several invoices, and an invoice can be paid by more than one method.

> The **network model** is similar to the hierarchical model, but records are organized differently. Unlike the hierarchical model, each record in the network model can have multiple parent and child records.

Exhibit 3.4
A network model

A **relational model** uses a two-dimensional table of rows and columns of data. Rows are records (also called tuples), and columns are fields (also referred to as attributes).

The **data dictionary** stores definitions, such as data types for fields, default values, and validation rules for data in each field.

A **primary key** uniquely identifies every record in a relational database. Examples include student ID numbers, account numbers, Social Security numbers, and invoice numbers.

A **foreign key** is a field in a relational table that matches the primary key column of another table. It can be used to cross-reference tables.

Normalization improves database efficiency by eliminating redundant data and ensuring that only related data is stored in a table.

3-2a The Relational Model

A **relational model** uses a two-dimensional table of rows and columns of data. Rows are records (also called *tuples*), and columns are fields (also referred to as *attributes*). To begin designing a relational database, you must define the logical structure by defining each table and the fields in it. For example, a Students table has fields for StudentID, StudentFirstName, StudentLastName, and so forth. The collection of these definitions is stored in the data dictionary. The **data dictionary** can also store other definitions, such as data types for fields, default values for fields, and validation rules for data in each field, as described in the following list:

- *Field name*—Student name, admission date, age, and major
- *Field data type*—Character (text), date, and number
- *Default value*—The value entered if none is available; for example, if no major is declared, the value is "undecided."
- *Validation rule*—A rule determining whether a value is valid; for example, a student's age cannot be a negative number.

In a relational database, every record must be uniquely identified by a **primary key**. Student ID numbers, Social Security numbers, account numbers, and invoice numbers are examples of primary keys. To establish relationships among tables so data can be linked and retrieved more efficiently, a primary key for one table can appear in other tables. In this case, it is called a **foreign key**. For example, a student ID number is the primary key for the Students table, and the code for a student's major (such as MKT, MIS, or FIN) is the primary key for the Majors table. Each student can have one major, and a number of students can be enrolled in each major. The primary key of the Majors table is a foreign key in the Students table.

To improve database efficiency, a process called **normalization** is used, which eliminates redundant data (e.g., ensuring customer names are stored in only one table) and ensures that only related data is stored in a table. Normalization can go through several stages, from first normal form (1NF) to fifth normal form (5NF). Typically, however, only stages 1NF through 3NF are used. For example, the following tasks are performed in the 1NF stage:

- Eliminate duplicated fields from the same table.
- Create separate tables for each group of related data.
- Identify each record with a unique field (the primary key).

Data stored in a relational model is retrieved from tables by using operations that pick and combine data from one or more tables. There are several operations, such as select, project, join, intersect, union, and difference. The first three are the most commonly used and are explained in the following paragraphs.

A select operation searches data in a table and retrieves records based on certain criteria (also called *conditions*). Table 3.1 shows data stored in the Students table. Using the select operation "Major=MIS," you can generate a list of only the students majoring in MIS, as Table 3.2 shows.

A project operation pares down a table by eliminating columns (fields) according to certain criteria. For example, say you need a list of students but do not want to include their ages. Using the project operation "PROJECT Student ID#, Name, Major, GPA (Table 3.1)," you can retrieve the data shown in Table 3.3. The "(Table 3.1)" in this statement means to use the data in Table 3.1.

Table 3.1 Data in the Students Table

Student ID	Name	Major	Age	GPA
111	Juan	MIS	18	4.00
222	Sue	CS	21	3.60
333	Debra	MGT	20	3.50
444	Alejandro	MKT	22	3.40
555	Mohammad	MIS	21	3.70

Table 3.2 Results of the Select Operation

Student ID	Name	Major	Age	GPA
111	Juan	MIS	18	4.00
555	Mohammad	MIS	21	3.70

Table 3.3   Results of the Project Operation

Student ID	Name	Major	GPA
111	Juan	MIS	4.00
222	Sue	CS	3.60
333	Debra	MGT	3.50
444	Alejandro	MKT	3.40
555	Mohammad	MIS	3.70

A join operation combines two tables based on a common field (e.g., the primary key in the first table and the foreign key in the second table). Table 3.4 shows data in the Customers table, and Table 3.5 shows data in the Invoices table. The Customer number is the primary key for the Customers table and is a foreign key in the Invoices table; the Invoice number is the primary key for the Invoices table. Table 3.6 shows the table resulting from joining these two tables.

Table 3.4   Customers Table

Customer	Name	Address
2000	ABC	Broadway
3000	XYZ	Jefferson
9000	TRY	Madison

Table 3.5   Invoices Table

Invoice	Customer	Amount	Payment
1110	2000	$2000.00	Cash
2220	3000	$4000.00	Credit
3330	3000	$1500.00	Cash
4440	9000	$6400.00	Cash
5550	9000	$7000.00	Credit

Table 3.6   Joining the Invoices and Customers Tables

Invoice	Customer	Amount	Payment	Name	Address
1110	2000	$2000.00	Cash	ABC	Broadway
2220	3000	$4000.00	Credit	XYZ	Jefferson
3330	3000	$1500.00	Cash	XYZ	Jefferson
4440	9000	$6400.00	Cash	TRY	Madison
5550	9000	$7000.00	Credit	TRY	Madison

Now that you have learned about the components of a database and a common data model, you can examine the software used to manage databases.

3-3 Components of a DBMS

DBMS software includes these components, as discussed in the following sections:

- Database engine
- Data definition
- Data manipulation
- Application generation
- Data administration

3-3a Database Engine

A database engine, the heart of DBMS software, is responsible for data storage, manipulation, and retrieval. It converts logical requests from users into their physical equivalents (e.g., reports) by interacting with other components of the DBMS (usually the data manipulation component). For example, say a marketing manager wants to see a list of the top three salespeople in the Southeast region (a logical request). The database engine interacts with the data manipulation component to find where these three names are stored and displays them on screen or in a printout (the physical equivalent). Because more than one logical view of data is possible, the database engine can retrieve and return data to users in many different ways.

3-3b Data Definition

The data definition component is used to create and maintain the data dictionary and define the structure of files in a database. Any changes to a database's structure, such as adding a field, deleting a field, changing a field's size, or changing the data type stored in a field, are made with this component.

3-3c Data Manipulation

The data manipulation component is used to add, delete, modify, and retrieve records from a database. Typically, a query language is used for this component. Many query languages are available, but Structured Query Language (SQL) and query by example (QBE) are two of the most widely used.

Structured Query Language (SQL) is a standard fourth-generation query language used by many DBMS packages, such as Oracle Database 12 and Microsoft SQL Server. SQL consists of several keywords that specify actions to take. The basic format of an SQL query is as follows:

SELECT *field* FROM *table or file* WHERE *conditions*

After the SELECT keyword, you list the fields you want to retrieve. After FROM, you list the tables or files from where the data is retrieved, and after WHERE, you list conditions (criteria) for retrieving the data. The following example retrieves the name, Social Security number, title, gender, and salary from the Employee

Graph Databases Move Relational Databases One Step Forward

➤ Finance | Technology in Society | Application

A **graph database** is a database that uses graph structures for query operation with nodes, edges, and properties to represent and store data. A typical relational database stores entities and their properties in tables, whereas a graph database also stores relations between entities. It focuses on connections between entities and navigates and manages connected data. This enables database operations across different but related entities. In the healthcare industry in particular, this has proven to be very helpful, as doctors may belong to multiple healthcare providers, diseases may have multiple symptoms, and there may be multiple relationships among organizations such as insurance companies, hospitals, and different employers. Healthcare providers such as Curaspan Health Group, GoodStart Genetics, SharePractice, and Janssen Pharmaceuticals use graph databases for patient management, drug research, genomics, clinical trials, and marketing.[3]

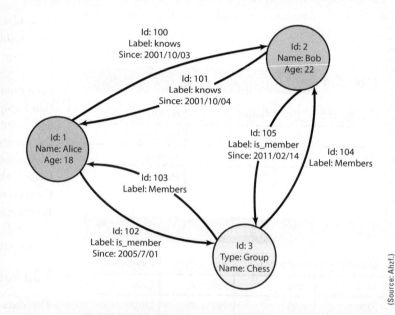

(Source: Ahzf.)

Online dating Web sites also use graph databases, and they believe this technology has increased the accuracy of the recommendations provided. The use of a graph database is beneficial because people in an extended social network—friends of friends and even friends of friends of friends—are much more likely to go on a date together than two complete strangers are.[4]

Social media companies such as LinkedIn, Facebook, and Twitter are also prime users of graph databases. In addition, companies such as Walmart, eBay, Lufthansa, and Deutsche Telekom use this technology. Problem areas such as fraud detection and asset management are also good candidates for graph databases because they provide the opportunity to better understand the connections between data and deriving meaning from the links among data items. Significant insights can be drawn from the existing data simply by reframing the problem and looking at it in a new way in a graph format.[5]

Major providers of graph databases include Neo Technology, GraphBase, HyperGraphDB, and Oracle Spatial and Graph.[6]

Questions and Discussions

1. What is the difference between a relational database and a graph database?
2. Which businesses benefit the most from graph databases?

and Payroll tables for all employees with the job title of engineer:

SELECT NAME, SSN, TITLE, GENDER, SALARY

FROM EMPLOYEE, PAYROLL

WHERE EMPLOYEE.SSN = PAYROLL.SSN AND TITLE = "ENGINEER"

> A database engine, the heart of DBMS software, is responsible for data storage, manipulation, and retrieval.

This query means that data in the NAME, SSN, TITLE, GENDER, and SALARY fields from the two tables EMPLOYEE and PAYROLL should be retrieved. Line 3 indicates on which field the EMPLOYEE and PAYROLL tables are linked (the SSN field) and specifies a condition for displaying data: only employees who are engineers. You can add many other conditions to SQL statements by using AND, OR, and NOT operators (discussed next).

With **query by example (QBE)**, you request data from a database by constructing a statement made up of query forms. With current graphical databases, you simply click to select query forms instead of having to remember keywords, as you do with SQL. You can add AND, OR, and NOT operators to the QBE form to fine-tune the query:

- *AND*—Means that all conditions must be met. For example, "Major = MIS AND GPA> 3.8" means a student must be majoring in MIS and have a GPA higher than 3.8 to be retrieved.

- *OR*—Means only one of the conditions must be met. For example, "Major = MIS OR GPA> 3.8" means that if a student has a GPA higher than 3.8, the student can be majoring in another field, such as accounting. Alternatively, if a student is majoring in MIS, the student can have a GPA of 3.8 or lower.

- *NOT*—Searches for records that do not meet the condition. For example, "Major NOT ACC" retrieves all students except accounting majors.

3-3d Application Generation

In the application generation component, a database is used to design elements of an application, such as data entry screens, interactive menus, and interfaces with other programming languages. These applications, for example, might be used to create a form or generate a report. If you are designing an order entry application for users, you could use the application generation component to create a menu system that makes the application easier to use. Typically, IT professionals and database administrators use this component.

3-3e Data Administration

The data administration component, also used by IT professionals and database administrators, is useful for tasks such as backup and recovery, security, and change management. In addition, this component is used to determine who has permission to perform certain functions, often summarized as **create, read, update, and delete (CRUD)**.

In large organizations, database design and management is handled by the **database administrator (DBA)**, although with complex databases this task is sometimes handled by an entire department. The DBA's responsibilities include the following:

- Designing and setting up a database
- Establishing security measures to determine users' access rights
- Developing recovery procedures in case data is lost or corrupted
- Evaluating database performance
- Adding and fine-tuning database functions

The "Graph Databases Move Relational Databases One Step Forward" box highlights graph databases that are more suitable for certain applications than the relational model.

> With **query by example (QBE)**, you request data from a database by constructing a statement made up of query forms. With current graphical databases, you simply click to select query forms instead of having to remember keywords, as you do with SQL. You can add AND, OR, and NOT operators to the QBE form to fine-tune the query.
>
> **Create, read, update, and delete (CRUD)** refers to a range of functions and the users who data administrators determine have permission to perform those functions.
>
> **Database administrators (DBA)** in large organizations design and set up databases, establish security measures, develop recovery procedures, evaluate database performance, and add and fine-tune database functions.

3-4 Recent Trends in Database Design and Use

Recent trends in database design and use include data-driven Web sites, natural language processing, distributed databases, and object-oriented databases. In addition to these trends, advances in artificial intelligence and natural language processing will have an impact on database design and use, such as improving user interfaces.[7] Module 13 covers natural language processing, and the other trends are discussed in the following sections.

3-4a Data-Driven Web Sites

With the popularity of e-commerce applications, data-driven Web sites are used more widely to provide dynamic content. A **data-driven Web site** acts as an interface to a database, retrieving data for users and allowing users to enter data in the database. Without this feature, Web site designers must edit the HTML code every time a Web site's data contents change. This type of site is called a "static" Web site. A data-driven Web site, on the other hand, changes automatically because it retrieves content from external dynamic data sources, such as MySQL, Microsoft SQL Server, Microsoft Access, Oracle, IBM DB2, and other databases.

A data-driven Web site improves access to information so users' experiences are more interactive, and it reduces the support and overhead needed to maintain static Web sites. A well-designed data-driven Web site is easier to maintain because most content changes require no change to the HTML code. Instead, changes are made to the data source, and the Web site adjusts automatically to reflect these changes. With a data-driven Web site, users can get more current information from a variety of data sources. Data-driven Web sites are useful for the following applications, among others:

- E-commerce sites that need frequent updates
- News sites that need regular updating of content
- Forums and discussion groups
- Subscription services, such as newsletters

3-4b Distributed Databases

The database types discussed so far use a central database for all users of an information system. However, in some situations, a **distributed database management system (DDBMS)**, in which data is stored on multiple servers placed throughout an organization, is preferable. Here are some of the reasons an organization would choose a distributed database:[8]

- The design better reflects the organization's structure. For example, an organization with several branch offices might find a distributed database more suitable because it allows faster local queries and can reduce network traffic.
- Local storage of data decreases response time but increases communication costs.
- Distributing data among multiple sites minimizes the effects of computer failures. If one database server goes down, it does not affect the entire organization.
- The number of users of an information system is not limited by one computer's capacity or processing power.
- Several small integrated systems might cost less than one large server.
- Accessing one central database server could increase communication costs for remote users. Storing some data at remote sites can help reduce these costs.
- Distributed processing, which includes database design, is used more widely now and is often more responsive to users' needs than centralized processing.
- Most important, a distributed database is not limited by the data's physical location.

There are three approaches to setting up a DDBMS, although these approaches can be combined:[9]

- *Fragmentation*—The **fragmentation** approach addresses how tables are divided among multiple locations. Horizontal fragmentation breaks a table into rows, storing all fields (columns) in different locations. Vertical fragmentation stores a subset of columns in different locations. Mixed fragmentation, which combines vertical and horizontal fragmentation, stores only site-specific

---

A **data-driven Web site** acts as an interface to a database, retrieving data for users and allowing users to enter data in the database.

A **distributed database management system (DDBMS)** stores data on multiple servers throughout an organization.

The **fragmentation** approach to a distributed DBMS addresses how tables are divided among multiple locations. There are three variations: horizontal, vertical, and mixed.

data in each location. If data from other sites is needed, the DDBMS retrieves it.

- *Replication*—With the **replication** approach, each site stores a copy of data in the organization's database. Although this method can increase costs, it also increases availability of data, and each site's copy can be used as a backup for other sites.

- *Allocation*—The **allocation** approach combines fragmentation and replication. Generally, each site stores the data it uses most often. This method improves response time for local users (those in the same location as the database storage facilities).

Security issues are more challenging in a distributed database because it has multiple access points from both inside and outside the organization. Security policies, scope of user access, and user privileges must be clearly defined, and authorized users must be identified. Distributed database designers should also keep in mind that distributed processing is not suitable for every situation, such as a company that has all its departments in one location.

3-4c Object-Oriented Databases

The relational model discussed previously is designed to handle homogenous data organized in a field-and-record format. Including different types of data, such as multimedia files, can be difficult, however. In addition, a relational database has a simple structure: Relationships between tables are based on a common value (the key). Representing more complex data relationships is sometimes not possible with a relational database.

To address these problems, **object-oriented databases** were developed. Like object-oriented programming, this data model represents real-world entities with database objects. An object consists of attributes (characteristics describing an entity) and methods (operations or calculations) that can be performed on the object's data. For example, as shown in Exhibit 3.5, a real-world car can be represented by an object in the Vehicle class. Objects in this class have attributes of year, make, model, and license number, for example. You can then use methods to work with data in a Vehicle object, such as the Add-Vehicle method to add a car to the database. Thinking of classes as categories or types of objects can be helpful.

Grouping objects along with their attributes and methods into a class is called **encapsulation**, which essentially means grouping related items into a single unit. Encapsulation assists in the handling of more complex types of data, such as images and graphs. Object-oriented databases can also use **inheritance**, which means new objects can be created faster and more easily by entering new data in

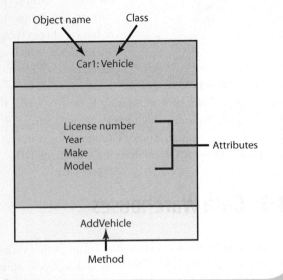

Exhibit 3.5
Objects, classes, attributes, and methods

attributes. For example, you can add a BMW as a Vehicle object by having it inherit attributes and methods of the Vehicle class. You do not have to redefine an object—in other words, specifying all its attributes and methods— every time you want to add a new one.

This data model expands on the relational model by supporting more complex data management, so modeling real-world problems is easier. In addition, object-oriented databases can handle storing and manipulating all types of multimedia as well as numbers and characters. Being able to handle many file types is useful in many fields. In the medical field, for example, doctors need to access X-ray images and graphs of vital signs in addition to patient histories consisting of text and numbers.

The **replication** approach to a distributed DBMS has each site store a copy of the data in the organization's database.

The **allocation** approach to a distributed DBMS combines fragmentation and replication, with each site storing the data it uses most often.

In **object-oriented databases**, both data and their relationships are contained in a single object. An object consists of attributes and methods that can be performed on the object's data.

Encapsulation refers to the grouping of various objects along with their attributes and methods into a class—in other words, grouping related items into a single unit. This assists in the handling of more complex types of data, such as images and graphs.

Inheritance refers to new objects being created faster and more easily by entering new data in attributes.

> A **data warehouse** is a collection of data from a variety of sources used to support decision-making applications and generate business intelligence.

In contrast to the query languages used to interact with a relational database, interaction with an object-oriented database takes place via methods, which are called by sending a message to an object. Messages are usually generated by an event of some kind, such as pressing Enter or clicking the mouse button. Typically, a high-level language such as C++ is used to create methods. Some examples of object-oriented DBMSs are Progress ObjectStore and Objectivity/DB.

3-5 Data Warehouses

A **data warehouse** is a collection of data from a variety of sources used to support decision-making applications and generate business intelligence.[10] Data warehouses store multidimensional data, so they are sometimes called *hypercubes*. Typically, data in a data warehouse is described as having the following characteristics, in contrast to data in a database:

- *Subject oriented*—Focused on a specific area, such as the home-improvement industry or a university, whereas data in a database is transaction/function-oriented

- *Integrated*—Comes from a variety of sources, whereas data in a database usually does not

- *Time variant*—Categorized based on time, such as historical information, whereas data in a database only keeps recent activity in memory

- *Type of data*—Captures aggregated data, whereas data in a database captures raw transaction data

- *Purpose*—Used for analytical purposes, whereas data in a database is used for capturing and managing transactions

Data Warehouse Applications at Marriott International

▶ Finance | Technology in Society | Application

Marriott International, one of the world's largest hospitality companies, operates over 7,000 properties under 30 hotel brands in 130 countries and territories.[11] The company, which encompasses 30 different brands, needed a campaign management tool to help it gather information from its various regions, brands, and franchises in order to effectively communicate and engage with customers.

To help achieve this goal, Marriott built a data warehouse that provides sales and marketing managers with critical information about its customers in a timely manner. The system collects all sorts of data

(Gorodenkoff/Shutterstock.com)

about the customers. Using this data, statistical models, and various algorithms, the system is able to present offers to individual customers based on their past preferences and their transaction histories. Marriott then knows exactly which service has been used by each customer. The system also provides the opportunity to tailor each offer to an individual customer. The new system includes Web-based tools for regional marketing managers and has enabled them to reduce campaign development from six weeks to two days. By using the new system, Marriott has exceeded its revenue goals, and it has been able to communicate more effectively with its customers by conducting more targeted communication.[12]

Questions and Discussions

1. What are two applications of the data warehouse at Marriott International?
2. How might this data give Marriott International a competitive advantage?

Designing and implementing a data warehouse is a complex task, but specific software is available to help. Oracle, Microsoft, Teradata, SAS, and Hewlett-Packard are market leaders in data-warehousing platforms. The "Data Warehouse Applications at Marriott International" box discusses how a data warehouse was used at Marriott International.

Exhibit 3.6 shows a data warehouse configuration with four major components: input; extraction, transformation, and loading (ETL); storage; and output. These components are explained in the following sections.

3-5a Input

Data can come from a variety of sources, including external data sources, databases, transaction files, enterprise resource planning (ERP) systems, and customer relationship management (CRM) systems. ERP systems collect, integrate, and process data that can be used by all functional areas in an organization. CRM systems collect and process customer data to provide information for improving customer service. (ERP and CRM systems are discussed in Module 11.) Together, these data sources provide the input a data warehouse needs to perform analyses and generate reports.

3-5b ETL

Extraction, transformation, and loading (ETL) refers to the processes used in a data warehouse. Extraction means collecting data from a variety of sources and converting it into a format that can be used in transformation processing. The extraction process can also parse data (divide it into pieces) to make sure it meets the data warehouse's structural needs. For example, parsing can be used to separate the street number, street name, city, and state in an address if you want to find out how many customers live in a particular region of a city.

Transformation processing is done to make sure data meets the data warehouse's needs. Its tasks include the following:

- Selecting only certain columns or rows to load
- Translating coded values, such as replacing *Yes* with *1* and *No* with *2*
- Performing select, project, and join operations on data

> **Extraction, transformation, and loading (ETL)** refers to the processes used in a data warehouse. It includes extracting data from outside sources, transforming it to fit operational needs, and loading it into the end target (database or data warehouse).

Exhibit 3.6
A data warehouse configuration

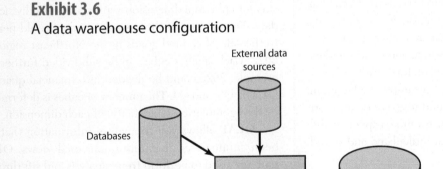

- Sorting and filtering data
- Aggregating and summarizing data before loading it in the data warehouse

Loading is the process of transferring data to the data warehouse. Depending on the organization's needs and the data warehouse's storage capacity, loading might overwrite existing data or add collected data to existing data.

3-5c Storage

Collected information is organized in a data warehouse as raw data, summary data, or metadata. Raw data is information in its original form. Summary data gives users subtotals of various categories, which can be useful. For example, sales data for a company's southern regions can be added and represented by one summary number. However, maintaining both raw data (disaggregated data) and summary data (aggregated data) is a good idea for decision-making purposes, as you learned in Module 1. Metadata is information about data—its content, quality, condition, origin, and other characteristics. Metadata tells users how, when, and by whom data was collected and how data has been formatted and converted into its present form. For example, metadata in a financial database could be used to generate a report for shareholders explaining how revenue, expenses, and profits from sales transactions are calculated and stored in the data warehouse.

3-5d Output

As Exhibit 3.6 shows, a data warehouse supports different types of analysis and generates reports for decision making. The databases discussed so far support **online transaction processing (OLTP)** to generate reports such as the following:[13]

- Which product generated the highest sales last month?

> **When Netflix recommends movies to you based on your viewing history, it is using information generated by data-mining tools.**

- Which region generated the lowest sales last month?
- Which salespersons increased sales by more than 30 percent last quarter?

Data warehouses, however, use online analytical processing and data-mining analysis to generate reports. These are discussed in the following sections.

Online Analytical Processing

Online analytical processing (OLAP), unlike OLTP, is used to quickly answer multidimensional analytical queries, thereby generating business intelligence. It uses multiple sources of information and provides multidimensional analysis, such as viewing data based on time, product, and location. For example, if you wanted to find out how Product X performed in the Northwest region during the previous quarter, you could use OLAP. Sometimes, this analysis is called "slicing and dicing data." In other words, OLAP breaks the entire body of data down into smaller parts or examines it from different viewpoints so that the user can understand it better. The hypercube in Exhibit 3.7 can be sliced in different directions. You can think of this hypercube as a multidimensional spreadsheet, with each side representing a dimension, such as a region ("Geography" in Exhibit 3.7). The advantage of a hypercube is that it enables fast manipulations and calculations. In the hypercube in Exhibit 3.7, each smaller cube in a dimension represents a subdivision of data. Data in one of these smaller cubes could pertain to the sale of canned goods in the Northeast region in 2022. Each smaller cube can be subdivided further; for example, 2022 could be divided into financial quarters: Q1, Q2, Q3, and Q4. The number of cubes is determined by the "granularity" (specificity) of each dimension.

OLAP allows you to analyze information that has been summarized in multidimensional views. OLAP tools are used to perform trend analysis and sift through massive amounts of statistics to find specific information. These tools usually have a "drill-down" feature for accessing multilayer information. For example, an OLAP tool might access the first layer of information to generate a report on sales performance in a company's eight regions. If a marketing executive is interested in more information on the Northwest region, the OLAP tool can access the next layer of information for a more

Exhibit 3.7
Slicing and dicing data

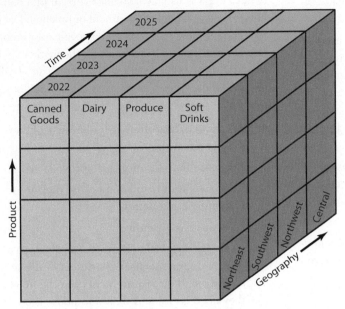

detailed analysis. OLAP tools are also capable of "drilling up," proceeding from the smallest unit of data to higher levels. For example, an OLAP tool might examine sales data for each region and then drill up to generate sales performance reports for the entire company.

Data-Mining Analysis

Data-mining analysis is used to discover patterns and relationships. For example, data-mining tools can be used to examine point-of-sale data to generate reports on customers' purchase histories. Based on this information, a company could better target marketing promotions to certain customers. Similarly, a company could mine demographic data from comment or warranty cards and use it to develop products that appeal to a certain customer group, such as teenagers or women over the age of 30. When Netflix recommends movies to you based on your viewing history, it is using information generated by data-mining tools. Netflix awarded a $1 million prize to the team that devised the best algorithm for substantially improving the accuracy of its movie recommendations (*www.Netflix.com*). American Express conducts the same type of analysis to suggest products and services to cardholders based on their monthly expenditures—patterns discovered by using data-mining tools. The following are typical questions you can answer by using data-mining tools:

- Which customers are likely to respond to a new product?

- Which customers are likely to respond to a new ad campaign?

- What product should be recommended to customers based on their past buying patterns?

Vendors of data-mining software include SAP Business Objects (*www.sap.com*), SAS (*www.sas.com*), IBM Cognos Analytics (*http://cognos.com*), and Informatica (*www.informatica.com*).

The information box "Data Mining and the Airline Industry" highlights the applications of data mining in the airline industry.

Text-Mining Analysis

Text-mining analysis or text data-mining analysis is the process of analyzing vast amounts of textual information to capture key concepts, trends, and hidden relationships. Businesses collect and process three types of data: structured (such as names, addresses, sales totals, and phone numbers), unstructured (such as social media data, product reviews, videos, and audio files), and semi-structured (a mix of structured and unstructured data, such as e-mail, electronic data interchange, and device IDs). It is estimated that 80 percent of data throughout the world is in unstructured format. Text-mining analysis of this massive amount of data could generate valuable information, which could result in improved decision-making processes and better business outcomes. Text-mining analysis could reduce operational costs, uncover previously unknown relationships, and reveal insights into future trends. There are numerous applications of text-mining analysis, including the following popular options:[14, 15]

- Customer service—Text-mining analysis of online reviews, social media profiles, likes and dislikes, call center transcripts, and online surveys enables businesses to respond to urgent issues in real time and increase customer satisfaction.

- Risk management— Text-mining analysis enables

> **Data-mining analysis** is used to discover patterns and relationships.

> **Text-mining analysis** or text data-mining analysis is the process of analyzing vast amounts of textual information to capture key concepts, trends, and hidden relationships.

businesses to monitor shifts in sentiment in the marketplace and to extract information from analyst reports, market reports, and white papers in a timely manner, which can reduce decision-making risks.

- Healthcare—Text-mining analysis could be used to provide an automated method for extracting valuable information from vast amounts of medical literature. This could result in better healthcare systems with reduced costs.

- Spam filtering—E-mail spam is a global problem. Text-mining analysis can be used to provide a filtering method to exclude spam from inboxes, which improves the overall user experience and system performance and minimizes the risk of phishing.

Popular text-mining analysis tools include Monkey-Learn, IBM Watson, Google Cloud NLP, and Amazon Comprehend.

Decision-Making Reports

A data warehouse can generate all types of information as well as reports used for decision making. The following are examples of what a data warehouse can allow you to do:

- Cross-reference segments of an organization's operations for comparison purposes—for example, compare personnel data with data from the finance department, even if they have been stored in different databases with different formats.

- Generate complex queries and reports faster and easier than when using databases.

- Generate reports efficiently using data from a variety of sources in different formats and stored in different locations throughout an organization.

- Find patterns and trends that cannot be found with databases.

- Analyze large amounts of historical data quickly.

- Assist management in making well-informed business decisions.

- Manage a high demand for information from many users with different needs and decision-making styles.

A **data mart** is usually a smaller version of a data warehouse, used by a single department or function.

A **data lake** gathers and stores data in its original format in a central location. The collected data can be structured as well as unstructured.

3-6 Data Marts

A **data mart** is usually a smaller version of a data warehouse, used by a single department or function. Data marts focus on business functions for a specific user group in an organization, such as a data mart for the marketing department. Despite being smaller, data marts can usually perform the same types of analysis as a data warehouse. Data marts have the following advantages over data warehouses:

- Access to data is often faster because of their smaller size.

- Response time for users is improved.

- They are easier to create because they are smaller and often less complex.

- They are less expensive.

- Users are targeted better because a data mart is designed for a specific department or division; identifying their requirements and the functions they need is easier. A data warehouse is designed for an entire organization's use.

Data marts, however, usually have more limited scope than data warehouses, and consolidating information from different departments or functional areas (such as sales and production) is more difficult.

3-7 Data Lakes

A **data lake** gathers and stores data in its original format in a central location. The collected data can be structured as well as unstructured. Data lakes are not intended to replace data warehouses; rather, the two alternatives are complementary. Compared with data warehouses, data lakes are more suitable for big data analytics and machine learning applications (discussed in Module 13). Table 3.7 highlights key differences between the two.[16]

Because data lakes are more flexible in gathering and storing all types of data, an organization must exercise tight access control; otherwise, a data lake may turn into a "data swamp" of unusable raw data.

A growing number of industries and businesses are using data lakes as a preferred alternative to data warehouses. The healthcare industry is a good example because of the nature of the data it collects and because its data processes include structured and unstructured data, such as physicians' notes, clinical data, and x-rays. The education and transportation industries are other beneficiaries of data lakes.

Data Mining and the Airline Industry

▶▶▶ Finance | Technology in Society | Application | Social and Ethical Issues

In the airline industry, data mining could improve customer service and, at the same time, increase revenue. Soon, an airline crew will know if, say, the customer in seat 19A is a vegetarian or is allergic to a certain food. The crew will also know which passengers lost their bags on a previous flight. Airline marketing is becoming more sophisticated, based on passengers' online browsing histories and the wealth of information available through social media. To sell products and services to their passengers, some airlines now combine the passenger's flight information (such as name, frequent flyer number, age, income, and address) with social media information (such as the number of "likes" on the passenger's Facebook page). All this information could be accessible to flight attendants equipped with tablets and smartphones in the cabin. Data mining could improve targeted in-flight sales by showing a passenger's destination, income, and social media interests. For example, show tickets, helicopter tours, and tickets for boxing matches could be sold to passengers en route to Las Vegas. However, airlines must make every effort to protect the privacy of their passengers. There must be a balance between providing excellent customer service and protecting the passengers' personal information.[17]

Questions and Discussions

1. How could data mining improve customer service and, at the same time, increase revenue in the airline industry?
2. What are some of the challenges in using data mining for this particular application?

Table 3.7	Key Differences Between Data Lakes and Data Warehouses	
Key Factors	**Data Lake**	**Data Warehouse**
Types of data	Raw (original format, structured as well as unstructured)	Processed (passed through ETL)
Application of collected data	Not yet determined	Currently in use
Key users	Data scientists	Any decision maker that needs it
Accessibility	Highly accessible	More complex and limited
Update procedure	Quick	Slow and costly
Storage space	More than a data warehouse	Less than a data lake
Cost	Less than a data warehouse	More than a data lake

Amazon is a prime user of data lakes. This platform enables Amazon to break down data silos, perform advanced data analytics, increase data access, and accelerate machine learning.[18] There are several platforms for a successful implementation of data lakes; the most popular include Amazon Web Services S3, Microsoft Azure Data Lake, and Google Cloud Storage.[19]

3-8 Business Analytics

Business analytics (BA) uses data and statistical methods to gain insight into the data and provide decision makers with information they can act on. BA is increasingly used for data-driven decision making that leverages and explores the data in a database, data warehouse, or data mart system. Compared to business intelligence, which was discussed earlier in this module, BA is more forward looking; it tells the user what is going to happen in the future rather than what has happened in the past.

BI can help determine what happened, what the problem is, and what decisions need to be made based on the available data. BA can help determine why something is happening, what it will mean if the trend continues, and what actions should be taken. BI uses dashboards, scorecards, OLAP, and query reports to support

> **Business analytics (BA)** uses data and statistical methods to gain insight into the data and provide decision makers with information they can act on.

decision-making activities, whereas BA uses statistical analysis, data-mining tools, and predictive modeling.

There are several types of BA methods. Three popular ones are descriptive, predictive, and prescriptive analytics. Descriptive analytics reviews past events, analyzes the data, and provides a report indicating what happened in a given period and how to prepare for the future. Thus, it is a reactive strategy. Predictive analytics, as the name indicates, is a proactive strategy; it prepares a decision maker for future events. As an example, it might indicate that if a current sales trend continues, a company will need a certain number of salespeople in the coming years. Prescriptive analytics goes beyond descriptive and predictive analytics by recommending a course of action that a decision maker should follow and showing the likely outcome of each decision. In other words, prescriptive analytics is more specific than predictive analytics by recommending a precise course of action.[20]

Amazon Analytics, Google Analytics, and Twitter Analytics are among the popular analytics platforms.

Mobile Analytics in Action: Airbnb

▶▶ Finance | Technology in Society | Application

Airbnb is a community marketplace for people to list, discover, and book accommodations around the world—online or from a mobile phone. It is active in more than 65,000 cities and in 191 countries.[21]

Airbnb needed an analytics tool to help the company optimize its mobile app for potential first-time hosts to list rental properties. The company used Mixpanel for this implementation. Mixpanel is an analytics platform for mobile and Web applications. It helps a Web site or a mobile app analyze the actions and activities its visitors take or perform. This is significantly different from measuring page views. Actions might include loading a photo, opening an application, adding comments, or reviewing a listing on a Web site. Airbnb used the Mixpanel platform to do the following on their mobile app:[22]

(Jirapong Manustrong/Shutterstock.com)

- Optimize their first-time listing and booking flows
- Measure the amount of time customers spent within the app
- Measure most frequent actions
- Measure the percentages of visitors who passively browsed versus actively managed a booking

According to Airbnb, Mixpanel's event-tracking and funnel analysis (using a series of events that lead to a defined goal) helped the company revamp the host listing process on its app, resulting in a 400 percent increase in conversion rate.

Airbnb also uses another analytics tool called Spark that assists hosts in listing their rental properties at a competitive price. Obviously, over- or underpricing is not desirable. The system uses 5 billion data points a day to come up with competitive prices. This tool should bring more listings to the site and generate more revenue for Airbnb, which collects 3 percent from each rental deal.[23]

Questions and Discussions

1. What are two applications of mobile analytics at Airbnb?
2. What are two tasks performed by the Mixpanel platform at Airbnb?

Within the general domain of analytics, two other terms are commonly used: Web analytics and mobile analytics. Web analytics collects and analyzes Web data to help determine the efficiency and effectiveness of a Web site. This may be done for market research and for assessing and improving the effectiveness of a Web site. On the other hand, mobile analytics is concerned with the mobile Web and mobile apps. It assesses and measures traffic among mobile devices and all the apps used by these mobile devices. There are three popular types of mobile analytics:[24]

- Advertising and marketing analytics—Determines which ad a user clicked that led the user to install the app on a device

- In-app analytics—Determines who users are and how they interact with the app

- Performance analytics—Ensures the app's functional and operational success by measuring the app's uptime and responsiveness

As the number of mobile users is increasing on a daily basis, mobile analytics is gaining in popularity. Some companies build tablet-specific Web sites; some design and optimize their regular Web sites to better fit the screen sizes, browsers, connection speeds, and other capabilities of mobile devices.[25, 26] See the information box on Airbnb.

The value that BA offers organizations is huge. Organizations that want to take full advantage of it, however, will need a chief analytics officer (CAO). This person should sift through enterprise-wide data in order to generate BI.[27]

Major providers of predictive analytics software include SAS, IBM, SAP, Microsoft, and Oracle. The "Mobile Analytics in Action" box describes how Airbnb is using mobile analytics.

3-9 The Big Data Era

Companies such as MasterCard and Visa have been involved in big data for years, processing billions of transactions on a typical holiday weekend. However, there has been an explosion in data growth throughout the business world in recent years. In fact, it has been estimated that the volume of business data worldwide doubles every 1.2 years.[28]

Predictive Analytics in Action

▶ Finance | Technology in Society | Application | Social and Ethical Issues | Reflective Thinking

Blue Cross and Blue Shield (BCBS), which provides healthcare insurance to nearly 33 percent of Americans, is a successful user of predictive analytics. BCBS has established a database that contains more than 100 million medical claims. To control increasing medical costs, BCBS uses predictive analytics to identify the risk factors that lead to several chronic diseases. It also uses predictive analytics to identify individuals who are at heightened risk of getting such diseases. The goal is to be able to use the data to get doctors to provide better, more targeted care for high-risk patients, reducing their need for expensive, long-term treatment.

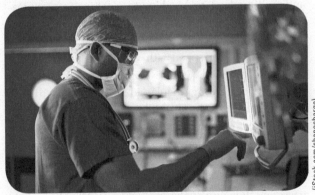

(iStock.com/shapecharge)

Match.com, an online dating service, is also a successful user of predictive analytics. The company collects data from subscribers during the registration process and by monitoring subscribers' interactions on the Web site. The goal is to find the best possible matches based on each subscriber's preferences. By using predictive analytics, Match.com matches its members not just by their expressed preferences but by their behavior and interactions on the Web site.[29]

Questions and Discussions

1. How do Blue Cross and Blue Shield and Match.com improve user outcomes with predictive analytics?
2. What are the benefits and challenges of using predictive analytics?

> **Big data** is data so voluminous that conventional computing methods are not able to efficiently process and manage it.

So, what is big data? The result of the exponential growth of data in both public and private organizations, **big data** is data so voluminous that conventional computing methods are not able to efficiently process and manage it. There are five dimensions to big data, known as the 5 Vs: volume, variety, velocity, veracity, and value.[30]

Volume—The sheer quantity of transactions, measured in petabytes (1,024 terabytes) or exabytes (1,024 petabytes). Here are four examples of big data volume:

- All the packages shipped through the U.S. Postal Service the week before Christmas
- The sales of all Walmart stores on Black Friday
- All the items purchased from Amazon on Cyber Monday
- The number of tweets sent or received around the world per day

Variety—The combination of structured data (e.g., customers' product ratings between 1 and 5) and unstructured data (e.g., call center conversations or customer complaints about a service or product). Most data available on social networks is unstructured. Businesses combine data collected from the Internet and various handheld and mobile devices with location-related data and multimedia data. Machine-to-machine communication data, which is collected and transmitted automatically, also plays a major role in big data operations.

Velocity—The speed with which data has to be gathered and processed. As an example, imagine a billboard that could display a particular ad as soon as a particular customer drives by it. The billboard would recognize the driver's face by comparing it with human faces in a huge database, integrate that data with the driver's social media data, find out what the driver's favorites are based on the number of likes and dislikes on the driver's Facebook page, and then display the applicable ad. All of this would need to happen in a nanosecond; otherwise, the window of opportunity will be lost!

Veracity—The trustworthiness and accuracy of the data. For example, social media posts, abbreviations, typos, and colloquial speech make this dimension important. However, in most cases, volume makes up for the lack of quality or accuracy.

Value—The value that the collected data brings to the decision-making process. If there is no value, then the entire process of data collection and analysis would be a waste of resources and miss the windows of opportunities. For that reason, value is the most important V of big data.[31]

3-9a Who Benefits from Big Data?

Many industries could benefit from big data analytics and gain a competitive advantage in the following areas:[32]

- *Retail*—Customer relationship management, tailoring retail offerings to customer needs, offering personalized service, finding optimum store locations and layouts[33, 34]
- *Financial services*—Risk analysis, fraud detection, attracting new customers
- *Advertising and public relations*—Targeted advertising, more effective messaging of the effectiveness of advertising campaigns, data-driven PR[35]
- *Government*—National security, airport security, weapon systems, and counterterrorism
- *Manufacturing*—Product research, process and quality analysis, route and distribution optimization
- *Media and telecommunications*—Customer scoring, network optimization, effective media programming
- *Energy*—Smart grids, customer segmentation, energy savings[36]
- *Healthcare*—Pharmaceutical research, developing effective medical treatments, genome research[37]

3-9b Tools and Technologies of Big Data

Many technologies and applications have contributed to the growth and popularity of big data. Mobile and wireless technology, the popularity of social networks, and the enhanced power and sophistication of smartphones and handheld devices are among the key factors. Significant improvements in storage technology as well as substantial cost reduction and improved capabilities and affordability of analytics tools have made big data analytics accessible to nearly all types of organizations.

The most commonly used platform for big data analytics is the open-source Apache Hadoop, which uses the Hadoop Distributed File System (HDFS) to manage storage. Distributed databases, including NoSQL and Cassandra, are also commonly associated with big data projects. Examples of big data commercial platforms include SAP Big Data Analytics (*www.sap.com/BigData*), Tableau (*www.tableausoftware.com*), SAS Big Data Analytics (*www.sas.com/big-data*), and QlikView (*www. qlikview.com*).

3-9c Big Data Privacy Risks

Big data analytics is able to provide key decision makers with unprecedented support and great potential for gaining a competitive advantage. However, this powerful tool could reveal and expose certain information that puts some people's privacy at risk. It also may create some legal and ethical concerns. The following list describes the risks associated with this technology. Key executives should make every effort to guard against these risks and eliminate or at least minimize their impact:[38, 39, 40]

- Discrimination: Big data analytics may reveal information that gives a decision maker—such as a banker—a reason to approve or decline an individual's loan application.

- Privacy breaches and embarrassments: Big data analytics may reveal that a retail customer, for example, is pregnant by sending promotional materials related to pregnancy. The person may not have made her pregnancy public yet, creating embarrassment and privacy issues.

- Unethical actions based on interpretations: Big data analytics may be misinterpreted and offer support for a decision that, while legal, may not be ethical.

- Loss of anonymity: Big data analytics, by combining several data sets and cross-referencing various data, could easily reveal the identity of individuals whose data was analyzed.

- Few legal protections exist for the involved individuals: There are, to date, few (if any) legal requirements for protecting privacy while using big data analytics.

The "Big Data in Action" information box explains how Express Scripts is using big data analytics.

3-9d Integration of IoT with Big Data Analytics

We talk about the Internet of Things (IoT) in detail in Module 7. IoT is the assortment of sensor-based devices that are used all over the world for diverse applications. They collect structured and unstructured data 24/7 from

Big Data in Action

▶▶ **Finance | Technology in Society | Application | Social and Ethical Issues | Reflective Thinking**

Based in St. Louis, Missouri, Express Scripts provides pharmacy benefits management. It processes nearly 1.5 billion prescriptions for approximately 100 million consumers per year. The company constantly analyzes its massive amounts of data on prescriptions and insurance claims in order to speed up delivery, reduce errors, and increase profitability. Big data analytics has enabled Express Scripts to quickly find out if customers are filling their prescriptions through mail order, which is cheaper, or going to a retail pharmacy. For customers not using mail order, the company can intervene and provide them with cost options.[41] By using analytics, the company can be proactive and present cost alternatives to customers who are taking drugs on a long-term basis.

Express Scripts has recently expanded into predictive analytics with a system called Screen Rx. The goal of the system is to screen and identify patients with chronic diseases (such as high blood pressure, diabetes, or high cholesterol) who are not taking their prescriptions. This system uses 400 factors (such as family history, past diseases, gender, and where the customer lives) to identify these patients and then offer proactive recommendations. Nonadherence to medical advice is the most expensive healthcare-related problem in the United States, with an annual cost of over $317 billion. The Screen Rx system can bring this cost down by intervening proactively.[42]

Questions and Discussions

1. What was achieved by big data analytics at Express Scripts?
2. What is the role of the Screen Rx analytics system?

the factory floor, from smart homes, and from everything in between. According to IDC, 90 ZB of data will be created on IoT devices by 2025.[43] IoT big data analytics can be a powerful tool for a variety of applications. They can do the following:[44]

- Examine various situations from the industrial field, the medical field, and others.

- Reveal trends that can be used for forecasting and planning.

- Find unseen patterns that can be used for marketing opportunities.

- Find hidden correlations that can be used for marketing opportunities and other managerial decision making.

- Reveal new information that can be used for competitive advantage.

Different industries will benefit in different ways from this integration. The following is a sample list of industry benefits.

1. It helps to increase return on investment (ROI) for any industry by providing real-time analytics of key variables and helping decision makers to implement real-time decisions with moderate costs.

2. It will improve the healthcare industry by enabling new methods of remote diagnosis with a better understanding of diseases, which will lead to timely development of new treatments.

3. It will help the manufacturing industry by enabling companies to find out which equipment needs repair before breakdown. This prevents more significant expenses by skipping downtime or replacement of the equipment.

4. It will help the transportation industry to monitor vehicles, fuel efficiency, and how drivers utilize their time and delivery routes. As a result, fleets will be optimized and organizational productivity will be improved.

5. IIoT (Industrial Internet of Things) big data analytics will improve nearly all operations of industrial devices by real-time monitoring, collection, exchange, and analysis of data and implementation of real-time decisions.

6. IoT big data analytics will raise self-service analytics that will enable most IT functions to be automated. As a result, analytics as a service will become commonplace.

3-10 Database Marketing

One of the main applications of databases and database systems is **database marketing**. For the purposes of this book, we define database marketing as using an organization's database of customers and potential customers to promote its products or services.

The main goal of a successful database marketing campaign is to use the information in the database to implement marketing strategies that eventually increase profits and enhance the competitiveness of the organization in the marketplace. The key motivation behind database marketing is establishing, building, and maintaining a long-term relationship with customers.

As you have seen in this module, customer information comes from a variety of internal and external sources, such as sales information, e-mail correspondence, warranty cards, club cards, promotional campaigns, and more recently, social media. The increasing popularity of social media makes the implementation of database marketing challenging and, at the same time, a very powerful strategic tool for making an organization more competitive in the marketplace.

Database marketing works by using multivariate analysis, data segmentation, and automated tools to transform marketing from a reactive process to a proactive process. It makes an organization more responsive to the needs and desires of its customers and allows the organization to better respond to changes in the marketplace.

The earliest use of automated marketing tools was by Reader's Digest, American Express, mail-order catalog companies, and credit bureaus. Database marketing made call centers and telemarketing popular. It also became popular with loyalty programs, such as grocery chain club cards, airline mileage programs, and My Starbucks Rewards.

The goal of a successful marketing campaign is to generate the highest possible revenue for the organization. Database marketing is the backbone of this process and is part of an integrated approach of analyzing profitability, segmenting customers, and using marketing tactics that build customer loyalty and increase sales.

Segmentation of customers is an important task; not all the products or services that an organization offers are suitable for all customers. Customers can be segmented by many variables, including demographics, geography, benefits sought, psychographics, price sensitivity, and socioeconomic characteristics.

While demographic data explains "who" buyers are, psychographics explain "why" they buy a product or service. Demographic information includes gender, age, income, and marital status. Psychographic information includes habits, hobbies, spending patterns, and values. The following tasks are usually performed by a successful database marketing campaign:[45]

- *Calculating customer lifetime value (CLTV)*—This model generates an estimate of what the lifetime relationship of a typical customer will be worth to a business. Based on this value, a business knows how much it should spend in order to keep the relationship.

- *Recency, frequency, and monetary analysis (RFM)*—This model generates an estimate that tells a business how valuable a customer is based on the recentness of purchases, frequency of purchases, and how much the customer spends. The theory behind this model is that 80 percent of business revenue comes from 20 percent of its customers. This means the business should pay more attention to those in the 20 percent group.

- *Customer communications*—Using different techniques to communicate effectively with customers increases loyalty, customer retention, and sales. In the Internet era, businesses use a number of tools to communicate with their customers, including e-mail, Web sites, a portal, and the intranet (discussed in Module 7).

- *Analytical software*—This means using different techniques to monitor customers' behavior across a number of retail channels, including Web sites, mobile apps, social media, and physical stores.

Database marketing offers several advantages to businesses, including improved profitability, increased sales, improved marketing communications, and improved product development. High startup costs, such as those for hardware and software, and ongoing operational costs are among the drawbacks of database marketing. Also, for effective use and operation of a successful database marketing program, employees with technical knowledge are needed. This may put the technology out of reach for small organizations that have limited budgets.[46, 47] Database marketing has helped many companies improve their bottom lines. Hearst Magazines, one of the world's largest publishers of monthly magazines (*https://www.hearst.com/magazines*), has used database marketing to generate a 200 percent ROI, a 25 percent increase in direct-mail response, and an 8 percent reduction in database records.[48]

The "Database Marketing in Action: Caterpillar Corporation" box highlights how Caterpillar Corporation is using database marketing.

3-11 Tableau and Power BI: Two Popular BI and Visualization Platforms

3-11a What Is Tableau?

Tableau is a data visualization tool used for generating business intelligence. It is used to analyze data for generating trends using graphs and charts. Tableau users can do the following:[49]

- Explore and find quick patterns in data.
- Reproduce and further analyze data patterns.
- Create multiple charts to get meaningful insight from data.

Tableau is a powerful platform for performing visual analytics that helps design visualizations that users with minimal analytics backgrounds can easily understand and use. It can utilize data from various sources including data files (with various formats such as Excel and PDF) and relational databases, as well as big data sources. It is extensively used by both private and public sectors, including academic researchers, businesses, and many government agencies. The Tableau product suite includes the following: Tableau Server, Tableau Desktop, Tableau Reader, Tableau Online, and Tableau Public. Some of the unique features of Tableau include the following:

- Superb visualizations—Users can switch between different

Tableau is a data visualization tool used for generating business intelligence. It is used to analyze data for generating trends using graphs and charts.

Database Marketing in Action: Caterpillar Corporation

▶▶▶ Finance | Application | Social and Ethical Issues | Reflective Thinking

In addition to its earth-moving equipment, Caterpillar Corporation builds the large truck engines used in 18-wheelers. These engines bring the company about $2 billion annually. Alan Weber and Frank Weyforth of Caterpillar built one of the first successful database marketing campaigns.

Prior to this campaign, Caterpillar had no information about who used its engines. The company had no database in place, and management could not get answers to critical questions, such as: To what truck fleets are we not trying to sell our engines? What fleets should test our new engines? How can we implement a marketing strategy that can be measured?[50]

Weber and Weyforth built four internal databases and gave laptops to each of Caterpillar's 260 salespersons. The company implemented a policy that sales staff would only be paid if customers' names, addresses, and sales information were entered into the database.

After two years, the company had 110,000 customer files and 42,000 fleet files—essentially the entire universe of all heavy trucks on the road at that time. Initially, the four databases were not compatible, so they were combined into one, and data analysis and modeling was started. The company used modeling techniques to select customers and predict their responses to certain variables. Caterpillar was able to predict which customers and prospects would buy engines, their trade cycles (the number of years before the engine would be traded in), and their maintenance needs by assigning scores to variables and their dependence on each other. This allowed the company to develop messages for prospects and customers based on their needs. Caterpillar developed sales incentives for staff based on this business intelligence; in the first year alone, sales increased by $500 million. Five hundred fleets were signed on that year and the company's market share went up by 5 percent.[51]

Questions and Discussions

1. How did Caterpillar Corporation benefit from database marketing?
2. What are additional applications of database marketing?

visualizations to zero in on a particular data point by drilling up and down.

- In-depth insights—Users can explore the visualizations and view the same data from different angles. Users can perform "what-if" analysis to explore the impact of each variable on the entire model.

- User-friendly interface—Most of the features and visualization in Tableau are accessed with the drag-and-drop technique; no programming is needed to use this platform.

- Works with disparate data sources—Users can connect, use, and analyze data from various sources, including data warehouses, data marts, spreadsheets, and big data sources.

> **Power BI** is a platform that allows a user to analyze and visualize data from different sources with different formats.

- Can add data sets to existing data—New data sets from various sources could easily be added to and blended with existing data for further analysis.

3-11b What Is Power BI?

Power BI from Microsoft is a platform that allows a user to analyze and visualize data from different sources with different formats.[52] Data may be from an Excel spreadsheet, from the cloud, or from data warehouses and data marts. Visualization allows the user to discover patterns and understand important points in the data that may not be easily understood otherwise. Power BI is for extensive modeling and real-time analytics. It allows users to create, share, and utilize business insights for effective decision making. It may be used for many different purposes by many different users. As an example, a finance executive may use it for number-crunching and creating business reports. A marketing executive may use it to monitor sales trends and achieve sales goals. A production and operation executive may use it to spot production efficiencies and meet production goals. Advantages of Power BI include the following:

- Seamless integration with other data and existing applications
- The ability to create personalized dashboards for different users with diverse information needs
- Delivery of actionable information with high speed, accuracy, and security

Major components of Power BI include the following:

- A Windows desktop application called Power BI Desktop
- An online SaaS (software as a service) product called the Power BI service
- Power BI mobile apps for Windows, iOS, and Android devices

The Industry Connection box summarizes Oracle Corporation's database products and services.

Industry Connection: Oracle Corporation[53]

Oracle offers database software and services. It is a major vendor of software for enterprise-level information management, and it was the first software company to offer Web-based products. In addition, Oracle offers "single-user versions" of some of its database products. The following list describes some of Oracle's database software and services:

Oracle Database: A relational DBMS that runs on Windows, Linux, and UNIX platforms and includes a variety of features for managing transaction processing, business intelligence, and content management applications.

Oracle OLAP: An option in Oracle Database Enterprise Edition that is a calculation engine for performing analyses such as planning, budgeting, forecasting, sales, and marketing reports. It improves the performance of complex queries with multidimensional data.

Oracle PeopleSoft: An enterprise-level product for customer/supplier relationship management and human capital management (HCM).

Oracle Fusion Middleware: A suite of products for service-oriented architecture (SOA), business process management, business intelligence, content management, identity management, and Web 2.0.

Other Oracle products and services include Oracle E-Business Suite as well as Siebel customer-relationship management applications. Oracle is also a major player in cloud computing by offering IaaS, PaaS, and SaaS services (discussed in Module 14).

Module Summary

3-1 Define a *database* and a *database management system*. A database is a collection of related data that is stored in a central location or in multiple locations. A database management system (DBMS) is software for creating, storing, maintaining, and accessing database files.

3-2 Explain logical database design and the relational database model. The logical view involves how information appears to users and how it can be organized and retrieved. A relational model uses a two-dimensional table of rows and columns of data.

Rows are records (also called tuples), and columns are fields (also referred to as attributes).

3-3 Define the five components of a database management system. They include the database engine, data definition, data manipulation, application generation, and data administration.

3-4 Summarize three recent trends in database design and use. They include data-driven Web sites, distributed database management systems (DDBMS), and object-oriented databases.

3-5 Analyze the four major components and functions of a data warehouse and their use for business. They include input; extraction, transformation, and loading (ETL); storage; and output.

3-6 Describe the functions of a data mart. A data mart is usually a smaller version of a data warehouse, used by a single department or function.

3-7 Compare and contrast data lakes with data warehouses. A data lake gathers and stores data in its original format in a central location. The collected data can be structured as well as unstructured. Data lakes are not intended to replace data warehouses; rather, the two alternatives are complementary.

3-8 Describe the role of business analytics in the decision-making process. Business analytics (BA) uses data and statistical methods to gain insight into the data and provide decision makers with information they can act on.

3-9 Examine the advantages and challenges of big data and predictive analytics for a business. Big data is data so voluminous that conventional computing methods are not able to efficiently process and manage it. There are five dimensions to big data, known as the 5 Vs: volume, variety, velocity, veracity, and value.

3-10 Explain database marketing and its business applications. Database marketing uses an organization's database of customers and potential customers to promote products or services.

3-11 Explain key features of Tableau and Power BI as two popular business intelligence and visualization platforms. Tableau is a data visualization tool used for generating business intelligence. It is used to analyze data for generating trends using graphs and charts. Power BI is a platform that allows a user to analyze and visualize data from different sources in different formats.

Key Terms

- Allocation
- Big data
- Business analytics (BA)
- Create, read, update, and delete (CRUD)
- Data dictionary
- Data hierarchy
- Data lake
- Data mart
- Data model
- Data warehouse
- Database
- Database administrators (DBA)
- Database management system (DBMS)
- Database marketing
- Data-driven Web site
- Data-mining analysis
- Distributed database management system (DDBMS)
- Encapsulation
- Extraction, transformation, and loading (ETL)
- Foreign key
- Fragmentation

- Graph database
- Hierarchical model
- Indexed sequential access method (ISAM)
- Inheritance
- Logical view
- Network model
- Normalization
- Object-oriented databases
- Online analytical processing (OLAP)
- Online transaction processing (OLTP)
- Physical view
- Power BI
- Primary key
- Query by example (QBE)
- Random access file structure
- Relational model
- Replication
- Sequential access file structure
- Structured Query Language (SQL)
- Tableau
- Text-mining analysis

Reviews and Discussions

1. Define a *database*.
2. What are the differences between physical and logical views of information?
3. What are five components of a DBMS?
4. What are three recent trends in database design and implementation?
5. What are two inputs and two outputs of a data warehouse?
6. What are two advantages and two disadvantages of a data mart compared to a data warehouse?
7. Explain business analytics and list the three popular types of business analytics.
8. What are the 5 Vs of big data?

Projects

1. After reading the information presented in this module and other sources, write a two-page paper that explains BI. Identify three companies not already mentioned in this module that have been using BI and explain the applications of BI in these companies. What are two differences between BI and information or data?

2. After reading the information presented in this module and other sources, write a one-page paper that identifies three companies not already mentioned in this module that are using data-mining tools. Explain how data mining has helped these companies with their bottom lines. Are data-mining tools beneficial to service companies, manufacturing companies, or both? Which companies or sectors may benefit from text-mining analysis?

3. After reading the information presented in this module and other sources, write a one-page paper that identifies two companies that use mobile analytics. How has mobile analytics helped these companies achieve their sales goals? What are two differences between mobile analytics and traditional analytics?

4. After reading the information presented in this module and other sources, write a two-page paper that explains database marketing. Identify two companies that have been using database marketing. What are three challenges in using database marketing? What are three advantages of using database marketing?

5. After reading the information presented in this module and other sources, write a two-page paper that identifies three companies that have been using big data analytics. Explain how big data analytics is helping these companies improve the efficiency of their operations. How could privacy risks from big data analytics be eliminated or minimized?

6. The following sample table shows 10 of the students enrolled in an MIS course. Organize the data in a relational format, and use Microsoft Access to list all ACC majors, all ACC majors with a GPA higher than 3.7, all students who are MIS or ACC majors, and all students who aren't ACC majors. Repeat this assignment, this time using Excel, and generate the same results.

Sample Table

Fname	Lname	ID	Major	GPA	Age	Status
Juan	Chavez	111-1	MIS	2.79	19	Freshman
Tom	Smith	222-7	ACC	3.60	22	Senior
Alan	Bidgoli	333-9	ACC	3.86	21	Junior
Mohammad	Alessa	444-6	MKT	3.45	20	Sophomore
Steve	Kline	555-6	MGT	3.75	24	Junior
Nooshin	Bidgoli	666-1	MIS	3.90	21	Junior
Moury	Bidgoli	777-2	MIS	3.90	22	Junior
Janet	Jeffrey	888-0	MGT	4.00	20	Junior
Jesus	Lopez	999-2	MKT	3.65	29	Senior
Luke	Galvez	234-1	ACC	3.92	23	Senior

Module Quiz

1. One of the main applications of databases and database systems is database marketing. True or False?

2. A data lake gathers and stores data in its original format in a central location. The collected data can be structured as well as unstructured. True or False?

3. In a data warehouse environment, ETL refers to extraction, transformations, and language. True or False?

4. Which of the following is not a type of mobile analytics?
   a. Advertising and marketing analytics
   b. In-app analytics
   c. Performance analytics
   d. Installation analytics

5. Which of the following is not among the 5 Vs of big data?
   a. Variance
   b. Value
   c. Variety
   d. Veracity

6. Tableau and Power BI are used for all of the following purposes except:
   a. Exploring and finding patterns in data
   b. Creating multiple charts to get meaningful insight into data
   c. Allowing analyzing data with different formats
   d. All of these options

Case Study 3-1
Data Mining Helps Students Enroll in Courses with Higher Chances of Success
➤ Finance | Technology in Society | Application | Social and Ethical Issues

Austin Peay State, a university in Clarksville, Tennessee, is applying a data-mining approach to higher education. Before students register for classes, a robot looks at their profiles and transcripts and recommends courses in which they are likely to be successful or have higher chances of success. The software takes an approach similar to the ones Netflix, eHarmony, and Amazon use to make their recommendations. It compares a student's transcripts with those of past students who had similar grades and SAT scores. When a student logs in, the program offers 10 "Course Suggestions for You." These recommendations are based on the student's major and other information related to that student. The goal is to steer students toward courses in which they will make better grades. According to Tristan Denley, a former programmer turned math professor turned provost, students who follow the recommendations

(Monkey Business Images/Shutterstock.com)

do substantially better. In one academic semester, 45 percent of the classes that students took had been on their list of top 10 recommendations. This data-mining concept is catching on. Three other Tennessee colleges now use Denley's software. Institutions outside the state are developing their own versions of the idea.[54]

Answer the following questions:

1. Which other companies are using approaches similar to the one used by Austin Peay State?
2. Based on which data does the system make a course recommendation to a student?
3. What are the benefits and drawbacks of this approach to course recommendations?
4. Is there any data that should or should not be included in data mining for this purpose? Why or why not?

Case Study 3-2
Big Data Analytics Helps Spotify Dominate Music Streaming Worldwide
Finance | Technology in Society | Application | Social and Ethical Issues

Spotify, the world's largest on-demand music service provider, is a Swedish company that provides commercial music streaming, podcasts, and video services. As of the second quarter of 2021, Spotify had 365 million users, including 165 million paid subscribers worldwide. The platform includes more than 70 million tracks and more than 2.9 million podcast titles, which are available either for free or with an upgrade to Spotify Premium. The platform can be used with many devices and allows users to browse through a catalog of music licensed through multiple record labels. Users can also create and share playlists with other users.[55]

The company effectively leverages information technology, including data-mining analysis, artificial intelligence, machine learning, and particularly big data analytics, to provide a personalized experience to each user. The company uses big data analytics to achieve the following five goals:[56, 57, 58]

- Developing personalized content—Big data analytics enables Spotify's Discover feature to generate a playlist of songs released by popular artists, and it serves as a recommendation tool based on information the platform has gathered about a particular user. In addition, the Discover Weekly feature examines songs liked or disliked by users and the amount of time they spent listening to particular tracks. This information helps Spotify make recommendations.

- Digitizing the taste of the user—Listeners' daily preferred songs are incorporated into Spotify's Daily Mixes playlists, while their Release Radar and Discover features constantly refresh users' playlists.

- Enhancing marketing through targeted ads—By analyzing the users' profile data, Spotify has been able to launch personalized advertising campaigns that have improved sales and engagement.

- Continuously updating the platform—Big data analytics has helped the company to improve the ease of use of its offerings based on feedback from users. Also, through mobile apps, artists can see the users' engagement on the platform and enhance their offerings.

- Implementing the Spotify Wrapped feature—This is a year-end report from Spotify that allows its users to share their musical tastes on social media. This feature has created more user engagement and has helped increase the number of users on the platform.

Answer the following questions:

1. How does Spotify recommend music to its listeners?
2. What is the function of the Discover feature on Spotify's platform?
3. What are the five goals that Spotify has achieved using big data analytics?

Module
4

Personal, Legal, Ethical, and Organizational Issues

Learning Objectives

After studying this module, you should be able to...

4.1 Discuss information privacy and methods for improving the privacy of information.

4.2 Explain the General Data Protection Regulation.

4.3 Explain the privacy issues of e-mail and data collection in a business setting.

4.4 Examine ethical issues and censorship in information technology.

4.5 Discuss the principles of intellectual property and issues related to the infringement of intellectual property.

4.6 Examine the impact of information technology on society: the digital divide, telecommuting, and health issues.

4.7 Describe green computing and the ways it can improve the quality of the environment.

This module examines privacy issues (including the privacy of e-mail), the General Data Protection Regulation, censorship, and data collection on the Web. It then discusses ethical issues of information technology, as well as intellectual property and copyright laws. Finally, the module reviews some broader issues of information technologies, including its impacts on the workplace, the digital divide, electronic publishing, health effects, and green computing.

4-1 Privacy Issues

Information technologies have brought many benefits, but they have also created concerns about privacy in the workplace. For example, employers now search social networking sites such as Facebook to find background information on job applicants, and this information can influence their hiring decisions. In fact, some recruiters and hiring managers use the extracted information to assign a potential employee a numeric rank between 0 and 100.[1]

Is this use of social networking sites legal or ethical? What about users' privacy? Because information posted on these sites is often considered to be in the public domain, you should be careful about what you post in case it comes back to haunt you. See the "Social Networking Sites and Privacy Issues" box for an example of what could happen.

Two relatively new ethical issues related to social media are fake news and deepfakes; each has potentially serious political and financial consequences. **Fake news** is a story or hoax created to intentionally misinform or deceive readers. Creation and dissemination of fake news could have economic and social consequences. **Deepfakes** are fake videos or audio recordings that look and sound just like the real thing. They may swap celebrities' faces into porn videos and put words in politicians' mouths. Unfortunately, creation of these types of videos is relatively easy; anyone can download deepfake software from the Web and create convincing fake videos in a short time. Is this legal or ethical?[2]

Variations of fake news include cheap fakes, misinformation, and disinformation. They are briefly explained in the following list:

- **Cheap fakes**, sometimes known as the new fake news, are audiovisual manipulations of events created with cheap software that's readily available on the Web and then modified using Photoshop and other tools and distributed through the Internet.

- **Misinformation** is fake information that is distributed to an audience, regardless of intent to mislead. The person spreading the information does not know that it is false. In most cases, it is sensational and intended to attract the attention of others.

- On the other hand, **disinformation** is fake information that is knowingly distributed.

Unfortunately, all these variations have legal, political, ethical, economical, and social consequences, and they are rampant on the Web, particularly during political campaigns and the COVID-19 pandemic. An MIT study found that fake stories on Twitter were 70 percent more likely to get retweeted than accurate stories.[3]

Be careful to make sure that the news stories you read on the Web are authentic. Here are a few tips to help you spot fake news:[4]

- Don't just read the headline—read the full story and assess the sources of the story.

- Search for evidence, not opinion.

- Search for replication and distribution of the story.

Fake news is a story or hoax created to intentionally misinform or deceive readers.

Deepfakes are fake videos or audio recordings that look and sound just like real events.

Cheap fakes, sometimes known as the new fake news, are audiovisual manipulations of events created with cheap software that's readily available on the Web and then modified using Photoshop and other tools and distributed through the Web.

Misinformation is fake information that is distributed to an audience, regardless of intent to mislead.

Disinformation is fake information that is knowingly distributed.

- Read about the Web site, the author, and the publisher that is the source of the story.

- Question the intentions of the author and ask, "What is the purpose of this news story?"

A recent survey conducted by IDC indicated that 84 percent of U.S. consumers are concerned about the privacy of their personal information, with 70 percent saying their concern is greater today than it was a few years ago. Major recent security breaches at Colonial Pipeline, Kroger, Yahoo!, Equifax, and Uber further increase this concern.[5] With employee-monitoring systems, managers can also supervise employees' performance—the number of errors they make, their work speed, and their time away from the desk. Naturally, this monitoring has made some workers concerned about their privacy. See the "Employee Monitoring: Improving Productivity or Invasion of Privacy?" box.

Healthcare organizations, financial institutions, legal firms, and even online-ordering firms gather a great deal of personal data and enter it in databases. Misuse and abuse of this information can have serious consequences. For this reason, organizations should establish comprehensive security systems (discussed in Module 5) to protect their employees' and clients' privacy.

Some "information paranoia" is valid because information about almost every aspect of people's lives is now stored on various databases, and misuse of extremely sensitive information (such as medical records) could prevent someone from getting employment, health insurance, or housing. Laws are in place to prevent these problems, but taking legal action is often costly, and by that point, the damage has often been done already.

You can probably give examples of things you expect to be private, such as your personal mail, your bank account balances, and your phone conversations. Defining privacy is difficult, however. In terms of electronic information, most people believe they should be able to keep their personal affairs to themselves and should be told how information about them is being used. Based on this definition, many practices of government agencies, credit agencies, and marketing companies using databases would represent an invasion of privacy. Unfortunately, information technologies have increased the ease of access to information for hackers as well as for legitimate organizations.

Social Networking Sites and Privacy Issues

▶ Social and Ethical Issues

Stacy Snyder, a former student at Millersville University of Pennsylvania, posted a photo of herself on social media that showed her wearing a pirate's hat while drinking. The photo was captioned "Drunken Pirate." Although Snyder was of legal drinking age at the time, Millersville administrators considered the image unprofessional and refused to grant her a degree in education and a teaching certificate. Instead, she was given a degree in English. Did the university violate Stacy's privacy?[6]

Recently, Harvard University withdrew acceptances for several prospective students due to offensive posts on social media. Two students were expelled from Colorado College for their offensive posting on Yik-Yak, an anonymous messaging app for college students. Paige Shoemaker was expelled from Kansas State University after an offensive Snapchat image of her and a friend was discovered. These cases illustrate the seriousness of offensive behavior on social media; students and young adults should become educated about social media etiquette and understand the consequences of their actions.[7] Follow these five recommendations before you post anything online:[8]

1. Think carefully before you post and think about the fact that it might follow you and impact your employment possibilities.
2. Do not post anything that you wouldn't want everyone to see.
3. Remember that once you post something online, it will be there forever.
4. Remember that there is no such thing as true anonymity on social media.
5. Only share information that you think others would enjoy or find useful.

Questions and Discussions

1. Why were these students penalized for their social media usage?
2. Should employers evaluate social media as part of the hiring process? Why or why not?

Employee Monitoring: Improving Productivity or Invasion of Privacy?

➤➤ Finance | Social and Ethical Issues

Workers in logistics and delivery trucks have long been monitored by their supervisors through global positioning system (GPS) devices. Today, Telematics, a more advanced version of GPS, can perform monitoring and even reduce a truck's speed if it gets too close to an adjacent vehicle. In general, employers now have a myriad of software tools with which to monitor their employees. For example, they can monitor every keystroke that their employees enter into their computers or handheld devices. In addition, managers can view their employees' photos, text messages, e-mail, call logs, and Web site visits. Using these monitoring tools, companies track their employees' locations, check their phone calls, find out if particular drivers are wearing their seat belts, or even find out if a driver is tailgating other cars. Employee monitoring software is expanding to incorporate wearable technology using cameras and microphones, which makes employee monitoring a universal process.

Without telling his drivers, a supervisor for Accurid Pest Solutions in southern Virginia installed GPS tracking software on the company-owned smartphones of five of its 18 drivers. The software allowed the supervisor, through his computer, to see a map of the drivers' movements, the number of stops, and the duration of the stops. The software disclosed that one driver was frequently visiting the same address. It was later revealed that the driver had been seeing a woman during work hours; he was fired.

Employees see these monitoring practices as an invasion of their privacy, but employers believe that they improve productivity, customer service, and safety as well as reduce theft and the loss of corporate secrets. Some employers tell their employees they are being monitored; some do not. However, employees should assume that they are always being monitored and that such practices are legal.[9]

Questions and Discussions

1. Is employee monitoring ethical?
2. What are three examples of information technology tools that can be used for employee monitoring?

Revelations of widespread surveillance and spying by the U.S. National Security Agency have helped bring the privacy discussion to the forefront.[10, 11]

The number of databases is increasing rapidly. In the United States, for example, the top three credit-rating companies—Experian, Equifax, and TransUnion—have records on nearly every person in the United States. In 2017, Equifax was hacked, impacting 148 million people. We talk about this case in detail in Module 5. Although these organizations and agencies are reputable and supply information to people using it for its intended purpose, many small companies buy information from credit-rating companies and use it in ways that were never intended. This action is clearly illegal, but enforcement of federal laws has been lax. You may have noticed the effects of this problem if you recently joined an organization and then began receiving mail from other organizations to whom you have not given your address.

Advances in computer technology have made it easy to do what was once difficult or impossible. Information in databases can now be cross-matched to create profiles of people and predict their behavior, based on their transactions with educational, financial, and government institutions. This information is often used for direct marketing and for credit checks on potential borrowers or renters.

The most common way to index and link databases is by using Social Security numbers (typically obtained from credit bureaus), although names are sometimes used to track transactions that do not require Social Security numbers. Such transactions include credit card purchases, charitable contributions, and movie rentals. Direct marketing companies are major users of this information. You may think that the worst result of this information sharing is an increase in junk mail (postal mail or e-mail), but there are more serious privacy issues. Should information you give to a bank to help establish a credit record be repackaged (i.e., linked with other databases) and used for other purposes?

In 1977, the U.S. government began linking large databases to find information. The Department of Health, Education, and Welfare decided to look for people collecting welfare who were also working for the government. (Collecting welfare while being employed is illegal.) By comparing records of welfare payments with the government payroll, the department was able to identify workers who were breaking the law. In this case, people abusing the system were discovered, so this use of databases was helpful.

The Department of Housing and Urban Development, which keeps records on whether mortgage borrowers are in default on federal loans, previously made this information available to large banking institutions, which added it to their credit files. This action led Congress to pass the first of several laws intended to protect people's rights to keep their credit records private.

Several federal laws now regulate the collection and use of information about people and corporations, but the laws are narrow in scope and contain loopholes. For example, the 1970 Fair Credit Reporting Act prohibits credit agencies from sharing information with anyone but "authorized customers." An authorized customer, however, is defined as anyone with a "legitimate need," and the act does not specify what a legitimate need is.

There are three important concepts when it comes to the Web and network privacy: **acceptable use policies**, **accountability**, and **nonrepudiation**. To guard against possible legal ramifications and the consequences of using the Web and networks, an organization usually establishes an acceptable use policy, which is a set of rules specifying the legal and ethical use of a system and the consequences of noncompliance. Having a clear, specific policy can help prevent users from taking legal action against an organization, as in cases of termination. Most organizations have new employees sign an acceptable use policy before they can access the network. The second concept, accountability, refers to issues involving both a user's and organization's responsibilities and liabilities. As for nonrepudiation, it is basically a method for binding all parties to a contract. It is covered in more detail in Module 5.

Because of concerns about privacy, hardware or software controls should be used to determine what personal information is provided on the Web. Module 5 explains these controls in more detail, but to minimize invasion of privacy, users and organizations should adhere to the following guidelines:

- Conduct business only on Web sites with privacy policies that are easy to find, read, and understand.

- Limit access to your personal information to those who have authorization.

- Any organization that creates, maintains, uses, or disseminates records of personal data must ensure the reliability of its systems and take precautions to prevent misuse of the data.

- Any data collection must have a stated purpose. Organizations should keep collected information only as long as it is needed for the stated purpose.

- People must have a way to prevent personal information from being gathered about them for one purpose and then being used for other purposes or disclosed to others without their consent.

An **acceptable use policy** is a set of rules specifying the legal and ethical use of a system and the consequences of noncompliance.

Accountability refers to issues involving both a user's and organization's responsibilities and liabilities.

Nonrepudiation is a method for binding all parties to a contract.

Rena Schild/Shutterstock.com

- Organizations should monitor data collection and entry and should use verification procedures to ensure data accuracy; they should also collect only the data that is necessary.

- Records kept on an individual should be accurate and up to date. Organizations must correct or delete incorrect data and delete data when it is no longer needed for the stated purpose.

- Users should be able to review their records and correct any inaccuracies.

- The existence of record-keeping systems that store personal data should not be kept secret. In addition, people must have a way to find out what information has been stored about them and how it is used.

- Organizations must take all necessary measures to prevent unauthorized access to data and misuse of data.

Privacy-protection software can take many forms. For example, to guard against cookies, which record your navigations around the Web, you can use the cookie control features contained in your browser. There are also commercial vendors that address this problem. Using privacy-protection software has some drawbacks, however. For example, eBay often has to contend with sellers who use different user accounts to bid on their own items and inflate the prices. Currently, eBay can trace these sellers' user accounts, but privacy-protection software would make this tracking impossible.

Three important federal data-protection laws include the Health Insurance Portability and Accountability Act (HIPAA), the Fair and Accurate Credit Transaction Act (FACTA), and the Children's Online Privacy Protection Act (COPPA). They are briefly explained here.

- *HIPAA*—The goal is to protect the confidentiality of a patient's medical information and establish safeguards to protect the privacy of health information. This includes medical providers' notes and records, health insurers' computer records, patients' billing information, and conversations between medical personnel concerning patient care and treatment.[12]

- *FACTA*—The goal is to protect consumers' credit information from the risks related to data theft and to ensure the proper disposal of information in consumer reports and records, which protects against unauthorized access or use of the information.[13]

- *COPPA*—The goal is to protect the privacy of children under the age of 13. Web sites directed to children must publish their privacy policies. Any information collected from children must have parental consent.[14]

4-1a General Data Protection Regulation (GDPR)

The General Data Protection Regulation replaced Data Protection Directive 95/46/ec and went into effect in May 2018. The **General Data Protection Regulation (GDPR)** covers a series of laws that protect European Union (EU) citizens' personal data, including genetic data, health records, racial or ethnic origin, and religious beliefs. The goal is to create more consistent protection of consumer and personal data across EU nations; the GDPR applies to each member state of the European Union. Any company that sells products or services to EU residents must be aware of this law and its consequences, regardless of the company's location. In this regard, there is no difference between EU-based companies and international companies. If any organization's Web site collects any regulated data from EU users, it is liable to comply to the GDPR. A violator could be fined up to 4 percent of the company's global annual revenue, depending on the nature of the violation. Under the GDPR, individuals can easily transfer their personal data between service providers; this practice is called "right to portability." The GDPR contains 11 modules and 91 articles. The key components include the following:

- User consent must be given for any type of processing of personal information.

- Collected data must be anonymized to protect privacy.

- Users must be notified of any types of data breaches within 72 hours of the breach's discovery. Companies must provide specific details of the breach, such as its nature and scope.

- Data transfer across borders must be safely done.

- Certain companies are required to appoint a data protection officer to oversee GDPR compliance.

Businesses that deal with EU citizens must

> The **General Data Protection Regulation (GDPR)** covers a series of laws that protect European Union (EU) citizens' personal data, including genetic data, health records, racial or ethnic origin, and religious beliefs.

designate a data protection officer who will build a data protection program to meet GDPR requirements. It is also important to stay informed of changes to the law, new developments, and enforcement methods because the law is evolving.[15] The following are major business benefits of GDPR compliance:[16]

- Improved consumer confidence
- Better data security
- Reduced maintenance costs by retiring any data inventory software and legacy applications that are no longer GDPR-compliant
- Better alignment with evolving technology
- Better decision making by using customer information effectively

In 2018, consumer groups across seven European countries filed GDPR complaints against Google's location tracking.[17] In the same year, Ireland's data privacy commissioner stated that the country would investigate Facebook over a security breach that affected 29 million accounts.[18]

4-1b E-mail

Although e-mail is widely used, it presents some serious privacy issues. One issue is junk e-mail, also known as **spam**—unsolicited e-mail sent for advertising purposes. Because sending spam is inexpensive, even a small response—a fraction of a percent, for example—is a worthwhile return on the investment. Usually, spam is sent in bulk using automated mailing software, and many spammers sell their address lists. For these reasons, the volume of spam can rise to an unmanageable level quickly, clogging users' in-boxes and preventing access to legitimate e-mail.

Another privacy concern is ease of access. Whether an e-mail is distributed through the Web or through a company network, people should assume that others have access to their messages. In addition, many organizations have policies stating that any e-mail sent on company-owned computers are the organization's property and that the organization has the right to access them. In other words, employees often have no right to privacy, although there is a lot of controversy over this point and several lawsuits have resulted.

> **Whether an e-mail is distributed through the Web or through a company network, people should assume that others have access to their messages.**

Spamming has also created concerns about its decency because spam often contains explicit language or nudity and can be opened by children. The following statistics for e-mail and spam illustrate how pervasive the problem has become:[19]

- 3.8 billion: E-mail accounts worldwide
- 281 billion: E-mails sent per day (expected to grow to more than 333 billion by 2022)
- 60 percent: E-mail read on mobile devices worldwide
- 49.7 percent: E-mail that is considered spam
- 2.3 percent: E-mail that has a malicious attachment
- The United States, China, and Russia are the top three countries for generating spam.

The "E-Mail and Corporate Data Leakage" box highlights other privacy issues related to e-mail.

4-1c Data Collection on the Web

The number of people shopping online is increasing rapidly because of its convenience, the array of choices, and lower prices. Many customers, however, are reluctant to make online purchases because of concerns about hackers getting access to their credit card numbers and charging merchandise to their accounts. To lessen consumers' concerns, many

iStock.com/lucadp

credit card companies reimburse fraudulent charges. In addition, other electronic payment systems are being developed, such as e-wallets and smart cards, that reduce the risks of exposing consumers' information on the Web (discussed in Module 8).

Some Web sites require you to enter your name, address, and employment information before you are allowed to use the site. Privacy issues include the concern that this personal information will be sold to telemarketing firms; consumers do not want to be bombarded with spam. Also, some consumers are concerned about their computers' contents being searched while they are connected to the Web, and that personal information could be used without their consent for solicitation and other purposes.

Information that users provide on the Web can be combined with other information and technologies to produce new information. For example, a financial profile can be created by collecting a person's employment information. Two commonly used technologies for data collection are cookies and log files.

Cookies are small text files with unique ID tags that are embedded in a Web browser and saved on the user's hard drive. Whenever a user returns to a previously visited Web site and accesses the same domain, the browser sends the saved information about the site to the Web server. Sometimes, cookies are useful or innocuous, such as those used by a Web page to welcome you to a site or those used by a Web site to remember your personal information for online ordering. Typically, users rely on

> **Cookies** are small text files with unique ID tags that are embedded in a Web browser and saved on the user's hard drive.

E-Mail and Corporate Data Leakage

➤➤ Finance | Social and Ethical Issues

Employees' lack of knowledge about e-mail or their reluctance to follow company policy can have significant consequences for an organization. For example, using the "Reply All" option instead of "Reply" can result in private information being sent to recipients who were not supposed to have access to the information. Also, printouts of confidential e-mail can end up in wastebaskets, hotel rooms, or airport terminals (or linger in the printer's memory), which introduces risks. Sending and receiving e-mail through smartphones, tablets, and other handheld devices further adds to the vulnerability of a company's private information. To increase the security of your e-mail communication and reduce the risks involved, follow these recommendations:[20]

- Encrypt sensitive e-mail.
- Do not send corporate information from personal (unsecured) e-mail accounts.
- Back up, save, or archive important e-mail.
- Don't use the "Reply All" option for all e-mail responses, and remember to delete prior threads within the e-mail.
- Train employees to consider every e-mail as potentially public.
- Avoid e-mailing from a shared or public computer.
- Watch for phishing e-mail.
- Do not respond to spam e-mail.
- Consider erasing all nonessential e-mail after 90 to 120 days.
- Understand the difference between the BCC and CC options. When using the blind carbon copy (BCC) option, e-mail addresses are hidden from view. When using carbon copy (CC), each recipient of an e-mail can view the e-mail addresses of all other recipients.

Questions and Discussions

1. How might corporate data leak out unintentionally?
2. What is the difference between BCC and CC?

Log files, which are generated by Web server software, record a user's actions on a Web site.

Web sites to keep this information from being compromised. Cookies also make it possible for Web sites to customize pages for users; this is why Amazon can recommend books based on your past purchases.

Cookies can sometimes be considered an invasion of privacy, and some people believe their information should be collected only with their consent. Cookies provide information about the user's location and computer equipment, and this information could be used for unauthorized purposes, such as corporate espionage.

For these reasons, many users disable cookies by installing a cookie manager, which can eliminate existing cookies and prevent additional cookies from being saved to a user's hard drive. Popular Web browsers such as Chrome, Safari, and Firefox provide a range of options for accepting and restricting cookies. However, there is another cookie called a *supercookie* that is

more challenging to deal with. A supercookie is a type of browser cookie that is designed to be permanently stored on a user's device and is much more difficult to remove. Its function is the same as a regular cookie that tracks a user's browsing activities, even in a privacy mode. However, utility programs are available to help guard against these types of cookies and remove them from a user's device.[21]

Log files, which are generated by Web server software, record a user's actions on a Web site. Sometimes, users give incorrect information on purpose—on chatting or dating sites, for example, or when opening e-mail accounts. If the information collected is not accurate, the user's identity could be misrepresented. For example, if someone claims to be younger than their actual age on an online dating site, demographic data collected from the site would be flawed. Similarly, if a network streaming service collects data on viewing trends through online surveys and people supply answers that are not truthful, any analyses the network attempts to conduct would not be accurate. Therefore, data collected on the Web must be used and interpreted with caution.

Unethical Behavior at Facebook

▶▶ Finance | Social and Ethical Issues

During the 2016 U.S. presidential election, Cambridge Analytica, a political data company hired by Donald Trump's election campaign, gained access to the private information of more than 50 million Facebook users. The company offered tools that could identify the personalities of American voters and influence their behavior. The company promised to target voters' "unconscious psychological biases" by using massive amounts of individual data collected from each user's profile. The data collected from the Facebook users included users' identities, friend networks, and "likes." The idea was to map personality traits based on what people had liked on Facebook, and then use that information to target audiences with digital ads. This massive data collection was used to create specific ads. Cambridge Analytica has been under scrutiny from government officials and regulators over its role in the 2016 election as well as the United Kingdom's Brexit campaign to leave the European Union in 2015. In 2018, Facebook suspended Cambridge Analytica for violating its terms of service by collecting and sharing the personal information of users without their consent.[22]

This is not the first time that users' personal information has been misused on Facebook. In 2012, a team of researchers from Facebook and Cornell University manipulated the news feeds of approximately 700,000 Facebook users to measure whether certain emotions could be spread on social media. Interestingly enough, they found that users who saw more positive posts tended to write more positive posts themselves, and vice versa. This created ethical concerns, as researchers were manipulating users' moods. The experiment created outrage and disappointment among users after results were published in 2014.

Alexandra Popova/Shutterstock.com

(Continued)

Facebook privacy violations go well beyond the two cases already discussed. Between 2004 and 2021, more than 25 cases showed how Facebook violated the privacy of users on its platform worldwide and was directed to pay millions of dollars in fines to various regulatory agencies. In one of these cases, for example, Facebook uploaded the e-mail contact information of 1.5 million users without their consent. In two other cases, the private information of various WhatsApp group members was made public via Google and information for 533 million Facebook users was found on a hackers' Web site.[23]

Some experts believe that Facebook has too much power and that its business model can lead to misuse of users' personal information. The cases filed against Facebook clearly underscore the online world's need for better ethical guidelines.[24]

Questions and Discussions

1. Discuss Cambridge Analytica's unethical use of Facebook data.
2. What are two examples of unethical behavior by Facebook?

4-2 Ethical Issues of Information Technologies

Problems at companies such as Enron, Arthur Andersen, WorldCom, and Tyco have highlighted the ethical issues that corporations face in the 21st century. In essence, ethics means doing the right thing, but what is "right" can vary from one culture to another and even from one person to another.[25]

The distinction between what is legal and what is illegal is usually clear, but drawing a line between ethical and unethical behavior is more difficult. Exhibit 4.1 shows a grid that can be used for assessing whether an action is legal and ethical.

Review the following situations and try to determine where they might fall within the grid shown in Exhibit 4.1:

1. You make two copies of a software package you just bought and sell one to a friend.

2. You make two copies of a software package you just bought for personal use, in case the original software fails and you need a backup.

3. A banker uses the information a client enters in a loan application to sell other financial products to the client.

4. A credit card company sells its customers' mailing addresses to its competitors.

5. A supervisor fires a programmer who has intentionally spread viruses to the organization's network.

Statement 1 is clearly illegal and unethical (quadrant IV). Statement 2 represents ethical behavior because you made the copy for your own use, but some software vendors who prohibit making copies might consider it illegal (quadrant II). Statements 3 and 4 are legal but not ethical (quadrant III). In statement 5, the supervisor's behavior is both legal and ethical. The supervisor has a clear legal reason for firing the programmer; allowing the programmer to continue working at the organization would not be ethical. As a future knowledge worker, watch your own actions, and make sure you behave both legally and ethically. Be careful about decisions you make that might affect coworkers so you can help maintain an ethical working environment.

Some information systems professionals believe that information technology offers many opportunities for unethical behavior, particularly because of the ease of collecting and disseminating information. Cybercrime, cyberfraud, identity theft, and intellectual property theft (discussed later in this module) are on the rise. Nearly 15 million U.S. residents have their identities stolen every year,

Exhibit 4.1
Ethical versus legal grid

	Legal	Illegal
Ethical	I	II
Unethical	III	IV

with a total loss of over $50 billion. This means one identity is stolen every two seconds, with an average loss of $3,500.[26]

To find out how quickly stolen data can spread throughout the world, a data protection company conducted an experiment. The company put sensitive information, including credit card numbers and Social Security numbers of 1,568 fictitious individuals, on sites that buy and sell stolen data. Within two weeks, the company found that the stolen data was viewed more than 1,000 times and downloaded 47 times by people in 22 countries on five continents.[27]

Another type of identity theft, called business identity theft, is on the rise. There are four main types of business identity theft: financial fraud, tax fraud, Web site defacement, and trademark ransom. Each of these can have significant financial consequences, including damage to reputation and customer relationships or even making a business go bankrupt. Thieves can alter business information online and then use it to apply for credit cards or make payments to other criminals.[28] Businesses are at risk for their brand, reputation, and trade secrets. According to the FBI, one prominent case of business identity theft cost the business $1 billion in market share and hundreds of jobs. Insiders can play a major role in committing business identity theft, and they are very difficult to control. Businesses should restrict data access only to workers who need it to perform their jobs. The security measures presented in Module 5 should help to guard against this type of identity theft.[29]

Many experts believe management can reduce employees' unethical behavior by developing and enforcing codes of ethics. Many associations promote the ethically responsible use of information systems and technologies and have developed codes of ethics for their members. The Association for Computing Machinery (ACM), for example, has a code of ethics and professional conduct that includes the following general moral imperatives:[30]

1. Contribute to society and to human well-being, acknowledging that all people are stakeholders in computing.
2. Avoid harm.
3. Be honest and trustworthy.
4. Be fair and take action not to discriminate.
5. Respect the work required to produce new ideas, inventions, creative works, and computing artifacts.
6. Respect privacy.
7. Honor confidentiality.

As a knowledge worker, you should consider the following questions and statements before making a work-related decision:

1. Does this decision comply with my organization's values?
2. How will I feel about myself after making this decision?
3. If I know this decision is wrong, I must not make it.
4. If I am not sure about this decision, I must ask my supervisor before making it.
5. Is the decision right?
6. Is the decision fair? How will I feel if somebody else makes this decision on my behalf?
7. Is the decision legal?
8. Would I want everyone to know about this decision after I make it?

Ten Commandments of Computer Ethics[31]

Thou shalt not use a computer to harm other people.

Thou shalt not interfere with other people's computer work.

Thou shalt not snoop around in other people's files.

Thou shalt not use a computer to steal.

Thou shalt not use a computer to bear false witness.

Thou shalt not use or copy software for which you have not paid.

Thou shalt not use other people's computer resources without authorization.

Thou shalt not appropriate other people's intellectual output.

Thou shalt think about the social consequences of the program you write.

Thou shalt use a computer in ways that show consideration and respect.

The "Ten Commandments of Computer Ethics" was created by the Computer Ethics Institute. You should observe the guidelines in the preceding box when using information technology for personal or professional reasons.

4-2a Computer Network Ethics

Computer network ethics includes two types of ethics: social media networking ethics and business networking ethics. **Social media networking ethics** advocates that social media should be open and provide fair access to all of its users. However, every user must understand that social media is a community and that users must treat others in the community with respect and kindness. For example, aggressive targeted marketing has no place in social media. Three main principles of social media ethics include:[32]

- *Authenticity*—Members should be trustworthy and sincere.
- *Transparency*—Members should be honest and open with no hidden agenda.
- *Communication*—Members should be open to knowing other members and be able to communicate openly.

Netiquette should also be considered a part of social media ethics and should be carefully exercised. Netiquette is short for "Internet etiquette," which is a code of good behavior on the Internet. It simply refers to good manners when you are online and using e-mail, the Internet, blogs, and social media. The following list specifies important netiquette that should be followed when you are online:[33]

- When typing, never write in all capital letters.
- Do not plagiarize. Always respect intellectual property.
- Use proper quotes and always use the entire quote in context.
- Do not gossip; keep personal information to yourself.
- If you use artwork from the Web, give the correct credit to the originator or get permission from the copyright holder.
- Use proper language with no profanity.
- Be patient with Internet newbies.
- Do not spam.
- Always use a header in e-mail communication that is relevant to the content of the e-mail.
- Do not use too many emoticons.

Business networking ethics advocates that to maintain a business network, not only should the organization provide open and fair access to all authorized users, it should also consider three types of networking, including utilitarian, emotional, and virtuous. These types are explained briefly as follows.[34]

- *Utilitarian networking*—Ensures that the networking is a true utility, truthful, and is not wasting its users' time.
- *Emotional networking*—Ensures that users will empathize with being ethical in all situations and that emotion should not play a role.
- *Virtuous networking*—Ensures that all parties will act in good faith by sharing honest goals and participating in legitimate activities.

There are six principles for the implementation of successful and ethical business networking:[35]

1. Consider the front-page rule. Would I want everyone to know about a particular decision after I made it? How would I feel if details of my decision appeared on the front page of the local newspaper?
2. Formulate ethical yet practical policies. Establish achievable ethical goals.
3. Educate users. Explain the consequences of unethical decision making to all users.
4. Make ethics part of the hiring process. Do not just look for technical skills in new hires. Put the new hires through an ethical test as well as a technical test.
5. Ensure that staff members know what to do when faced with an ethical dilemma. If they are not sure about a decision, they must ask their supervisors before making it.
6. Enforce ethical standards strictly and evenly. Violators must be punished.

To minimize the ethical and legal problems of information technology, we must become good digital citizens. Digital citizenship must be taught to children and young adults early in their education and should be practiced by everyone who uses information

Social media networking ethics advocates that social media should be open and provide fair access to all of its users.

Business networking ethics advocates that to maintain a business network, not only should the organization provide open and fair access to all authorized users, it should also consider three types of networking: utilitarian, emotional, and virtuous.

technology in society. **Digital citizenship** means using information technology safely, ethically, and responsibly. The following seven principles should be taught and practiced by a good digital citizen:[36]

- The importance of online etiquette
- The importance of privacy protection
- The importance of knowing how to stay safe online
- The importance of the "dos and don'ts" of information technology
- The importance of protecting and respecting intellectual property
- The importance of understanding one's digital footprint—thinking before posting something on the Web
- The importance of healthy usage patterns—a balance between screen time and offline time

4-2b Censorship

No organization controls the whole Web, so who decides what content should be on it? Two types of information are available on the Web: public and private. Public information posted by an organization or public agency can be censored for public policy reasons—for example, military secrets should not be published, lest the information fall into enemy hands. Public information can also be censored if the content is deemed offensive to a political, religious, or cultural group. However, private information—what is posted by a person—is not subject to censorship because of the person's constitutional freedom of expression. Of course, whether or not something can be censored depends in part on who is doing the censoring. For example, if you agree to abide by an organization's or Internet service provider's policies and then post something that violates the terms, you might be censored or denied access.

Some countries, such as China, Myanmar (Burma), and Singapore, restrict or forbid their citizens' access to the Web or try to censor information posted on the Web. Governments in these countries believe that the racist, pornographic, and politically extreme content of some Web sites could affect national security. In other

> **Public information posted by an organization or public agency can be censored for public policy reasons.**

countries, only employees of multinational corporations have direct access to the Web. Some countries censor parts of the Web or the entire Internet for political or social reasons. As of 2021, the top 10 Internet-censored countries were North Korea, China, Turkey, Russia, the United Arab Emirates, Pakistan, Iran, Turkmenistan, India, and Iraq.[37]

Most experts believe that Internet neutrality (also known as "net neutrality") must be practiced in all cases. According to this principle, Internet service providers and government agencies should treat all data on the Internet equally—that is, they should not block traffic, charge different rates, or discriminate in any way based on the user, content, Web site, type of equipment in use, telecommunication provider, platform, or application.[38]

A non-neutral network would have an impact on nearly all individuals and businesses, regardless of the type of business they are engaged in. A non-neutral network would increase the cost of Internet connectivity for nearly all of us. Companies and individuals that wanted faster access in a non-neutral network would have to pay a much higher rate to get to the "fast lane."[39]

Although U.S. citizens do not want the government controlling Web access, many parents are concerned about their children being exposed to pornography, violence, and adult language while using the Web.

Another concern is children searching for information on the Web. If a search includes keywords such as *toys*, *pets*, *boys*, or *girls*, for example, the results could list pornography sites. Guidelines for Web use have been published to inform parents of the benefits and hazards of the Web, and parents can use these guidelines to teach their children to use good judgment while on the Web. For example, Microsoft posts a guideline called "Online Safety Information and Tips | Microsoft" (*https://www.microsoft.com/en-us/digital-skills/online-safety-resources*). In addition, many parents use programs such as CyberPatrol, CYBERSitter, Net Nanny, and SafeSurf to prevent their children from accessing certain Web sites.

Web browser software has also been developed with children in mind. For example, a Web browser might accept e-mail only from an address that uses the same Web browser software. This helps ensure that children receive e-mail only from other children. As an example, Facebook released a version of its Messenger chat app designed for children between ages 6 and 12. Because kids under the age of 13 cannot sign up for a Facebook account, parents can manage a child's Messenger Kids app from their own Facebook account, controlling which friends and family members the child is able to contact.[40] Another control option is to create different levels of user access, similar to movie ratings, to prevent children from accessing controversial or pornographic information. This system could use control techniques such as passwords or biometrics, including fingerprints or retinal scans (discussed in Module 5).

4-2c Intellectual Property

Intellectual property is a legal umbrella covering protections that involve copyrights, trademarks, trade secrets, and patents for "creations of the mind" developed by people or businesses.[41] Intellectual property can be divided into two categories: industrial property (inventions, trademarks, logos, industrial designs, and so on) and copyrighted material, which covers literary and artistic works.

Generally, copyright laws protect tangible material, such as books and drawings. However, they also cover online materials, including Web pages, HTML code, and computer graphics, as long as the content can be printed or saved on a storage device. Copyright laws give the material's creator exclusive rights, meaning no one else can reproduce, distribute, or perform the work without permission.[42]

Copyright laws do have some exceptions, however, usually under the Fair Use Doctrine. These exceptions mean you can use copyrighted material for certain purposes, such as quoting passages of a book in literary reviews. There are limits on how much material you can use. In addition, some copyrighted material can be used to create new work, particularly for educational purposes. Checking copyright laws carefully before using such material is strongly recommended. The U.S. Copyright Office (*www.copyright.gov*) offers detailed information on copyright issues. Exhibit 4.2 shows its home page.

Other intellectual property protections include trademarks and patents. A trademark protects product names and identifying marks (logos, for example). A patent protects new processes. (Note that laws governing trademarks, patents, and copyrights in the United States might not apply in other countries.) The length of a copyright varies based on the type of work. In general, copyrights last the author's lifetime plus 70 years and do not need to be renewed; U.S. design patents resulting from applications filed on or after May 13, 2015, have a 15-year term from the date of grant.

> **Intellectual property**
> is a legal umbrella covering protections that involve copyrights, trademarks, trade secrets, and patents for "creations of the mind" developed by people or businesses.

Exhibit 4.2
U.S. Copyright Office home page

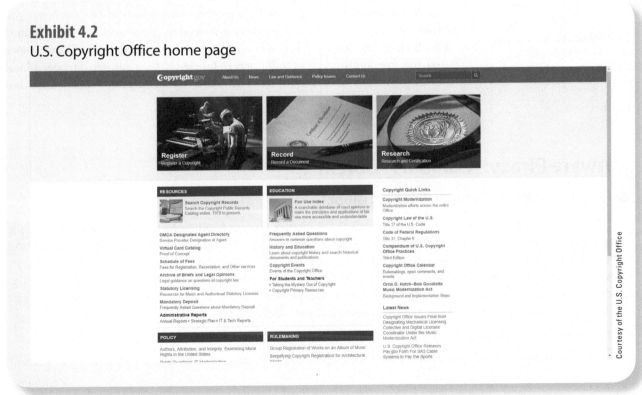

Courtesy of the U.S. Copyright Office

An organization can benefit from a patent in at least three ways:[43]

1. It can generate revenue by licensing its patent to others.
2. It can use the patent to attract funding for further research and development.
3. It can use the patent to keep competitors from entering certain market segments.

Another copyright concern is software piracy (see the information box "Software Piracy: A Global Problem"), but the laws covering it are very straightforward. The 1980 revisions to the Copyright Act of 1976 include computer programs, so both people and organizations can be held liable for unauthorized duplication and use of copyrighted programs. Sometimes, contracts are used to supplement copyrights and give the software originator additional protection. For example, a software vendor might require that a university sign a contract specifying how many people can use the software. Companies also make use of laws on trade secrets, which cover ideas, information, and innovations, to afford themselves extra protection.

Most legal issues related to information technologies in the United States are covered by the Telecommunications Act of 1996, the Communications Decency Act (CDA), and laws against spamming. The CDA was partially overturned in the 1997 *Reno v. ACLU* case, in which the U.S. Supreme Court unanimously voted to strike down the CDA's anti-indecency provisions, finding they violated the freedom of speech provisions of the First Amendment.

> **Cybersquatting** is registering, selling, or using a domain name to profit from someone else's trademark.

To avoid the following legal risks, organizations should have an Internet use policy:[44]

- *Risk 1*—If employees download pornographic materials to their office computers over the corporate network, the organization could be liable for harassment charges as well as infringement of privacy and even violation of copyright laws.

- *Risk 2*—Indecent e-mail exchanges among employees can leave a corporation open to discrimination and sexual harassment charges.

- *Risk 3*—Employees using a corporate network to download and distribute unlicensed software can leave the corporation open to serious charges of copyright infringement and other legal issues.

One aspect of intellectual property that has attracted attention is **cybersquatting**, also known as domain squatting, which is registering, selling, or using a domain name to profit from someone else's trademark. Often, it involves buying domains containing the names of existing businesses and then selling the names for a profit. A variation of cybersquatting is typosquatting, also called URL hijacking. This technique relies on typographical errors made by Web users when typing a Web site address into a Web browser. If the user accidentally enters an incorrect Web site address, the user may be directed to an alternative Web site owned by a typosquatter. In such a case, the legitimate site does not get the intended traffic. Examples include *whitehouse.org* instead of *whitehouse.gov* and *goggle.com* instead of *google.com*. To guard against this, major Web sites register variations of their names so traffic gets redirected to the main site if typographical errors are made. The "Cybersquatting Is on the Rise" box describes such a case.

Software Piracy: A Global Problem

➤➤ Social and Ethical Issues | Finance | Global

Globally, two of every five copies of a software product are pirated; Microsoft Office, Microsoft Windows, and Adobe Photoshop are among the top three pirated software products.[45] The top three countries with the highest piracy rates are Venezuela at 88 percent, Indonesia at 86 percent, and China at 77 percent.[46] According to the 2018 Global Software Survey, the commercial value of unlicensed software globally is $46.3 billion, and 37 percent of software installed on personal computers is unlicensed. Users should be aware that there is a one-in-three chance that unlicensed software carries some type of malware. Here are some important statistics related to piracy:[47, 48]

- 57 percent of the world's computer users confess to pirating software.

- The United States has the largest market for software, spending $42 billion, and the lowest piracy rate at 19 percent.

(Continued)

- Unlicensed software was found in 194 of 195 countries surveyed.
- China, the United States, Iran, Russia, and India are among the top 20 countries for software license misuse and piracy hotspots.

Questions and Discussions

1. What are the top three pirated software products? What is the commercial value of unlicensed software globally?
2. Why is software pirated? What might be some effective ways of preventing software piracy?

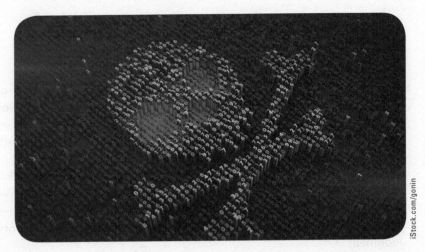

iStock.com/gonin

As a knowledge worker, you should be familiar with two additional concepts that are related to intellectual property: open source and Creative Commons. *Open source* software is created by designers and programmers who write programs or applications and then make the original source code freely available. This code may be used or redistributed and modified freely. Some experts argue that there are ethical issues involved in the open source platform. For example, who develops this software? Is there a balance between male and female developers? Is any minority group involved in the design process? What if open source software is modified and sold later? Who actually gains the most benefit from open source? These issues should be examined before widespread adoption and implementation of such code.[49]

A *Creative Commons (CC)* license is one of several public copyright licenses that enable the free distribution of an otherwise copyrighted work. CC licenses are used when creators allow other people the right to share, use, and build upon a work they created. Under CC, the creator has freedom and flexibility to select beneficiaries of the work. For example, the creator might choose to allow only educational institutions to use the work freely. The group specified by the creator can use the work without violating any copyright agreement.[50]

4-2d Social Divisions and the Digital Divide

Some believe that information technology and the Internet have created a **digital divide** between the information-rich and the information-poor. Although their prices have been decreasing steadily, computers are still not affordable for many people. In addition, a type of economic "red-lining" can occur when companies that install coaxial and fiber-optic cable for Internet connections focus on higher-income communities, where more residents are expected to use the Internet.[51]

Children in particular are often victims of the digital divide. Those without computers or Web access at home, as well as students who cannot afford computer equipment, are at a disadvantage and can often fall behind in their education. Students without access to the wide array of resources on the Web have more difficulty writing papers and learning about topics that interest them. Lack of access to interactive and virtual-reality educational games on the Web can widen the gap more. The speed of the Internet connection also plays a role in the digital divide discussion. Because of the availability of multimedia information on the Web, those who have faster connections may benefit more than people with a slower connection. Increasing funding for computer equipment at schools and adding more computers in public places, such as libraries, can help offset this divide. Some schools have even started loaner programs so students can have a portable computer to use after school hours.

The "Digital Divide in Action" box highlights some interesting facts related to the digital divide in the United States and the rest of the world.

> Information technology and the Internet have created a **digital divide**. Computers are still not affordable for many people. The digital divide has implications for education.

Cybersquatting Is on the Rise

➤ Social and Ethical Issues | Finance

According to the World Intellectual Property Organization (WIPO), cybersquatting cases grew by 12 percent to reach a new record of 3,447 cases in 2018.[52] In 2018, DreamWorks Animation won a cybersquatting case in which a person had registered two domain names illegally: *orientaldreamworks.com* and *shanghaidreamworks.com*. The same person had registered more than 200 other domain names. Most frequently, squatters use domain names to offer counterfeit goods or for phishing attacks.

Verizon sued a company called OnlineNic, accusing it of trademark infringement and illegal cybersquatting. According to Verizon, OnlineNic registered domain names containing Verizon trademarks. The registered names included *myverizonwireless.com*, *iphoneverizonplans.com*, and *verizon-cellular.com*, among others, and Verizon was concerned that the names would mislead consumers. Verizon won the suit and was awarded a $33 million judgment.[53, 54]

Questions and Discussions

1. Which company was sued by Verizon for cybersquatting? What is the difference between cybersquatting and typosquatting?
2. Is cybersquatting unethical? Why or why not?

4-3 The Impact of Information Technology in the Workplace

Although information technology has eliminated some clerical jobs, it has created many new jobs (described in Module 1) for programmers, systems analysts, database and network administrators, network engineers, Webmasters, Web page developers, e-commerce specialists, chief information officers, and technicians. In e-commerce, jobs for Web designers, Java programmers, and Web troubleshooters have been created as well. Some argue that the new jobs have been mostly technical, requiring extensive training. Others believe that information technologies have reduced production costs and improved consumers' purchasing power, resulting in a stronger economy.

Information technologies have a direct effect on the nature of jobs. Telecommuting, also known as virtual work, has enabled some people to perform their jobs from home. With telecommunications technology, a worker can send and receive data to and from the main office, and organizations can use the best and most cost-effective human resources to cover a large geographical region. Table 4.1 lists some potential benefits and drawbacks of telecommuting.

By handling repetitive and boring tasks, information technologies have made many jobs more interesting, resulting in more worker satisfaction. Information technologies have also led to "job deskilling." This occurs when skilled labor is eliminated by high technology or when a job is downgraded from a skilled to a semiskilled or unskilled position. Job deskilling usually happens when a job is automated or when a complex job is fragmented into a sequence of easily performed tasks. An example is a computer-aided design (CAD) program that performs technical tasks once performed by a human designer. Information technologies have also created "job upgrading," as when clerical workers use computers for word-processing tasks. This upgrading makes it possible to add new tasks to employees' responsibilities, too; for example, clerical workers could be responsible for updating the company's Web site. Job upgrading has some limitations, however. Even with information technologies, training clerical workers to write programs for the company Web site could be difficult.

With information technologies, one skilled worker might be capable of doing the job of several workers. For example, with mail-merge programs, an office worker can generate thousands of letters, eliminating the need for additional workers. Information technologies can also make workers more efficient—they can send a message

The Digital Divide in Action

🡆 Social and Ethical Issues | Finance

As of 2021, 7 percent of U.S. adults (about 23 million) did not use the Internet.[55] However, this is a significant improvement when compared to the year 2000, when the usage was only 48 percent. Internet adoption and use is highly correlated to a number of factors, including age, household income, educational background, race and ethnicity, and community.[56] As of 2021, nearly 34 percent of the world's population did not have access to the Internet.

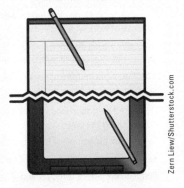

Broadband Internet access is a key factor in improving the digital divide because it can bring a wealth of information and economic opportunities to people, regardless of where they live. In rural America, 35 percent of schools do not have access to broadband Internet, compared with 3 percent in urban areas.[57] Bringing broadband communication to rural schools and libraries will help narrow the gap. Bridging the digital divide and broadening high-speed access will benefit the entire society and help economic growth. In particular, it will offer the following three benefits:[58]

- *Education*—All students throughout the country will have access to the same educational resources.
- *Economic development*—Broadband Internet could encourage companies to open shops all over the country and hire workers to produce goods and services. An interesting study conducted by Brookings Institution indicates that for every 1 percent increase in high-speed Internet penetration, employment expands by nearly 300,000 jobs.
- *Public health*—High-speed communication will provide health-related services such as telemedicine and make them more cost-effective to the entire nation.

Smartphones and mobile devices for accessing the Internet help to bridge the digital divide, particularly in economically developing nations, where there are few established wired networks. Wireless and mobile networks are easier and cheaper to install.

Questions and Discussions

1. As of 2021, what percentage of U.S. adults did not use the Internet?
2. Bridging the digital divide and broadening high-speed access will benefit the entire society. Discuss.

---

throughout an organization by using e-mail instead of interoffice memos, for example. Similarly, mass-marketing efforts for new product announcements have been streamlined, reducing the expense and personnel needed to reach millions of customers.

Another impact of information technology is the creation of **virtual organizations**, which are networks of independent companies, suppliers, customers, and manufacturers that can share skills and costs and have access to each other's markets.[59] A virtual organization does not need central offices or an organizational hierarchy for participants to contribute their expertise. Advantages of virtual organizations include the following:[60]

- Each participating company can focus on what it does best, thus improving the ability to meet customers' needs.

- Because skills are shared among participating companies, the cost of hiring additional employees is reduced.

- Companies can respond to customers faster and more efficiently.

- The time needed to develop new products is reduced.

- Products can be customized more to respond to customers' needs.

In one example, Dell, Microsoft, and Unisys Corporation created a partnership to design

> **Virtual organizations** are networks of independent companies, suppliers, customers, and manufacturers connected via information technology so they can share skills and costs and have access to each other's markets.

Table 4.1 Potential Benefits and Drawbacks of Telecommuting

Potential Benefits	Potential Drawbacks
Better ability to care for small children or elderly parents and spend more time with family	Possibility of becoming a workaholic (no hard boundaries between "at work" and "at home")
Fewer restrictions on clothing for work, thereby saving the expense of work wear	No regulated work routine
No commute, so distance and time factors are reduced as well as the effects of car emissions on air quality	Less interaction with coworkers
Ability to work in more pleasant surroundings	No separation between work and home life
Increased productivity	Potential legal issues about workers' injuries
Decreased neighborhood crime because more people are home during the day	Family interruptions and household distractions
Easier work environment for employees with disabilities	Lack of necessary supplies or equipment
Reduced costs for office space and utilities	Possibility of creating a two-tiered workforce—telecommuters and on-site workers—that affects promotions and raises
Reduced employee turnover and absenteeism	Security and privacy issues
Ability to find and hire people with special skills, regardless of where they are located	
Fewer interruptions from coworkers	

a voting system for several U.S. states. Microsoft offered software, Dell offered hardware, and Unisys served as the systems integrator. This example illustrates the principle of virtual organizations—the idea that several organizations working together can do what one organization cannot.

4-3a Information Technology and Health Issues

Although there have been reports of health problems caused by video display terminals (VDTs), no conclusive study indicates that VDTs are the cause, despite all the complaints. Work habits can cause physical problems, however, and so can some aspects of the work environment in which computers are used—for example, static electricity, inadequate ventilation, poor lighting, dry air, unsuitable furniture, and too few rest breaks.

The increasing popularity of touchscreens on smartphones, tablets, and some PCs may result in more stress-related injuries to users' hands, arms, back, and eyes. Because these devices can be accessed almost anywhere and are used with any number of body positions (most of which involve poor posture), users should exercise caution and take frequent breaks.[61] *Text neck* is a relatively new term that describes neck pain and damage caused from looking down frequently at smartphones, tablets, or other handheld devices. It is affecting millions of people all over the world, particularly teenagers and young adults.[62]

Repetitive typing with thumbs or continually navigating through various pages and apps is causing another health issue called "smartphone thumb" or *tendinitis* for many smartphone users. This condition was seen among factory workers in the past. Using the speech feature available on most smartphones, taking periodic breaks, and performing stretching exercises could alleviate this problem to a degree.[63, 64]

Mobile devices, particularly smartphones, may create serious health issues and other negative impacts for teenagers. Half of all teenagers believe they're addicted to their smartphones.[65] Here are the major negative impacts:[66]

- *Teen tendinitis:* Too much texting and poor posture can cause pain in the hands, back, and neck.

- *Stress:* Too much time spent on handheld devices causes stress and fatigue.

- *Sleep loss:* Because most teenagers (and many adults) keep their smartphones nearby while sleeping, sleep interruption and sleep deprivation may result.

- *Accidents:* Some teens use their smartphones while driving and answer calls or texts; this may cause accidents.

- *Increased anxiety:* Delays in response or no response to their communications causes anxiety for teens.

- *Cyberbullying:* Studies show that nearly one-third of teens are victims of cyberbullying; the perpetrators are anonymous and cannot be recognized.

- *Risk of cancer:* Compared with adults, teenagers might have a greater risk of developing brain cancer from excessive use of smartphones.

Also, according to some reports, a disorder called "Snapchat dysmorphia" is developing in young adults. Snapchat offers several features that can animate a human face with special filtered effects, and some doctors say young adults are seeking plastic surgery to permanently look like the filtered versions of themselves, which is quite dangerous.[67]

Other reports of health problems related to computer equipment include vision problems, such as eye fatigue, itching, and blurriness; musculoskeletal problems (back strain and wrist pain); skin problems, such as rashes; reproductive problems, such as miscarriages; and stress-related problems (headaches and depression). Ergonomics experts believe that using better-designed furniture, flexible or wireless keyboards, correct lighting, and special monitors for workers with vision problems can solve many of these problems.

Another relatively new health issue involves the amount of time some people spend on the Web playing games or participating in chat rooms and other activities. Although the Internet can provide valuable educational resources, too much time spent on the Web can create psychological, social, and health problems, especially for young people. Another issue is related to the well-being of children. Recent research revealed that children feel "hidden sadness" when their parents spend too much time on their digital gadgets, including smartphones. Children indicated that they have a hard time getting time or attention from their parents.[68]

Research conducted by the security company AVG found that one-third of children indicated that their parents spend as much time or more time with their gadgets than with them, and one-third said they feel unimportant when their parents are distracted by their phones. Parental inattention to children can be dangerous; there has been nearly a 22 percent increase in preventable accidents suffered by young children when their parents are using their gadgets.[69]

Another health-related issue is Internet addiction, of which there are five types:[70]

- *Cybersexual*—Cybersex and Internet porn
- *Web compulsions*—Online gambling, shopping, or stock trading

Health and Social Issues of Online Gaming

⏩ Social and Ethical Issues | Finance | Global

World of Warcraft and EverQuest, two massively multiplayer online role-playing games (MMORPG), have been blamed for a host of problems, including poor academic performance, divorce, suicide, and even the death of a child because of parental neglect. Mental health professionals believe the fantasy worlds in online games can be addictive and affect marriages and careers. According to Dr. Timothy Miller, a clinical psychologist, it is a growing problem with teenaged boys and young adult men.[71]

In June 2018, the World Health Organization (WHO) classified gaming disorder as a disease and stated that compulsively playing video games now qualifies as a mental health condition.[72]

According to *Global Times*, a 33-year-old man died after playing online games at an Internet café for 27 days in a row. That's nearly 650 hours of playing while barely eating or sleeping.[73] Also, an Xbox addict died from a blood clot; according to reports, he had been playing games on his Xbox for up to 12 hours a day.[74] In 2021, a 16-year-old boy collapsed and died after he reportedly played the online game Fire Wall continuously for several hours.[75]

sezer66/Shutterstock.com

Questions and Discussions

1. The World Health Organization has classified gaming disorder as a disease. Discuss.
2. How could playing online games cause serious health issues or even death? Discuss.

- *Cyber relationships*—Social media, online dating, and other virtual communication
- *Gaming*—Online game playing
- *Information seeking*—Web surfing or database searches

Internet addiction is a type of compulsive behavior that interferes with a person's normal activities and causes stress and other health issues. Researchers estimate that about 7 percent of the world's 4.88 billion Internet users are addicted to the Internet—more than 330 million people in 2022.[76] Experts believe that many of us, particularly millennials, are addicted to their smartphones. The following statistics back up this claim:[77]

- People typically check their smartphones 100 times a day.
- Forty percent of people check their smartphones while using the bathroom.
- One in 10 people use their smartphones in the shower.

Another health-related issue is "distracted walking," which causes 11,000 injuries a year in the United States alone. This term refers to walking while using a smartphone for texting, watching videos, and other activities.[78] Common risks associated with distracted walking include injuring someone else, injuring oneself, and even death in some cases.[79]

Another relatively new problem is the number of selfie deaths around the world. A recent report indicated that 259 people died within a six-year period after stepping in front of a smartphone camera in often dangerous places to take a selfie.[80]

Experts offer several recommendations for overcoming addiction to the Internet, smartphones, or other computing devices:[81, 82]

- Admit that you have a problem.
- Limit your Internet and smartphone use.
- Change communication patterns by not using mobile devices for a while.
- Socialize with family and friends more.
- Find interests that do not involve mobile devices.
- Set and adhere to a schedule for mobile device use.
- Keep mobile devices inaccessible at times.

Green computing involves the design, manufacture, use, and disposal of computers, servers, and other computing devices so that there is minimal impact on the environment.

- Turn off your mobile devices at certain times of the day.
- Don't bring your mobile device to bed.
- Ask for professional help!

The "Health and Social Issues of Online Gaming" box discusses some of these problems.

4-4 Green Computing

Green computing is computing that promotes a sustainable environment and consumes the least amount of energy. Information and communications technology (ICT) generates approximately 2 percent of the world's carbon dioxide emissions, roughly the same amount as the aviation industry.[83] Although ICT is a part of the problem, it could also be part of the solution. Many IT applications and tools can help reduce carbon dioxide emissions. Green computing not only helps an organization save on energy costs, it also improves the quality of the environment in which you live and work.

Green computing involves the design, manufacture, use, and disposal of computers, servers, and other computing devices so that there is minimal impact on the environment.[84] It is one of the methods for combating global warming. In some states, certain computer manufacturers collect a fee from their customers, called an *advance recovery fee*, in order to dispose of a computer after its useful life. A successful green computing strategy cannot be fully implemented without the cooperation of both the private and public sectors. Furthermore, employees and top management both must be involved.

To implement a successful green computing program, the following four approaches are generally used:[85]

1. Green design—Designing energy-efficient computers, servers, handheld devices, printers, and other digital devices
2. Green manufacturing—Minimizing waste during the manufacturing of computers and other digital devices to reduce the environmental impact of these activities
3. Green use—Minimizing the electricity consumption of computers and other digital devices and using them in an eco-friendly manner
4. Green disposal—Remaking an existing digital device or properly disposing of or recycling unwanted digital devices

There are a number of ways to pursue a green computing strategy. Some can be easily done with no cost to the organization. Others are more challenging and require an initial investment. Here are some of the ways that green computing can be achieved:

1. Design products that last longer and are modular in design so certain parts can be upgraded without replacing the entire system.

2. Design search engines and other computing routines that are faster and consume less energy. In October 2021, Google announced plans to update its Maps, Search, and other products to help consumers save energy and reduce emissions.[86]

3. Replace several underutilized smaller servers with one large server using a virtualization technique. Using this method, multiple operating systems are hosted on a single hardware platform and can share it. IBM's Project Big Green is an example of virtualization, with energy savings of approximately 42 percent for an average data center.[87]

4. Use computing devices that consume less energy and are biodegradable.

5. Allow certain employees to work from their homes, resulting in fewer cars on the roads. Telecommuting gained in popularity during the COVID-19 pandemic and afterward.

6. Replace face-to-face meetings with meetings over computer networks (discussed in Module 6).

7. Use video conferencing, electronic meeting systems, and collaboration software (discussed in Module 12). These technologies can also reduce business travel.

8. Use a virtual world (discussed in Module 14). This technology can also reduce face-to-face meetings, resulting in less travel.

9. Use cloud computing as promoted by companies such as Amazon (discussed in Module 14). This platform can also reduce energy consumption.

10. Turn off idle PCs, recycle computer-related materials, and encourage carpooling and nonmotorized transportation for employees.

Increasingly, electronic devices and computers use either corporate or cloud data centers for computing tasks. Efficient operations of these data centers play a major role in the implementation of a green computing program. Currently, data centers in the United States consume approximately 2 percent of the total power produced in the country—about 70 billion kilowatt hours. With global data traffic more than doubling every four years, data centers are playing a major role. Experts offer two possible solutions: (1) look to renewable sources for energy consumption and (2) introduce major improvements in the energy efficiency of servers, storage devices, and other ICT equipment.[88]

Improving the efficiency of these data centers plays a significant role in reducing the carbon footprint. Several companies, including Apple, eBay, Amazon, and Facebook, have improved the efficiency of their data centers using different techniques.[89] There are new and innovative techniques for improving the efficiency of data centers. Google uses artificial intelligence (AI, discussed in Module 13) for this purpose. According to Google, using AI has resulted in an overall power consumption reduction of approximately 40 percent. Microsoft's Project Natick operates underwater data centers that use cold ocean water to cool hardware infrastructure. Facebook employs a free cooling technique that uses ocean breezes to cool its servers and network infrastructure.[90]

The Industry Connection highlights the monitoring software offered by InterGuard, Inc.

Industry Connection: InterGuard, Inc.[91]

Founded in 2002, InterGuard develops and sells monitoring software that records and controls user activities on PC, Mac, iOS, and Android devices. This software enables employers to measure and score employee productivity. The company offers on-premises and SaaS-based services (discussed in Module 14) at a moderate cost. The following products and services are offered by InterGuard:

Employee Monitoring Software: Allows employers to track employee activity from anywhere as long as the employees are connected to the network. Monitoring employee activity enables employers to identify which employees are being productive and determine the amount of time they are idle or engaged in activity not related to their jobs.

(Continued)

Employee Computer Monitoring Software for PC and Macs: Allows employers to remotely monitor employees' computers and review their productivity, active time, and idle time. This product includes e-mail monitoring, IM/chat monitoring, and logging of time spent on the Web.

Employee Smartphone Monitoring: Allows employers to make sure employees are using their smartphones for business-related tasks and lets employers view employee app usage, texts, Web site visits, Web searches, call logs, GPS use, and so forth.

Web Filtering and Internet Activity Monitoring: Allows employers to block employee Internet access to sites that contain inappropriate content.

Endpoint Lockdown and Data Retrieval: Allows employers to take complete remote control of compromised devices by using remote lockdown, activity monitoring, and geolocation.

Endpoint-Based Data Loss Prevention Solution: Allows employers to block or report on data leakage via e-mail, Web forms, e-mail attachments, removable media, USB devices, and data saved on local drives, including remote laptops.

Module Summary

4-1 Discuss information privacy and methods for improving the privacy of information. Defining privacy is difficult; however, most people believe they should be able to keep their personal affairs to themselves and should be told how information about them is being used. One method for improving the privacy of information is to conduct business only on Web sites with privacy policies that are easy to find, read, and understand.

4-2 Explain the General Data Protection Regulation (GDPR). GDPR covers a series of laws that protect EU citizens' personal data, including genetic data, health records, racial or ethnic origin, and religious beliefs. The GDPR contains 11 modules and 91 articles.

4-3 Explain the privacy issues of e-mail and data collection in a business setting. User education and enforcing the organization's e-mail policy can significantly reduce the risk of invading privacy and maintaining the confidentiality of e-mail.

4-4 Examine ethical issues and censorship in information technology. In essence, ethics means doing the right thing, but what is "right" can vary from one culture to another and even from one person to another. As a future knowledge worker, watch your own actions, and make sure you behave both legally and ethically. Be careful about decisions

you make that might affect coworkers so you can help maintain an ethical working environment.

4-5 Discuss the principles of intellectual property and issues related to the infringement of intellectual property. Intellectual property is a legal umbrella covering protections that involve copyrights, trademarks, trade secrets, and patents for "creations of the mind" developed by people or businesses.

4-6 Discuss information system issues that affect organizations, including the digital divide, electronic publishing, and the connection between the workplace and employees' health. Information technology and the Internet have created a digital divide between the information-rich and the information-poor. Although their prices have been decreasing steadily, computers are still not affordable for many people. One common health issue is repetitive typing with thumbs or continual navigation through various pages and apps, which causes a problem called "smartphone thumb" for many users.

4-7 Describe green computing and the ways it can improve the quality of the environment. Green computing involves the design, manufacture, use, and disposal of computers, servers, and other computing devices so that there is minimal impact on the environment.

Key Terms

- Acceptable use policies
- Accountability
- Business networking ethics

- Cheap fakes
- Cookies
- Cybersquatting

- Deepfakes
- Digital citizenship
- Digital divide
- Disinformation
- Fake news
- General Data Protection Regulation (GDPR)
- Green computing
- Intellectual property
- Log files
- Misinformation
- Nonrepudiation
- Social media networking ethics
- Spam
- Virtual organizations

Reviews and Discussions

1. What are three recommendations for improving the privacy of your information?
2. What are four key components of GDPR?
3. What are three recommendations for improving the privacy of e-mail?
4. What are the 10 commandments of computer ethics?
5. What are three examples of intellectual property?
6. What are four health-related issues of information technology?
7. What are three strategies for implementation of a green computing program?
8. Define *digital divide*. Offer three recommendations for bridging the gap.

Projects

1. After reading the information presented in this module and other sources, write a one-page paper that outlines five recommendations for improving the privacy of e-mail in an organization. Your recommendations should also highlight ways that minimize or eliminate corporate data leakage.

2. After reading the information presented in this module and other sources, write a one-page paper that describes GDPR. Describe how businesses may benefit from this compliance. Research three companies that have been sued by the European Union. Which privacy issues were violated by each company?

3. The admissions office of Southern State University needs a simple and easy-to-follow Web policy document to send to its incoming freshmen. The document should tell students how to behave while on the Web. After reading the information presented in this module and other sources, create a document that includes a 10-item bulleted list highlighting the key issues of which incoming students should be aware.

4. An oil company in central Texas with more than 2,000 employees needs a document about green computing to send to all its key employees. After reading the information presented in this module and other sources, create a one-page document that includes an eight-item bulleted list highlighting the key issues of which all division managers should be aware. Give three examples of information technologies that can play a role in this green computing implementation.

5. Southern Tech, a major distributor of electronic devices, needs your advice. With more than 1,500 employees who use tablets and smartphones to perform their jobs, the company needs a document that highlights key health-related issues with these devices. The document will be distributed to employees to improve efficiency and reduce work-related injuries. After reading the information presented in this module and other sources, create a one-page document that includes a five-item bulleted list highlighting key health-related issues of which employees need to be aware. Why could tablets and smartphones potentially create more work-related injuries than desktop computers?

6. An Internet company in Northern California is receiving frequent requests from employees who want to telecommute. The company's CTO

wants to be flexible and accommodate as many employees as possible. At the same time, the CTO wants to achieve productivity goals and keep to a minimum any legal issues that may arise from this new work alternative. After reading the information presented in this module and other sources, create a one-page document that includes three guidelines that telecommuters need to follow and three guidelines that the company needs to follow to achieve both personal and organizational objectives. What are three examples of information technologies that could help this company monitor telecommuters?

Module Quiz

1. Digital citizenship means using information technology safely, ethically, and responsibly. True or False?

2. Repetitive typing with thumbs or continual navigation through various pages and apps is causing a health issue for many smartphone users called "smartphone thumb," or *tendinitis*. True or False?

3. Public information posted by an organization or public agency cannot be censored for public policy reasons. True or False?

4. All of the following are among the potential drawbacks of telecommuting except:
   a. The ability to work in more pleasant surroundings
   b. No regulated work routine
   c. Less interaction with coworkers
   d. Potential legal issues about workers' injuries

5. Registering, selling, or using a domain name to profit from someone else's trademark is called:
   a. Cybersquatting
   b. Typosquatting
   c. Cyberspinach
   d. Cybercrime

6. One of the following is not among the important concepts related to the Web and network privacy:
   a. Acceptable use policies
   b. Nonrepudiation
   c. Data integrity
   d. Accountability

Case Study 4-1
Telecommuting with a New Twist
▶▶ **Social and Ethical Issues | Finance | Global | Technology in Society**

Without a doubt, the COVID-19 pandemic has been a boost to telecommuting as a work alternative. Even prior to the pandemic, this work alternative was gaining in popularity. A global survey published in 2019 indicated that 99 percent of respondents would like to work remotely at least some of the time, and 95 percent of respondents indicated that they encourage others to work remotely.[92] In another survey published the same year, 47 percent of respondents indicated that a remote work policy is important to them when looking for a new job. Also, 40 percent indicated they would consider a pay cut for a job that allows them to work from anywhere. Appen, Dell, Appiro, Cisco, Salesforce, ConsenSys, GitHub, Lenovo, Ultimate Software, and Rackspace are among the top tech companies hiring remote workers. The job titles for telecommuters include search engine evaluator, voice data collector, digital project lead, software engineer, and AR/VR solutions architect.[93]

Working from home offers some clear advantages for both employees and employers. It also creates some disadvantages, such as lack of control and monitoring; however, this is changing. Using computer-monitoring software, employers can check if employees are working or slacking off. One such software application is InterGuard, from Awareness Technologies.[94] To make telecommuting more productive, some employers set targets for each employee to accomplish in a given period. Other employers review summaries of different Web sites that employees have visited and the amount of time that employees have spent on various Web sites.

Some employers track projects and schedule meetings on shared calendars to monitor their employees. Still other employers require "virtual face time" via e-mail, instant messaging, video chat, or calls.[95]

Answer the following questions:

1. Is a telecommuting policy essential to attracting top employees to a company? Why or why not?
2. What types of job functions are suitable for telecommuters?
3. What are some methods that employers use to monitor their employees?
4. What is an example of a software tool that is used for employee monitoring? What are the benefits and drawbacks of using employee monitoring software?

Zivica Kerkez/Shutterstock.com

Case Study 4-2
Privacy and Other Legal Issues at Google
➤ **Social and Ethical Issues | Finance | Global | Technology in Society**

With the widespread adoption of intelligent assistants such as Amazon Alexa, Apple's Siri, and Google Home, the issue of privacy has reached a new level. How do we make these devices as private as possible?[96]

In general, Google knows a lot about us that could put our privacy at risk, including the history of our voice commands, number of Gmail conversations, a full history of everywhere we have ever been, sites that we have visited in Chrome, number of Google searches made, and much more.[97, 98] Google was sued in 2018 for continuing to collect location data even when users turned off location services.

Two Google services, Google Maps and Google Books, have created legal and privacy issues for the company. Google Maps' Street View option shows 360-degree street-level imagery, which enables users to see homes, businesses, streets, and other scenery. After inquiries by German privacy authorities, Google announced that it had been unknowingly collecting private data from unencrypted Wi-Fi networks. The collected material included a list of people with certain medical conditions, e-mail addresses, video files, and lists of visited Web pages. According to Google, the data collection was an accident due to a programming error.[99, 100]

In another case, a woman claimed that by following Google Maps, she got run over by a car.[101] In still another case, a couple was upset because they had been trying for three years to get Google to alter the directions it supplies to Round Valley State Park in New Jersey. The couple owns one of the three log cabins positioned at the back of the park, and because of incorrect directions supplied by Google Maps, they had annually been subjected to dozens of people coming into their yard or knocking on their door looking for an entrance to the park.[102]

Natee Meepian/Shutterstock.com

Google Books has created some legal issues as well. By searching the full text of books, the service attempts to provide an online catalog of all the books contained in its vast database, but some people have claimed that the application has violated copyright protections.[103]

Although most of these lawsuits and technical issues have been resolved, it remains to be seen whether Google can steer clear of privacy and legal issues.

In June 2014, the U.S. Supreme Court declined to throw out a class-action lawsuit against Google for sniffing Wi-Fi networks with its Street View cars.[104]

Answer the following questions:

1. What are some business applications of Google Maps' Street View?
2. How has Google Maps' Street View created privacy issues and other legal issues?
3. What is Google Books, and how has it created copyright protection issues and other legal issues?

Module

5 Protecting Information Resources

Learning Objectives

After studying this module, you should be able to…

5.1 Explain cybercrime and its impact on the global economy.

5.2 Describe information technologies that could be used in computer crimes.

5.3 Describe basic safeguards in computer, network, and cyber security.

5.4 Identify the ten most common intentional security threats.

5.5 Describe the nine security measures and enforcement that a comprehensive security system should include.

5.6 Summarize the guidelines for a comprehensive security system, including business continuity planning.

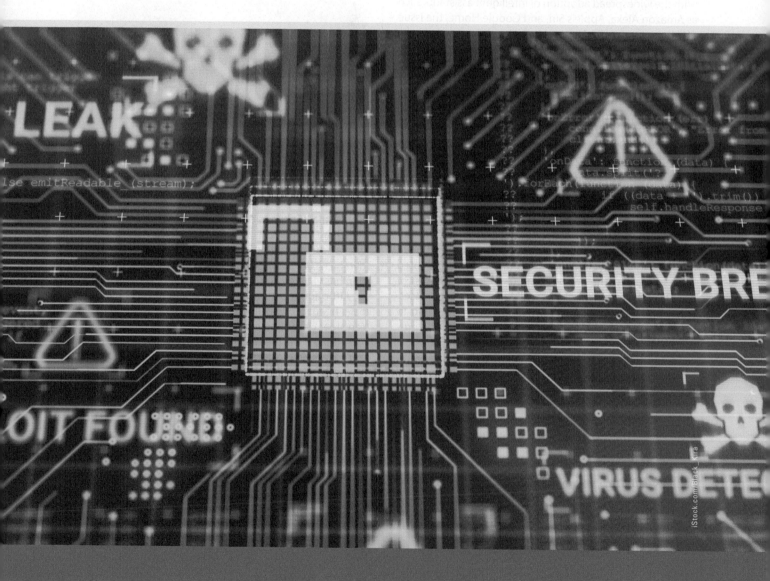

This module begins by discussing the impact of information technology tools on privacy and how these tools can be used to commit computer crimes. The module discusses security threats and measures related to computer, network, and cyber environments. A comprehensive security system can protect an organization's information resources, which are its most important asset after human resources. The module then discusses major types of security threats and a variety of measures designed to protect against those threats. Some organizations even use the resources of a computer emergency response team (CERT) to handle threats and their effects. A review of zero trust security will be presented and, finally, the module covers the principles behind devising a comprehensive security system and the use of business continuity planning to help an organization recover from a disaster.

> **Information technologies can be misused to invade users' privacy and commit computer crimes.**

5-1 Risks Associated with Information Technologies

Information technologies can be misused to invade users' privacy and commit computer crimes. The following sections describe some of these misuses and discuss related privacy issues. Keep in mind, however, that you can minimize or prevent many of these risks by installing operating system updates regularly, using antivirus and antispyware software, and using e-mail security features.

5-1a The Costs of Cybercrime to the Global Economy

According to research published by Cybersecurity Ventures in 2020, cybercrime will cost the world economy $10.5 trillion annually by 2025.[1]

The costs will include loss of revenue from the theft of identities, intellectual property, and trade secrets as well as the damage done to companies' and individuals' reputations. A recent survey indicates that 19 percent of shoppers would abandon a retailer that has been hacked. The survey also found that the majority of retailers have not invested in cyber security.[2] The total cost of cybercrime also includes the expense of enhancing and upgrading a company's network and cyber security after an attack. The CSIS (Center for Strategic and International Studies) issued a report that went further than the research from Cybersecurity Ventures; it included the opportunity costs associated with downtime and lost trust as well as the loss of sensitive business information. Job losses would include manufacturing jobs as well as those in which stolen trade secrets and other intellectual properties resulted in jobs being moved overseas. In fact, the total cost may even be higher than the CSIS report projected, given that businesses often do not reveal or admit certain cybercrimes or realize the amount of damage that has been caused by computer criminals and cyber criminals.[3]

5-1b Spyware and Adware

Spyware is software that secretly gathers information about users while they are connected to the Internet. This information could be used for malicious purposes. Spyware can also interfere with users' control of their computers through such methods as installing additional software and redirecting Web browsers. Some

> **Spyware** is software that secretly gathers information about users while they browse the Web.

spyware changes computer settings, resulting in slow Internet connections, changes to users' default home pages, and loss of functions in other programs. To protect against spyware, you should install antivirus software that also checks for spyware or you should install antispyware software, such as Spy Sweeper, CounterSpy, and STOPzilla.

Adware is a form of spyware that collects information about the user (without the user's consent) to determine which advertisements to display in the user's Web browser. In addition to antivirus software, you can install an ad-blocking feature in your Web browser to protect against adware.

5-1c Phishing, Pharming, Baiting, Quid Pro Quo, SMiShing, and Vishing

Phishing is the transmission of fraudulent e-mails that seem to come from legitimate sources, such as a bank or university. The e-mails usually direct recipients to false Web sites that look like the real thing for the purpose of capturing personal information, such as Social Security numbers, passwords, bank account numbers, and credit card numbers. Spear phishing is the same as phishing; the difference is that the attack is targeted toward a specific person or group.

Pharming is similar to phishing in that Internet users are directed to fraudulent Web sites with the intention of stealing their personal information, such as Social Security numbers, passwords, bank account numbers, and credit card numbers. The difference is that pharmers usually hijack an official Web site address by hacking a domain name system server (discussed in Module 7), then alter the legitimate Web site IP address so that users who enter the correct Web address are directed to the pharmer's fraudulent site.

Baiting is similar to phishing attacks. What distinguishes it from phishing is the promise that the baiter gives to the recipient. For example, users might be told they will receive free software or a gift card after completing a form. Similar to baiting, **quid pro quo** involves a hacker requesting the exchange of critical data or login information for a service or prize.

SMiShing (SMS phishing)—This technique tricks users into downloading malware to their smartphones or other mobile devices.

Vishing (voice or VoIP phishing)—This technique tricks a user into revealing important financial or personal information to unauthorized entities. It is similar to phishing but uses voice technology such as voice e-mail, VoIP (voice over IP), landline phones, or cell phones.

5-1d Keystroke Loggers

Keystroke loggers are software or hardware devices that monitor and record keystrokes. Sometimes, companies use these devices to track employees' use of e-mail and the Internet; this use is legal. However, keystroke loggers also can be used for malicious purposes, such as collecting credit card numbers that users enter while shopping online. Some antivirus and antispyware programs guard against software keystroke loggers, and utilities are available to install as additional protection.

5-1e Sniffing and Spoofing

Sniffing is capturing and recording network traffic. Although it can be done for legitimate reasons, such as monitoring network performance, hackers often use it to intercept information. **Spoofing** is an attempt to gain access to a network by posing as an authorized user in order to find sensitive information, such as passwords and credit card information. Spoofing also happens when an illegitimate program poses as a legitimate one.

5-1f Computer Crime and Fraud

Computer fraud is the unauthorized use of computer data for personal gain, such as transferring money from another's account or charging purchases to someone else's account. Many of the technologies discussed previously can be used for committing computer crimes. In addition, social networking sites such as Facebook and Instagram have been used for committing computer crimes.

In addition to phishing, pharming, and spoofing, computer crimes include the following:

- Denial-of-service attacks, which inundate a Web site or network with e-mails and other network traffic so that it becomes overloaded and cannot handle legitimate traffic
- Identity theft, such as stealing Social Security numbers for unauthorized use (see the information box titled "Identity Theft at the Internal Revenue Service")
- Software piracy and other infringements of intellectual property
- Distributing child pornography
- E-mail spamming
- Writing or spreading viruses, worms, Trojan programs, and other malicious code
- Stealing files for industrial espionage
- Changing computer records illegally

Andrey_Popov/Shutterstock.com

- Virus hoaxes, in which individuals intentionally spread false statements or information through the Internet in an attempt to trick readers

Another computer crime is sabotage, which involves destroying or disrupting computer services. Computer criminals change, delete, hide, or use computer files for personal gain. Usually called *hackers*, many of them break into computer systems for personal satisfaction, but others seek financial gain. Surprisingly, most computer crimes are committed by company insiders (see the "Challenges of Insiders' Threats" box), which makes protecting information resources even more difficult.

Challenges of Insiders' Threats

▶▶▶ Finance | Technology in Society | Social and Ethical Issues

Insiders such as employees, contractors, and trusted business partners pose serious security challenges to any organization. Some insider acts are malicious, and some are simply caused by incompetent employees. Many organizations do not report damages caused by insiders for legal or public relations reasons. In a MeriTalk survey of 150 federal IT managers, 45 percent of respondents indicated that they have been a target of insider attacks, 20 percent lost data, and 40 percent of the incidents were unintentional.

Among the common unintentional actions are e-mailing a file to the wrong recipient, data leaks, losing a laptop or USB drive, putting sensitive data on publicly accessible FTP servers, or not following the security standards and protocols established by the organization, such as e-mailing sensitive data to personal accounts. An effective security training and awareness program should resolve most of these unintentional threats. This program should also teach employees the basics of social engineering.

Stopping employees' malicious acts is more challenging and requires an effective access control. One of the most difficult problems to stop or catch is former employees who go to work for a competitor with their previous company's intellectual property, such as customer data, design of a new product, or pricing lists. In one case, three ex-employees of AT&T were sued for unauthorized software installations on AT&T networks after unlocking customer devices. These former employees received between $10,500 to $20,000 as a fee for performing the software installations.[4]

Questions and Discussions

1. What are three examples of unintentional threats committed by insiders?
2. Why is it a challenge to stop employees' malicious acts? Discuss ways to prevent such acts.

Identity Theft at the Internal Revenue Service

▶▶ Finance | Technology in Society | Social and Ethical Issues

Identity theft has been a major problem at the Internal Revenue Service (IRS) in recent years. Taxpayers' personal information has been stolen both by domestic and international hackers. According to the IRS, 655 tax refunds were sent to a single address in Lithuania one year, and 343 refunds went to a single address in Shanghai.

The IRS sent $5.8 billion in fraudulent refunds to identity thieves in one year. Two years later, a total of 334,000 people became victims of identity theft at the IRS. The next year, the IRS reported 700,000 victims.[5] The ID thieves accessed a system called "Get Transcript," where taxpayers can obtain their tax returns and other filing information related to previous years. To access this system, thieves must have personal information such as Social Security numbers, addresses, and dates of birth; these were stolen from other sources. The IRS did notify potential victims and offered free credit monitoring services. The IRS said these ID thieves were part of a sophisticated criminal operation based in Russia, and said the agency was taking additional measures to protect the identity of taxpayers.[6,7]

Questions and Discussions

1. What was the IRS's response to this fraud? Do you think the response was appropriate?
2. Which system was accessed by ID thieves at the IRS? Why might the IRS maintain this system?

In some cases, computer criminals and hackers steal a company's critical data and then ask for ransom. If the money is not paid through PayPal or Coinbase, they destroy the data. Code Spaces, a company that did not pay the specified amount, was put out of business in 12 hours.[8]

A report published in 2021 indicated that paying a ransom doesn't guarantee data recovery. According to the report, 92 percent of parties that paid the requested ransom did not get their data back.[9]

In recent years, an insidious form of software has been created. Ransomware is a type of malware designed to block access to a computer system until a sum of money is paid. Hackers and computer criminals use ransomware to extort money both from individuals and corporations.

In 2021, more than 2,300 local governments, schools, and healthcare organizations in the United States were attacked by ransomware. More than 1,200 of these organizations were healthcare providers. These attacks also led to 118 data breaches that exposed substantial amounts of sensitive information. According to one report, the average ransomware incident cost $8.1 million and required 287 days to recover.[10]

The healthcare industry and financial institutions are the top two targets for ransomware attacks. A study published in 2021 revealed some interesting statistics about these attacks:[11]

- In 2021, ransomware cost the world economy $20 billion.
- That cost is expected to rise to $265 billion by 2031.
- In 2021, 37 percent of all organizations were hit by ransomware.
- In 2021, recovering from a ransomware attack cost businesses $1.85 million on average.
- Only 57 percent of businesses were successful in recovering their data using a backup.
- 32 percent paid the ransom, but they got only 65 percent of their data back.

The number of ransomware attacks in the first half of 2021 exceeded that for all of 2020. High-profile ransomware attacks in the first six months of 2021 included those on Colonial Pipeline, Kia Motors, CD Projekt Red, Acer, and the Washington, DC, police department.[12]

Many of the security guidelines discussed in this module could help hospitals and other organizations guard against ransomware. Specifically, they should do the following:[13, 14]

- Provide user education.
- Back up data frequently.
- Be skeptical: Don't click on any suspicious e-mail with an attachment.
- Have a continuity plan in place.
- Install the latest patches for all software.
- Block popups.

Types of Hackers

➤ Technology in Society | Social and Ethical Issues

Script kiddies—Inexperienced, usually young hackers who use programs that others have developed to attack computer and network systems and deface Web sites.

Black hats—Hackers who specialize in unauthorized penetration of information systems. They attack systems for profit, fun, or political motivation or as part of a social cause. These penetration attacks often involve modifying and destroying data.

White hats—Also known as ethical hackers, these are computer security experts who specialize in penetration testing and other testing methods to ensure that a company's information systems are secure.

Gray hats—As you might imagine, they are a mixture of black and white hacking. Gray hats may violate laws or ethical standards, but they do not have the malicious intent to harm a person or a system. They look for vulnerabilities in a system without the owner's permission or knowledge. They may inform the owner that they have found vulnerabilities and will fix them for a small fee.

Questions and Discussions

1. What are four types of hackers?
2. Which type is the most dangerous?

5-2 Computer, Network, and Cyber Security: Basic Safeguards

Computer, network, and cyber security have become critical for most organizations, especially in recent years, with hackers becoming more numerous and more adept at stealing and altering private information. The various types of hackers are described in the previous information box. To break into networks, hackers use a variety of tools, such as sniffers, password crackers, rootkits, and many others; all can be found free on the Web. Also, journals such as *Phrack* and *2600: The Hacker Quarterly* offer hackers informative tips. A rootkit is a software application that hides its presence on the computer, making it nearly undetectable by common antimalware software. (Rootkits will be further explained later in the module.) The "Nearly All Organizations Get Hacked" box highlights the widespread problem of hacking.

A comprehensive security system protects an organization's resources, including information, computers, and network equipment. The information an organization needs to protect can take many forms: e-mails, invoices transferred via electronic data interchange (EDI), new product designs, marketing campaigns, and financial statements. Security threats involve more than stealing data; they include such actions as sharing passwords with coworkers, leaving a computer unattended while logged on to the network, or even spilling coffee on a keyboard. A comprehensive security system includes hardware, software, procedures, and personnel that collectively protect information resources and keep intruders and hackers at bay. There are three important aspects of computer, network, and cyber security: confidentiality, integrity, and availability, collectively referred to as the *CIA triangle*.[15]

Confidentiality means that a system must not allow the disclosure of information to anyone who is not authorized to access it. In highly secure government agencies, such as the U.S. Department of Defense, the Central Intelligence Agency (CIA), and the IRS, confidentiality ensures that the public cannot access private information. In businesses, confidentiality ensures that private information, such as payroll and personnel data, is protected from competitors and other organizations. In the e-commerce world, confidentiality

> **Confidentiality** means that a system must prevent disclosing information to anyone who is not authorized to access it.

ensures that customers' data cannot be used for malicious or illegal purposes.

Integrity refers to the accuracy of information resources within an organization. In other words, the security system must not allow data to be corrupted or allow unauthorized changes to a corporate database. In financial transactions, integrity is probably the most important aspect of a security system because incorrect or corrupted data can have a huge impact. For example, imagine a hacker breaking into a financial network and changing a customer's balance from $10,000 to $1,000—a small change, but one with a serious consequence. Database administrators and Webmasters are essential in this aspect of security. In addition, part of ensuring integrity is identifying authorized users and granting them access privileges.

Availability means that computers and networks are operating and authorized users can access the information they need. It also means a quick recovery in the event of a system failure or disaster. In many cases, availability is the most important aspect of the CIA triangle for authorized users. If a system is not accessible to users, the confidentiality and integrity aspects cannot be assessed.

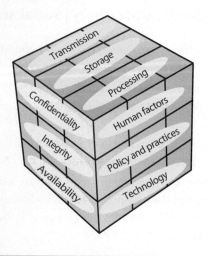

Exhibit 5.1
McCumber cube

The Committee on National Security Systems (CNSS) has proposed another security model, called the *McCumber cube*. John McCumber created this framework for evaluating information security. Represented as a three-dimensional cube (see Exhibit 5.1), it defines nine characteristics of information security.[16] The McCumber cube is more specific than the CIA triangle and helps designers of security systems consider many crucial issues for improving the effectiveness of security measures. Note that this model includes the different states

Nearly All Organizations Get Hacked

▶ Finance | Technology in Society | Social and Ethical Issues

Several major private- and public-sector organizations have been hacked, including Marriot International, Yahoo!, Sony Pictures, the Home Depot, Anthem (a major health insurer), Target, Neiman Marcus, Adobe, RSA, Lockheed Martin, Oak Ridge National Laboratories, and the International Monetary Fund. Ponemon Research conducted a survey of 583 U.S. companies ranging from small organizations with fewer than 500 employees to enterprises with workforces of more than 75,000. Ninety percent of the respondents indicated that their organizations' computers and network systems had been compromised by hackers at least once in the previous 12 months; nearly 60 percent reported two or more breaches within that period. Over half the respondents indicated they had little confidence in their organization's ability to avoid further attacks. Roughly half blamed a lack of resources for their security problems, and about the same percentage said network complexity was their main challenge to implementing security protections.[17]

Questions and Discussions

1. Five examples of companies that have been hacked in recent years are shared in this feature box. What other companies have been hacked recently?
2. What were two major issues with security protection expressed by the survey participants?

in which information can exist in a system: Transmission, Storage, and Processing.

In addition, a comprehensive security system must provide three levels of security:

- *Level 1*—Front-end servers, those available both to internal and external users, must be protected against unauthorized access. Typically, these systems are e-mail and Web servers.

- *Level 2*—Back-end systems (such as users' workstations and internal database servers) must be protected to ensure the confidentiality, accuracy, and integrity of data.

- *Level 3*—The corporate network must be protected against intrusion, denial-of-service attacks, and unauthorized access.

When planning a comprehensive security system, the first step is designing **fault-tolerant systems**, which use a combination of hardware and software for improving reliability—a way of ensuring availability in case of a system failure. Commonly used methods include the following:

- *Uninterruptible power supply (UPS)*—This backup unit continues to provide electrical power in the event of blackouts and other power interruptions and is most often used to protect servers. It performs two crucial tasks: It serves as a power source to continue running the server (usually for a short period), and it safely shuts down the server. More sophisticated UPS units can prevent users from accessing the server and send an alert to the network administrator.

- *Redundant array of independent disks (RAID)*—As you learned in Module 2, a RAID system is a collection of disk drives used to store data in multiple places. RAID systems also store a value called a *checksum*, which is used to verify that data has been stored or transmitted without error. If a drive in the RAID system fails, data stored on it can be reconstructed from data stored on the remaining drives. RAID systems vary in cost, performance, and reliability.

- *Mirror disks*—This method uses two disks containing the same data; if one fails, the other is available, allowing operations to continue. Mirror disks are often a relatively inexpensive, level-1 RAID system, and can be a suitable solution for small organizations.

> **A recent study estimates that the cost of cybercrime to the global economy is expected to reach $10.5 trillion by 2025.**

5-3 Security Threats: An Overview

Computer, network, and cyber security are important to prevent the loss of important information resources or unauthorized access to them. Some threats can be controlled completely or partially, but some cannot be controlled. For example, you can control power fluctuations and blackouts to some degree by using surge suppressors and UPSs, but you cannot control whether natural disasters strike. You can, however, minimize the effects of a natural disaster by making sure fire suppression systems are up to code or by making structural changes to your organization's facility for earthquake protection—such as bolting the foundation.

Threats can also be categorized by whether they are unintentional (such as natural disasters, a user's accidental deletion of data, and structural failures) or intentional. Intentional threats include hacker attacks and attacks by disgruntled employees—such as spreading a virus on the company network. The following sections describe the most common intentional threats.

5-3a Intentional Threats

Intentional computer, network, and cyber threats include the following:

- Viruses
- Worms
- Trojan programs
- Logic bombs
- Backdoors
- Blended threats (e.g., a worm launched by a Trojan)
- Rootkits
- Denial-of-service attacks
- Social engineering
- Cryptojacking

Viruses

Viruses are the best-known computer, network, and cyber threats; you have probably heard of the I Love You and Michelangelo viruses. Viruses are a type of malware (short for *malicious software*), which is any program or file that is harmful to computers or networks.

> **Fault-tolerant systems**
> ensure availability in the event of a system failure by using a combination of hardware and software.

A **virus** consists of self-propagating program code that is triggered by a specified time or event. When the infected program or operating system is used, the virus attaches itself to other files, and the cycle continues.

A **worm** travels from computer to computer in a network, but it does not usually erase data. Unlike viruses, worms are independent programs that can spread themselves without having to be attached to a host program.

A **Trojan program** contains code intended to disrupt a computer, network, or Web site, and it is usually hidden inside a popular program. Users run the program, unaware that the malicious program is also running in the background.

A **logic bomb** is a type of Trojan program used to release a virus, worm, or other destructive code. Logic bombs are triggered at a certain time (sometimes the birthday of a famous person) or by a specific event, such as a user pressing the Enter key or running a certain program.

Estimating the dollar cost of viruses can be difficult. Many organizations are reluctant to report their losses because they do not want to publicize how vulnerable they are.

A **virus** consists of self-propagating program code that is triggered by a specified time or event. When the infected program or operating system is used, the virus attaches itself to other files, and the cycle continues. The seriousness of viruses varies; some are just pranks, such as displaying a funny (but usually annoying) image on the user's screen, but some viruses can destroy programs and data.

Viruses can be transmitted through a network or through e-mail attachments. Some of the most dangerous ones come through bulletin boards or message boards because they can infect any system that's using the board. Experts believe viruses that infect large servers, such as those used by air traffic control systems, pose the most risk to national security.

Virus hoaxes can also be spread as well. Such hoaxes are e-mails or reports about viruses that turn out not to exist; they can cause panic and even prompt organizations to shut down their networks. In some ways, virus hoaxes can cause as much damage as real viruses.

The following list describes some of the indications that a computer might be infected by a virus:

- Some programs have suddenly increased in size.
- Files have been corrupted or the user is unable to open some files.
- A hard disk's free space is reduced drastically.
- The keyboard locks up or the screen freezes.
- Available memory dips down more than usual.
- Disk access is slow.

- The computer takes longer than normal to start.
- There is unexpected disk activity, such as the disk drive light flashing even though the user is not trying to save or open a file.
- There are unfamiliar messages on the screen.

Installing and updating an antivirus program is the best measure against viruses. Widely used antivirus programs include McAfee VirusScan (*www.mcafee.com/us*), Norton Antivirus (*www.norton.com*), and Intrusta (*https://intrusta.com*). You can even download free or inexpensive programs from the Internet. The top two free antivirus programs are TotalAV (*https://www.totalav.com*) and PCPROTECT (*https://www.pcprotect.com*). Most computers now have antivirus software already installed, but you should check to ensure that you have the most current version of it. New viruses are released constantly, so use automatic updating to make sure your computer's protection is current.

Worms

A **worm** travels from computer to computer in a network, but it does not usually erase data. Unlike a virus, it is an independent program that can spread itself without having to be attached to a host program. It might corrupt data, but it usually replicates itself into a full-blown version that eats up computing resources, eventually bringing a computer or network to a halt. Well-known worms include Code Red, Melissa, and Sasser. The Conficker worm has infected millions of Windows computers.

Trojan Programs

Trojan programs are named after the Trojan horse that the Greeks used to enter Troy during the Trojan War. This program contains code intended to disrupt a computer, network, or Web site, and it is usually hidden inside a popular program. Users run the program, unaware that the malicious program is also running in the background. Disgruntled programmers seeking revenge on an organization have created many Trojan programs. They can erase data and wreak havoc on computers and networks, but they do not replicate themselves, as viruses and worms do.

Logic Bombs

A **logic bomb** is a type of Trojan program used to release a virus, worm, or other destructive code. Logic bombs are triggered at a certain time (sometimes the birthday of a famous person) or by a specific event, such as a user pressing the Enter key or running a certain program.

Backdoors

A **backdoor** (also called a *trapdoor*) is a programming routine built into a system by its designer or programmer. This routine enables the designer or programmer to bypass system security and sneak back into the system later to access programs or files. Usually, system users are not aware that a backdoor has been activated; a user logon or combination of keystrokes can be used to activate backdoors.

Blended Threats

A **blended threat** is a security threat that combines the characteristics of computer viruses, worms, and other malicious codes with vulnerabilities found on public and private networks. Blended threats search for vulnerabilities in computer networks and then take advantage of these vulnerabilities by embedding malicious codes in the server's HTML files or by sending unauthorized e-mails from compromised servers with a worm attachment. They may launch a worm through a Trojan horse or launch a denial-of-service (DoS) attack at a targeted IP address. Their goal is not just to start and transmit an attack but to spread it. A multilayer security system, as discussed later in this module, can guard against blended threats.

Rootkits

A **rootkit** is a series of software tools that enable an unauthorized user to gain access to a computer or network system without being detected. Generally speaking, rootkits are a type of malware similar to Trojan programs, worms, and viruses that conceal their presence and actions from the users and other system processes. After a rootkit has been installed on a user's computer, the controller part of the rootkit program has the ability to remotely execute files and change system configurations on the user's computer. The best way to guard against rootkits is to install the latest patches for all software, including OSs, application software, and antivirus programs.

Denial-of-Service Attacks

A **denial-of-service (DoS) attack** floods a network or server with service requests to prevent legitimate users' access to the system.

A **backdoor** (also called a trapdoor) is a programming routine built into a system by its designer or programmer. It enables the designer or programmer to bypass system security and sneak back into the system later to access programs or files.

A **blended threat** is a security threat that combines the characteristics of computer viruses, worms, and other malicious codes with vulnerabilities found on public and private networks.

A **rootkit** is a series of software tools that enable an unauthorized user to gain access to a computer or network system without being detected.

A **denial-of-service (DoS) attack** floods a network or server with service requests to prevent legitimate users' access to the system.

Protecting Against Data Theft and Data Loss

➤ **Finance | Technology in Society | Social and Ethical Issues**

USB flash drives, CDs, smartphones, and other portable storage media pose a serious security threat to organizations' data resources. Theft or loss of these devices is a risk, of course, but disgruntled employees can also use these devices to steal company data. The following guidelines are recommended to protect against these potential risks:[18]

- Do a risk analysis to determine the effects of confidential data being lost or stolen.
- Ban portable media devices and remove or block USB ports, particularly in organizations that require tight security. This measure might not be practical in some companies, however.
- Make sure employees have access only to data they need for performing their jobs, and set up rigorous access controls.
- Store data in databases instead of spreadsheet files for better access control.
- Have clear, detailed policies about what employees can do with confidential data, including whether data can be removed from the organization.
- Encrypt data downloaded from the corporate network.

Questions and Discussions

1. What are three recommendations for protecting against data theft and data loss?
2. How might data be stolen from a company? Discuss.

BeeBright/Shutterstock.com

Think of it as 5,000 people surrounding a store and blocking customers who want to enter; the store is open, but it cannot provide service to legitimate customers. Typically, DoS attackers target Internet servers (usually Web, FTP, or mail servers), although any system connected to the Internet that's running Transmission Control Protocol services is subject to attack.

Another type of DoS is a distributed denial-of-service (DDoS) attack, which occurs when hundreds or thousands of computers work together to bombard a Web site with thousands of requests for information in a short period, causing it to grind to a halt. Because DDoS attacks come from multiple computers, they are difficult to trace.

A major DDoS attack in October 2016 affected such Web sites as Twitter, Netflix, Spotify, Airbnb, Reddit, Etsy, SoundCloud, and the *New York Times*.[19]

At least one major DDoS attack is reported almost every year. For example, the Google Amplification DDoS attack took place in 2017; at its peak, this attack saw incoming traffic at a rate of 2.5 terabits per second (2.5 Tbps). The GitHub attack occurred in 2018 (1.35 Tbps), and the AWS attack occurred in 2020 (2.3 Tbps).[20]

The aforementioned DDoS attack in 2016 infected Internet of Things (IoT) devices—such as game consoles, baby monitors, webcams, DVRs, and routers—all over the world with malware. (IoT is discussed in Module 7.) Once infected, those Internet-connected devices become part of a botnet army, driving malicious traffic toward a given target. In this case the target was Dyn, whose servers monitor and reroute Internet traffic to several major Web sites.[21] A *botnet* is a network of computers and IoT devices infected with malicious software and controlled as a group without the owners' knowledge. DDoS attacks are on the rise and are becoming bigger and more devastating than ever before. Nearly every business is a target, from a small firm to multinational banks and financial institutions. According to Cisco, the number of worldwide DDoS attacks will likely double from 7.9 million in 2018 to roughly 15.4 million by 2023.[22]

Recently, emergency-service providers and many other organizations have been targeted by a new type of DoS attack called a *TDoS (telephony denial-of-service) attack*. These attacks use high volumes of automated calls to tie up a target phone system, halting incoming and outgoing calls. In some cases, the attacker demands a ransom. If the ransom is not paid, the TDoS begins, perhaps lasting for several hours.[23]

Google and Facebook Were Victims of Social Engineering

➤ Finance | Technology in Society | Social and Ethical Issues

Social engineering attacks come in many forms and shapes and arise from diverse sources, such as impersonation in an office visit, targeted e-mails, phone call pretexting, or acting like a service technician to get access to IS resources.[24] In 2018, more organizations than ever before were affected by all types of social engineering attacks, including phishing, spear phishing, SMS phishing, voice phishing, and USB drops, where computer criminals leave USB devices for people to find and plug into their computers. For the first time, compromised accounts bypassed malware infections as the most commonly identified impact of successful phishing attacks.[25]

According to a report published in 2022, data compromises increased 68 percent nationwide in 2021 from the previous year. A total of 1,862 data breaches, exposures, and leaks affected 294 million people nationwide in 2021.[26] Cybercriminals used social engineering in 98 percent of the attacks; more than 70 percent of all data breaches have involved social engineering.[27]

Google and Facebook paid out $23 million and $100 million, respectively, to a cybercriminal from Lithuania. Business e-mail compromise (BEC) attacks or invoice fraud costs small businesses billions of dollars every year, and many of them go out of business completely. Using these techniques, cybercriminals pose as vendors or business partners and convince a company to wire a huge sum of money to an offshore account as payment for products or services. Although

Google and Facebook claimed that they recovered most of this money, they did not specify how, and many smaller companies are not as lucky. In the Google and Facebook cases, a Lithuanian national named Evaldas Rimasauskas, who pleaded guilty to wire fraud in March 2019, spent two years posing as a third party who conducted business with the two companies and finally succeeded in convincing them to wire the money.[28] To avoid or minimize these types of attacks, the FBI offers the following recommendations:[29]

- Do not use free Web-based e-mail.
- Be careful and restrictive about posting the business credentials and duties of employees on social media.
- Use the Forward option rather than the Reply option on business correspondences.
- Be careful with unsolicited e-mails and do not click on attachments.
- Deploy a two-step verification process for financial transactions—for example, an e-mail and a phone call.
- Be careful of requests for confidential information.
- Be cautious about requests that require prompt action.
- Victims can file a complaint at *https://www.ic3.gov* to protect others.

Questions and Discussions

1. What are five popular techniques used in social engineering?
2. How were social engineering attacks committed at Google and Facebook?

Social Engineering

In the context of security, **social engineering** means using "people skills"—such as being a good listener and assuming a friendly, unthreatening air—to trick others into revealing private information. This is an attack that takes advantage of the human element of security systems. Social engineers use the private information they have gathered to break into servers and networks and steal data, thus compromising the integrity of information resources. Social engineers use a variety of tools and techniques to gather private information and publicly available sources of information—Google Maps, company Web sites, newsgroups, and blogs, for example.

In addition, five commonly used social-engineering techniques are called *dumpster diving, shoulder surfing, tailgating, scareware,* and *pretexting.* In the first of these techniques, social engineers often search through dumpsters or trash cans looking for discarded material (such as phone lists and bank statements) that they can use to help them break into a network. For example, a social engineer might look up the phone number of a receptionist and then call and pretend to be someone else in the organization. Shoulder surfing—that is, looking over someone's shoulder—is the easiest form of collecting information. Social engineers use this technique to observe an employee entering a password or a person

entering a PIN at an ATM, for example. A different type of shoulder surfing is called "shoulder snooping" or "visual hacking"; this technique is used in crowded spaces. A user can guard against this by avoiding sensitive transactions in public places, such as entering passwords or credit card numbers. Another solution is to get a privacy screen—a tempered glass cover for a smartphone that is similar to a tinted window—that allows you to view your screen but keeps screen snoopers at bay.[30]

Tailgating or "piggybacking" takes place when an unauthorized person follows an employee into a restricted area (e.g., an individual impersonates a help desk employee). Scareware is malware that uses pop-up security alerts and other social engineering tricks to frighten users into paying for what they mistakenly think is cyber-security protection. Pretexting occurs when a hacker creates a false sense of trust with a user by impersonating a coworker or a high official in a company to gain access to login information. The information box "Google and Facebook Were Victims of Social Engineering" illustrates the costly outcome of one social engineering incident.

In addition to these intentional threats, loss or theft of equipment and computer media

> **Social engineering**
> takes advantage of the human element of a security system to trick others into revealing private information.

is a serious problem, particularly when a computer or flash drive contains confidential data. The "Protecting Against Data Theft and Data Loss" box discusses this problem and offers some protective measures.

Cryptojacking

Because of the popularity of cryptocurrency (discussed in Module 14), a new type of threat called cryptojacking has been created, in which hackers secretly use the computing power of a user to mine cryptocurrency. **Cryptojacking** reduces the performance of the victim's computer. A computer gets infected by this threat, similar to a virus attack, when the user clicks a malicious link in an e-mail that downloads cryptomining code or the user accesses an infected Web site or an online ad with JavaScript code that auto-executes once loaded in the user's browser.[31] Installation of ad-blocking software or an anticryptomining extension on Web browsers could guard against cryptojacking.

5-4 Security Measures and Enforcement: An Overview

In addition to backing up data and storing it securely, organizations can take many other steps to guard against threats. A comprehensive security system should include the following:

- Biometric security measures
- Nonbiometric security measures
- Physical security measures
- Access controls
- Virtual private networks
- Data encryption
- E-commerce transaction security measures
- Computer emergency response team
- Zero trust security

5-4a Biometric Security Measures

Biometric security measures use a physiological element that is unique to a person and cannot be stolen, lost, copied, or passed on to others. The following list

describes some biometric devices and measures, some of which are shown in Exhibit 5.2:

- *Facial recognition*—Identifies users by analyzing the unique shape, pattern, and positioning of facial features.

- *Fingerprints*—Scans users' fingerprints and verifies them against prints stored in a database.

- *Hand geometry*—Compares the length of each finger, the translucence of fingertips, and the webbing between fingers against stored data to verify users' identities.

- *Iris analysis*—Uses a video camera to capture an image of the user's iris, then uses software to compare the data against stored templates. Smartphones, ATMs, and automobiles will be the prime users of iris scan technology for ID verification.[32]

- *Palm prints*—Uses the palm's unique characteristics to identify users. A palm reader uses near-infrared light to capture a user's vein pattern, which is unique to each individual. This is compared to a database that contains existing patterns. This method is often used by law enforcement agencies.

- *Retinal scanning*—Scans the retina using a binocular eye camera, then checks against data stored in a database.

- *Signature analysis*—Checks the user's signature as well as deviations in pen pressure, speed, and length of time used to sign the name.

- *Vein analysis*—Analyzes the pattern of veins in the wrist and back of the hand without making any direct contact with the veins.

- *Voice recognition*—Translates words into digital patterns, which are recorded and examined for tone and pitch. Using voice to verify user identity has one advantage over most other biometric measures: It can work over long distances via ordinary telephones. A well-designed voice-recognition security system can improve the security of financial transactions conducted over the phone.

Although biometric techniques are effective security measures, they might not be right for all organizations. Some drawbacks of biometrics are their high cost, user reluctance, and complex installation procedures. However, with improvements being made to address these drawbacks, biometrics can be a viable alternative to traditional security measures. The

Exhibit 5.2
Examples of biometric devices

Dmitry Zimin/Shutterstock.com

Vlasov Yevhenii/Shutterstock.com

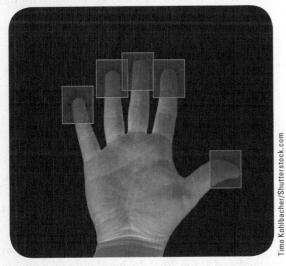

Timo Kohlbacher/Shutterstock.com

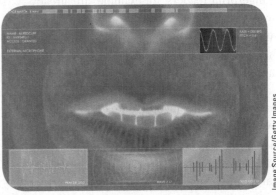

Image Source/Getty Images

information box titled "Biometrics at Phoebe Putney Memorial Hospital" presents a real-life application of biometrics.

Other Applications of Biometrics

Since September 11, 2001, biometrics have become more widespread in forensics and related law enforcement fields, such as criminal identification, prison security, and airport security. Because biometrics offer a high degree of accuracy that is not possible with other security measures, they have the potential to be used in many civilian fields, too. They are already employed in e-commerce and banking by phone, for example, using voice synthesizers and customers' voices as the biometric element that identifies them remotely. Here are some current and future applications of biometrics:

- *ATM, credit, and debit cards*—Even if users forget their PINs, they can use their cards if their biometric attributes are stored. Biometrics make ATM and credit/debit cards more secure, too, because they cannot be used by others if they are lost or stolen. Using "face ID" or "finger ID" on a smartphone as part of the login process is increasingly common.

Biometrics at Phoebe Putney Memorial Hospital

▶ Finance | Technology in Society | Application

Phoebe Putney Memorial Hospital, a 443-bed community hospital in Albany, Georgia, needed to improve its electronic health record (EHR) system. Doctors and nurses were complaining about the number of passwords required to access clinical records, so the hospital switched to fingerprint scanners, which, along with a single sign-on application, made the EHR system both easier to use and more secure. With the scanners, it is possible to audit usage, thereby ensuring that only authorized users have access to sensitive information. Another advantage of fingerprint scanners: Fingerprints do not get lost, unlike smart cards.[33]

Questions and Discussions

1. Why was biometrics security implemented at Phoebe Putney Memorial Hospital? Which type of biometrics security was deployed there?
2. What are the advantages and challenges of using biometrics security?

- *Network and computer login security*—Other security measures, such as ID cards and passwords, can be copied or stolen, which is not likely with biometric security measures. Fingerprint readers, for example, are already available at moderate prices.

- *Web page security*—Biometric measures could add another layer of security to Web pages to guard against attacks and eliminate or reduce defacing (a kind of electronic graffiti). For example, a stock-trading Web site might require customers to log on with a fingerprint reader.

- *Voting*—Biometrics could be used to make sure people do not vote more than once, for example, and could be useful for authentication purposes in voting via the Internet.

- *Employee time clocks*—Biometrics could uniquely identify each employee and verify clock-in and clock-out times. This technology could also prevent one coworker from checking in for another.

- *Member identification in sports clubs*—Fingerprint scanners are used in some sports clubs to allow members admittance. This technology improves convenience and security.

- *Airport security and fast check-in*—Israeli airports have been using biometrics for this purpose for years. Ben Gurion International Airport in Tel Aviv has a frequent flyer check-in system based on smart cards that stores information on users' hand geometry. With this system, travelers can pass through check-in points in less than 20 seconds.[34]

- *Passports and highly secured government ID cards*—A biometrically authenticated passport or ID card can never be copied and used by an unauthorized person. Citizens of Germany, Canada, the United States, and other countries can apply for an ePass, a passport containing a chip that stores a digital photograph and fingerprints. Other biometric identifiers, such as iris scans, could be added. Such technology is used at immigration kiosks to enter the United States.

- *Sporting events*—Facial recognition terminals were deployed at the 2022 Beijing Winter Olympics to provide convenient identity verification during the COVID-19 pandemic without requiring people to remove their masks.[35] Facial recognition technology was also used for the 2021 Tokyo Summer Olympics.[36]

- *Cell phones and smart cards*—Biometrics can be used to prevent unauthorized access to cell phones and smart cards and prevent others from using them if they are lost or stolen. An example is Apple's iPhone, which uses a fingerprint sensor and face ID scan.

The "Face Recognition Technology in Action" box highlights several potential real-life applications of face recognition technology.

Face Recognition Technology in Action

➤ Finance | Technology in Society | Social and Ethical Issues

Companies such as Apple, Google, Facebook, and Tesco are increasingly using face recognition technology for security and other purposes. Google uses it for image searches of billions of photos that exist online to recognize its users. It is also used in Google Glass. Facebook uses it to identify its users and for potential target marketing. Apple uses it to identify users of its devices.

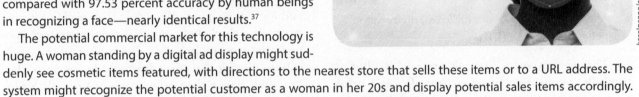

karelnoppe/shutterstock.com

According to Facebook, its facial recognition technology, DeepFace, demonstrated 97.25 percent accuracy, as compared with 97.53 percent accuracy by human beings in recognizing a face—nearly identical results.[37]

The potential commercial market for this technology is huge. A woman standing by a digital ad display might suddenly see cosmetic items featured, with directions to the nearest store that sells these items or to a URL address. The system might recognize the potential customer as a woman in her 20s and display potential sales items accordingly. The technology enables the system to tailor its messages to a particular person.

Kraft Foods Inc. and Adidas are planning to use face recognition technology to promote their products. A group of bar owners in Chicago use face recognition technology to keep tabs on the male/female ratios and age mixes of their crowds.[38]

Face recognition technology as a biometric measure is fundamentally different from other biometric measures, such as fingerprint or retina identification, because an individual does not need to opt in to be recognized by the system. Any camera in a public place can take a picture of a person and recognize the person with a high degree of accuracy. For that reason, security and privacy concerns with this technology are challenging, and careful consideration must be given to its potential use.[39]

Questions and Discussions

1. What are examples of three companies that use face recognition technology for security and other purposes?
2. For what purpose is a group of bar owners in Chicago using face recognition? Do you see any ethical issues related to this type of use? Discuss.

5-4b Nonbiometric Security Measures

The three main nonbiometric security measures are callback modems, firewalls, and intrusion detection systems.

Callback Modems

A **callback modem** verifies whether a user's access is valid by logging the user off (after the user attempts to connect to the network) and then calling the user back at a predetermined number. This method is useful in organizations that have many employees who work off-site and who need to connect to the network from remote locations.

Firewalls

A **firewall** is a combination of hardware and software that acts as a filter or barrier between a private network and external computers or networks, including the Internet. A network administrator defines rules for access, and all other data transmissions are

A **callback modem** verifies whether a user's access is valid by logging the user off (after the user attempts to connect to the network) and then calling the user back at a predetermined number.

A **firewall** is a combination of hardware and software that acts as a filter or barrier between a private network and external computers or networks, including the Internet. A network administrator defines rules for access, and all other data transmissions are blocked.

blocked. An effective firewall should protect data going from the network as well as data coming into the network. Exhibit 5.3 shows a basic firewall configuration.

A firewall can examine data passing into or out of a private network and decide whether to allow the transmission based on users' IDs, the transmission's origin and destination, and the transmission's contents. Information being transmitted is stored in what's called a *packet*; after examining a packet, a firewall can take one of the following actions:

- Reject the incoming packet
- Send a warning to the network administrator
- Send a message to the packet's sender that the attempt failed
- Allow the packet to enter (or leave) the private network

The main types of firewalls are packet-filtering firewalls, application-filtering firewalls, and proxy servers. Packet-filtering firewalls control data traffic by configuring a router to examine packets passing into and out of the network. The router examines the following information in a packet: source IP address and port, destination IP address and port, and protocol used. Based on this information, rules called *packet filters* determine whether a packet is accepted, rejected, or dropped. For example, a packet filter can be set up to deny packets coming from specific IP addresses. A packet-filtering firewall informs senders if packets are rejected but does nothing if packets are dropped; senders have to wait until their requests time out to learn that the packets they sent were not received.

In addition, these firewalls record all incoming connections; packets that are rejected might be a warning sign of an unauthorized attempt. Packet-filtering firewalls are somewhat inefficient, however, because they have to examine packets one by one, and they might be difficult to install. In addition, they cannot

usually record every action taking place at the firewall, so network administrators could have trouble finding out whether and how intruders are trying to break into the network.

Application-filtering firewalls are generally more secure and flexible than packet-filtering firewalls, but they are also more expensive. Typically, they are software that is installed on a host computer (a dedicated workstation or server) to control use of network applications, such as e-mail, Telnet, and FTP. In addition to checking which applications are requested, these firewalls monitor the time when application requests take place. This information can be useful because many unauthorized attempts take place after normal work hours. Application-filtering firewalls also filter viruses and log actions more effectively than packet-filtering firewalls, which help network administrators spot potential security breaches. Because of all the application filtering that these firewalls do, however, they are often slower than other types of firewalls, which can affect network performance.

A proxy server, shown in Exhibit 5.4, is software that acts as an intermediary between two systems—between network users and the Internet, for example. It is often used to help protect the network against unauthorized access from outside the network by hiding the network addresses of internal systems. A proxy server can also be used as a firewall that scans for malware and viruses, speeds up network traffic, or takes some load off internal servers (which firewalls cannot do). It can also block requests from certain servers.

Although firewalls can do a lot to protect networks and computers, they do not offer complete security. Sophisticated hackers and computer criminals can circumvent almost any security measure. For example, some hackers use a technique called *IP spoofing* to trick firewalls into treating packets as coming from legitimate IP addresses. This technique is the equivalent of forgery. To provide comprehensive security for data resources, firewalls should be used along with other security measures.

Exhibit 5.3
Basic firewall configuration

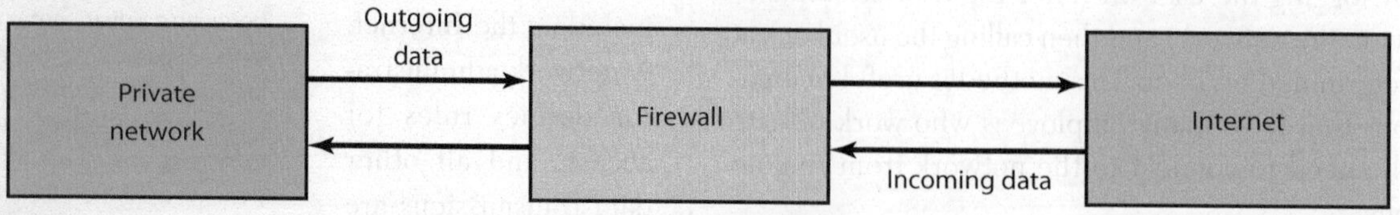

Exhibit 5.4
Proxy server

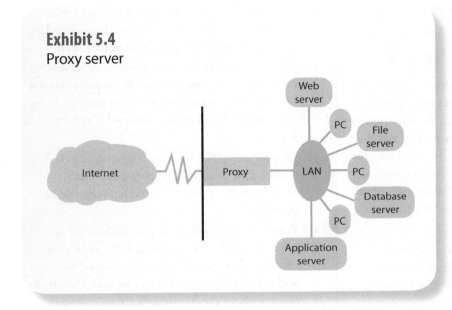

Other guidelines for improving a firewall's capabilities include the following:

- Identify what data must be secured and conduct a risk analysis to assess the costs and benefits of a firewall.

- Compare a firewall's features with the organization's security needs. For example, if your organization uses e-mail and FTP frequently, make sure the application-filtering firewall you are considering can handle these network applications.

- Compare features of packet-filtering firewalls, application-filtering firewalls, and proxy servers to determine which of these addresses your network's security needs the best.

- Examine the costs of firewalls, keeping in mind that the most expensive firewall is not necessarily the best. Some inexpensive firewalls might be capable of handling everything your organization needs.

- Compare the firewall's security with its ease of use. Some firewalls emphasize accuracy and security rather than ease of use and functionality. Determine what is most important to your organization when considering the trade-offs.

- Check the vendor's reputation, technical support, and update policies before making a final decision. As the demand for firewalls has increased, so has the number of vendors, and not all vendors are equal. Keep in mind that you might have to pay more for a product from a vendor with a good reputation that offers comprehensive technical support.

Another alternative is to build a firewall instead of purchasing one. This option might be more expensive (and requires having an employee with the necessary skills), but the customized features and flexibility offered by a firewall developed in-house could outweigh the cost.

Intrusion Detection Systems

Firewalls protect against external access, but they leave networks unprotected from internal intrusions. An **intrusion detection system (IDS)** can protect against both external and internal access. It is usually placed in front of a firewall and can identify attack signatures, trace patterns, generate alarms for the network administrator, and cause routers to terminate connections with suspicious sources. These systems can also prevent DoS attacks. An IDS monitors network traffic and uses the "prevent, detect, and react" approach to security. Although it improves security, it requires a great deal of processing power and can affect network performance. It might also need additional configuration to prevent it from generating false-positive alarms.

A number of third-party tools are available for intrusion detection. The vendors listed in Table 5.1 offer comprehensive IDS products and services.

Table 5.1	IDS Vendors
Vendor	**URL**
Enterasys Networks	www.enterasys.com
Cisco Systems	www.cisco.com
Juniper Networks	www.juniper.net/us/en
Check Point Software Technologies	www.checkpoint.com

5-4c Physical Security Measures

Physical security measures primarily control access to computers and networks, and they include devices for securing computers and peripherals from theft. As shown in Exhibit 5.5, common physical security measures can include the following:

- *Cable shielding*—Braided layers around the conductor cable protect it from electromagnetic interference (EMI), which could corrupt data or data transmissions.

- *Corner bolts*—An inexpensive way to secure a computer to a desktop or counter, these often have locks as an additional protection against theft.

- *Electronic trackers*—These devices are secured to a computer at the power outlet. If the power cord is disconnected, a transmitter sends a message to an alarm that goes off or to a camera that records what happens.

- *Identification (ID) badges*—These are checked against a list of authorized personnel, which must be updated regularly to reflect changes in personnel.

- *Proximity-release door openers*—These are an effective way to control access to the computer room. A small radio transmitter is placed in authorized employees' ID badges, and when they come within a predetermined distance of the computer room's door, a radio signal sends a key number to the receiver, which unlocks the door.

  - *Room shielding*—A nonconductive material is sprayed in the computer room, which reduces the number of signals transmitted or confines the signals to the computer room.

  - *Steel encasements*—These fit over the entire computer and can be locked.

With the increasing popularity of laptops, theft has become a major security risk. Laptops can store confidential data, so a variety of security measures should be used. For example, a cable lock on the laptop could be combined with a fingerprint scan to make sure only the laptop's owner can access files. The information box titled "Lost and Stolen Laptops" discusses this security threat in more detail.

Exhibit 5.5
Common physical security measures

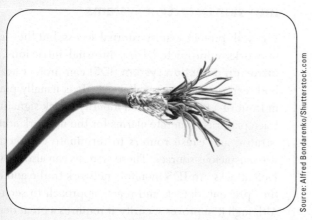

Source: Alfred Bondarenko/Shutterstock.com

Cable shielding

Source: igor kisselev/Shutterstock.com

Lock for securing a computer

5-4d Access Controls

Access controls are designed to protect systems from unauthorized access in order to preserve data integrity. The following sections describe two widely used access controls: terminal resource security and passwords.

Terminal Resource Security

Terminal resource security is a software feature that erases the screen and signs the user off automatically after a specified length of inactivity. This method of access control prevents unauthorized people from using an unattended computer to access the network and data. Some programs also allow users to access data only during certain times, which reduces break-in attempts during off hours.

Passwords

A **password** is a combination of numbers, characters, and symbols that a user enters to gain access to a system. A password's length and complexity determines its vulnerability to discovery by unauthorized users. For example, *p@s$w0rD* is much harder to guess than *password*. The human element is one of the most notable weaknesses of password security because users can forget passwords or give them to an unauthorized user (intentionally or unintentionally). To increase the effectiveness of passwords, follow these guidelines:

- Change passwords frequently.
- Passwords should be 12 characters or longer.
- Passwords should be a combination of uppercase and lowercase letters, numbers, and special symbols, such as @ or $.
- Passwords should not be written down.

- Passwords should not be common names, such as the user's first or last name, obvious dates (such as birthdays or anniversaries), or words that can be found in a dictionary.

> A **password** is a combination of numbers, characters, and symbols that a user enters to gain access to a system.

- Passwords should not be increased or decreased sequentially or follow a pattern (e.g., 222ABC, 224ABC, 226ABC).
- Before employees are terminated, make sure their passwords have been deleted.
- Do not use passwords that you have used before.

Because of the obvious limitations and shortcomings of passwords, researchers are hard at work to replace passwords with other authentication methods that are less vulnerable. Experts predict that passwords will be phased out by 2025.[40] Various types of biometrics, including those that analyze fingerprints, irises, voices, and faces, are among the front-runners to replace passwords.[41, 42]

Lost and Stolen Laptops

⏩ Finance | Technology in Society | Social and Ethical Issues

With wireless connections now available in many public places, laptops are more popular than ever. However, they can easily be lost or stolen. Replacing the laptop is not the only problem; you also have to replace the data stored on it, which can be quite a serious loss. A recent survey reveals some alarming statistics about laptops:[43]

- A laptop is stolen every 53 seconds.
- Eight-six percent of IT practitioners report that someone in their organization has had a laptop lost or stolen, with 56 percent of them reporting that it resulted in a data breach.
- Fifty-two percent of business managers sometimes or often leave their laptop with a stranger when traveling.
- Forty-five percent of healthcare information breaches occur on stolen laptops.
- The average total cost to a business from a single laptop loss is $47,000.

In one case, an employee of the U.S. Department of Veterans Affairs lost a laptop that contained personal information for 26 million veterans. Later the same year, an employee of the American Institute of Certified Public Accountants (AICPA) lost a laptop that stored the Social Security numbers of AICPA's members. If unauthorized users gain access to this kind of confidential information, identity theft and other crimes can result. In a third case, the California Department of Justice revealed that in the healthcare industry, 70 percent of data breaches were related to "lost or stolen hardware or portable media containing unencrypted data." The report concluded that device loss, not hacking, posed the greatest risk to healthcare data.[44] To make laptops more secure, consider the following recommendations:[45]

- Install cable locks on laptops and use biometric security measures.
- Make sure confidential data is stored on laptops only when absolutely necessary.

- Use logon passwords, screensaver passwords, and passwords for confidential files.
- Encrypt data stored on the laptop.
- Install security chips that disable a laptop if unauthorized users try to access it. Some chips send out an audio distress signal and a GPS alert showing the laptop's location.

Questions and Discussions

1. How often might a laptop be lost or stolen?
2. What are three recommendations for making laptops more secure?

In addition to the inherent weaknesses of passwords, managing them is a time-consuming and sometimes risky task. Most of us have a dozen or so passwords for different businesses and Web sites. Every time an organization gets hacked, we have to change our password. Remembering all these different passwords is a challenging task. A password manager is a good solution.

A password manager generates secure, random passwords for you and remembers them so you don't need to remember them yourself. A password manager allows you to sync your passwords among different devices, including computers, tablets, and smartphones.

These managers also encrypt your password database with a master password, so it's the only password you have to remember.

Password managers allow you to store other types of data, including credit and debit card numbers. All data in a password manager is encrypted so that no one but you can access it.

Most password managers assist you in avoiding phishing, as they recognize phishing sites even if the domain names appear to be identical to those of your bank or organizations with whom you usually communicate.

There are several dedicated password managers on the market with different capacities. Some are free for a single device and some have a cost, which varies from $12 to $50. Among the most popular password managers on the market are 1Password, Dashlane, LastPass, PasswordBox, and KeePass.[46, 47]

In addition to using biometric measures as replacements for passwords, five other techniques are potential candidates to replace passwords, including zero login, brain passwords, DNA identification, authentication tokens, and implanted microchips. These techniques are briefly explained in the following list:

- **Zero login** assumes that devices will be smart and secure enough to quickly recognize users by their unique features, such as their voice and their typing patterns. The zero-login technique may also identify users from their other possessions that are connected to a network, such as their car, wearable devices, and headphones.[48]
- A **brain password** is a digital reading of a user's brain activity while looking at a series of images. These brain activities are recorded in a database. To log in to a system or enter a secure room, the user puts on a special hat and again watches the sequence of images. The new brain activities are compared with the ones in the database and then access is given or denied.[49]
- **DNA identification** gathers a user's unique behavioral characteristics and then creates an "eDNA" profile. This profile is then used for identification when the user tries to log in to a system.[50]

Zero login assumes that devices will be smart and secure enough to quickly recognize users by their unique features, such as their voice and their typing patterns.

A **brain password** is a digital reading of a user's brain activity while looking at a series of images. These brain activities are recorded in a database. To log in to a system or enter a secure room, the user puts on a special hat and again watches the sequence of images. The new brain activities are compared with the ones in the database and then access is given or denied.

DNA identification gathers a user's unique behavioral characteristics and then creates an "eDNA" profile that is used for identification when the user tries to log in to a system.

- **Authentication tokens** improve security by transmitting a security token among connected applications. The user logs in once with approved credentials, and then a unique token is generated and shared with connected applications or Web sites to verify the user's identity for a given period.[51]
- **Implanted microchips**, a controversial technology, are microchips the size of a grain of rice that are inserted between the thumb and the index finger. The microchip can store various information, including that for a user's ID cards, credit cards, Social Security account, and passwords, which could be used to log in to Web sites and to enter a secure room.[52]

5-4e Virtual Private Networks

A **virtual private network (VPN)** provides a secure "tunnel" through the Internet for transmitting messages and data via a private network (see Exhibit 5.6). It is often used so that remote users have a secure connection to the organization's network. VPNs can also be used to provide security for extranets, which are networks set up between an organization and an external entity, such as a supplier (see Module 7). Data is encrypted before it is sent through the tunnel with a protocol, such as Layer Two Tunneling Protocol (L2TP) or Internet Protocol Security (IPSec). The cost of setting up a VPN is usually low, but transmission speeds can be slow, and lack of standardization can be a problem.

Typically, an organization leases the media used for a VPN on an as-needed basis, and network traffic can be sent over the combination of a public network (usually the Internet) and a private network. VPNs are an alternative to private leased lines or dedicated Integrated Services Digital Network (ISDN) lines and T1 lines.

5-4f Data Encryption

Data encryption transforms data, called *plaintext* or *cleartext*, into a scrambled form called *ciphertext* that cannot be read by others. The rules for encryption, known as the encryption algorithm,

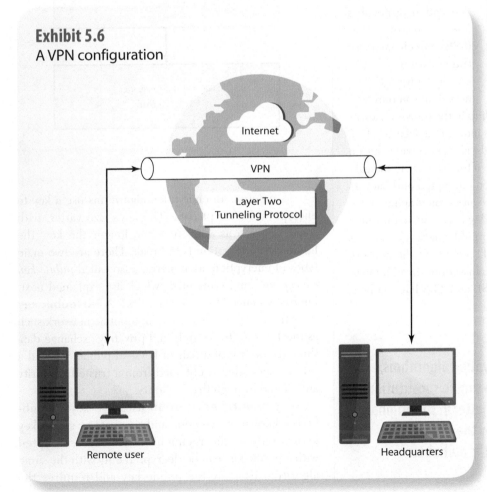

Exhibit 5.6
A VPN configuration

Internet

VPN

Layer Two
Tunneling Protocol

Remote user

Headquarters

Secure Sockets Layer (SSL) is a commonly used encryption protocol that manages transmission security on the Internet.

Transport Layer Security (TLS) is a cryptographic protocol that ensures data security and integrity over public networks, such as the Internet.

A **PKI (public key infrastructure)** enables users of a public network such as the Internet to securely and privately exchange data through the use of a pair of keys—a public one and a private one—that is obtained from a trusted authority and shared through that authority.

Asymmetric encryption uses two keys: a public key known to everyone and a private or secret key known only to the recipient. A message encrypted with a public key can be decrypted only with the same algorithm used by the public key and requires the recipient's private key, too. Any people who intercept the message cannot decrypt it because they do not have the private key.

determine how simple or complex the transformation process should be. The receiver then unscrambles the data by using a decryption key.

There are many different encryption algorithms. One of the oldest encryption algorithms, used by Julius Caesar, is a simple substitution algorithm in which each letter in the original message is replaced by the letter three positions later in the alphabet. For example, the word *top* is transmitted as *wrs*. Exhibit 5.7 shows a simple example of encryption with a substitution algorithm.

A commonly used encryption protocol is **Secure Sockets Layer (SSL)**, which manages transmission security on the Internet. The next time you purchase an item online, notice that the *http* in the browser address bar changes to *https*. The *https* indicates a Secure HTTP connection over SSL. You might also see a padlock icon in the status bar at the bottom of the browser to indicate that your information has been encrypted and hackers cannot intercept it. A more recent cryptographic protocol is **Transport Layer Security (TLS)**, which ensures data security and integrity over public networks, such as the Internet. Similar to SSL, TLS encrypts the network segment used for performing transactions. In addition to being encryption protocols, SSL and TLS have authentication functions.

> One of the oldest encryption algorithms, used by Julius Caesar, is a simple substitution algorithm in which each letter in the original message is replaced by the letter three positions later in the alphabet.

Exhibit 5.7
Using encryption

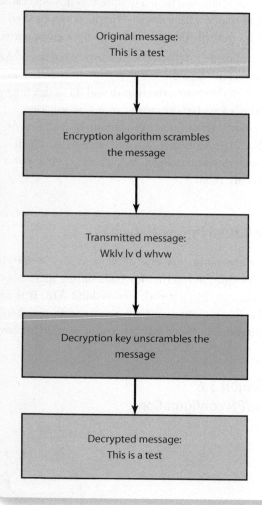

As mentioned, encryption algorithms use a key to encrypt and decrypt data. The key's size varies, with some as large as 4096 bits; the longer the key, the harder the encryption is to break. There are two main types of encryption: asymmetric (also called *public key encryption*) and symmetric, which are explained next, but first you need to understand PKI. A **PKI (public key infrastructure)** enables users of a public network such as the Internet to securely and privately exchange data through the use of a pair of keys—a public one and a private one—that is obtained from a trusted authority and shared through that authority.

Asymmetric encryption uses two keys: a public key known to everyone and a private or secret key known only to the recipient. A message encrypted with a public key can be decrypted only with the same algorithm used by the public key and requires the recipient's private key, too. Any people who intercept the message cannot decrypt it because they do not have the private key.

This encryption usually works better for public networks, such as the Internet. Each company conducting transactions or sending messages gets a private key and a public key; a company keeps its private key and publishes its public key for others to use. One of the first public key algorithms, RSA (named after its creators—Rivest, Shamir, and Adleman), is still widely used today. The main drawback of asymmetric encryption is that it is slower and requires a large amount of processing power.

> In e-commerce transactions, three factors are critical for security: authentication, confirmation, and nonrepudiation.

In **symmetric encryption** (also called *secret key encryption*), the same key is used to encrypt and decrypt a message. The sender and receiver must agree on the key and keep it secret. Advanced Encryption Standard (AES), a symmetric encryption algorithm with a key size of up to 256 bits, is the one used by the U.S. government. The problem with symmetric encryption is that sharing the key over the Internet is difficult.

Encryption can also be used to create digital signatures that authenticate senders' identities and verify that the message or data has not been altered. Digital signatures are particularly important in online financial transactions. They also provide nonrepudiation, as discussed in the next section. Here is how they work: You encrypt a message with your private key and use an algorithm that hashes the message and creates a message digest. The message digest cannot be converted back to the original message, so anyone intercepting the message cannot read it. Then you use your private key to encrypt the message digest, and this encrypted piece is called the *digital signature.*

You then send the encrypted message and digital signature. The recipient has your public key and uses it to decrypt the message, and then uses the same algorithm that you did to hash the message and create another version of the message digest. Next, the recipient uses your public key to decrypt your digital signature and get the message digest you sent. The recipient then compares the two message digests. If they match, the message was not tampered with and is the same as the one you sent.

5-4g E-Commerce Transaction Security Measures

In e-commerce transactions, three factors are critical for security: authentication, confirmation, and nonrepudiation. Authentication is important because the person using a credit card number in an online transaction is not necessarily the card's legitimate owner, for example. Two factors are important: what the receiver knows to be accurate and what the sender is providing. Passwords and personal information, such as your mother's maiden name, your Social Security number, or your date of birth, can be used for authentication. Physical proof, such as a fingerprint or retinal scan, works even better.

Confirmation must also be incorporated into e-commerce transactions—to verify orders and receipt of shipments, for example. When an electronic document, such as a payment, is sent from a customer to a vendor, a digitally signed confirmation with the vendor's private key is returned to verify that the transaction was carried out.

Nonrepudiation is needed in case a dispute is raised over a transaction. Digital signatures are used for this purpose and to bind partners in a transaction. With this process, the sender receives proof of delivery and the recipient is assured of the sender's identity. Neither party can deny having sent or received the information.

E-commerce transaction security includes the following issues:

- *Confidentiality*—How can you ensure that only the sender and intended recipient can read the message?
- *Authentication*—How can the recipient know that data is actually from the sender?
- *Integrity*—How can the recipient know that the data's contents have not been changed during transmission?
- *Nonrepudiation of origin*—The sender cannot deny having sent the data.
- *Nonrepudiation of receipt*—The recipient cannot deny having received the data.

5-4h Computer Emergency Response Team

The Computer Emergency Response Team (CERT) was developed by the Defense Advanced Research Projects Agency (part of the U.S. Department of Defense) in response to the 1988 Morris worm attack, which disabled 10 percent of the computers connected to the Internet. Many organizations now follow the CERT model to form teams that can handle network intrusions and attacks quickly and effectively. Currently, CERT focuses on security breaches and DoS attacks and offers guidelines on handling and preventing these incidents. CERT also conducts a public awareness campaign and researches Internet security vulnerabilities and ways to improve security systems. Network administrators and e-commerce site managers should check the CERT Coordination Center for updates on protecting network and information resources.

In addition, the Office of Cybersecurity at the Department of Energy offers a security service, Cyber Incident Response Capability (CIRC), which you can learn more about at *http://energy.gov/cio/office-chief-information-officer/services/incident-management*. CIRC's main function is to provide information on security incidents, including information systems' vulnerabilities, viruses, and malicious programs. CIRC also provides awareness training, analysis of threats and vulnerabilities, and other services.

> An organization's employees are an essential part of the success of any security system, so training on security awareness and security measures is important.

5-4i Zero Trust Security

Zero trust security is a relatively new security model that requires every person and every device that accesses a network to be secure, regardless of whether the access is within the organization or outside of it. To achieve this security, zero trust incorporates several different principles.[53] The traditional security model is based on the castle-and-moat concept, which emphasizes securing a network from outside threats. If an intruder gets to the network, the intruder might have access to the entire network. In addition to external threats, as discussed earlier, insiders pose a serious threat to computers and network infrastructure. In today's modern computing world that is dominated by cloud computing, information is often spread across cloud vendors in different locations, which makes it more difficult to have a single security control for the entire network. The term "zero trust" was coined in 2010 by John Kindervag, an analyst at Forrester Research Inc.[54] A few years later, Google announced that it had implemented zero trust security in its network, which led to a growing interest in adoption within the computing community. The main principles of the zero-trust model include the following:[55]

- Every device and every person that wants to have access to the network must be verified before the access is given. This is based on the well-known principle "trust but verify."

- Least-privilege access must be established, which means a user must only be given access to the information needed to perform the job.

- Microsegmentation must be established. This is the practice of breaking up security perimeters into small zones to maintain separate access for separate parts of the network. As an example, consider dividing the network into four segments or into departments, such as marketing, human resources, manufacturing, and finance. Based on this principle, the marketing department will not have access to human resources computing or vice versa.

- Multifactor authentication (MFA) must be established, meaning that a single access method such as a password is not adequate. At least one other factor has to be added. This technique is very helpful to counter credential-based attacks. A popular type of two-factor authentication (2FA) is employed by many social media users; they log on to Facebook or Google with a password, which triggers a code to be sent to the user's mobile device.

5-5 Guidelines for a Comprehensive Security System

An organization's employees are an essential part of the success of any security system, so training employees about security awareness and security measures is important. Some organizations use a classroom setting for training, and others conduct it over the organization's intranet. Tests and certificates should be given to participants at the end of training sessions. In addition, making sure management supports security training is important to help promote security awareness throughout the organization.

Organizations should understand the principles of the Sarbanes-Oxley Act of 2002 (described in the box titled "Sarbanes-Oxley and Information Security") and conduct a basic risk analysis before establishing a security program. This analysis often makes use of financial and budgeting techniques, such as return on investment (ROI), to determine which resources are most important and should have the strongest protection. This information can also help organizations weigh the cost of a security system.

> A disaster recovery plan lists the tasks that must be performed to restore damaged data and equipment as well as steps to prepare for a disaster.

The following steps should be considered when developing a comprehensive security plan:[56]

1. Set up a security committee with representatives from all departments as well as upper management. The committee's responsibilities include the following:

   - Developing a clear, detailed security policy and procedures
   - Providing security training and security awareness for key decision makers and computer users
   - Periodically assessing the security policy's effectiveness, including the basics of social engineering
   - Developing an audit procedure for system access and use
   - Overseeing enforcement of the security policy
   - Designing an audit trail procedure for incoming and outgoing data

2. Post the security policy in a visible place or post copies next to all workstations.

3. Raise employees' awareness of security problems.

4. Use strong passwords and don't use the same passwords across systems or Web sites.

5. Install software patches and updates on operating systems on a regular basis.

6. Revoke terminated employees' passwords and ID badges immediately to prevent attempts at retaliation.

7. Keep sensitive data, software, and printouts locked in secure locations.

8. Exit programs and systems promptly, and never leave logged-on workstations unattended.

9. Limit computer access to authorized personnel only.

10. Compare communication logs with communication billing periodically. The log should list all outgoing calls with users' names, call destinations, and time of call. Investigate any billing discrepancies.

11. Install antivirus programs and make sure they are updated automatically.

12. Install only licensed software purchased from reputable vendors.

13. Make sure fire protection systems and alarms are up to date and test them regularly.

14. Check environmental factors, such as temperature and humidity levels.

15. Use physical security measures, such as corner bolts on workstations, ID badges, and door locks.

16. Install firewalls and intrusion detection systems. If necessary, consider biometric security measures.

17. Before you recycle or donate any computing device, make sure that it is properly cleared of data (wiped). Research indicates that only 3 percent of such devices are completely and properly wiped.[57]

18. Consider implementing zero trust security, as discussed earlier.

These steps should be used as a guideline. Not every organization needs to follow every step; however, some might need to include even more steps to fit their needs.

Sarbanes-Oxley and Information Security

▶ Finance | Technology in Society | Social and Ethical Issues

Section 404 of the Sarbanes-Oxley Act of 2002 requires IT professionals to document and test the effectiveness of security measures that protect information technology and systems, including general computer controls, application controls, and system software controls. IT professionals must be familiar with this legislation and incorporate it into their organizations' security policies. In addition, companies must set up a security system that protects vital records and data and prevents them from being destroyed, lost, corrupted, or altered by unauthorized users. The purpose of this act is to maintain data integrity and availability of business operations, which are particularly critical in financial organizations.[58]

Questions and Discussions

1. What is the impact of the Sarbanes-Oxley Act on information security?
2. In addition to information security, what else is covered by this act?

5-5a Business Continuity Planning

To lessen the effects of a natural disaster or a network attack or intrusion, planning the recovery is important. This should include **business continuity planning**, which outlines procedures for keeping an organization operational. A disaster recovery plan (DRP) lists the tasks that must be performed to restore damaged data and equipment as well as steps to prepare for a disaster, such as the following:

- Back up all files.
- Periodically review security and fire standards for computer facilities.
- Periodically review information from CERT and other security agencies.
- Make sure staff members have been trained and are aware of the consequences of possible disasters and steps to reduce their effects.
- Test the disaster recovery plan with trial data.
- Identify vendors of all software and hardware used in the organization, and make sure their mailing addresses, phone numbers, and Web site addresses are up to date.
- Document all changes made to hardware and software.
- Get a comprehensive insurance policy for computers and network facilities. Periodically review the policy to make sure coverage is adequate and up to date.

> **Business continuity planning** outlines procedures for keeping an organization operational after a natural disaster or network attack.

- Set up alternative sites to use in case of a disaster. Cold sites have the right environment for computer equipment (such as air conditioning and humidity controls), but no equipment is stored in them. Hot sites, on the other hand, have all the needed equipment and are ready to go.
- Investigate using a co-location facility, which is rented from a third party and usually contains telecommunication equipment.
- Check sprinkler systems, fire extinguishers, and halon gas systems.
- Keep backups in off-site storage, periodically test data recovery procedures, and keep a detailed record of machine-specific information, such as model and serial numbers. Backup facilities can be shared to reduce costs.
- Keep a copy of the disaster recovery plan off-site.
- Go through a mock disaster to assess response time and recovery procedures.

If disaster strikes, organizations should follow these steps to resume normal operations as soon as possible:

1. Put together a management crisis team to oversee the recovery plan.
2. Contact the insurance company.
3. Restore phone lines and other communication systems.
4. Notify all affected people, including customers, suppliers, and employees.
5. Set up a help desk to assist affected people.

6. Notify the affected people that recovery is underway.

7. Document all actions taken to regain normal operations so organizations know what worked and what did not work; revise the disaster recovery plan, if needed.

The Industry Connection highlights the McAfee Corporation, which offers several security products and services.

Industry Connection: McAfee Corporation[59]

McAfee is a leading vendor of antivirus software that uses the Internet as a distribution medium for its products and services, although products can also be purchased through other outlets, such as retailers. In addition to antivirus software, McAfee offers network management software that includes virus scanning, firewalls, authentication, and encryption capabilities. McAfee also has an online bug-tracking system. The following list describes some popular McAfee products:

Antivirus: Protects data and devices from threats such as ransomware, malware, and phishing.

Identity: Protects personal information with 24/7 monitoring of e-mail addresses and bank accounts, with up to $1 million of ID theft coverage.

VPN: Protects personal data and credit card information and offers smart VPN that automatically turns on when the user needs it.

Total Protection: Includes features for antivirus, antispyware, antispam, and antiphishing protection, as well as two-way firewalls, advanced Web site safety ratings, identity protection, parental controls, and data backup.

McAfee also offers several products and services for free. Selected free services include:

FreeScan: Searches for the most recent viruses and displays a detailed list of any infected files.

World Virus Map: Shows where recent viruses are infecting computers worldwide.

Virus Removal Tools: Removes viruses and repairs damage.

Security Advice Center: Offers tips and advice on keeping your computer and network safe and preventing attacker intrusions.

Free PC and Internet Security Newsletter: Includes virus alerts, special offers, and breaking news.

Internet Connection Speedometer: Tests your Internet connection to see how fast or slow it is.

Module Summary

5-1 Explain cybercrime and its impact on the global economy. According to research published by Cybersecurity Ventures in 2020, cybercrime will cost the world economy $10.5 trillion annually by 2025. The costs will include loss of revenue from the theft of identities, intellectual property, and trade secrets as well as the damage done to companies' and individuals' reputations. A recent survey indicates that 19 percent of shoppers would abandon a retailer that has been hacked.

5-2 Describe information technologies that could be used in computer crimes. Information technologies can be misused to invade users' privacy and commit computer crimes. Spyware, adware, phishing, pharming, keystroke loggers, and baiting are just a few examples of information technologies that can be used for this purpose.

5-3 Describe basic safeguards in computer, network, and cyber security. There are three important aspects of these types of security: confidentiality, integrity, and availability, collectively referred to as the CIA triangle. In addition, a comprehensive security system must provide three levels of security: Level 1 (front-end servers), Level 2 (back-end systems), and Level 3 (the corporate network).

5-4 Identify the ten most common intentional security threats. Intentional computer, network, and cyber threats include viruses, worms, Trojan programs, logic bombs, backdoors, blended threats (e.g., a worm launched by a Trojan), rootkits, denial-of-service attacks, social engineering, and cryptojacking.

5-5 Describe the nine security measures and enforcement that a comprehensive security system should have. They include biometric security measures, nonbiometric security measures, physical security measures, access controls, virtual private networks, data encryption, e-commerce transaction security measures, a computer emergency response team (CERT), and zero trust security.

5-6 Summarize the guidelines for a comprehensive security system, including business continuity planning. An organization's employees are an essential part of the success of any security system, so training employees about security awareness and security measures is important. Business continuity planning outlines procedures for keeping an organization operational after a natural disaster or network attack.

Key Terms

- Access controls
- Adware
- Asymmetric encryption
- Authentication tokens
- Availability
- Backdoors
- Baiting
- Biometric security measures
- Black hats
- Blended threats
- Brain passwords
- Business continuity planning
- Callback modem
- Computer fraud
- Confidentiality
- Cryptojacking
- Data encryption
- Denial-of-service attacks
- DNA identification
- Fault-tolerant systems
- Firewall
- Gray hats
- Implanted microchips
- Integrity
- Intrusion detection system (IDS)

- Keystroke loggers
- Logic bombs
- Password
- Pharming
- Phishing
- Physical security measures
- PKI (public key infrastructure)
- Quid pro quo
- Rootkits
- Script kiddies
- Secure Sockets Layer (SSL)
- Sniffing
- Social engineering
- Spoofing
- Spyware
- Symmetric encryption
- Transport Layer Security (TLS)
- Trojan programs
- Virtual private network (VPN)
- Virus
- White hats
- Worm
- Zero login
- Zero trust security

Reviews and Discussions

1. What are six examples of information technologies that could be used in computer crimes?
2. What is the CIA triangle?
3. What are the three most common security threats?
4. What are the three most common security measures?
5. What are 10 guidelines that should be included in a comprehensive security system?
6. Explain business continuity planning.
7. What are five examples of biometric security measures?
8. Define *zero trust security*. What are three of its principles?

Projects

1. The computer lab of a local college needs a one-page document that it will distribute to its incoming students to increase their security awareness. After reading the information presented in this module and other sources, prepare a document that includes a 10-item bulleted list of guidelines students must remember to reduce the risks of using information technology.

2. After reading the information presented in this module and other sources, write a one-page paper about three high-profile companies that faced security breaches in the last two years. Identify two vulnerabilities that enabled hackers to break into these companies' systems.

3. Denial of service (DoS) is among the security threats that have been on the rise in recent years. After reading the information presented in this module and other sources, write a one-page paper that outlines four recommendations for dealing with a DoS attack. Cite three U.S. companies that have been victimized by this security threat. What is the relationship between DDoS and IoT devices? Discuss.

4. After reading the information presented in this module and other sources, write a one-page paper that lists three antivirus software applications; include one advantage and one disadvantage of each. Which one do you recommend for the student lab mentioned in Project 1? What are the bases for your recommendation? Is antivirus software alone sufficient to protect the security of a network? Why or why not?

5. After reading the information presented in this module and other sources, write a one-page paper that identifies three companies (in addition to those mentioned in this book) that are using biometric security measures for authentication. Why has each company chosen this alternative over other security measures? What are two advantages and two disadvantages of biometrics as a security measure?

6. After reading the information presented in this module and other sources, write a two-page paper that offers five recommendations for improving the security of online transactions. List two companies that provide preventive measures for e-commerce sites. What is included in their offerings? What are the costs? When you purchase from online businesses, how do you know that a Web site is secure?

Module Quiz

1. Symmetric encryption is also called secret key encryption. True or False?

2. An intrusion detection system is a combination of hardware and software that acts as a filter or barrier between a private network and external computers or networks, including the Internet. True or False?

3. Keystroke loggers monitor and record keystrokes, and can be software or hardware devices. True or False?

4. Software that gathers information about users while they browse the Web is called:
   a. Spyware
   b. Adware
   c. A virus
   d. A worm

5. All of the following are a part of the CIA triangle except:
   a. Confidentiality
   b. Integrity
   c. Availability
   d. Consistency

6. Which one of the following is not among the candidates to replace passwords?
   a. Zero login
   b. Biometrics
   c. DNA identification
   d. They all are.

Case Study 5-1
Vulnerabilities of Medical Devices

➤➤➤ Finance | Technology in Society | Application | Reflective Thinking | Social and Ethical Issues

Medical devices that are controlled by computer software—from heart monitors and pacemakers to mammogram and X-ray machines—are new targets for computer viruses and malware.[60] This could put patients at risk, although no injuries or deaths have been reported so far. A recent survey reveals some interesting facts:[61]

- Connected medical devices, also called Internet of Medical Things (IoMT), are becoming a key part of healthcare infrastructure, with the average hospital room containing 15 to 20 of them. The number of IoMT devices in use is expected to reach more than 142 billion by 2026.[62]
- The number of IoMT devices in a hospital can be more than twice the number of traditional networked devices, such as laptops and smartphones.
- 18 percent of providers reported that their medical devices were affected by malware or ransomware.

The U.S. Food and Drug Administration (FDA) is warning manufacturers of medical devices about the problem and is asking them to review the relevant parts of their security plans when they seek FDA approval for their products. In October 2016, Johnson & Johnson warned users of its insulin pumps to exercise caution, as it had learned of a security vulnerability that a hacker could exploit to overdose diabetic patients with insulin, although the risk was low.[63]

A Department of Veterans Affairs (VA) report has shown that 327 devices at VA hospitals have been infected by malware since 2009. In January 2010, a VA catheterization laboratory was temporarily closed due to infected computer equipment that is used to open blocked arteries. In a case at a private Boston Hospital, computer viruses exposed sensitive patient data by sending it to outside servers. The increased applications of electronic record systems as a part of the 2009 U.S. stimulus package is adding to this risk.

In addition to privacy issues, hackers can change patients' medical records and treatment plans. If the system does not have a strong login access, some patients can access a system and alter their own medications, including narcotic substances. Hackers could use Shodan, a search engine for locating Internet-connected devices, using terms such as "radiology" and "X-ray."[64]

Manufacturers must improve the security features of these devices and make them more difficult for hackers to break into. There needs to be close coordination between manufacturers and healthcare providers to further enhance security. Also, hospitals and medical facilities must make sure that all software running these devices is up to date and that any updates have been installed. Finally, these devices must be blocked from Internet access.[65]

Answer the following questions:

1. What are three examples of devices that could be attacked by computer viruses?
2. What are the risks related to using electronic health records in hospitals and medical facilities?
3. What are three pieces of advice for reducing the risk associated with using these devices?

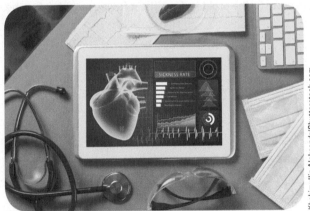

Khakimullin Aleksandr/Shutterstock.com

Case Study 5-2
Security Breach at Equifax

➤ **Finance | Technology in Society | Application | Social and Ethical Issues | Global**

In May 2017, it was revealed that Equifax joined other high-profile companies, including Marriott, Home Depot Inc., Target Corporation, Anthem, Blue Cross, and Yahoo!, as a victim of cyberattacks. Equifax is one of the largest credit-rating companies in the United States; it operates or has investments in 24 countries and employs over 11,000 employees worldwide.[66]

Hackers gained access to the Equifax network in May 2017 and attacked the company for 76 days. In July, Equifax staff discovered the intrusion during routine checks of the operating status and configuration of IT systems. This was 76 days after the initial attack. Hackers accessed Social Security numbers, dates of birth, home addresses, and some driver's license numbers and credit card numbers, impacting over 148 million people. The company's security system did not keep up with corporate growth, and Equifax failed to modernize the system. According to the report, the company did not take action to address vulnerabilities that it was aware of prior to the attack. According to Equifax, hackers exploited a software vulnerability known as Apache Struts CVE-2017-5638, which was disclosed back in March 2017. There were clear and simple instructions for how to fix the problem from the software provider, Apache.

It was the responsibility of Equifax to immediately follow the recommendations offered by Apache. According to Apache, software patches were made available in March, two months before hackers began accessing Equifax data. In addition to the previously mentioned vulnerability, the hackers found a file containing unencrypted usernames and passwords. They also found an expired security certificate on a device for monitoring network traffic. This discovery indicated that Equifax did not detect the data theft.[67]

The Government Accountability Office (GAO) report indicated that the hack took place because Equifax failed to segment its databases into smaller networks. This, in turn, allowed the attackers direct and easy access to customer data. As part of fixing the security issues, the company hired a new chief information security officer, Jamil Farshchi, and invested $200 million on data security infrastructure.[68]

Answer the following questions:

1. Which vulnerability enabled hackers to breach the security system at Equifax?
2. Was the breach preventable? Discuss.
3. How will the company stop future attacks?

Data Communication, the Internet, E-Commerce, and Global Information Systems

Module 6

Data Communication: Delivering Information Anywhere and Anytime

Learning Objectives

After studying this module, you should be able to...

6.1 Describe the major applications of a data communication system.

6.2 Explain the three major components of a data communication system.

6.3 Describe the three major types of processing configurations.

6.4 Explain the three types of networks.

6.5 Describe the five main network topologies.

6.6 Explain important networking concepts, including protocols, TCP/IP, routing, routers, and the client/server model.

6.7 Examine wireless and mobile technologies and networks in a business setting.

6.8 Describe networking trends such as Wi-Fi, WiMAX, and Bluetooth.

6.9 Discuss the importance of wireless security and the five techniques used.

6.10 Summarize the concept of convergence and its applications for business and personal use.

This module explains the role of data communication systems in delivering information for decision making, although you can see applications of data communication systems everywhere, from within your own home to multinational corporations. The module starts with the basics of data communication systems, including components, processing configurations, and types of networks and topologies. The module also covers important concepts in data communication, such as bandwidth, routing, routers, and the client/server model. Next, the module gives an overview of wireless and mobile networks and the technologies they use. Finally, the module takes a look at a growing phenomenon—the convergence of voice, video, and data—and its importance in the business world.

6-1 Defining Data Communication

Data communication is the electronic transfer of data from one location to another. An information system's effectiveness is measured in part by how efficiently it delivers information, and a data communication system is what enables an information system to carry out this function. In addition, because most organizations collect and transfer data across great geographic distances, an efficient data communication system is critical. A data communication system can also improve the flexibility of data collection and transmission. For example, many workers use portable devices such as laptops and smartphones to communicate with the office at any time and from any location.

Data communication is also the basis of virtual organizations, as discussed in Module 4. By using the capabilities of a data communication system, organizations are not limited by physical boundaries. They can collaborate with other organizations, outsource certain functions to reduce costs, and provide customer services via data communication systems.

E-collaboration is another main application of data communication. Decision makers can be located throughout the world but can still collaborate with their colleagues, no matter where they are.

> Data communication systems make virtual organizations possible; they can cross geographic boundaries to develop products more quickly and effectively.

6-1a Why Managers Need to Know about Data Communication

Data communication has become so woven into the fabric of corporate activity that separating an organization's core functions from the data communication systems that enable and support them is difficult. When a new product is introduced, for example, the executives who are the key decision makers might be scattered throughout the world in a multinational corporation. However, they can use data communication systems to collaborate and coordinate their efforts to introduce the new product in a timely manner.

Data communication applications can enhance decision makers' efficiency and effectiveness in many ways. For example, data communication applications support just-in-time delivery of goods, which reduces inventory costs and improves the competitive edge. As you learned in previous modules, many large corporations, such as Walmart, Home Depot, and United Parcel Service (UPS), use data communication technologies to stay ahead of their competitors. As mentioned earlier, data communication systems also make virtual organizations possible; they can cross geographic boundaries to develop products more quickly and effectively.

> **Data communication** is the electronic transfer of data from one location to another.

GoToMeeting: Example of an E-Collaboration Tool

⏩ Finance | Technology in Society | Application

GoToMeeting is a Web-conferencing service hosted by Citrix Online, a division of Citrix Systems. Capable of running on both PCs and Macs, it offers high-definition video conferencing that enables you to see your fellow meeting attendees. It also allows you to show them the applications and files that are currently running on your desktop. The other attendees can share their desktops as well. Users can either chat with all the attendees or speak privately with an individual participant. They also have the option of choosing free VoIP, phone conferencing, or both. GoToMeeting allows users to save, replay, post, or e-mail important interactions and presentations, with audio. It also offers comprehensive security and privacy features. Meetings cannot be viewed by anyone except meeting attendees.

Zoom Video Communication, Inc., WebEx (Cisco), My Web Conferences (MyTrueCloud), Chime (Amazon), Workspace (Google), and Skype (Microsoft) are six alternatives to GoToMeeting.[1, 2]

Questions and Discussions

1. What are two features of GoToMeeting as a Web-conferencing service?
2. What are the advantages of using a Web-conferencing tool? Have you used one of these tools?

> **Bandwidth** is the amount of data that can be transferred from one point to another in a certain time period, usually one second.

Data communication systems also enable organizations to use e-mail and electronic file transfer to improve efficiency and productivity. A communication network, a crucial part of an organization's information system, shortens product and service development life cycles and delivers information to those who need it faster and more efficiently. Here are some of the ways data communication technologies affect the workplace:

- Online training for employees can be provided via virtual classrooms. In addition, employees get the latest technology and product information immediately.

- Internet searches for information on products, services, and innovations keep employees up to date.

- The Internet and data communication systems facilitate lifelong learning, which will be an asset for knowledge workers of the future.

- Boundaries between work and personal life are less clear-cut because data communication is more available in both homes and businesses. The increase in telecommuters is an example of this trend.

- Web and video conferencing are easier, which can reduce the costs of business travel.

Managers need a clear understanding of the following areas of data communication:

- The basics of data communication and networking
- The Internet, intranets, and extranets

- Wired and wireless networks
- Network security threats and measures
- Organizational and social effects of data communication
- Globalization issues
- Applications of data communication systems

E-collaborations and virtual meetings are other important applications of data communication systems for managers. These applications are cost effective and improve customer service. One example of an e-collaboration tool is GoToMeeting, as described in the box titled "GoToMeeting: Example of an E-Collaboration Tool."

6-2 Basic Components of a Data Communication System

A typical data communication system includes the following components:

- Sender and receiver devices
- Modems or routers
- A communication medium (channel)

Before examining these components, you need to review some basic concepts in data communication. **Bandwidth** is the amount of data that can be transferred from one point to another in a certain time period, usually one second. Bandwidth is often expressed in terms of bits per second (bps). Other measurements include kilobits per second (Kbps), megabits per second (Mbps), and gigabits per second (Gbps). **Attenuation** is the loss of power in a signal as it travels from the sending device to the receiving device.

Data transmission channels are generally divided into two types: broadband and narrowband. In **broadband** data transmission, multiple pieces of data are sent simultaneously to increase the transmission rate. As of January 2020, about 94 percent of all Americans had access to broadband communication (25 Mbps/3 Mbps service).[3]

Narrowband is a voice-grade transmission channel capable of transmitting a maximum of 56,000 bps, so only a limited amount of information can be transferred in a specific period of time.

Before a communication link can be established between two devices, they must be synchronized, meaning that both devices must start and stop communicating at the same point. Synchronization is handled with **protocols**, rules that govern aspects of data communication, including error detection, message length, and transmission speed. Protocols also help ensure compatibility between different manufacturers' devices.

6-2a Sender and Receiver Devices

A sender and receiver device can take various forms:

- *Input/output device, or "thin client"*—Used only for sending or receiving information; it has no processing power.
- *Smart terminal*—An input/output device that can perform certain processing tasks but is not a full-featured computer. This type of device is often used on factory floors and assembly lines for collecting data and transmitting it to the main computer system.
- *Intelligent terminal, workstation, or personal computer*—These serve as input/output devices or as stand-alone systems. Using this type of device, a remote computer can perform certain processing tasks without the main computer's support. Generally, an intelligent terminal is considered a step up from a smart terminal.
- *Netbook computer*—A low-cost, diskless computer used to connect to the Internet or a local area network (LAN). Netbook computers run software off servers and save data to servers. According to Forrester Research, however, the iPad and other tablet devices have significantly reduced the demand for netbooks.[4]
- *Minicomputers, mainframes, and supercomputers*— These process data and send it to other devices, or they receive data that has been processed elsewhere,

process it, and then transmit it to other devices.

- *Smartphones*— Briefly described in Module 1, these are mobile phones with advanced capabilities, such as e-mail and Web browsing; most have a built-in keyboard or an external USB keyboard.

6-2b Modems

A **modem** (short for "modulator-demodulator") is a device that connects a user to the Internet. Not all Internet connections require a modem; for example, wireless users connect via access points, and satellite users use a satellite dish. However, dial-up, digital subscriber line (DSL), and cable access require modems to connect.

When phone lines are used for Internet connections, an analog modem is necessary to convert a computer's digital signals to analog signals that can be transferred over analog phone lines. In today's broadband world, however, analog modems are rarely used. Instead, DSL or cable modems are common. **Digital subscriber line (DSL)**, a common carrier service, is a high-speed service that uses ordinary phone lines. With DSL connections, users can receive data at up to 35 Mbps and send data at 1 to 10 Mbps, although the actual speed is determined by proximity to the provider's location. Also, different providers might offer different speeds. Cable modems, on the other hand, use the same cable that connects to TVs for Internet connections; they can usually reach transmission speeds of up to 500 Mbps.

6-2c Communication Media

Communication media, or channels, connect sender and receiver devices. They can be conducted (wired or guided) or radiated (wireless), as shown in Exhibit 6.1.

Attenuation is the loss of power in a signal as it travels from the sending device to the receiving device.

In **broadband** data transmission, multiple pieces of data are sent simultaneously to increase the transmission rate.

Narrowband is a voice-grade transmission channel capable of transmitting a maximum of 56,000 bps, so only a limited amount of information can be transferred in a specific period of time.

Protocols are rules that govern aspects of data communication, including error detection, message length, and transmission speed.

A **modem** (short for "modulator-demodulator") is a device that connects a user to the Internet.

Digital subscriber line (DSL), a common carrier service, is a high-speed service that uses ordinary phone lines.

Communication media, or channels, connect sender and receiver devices. They can be conducted or radiated.

Exhibit 6.1
Types of communication media

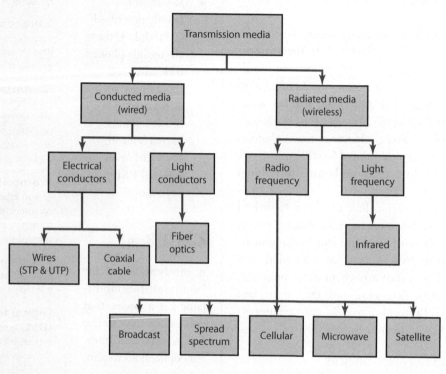

Conducted media provide a physical path along which signals are transmitted; paths include twisted-pair copper cable, coaxial cable, and fiber optics.

Radiated media use an antenna for transmitting data through air or water.

Conducted media provide a physical path along which signals are transmitted; paths include twisted-pair copper cable, coaxial cable, and fiber optics. Twisted-pair copper cable consists of two copper lines twisted around each other and is either shielded or unshielded; it is used in telephone networks and for communication within buildings. Coaxial cables are thick cables that can be used for both data and voice transmissions. They are used mainly for long-distance telephone transmissions and local area networks. Fiber-optic cables are glass tubes (half the diameter of a human hair) surrounded by concentric layers of glass, called "cladding," that form a light path through wire cables. At the core is the central piece of glass that carries the light, and surrounding the core is a second layer of glass that keeps the light from escaping the core. Around both of these layers lies the buffer, an outer layer of plastic, which provides protection and strength. Fiber-optic cables have a higher capacity, smaller size, lighter weight, lower attenuation, and better security than other cable types; they also have the highest bandwidth of any communication medium and are immune to electromagnetic interference (EMI).

Radiated media use an antenna for transmitting data through air or water. Some of these media are based on "line of sight" (an open path between sending and receiving devices or antennas), including broadcast radio, terrestrial microwave, and satellite. Satellites link ground-based microwave transmitters/receivers, known as Earth stations, and are commonly used in long-distance telephone transmissions and TV signals. Terrestrial microwave systems use Earth-based transmitters and receivers and are often used for point-to-point links between buildings.

A communication medium can be a point-to-point or multipoint system. In a point-to-point system, only one device at a time uses the medium. In a multipoint system, several devices share the same medium, and a transmission from one device can be sent to all other devices sharing the link. The information box titled "Google and Facebook Invest in Communication Media" highlights the companies' investments in communication media and satellite technology.

6-3 Processing Configurations

Data communication systems can be used in several different configurations, depending on users' needs, types of applications, and responsiveness of the system. During the past 60 years, three types of processing configurations have emerged: centralized, decentralized, and distributed.

6-3a Centralized Processing

In a **centralized processing** system, all processing is done at one central computer. In the early days of computer technology, this type of processing was justified because data-processing personnel were in short supply, hardware and software were expensive, and only large organizations could afford computers. The main advantage of this configuration is being able to exercise tight control over system operations and applications. The main disadvantage is lack of responsiveness to users' needs because the system and its users could be located far apart from each other. This configuration is not used much anymore.

6-3b Decentralized Processing

In **decentralized processing**, each user, department, or division has its own computer (sometimes called an "organizational unit") for performing processing tasks. A decentralized processing system is certainly more responsive to users than a centralized processing system. Nevertheless, decentralized systems have some drawbacks, including lack of coordination among organizational units, the high cost of having many systems, and duplication of efforts.

6-3c Distributed Processing

Distributed processing solves two main problems—the lack of responsiveness in centralized processing and the lack of coordination in decentralized processing—by

> In a **centralized processing** system, all processing is done at one central computer.
>
> In **decentralized processing**, each user, department, or division has its own computer (sometimes called an "organizational unit") for performing processing tasks.
>
> **Distributed processing** maintains centralized control and decentralized operations. Processing power is distributed among several locations.

Google and Facebook Invest in Communication Media

▶▶ Finance | Technology in Society | Global

As of 2021, nearly 50 percent of the world's population did not have access to the Internet. Satellites and drones are two attractive alternatives to reach remote parts of the world. A project named Loon, by Google, uses high-altitude balloons to provide wireless broadband service to remote regions. Google also deploys solar-powered drones for the same purpose. These projects could connect hundreds of millions of additional people to the Internet.

Drones and satellites are two complementary technologies; drones offer better high-capacity service in smaller areas, and satellites offer much broader coverage. On the other hand, satellites offer more flexibility and provide greater capacity. Satellite costs have also come down significantly in recent years.[5]

Google has teamed up with five East Asian companies to build a 6,000-mile fiber-optic underwater cable. This cable spans the Pacific Ocean and connects the East Coast of the United States to two cities in Japan. It is expected to deliver speeds of 60 terabytes per second—a speed that is about 10 million times faster than a typical cable modem.[6]

In 2019, Google built three underwater cables to help expand its cloud business to new regions. The first cable goes from Chile to Los Angeles, the second connects the United States to Denmark and Ireland, and the third connects Hong Kong to Guam.[7]

Since 2020, Facebook has been building an undersea cable called "2Africa" around the African continent. The cable will be 37,000 km long and will provide better connectivity for more than 1.3 billion Africans.[8]

Questions and Discussions

1. What is the purpose of Google's Loon project?
2. Why has Google invested in underwater cables? Is it worth the investment? Discuss.

maintaining centralized control and decentralizing operations. Processing power is distributed among several locations. For example, in the retail industry, each store's network does its own processing but is under the centralized control of the store's headquarters.

Databases and input/output devices can also be distributed.

The advantages of distributed processing include the following:

- Unused processing power might be accessible.
- Modular design means computer power can be added or removed, based on need.
- Distance and location are not limiting.
- It is more compatible with organizational growth because workstations can be added easily.
- Fault tolerance is improved because of the availability of redundant resources.

- Resources such as high-quality laser printers can be shared to reduce costs.
- Reliability is improved because system failures can be limited to only one site.
- The system is more responsive to user needs.

The disadvantages of distributed processing include the following:

- There may be more security and privacy challenges.
- There may be incompatibility between the various pieces of equipment.
- Managing the network can be challenging.

6-3d Open Systems Interconnection Model

The **Open Systems Interconnection (OSI) model** is a seven-layer architecture for defining how data is transmitted from computer to computer in a network. OSI also standardizes interactions between network computers exchanging information. Each layer in the architecture performs a specific task (see Exhibit 6.2):

Exhibit 6.2
Seven-layer OSI model

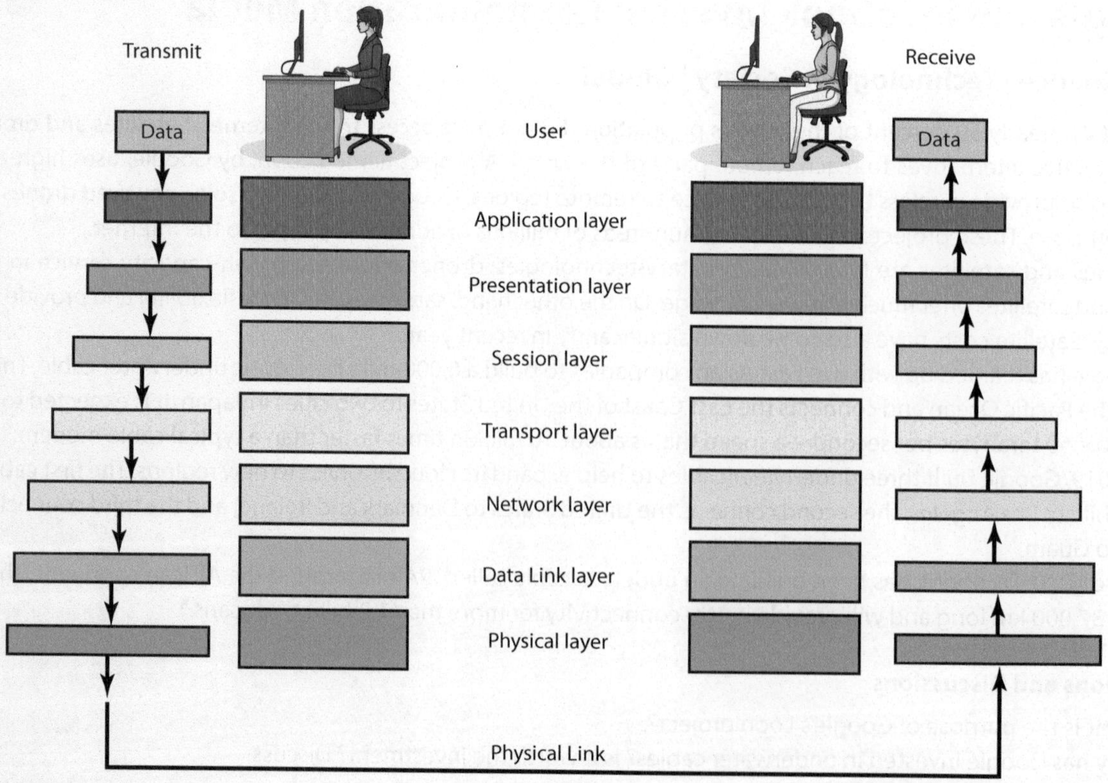

Transmit — Receive

Data — User — Data

- Application layer
- Presentation layer
- Session layer
- Transport layer
- Network layer
- Data Link layer
- Physical layer

Physical Link

- *Application layer*—Serves as the window through which applications access network services. It performs different tasks, depending on the application, and provides services that support users' tasks, such as file transfers, database access, and e-mail.
- *Presentation layer*—Formats message packets.
- *Session layer*—Establishes a communication session between applications.
- *Transport layer*—Uses a port number to identify the service being requested on the receiver and ensures the integrity of messages by making sure packets are delivered without error, in sequence, and with no loss or duplication. This layer provides methods for controlling data flow, ordering received data, and acknowledging received data.
- *Network layer*—Routes messages.
- *Data Link layer*—Oversees the establishment and control of the communication link.
- *Physical layer*—Specifies the electrical connections between computers and the transmission medium; defines the physical medium used for communication. This layer is primarily concerned with transmitting binary data, or bits, over a communication network.

6-4 Types of Networks

There are three major types of networks: local area networks, wide area networks, and metropolitan area networks. In all these networks, computers are usually connected via a **network interface card (NIC)**, a hardware component that enables computers to communicate. A NIC, also called an adapter card, is the physical link between a network and a workstation, so it operates at the OSI model's Physical and Data Link layers. NICs are available from many vendors, and the most common type of local area network, Ethernet, can use NICs from almost any vendor. In addition, to operate a server in a network, a network operating system (NOS) must be installed, such as Windows Server 2020 or Linux.

6-4a Local Area Networks

A **local area network (LAN)** connects workstations and peripheral devices that are in close proximity (see Exhibit 6.3). Usually, a LAN covers a limited geographical area, such as a building or campus, and one company owns it. Its data transfer speed varies from 100 Mbps to 10 Gbps.

LANs are used most often to share resources, such as peripherals, files, and software. They are also used to integrate services, such as e-mail and file sharing. In a LAN environment, there are two basic terms to remember:

Ethernet and *Ethernet cable*. Ethernet is a standard communication protocol embedded in software and hardware devices used for building a LAN. An Ethernet cable is used to connect computers, switches, and routers to a network. Assessing information needs and careful planning are important in setting up a LAN.

> A **network interface card (NIC)** is a hardware component that enables computers to communicate over a network.
>
> A **local area network (LAN)** connects workstations and peripheral devices that are in close proximity.
>
> A **wide area network (WAN)** can span several cities, states, or even countries, and is usually owned by several different parties.

6-4b Wide Area Networks

A **wide area network (WAN)** can span several cities, states, or even countries, and is usually owned by several different parties (see Exhibit 6.4). The data transfer speed depends on the speed of its interconnections (called "links") and can vary from 28.8 Kbps to 155 Mbps. For example, a WAN can be useful for a company headquartered in Washington, D.C., with 30 branch offices in 30 states. The WAN makes it possible for all branch offices to communicate with headquarters and send and receive information.

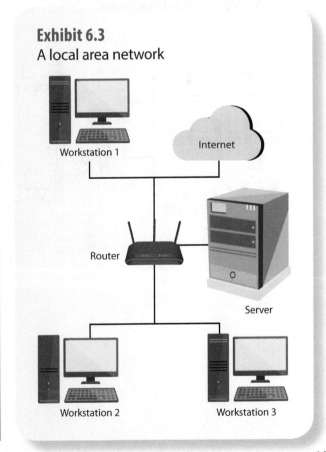

Exhibit 6.3
A local area network

Workstation 1

Internet

Router

Server

Workstation 2

Workstation 3

A WAN can use many different communication media (coaxial cables, satellite, and fiber optics) and terminals of different sizes and sophistication (PCs, workstations, and mainframes); it can also be connected to other networks.

6-4c Metropolitan Area Networks

The Institute of Electrical and Electronics Engineers (IEEE) developed specifications for a public, independent, high-speed network that connects a variety of data communication systems, including LANs and WANs, in metropolitan areas. This network, called a **metropolitan area network (MAN)**, is designed to handle data communication for multiple organizations in a city and sometimes nearby cities as well (see Exhibit 6.5). The data transfer speed varies from 34 Mbps to 155 Mbps. Table 6.1 compares LANs, WANs, and MANs.

Exhibit 6.4
A wide area network

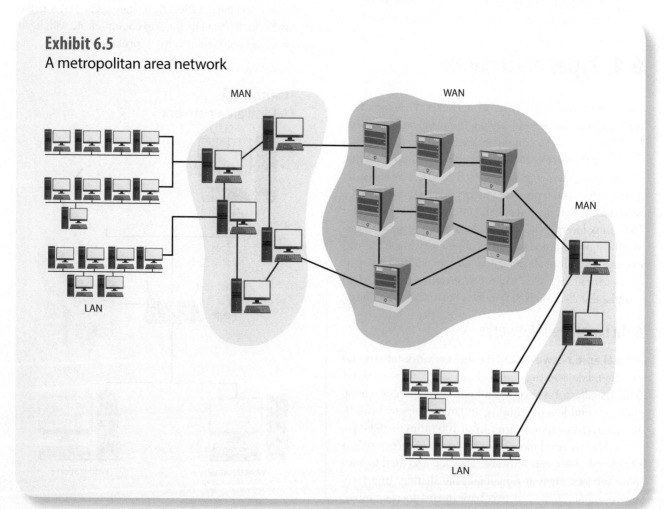

Exhibit 6.5
A metropolitan area network

MAN · WAN · MAN · LAN · LAN

Table 6.1	Comparison of LANs, WANs, and MANs			
Network Type	**Ownership**	**Data Transfer Speed**	**Scope**	
LAN	Usually one party	100 Mbps to 10 Gbps	A building or a campus	
WAN	More than one party	28.8 Kbps to 155 Mbps	Intercity to international	
MAN	One to several parties	34 Mbps to 155 Mbps	One city to several contiguous cities	

6-5 Network Topologies

A **network topology** represents a network's physical layout, including the arrangement of computers and cables. Five common topologies are discussed in the following sections: star, ring, bus, hierarchical, and mesh.

6-5a Star Topology

The **star topology** usually consists of a central computer (the host computer, often a server) and a series of nodes (typically, workstations or peripheral devices). The host computer supplies the main processing power. If a node fails, it does not affect the network's operation, but if the host computer fails, the entire network goes down.

Advantages of the star topology include the following:

- Cable layouts are easy to modify.
- Centralized control makes detecting problems easier.

- Nodes can be added to the network easily.
- It is more effective at handling heavy but short bursts of traffic.

Disadvantages of the star topology include the following:

- If the central host fails, the entire network becomes inoperable.
- Many cables are required, which increases cost.

> A **network topology** represents a network's physical layout, including the arrangement of computers and cables.
>
> The **star topology** usually consists of a central computer (the host computer, often a server) and a series of nodes (typically, workstations or peripheral devices).
>
> In a **ring topology**, no host computer is required because each computer manages its own connectivity.

6-5b Ring Topology

In a **ring topology**, no host computer is required because each computer manages its own connectivity. Computers and devices are arranged in a circle so each node is connected to two other nodes: its upstream neighbor and its downstream neighbor. Transmission is in one direction, and nodes repeat a signal before passing it to the downstream neighbor. If any link between nodes is severed, the entire network is affected, and failure of a single node

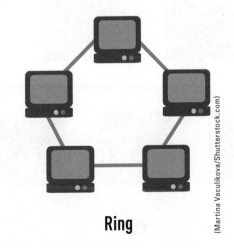

Star (Martina Vaculikova/Shutterstock.com)

Ring (Martina Vaculikova/Shutterstock.com)

disrupts the entire network. A ring topology is a LAN protocol, specified in IEEE 802.5, in which all stations are connected in a ring and each station can directly receive transmissions only from its immediate neighbor. Permission to transmit is granted by a message (token) that circulates around the ring. Ring topologies, such as Fiber Distributed Data Interface (FDDI), are capable of bidirectional transmission (clockwise and counterclockwise), which prevents the problems caused by a single node failure.

A ring topology needs less cable than a star topology, but it is similar to a star topology in that it is better for handling heavy but short bursts of traffic. Also, diagnosing problems and modifying the network are more difficult than with a star topology.

6-5c Bus Topology

The **bus topology** (also called "linear bus") connects nodes along a network segment, but the ends of the cable are not connected, as they are in a ring topology. A hardware device called a terminator is used at each end of the cable to absorb the signal. Without a terminator, the signal would bounce back and forth along the length of the cable and prevent network communication.

A node failure has no effect on any other node. Advantages of the bus topology include the following:

- It is easy to extend.
- It is very reliable.
- The wiring layout is simple and uses the least amount of cable of any topology, which keeps costs down.
- It handles steady (even) traffic well.

Disadvantages of the bus topology include the following:

- Fault diagnosis is difficult.
- The bus cable can be a bottleneck when network traffic is heavy.

6-5d Hierarchical Topology

A **hierarchical topology** (also called a "tree") combines computers with different processing strengths in different organizational levels. For example, the bottom level might consist of workstations, with minicomputers in the middle and a server at the top. Companies that are geographically dispersed and organized hierarchically are good candidates for this type of network. Failure of nodes at the bottom might not have a big impact on network performance, but the middle nodes and especially the top node (which controls the entire network) are crucial for network operation.

Traditional mainframe networks also use a hierarchical topology. The mainframe computer is at the top, front-end processors (FEPs) are at the next level, controllers and multiplexers are at the next level, and terminals and workstations are at the bottom level. A **controller** is a hardware and software device that controls data

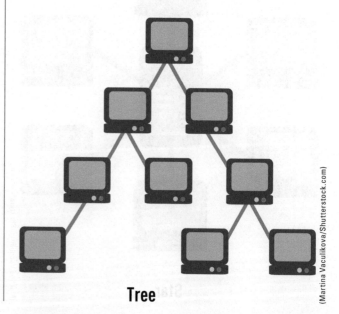

Bus

Tree

(Martina Vaculikova/Shutterstock.com)

transfer from a computer to a peripheral device (for example, a monitor, a printer, or a keyboard) and vice versa. A **multiplexer** is a hardware device that allows several nodes to share one communication channel. The intermediate-level devices (FEPs and controllers) reduce the host's processing load by collecting data from terminals and workstations.

The hierarchical topology offers a great deal of network control and lower costs, compared to a star topology. Its disadvantages are that network expansion may pose a problem and there could be traffic congestion at the root and higher-level nodes.

6-5e Mesh Topology

In a **mesh topology** (also called "plex" or "interconnected"), every node is connected to every other node. The nodes can differ in their size and configuration. The mesh topology is highly reliable. Failure of one or a few nodes does not usually cause a major problem in network operation because many other nodes are available. However, this topology is costly and difficult to maintain and expand.

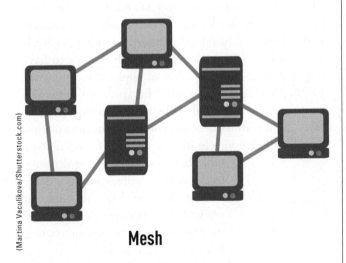

(Martina Vaculikova/Shutterstock.com)

Mesh

6-6 Major Networking Concepts

The following sections explain important networking concepts, including protocols, TCP/IP, routing, routers, and the client/server model.

6-6a Protocols

As mentioned earlier, protocols are agreed-upon methods and rules that electronic devices use to exchange information. People need a common language to communicate, and the same is true of computers and other electronic devices. Some protocols deal with hardware connections, and others control data transmission and file transfers. Protocols also specify the format of message packets sent between computers. In today's networks, multiple protocol support is becoming more important, as networks need to support protocols of computers running different operating systems, such as macOS, Linux/UNIX, and Windows. The following section describes the most widely used network protocol, TCP/IP.

6-6b Transmission Control Protocol/ Internet Protocol

Transmission Control Protocol/Internet Protocol (TCP/IP) is an industry-standard suite of communication protocols. TCP/IP's main advantage is that it enables interoperability—in other words, it allows the linking of devices running on many different platforms. TCP/IP was originally intended for Internet communication, but because it addresses issues such as portability, it also became the standard protocol for UNIX network communication.

Two of the major protocols in the TCP/IP suite are Transmission Control Protocol (TCP), which operates at the OSI model's Transport layer, and Internet Protocol (IP), which operates at the OSI model's Network layer. TCP's primary functions are establishing a link between hosts, ensuring message integrity, sequencing and acknowledging packet delivery, and regulating data flow between source and destination nodes.

IP is responsible for packet forwarding. To perform this task, it must be aware of the available data link protocols and the optimum size of each packet. After it recognizes the size of each packet, it must be able to divide data into packets of the correct size. An IP address consists of 4 bytes in IPv4 or 16 bytes in IPv6 (32 bits or 128 bits), and is divided into two parts: a network address and a node address. Computers on the same network must use the same network address, but each computer must have a unique node address. IP networks combine network and node addresses into one IP address; for example, 131.255.0.0 is a valid IP address.

A **multiplexer** is a hardware device that allows several nodes to share one communication channel.

In a **mesh topology** (also called "plex" or "interconnected"), every node is connected to every other node.

Transmission Control Protocol/Internet Protocol (TCP/IP) is an industry-standard suite of communication protocols that enables interoperability.

6-6c Routing

To understand routing better, you will first examine packet switching, a network communication method that divides data into small packets and transmits them to an address, where they are reassembled. A **packet** is a collection of binary digits—including message data and control characters for formatting and transmitting—sent from computer to computer over a network. Packets are transmitted along the best route available between sender and receiver (see Exhibit 6.6). Any packet-switching network can handle multimedia data, such as text, graphics, audio, and video.

The path or route that data takes on a network is determined by the type of network and the software used to transmit data. The process of deciding which path that data takes is called **routing**. Routing is similar to the path you take from home to work. Although you probably take the same path most of the time, sometimes you have to change your path, depending on road and weather conditions, traffic, and time of day. Similarly, a packet's route can change each time a connection is made, based on the amount of traffic and the availability of the circuit. The decision about which route to follow is made in one of two ways: at a central location (centralized routing) or at each node along the route (distributed routing). In most cases, a **routing table**, generated automatically by software, is used to determine the best possible route for the packet. The routing table lists nodes on a network and the path to each node, along with alternate routes and the speed of existing routes.

In **centralized routing**, one node is in charge of selecting the path for all packets. This node, considered the network routing manager, stores the routing table, and any changes to a route must be made at this node. All network nodes periodically forward status information on the number of inbound, outbound, and processed messages to the network routing manager. The network routing manager, therefore, has an overview of the network and can determine whether any part of it is underused or overused. As with all centralized configurations, there are disadvantages to having control at one node. For example, if the network routing manager is at a point far from the network's center, many links and paths that make up the network are far from the central node. Status information sent by other nodes to initiate changes to the routing table have to travel a long distance to the central node, causing a delay in routing some data and reducing network performance. In addition, if the controlling node fails, no routing information is available.

Distributed routing relies on each node to calculate the best possible route. Each node contains its own routing table with current information on the status of adjacent nodes so packets can follow the best possible route. Each node also sends status messages periodically so adjacent nodes can update their tables. Distributed routing eliminates the problems caused by having the routing table at a centralized site. If one node is not operational, routing

Exhibit 6.6
Packet-switching network

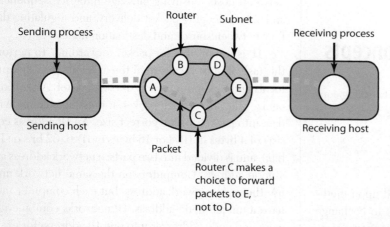

tables at other nodes are updated, and the packet is sent along a different path.

6-6d Routers

A **router** is a network connection device containing software that connects network systems and controls traffic flow between them. The networks being connected can operate on different protocols, but they must use a common routing protocol. Routers operate at the Network layer of the OSI model and handle routing packets on a network. Cisco Systems and Juniper Networks are two major router vendors.

A router performs the same functions as a bridge but is a more sophisticated device. A bridge connects two LANs using the same protocol, and the communication medium does not have to be the same on both LANs.

Routers can also choose the best possible path for packets based on distance or cost. They can prevent network jams that delay packet delivery, and they can handle packets of different sizes. A router can also be used to isolate a portion of the LAN from the rest of the network; this process is called "segmenting." For example, you might want to keep information about new product development or payroll information isolated from the rest of the network for confidentiality reasons.

A router typically forwards packets using either static routes or dynamic routes. **Static routes** are manually configured and give the router information about available networks in the form of IP addresses. Static routes are ideal for smaller networks. **Dynamic routes** are learned dynamically (automatically) and added to the routing table using a dynamic routing protocol such as RIP (Routing Information Protocol) or OSPF (Open Shortest Path First); they are ideal for larger networks.

6-6e Client/Server Model

In the **client/server model**, software runs on the local computer (the client) and communicates with the remote server to request information or services. A server is a remote computer on the network that provides information or services in response to client requests. For example, on your client computer, you might make this request: "Display the names of all marketing majors with a grade point average (GPA) greater than 3.8." The database server receives your request, processes it, and returns the following names: Alan Bidgoli, Moury Jones, and Jasmine Thomas.

In the most basic client/server configuration, the following events usually take place:

1. The user runs client software to create a query.
2. The client accepts the request and formats it so the server can understand it.
3. The client sends the request to the server over the network.
4. The server receives and processes the query.
5. The results are sent to the client.
6. The results are formatted and displayed to the user in an understandable format.

A **router** is a network connection device containing software that connects network systems and controls traffic flow between them.

Static routes are manually configured and give the router information about available networks in the form of IP addresses. Static routes are ideal for smaller networks.

Dynamic routes are learned dynamically (automatically) and added to the routing table using a dynamic routing protocol such as RIP (Routing Information Protocol) or OSPF (Open Shortest Path First); they are ideal for larger networks.

In the **client/server model**, software runs on the local computer (the client) and communicates with the remote server to request information or services. A server is a remote computer on the network that provides information or services in response to client requests.

The main advantage of the client/server architecture is its scalability, meaning its ability to grow. Client/server architectures can be scaled horizontally or vertically. Horizontal scaling means adding more workstations (clients), and vertical scaling means migrating the network to larger, faster servers.

To better understand client/server architecture, you can think of it in terms of these three levels of logic:

- Presentation logic
- Application logic
- Data management logic

Presentation logic, the top level, is concerned with how data is returned to the client. The Windows graphical user interface (GUI) is an example of presentation software. An interface's main function is to translate tasks and convert them to something users can understand. Application logic is concerned with software processing requests for users. Data management logic is concerned with data management and storage operations. The real challenge in a client/server architecture is how to divide these three types of logic between the client and server.

The following sections describe some typical architectures used for this purpose.

Two-Tier Architecture

In the **two-tier architecture**, a client (tier one) communicates directly with the server (tier two), as shown in Exhibit 6.7. The presentation logic is always on the client, and the data management logic is on the server. The application logic can be on the client, on the server, or split between them, although it is usually on the client side.

This architecture is effective in small workgroups (i.e., groups of 50 clients or less). Because application logic is usually on the client side, a two-tier architecture has the advantages of application development speed, simplicity, and power. On the downside, any changes in application logic, such as stored procedures and validation rules for databases, require major modifications of clients, resulting in upgrade and modification costs. However, this depends on the application.

N-Tier Architectures

If the application logic is modified in a two-tier architecture, it can affect the processing workload. For example, if application software is placed on the client, changing the data management software requires modifying the software on all clients. An **n-tier architecture** attempts to balance the workload between client and server by removing application processing from both the client and server and placing it on a middle-tier server, as shown in Exhibit 6.8. The most common n-tier architecture is the three-tier architecture. This arrangement leaves the presentation logic on the client and the data management logic on the server (see Exhibit 6.9).

Improving network performance is a major advantage of this architecture. However, network management is more challenging because there is more network traffic, and testing software is more difficult in an n-tier architecture because more devices must communicate to respond to a user request.

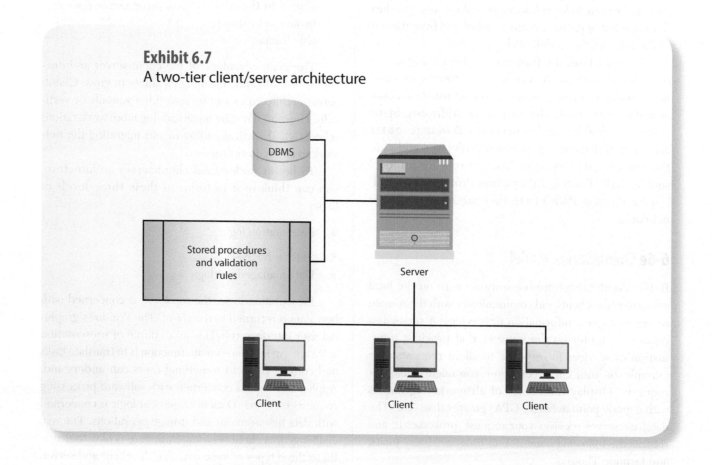

Exhibit 6.7
A two-tier client/server architecture

DBMS

Stored procedures and validation rules

Server

Client   Client   Client

Exhibit 6.8
An n-tier architecture

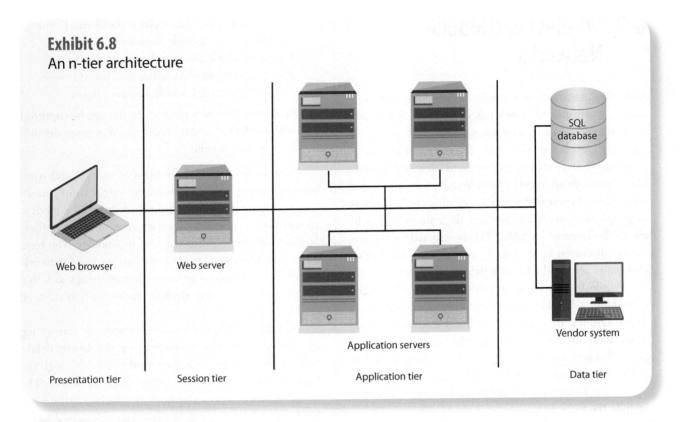

Web browser

Web server

Application servers

SQL database

Vendor system

Presentation tier

Session tier

Application tier

Data tier

Exhibit 6.9
A three-tier architecture

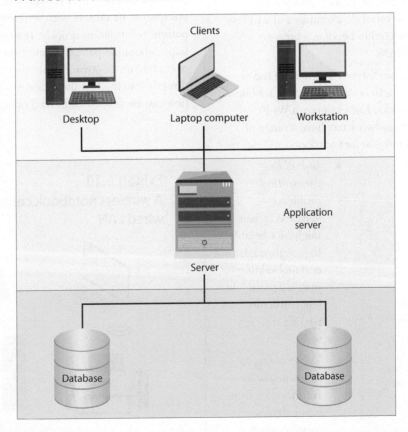

Clients

Desktop

Laptop computer

Workstation

Application server

Server

Database

Database

6-7 Wireless and Mobile Networks

A **wireless network** uses wireless instead of wired technology. A **mobile network** (also called a cellular network) operates on a radio frequency (RF) and consists of radio cells, each served by a fixed transmitter known as a cell site or base station, as discussed later in this module. These cells are used to provide radio coverage over a wider area. It is estimated that approximately 72 percent of people worldwide will use just their smartphones to access the Internet by 2025.[9] This is essential for e-commerce (discussed in Module 8), as a growing number of customers buy products using their smartphones.

Wireless and mobile networks have the advantages of mobility, flexibility, ease of installation, and low cost. These systems are particularly effective when no communication infrastructure or established networks are in place; this is common in many developing nations and in old buildings that do not have the necessary wiring for a network. Drawbacks of mobile and wireless networks include the following:

- *Limited throughput*—**Throughput** is similar to bandwidth. It is the amount of data transferred or processed in a specified time, usually one second. Unlike the other disadvantages of wireless, throughput is expected to become a bigger problem in the future.

- *Limited range*—The distance a signal can travel without losing strength is more limited in mobile and wireless networks. For example, a Wi-Fi (Wireless Fidelity) network can have a range of 150 feet indoors and 300 feet outdoors.

- *In-building penetration problems*—Wireless signals might not be able to pass through certain building materials or might have difficulty passing through walls.

- *Vulnerability to frequency noise*—Interference from other signals, usually called "noise," can cause transmission problems. Common sources of noise include thunderstorms and lightning, which create radio waves (the same waves used by wireless networks); transformers; high-voltage cables; and fluorescent lights.

- *Security*—Wireless network traffic can be captured with sniffers. (Security is discussed in more detail later in this module.)

There are various definitions of mobile and wireless computing. Mobile computing might simply mean using a laptop away from the office or using a modem to access the corporate network from a client's office. Neither activity requires wireless technology. The term *wireless LAN* is used to describe any wireless network. Wireless LANs have the same characteristics as wired LANs, except they use wireless media, such as infrared (IR) light or RF.

Exhibit 6.10 shows a wireless notebook connecting to a wired LAN. The transceiver on the laptop establishes radio contact with the wired LAN (although the figure does not show the entire wired network). The transceiver/receiver can be built in, attached to the notebook, mounted on a wall, or placed on a desk next to the notebook.

Wireless networks have many advantages. For example, healthcare workers who use handheld notebook computers or tablets with wireless capabilities can get patient information quickly. Instead of writing notes on paper about the patient's condition, then transcribing the notes into an electronic form, they can enter information directly into the handheld devices. Because the information can be sent to and saved on a centralized database,

A **wireless network** uses wireless instead of wired technology.

A **mobile network** (also called a cellular network) operates on a radio frequency (RF) and consists of radio cells, each served by a fixed transmitter known as a cell site or base station.

Throughput is similar to bandwidth. It is the amount of data transferred or processed in a specified time, usually one second.

Exhibit 6.10
A wireless notebook connecting to a wired LAN

Mobile Computing and Mobile Apps

Finance | Technology in Society | Application | Reflective Thinking

Mobile computing has become a familiar term because of the popularity of mobile apps. An app is designed to perform a specific task and can run on mobile devices such as smartphones and tablets. Today, there is an app available for just about any task or application that has a general audience, including such areas as games, social media, retail, banking, finance, and medicine. Many of the apps are free; some must be purchased.

As of September 2021, there were more than 2.79 million apps for Android devices at Google Play.[10] As of August 2021, there were more than 3.74 million apps for iOS devices at the App Store. Apple Watch and Apple TV apps aren't counted as part of the total apps because they have slightly separate app stores.[11]

As of March 2021, the 10 most downloaded apps in the world were:[12]

- TikTok—Short-form video sharing
- Facebook—Social media
- Instagram—Social media
- WhatsApp—Secure messaging and calling
- Telegram—Secure messaging and calling
- Moj—India's own short-video app
- Zoom—A popular video conference platform
- Snapchat—A multimedia messaging app
- Messenger—Instant messaging
- MX TakaTak—A short-video app from India

(BigTunaOnline/Shutterstock.com)

Here are more examples of popular apps in use:

- *EPOCRATES (Epocrates Inc.)*—Gives doctors basic information about drugs, the right dosing for adults and children, and warnings about harmful interactions.[13]
- *ALIVECOR (AliveCor Inc.)*—Produces electrocardiograms when patients place their fingers over the monitor's sensors.
- *Google Shopper*—Provides information such as prices, reviews, and videos for millions of products.[14]
- *RBS (Citizens Bank)*—Performs various online banking tasks.[15]
- *Spotify*—Streams millions of songs from the Internet.[16]
- *Calm (www.calm.com)*—One of the best apps for anxiety treatment.[17]

Questions and Discussions

1. How many apps are available for iOS and Android devices?
2. What are three examples of popular apps? What are their functions? What are two examples of apps for anxiety treatment?

it is available to other workers instantly. In addition, entering notes directly prevents errors that are common during the transcription process, improving the quality of information. The information box titled "Mobile Computing and Mobile Apps" discusses mobile apps, which have further enhanced the popularity of mobile computing.

A strategy used by some companies called BYOD (bring your own device) has helped the popularity of mobile and wireless networks. This strategy allows employees of an organization to use their own computers, tablets, smartphones, or other devices for work purposes. Advantages of this strategy include cost savings, increased flexibility, increased productivity, and attractiveness for some job-seekers. Disadvantages include privacy and security issues related to an organization's information resources.

6-7a Wireless Technologies

The use of wireless and mobile devices is on the rise. In 2021, the number of mobile devices worldwide totaled approximately 15 billion, up from over 14 billion in 2020. The number of mobile devices is expected to reach 18.22 billion by 2025, a significant increase from just five years before.[18]

In a wireless environment, portable computers use small antennas to communicate with radio towers in the surrounding area. Satellites in near-Earth orbit pick up low-powered signals from mobile and portable network devices. The wireless communication industry has many vendors and is changing rapidly, but wireless technologies generally fall into two groups:

- *Wireless LANs (WLANs)*—These networks are becoming an important alternative to wired LANs in many companies. Like their wired counterparts, WLANs are characterized by having one owner and covering a limited area.

- *Wireless WANs (WWANs)*—These networks cover a broader area than WLANs and include the following devices: cellular networks, cellular digital packet data (CDPD), paging networks, personal communication systems (PCS), packet radio networks, broadband personal communications systems (BPCS), microwave networks, and satellite networks.

WLANs and WWANs rely on the RF spectrum as their communication medium, but they differ in the

(iQoncept/Shutterstock.com)

ways that are outlined in Table 6.2. Some of the popular variations of 802.11 wireless standards are listed in Table 6.3.[19]

6-7b Wi-Fi

Wi-Fi, officially called the IEEE 802.11 standard and unofficially called **Wireless Fidelity**, is a broadband wireless technology that allows computers and other devices to communicate over a wireless signal. Information can be transmitted over short distances—typically 150 feet indoors and 300 feet outdoors—in the form of radio waves. You can connect computers, mobile devices, smartphones, and game consoles to the Internet with Wi-Fi. Some restaurants, coffee shops, and university campuses provide Wi-Fi access; these are called "hotspots." Wi-Fi connections are easy to set up, they have fast data transfer rates, and they offer mobility and flexibility. However, they are susceptible to interference from other devices and to being intercepted, which raises security concerns.

> **Wireless Fidelity (Wi-Fi)** is a broadband wireless technology. Information can be transmitted over short distances—typically 150 feet indoors and 300 feet outdoors—in the form of radio waves.

Table 6.2	WLANs versus WWANs	
	WLANs	**WWANs**
Coverage	About 100 meters	Much wider area than for WLANs; capable of a regional, nationwide, or international range
Speed	With the 802.11b wireless standard, data transfer rates of up to 11 Mbps; with 802.11a, up to 54 Mbps; with 802.11n, up to 100 Mbps	Varies from 115 Kbps to 14 Mbps, depending on the technology
Data security	Usually lower than for WWANs	Usually higher than for WLANs

Table 6.3 Selected Wireless Standards

Standard	Release Date	Frequency (GHz)	Speed (Data transfer rate)	Range
Wi-Fi 3/IEEE 802.11g	2003	2.4	54 Mbps	Indoors: 38 m, Outdoors: 140 m
Wi-Fi 4/IEEE 802.11n	2009	2.4/5	600 Mbps	Indoors: 70 m, Outdoors: 250 m
Wi-Fi 5/IEEE 802.11ac	2013	2.4/5	450 Mbps/1300 Mbps	Indoors: 35 m
IEEE 802.11ad (WiGig)	2012	60	6.7 Gbps	3.3 m
IEEE 802.11ah (HaLow)	2016	0.9	347 Mbps	1 km
Wi-Fi 6/IEEE 802.11ax	2019 (est.)	2.4/5	450 Mbps/10.53 Gbps	TBD

6-7c WiMAX

Worldwide Interoperability for Microwave Access (WiMAX) is a broadband wireless technology based on the IEEE 802.16 standards. It is designed for wireless metropolitan area networks and usually has a range of about 30 miles for fixed stations and 3–10 miles for mobile stations. Compared with Wi-Fi, WiMAX theoretically has faster data transfer rates and a longer range. In addition, it is fast and easy to install and enables devices using the same frequency to communicate. A single station can serve hundreds of users.

Disadvantages of WiMAX include interference from other wireless devices, high costs, and interruptions from weather conditions, such as rain. This technology also requires a lot of power; when bandwidth is shared among users, transmission speed decreases.

6-7d Bluetooth

Bluetooth is a wireless technology that allows fixed and mobile devices to transfer data over short distances. Bluetooth 5 offers a range of 800 feet (240 meters) with direct line of sight, or about 131 feet (40 meters) for typical indoor use. Bluetooth 5 offers four data rates to accommodate a variety of transmission ranges: 2 Mbps, 1 Mbps, 500 kbps, and 125 kbps.[20]

It can also be used to create a personal area network (PAN) for communication among computerized devices, including smartphones and game consoles. (PANs can be used for communication among the devices themselves or for connecting to the Internet.) Used with mobile headsets, Bluetooth has become popular as a safer method of talking on cell phones while driving. Bluetooth uses a radio technology called frequency-hopping spread spectrum (FHSS), which separates data into chunks and transmits each chunk on a different frequency, if needed. Bluetooth is also used to connect devices such as computers, global positioning systems (GPSs), smartphones, laptops, printers, and digital cameras. Unlike infrared devices, Bluetooth has no line-of-sight limitations. Similar to other wireless devices, its susceptibility to interception is a security concern.

Bluetooth can also be used in the following ways:

- Video game consoles, such as Nintendo and Sony PlayStation, can use it in their wireless controllers.

- Companies can use it to send short advertisements to Bluetooth-enabled devices. For example, a restaurant can send announcements of dinner specials.

- A wireless device, such as a mouse, keyboard, printer, or scanner, can be connected via Bluetooth.

- Computers that are close together can network via Bluetooth.

- Contact information, to-do lists, appointments, and reminders can be transferred wirelessly between devices with Bluetooth and OBject EXchange (OBEX), a communication protocol for transmitting binary data.

6-7e Mobile Networks

Mobile networks have a three-part architecture, as shown in Exhibit 6.11:

- Base stations send and receive transmissions to and from subscribers.

- Mobile telephone switching offices (MTSOs) transfer

Exhibit 6.11
Mobile network architecture

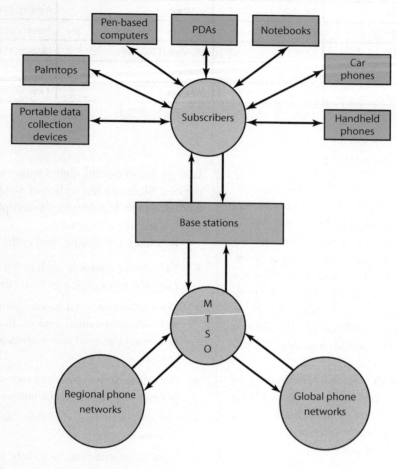

To improve the efficiency and quality of digital communications, **Time Division Multiple Access (TDMA)** divides each channel into six time slots. Each user is allocated two slots: one for transmission and one for reception. This method increases efficiency by 300 percent, as it allows carrying three calls on one channel.

To improve the efficiency and quality of digital communications, **Code Division Multiple Access (CDMA)** transmits multiple encoded messages over a wide frequency and then decodes them at the receiving end.

calls between national or global phone networks and base stations.

- Subscribers (users) connect to base stations by using mobile communication devices.

Mobile devices register by subscribing to a carrier service (provider) licensed for certain geographic areas. When a mobile unit is outside its provider's coverage area, roaming occurs. *Roaming* is using a cellular phone outside of a carrier's limited service area. By doing this, users are extending the connectivity service in a location that is different from the home location where the service was first registered.

To improve the efficiency and quality of digital communications, two technologies have been developed: Time Division Multiple Access and Code Division Multiple Access. **Time Division Multiple Access (TDMA)** divides each channel into six time slots. Each user is allocated two slots: one for transmission and one for reception. This method increases efficiency by 300 percent, as it allows carrying three calls on one channel. **Code Division Multiple Access (CDMA)** transmits multiple encoded messages over a wide frequency and then decodes them at the receiving end.

Table 6.4 describes the various generations of cellular networks.

Table 6.4 Generations of Cellular Networks

Generation	Description
1G	Analog transmission with limited bandwidth
2G	Support for voice, data, paging, and fax services added
2.5G	Added packet-switching technology, which transmits data packets over radio signals; different from the phone system's circuit-switching technology, which transmits data as a continuous stream of bits
3G	Supports transmission of high-quality multimedia data, including voice and video
4G	Advanced version of 3G that provides broadband, large-capacity, high-speed data transmission and high-quality interactive multimedia services
5G	Fifty times higher throughput than 4G, the capability to handle more devices, very low latency (the time it takes one device to send a packet of data to another device), and support for IoT (Internet of Things, discussed in Module 7)[21, 22]

5G, a fifth-generation wireless data transmission technology, offers the highest speeds consumers have ever seen, and it should significantly benefit several industries as follows:[23]

- Healthcare—Widespread applications of wearable medical devices, including IoMT (Internet of Medical Things) and medical applications for augmented reality and virtual reality (AR/VR)

- Transportation and mobility—Autonomous and semi-autonomous cars, dynamic traffic management, smart parking meters, and smarter road infrastructure

- Energy—Smart meters, smart grid systems, electric cars, and growth in charging points

- Manufacturing—Smart factories and collaborative manufacturing systems operating in real time

- Media and entertainment—Faster delivery of video and audio, increased applications of AR/VR, and improved gaming platforms and game delivery systems

Table 6.5 compares key features of 4G with 5G.[24]

Industry experts predict that 6G will be launched by 2030, and that it will resolve some of 5G's shortcomings. The following are some characteristics of 6G.[25]

- Much higher data rates
- Much lower latency
- Higher network reliability and accuracy
- Higher energy efficiency
- Availability of AI-driven wireless communication tools
- Improved personalized network experience

Many businesses use wireless and mobile networks to improve customer service and reduce operational costs. The box titled "Mobile Computing in Action: The Apple iPhone" provides an overview of the Apple iPhone and its business applications.

6-8 Wireless Security

Security is important in any type of network, but it is especially important in a wireless network because anyone walking or driving within the range of an access

Table 6.5 4G versus 5G

Key Features	4G	5G
Data rate (downlink)	1 Gbps	20 Gbps
User-experienced data rate	10 Mbps	100 Mbps
Latency	10 ms	1 ms
Connection density	100,000 devices/sq km	1,000,000 devices/sq km
Energy efficiency	1x	100x
Area traffic capacity	0.1 Mbps/sq m	10 Mbps/sq m
Bandwidth efficiency	1x	3x

Mobile Computing in Action: The Apple iPhone

➤ Finance | Technology in Society | Application

Since its inception in 2007, Apple has released over 17 iPhone models. They are used for diverse personal and business applications. Here are some of the business benefits of using the iPhone:[26]

- It integrates with Microsoft Exchange so you can check your e-mail, your contacts, and your calendar, staying up to date no matter where you are.
- The Safari browser gives you access to your company's resources anytime and anywhere.
- It includes innovative apps like Maps, Voice Memos, and Voice Control.
- You can send SMS messages to multiple recipients.
- You can check stocks from anywhere or get a quick weather report before heading off on your next business trip.

Questions and Discussions

1. What are three features of an iPhone?
2. What are three business applications of iPhones?

---

point (AP) can use the network. An AP is the part of a WLAN that connects it to other networks. Finding WLANs is an easy task. A user can simply walk or drive around office buildings or homes that have a WLAN-equipped computer and try to pick up a signal. Wireless signals can be intercepted, and they are susceptible to the same DoS attacks (discussed in Module 5) to which wired networks are susceptible.

There are several techniques for improving the security of a wireless network:

- *SSID (Service Set Identifier)*—All client computers that try to access the AP are required to include an SSID in all their packets. A packet without an SSID is not processed by the AP. The major weakness of using an SSID is that it can be picked up by other devices within range, given the right software.

- *WEP (Wired Equivalent Privacy)*—A key must be manually entered into the AP and the client computer. The key encrypts messages before transmission. Because this manual process is complex and time-consuming, the WEP technique is not suitable for large networks. More importantly, however, it has too many inherent vulnerabilities to be considered secure.

- *EAP (Extensible Authentication Protocol)*—EAP keys are dynamically generated based on the

user's ID and password. When the user logs out of the system, the key is discarded. A new key is generated when the user logs back in to the network.

- *WPA (Wi-Fi Protected Access)*—This technique combines the strongest features of WEP and EAP. Keys are fixed, as in WEP, or dynamically changed, as in EAP. However, the WPA key is longer than the WEP key; therefore, it is more difficult to break. Also, the key is changed for each frame (a distinct and identifiable data set) before transmission.

- *WPA2 or 802.11i*—This technique uses EAP to obtain a master key. With this master key, a user's computer and the AP negotiate for a key that will be used for a session. After the session is terminated, the key is discarded. This technique uses the Advanced Encryption Standard, which is more complex than WPA and much harder to break.

Securing a Wi-Fi network, particularly for home networks, is a challenging task. An unsecured Wi-Fi network could create privacy and legal issues. Imagine that a hacker breaks into your network and downloads copyrighted materials or sends phishing and scam e-mails to other users—all in your account. Listed next are some security guidelines for a Wi-Fi network.[27, 28]

Privacy and Ethical Issues of Mobile Devices

Some mobile devices, including iPhones, iPads, and Android devices, track the locations of their users. These location data points are saved either on the device itself or on other computers and networks. Although the users of these devices are able to turn off the GPS feature, many do not. In fact, having GPS capability is probably one of the reasons many people buy these devices in the first place. However, location tracking can create privacy concerns for users and ethical issues for IT personnel. Today, many corporations issue mobile devices to their employees to help them perform their jobs more efficiently. Of course, the employers have a legal right to monitor how these devices are used by their employees. This can include monitoring the Web sites their employees visit, the e-mails they send or receive, and their telephone conversations. Many corporations require their employees to carry company-issued devices at all times, which means that the employees' movements are tracked outside of work hours. Is it ethical for an employer to monitor its employees' movements in this way?[29, 30]

iStock.com/Михаил Руденко

Questions and Discussions

1. What are three privacy and ethical issues of mobile devices?
2. Do employers have a legal right to monitor company-issued mobile devices used by their employees? Discuss.

---

1. Open your router settings page and change the default password on your router to a strong password, as discussed in Module 5.

2. Change your network's SSID default name to a name that you choose.

3. Enable network encryption to WPA2.

4. Filter MAC (media access control) addresses on your router.

5. If your wireless device is in a small place (such as a small apartment), reduce the range of the wireless signal.

6. As you do with antivirus software, upgrade your router's firmware to the latest version.

7. Disable SSID broadcasts to hide your Wi-Fi network. This will improve your home network security.

The information box titled "Privacy and Ethical Issues of Mobile Devices" highlights privacy and ethical issues related to wireless devices.

6-9 Convergence of Voice, Video, and Data

In data communication, **convergence** refers to integrating voice, video, and data so that multimedia information can be used for decision making. In the past, separate networks were used to transmit voice, video, and data, but as the demand for integrated services increased, technology was developed to meet this demand.

Convergence can require major network upgrades because video requires much more bandwidth. This has changed, however, with the availability of high-speed technologies such as Asynchronous Transfer Mode (ATM); Gigabit Ethernet; 3G, 4G, and 5G networks;

> In data communication, **convergence** refers to integrating voice, video, and data so that multimedia information can be used for decision making.

Telepresence: A New Use of Data Communication and Convergence

➤➤ Finance | Technology in Society | Application

Telepresence has attracted a lot of attention in recent years, particularly because companies have found that they can reduce business travel and business meeting expenses. Telepresence technology integrates audio and video conferencing into a single platform, and recent improvements have resulted in higher quality, greater ease of use, and better reliability.

Telepresence systems can be used to record meetings for later use or to incorporate multimedia technologies into presentations. They can also offer plug-and-play collaboration applications. Some products offer a telepresence room with customized lighting and acoustics as well as large high-density (HD) screens that can be configured for up to 20 users. Other products operate on a smaller scale and have a single HD screen. Major vendors of telepresence products include Cisco, Poly, Teliris, and HP.[31]

Questions and Discussions

1. What are three business applications of telepresence systems?
2. What are other possible business applications for this technology?

and more demand for applications using these technologies. Gigabit Ethernet is a LAN transmission standard capable of 1 Gbps and 10 Gbps data transfer speeds. ATM is a packet-switching service that operates at 25 Mbps and 622 Mbps, with a maximum speed of up to 10 Gbps. As mentioned earlier, the 3G network is the third generation of mobile networking and telecommunications. It featured a wider range of services and a more advanced network capacity than the 2G network. The 3G network increased the rate and quality of information transfer, video transfers, and broadband wireless data transfers, and increased the quality of Internet telephony or Voice over Internet Protocol (VoIP). It also made streaming video possible, as well as much faster uploads and downloads. The 4G and particularly 5G networks have further enhanced all these features.

More content providers, network operators, telecommunication companies, and broadcasting networks, among others, have moved toward convergence. Even smaller companies are now taking advantage of this fast-growing technology by offering multimedia product demonstrations and using the Internet for multimedia presentations and collaboration. Convergence is possible now because of a combination of technological innovation, changes in market structure, and regulatory reform. Common applications of convergence include the following:

- E-commerce
- More entertainment options as the number of TV channels substantially increases and movies and videos on demand become more available

(bloomua/Shutterstock.com)

- Increased availability and affordability of video and computer conferencing
- Consumer products and services, such as virtual classrooms, telecommuting, and virtual reality

As a tool for delivering services, the Internet is an important contributor to the convergence phenomenon. Advances in digital technologies are helping to move convergence technologies forward, and when standards in data collection, processing, and transmission become more available and acceptable, their use should increase even further. See the "Telepresence: A New Use of Data Communication and Convergence" box.

The Industry Connection box on Cisco Systems describes some of the products and services used in data communication systems.

Industry Connection: Cisco Systems, Inc.[32]

The main goal of Cisco Systems, Inc., the world's largest vendor of networking equipment, is to make it easier to connect different computers. Cisco offers a wide variety of products, including routers, switches, network management tools, optical networking, security software, VPNs, firewalls, and collaboration and telepresence products. The variety of products makes it possible for organizations to get everything they need for networking solutions from one vendor. Cisco's products and services include the following:

PIX Firewall Series: Allows corporations to protect their internal networks from outside intruders.

Network Management Tools: Allow network managers to automate, simplify, and integrate their networks to reduce operational costs and improve productivity.

Identity Management Tools: Protect information resources through identity policies, access control, and compliance features.

TelePresence Network Management: Integrates audio, high-definition video, and interactive features to deliver face-to-face collaboration capabilities.

Cisco 900 Series Integrated Services Routers (ISRs): Combine Internet access, comprehensive security, and wireless services in a single high-performance device that is easy to deploy and manage. The routers are suited for deployment as customer premises equipment (CPE) in small branch offices and in environments managed by service providers.

The routing system CRS-3 (Cisco Carrier Routing System-3) delivers Internet speeds of up to 322 terabits per second, which means it can offer video and other content 12 times faster than its rivals' systems.

Module Summary

6-1 Describe the major applications of a data communication system. Data communication is the electronic transfer of data from one location to another. An information system's effectiveness is measured in part by how efficiently it delivers information, and a data communication system is what enables an information system to carry out this function. In addition, because most organizations collect and transfer data across great geographic distances, an efficient data communication system is critical.

6-2 Explain the three major components of a data communication system. A typical data communication system includes the following components: sender and receiver devices, modems or routers, and a communication medium (channel).

6-3 Describe the three major types of processing configurations. During the past 60 years, three types of processing configurations have emerged: centralized, decentralized, and distributed.

6-4 Explain the three types of networks. There are three major types of networks: local area networks, wide area networks, and metropolitan area networks. In all these networks, computers are usually connected to the network via a network interface card (NIC), a hardware component that enables computers to communicate over a network.

6-5 Describe the five main network topologies. A network topology represents a network's physical layout, including the arrangement of computers and cables. Five common topologies are star, ring, bus, hierarchical, and mesh.

6-6 Explain important networking concepts, including protocols, TCP/IP, routing, routers, and the client/server model. Transmission Control Protocol/Internet Protocol (TCP/IP) is an industry-standard suite of communication protocols. TCP/IP's main advantage is that it enables interoperability—in other words, it allows the linking of devices running on many different platforms. In the client/server model, software runs on the local computer (the client) and communicates with the remote server to request information or services.

6-7 Examine wireless and mobile technologies and networks in a business setting. A wireless network uses wireless instead of wired technology. A mobile network (also called a cellular network) operates on a radio frequency (RF) and consists of radio cells, each served by a fixed transmitter known as a cell site or base station.

6-8 Describe networking trends such as Wi-Fi, WiMAX, and Bluetooth. Wireless Fidelity (Wi-Fi) is a broadband wireless technology. Information can be transmitted over short distances—typically 150 feet indoors and 300 feet outdoors—in the form of radio waves. Worldwide Interoperability for Microwave Access (WiMAX) is a broadband wireless technology based on the IEEE 802.16 standards. It is designed for wireless metropolitan area networks and usually has a range of about 30 miles for fixed stations and 3–10 miles for mobile stations. Bluetooth, which can be used to create a personal area network (PAN), is a wireless technology for transferring data over short distances. Bluetooth 5 offers a range of 800 feet (240 meters) with direct line of sight, or about 131 feet (40 meters) for typical indoor use.

6-9 Discuss the importance of wireless security and the five techniques used. There are several techniques for improving the security of a wireless network, including SSID (Service Set Identifier), WEP (Wired Equivalent Privacy), EAP (Extensible Authentication Protocol), WPA (Wi-Fi Protected Access), and WPA2 or 802.11i.

6-10 Summarize the concept of convergence and its applications for business and personal use. In data communication, convergence refers to integrating voice, video, and data so that multimedia information can be used for decision making. In the past, separate networks were used to transmit voice, video, and data, but as the demand for integrated services increased, technology was developed to meet this demand. Common applications of convergence include e-commerce, entertainment, and video and computer conferencing.

Key Terms

- Attenuation
- Bandwidth
- Bluetooth
- Broadband
- Bus topology
- Centralized processing
- Centralized routing
- Client/server model
- Code Division Multiple Access (CDMA)
- Communication media
- Conducted media
- Controller
- Convergence
- Data communication
- Decentralized processing
- Digital subscriber line (DSL)
- Distributed processing
- Distributed routing
- Dynamic routes

- Hierarchical topology
- Local area network (LAN)
- Mesh topology
- Metropolitan area network (MAN)
- Mobile network
- Modem
- Multiplexer
- Narrowband
- Network interface card (NIC)
- Network topology
- N-tier architecture
- Open Systems Interconnection (OSI) model
- Packet
- Protocols
- Radiated media
- Ring topology
- Router
- Routing
- Routing table

- Star topology
- Static routes
- Throughput
- Time Division Multiple Access (TDMA)
- Transmission Control Protocol/Internet Protocol (TCP/IP)

- Two-tier architecture
- Wide area network (WAN)
- Wireless Fidelity (Wi-Fi)
- Wireless network
- Worldwide Interoperability for Microwave Access (WiMAX)

Reviews and Discussions

1. What are three applications of data communication systems?
2. In order to have a data communication system, three major components are needed. Explain these three components.
3. What are one advantage and one disadvantage of each processing configuration?
4. Which of the three types of networks is the fastest? Which one is the slowest?
5. Which network topology is the most reliable? Discuss.
6. What is TCP/IP? What does it do?
7. What are three advantages of a wireless network compared to a wired one?
8. What are the five techniques used for wireless security?

Projects

1. A newly established Internet company with 40 employees needs your advice. They are looking for a collaboration tool and have narrowed their choices to GoToMeeting, WebEx, and Zoom. After reading the information presented in this module and other sources, prepare a two-page document that includes two advantages and two disadvantages of each tool. Which tool is your final recommendation? Why did you choose that tool over the other two?

2. Cisco and Poly are two major vendors of telepresence products. After reading the information presented in this module and other sources, write a one-page paper that identifies a top-of-the-line product from each company. Which product would you recommend to the company referenced in Project 1? Explain the reasons for your recommendation. What are two advantages of using a telepresence system compared to a face-to-face meeting? What are two disadvantages?

3. Mobile and wireless devices are increasingly used in the healthcare industry. After reading the information presented in this module and other sources, write a

two-page paper that outlines five applications of these devices in this industry. Also, identify three mobile apps that could be used by medical personnel to increase their productivity.

4. After reading the information presented in this module and other sources, write a two-page paper that identifies five mobile apps that could be used in the banking industry. How do these apps increase the productivity of bankers and their customers? Do you see any drawbacks in using these apps?

5. After reading the information presented in this module and other sources, write a one-page paper that includes a six-item bulleted list for improving the privacy and security of your smartphone. Generally speaking, are iOS devices more or less secure than Android devices?

6. After reading the information presented in this module and other sources, write a two-page paper that describes five business applications of convergence. Which industries are expected to gain the most from the convergence trend?

Module Quiz

1. In data communication, convergence refers to integrating voice, video, and data so that multimedia information can be used for decision making. True or False?

2. To improve the efficiency and quality of digital communications, Time Division Multiple Access divides each channel into two time slots. True or False?

3. In the two-tier architecture of the client/server model, a client (tier one) communicates directly with the server (tier two). True or False?

4. Which of the following layers of the OSI model is responsible for formatting message packets?
   a. Presentation
   b. Application
   c. Session
   d. Transport

5. A typical data communication system includes all of the following components except:
   a. Sender and receiver devices
   b. Modems or routers
   c. Communication medium (channel)
   d. A local area network

6. Which of the following has the highest bandwidth of any communication medium?
   a. Coaxial cable
   b. Fiber-optic cable
   c. Twisted-pair copper cable
   d. Microwave

Case Study 6-1
Data Communication at Walmart
➤ Finance | Technology in Society | Application

Walmart has made several changes in its data communication systems to improve its suppliers' access to sales and inventory data. For example, the company added a customized Web site for its suppliers, such as Mattel, Procter & Gamble, and Warner-Lambert. Walmart's goal is to improve efficiency in order to keep prices low and maintain a high level of customer service. With Walmart's network, suppliers can access sales, inventory, and forecasting data over extremely fast connections. To ensure confidentiality of data, a sophisticated security system has been implemented to prevent suppliers from accessing data about one another's products.

Walmart has also added Web-based access to its Retail-Link system so suppliers can use information in the database. Other data communication applications at Walmart include automated distribution, computerized routing, and electronic data interchange (EDI).[33, 34]

Walmart uses the latest wireless technology in its operations for warehouse management systems to track and manage the flow of goods through its distribution centers. Another application of wireless technology is for controlling and monitoring forklifts and industrial

(Vdovichenko Denis/Shutterstock.com)

vehicles that move merchandise inside distribution centers. The Vehicle Management System (VMS) is the latest application of data communication at Walmart. Among other features, the VMS includes a two-way text-messaging system that enables management to effectively divert material-handling resources to where they are needed the most. (The VMS works effectively with RFID-based systems.) According to Walmart, the VMS has improved safety and significantly improved the productivity of its operations.[35]

Answer the following questions:

1. How has Walmart improved its data communication systems for suppliers?
2. What are some typical data communication applications at Walmart?
3. What are some of the applications of wireless technology at Walmart?
4. What are some of the features and capabilities of the VMS?

Case Study 6-2
Protecting the Security and Privacy of Mobile Devices
➤➤ **Finance | Technology in Society | Social and Ethical Issues | Application**

As the number of smartphones and tablet devices increases, so does the risk that hackers and computer criminals will target these devices. Since they were first introduced, certain mobile devices have been vulnerable to eavesdropping and incurring fraudulent charges. In addition, many of them automatically track a user's location.[36]

The major security risks associated with mobile devices include the following:[37]

Malware—Android apps, in particular, are vulnerable to malware because of the platform's openness. To guard against malware threats, users have to upload the most recent versions of the operating system and use mobile security tools.

Premium SMS billing—Smartphone users face an added risk of subscribing to premium text-messaging services that charge every time users interact with them. Most cell phone carriers allow subscribers to block premium SMS messaging, however.

E-mail and SMS phishing—Because it is more difficult to establish a link's legitimacy on a mobile device, mobile users are more likely to click on them, which is a phisher's dream come true. Mobile users should therefore exercise caution when using e-mail on mobile devices.

Spyware—Commercially available software can be used by intruders to track and control a user's mobile activities.

Malicious Web sites—These could pose a threat in the future, given that many smartphone browsers are based on a browser engine that has vulnerabilities.

In addition, many apps on your smartphone are tracking everywhere you go. To stop them, open Settings, tap Privacy, and then select Location Services. If you want to stop all apps from using your location, turn Location Services off. If you want to manage settings app by app, tap each app and choose Never or While Using. Make sure apps that do not need your location, such as most games, are set to Never. Other apps should be set to track your location only while you are using them.[38] Many of the recommendations

(Art Alex/Shutterstock.com)

discussed in Modules 4 and 5 apply here. Never leave your mobile device unlocked, never leave it unattended, and always protect it with a password.

Answer the following questions:

1. What are some examples of security risks associated with a mobile device?
2. How can these devices automatically track a user's location?
3. What are two recommendations for protecting your mobile device against these threats?
4. How do you stop the tracking feature of an app on your smartphone? Are you concerned about this? Why or why not?

Module
7
A Connected World

Learning Objectives

After studying this module, you should be able to…

7.1 Describe the makeup of the Internet and the Web.

7.2 Discuss navigational tools, search engines, and directories.

7.3 Describe four common Internet services and how they are used in a business environment.

7.4 Explain business applications of the Internet.

7.5 Describe the role of intranets in various business functions.

7.6 Describe the role of extranets in various business functions.

7.7 Analyze Web trends and their impact on business.

7.8 Analyze the Internet of Everything and its business applications.

This module introduces you to the Internet and Web technologies. It provides an overview of the Domain Name System and various types of Internet connections. You learn how navigational tools, search engines, and directories are used on the Internet, and there is a brief survey of common Internet services and Web applications. This module also explains intranets and extranets and how they are used. Finally, you learn about Web trends, the Internet of Everything, the Internet of Things, and the Internet of Me.

7-1 The Internet

The **Internet** is a worldwide collection of billions of computers and networks of all sizes. The term *Internet* is derived from *internetworking*, which means connecting networks. Simply put, the Internet is a network of networks. No one actually owns or runs the Internet, and each network is administered and funded locally.

The Internet is playing an increasingly major role in our personal and professional lives. The number of Internet users is growing daily around the globe. As of January 2022, there were 307.2 million Internet users in the United States, and 92 percent of the total U.S. population used the Internet. This data shows that 26.71 million people in the United States did not use the Internet at the start of 2022.[1]

The Internet started in 1969 as a U.S. Department of Defense project called the **Advanced Research Projects Agency Network (ARPANET)** that connected four nodes: the University of California at Los Angeles, the University of California at Santa Barbara, the Stanford Research Institute at Stanford University in California, and the University of Utah at Salt Lake City. Other nodes composed of computer networks from universities and government laboratories were added to the network later. These connections were linked in a three-level hierarchical structure: backbones, regional networks, and local area networks.

> **The Internet started in 1969 as a U.S. Department of Defense project.**

In 1987, ARPANET evolved into the National Science Foundation Network (NSFNET), which is considered the first Internet backbone. The NSF initially restricted Internet use to research and educational institutions; commercial use was not allowed. Eventually, because of increased demand, other backbones were allowed to connect to NSFNET.

The **Internet backbone** is a foundation network linked with fiber-optic cables that can support very high bandwidth. It is called a *backbone* because it supports all the other networks that form the Internet, just as the human backbone is the foundation of the nervous system. The Internet backbone is made up of many interconnected government, academic, commercial, and other high-capacity data routers.

Several private companies operate their own Internet backbones that interconnect at network access points (NAPs). Exhibit 7.1 shows IBM's backbone. NAPs determine how traffic is routed over the Internet. As you learned in Module 6, local area networks (LANs) serve as localized Internet connections, and they use NAPs to connect to the Internet backbone.

The Web changed the Internet in 1989 by introducing a graphical interface to the largely text-based system. The Web was proposed by Tim Berners-Lee at the European Organization for Nuclear Research (CERN), the world's largest particle physics center. (CERN stands for *Conseil Europeen pour la Recherche Nucleaire*.)

The Web organizes information by using **hypermedia**, which are documents that include embedded references to

The **Internet** is a worldwide collection of billions of computers and networks of all sizes. It is a network of networks.

The **Advanced Research Projects Agency Network (ARPANET)**, a project started in 1969 by the U.S. Department of Defense, was the beginning of the Internet.

The **Internet backbone** is a foundation network linked with fiber-optic cables that can support very high bandwidth. It is made up of many interconnected government, academic, commercial, and other high-capacity data routers.

With **hypermedia**, documents include embedded references to audio, text, images, video, and other documents.

Exhibit 7.1
IBM's backbone

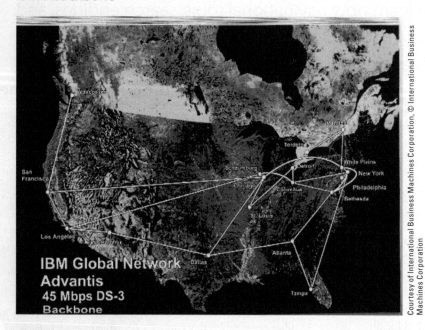

audio, text, images, video, or other documents. Composed of billions of hypermedia documents, the Web constitutes a large portion of the Internet. The embedded references in hypermedia documents are called **hypertext**; they consist of links that users can click to follow a particular thread (topic). By using hypertext links, users can access files, applications, and other computers in any order they like (unlike in paper documents) and retrieve information with the click of a button. In essence, hypertext is an approach to data management, in which data is stored in a network of nodes connected by links. Data in these nodes is accessed with an interactive browsing system, meaning the user determines the order in which information is accessed.

Any computer that stores hypermedia documents and makes them available to other computers on the Internet is called a server or Web server, and computers that request these documents are called clients. A client can be a home computer or a node in an organization's LAN. The most exciting feature of the Web is that hypermedia documents can be stored anywhere in the world, so users can jump from a site in the United States to a site in Paris in a few milliseconds. The "Major Events in the Development of the Internet" box summarizes major events in the development of the Internet.

7-1a The Domain Name System

Domain names, such as *IBM. com* or *whitehouse.gov*, are unique identifiers of computer or network addresses on the Internet. Each computer or network also has an Internet Protocol (IP) address, such as 208.77.188.166, which is assigned by the Internet Corporation for Assigned Names and Numbers (ICANN). These numbers are difficult to remember, however, so language-based domain names are used more often to access Web sites. When information is transferred from one network to another, domain names are converted to IP addresses by the **Domain Name System (DNS)** protocol. Servers that use this protocol (called DNS servers) maintain lists of computer and Web site addresses and their associated IP addresses. DNS servers translate all domain names into IP addresses.

You see domain names used in **uniform resource locators (URLs)**, also called *universal resource locators*, to identify a Web page. A URL is the address of a document or site on the Internet. For example, in the URL *http://www.csub.edu*, the domain name is *csub.edu*. Every domain name has a suffix indicating its top-level domain (TLD). In this example, the suffix is .edu, which stands for "educational institutions." Combinations of letters, the numerals 0 through 9, and hyphens can be used in domain names, too. Spaces are not allowed.

The TLD denotes the type of organization or the country the address specifies. TLDs are divided into organizational domains (generic top-level domains, or gTLDs) and geographic domains (country code top-level domains, or ccTLDs). Table 7.1 lists common gTLDs.

The embedded references in hypermedia documents are called **hypertext**; they consist of links that users can click to follow a particular thread (topic).

When information is transferred from one network to another, domain names are converted to IP addresses by the **Domain Name System (DNS)** protocol. Servers that use this protocol (called DNS servers) maintain lists of computer and Web site addresses and their associated IP addresses.

Uniform resource locators (URLs), also called *universal resource locators*, identify a Web page. A URL is the address of a document or site on the Internet.

Major Events in the Development of the Internet

▶ Finance | Technology in Society | Global

September 1969: ARPANET is born.

1971: Ray Tomlinson of BBN invents an e-mail program to send messages across a network.

January 1983: A transition occurs from Network Control Protocol (NCP) to Transmission Control Protocol/Internet Protocol (TCP/IP), the protocol for sending and receiving packets.

1987: The National Science Foundation creates a backbone to the National Research and Education Network called NSFNET; it signifies the birth of the Internet.

November 1988: A worm attacks more than 6,000 computers, including those at the Department of Defense.

1989: The Web is developed at CERN.

February 1991: The Bush administration approves Senator Al Gore's idea to develop a high-speed national network, and the term "information superhighway" is coined.

November 1993: Pacific Bell announces a plan to spend $16 billion on the information superhighway.

January 1994: MCI announces a six-year plan to spend $20 billion on an international communication network.

April 1995: Netscape becomes the most popular graphical navigator for surfing the Web.

August 1995: Microsoft releases the first version of Internet Explorer.

February 2000: A denial-of-service (DoS) attack shuts down several Web sites (including Yahoo!, Ameritrade, and Amazon) for several hours.

2004: A worm called MyDoom or Novarg spreads through Web servers. About 1 of every 12 e-mail messages is infected.

2005: YouTube is launched.

2009: The number of worldwide Internet users surpasses 1 billion per month.[2]

2021: Internet users top the 5.17 billion mark.

Questions and Discussions

1. Why was the information superhighway a strategic objective of the U.S. government?
2. What are some of the challenges facing Internet users today?

Many new gTLDs have been proposed, including .aero (aviation industry), .museum, .law, and .store. Some are already in use, such as .info for organizations providing information services, .biz for businesses, and .news for news-related sites.

In addition, most countries have geographic domains. These ccTLDs include .au for Australia, .ca for Canada, .fr for France, .jp for Japan, and .uk for the United Kingdom. You can find a complete list of ccTLDs at *www. ionos.com/digitalguide/domains/domain-extensions/ cctlds-a-list-of-every-country-domain/*.

Corporations and individuals can now choose from an expanded list of TLDs that has been approved by ICANN. Before the expansion, there were only 22 generic TLDs, such as .com and .edu. Now, Internet address names can end with almost any word in any language, giving organizations around the world the opportunity to market their brands, products, or causes in new and creative ways. The TLDs can use any character set and can contain any phrase, including a company or brand name. The new gTLDs fall into four categories:[3,4]

- Generic word TLDs (e.g., .company or .TV)
- Corporate TLDs (e.g., .Microsoft or .Intel), owned by corporations to control use of their brands

7-1b Types of Internet Connections

As you learned in Module 6, there are several methods for connecting to a network, including the Internet. These methods include dial-up and cable modems as well as digital subscriber lines (DSL). Several types of DSL services are available:

- *Symmetric DSL (SDSL)*—SDSL has the same data transmission rate to and from the phone network (called upstream and downstream), usually up to 1.5 Mbps (million bits per second) in both directions.

- *Asymmetric DSL (ADSL)*—ADSL has a lower transmission rate upstream (3.5 Mbps) than downstream (typically 24 Mbps)—for example, the ITU G.992.5 Annex M standard.

- *Very High-Speed DSL (VDSL)*—VDSL has a downstream/upstream transmission rate of up to 100 Mbps over short distances—for example, the ITU G.993.2 standard.

You can always measure the speed of your connection by entering "*www.speedtest.net*" into your Web browser.

- Community TLDs (e.g., .Spanish or .Persian), limited to members of a defined community

- Geographic TLDs (e.g., .London or .Madrid), owned by cities and geographic regions and used to promote business and tourism

Here are brief explanations of each part of a URL, using *http://www.csub.edu/~hbidgoli/books.html* as an example:

- *http*—Stands for Hypertext Transfer Protocol, the protocol used for accessing most Web sites.

- *www.csub.edu*—*www* stands for *World Wide Web* or *the Web*. The *csub* stands for California State University at Bakersfield, and *.edu* is the suffix for educational institutions. Together, *csub.edu* uniquely identifies this Web site.

- */~hbidgoli*—This part is the name of the directory where the author has stored files pertaining to the books he has written. A server can be divided into directories for better organization.

- *books.html*—This part is the document itself. The .html extension means it is a Hypertext Markup Language (HTML) document. (See the information box "What Is HTML?" for more on HTML.) Servers that do not support long extensions display just *.htm*; other servers display *.html*.

Table 7.1 | Generic Top-Level Domains

gTLD	Purpose
.com	Commercial organizations (such as Microsoft)
.edu	Educational institutions (such as California State University)
.int	International organizations (such as the United Nations)
.mil	U.S. military organizations (such as the U.S. Army)
.gov	U.S. government organizations (such as the Internal Revenue Service)
.net	Backbone, regional, and commercial networks (e.g., the National Science Foundation's Internet Network Information Center)
.org	Other organizations, such as research and nonprofit organizations (e.g., the Internet Town Hall)

What Is HTML?

Technology in Society | Application

Hypertext Markup Language (HTML) is the language used to create Web pages. It defines a page's layout and appearance by using tags and attributes. A tag delineates a section of the page, such as the header or body; an attribute specifies a value, such as a font color, for a page component.

JavaScript (JS) is another important language for Web page design. It is not a markup language but a scripting language, which includes series of commands that can be executed without the need for compiling—the transformation from human-readable source code into object code that is in computer-executable format.

A typical structure for an HTML document is as follows:

```
<html>
<head>
(Enter the page's description.)
</head>
<body>
(Enter the page's content.)
</body>
</html>
```

iinspiration/Shutterstock.com

Questions and Discussions

1. What is Hypertext Markup Language (HTML)?
2. What is a tag in HTML?

Organizations often use T1 or T3 lines. These are provided by the telephone company and are capable of transporting the equivalent of 24 conventional telephone lines using only two pairs of copper wires. T1 uses two pairs of copper wires to carry up to 24 simultaneous conversations (called channels) and has a transmission rate of 1.544 Mbps; it is more widely used than T3. (In other countries, T1 is called E1 and has a transmission rate of 2.048 Mbps.) A T3 line is a digital communication link that supports transmission rates of 43–45 Mbps. A T3 line actually consists of 672 channels, each supporting rates of 64 Kbps.

As of 2021, the 10 countries with the fastest *mobile Internet* speeds were the United Arab Emirates, South Korea, Norway, Qatar, China, Kuwait, Saudi Arabia, Cyprus, Bulgaria, and Switzerland. The 10 countries with the fastest *broadband Internet* speeds were Monaco, Singapore, Hong Kong (China), Romania, Switzerland, Denmark, Thailand, Chile, France, and South Korea.[5]

7-2 Navigational Tools, Search Engines, and Directories

Now that you know what the Internet is and how to connect to it, you will need tools to get around and find what you are looking for. These tools can be divided into three categories:

- **Navigational tools**—These are used to travel from Web site to Web site (i.e., "surf" the Internet).

Hypertext Markup Language (HTML) is the language used to create Web pages. It defines a page's layout and appearance by using tags and attributes. A tag delineates a section of the page, such as the header or body; an attribute specifies a value, such as a font color, for a page component.

Navigational tools are used to travel from Web site to Web site—as in "surf" the Internet.

- **Search engines**—These allow you to look up information on the Internet by entering keywords related to your topic of interest.

- **Directories**—These are indexes of information, based on keywords embedded in documents, that allow search engines to find what you are looking for. Some Web sites such as Yahoo! also use directories to organize content into categories.

Originally, Internet users entered text-based commands for simple tasks, such as downloading files or sending e-mail. However, it was tedious to type commands at the command line, and users also had to have certain programming skills to use these systems. Graphical browsers changed all this by providing menus and graphics-based tools that allowed users to point and click. These systems make the user–system interface easier to use, and graphical browsers also support multimedia information such as images and sound.

The three common tools for getting around the Internet and finding information are described in more detail in the following sections.

7-2a Navigational Tools

Many graphical Web browsers are available, such as Microsoft Edge, Mozilla Firefox, Google Chrome, Apple Safari, and Opera. Typically, these browsers have menu options you have seen in word-processing programs, such as File, Edit, and Help. They also include options for viewing your browsing history, bookmarking favorite Web sites, and setting viewing preferences, as well as navigation buttons to move backward and forward in Web pages you visit. With some browsers, you can also set up specialized toolbars for accessing frequently visited sites or conducting searches.

7-2b Search Engines and Directories

A search engine, such as Google, Bing, DuckDuckGo, Neeva, or Ask, is an information system that enables users to retrieve data from the Web by using search terms. All search engines follow a three-step process:

1. *Crawling the Web*—Search engines use software called *crawlers, spiders, bots*, and other similar names. These automated modules search the Web continuously for new data. When you post a new Web page, crawlers find it (if it is public), and when you update it, crawlers find the new data. Crawlers also check to see what links are on your page and make sure they work; if a link is broken, crawlers identify it and include this information as part of the data about that page. In addition, crawlers can go through the other pages that are part of your Web site, as long as there are links to those pages. All the gathered data is sent back to the search engine's data center so the search engine always has the most current information on the Web.

2. *Indexing*—Housed at server farms, search engines use keywords to index data coming in from crawlers. Each keyword has an index entry that is linked to all Web pages containing that keyword. For example, a company selling picture frames includes the term *picture frame* on its Web site several times. The indexing process recognizes the frequency of use and creates an index entry for the term *picture frame*. This index entry is linked to the company's Web site, along with all other sites containing the term *picture frame*. Indexing makes it possible for search engines to retrieve all related Web pages when you enter a search term.

3. *Searching*—When you enter a search term, the search engine uses the index created in Step 2 to look up the term. If the term exists in the index, the search engine identifies all Web pages linked to the term. However, it needs some way of prioritizing Web pages based on how close each one is to the search term. For example, say your Aunt Emma makes picture-frame cookies and has a Web site for selling them. Someone searching on the term *picture frame* might see Aunt Emma's site listed, too. Because search engines are programmed to try to differentiate various types of search requests, they can use other terms, such as *posters, photos,* and *images*, to give a higher priority to Web pages containing these additional terms. A lower priority is given to Web pages containing terms such as *cookies* or *baked goods* along with *picture frame*. Search engines vary in intelligence, which is why you can use the same search term and get different results with two different search engines.

In recent years, two new types of searches are gaining in popularity: Graph Search by Facebook and Knowledge Graph by Google. Graph Search allows Facebook users to find people, photos, places, and interests that are relevant to them. Example searches using this method include the following:[6]

- People who like sausage and live in the southwest part of the city I live in

A search engine, such as Google or Bing, is an information system that enables users to retrieve data from the Web by using search terms.

Directories are indexes of information based on keywords embedded in documents, which make it possible for search engines to find what you are looking for.

- Photos of a particular friend of mine that were taken after 2019

- Photos of all my friends who live in Los Angeles

- Chinese restaurants in Boston that my friends have liked

- Tourist attractions in southern France visited by my friends

panuwat phimpha/Shutterstock.com

The Graph Search feature is not turned on automatically. The user has to activate it first in the search bar. Once the Graph Search feature is on, Facebook allows the user to search for people, places, and things.[7]

In a traditional Google search, users type in keywords and Google displays the most relevant Web pages, based mostly on the number of times those Web pages have been linked to. With Facebook's Graph Search, the objects that users are searching for are not Web pages; instead, they're searching for the virtual representations of real-world objects: people, places, photos, and so forth. The results of the search are determined by Facebook "likes."[8]

According to Google, Knowledge Graph provides answers, not just links. So, along with the usual results, there are panels containing important facts about people, places, and things. The goal is to return pages that match the entities or concepts that the keywords evoke.

Another type of search, Google Voice Search, has become popular on mobile devices. This can be activated by saying "Okay, Google." You can use an Android or iOS device and conduct a search using your voice. This search works quickly and overcomes difficulties that some people have with typing on handheld devices. Using Voice Search, you can generate queries, ask for help, get directions, and so forth. You can also use your voice to generate reminders that can be added in a note to Google Keep or Evernote. Here are some examples:[9]

- How many inches are in a foot

- Show me a video of how to fix my garage door opener

- Show me a picture of the new iPhone

- When is Veteran's Day

- Where is a good Chinese restaurant close to our university

- Where is the capital of Ecuador

- Remind me to buy milk tomorrow

- Remind me to pay my tuition on January 15

Directories organize information into categories. There are two kinds of directories on the Web. The first is the automated, or crawler-based, directory that search engines use; it creates indexes of search terms and collects these terms automatically by using crawlers. Google, Yahoo!, Ask, and others fall into this category. When your Web page changes, for example, these directories update their indexes and databases automatically to reflect the change. The second type of directory is the human-powered directory. If you want your Web page to be listed in a search engine's results, you have to manually submit keywords to a human-powered directory. It does not use crawlers to collect data; instead, it relies on users to supply the data. After keywords are submitted, they are indexed with search engines and can then be listed in search results. The main difference is that if your Web page changes, the directory does not have the updated content until you submit changes to the directory. Open Directory is an example of a human-powered directory. However, Google has made many directories obsolete, and directories in general are not as relevant as they used to be.

Crawler-based directories are based on index terms, just as the database for a large multinational corporation is based on the last names and first names of people. Some search engines, in addition to their index term–based directory, offer directories based on popular categories, such as business, sports, entertainment, travel, and dining. Each category can have subcategories; for example, an Entertainment category might contain Movies, Music, and Theater subcategories. Yahoo! Travel, Yahoo! Finance, and Yahoo! News are some categories in the Yahoo! directory, which is considered an excellent source both by users and experts.

7-3 Internet Services

Many services are available via the Internet, and most are made possible by the TCP suite of protocols in the Application layer (introduced in Module 6). For instance, TCP/IP provides several useful e-mail protocols, such as Simple Message Transfer Protocol (SMTP) for sending e-mail and Post Office Protocol (POP) for retrieving messages. Popular services include e-mail, newsgroups and discussion groups, instant messaging, and Internet telephony. All are discussed in the following sections.

7-3a E-Mail

E-mail is one of the most widely used services on the Internet. In addition to personal use, many companies use e-mail for product announcements, payment confirmations, and newsletters. Some businesses also send e-mail receipts for items that customers purchase. This helps reduce costs and is more environmentally friendly than using paper.

There are two main types of e-mail. Web-based e-mail enables you to access your e-mail account from any computer and, in some cases, store your e-mails on a Web server. Microsoft Outlook and Google Gmail are two examples of Web-based e-mail services. The other type of e-mail is client-based e-mail, which consists of an e-mail program you install on your computer; e-mail is downloaded and stored locally on your computer. Examples of client-based e-mail programs include Microsoft Outlook, Mozilla Thunderbird, and Apple Mail.

Most e-mail programs include a folder system for organizing your e-mails and an address book in which to store e-mail addresses. Many address books include an autocompletion feature that fills in an e-mail recipient's name automatically after you type the first few letters. You can also set up distribution groups for sending an e-mail to several people at the same time. Other commonly available features are spell checkers and delivery notifications. You can also attach documents and multimedia files to e-mails.

7-3b Newsgroups and Discussion Groups

The Internet serves billions of people with diverse backgrounds and interests. Discussion groups and newsgroups are a great way for people with similar interests to find one another. Although newsgroups and discussion groups are similar in many ways, **discussion groups** are usually for exchanging opinions and ideas on a specific topic, usually of a technical or scholarly nature. Group members post messages or articles that others in the group can read. **Newsgroups** are typically more general in nature and can cover any topic; they allow people to get together for fun or for business purposes. For example, you could join a newsgroup for people interested in ancient civilizations or one that helps people write and debug computer programs. Newsgroups can also serve as an effective advertising medium in e-commerce.

Another type of discussion is a discussion thread, which is a chain of written ideas or opinions exchanged among two or more participants online. By using hypertext, discussion threads allow participants to start at any point and follow the entire discussion from its beginning to its latest idea or opinion. There are many platforms available for discussion threads, including Reddit, Facebook, Instagram, and Quora.

7-3c Instant Messaging

Instant messaging (IM) is a service for communicating with others via a private "chat room" on the Internet. It can be a private message between individuals, with a group, or with a broader audience. Many IM applications are available, such as Facebook Messenger, WhatsApp Messenger (owned by Facebook), Windows Messenger, and Google Chat; their capabilities and features vary depending on the application. For example, some IM applications notify you when someone on your chat list comes online; others have features for audio or video conversations.

Also, mmhmm (*www.mmhmm.app/about/*) is a relatively new video chat platform for personal and business use. It offers several unique features and can be used in real-time mode as well as in asynchronous mode.

Facebook Messenger has over 300,000 chatbots. These chatbots offer flexibility in order to automate tasks and assist in retrieving data. They improve the user experience and user productivity. For example, chatbots can now send videos, audio clips, GIFs, and other files automatically.[10]

Discussion groups are usually for exchanging opinions and ideas on a specific topic, usually of a technical or scholarly nature. Group members post messages or articles that others in the group can read.

Newsgroups are typically more general in nature and can cover any topic; they allow people to get together for fun or for business purposes.

Instant messaging (IM) is a service for communicating with others via a private "chat room" on the Internet. It can be a private message between individuals, with a group, or with a broader audience.

Another type of messaging is offered by a mobile app called Snapchat. Here, users combine pictures, videos, text, and drawings into "Snaps" that are sent to other Snapchat users. Facebook and Instagram also have this functionality. The Snaps self-destruct in a matter of seconds, seeming not to leave a trace. However, while they are on the screen, they can be captured or somebody can take a screenshot of them. They can also be undeleted and restored using recently developed tools. Some people have used Snapchat for sexting or to send nude pictures of themselves to others, which may cause them legal issues.[11]

A newer function of Snapchat, Instagram, and Facebook is the "stories" feature. The Facebook Stories feature is a type of news feed that uses visual information rather than written information. It adds new filters and effects to the user's camera and requires the user to select the Stories section rather than just posting to Facebook as usual.[12]

Five additional popular messaging systems include WeChat (Tencent, China), Popcorn Buzz (Line Corp., Japan), Kik, Allo (Google), and iMessage (Apple).

Alexey Boldin/Shutterstock.com

> **Many businesses use VoIP to offer hotlines, help desks, and other services at far lower costs than those of telephone networks.**

7-3d Internet Telephony

Internet telephony uses the Internet rather than the telephone network to exchange spoken conversations. The protocol used for this capability is **Voice over Internet Protocol (VoIP)**. To use VoIP, you need a high-speed Internet connection and usually a microphone or headset. Some companies have special adapters that connect to your high-speed modem and allow you to use your regular phone. Because access to the Internet is available at local phone connection rates, international and other long-distance calls are much less expensive. Many businesses use VoIP

to offer hotlines, help desks, and other services at far lower costs than those of telephone networks.

VoIP is also used to route traffic starting and ending at conventional public switched telephone network (PSTN) phones. The only drawback is the call quality, which is not as good as with regular phone lines. However, the quality has been improving steadily. In addition to cost savings, VoIP offers the following advantages:

- Users do not experience busy lines.
- Voicemails can be received on the computer.
- Users can screen callers, even if a caller has caller ID blocked.
- Users can have calls forwarded from anywhere in the world.
- Users can direct calls to the correct departments and take automated orders.

7-4 Web Applications

Several service industries use the Internet and its supporting technologies to offer services and products to a wide range of customers at more competitive prices and with increased convenience. The Internet is playing an important role in helping organizations reduce expenses because Web applications can be used with minimal costs. The following sections describe how a variety of service industries use Web applications.

7-4a Tourism and Travel

The tourism and travel industry has benefited from e-commerce Web applications. Many travel Web sites allow customers to book tickets for plane trips and cruises as well as make reservations for hotels and rental cars. *Expedia.com, Travel. com, Travelocity.com,*

> **Internet telephony** uses the Internet rather than the telephone network to exchange spoken conversations.
>
> **Voice over Internet Protocol (VoIP)** is the protocol used for Internet telephony.

Priceline.com, Hotels.com, Google.com/flights/, and Yahoo! Travel are examples of sites that offer tourism and travel services. Yet another example, TripAdvisor (*www.tripadvisor. com*), features reviews and advice on hotels, resorts, flights, vacation rentals, vacation packages, travel guides, and much more.

7-4b Publishing

Many major publishers in the United States and Europe have Web sites that offer descriptions of forthcoming books, sample modules, online ordering, and search features for looking up books on certain topics or by specific authors. Some publishers offer books that can be read online free for 90 days or allow you to buy e-book versions of their products.

An innovative application of Web publishing has been implemented by the publisher of this textbook, Cengage Learning. Cengage Unlimited is a first-of-its-kind digital subscription that gives students total and on-demand access to all of Cengage's digital learning platforms, ebooks, online homework, and study tools (*https:// www.cengage.com/unlimited/*).

7-4c Higher Education

Most universities have Web sites with information about departments, programs, faculty, and academic resources. Some offer virtual tours of their campus for prospective students, and more universities are creating virtual divisions that offer entire degree programs via the Internet. Online degree programs help colleges and universities that are facing enrollment declines, because the programs enable students to enroll in classes when they otherwise could not attend school. With online classes, universities can also have renowned experts give lectures or seminars, usually at a reduced cost because travel expenses are not a factor. In addition, many professional certification programs are offered through the Internet, which is convenient for people who live in remote areas or cannot attend regular classes.

Because an increasing number of colleges, universities, and third parties offer online courses, an interesting question is raised: Can massive open online courses (MOOCs) replace traditional university systems? The simple answer is "no." MOOCs certainly will bring down costs and offer flexibility, but at the expense of losing the personal touch and interaction that exists in campus-based learning. MOOCs are suitable for retraining, job-related credentials, and updating skills. A blended or hybrid model of teaching and learning will most likely emerge. Using this model, some courses will be taught online and some on campus; the line between campus offerings and online learning will become blurred in the years ahead.[13] The growth of online degrees from companies like Coursera and 2u has been steady. As a result, Coursera's market value has surpassed $4.8 billion as of November 2021.[14]

7-4d Real Estate

Real-estate Web sites provide millions of up-to-date listings of homes for sale. Buyers can review neighborhoods, schools, and local real-estate prices, and customers can use these sites to find realtors and brokerage firms and learn home-buying tips. Some sites have virtual tours of houses for sale, which is convenient for buyers who are moving to another state. (Module 14 covers virtual reality technologies.) Other services include appraisals, neighborhood and school profiles, financing options, and home-improvement advice. Major real-estate Web sites include Remax (*www.remax.com*), Century 21 (*www.century21.com*), Prudential (*www.prudential.com*), ERA (*www.era. com*), and Zillow (*www.zillow.com*). Zillow is a home and real-estate marketplace that assists its users in making home-related decisions. Apps are also available for iPhone and Android devices that can simplify real-estate decisions. One popular example is the free iPhone app called HomeSnap, which uses the Multiple Listing Service (MLS) and public records to offer home prices and other information about houses both on and off the market.[15] Companies such as Redfin bring e-commerce to home buying by allowing buyers to bid on properties directly through their Web sites.[16]

7-4e Employment

Employment services are widely available on the Internet. You might be familiar with *LinkedIn* or *Monster*, for example. These sites offer comprehensive services to job seekers, including the following:

- Expert advice and tools for managing your career
- Resume assistance, including tools for creating professional-looking resumes
- Job search tutorials
- Resume posting and distribution
- Searches by company, industry, region, or category
- Announcements of job fairs
- Career tests to see what career is right for you
- Salary calculators

7-4f Financial Institutions

Almost all U.S. and Canadian banks and credit unions, and many others worldwide, offer online banking services and use e-mail to communicate with customers and send account statements and financial reports. E-mail helps banks reduce the time and costs of communicating via phone (particularly long-distance calls) and postal mail. Customers can get up-to-date account information and check their balances at any time of the day or night.

Measures are being taken to ensure that a secure nationwide electronic banking system is in place. For example, digital signatures (discussed in Module 5) are a key technology because they provide an electronic means of guaranteeing the authenticity of involved parties and verifying that encrypted documents have not been changed during transmission.

The following list describes some banking services available via the Internet:

- Accessing customer service by e-mail around the clock
- Viewing current and old transactions
- Online mortgage applications
- Interactive tools for designing a savings plan, choosing a mortgage, or getting insurance quotes online
- Finding loan status and credit card account information online
- Paying bills and credit card balances
- Transferring funds
- Viewing digital copies of checks

7-4g Software Distribution

Many vendors distribute software on the Internet as well as drivers and patches. For example, most antivirus vendors make updates available for download in order to keep up with new viruses and worms. Typically, patches, updates, and small programs such as new browser versions are fast and easy to download. Microsoft Office, the Adobe suite, and many other popular programs are available via download. However, most software vendors, including Microsoft and Adobe, have moved

Gil C/Shutterstock.com

their software to the cloud and distribute it based on a subscription model, in which a user pays a monthly fee to use the latest version of the software. As you will learn in Module 14, software as a service (SaaS) is gaining popularity among major software vendors. Online software distribution provides an inexpensive, convenient, and fast way to sell software.[17]

7-4h Healthcare

With patient records stored on the Internet, healthcare workers can order lab tests and prescriptions, admit patients to hospitals, and refer patients to other physicians more easily. Also, test results and consultation results can be directed to patient records automatically. All patient information can be accessible from one central location, so finding critical health information is faster and more efficient, especially if a patient falls ill while away from home. However, these systems have potential problems related to information privacy, accuracy, and currency. Popular health-related Web sites include the following:

- National Institutes of Health (*www.nih.gov*)
- KidsHealth (*kidshealth.org*)
- WebMD (*www.webmd.com*)
- Drugs.com (*www.drugs.com*)

There are other uses for healthcare Web sites. Telemedicine, for example, enables medical professionals to conduct remote consultations, diagnoses, and conferencing, which can save on office overhead and travel costs. All you need is a smartphone, laptop, or computer to connect to a healthcare provider. Telemedicine is a part of telehealth, which provides healthcare monitoring, virtual clinical visits, and healthcare education services using data communication and related technologies. Most insurance companies cover telemedicine services. In addition, Medicare covers telemedicine services, including nurse practitioners, doctors, licensed social workers, and clinical psychologists.[18] In addition, personal health information systems (PHISs) can make interactive medical tools available to the public. These systems use public kiosks (often in shopping malls) equipped with Internet-connected computers and a diagnostic procedure that prompts patients with a series of questions. These systems can be useful in detecting the early onset of diseases.[19]

Also, virtual medicine on the Internet enables specialists at major hospitals to operate on patients remotely. Telepresence surgery allows surgeons to operate all over the world without physically traveling anywhere. A robot performs the actual surgery based on digitized information sent by the surgeon via the Internet. These robots are equipped with stereoscopic cameras to create

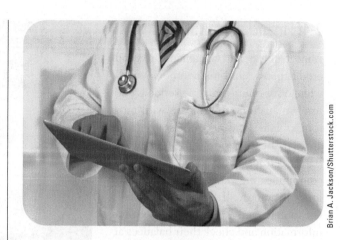

Brian A. Jackson/Shutterstock.com

three-dimensional images for the surgeon's virtual reality goggles and tactical sensors that provide position information to the surgeon.

The next information box discusses a successful implementation of electronic health records at Kaiser Permanente.

Electronic Health Records Pay Off for Kaiser Permanente

➤➤ **Finance | Technology in Society | Application | Reflective Thinking**

According to an article in *InfoWorld*, only 9 percent of U.S. hospitals were using even a basic form of electronic health records (EHRs) in 2009, but that has changed. For example, Kaiser Permanente, a managed-care consortium with over 9 million members, implemented an EHR system that became fully operational in 2010. It took Kaiser 10 years to implement the system, at a total cost of $4 billion ($444 per member).

The Kaiser system, called HealthConnect, uses data mining and analytics to improve patient service and reduce their bills. For example, the system reminds a patient about a particular upcoming test or the need to refill a prescription. According to Kaiser, duplicate testing accounts for 15 to 17 percent of total healthcare costs, and HealthConnect eliminates this cost by integrating all of a patient's medical records, including X-rays and ER visits. The system also

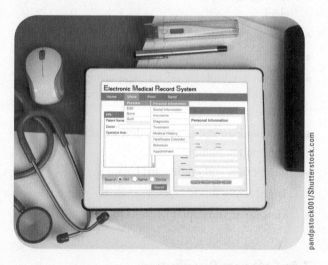

pandpstock001/Shutterstock.com

allows patients to access their medical records (including lab results) from iOS and Android devices, and they can e-mail their doctors directly through the system. Kaiser has already launched the next phase of its EHR system, Health360, which embraces the latest in mobile technology.[20]

Questions and Discussions

1. What are two applications of electronic health records at Kaiser Permanente?
2. How can electronic health records help an organization achieve cost leadership?

7-4i Politics

Most political candidates now make use of Web sites in campaigns. The sites are a helpful tool for announcing candidates' platforms, publicizing their voting records, posting notices of upcoming appearances and debates, and even raising campaign funds. Fundraising efforts in presidential campaigns and U.S. congressional races are good examples of how successful Web sites can be in politics.

Some people claim that the Internet has helped empower voters and revitalize the democratic process. Being well informed about candidates' stances on political issues is much easier with Web sites, for example, and online voting can benefit people who could not make it to polling sites in the past. However, there are some challenges that must be overcome, including hacking on government sites, the security of voting machines, and the prevalence of fake news and deepfakes, as discussed in Module 4.

In addition, U.S. legislators might be able to remain in their home states, close to their constituents, and vote on bills via an online system. However, a stringent ID system would have to be in place, one that most likely would use biometric security measures. Currently, the U.S. House of Representatives is attempting to put all pending legislation online. Presidential documents, executive orders, and other materials are available on the White House's Web site. You can also find full-text versions of speeches, proclamations, press briefings, daily schedules, the proposed federal budget, healthcare reform documents, and the Economic Report of the President.

7-5 Intranets

Many of the applications and services made possible with the Internet can be offered to an organization's users by establishing an intranet. An **intranet** is a network within an organization that uses Internet protocols and technologies (e.g., TCP/IP, which includes File Transfer Protocol, SMTP, and others) for collecting, storing, and disseminating useful information that supports business activities, such as sales, customer service, human resources, and marketing. Intranets are also called *corporate portals*. You might wonder what the difference is between a company's Web site and its intranet. The main difference is that the company Web site is usually public; an intranet is for internal use by employees. However, many companies also allow trusted business partners to access their intranets, usually with a password or another authentication method to protect confidential information.

An intranet uses Internet technologies to solve organizational problems that have been solved in the past by proprietary databases, scheduling, and workflow applications. An intranet is different from a LAN, although it uses the same physical connections. An intranet is an application or service that uses an organization's computer network. Although intranets are physically located in an organization, they can span the globe, allowing remote users to access the intranet's information. However, carefully defining and limiting access is important for security reasons, so intranets are typically set up behind a firewall.

In a typical intranet configuration (see Exhibit 7.2), users in the organization can access all Web servers, but the system administrator must define each user's level of access. Employees can communicate with one another and post information on their departmental Web servers.

Departmental Web servers can be used to host Web sites. For example, the Human Resources Department might have a separate Web site containing information that employees need to access frequently, such as benefits information or 401K records. Similarly, the Marketing Department could have a Web site with the latest product information. Employees can also bookmark important sites in the intranet.

7-5a The Internet versus Intranets

The Internet is a public network; an intranet is a private network. Any user can access the Internet, but access to an intranet is only for certain users and must be approved. Table 7.2 summarizes the major differences between the Internet and intranets.

Despite these differences, both use the same protocol, TCP/IP, and both use browsers for accessing information. Typically, they use similar languages for developing applications, such as Java, and offer files in similar formats.

An advantage of an intranet is that because the organization can control which browser is used, it can specify a browser that supports the technologies the organization uses, such as Internet telephony or video conferencing. In addition, the organization knows that documents will be displayed the same way in all users' browsers; on the Internet, there is no assurance that a Web page will be displayed the same way for every user who views it.

> An **intranet** is a network within an organization that uses Internet protocols and technologies (e.g., TCP/IP, which includes File Transfer Protocol, SMTP, and others) for collecting, storing, and disseminating useful information that supports business activities, such as sales, customer service, human resources, and marketing.

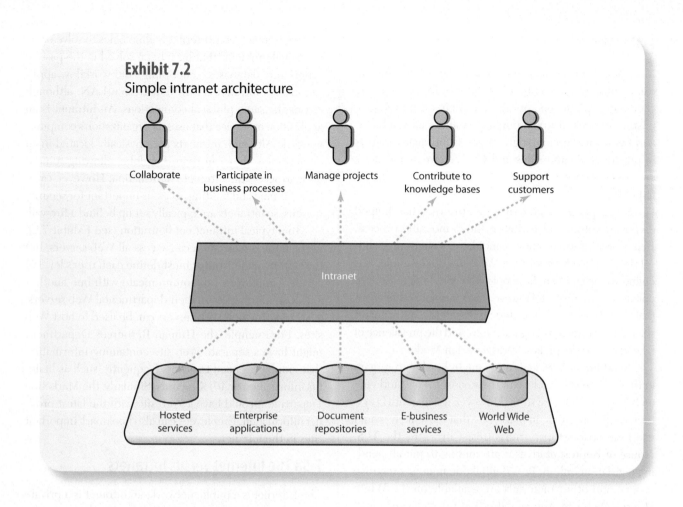

Exhibit 7.2
Simple intranet architecture

Collaborate

Participate in business processes

Manage projects

Contribute to knowledge bases

Support customers

Intranet

Hosted services

Enterprise applications

Document repositories

E-business services

World Wide Web

Intranets also enable organizations to share software, such as an office suite or a DBMS.

7-5b Applications of an Intranet

A well-designed intranet can make the following types of information available to the entire organization in a timely manner to improve its efficiency and effectiveness:[21]

- *Human resources management*—401K plans, upcoming events, the company's mission statement and policies, job postings, medical benefits, orientation materials, online training sessions and materials, meeting minutes, vacation time

- *Sales and marketing*—Call tracking, information on competitors, customer information, order tracking and placement, product information

- *Production and operations*—Equipment inventory, facilities management, industry news, product catalogs, project information

- *Accounting and finance*—Budget planning, expense reports

Intranets can also help organizations move from a calendar- or schedule-based document publishing strategy to one that is based on events or needs. In the past, for example, a company usually published an employee handbook once a year, and it was not updated until the following year, even if major changes happened that required updating, such as organizational restructuring. The company might occasionally have sent single pages as updates, and employees would have to insert these pages in a binder. Needless to say, these binders were often out of date and difficult to use. With an intranet, however, a company can make updates as soon as they are needed.

Intranets reduce the costs and time of document production, too. In the past, document production required several steps, such as creating content, producing and revising drafts, migrating content to desktop publishing, duplicating, and distributing. Intranets eliminate the duplication and distribution steps, and often the step of migrating to a publishing application can be streamlined or eliminated. The next information box lists the top 10 intranets in the world in 2021.

Table 7.2 The Internet versus Intranets

Key Feature	Internet	Intranet
User	Anybody	Approved users only
Geographical scope	Unlimited	Limited or unlimited
Speed	Slower than an intranet	Faster than the Internet
Security	Less than an intranet's	More than the Internet's; user access more restricted

7-6 Extranets

An **extranet** is a secure network that uses the Internet and Web technologies to connect intranets of business partners and enable communication between organizations or between consumers. Extranets are considered a type of interorganizational system (IOS). These systems facilitate information exchange among business partners. Some of these systems, such as electronic funds transfer (EFT) and e-mail, have been used in traditional businesses as well as in e-commerce. Electronic data interchange (EDI) is another common IOS.

> An **extranet** is a secure network that uses the Internet and Web technologies to connect intranets of business partners and enable communication between organizations or between consumers.

10 Best Intranets of 2021

➤➤ Finance | Technology in Society | Application | Global

Every year, Nielsen Norman Group publishes its list of the top 10 best intranets in the world. They use several criteria for selecting a winner. Some of the criteria include mobility, social features, personalization and customization, quality images and graphics, and support and help for users. These intranets increasingly serve as the hub of the digital workplace by providing easy access to applications and information that employees need to perform their jobs. Also, the currency of content is very important, and the following winners have carefully implemented it in their design. These intranets support user bases of 1,200 to 380,000 employees, with an average organization size of 72,330 employees. The 2021 winners, listed in alphabetical order, were as follows:[22,23]

- Baker Hughes (U.S.), a leading energy technology company
- Cathay Pacific Airways Ltd. (Hong Kong), one of the world's largest international airlines
- Commonwealth Care Alliance, Inc. (U.S.), a not-for-profit, community-based healthcare organization
- ConocoPhillips (U.S.), one of the world's largest independent energy exploration and production (E&P) companies
- Deutsche Vermögensberatung AG (DVAG), Germany's largest financial consultancy
- Johnson & Johnson (U.S.), the world's largest healthcare company
- Keysight Technologies, Inc. (U.S.), the world's leading electronic measurement company
- Snam S.p.A. (Italy), one of the world's leading energy infrastructure operators
- VMware, Inc. (U.S.), a publicly traded software company
- The World Bank (U.S.), a unique global partnership with 189 countries

Questions and Discussions

1. How are the best intranets selected?
2. Which factors and features differentiated these winners from the others?

As mentioned earlier, some organizations allow customers and business partners to access their intranets for specific purposes. For example, a supplier might want to check inventory status, or a customer might want to check an account balance. Often, an organization makes a portion of its *intranet* accessible to external parties as its *extranet*. Comprehensive security measures must ensure that access is granted only to authorized users and trusted business partners. Exhibit 7.3 shows a simple extranet. In Exhibit 7.3, *DMZ* refers to the demilitarized zone, an area of the network that is separate from the organization's LAN, where the extranet server is placed. Table 7.3 compares the Internet, intranets, and extranets.[24]

There are numerous applications of extranets. For example, Toshiba America, Inc., has designed an extranet for timely order-entry processing. Using this extranet, more than 300 dealers can place orders for parts until 5 p.m. for next-day delivery. Dealers can also check accounts-receivable balances and pricing arrangements, read press releases, and more. This secure system has decreased costs and improved customer service.[25]

Another example of an extranet is the FedEx tracking system (*www.fedex.com*). FedEx uses its extranet to collect information and make it available to customers over the Internet. Customers can enter a package's tracking number and locate any package still in the system as well as prepare and print shipping forms, get tracking numbers, and schedule pickups.

Extranets not only allow companies to reduce internetworking costs, they also give companies a competitive advantage, which can lead to increased profits. A successful extranet requires a comprehensive security system and management control, however. The security system should include access control, user-based authentication, encryption, and auditing and reporting capabilities.

An extranet offers an organization the same benefits as an intranet but provides other advantages, such as the following:[26]

> **Web 3.0 focuses on "intelligent" Web applications using various artificial intelligence technologies.**

- *Coordination*—Improves coordination between business partners, such as suppliers, distributors, and customers. Critical information can be made available quickly so decisions can be made without delays. For example, a manufacturer can coordinate production by checking inventory status.

- *Feedback*—Provides instant feedback from customers and other business partners to an

Exhibit 7.3
Simple extranet architecture

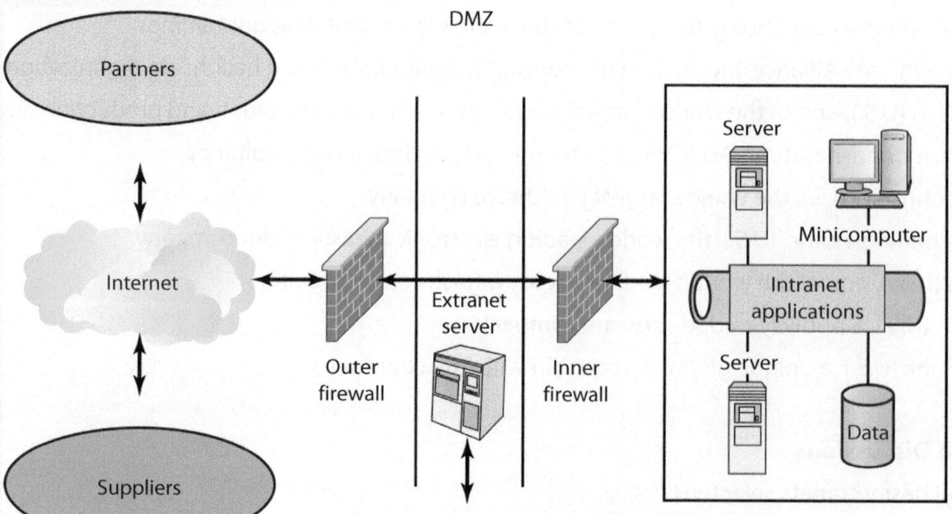

Table 7.3 — Comparison of the Internet, Intranets, and Extranets

	Internet	Intranet	Extranet
Access	Public	Private	Private
Information	General	Typically confidential	Typically confidential
Users	Everybody	Members of an organization	Groups of closely related companies, users, or organizations

organization and gives consumers an opportunity to express opinions on new products or services before they are introduced to the market.

- *Customer satisfaction*—Links customers to an organization so they can get more information on products and services. Customers can also order products online, expediting B2B (business-to-business). E-commerce is a major beneficiary of an extranet.

- *Cost reduction*—Reduces inventory costs by providing information to participants in a supply network program. For example, Mobil Corporation designed an extranet that allows its distributors to submit purchase orders, which has increased efficiency and expedited delivery of goods and services.

- *Expedited communication*—Improves communication by linking intranets for access to critical information. A traveling salesperson can get the latest product information remotely before going to a sales meeting, for example.

7-7 Web Trends

There have been three generations of Web applications so far: Web 1.0 (static content), Web 2.0 (dynamic content), and Web 3.0 (the Semantic Web). Table 7.4 compares various Web 2.0 and Web 3.0 features.[27]

Key features of Web 3.0 include the Semantic Web, artificial intelligence, 3D graphics, connectivity, and ubiquity. The Semantic Web provides personalization that allows users to access the Web more intelligently. Computers, not their users, will perform the tedious work involved in finding, combining, and acting upon information on the Web. Web 3.0 focuses on "intelligent" Web applications using various artificial intelligence technologies (discussed in Module 13). These include natural language processing, artificial neural networks, and intelligent agents. The goal is to tailor online searching and requests to users' specific search patterns, preferences, and needs. Microsoft's Bing and Google Search already offer many Web 3.0 features. Some of the key features and applications of Web trends are discussed in the following paragraphs.

7-7a Blogs

A **blog** (short for *Weblog*) is a journal or newsletter that is updated frequently and intended for the general public. Blogs reflect their authors' personalities and often include philosophical reflections and opinions on social or political issues. Sometimes, they are simply used as a way for families or groups of friends to keep in touch with one another. Automated tools have made creating and maintaining blogs easy, so even people with very little technical background can have blogs. In addition, many Web sites, such as *Blogger.com*, offer free space for blogs and even allow bloggers to post photos. One popular blogging tool is Tumblr (*www.tumblr.com*), which allows users to post anything—text, photos, quotes, links, music, and videos—from their browsers, phones, desktops, and e-mail programs. Another popular site is Pinterest (*http://pinterest.com*).

There are also blogs on Web sites that are dedicated to particular topics or organizations; these are periodically updated with the latest news and views. For example, on the CNN Web site, you can find blogs written by Anderson Cooper and Wolf Blitzer, among others. Blogs are a popular source of online publications, too, especially for political information, opinions, and alternative news coverage; some examples can be found at *www.huffingtonpost.com* and *www.buzzfeed.com/*. Microblogs, a newer version of traditional blogs, enable users to create smaller versions of blog posts (known as *microposts*); these can take the form of short sentences or individual images or links. Examples of microblogging sites include Twitter, Tumblr, Plurk, Twister, and Soup.io.

> A **blog** (short for *Weblog*) is a journal or newsletter that is updated frequently and intended for the general public. Blogs reflect their authors' personalities and often include philosophical reflections and opinions on social or political issues.

Table 7.4 Web 2.0 versus Web 3.0

Feature	Web 2.0	Web 3.0
Interaction with the user	Mostly read–write	Portable and personal
Focus	Community	Individual
Sharing information	Blogs and wikis	Livestreams
Content	Sharing	Consolidating
Applications	Web applications	Smart applications
Information transfer	Tagging	User behavior
Advertising method	Cost per click	User engagement
Advertising mode	Interactive	Behavioral
Content editing	Wikipedia	The Semantic Web
Data representation and programming language	XML/RSS	RDF*/OWL**

*RDF: Resource Description Framework, the current W3C standard for representing data on the Web.
**OWL: Web Ontology Language, a Web language that is designed to process and integrate information over the Web.

7-7b Wikis

A **wiki** is a type of Web site that allows users to add, delete, and sometimes modify content. One of the best-known examples is the online encyclopedia Wikipedia. What is unique about wikis is that an information user can also be an information provider. The most serious problem with wikis is the quality of information because allowing anyone to modify content affects its accuracy. Wikipedia is currently working on methods to verify the credentials of contributing users because of past problems with contributors falsifying credentials.

Wikis have caught on at many companies, too. For example, an Intel employee developed Intelpedia as a way for employees around the world to share

> A **wiki** is a type of Web site that allows users to add, delete, and sometimes modify content.

LinkedIn: A Professional Social Networking Site

▶▶ Finance | Technology in Society | Application | Global

LinkedIn (a part of Microsoft) is the world's largest professional networking site, with over 740 million members from around the world. LinkedIn allows its members to connect with professional partners to exchange ideas, opportunities, and knowledge.[28] As a future knowledge worker, you can use LinkedIn to network with industry professionals, maintain current professional relationships, create new relationships, build your personal network of industry experts, gain technical information, search for jobs, bookmark jobs for which you want to apply, and enhance your career opportunities. You can use LinkedIn's search tool to look for jobs and professional expertise, you can join LinkedIn groups for a particular interest, and much more. Over 57 million companies have a profile

on LinkedIn. Businesses can use LinkedIn to acquire new customers, keep in touch with existing customers, find the right vendors, build their industry networks, list jobs and search for potential candidates, get answers to technical questions, and do fund-raising. This book also has a LinkedIn page.[29]

With its recent acquisition of *Lynda.com*, LinkedIn is now able to match its users with courses that will prepare them for the jobs they are looking for.[30]

Questions and Discussions

1. What are two business applications of LinkedIn?
2. How has LinkedIn differentiated itself from other social networking sites?

information on company history, project progress, and more. However, some employees do not like their content being edited by others. For this reason, "corporate wikis" were developed; these include tighter security and access controls. Corporate wikis are used for a variety of purposes, such as posting news about product development. Many open-source software packages for creating wikis are available, such as MediaWiki and TWiki. Companies also create wikis to give customers information. For example, Motorola and T-Mobile have set up wikis about their products that function as continually updated user guides, and eBay has formed eBay Wiki, where buyers and sellers can share information on a wide range of topics.[31]

7-7c Social Networking Sites

Social networking refers to a broad class of Web sites and services that allow users to connect with friends, family, and colleagues online as well as meet people with similar interests or hobbies. As of September 2021, based on the number of active users, the following social media sites were the 15 most popular in the world: Facebook, YouTube, WhatsApp, Messenger, Instagram, WeChat, Qzone, Tumblr, Twitter, Reddit, LinkedIn, Snapchat, Skype, Pinterest, and Line.[32]

According to a study conducted by Experian Marketing Services, 16 minutes of every hour that Americans spend online takes place on social networks.[33] More than 100 of these social networks are available on the Internet. Two of the most popular are Facebook and Twitter. In addition, LinkedIn is a professional networking site where you can connect with professional contacts and exchange ideas and job opportunities with a large network of professionals. Many people use both LinkedIn and Facebook to keep their professional and social contacts separate. The information box titled "LinkedIn:

A Professional Social Networking Site" discusses some additional features of LinkedIn.

Social networking sites are also popular for business use. For example, many companies use Twitter to keep track of customer opinions about their products. (See the information box titled "Social Media Applications at Walmart.") Comcast, Dell, General Motors, and H&R Block are some additional examples.[34] Companies also use social networking sites for advertising; they might include links to their company Web sites or use pay-per-click (PPC) features. PPC is an Internet advertising method used on Web sites, in which advertisers pay their host only when their ad is clicked.

Twitter is a popular tool, especially among politicians and celebrities. The term *tweet* is used for a response or comment no longer than 280 characters, the maximum length allowed for a Twitter post. Even this book has a Twitter account! Follow it at *https://twitter.com/MIS_daily*.

7-7d Business Applications of Social Networks

We have already mentioned several business applications of social networks. Because of the importance of this topic, we provide a quick summary here that shows how social media can help a business.

As of 2021, more than 4.48 billion consumers across the world were using social networks, and the number is increasing daily.[35]

Social networks similar to the Internet put small businesses on the same footing as large organizations by providing an inexpensive platform for interacting with customers and selling products and services.

> **Social networking** refers to a broad class of Web sites and services that allow users to connect with friends, family, and colleagues online as well as meet people with similar interests or hobbies.

Social Media Applications at Walmart

➤➤ Finance | Technology in Society | Application

Walmart, the world's largest retailer, uses social media as marketing channels for brands as well as for constant communications with its customers. Walmart has created a timeline in Facebook that highlights how the brand has grown since its inception in 1962. With over 33 million Facebook fans (*https://www.facebook.com/walmart*), Walmart's Facebook account showcases new store openings and highlights the company's sustainability credentials. However, the majority of its posts are product suggestions and conversations with its customers.[36]

Walmart uses Twitter to post questions, with topics such as sports contests, healthy food, charities, community programs, and requests for retweets if customers agree with a certain topic. It has over 1.2 million followers (*https://twitter.com/hashtag/walmart?lang=en*). Walmart manages seven different Twitter accounts, each related to a specific issue such as sustainability, philanthropic efforts, and public policy.[37]

Walmart also uses Twitter for livestream shopping.

Walmart uses Pinterest for product ideas and for promoting green living; it has over 1.7 million followers and nearly 3,000 "Pins." A majority of these Pins link back to the Walmart e-commerce site. Occasionally, Walmart offers competitions on Pinterest; for example, it might ask customers to share images of products that help them lead more environmentally friendly lives. Pinterest enables Walmart to showcase its products for special events such as Mother's Day, Easter, and Christmas (*www.pinterest.com/walmart/*).

Walmart also uses TikTok for livestream events where customers can shop for Walmart fashion items featured by TikTok creators without having to leave the app. According to Walmart, this is a new way to engage with current customers and reach potential new customers. Using TikTok enhances digital advertising and enables Walmart to get closer to younger shoppers.[38]

Questions and Discussions

1. What are two applications of social media at Walmart?
2. What are three social media platforms used by Walmart? What is the purpose of each? Discuss.

Here are some specific examples that show how a business can use social networks to promote its products and services:

- Facebook—A business can create a Facebook business fan page.

- Twitter—A business can connect with its customers in real time.

- Pinterest—A business can showcase its product offerings.

- LinkedIn Groups—This is a good venue for businesspeople to enter into a professional dialogue with people in similar industries. Groups provide a place to share content with people and businesses with similar interests.

- YouTube—Using this platform, a business can create video content and "how-to" videos.

- TikTok—With over 1 billion annual users throughout the world, TikTok has generated a lot of interest among younger shoppers. Businesses can take advantage of this popular platform to promote their products and services in several ways. They can create their own content on TikTok, create and share user-generated content, advertise, and develop influencer-created content with audio, video, and animation.[39]

- Social media platforms like Yelp, Foursquare, and Level Up are great for brick-and-mortar businesses. A business should register on these sites to claim a location spot. Businesses should offer incentives, such as check-in rewards or special discounts. Customer reviews on these sites are very helpful for attracting new customers.

The "Social Media Applications at Walmart" box highlights the applications of social media at Walmart.

7-7e RSS Feeds

RSS (Really Simple Syndication) feeds are a fast, easy way to distribute Web content in eXtensible Markup Language (XML) format. RSS is a subscription service; new content from Web sites you have selected is delivered via a feed reader. The content all goes to one convenient spot where you can read "headlines." With this service, you do not have to keep checking a site for updates.

XML, a subset of the Standard Generalized Markup Language (SGML), is a flexible method for creating common formats for information. Unlike HTML tags that specify layout and appearance, XML tags represent the kind of content being posted and transmitted. Although HTML contains some layout and appearance features, these "presentational attributes" are deprecated by the W3C, which suggests that HTML should only be used for creating structured documents through markup. Layout and appearance should be handled by CSS (Cascading Style Sheets).

Data can be meaningless without a context for understanding it. For example, consider the following: "Information Systems, Smith, John, 357, 2021, Cengage, 45.00, 02-139-4467-X." From this string of data, you might make an educated guess that it refers to a book, including the title, author name, number of pages, year of publication, publisher, price, and ISBN. A computer, however, might interpret this same data as indicating that Smith John spoke about information systems for 357 minutes at a conference organized by Cengage in 2021 and received 45 euros as compensation, with a transaction ID of 02-139-4467-X for the payment.

XML prevents this kind of confusion by defining data with a context. So, you would format the preceding data string as follows:

```
<book>
<title>Information Systems</title>
<authorlastname>Smith</authorlastname>
<authorfirstname>John</authorfirstname>
<pages>357</pages>
<yearofpub>2021</yearofpub>
<publisher>Cengage</publisher>
<pricein$>45.00</pricein$>
<isbn>02-139-4467-X</isbn>
</book>
```

As you can see, each piece of data is defined with its context by using tags, which makes the data much easier to interpret. Although both HTML and XML are tag-based languages, they have different purposes. XML was designed to improve interoperability and data sharing between different systems, which is why RSS feeds are in XML. Any system can correctly interpret the data in an RSS feed because it is based on the data's meaning, not its format and layout.

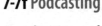

> Financial institutions offer podcasts to inform customers about investment strategies, market performance, and trading.

7-7f Podcasting

A **podcast** is an electronic audio file that is posted on the Web for users to download to their mobile devices or their computers. Users can also listen to podcasts over the Web. A podcast has a specific URL and is defined with an XML item tag.

Podcasts are usually collected by an "aggregator," such as iTunes or iPodder. You can also subscribe to various podcasts; NPR, *The Economist*, and ESPN all offer podcast subscriptions. What differentiates a podcast from a regular audio file is that users can subscribe to it. Each time a new podcast is available, the aggregator collects it automatically using the URL and makes it available for subscribers. Subscribers can then "sync" the podcast with their mobile devices and listen to it whenever they want.

Twitter: Real-Time Networking with Your Followers

⯈ Finance | Technology in Society | Application | Global

Twitter is a social network that connects you to the latest stories and to people you like to follow. As of January 2022, there were 396 million users around the world.[40] Each tweet is no more than 280 characters long; you can also see photos, videos, and conversations directly in tweets. In September 2016, Twitter relaxed its character count limits, but in Chinese, Japanese, and Korean, the limit for a tweet is still 140 characters.[41] Tagging someone doesn't reduce the character limit. Users are able to retweet themselves and bump a tweet back to the top of their feed, which provides a complete picture of a tweet in one place.[42]

Businesses use Twitter to connect with their customers, and individuals use it to connect with their followers in real time. Using Twitter, businesses can gather real-time market information and feedback as well as create relationships with their customers.[43]

The following list highlights some of the organizations that use Twitter to stay connected with their customers and promote their products and services:[44]

- The U.S. Chamber of Commerce uses Twitter to reach an influential audience.
- MTV incorporates Twitter into its Video Music Awards.
- The Fox television network integrates a real-time Twitter feed into its TV ads.
- The professional soccer team LA Galaxy uses Twitter to guide conversations and build awareness.
- The Red Cross uses Twitter for donor support and to mobilize communities in times of need.
- The United Nations Foundation extends the reach of its events globally with Twitter.

Questions and Discussions

1. What are two business applications of Twitter?
2. What are some of the challenges of Twitter?

The **Internet of Everything (IoE)** refers to Web-based development in which people, processes, data, and things are interconnected via the Internet using various means, such as RFID devices, barcodes, wireless systems (using Bluetooth and Wi-Fi), and QR codes.

The subscription model makes podcasts more useful and popular and increases their accessibility. Syndication feeds are one way of announcing a podcast's availability. Organizations use podcasts to update people on their products and services, new trends, changes in organizational structure, and merger/acquisition news. Financial institutions, for example, offer podcasts to inform customers about investment strategies, market performance, and trading. When multimedia information is involved, the terms *video podcast*, *vodcast*, or *vidcast* are sometimes used.

> With more than 330 million monthly active users as of the first quarter of 2021, Twitter is one of the biggest social networks worldwide.

7-8 The Internet of Everything and Beyond

The **Internet of Everything (IoE)** refers to Web-based development in which people, processes, data, and things are interconnected via the Internet using various means, such as RFID devices, barcodes, wireless systems (using Bluetooth and Wi-Fi), and QR codes. It is a network of networks in which billions of connections create unparalleled opportunities and challenges.

Although "IoE" refers to all the connections that can be made, the **Internet of Things (IoT)** refers to physical objects that are connected to the Internet and to other physical objects. As an example, consider a smart refrigerator that signals when your milk has reached its expiration date. By 2025, over 75 billion objects will be connected to the Internet, according to one estimate, and they will likely be smart devices that are uniquely identified through IP addresses, RFIDs, QR codes, or sensors.[45,46]

According to McKinsey, IoT applications could have an $11 trillion impact on the world economy by 2025. The IoT has key impacts on the supply chain by tracking and monitoring everything on the network, encouraging applications for automated checkout, monitoring machine performance, and scheduling maintenance.[47]

As an example, smart sensors helped the city of Copenhagen to reduce water loss due to leaking pipes. The city installed leak-detection sensors that can report leaks. Copenhagen's water loss was reduced to 7 percent from about 40 percent.[48]

Because of the popularity and the fast growth of IoT projects, we may soon see a new IT job called Chief IoT Officer. Among the responsibilities of this job would be to coordinate connected-product development. This individual would serve as the liaison between IoT research and development and the IT department in developing and managing connected products.[49]

The technology behind IoT will facilitate, among other things, automated inventory systems in the retail industry, automated and programmable appliances in domestic households, and road and bridge systems that will be able to detect a problem as soon as it occurs and notify the authorities. Consumers and businesses will save money by preserving energy when they control their room temperatures onsite or remotely through smart devices. Companies will save time and money on labor due to automation.

In general, the IoT could help solve many 21st-century social problems, such as hunger, water pollution, adverse climate change, and increasing energy costs. Other benefits could include people taking effective preventative measures for their health by wearing sensor-embedded clothing that measures vital signs; the resulting data can be securely and quickly transmitted to doctors.[50]

iStock.com/sdecoret

Many smart objects are currently on the market, such as 94Fifty's Bluetooth basketball, which can sense dribble force and shot angle; Nike Hyperdunk Plus basketball shoes, which can tell users how fast they are running and how high they are jumping; and the Under Armour Armour39 shirt, which can read a user's heart rate and lung capacity. Currently, these smart objects cannot be connected to one another, however; if all three devices were on the same person's body, they would not be aware of each other's existence. The IoT should change this by creating connectivity and communication.[51]

Individuals, businesses, and governments around the globe will benefit from IoE technology; security, privacy, and reliability will play a major role in the success of this technology, as they do for any network. There must be close coordination and communication among these three key elements to protect the privacy and integrity of the information being shared. The information box titled "The Internet of Things in Action" highlights two real-life examples of IoT as it exists today.

Additional real-world applications of IoT include IoT sensors, IoT data analytics, IoT tracking and monitoring systems, IoT-connected factories, smart supply chain management, smart barcode readers, smart grids, connected healthcare systems, and smart farming.[52]

A technology related to IoT is the **Internet of Me (IoM)**. The Internet of Me refers to a personalized Internet that gathers and processes information for a given user from the entire Internet, including IoT devices. The goal of IoM is to deliver a personalized Web

The **Internet of Things (IoT)** refers to physical objects that are connected to the Internet and to other physical objects.

The **Internet of Me (IoM)** is a subset of the Internet that gathers and processes information for a given user from the entire Internet and IoT devices to deliver a personalized experience.

experience, whether it is a search result, receiving news that a user likes, or receiving personalized medical care. For example, in an IoM environment, if a computer game enthusiast and a police officer search for "grand theft auto," the search engine will generate two sets of results based on what it knows about the two people searching.[53]

Healthcare and personalized medical care will be major beneficiaries of IoM. In the IoM environment, "my diet," "my health," "my fitness," and "my electronic medical record" all come together. A recent survey of health executives indicated that 73 percent see a positive ROI from personalization technology. IoM will enable health insurers to recommend personalized plan options, including some that offer savings for using a wearable device. An IoM device could signal something going wrong, such as a high blood pressure spike, and then preventative medicine could take over.[54] IoM should make treatment more effective by enabling the data gathering needed to create personalized care.[55]

In addition to Google, Amazon, and Netflix, which have delivered personalized services for years to their users, other companies are using personalization technology and connected devices in creative ways. The Internet of Me presents a unique opportunity for a broad range of businesses to build brand loyalty and increase customer satisfaction. To gain the full benefit of IoM, the following three challenges and recommendations should be considered:[56]

1. Companies should constantly gather accurate data about their customers and leverage this data to offer products and services that their customers want. A popular example is TaskRabbit (*www.taskrabbit. com*), which makes on-demand scheduling possible for just about any request. By not gathering data, a company loses a window of opportunity to grow its business. In the era of IoM, companies should offer what their customers want on a 24/7 basis.

2. Companies should create a platform that seamlessly syncs wired and wireless devices. They should offer products and services that are customized for specific customers. For example, a coupon stored on a customer's smartphone should automatically be applied at the cash register to the item that the customer has purchased.

3. In the connected world of IoM, trust is extremely important. Because customers share all sorts of private information with their business partners, businesses must make sure that this data is kept with the highest degree of accuracy and confidentiality and that the data will not get into the hands of unauthorized users.

The Internet of Things in Action

➤ Finance | Technology in Society | Application | Reflective Thinking

In parts of Africa, people used to go from well to well to get drinking water. After hiking miles to get to a particular well, they often found out that it was not operational. German pump manufacturer Grundfos installed sensors in these wells and developed an app so that people could use their smartphones to check a well's condition before hiking miles to get there.[57]

Elsewhere, the City24/7 project is designed to help revitalize large cities by gathering and sharing useful information with people through multiple devices. In collaboration with Cisco IBSG and the city of New York, the interactive platform was launched in 2012. Gathered information is displayed on large screens in public places such as bus stations, subways, and telephone booths. The information is location-based and is displayed as soon as it becomes available so that citizens can access it. First responders, including police and fire departments, can use this information and respond as needed. The next phase of the project is expansion into other large cities.[58]

metamorworks/Shutterstock.com

Questions and Discussions

1. How is IoT used in the City24/7 project?
2. How did the German pump manufacturer Grundfos use IoT?
3. What are some additional applications of IoT?

A growing application of IoT is **industrial IoT or IIoT**. IIoT is used to enhance manufacturing and industrial processes such as predictive maintenance and data analytics on factory floors. Popular applications of IIoT include the following:[59,60]

- Smart and connected factory—IoT-enabled machinery can transmit operational and real-time data to all members of a group for remote decision making, enabling process automation and optimization.

- Facility management—IoT sensors in manufacturing equipment enable condition-based maintenance alerts when the equipment deviates from its specified parameters.

- Production flow monitoring—IoT-enabled sensors highlight lags in production (if any), eliminating waste and unnecessary work-in-process inventory.

- Inventory management—IoT sensors enable the monitoring of events across the entire supply chain to optimize supply and reduce costs in the value chain network.

- Plant safety and security—IoT combined with big data analytics collects and analyzes all relevant data, such as numbers of injuries and illness rates, near misses, and vehicle incidents, and enables decision makers to react in real time, resulting in improved plant safety and security.

- Quality control—IoT sensors collect and analyze relevant data in the entire supply chain network, including customer sentiments about using a product, which helps to improve quality.

- Packaging optimization—By using IoT sensors in packaging, manufacturers can gain insights into the usage patterns and handling of products from multiple customers. This helps decision makers to re-engineer products and packaging for better performance.

- Logistics and supply chain optimization—IoT sensors provide real-time supply chain information that helps manufacturers predict issues, reduce inventory, and potentially reduce capital requirements.

Another recent application of IoT, particularly among millennials, is using it to create a smart home. A **smart home** automates many of the tasks that traditionally were handled manually by humans. Saving energy, improving security and safety, automating household tasks, and making the home more entertaining are among the key advantages of a smart home. A typical smart home may use the following IoT-enabled devices:[61]

- You can manage your home using voice commands with Amazon Echo and the Alexa digital assistant or with Google Home and Google Assistant. For example, you can use voice commands to play a song or order a pizza.

- Alphabet's Nest thermostat or a similar product enables you to remotely control the temperature of your home and use energy more efficiently.

- Phillips Hue or a competing product assists you in managing the lighting system in your home. You can turn lights on and off using your smartphone.

- The Ring video doorbell or a similar product enables you to use your smartphone to view visitors at your door.

- The Nest smart camera or a similar product enables you to manage the security of your home. You can see and record any activity in your house with Nest cameras.

- A hub device such as Wink Hub 2 allows you to connect all your smart devices to a central hub. A hub helps you manage devices centrally and should improve their security.

Many other IoT-enabled devices can be connected to your smart home, such as smart coffeemakers, smart toasters, and smart TVs. A smart home can include a smart refrigerator, which usually has a touchscreen interface that allows you to look inside the fridge without opening the door. A smart refrigerator can perform a number of tasks:[62]

- Create grocery lists that sync to your smartphone in real time.

- Set expiration dates and share notifications to use food while it is fresh.

- Customize temperatures by drawer or compartment.

- Use interior cameras to show if you are low on any grocery items while you're shopping at the market.

- Alert you when the water filter needs to be changed.

- Turn the ice maker on or off from your smartphone.

Haier, LG, Samsung, and GE are among the companies offering IoT-enabled

Industrial IoT or IIoT is used to enhance manufacturing and industrial processes such as predictive maintenance and data analytics on factory floors.

A **smart home** automates many of the tasks that traditionally were handled manually by humans.

refrigerators, which can monitor your food supply and automatically suggest updates for your shopping list.[63] LG Electronics sells a smart refrigerator embedded with Amazon's Alexa virtual assistant that allows users to buy groceries through Amazon Prime by speaking their orders to the appliance.[64]

With the ever-increasing popularity of IoT devices, users and designers should be aware of the security threats and risks that these devices present and implement security measures that eliminate or at least minimize the threats. The following are some common security threats and risks associated with IoT devices:[65]

- An IoT device could be hijacked and then send spam e-mails.

- An IoT device could be hijacked and then deployed into botnets and used for DDoS attacks.

- The Shodan search engine on an unsecured IoT device provides substantial information that can be used by hackers for criminal activities.

- An IoT device could leak out private information, such as residential locations.

- A typical IoT device is unsecured when purchased from vendors; the user has to change the default network name and secure it with a strong password.

- Remote car hijacking is possible if an IoT device used in a car is not secured.

General security policies, such as those discussed in Module 5, could also be helpful here. The following list provides some specific guidelines for improving the security and privacy of IoT devices:[66,67]

1. Secure and centralize the access logs of IoT devices. Network administrators should know which device is connected to the network and by whom.

2. Use encrypted protocols to secure communications so that even if the signal is intercepted, a hacker will not pose a threat.

3. Create sound password policies. As discussed in Module 5, users should have strong passwords and should always change the default passwords that come from manufacturers.

4. Implement restrictive network communication policies and set up virtual LANs. A virtual LAN isolates IoT devices in a logical subnetwork that will group together a collection of devices from different physical LANs. If an IoT device gets hacked in this arrangement, the hacker will not have access to the entire network.

5. Install IoT devices that have secure firmware (software) update policies and make sure that you have the latest firmware. Also, educate network users on how to secure home routers.

6. Turn off universal plug and play (UPnP), a set of networking protocols that allows networked devices to automatically discover each other and establish functional network services for data sharing. Hackers can potentially discover these devices and hack the network.

7. Keep personal devices out of the workplace. If such a connection is essential, use the established BYOD policies of the organization before connecting to its network.

The Industry Connection for this module highlights the role of Google as a leader in search technology and Web advertising platforms.

Industry Connection: Google, Inc.[68]

Google, founded in 1998, offers one of the most widely used search engines in the world. It also offers products and services in the following categories:

Search: There are more than 20 search categories, including the Web, blogs (by blog name, posts on a certain topic, a specific date range, and more), catalogs (for mail-order catalogs, many previously unavailable online), images, books (the full text of books and magazines that Google has scanned), and maps. There is also Google Earth, an exciting feature that combines searching with the viewing of satellite images, terrain maps, and 3D models.

Ads: AdSense, AdWords, and Analytics are used for displaying ads on your Web site or with Google search results. For example, with AdWords, you create an ad and choose keywords related to your business. When people search Google with one of your keywords, your ad is displayed next to the search results, so you are reaching an audience that is already interested in your product or service.

Applications: Google has many applications for account holders, such as Gmail, Google Talk (instant messaging and voice calls), Google Groups, YouTube, Blogger, Google Checkout (for shopping online with just a single Google sign-in), and Google Docs, a free, Web-based word-processing and spreadsheet program.

YouTube: A video-sharing Web site on which users can upload, share, and view videos.

Enterprise: Google has applications for organizations, such as Google Maps for Enterprise, which is particularly useful for planning operations and logistics, and SketchUp

Pro, a 3D modeling tool for architects, city planners, game developers, and others that can be used in presentations and documents.

Mobile: Many of Google's services and applications, such as Blogger, YouTube, and Gmail, are available on mobile devices. You can also use text messaging to get real-time information from Google on a variety of topics, including weather reports, sports scores, and flight updates. Google also offers Android OS for smartphone and mobile devices.

Google Wave: This collaboration and communication tool is designed to consolidate features from e-mail, instant messaging, blogging, wikis, and document sharing while offering a variety of social networking features.

Google Now: Available on smartphones and tablets, this product serves as a personal assistant by providing relevant information on weather, sports, traffic, and much more.

Module Summary

7-1   Describe the makeup of the Internet and the Web. The Internet is a worldwide collection of billions of computers and networks of all sizes. The term *Internet* is derived from *internetworking*, which means connecting networks. Simply put, the Internet is a network of networks.

7-2   Discuss navigational tools, search engines, and directories. Navigational tools are used to travel from Web site to Web site (i.e., "surf" the Internet). Search engines allow you to look up information on the Internet by entering keywords related to your topic of interest. Directories are indexes of information, based on keywords embedded in documents, that allow search engines to find what you are looking for. Some Web sites such as Yahoo! also use directories to organize content into categories.

7-3   Describe four common Internet services and how they are used in a business environment. Popular services include e-mail, newsgroups and discussion groups, instant messaging, and Internet telephony.

7-4   Explain business applications of the Internet. Popular Web applications include those for tourism and travel, publishing, higher education, real

estate, employment, financial institutions, software distribution, healthcare, and politics.

7-5   Describe the role of intranets in various business functions. An intranet is a network within an organization that uses Internet protocols and technologies (e.g., TCP/IP, which includes File Transfer Protocol, SMTP, and others) for collecting, storing, and disseminating useful information that supports business activities, such as sales, customer service, human resources, and marketing. Intranets are also called *corporate portals*.

7-6   Describe the role of extranets in various business functions. An extranet is a secure network that uses the Internet and Web technologies to connect intranets of business partners and enable communication between organizations or between consumers. Extranets are considered a type of interorganizational system (IOS). These systems facilitate information exchange among business partners.

7-7   Analyze Web trends and their impact on business. We have seen three generations of Web applications: Web 1.0 (static content), Web 2.0

(dynamic content), and Web 3.0 (the Semantic Web). Key features of Web 3.0 include the Semantic Web, artificial intelligence, 3D graphics, connectivity, and ubiquity. The Semantic Web provides personalization that allows users to access the Web more intelligently.

7-8 Analyze the Internet of Everything and its business applications. The Internet of Everything (IoE) refers to Web-based development in which people, processes, data, and things are interconnected via the Internet using various means, such as RFID devices, barcodes, wireless systems (using Bluetooth and Wi-Fi), and QR codes. The Internet of Things (IoT) refers to physical objects that are connected to the Internet and to other physical objects. The Internet of Me refers to a subset of the Internet that gathers and processes personalized information for a given user from the entire Internet and IoT devices.

Key Terms

- Advanced Research Projects Agency Network (ARPANET)
- Blog
- Directories
- Discussion groups
- Domain Name System (DNS)
- Extranet
- Hypermedia
- Hypertext
- Hypertext Markup Language (HTML)
- Industrial IoT (IIoT)
- Instant messaging (IM)
- Internet
- Internet backbone
- Internet of Everything (IoE)

- Internet of Me (IoM)
- Internet of Things (IoT)
- Internet telephony
- Intranet
- Navigational tools
- Newsgroups
- Podcast
- RSS (Really Simple Syndication) feeds
- Search engines
- Smart home
- Social networking
- Uniform resource locators (URLs)
- Voice over Internet Protocol (VoIP)
- Wiki

Reviews and Discussions

1. Describe the Internet.
2. What is a search engine?
3. Among the four services offered by the Internet, which one is the most popular? Discuss.
4. Explain four business applications of the Internet.
5. What is an intranet? What are two differences between the Internet and an intranet?
6. What are two applications of an extranet?
7. What are two applications or features of Web trends?
8. What are three applications of IoT?

Projects

1. A properly designed extranet allows companies to reduce internetworking costs and gives participating companies a competitive advantage, which can lead to increased profits. After reading the information presented in this module and other sources, write a two-page paper that identifies three companies that are using extranets as an internetworking platform. List two applications of this platform in each company. What are two challenges that must be overcome for designing a successful extranet?

2. AskMD (*www.sharecare.com/askmd/get-started*) is a popular medical app. After reading the information presented in this module and other sources, write a one-page paper that summarizes some of the features of this app. What are three other examples of medical apps for iOS and Android devices?

3. The human resources departments of many organizations are creating intranets to improve the efficiency and effectiveness of the departments' operations. After reading the information presented in this module and other sources, write a one-page paper that summarizes the applications of intranets in HR operations. What are some of the challenges in

designing and using such an application? Which other departments in a business firm can use intranets and for which applications?

4. Small and large businesses can use social networks to improve their efficiency and help their bottom lines. After reading the information presented in this module and other sources, write a two-page paper that identifies two applications of Twitter, Facebook, Pinterest, and Yelp in running a small business.

5. The Internet of Me has created a lot of excitement in the business world. After reading the information presented in this module and other sources, write a one-page paper that lists five business applications of this new platform. What are some of the legal and social issues related to the Internet of Me?

6. IoT security and privacy concerns are two issues that must be carefully considered before an organization introduces a comprehensive IoT application. After reading the information presented in this module and other sources, write a two-page paper that identifies five major threats posed by IoT. Offer five recommendations that could help the organization to guard against these threats.

Module Quiz

1. The Internet of Things (IoT) refers to physical objects that are connected to the Internet and to other physical objects. True or False?

2. A smart home does not use voice commands through devices such as Amazon's Alexa. True or False?

3. IIoT is used to enhance manufacturing and industrial processes such as predictive maintenance and data analytics on factory floors. True or False?

4. All of the following are correct except:
   a. An IoT device could be hijacked and then send spam e-mails.
   b. An IoT device could be hijacked and then deployed into botnets and used for DDoS attacks.
   c. IoT devices are vulnerable to the threat posed by the Shodan search engine.
   d. They are all correct.

5. All of these choices are examples of Web browsers except:
   a. Bing
   b. Chrome
   c. Firefox
   d. Safari

6. All of these choices are features or applications of Web 2.0 except:
   a. Tagging
   b. Livestreams
   c. Cost per click
   d. Wikipedia

Case Study 7-1
Scotts Miracle-Gro's Intranet: The Garden
➤ **Finance | Application | Reflective Thinking**

Scotts Miracle-Gro is a major provider of lawn, garden, and outdoor-living products and services. Its headquarters is in Marysville, Ohio, and it has over 8,000 employees.[69] In 2012, the company's internal network, called "The Garden," was chosen by the Nielsen Norman Group as one of the Ten Best Intranets of 2012. Since its launch in 2011, The Garden has served as an effective internal communication tool for Scotts employees. On any given day, some 2,250 employees visit the site to get the latest news about the company, among other things.

In fact, the system was developed based on employee needs and through close communication between employees and the IT department.[70] According to Tyler Kerr, Manager of Electronic Communications at Scotts, the company conducted surveys, engaging its stakeholders in discussions about their needs and opinions. As a result, The Garden is very user friendly, and employees are constantly asked about features they would like to see added.

The Garden gives Scotts employees fast access to important and frequently used documents, such as travel expense forms and human resources forms. Employees can also organize their important links into "My Favorites" lists. In October 2011, Scotts further enhanced The Garden by designing "The Vine," an internal social media site. Using The Vine, employees are able to communicate

Bochkarev Photography/Shutterstock.com

with one another through their profile categories, such as job title, location, years of experience, and other relevant information.[71]

Answer the following questions:
1. What are some key features of The Garden?
2. Why has The Garden been so successful?
3. What is the purpose of The Vine?
4. How can an intranet impact a company's success?

Case Study 7-2
Social Networking in Support of Small Businesses
➤ **Finance | Technology in Society | Application | Reflective Thinking**

The Internet puts small businesses on the same footing as large organizations by providing an inexpensive platform for interacting with customers and selling products and services. With their global reach, social networking sites are a good example of how the Internet can level the playing field. Here are five ways that small businesses can take advantage of these sites:

- *Creating local social networks*—Small businesses can use sites such as Yelp (*www.yelp.com*), which help people find local restaurants, dentists, hairstylists, mechanics, and so on. People also use these sites to find out about upcoming events, take advantage of special offers, and talk to other customers.

iStock.com/YinYang

- *Creating a blog or social hub*—This allows small businesses to keep customers engaged by creating useful content such as how-to lists or industry insights.
- *Using Twitter*—Small businesses can connect with their consumers in real time.
- *Creating a Facebook fan page*—Small businesses can visualize and build a community that can be customized by adding maps, coupons, and so forth.
- *Using a custom wiki*—A wiki can be used as a public forum that alerts customers to problems and concerns related to the company's products and services and resolves issues or answers questions to keep customers engaged.[72]

Answer the following questions:

1. How does the Internet put small businesses on the same footing as large organizations?
2. What are two ways that social networking sites such as Twitter can help a small business?
3. How can a site such as Yelp help small businesses?

Module

8 E-Commerce

Learning Objectives

After studying this module, you should be able to…

8.1 Define e-commerce and its advantages, disadvantages, and business models.

8.2 Explain the major categories of e-commerce.

8.3 Describe the five major activities of the business-to-consumer e-commerce cycle.

8.4 Summarize the four major models of business-to-business e-commerce.

8.5 Describe mobile-based and voice-based e-commerce.

8.6 Explain four supporting technologies for e-commerce.

8.7 Explain social commerce and the reasons for its popularity.

8.8 Explain hypersocial organizations and their growing popularity.

8.9 Explain social media information systems.

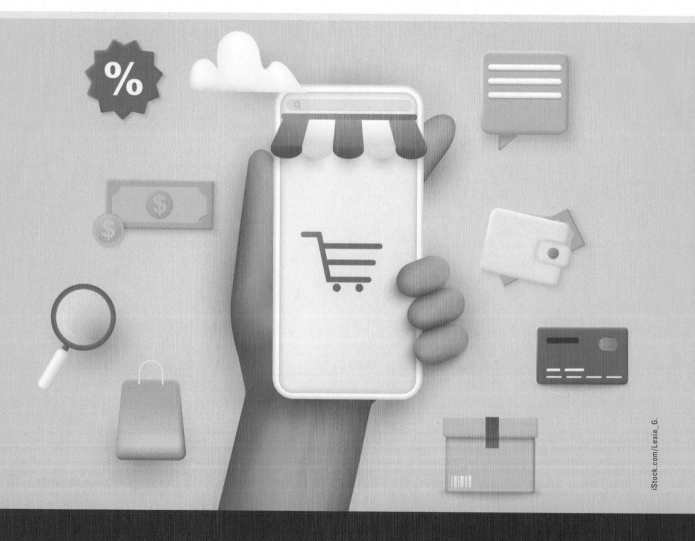

This module provides an overview of e-commerce and value chain analysis, then compares e-commerce with traditional commerce. It explains e-commerce business models and the major categories of e-commerce. Along the way, it illustrates the major activities in the business-to-consumer e-commerce cycle and the major models of business-to-business e-commerce as well as mobile-based and voice-based e-commerce. The module provides an overview of electronic payment systems, digital marketing, mobile marketing, and search engine optimization—four supporting technologies for e-commerce operations. Finally, it describes social commerce, hypersocial organizations, and social media information systems and the reasons for their popularity.

8-1 Defining E-Commerce

E-commerce and e-business differ slightly. **E-business** encompasses all the activities a company performs in buying and selling products and services using computers and communication technologies. In broad terms, e-business includes several related activities, such as online shopping, sales force automation, supply chain management, electronic procurement (e-procurement), electronic payment systems, Web advertising, and order management. **E-commerce** is buying and selling goods and services over the Internet. In other words, e-commerce is part of e-business. However, the two terms are often used interchangeably.

E-business includes not only transactions that center on buying and selling goods and services to generate revenue, but also transactions that generate demand for goods and services, offer sales support and customer service, and facilitate communication between business partners.

E-commerce builds on traditional commerce by adding the flexibility that networks offer and the availability of the Internet. The following are common business applications that use the Internet:

- Buying and selling products and services
- Collaborating with other companies
- Communicating with business partners
- Gathering business intelligence on customers and competitors
- Providing customer service
- Making software updates and patches available
- Offering vendor support
- Publishing and disseminating information

8-1a The Value Chain and E-Commerce

One way to examine e-commerce and its role in the business world is through value chain analysis. Michael Porter introduced the **value chain** concept in 1985.[1] It consists of a series of activities designed to meet business needs by adding value (or cost) in each phase of the process. Typically, a division within a business designs, produces, markets, delivers, and supports its products or services. Each activity adds cost and value to the product or service delivered to the customer (see Exhibit 8.1).

In Exhibit 8.1, the top four components—organizational infrastructure, human resource management, technological development, and procurement (gathering input)—are supporting activities. The "margin" represents the value added by supporting primary activities (the components shown at the bottom). The following list describes primary activities:

- *Inbound logistics*— Movement of materials and parts from suppliers and vendors

E-business encompasses all the activities a company performs in buying and selling products and services using computers and communication technologies.

E-commerce is buying and selling goods and services over the Internet.

A **value chain** is a series of activities designed to meet business needs by adding value (or cost) in each phase of the e-commerce process.

Exhibit 8.1
Michael Porter's value chain

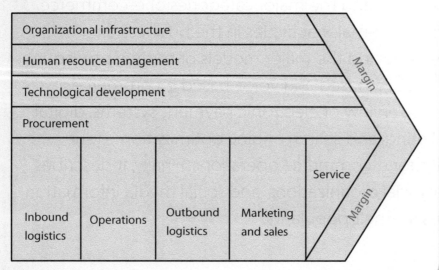

ships the finished products to retailers, distributors, or customers, and markets these products. The company can continue the value chain after delivering the chairs to furniture stores by offering other products and services. Value chain analysis can also help the furniture company spot manufacturing opportunities. For example, it could cut costs of raw materials if it owned or formed a partnership with a lumber company. In any industry, a company is part of a value chain when it buys goods or services from suppliers, adds features to increase value, and sells the goods or services to customers. As another example, a computer vendor can buy components from different vendors and then assemble them into complete PCs. The vendor has added value by assembling the components and can then charge a higher price than the combined cost of the components.

E-commerce, its applications, and its supporting technologies, as discussed in this module, are an example of using Porter's value chain concept. The Internet can increase the speed and accuracy of communication between suppliers, distributors, and customers. Moreover, the Internet's low cost means companies of any size can take advantage of value chain integration, which is the process of multiple companies in a shared market working together to plan and manage the flow of goods, services, and information from manufacturers to consumers. This process optimizes the value chain's efficiency, thus creating a competitive advantage for all companies involved.

to production or storage facilities; includes tasks associated with receiving, storing, and disseminating incoming goods or materials.

- *Operations*—Processing raw materials into finished goods and services.
- *Outbound logistics*—Storing and moving products from the end of the production line to end users or distribution centers.
- *Marketing and sales*—Activities for identifying customer needs and generating sales.
- *Service*—Activities to support customers after the sale of products and services.

For instance, by having superior relationships with suppliers, the company can ensure timely delivery and a high quality of raw materials. These, in turn, add value for customers by providing a high-quality product at a lower cost. If good quality and lower costs are top priorities for customers, the company knows where to focus efforts on the value chain—for example, the company might need better suppliers to ensure quality and reduce costs, superior operations to ensure quality, better distribution to reduce costs, and better after-sales service to ensure quality with warranties. So, the value chain is really about understanding what aspects of an organization's business add value for customers and then maximizing those aspects.

A furniture manufacturing company, for example, buys raw materials (wood) from a logging company, converts the raw materials into finished products (chairs),

> **The value chain is really about understanding what aspects of an organization's business add value for customers and then maximizing those aspects.**

Using Instagram to Promote Your Products and Services

➤➤ Finance | Technology in Society | Application

Instagram, with over 1 billion highly engaged monthly users who are viewing and producing millions of pictures and videos daily, has become a powerful tool for all sorts of businesses to promote their products and services. According to experts, Instagram is the digital equivalent of a magazine ad that also provides millions of pieces of data for analytics. Many different types of businesses have an Instagram page, including Shake Shack, Starbucks, Ben & Jerry's, Nike, and MAC Cosmetics, to mention a few.[2] Below are some interesting Instagram statistics as of 2021:[3,4]

- Seventy-one percent of monthly active users are under the age of 35.
- Users spend an average of 53 minutes per day on Instagram.
- Seventy-one percent of U.S. businesses use Instagram.
- Instagram helps 80 percent of its users to decide to buy a product or service.
- Half of all users follow at least one business.
- Eighty-eight percent of users are outside the United States.
- More than 130 million Instagram users tap on shopping posts every month.
- More than 500 million users use Instagram Stories every day.

To effectively market your products and services on Instagram, follow these nine recommendations:[5]

1. Optimize your Instagram business profile. Because this profile is usually the first point of contact a customer will have with your brand, it is important to make a good impression and entice potential customers to follow your business. At the very least, it should include a profile photo that makes your business easy to identify, an informative bio, and a link to your shop.
2. Use Instagram ads to reach your target audience.
3. Decide on a budget.
4. Create Instagram stories with product links.
5. Build a shoppable Instagram feed.
6. Offer Instagram-only promotions.
7. Establish partnerships with Instagram influencers.
8. Use the right hashtags—those that are used by your influencers.
9. Use the right caption that best describes an image; it could make or break your marketing efforts for a particular product.

Questions and Discussions

1. How and why has Instagram become such a powerful marketing tool? Discuss.
2. What are three recommendations for effectively using Instagram to promote a product or service?

E-commerce can enhance a value chain by offering new ways to reduce costs or improve operations:

- Using e-mail rather than regular mail to notify customers of upcoming sales can reduce costs.
- Selling to customers via the company Web site can generate new sources of revenue, particularly from customers who live far away from the company's headquarters or physical store.
- Offering online customer service can make products or services more appealing to customers.

As discussed throughout this book, many companies have taken advantage of the Web and e-commerce to reduce costs, increase revenue, and improve customer service. For example, Dell Computer generates a large portion of its revenue through the Web and eliminates the middleman in the process. Similarly, Cisco Systems sells networking hardware and software over the Web, and customers can track packages on the Web through United Parcel Service (UPS) and FedEx. The "Using Instagram to Promote Your Products and Services" box describes how Instagram, a popular social networking site, can help businesses.

Showrooming and Webrooming

➤➤ Finance | Technology in Society

Brick-and-mortar and "click-and-brick" businesses have to be able to manage both showrooming and webrooming to increase their total sales. *Showrooming* occurs when consumers physically inspect a product in a store to get a look and feel for it—and then buy it from an online store because it is cheaper to do so. *Webrooming* is the opposite of showrooming: consumers see a product online and do all their research online, but for a final check and purchase, they go to a store. To combat webrooming and showrooming, retailers can create an omnichannel, which integrates online services, social media, mobile technology, and the physical store. By doing this, a retailer is flexible enough to generate a sale regardless of where a customer wants to initiate the sale.[6] As an example, consider a customer who sees a product on the Target Web site. Using a smartphone, the customer orders the product and goes to a Target location to pick up the merchandise a few hours later. We discuss this in the "B2C E-Commerce Evolution: Multichannel, Cross-channel, and Omnichannel" section later in the module.

Questions and Discussions

1. When consumers physically inspect a product in a store to get a look and feel for it—and then buy it from an online store—is this showrooming or webrooming? How are these practices detrimental to retailers?

2. How does an omnichannel approach combat webrooming and showrooming? What are some examples of the omnichannel approach?

The "Showrooming and Webrooming" box highlights the differences between showrooming and webrooming.

8-1b E-Commerce versus Traditional Commerce

Click-and-brick e-commerce mixes traditional commerce and e-commerce. It capitalizes on the advantages of online interaction with customers yet retains the benefits of having a physical store location.

Although the goal of e-commerce and traditional commerce is the same—selling products and services to generate profit—they do it quite differently. In e-commerce, the Web and telecommunication technologies play a major role. Often, there is no physical store, and the buyer and seller do not see each other. Many companies now operate as a mix of traditional commerce and e-commerce, however, and have some kind of e-commerce presence. These companies, referred to as **click-and-brick e-commerce**, capitalize on the advantages of online interaction with their customers yet retain the benefits of having a physical store location. For example, customers can buy items from the company's Web site but take them to the physical store if they need to return items. Table 8.1 compares e-commerce and traditional commerce.

Table 8.1 E-Commerce versus Traditional Commerce

Activity	Traditional Commerce	E-Commerce
Product information	Magazines, flyers	Web sites, online catalogs
Business communication	Regular mail, phone calls	E-mail
Checking product availability	Phone calls, faxes, and letters	E-mail, Web sites, and extranets
Order generation	Printed forms	E-mail, Web sites
Product acknowledgments	Phone calls, faxes	E-mail, Web sites, and electronic data interchange (EDI)
Invoice generation	Printed forms	Web sites

8-1c Advantages and Disadvantages of E-Commerce

Businesses of all sizes use the Internet and e-commerce applications to gain a competitive edge. For example, IBM does business with more than 12,000 suppliers over the Web and uses the Web for sending purchase orders, receiving invoices, and paying suppliers. In addition, IBM uses the Internet and Web technologies for its transaction-processing network.

E-commerce has many advantages and disadvantages. If e-commerce is based on a sound business model (as discussed in the next section), its advantages outweigh its disadvantages. Advantages of e-commerce include the following:

- Creating better relationships with suppliers, customers, and business partners
- Creating "price transparency," meaning that all market participants can trade at the same price
- Being able to operate around the clock and around the globe
- Gathering more information about potential customers
- Increasing customer involvement (e.g., offering a feedback section on the company Web site)
- Improving customer service
- Increasing flexibility and ease of shopping

- Increasing the number of customers
- Increasing opportunities for collaboration with business partners
- Increasing return on investment because inventory needs are reduced
- Offering personalized services and product customization
- Reducing administrative and transaction costs

E-commerce also has the following disadvantages, although many of these should be eliminated or reduced in the near future:

- Bandwidth capacity problems (in certain parts of the world)
- Security and privacy issues
- Accessibility (not everybody is connected to the Web yet)
- Acceptance (not everybody accepts this technology)

> **The Internet has improved productivity in many organizations, but this improvement must be converted to profitability.**

The Home Depot Gets into E-Commerce

➤➤ Finance | Technology in Society | Application | Reflective Thinking

Changing shopper habits and diminishing returns from new store openings are among the major reasons that Home Depot opened its first distribution center in 2014. The company opened two distribution centers and only one traditional store in 2014. This is a sharp contrast to its history as a major supplier of home improvement products and services.

Home Depot and its e-commerce business offers more than 1 million products for do-it-yourself (DIY) customers and professional contractors. Home Depot is also the industry's largest installation business for do-it-for-me (DIFM) customers. From these statistics you can see that customers have a broad range of products and services to choose from. The company also allows customers to order items online and pick them up in a nearby store.

Rob Wilson/Shutterstock.com

(Continued)

Home Depot is hoping that its online store, in addition to attracting customers, will attract more contractors and builders because they account for 35 percent of its total sales. Due to the variety, size, and weight of many of the products that the company carries, logistics play a major role in sales; the company has to be able to deliver items to customers in a timely manner.

To improve logistics, Home Depot invested $1.5 billion in supply chain and technology improvements in 2014 to better connect its stores and Internet businesses. This included a new online fulfillment center. In 2016, Internet sales accounted for 5.6 percent of the company's total sales. In the third quarter of 2018, Home Depot's online sales surged by 28 percent compared with the same period in the previous year, indicating that online sales were growing faster than traditional sales.[7,8,9,10]

To enhance its e-commerce operations and resolve some of the challenges in online business, Home Depot has been heavily investing in artificial intelligence (AI) and data science techniques. It uses statistical analysis to discover relationships between different categories. It uses NLP (natural language processing, discussed in Module 13) to understand customers' reviews and their opinions about the pros and cons of products. These data-driven techniques have enabled Home Depot to improve its recommendation algorithm and offer a personalized customer experience.[11]

Questions and Discussions

1. What were two major reasons for Home Depot to get into e-commerce?
2. What major investments were required to grow the online business? Was it worth it? Discuss.

The **merchant model** transfers the old retail model to the e-commerce world by using the medium of the Internet.

Using the **brokerage model** brings sellers and buyers together on the Web and enables commissions on transactions between these parties.

The "The Home Depot Gets into E-Commerce" box illustrates how a brick-and-mortar company integrates e-commerce into its operations.

8-1d E-Commerce Business Models

To achieve profitability, e-commerce companies focus their operations on different parts of the value chain, as discussed earlier. To generate revenue, for example, an e-commerce company might decide to sell only products or services or cut out the middleman in the link between suppliers and consumers. Many business-to-consumer (B2C) business models do the latter by using the Web to deliver products and services to customers, which helps reduce prices and improve customer service. As you learned in the discussion of Michael Porter's differentiation strategies in Module 1, companies can increase their market shares as well as customer loyalty by differentiating themselves from their competitors.

The products that e-commerce companies sell could be traditional products, such as books and apparel, or digital products, such as music, software, and e-books.

Similarly, e-commerce models can be traditional or "digital." A traditional e-commerce model is usually an extension or revision of a traditional business model, such as advertising or merchandising, or a new type of model suitable for Web implementation, such as an infomediary (as described in the following list). The following are the most widely used business models in e-commerce:[12]

- *Merchant*—The **merchant model** transfers the old retail model to the e-commerce world by using the medium of the Internet. In the most common type of merchant model, an e-commerce company uses Internet technologies and Web services to sell goods and services over the Web. Companies following this model offer good customer service and lower prices to establish a presence on the Web. Amazon uses this model, but traditional businesses, such as Nike, Dell, Cisco, and Hewlett-Packard, have adopted the model to eliminate the middleman and reach new customers.

- *Brokerage*—Using the **brokerage model** brings sellers and buyers together on the Web and enables commissions on transactions between these parties. The best example of this model is an online auction site, such as eBay (*www.ebay.com*), DealDash (*www.dealdash.com*), or QuiBids (*www.quibids. com*). Auction sites can generate additional revenue by selling banner advertisements. Other examples of the brokerage model are online stockbrokers, such as *TDAmeritrade.com*, *Coinbase.com*, and *Schwab.com*, which generate revenue by collecting commissions from buyers and sellers of securities.

- *Advertising*—The **advertising model** is an extension of traditional advertising media, such as radio and television. Directories such as Yahoo! provide content (similar to radio and TV) to users for free. By creating more traffic with this free content, directories can charge companies for placing banner ads or leasing spots on their sites. Google, for example, generates revenue from AdWords, which offers pay-per-click (PPC) advertising and site-targeted advertising for both text and banner ads.

- *Mixed*—The **mixed model** refers to generating revenue from more than one source. For example, Amazon generates revenue from Amazon Prime subscription fees and from selling products and services to its customers. An auction site can also generate revenue from commissions collected from buyers and sellers and from advertising.

- *Infomediary*—E-commerce sites that use the **infomediary model** collect information on consumers and businesses and then sell this information to other companies for marketing purposes. For example, Bizrate (*bizrate.com*) collects information about the performance of other sites and sells this information to advertisers.

> The **advertising model** is an extension of traditional advertising media, such as radio and television. Directories such as Yahoo! provide content (similar to radio and TV) to users for free. By creating more traffic with this free content, directories can charge companies for placing banner ads or leasing spots on their sites.

> The **mixed model** refers to generating revenue from more than one source.

> Under the **infomediary model**, e-commerce sites collect information on consumers and businesses and then sell this information to other companies for marketing purposes.

E-Commerce in 2025

▶ Finance | Technology in Society | Application | Reflective Thinking | Global

According to Meticulous Research, the global e-commerce market will continue growing to reach $24.3 trillion by 2025. The driving forces behind this continued growth are mobile e-commerce, increasing numbers of Internet users throughout the world, advanced shipping and logistics, and the rise in disposable income. By providing access and ease of use, online payment systems are playing a significant role in the growth of the global e-commerce market.[13] A report from FTI Consulting predicts that U.S. online retail sales will reach $1 trillion by 2025.[14]

Peer reviews and the opinions of shoppers who post on social media will have an increasing impact on customers' buying decisions. Smartphones will play a major role in this trend as well. Social networking sites such as Facebook, Instagram, Twitter, Foursquare, and Groupon will continue to influence shopping decisions. Google searches through mobile devices will continue to influence online shoppers.[15]

It also looks like new online shopping models, such as "flash sales" and "daily deal" services, will become more popular. Flash sales, which last only a brief period of time, are invitation-only events that offer name-brand merchandise.[16]

Reservoir Dots/Shutterstock.com

Questions and Discussions

1. What are three forces that drive the continued growth of global e-commerce?
2. How do flash sales work? Why are some e-commerce businesses using this strategy?

- *Subscription*—Using the **subscription model**, e-commerce sites sell digital products or services to customers. For example, the *Wall Street Journal* and *Consumer Reports* offer online subscriptions, and antivirus vendors use this model to distribute their software and updates. As mentioned in Module 7, Cengage Unlimited is another good example of a subscription model. The information box "E-Commerce in 2025" predicts where e-commence will be in 2025.

8-2 Major Categories of E-Commerce

E-commerce transactions occur among consumers, businesses, and government, resulting in nine major categories that are summarized in Table 8.2. These categories are described in the following sections.

8-2a Business-to-Consumer E-Commerce

Business-to-consumer (B2C) companies—such as Amazon, *Barnesandnoble.com*, and *Overstock.com*—sell directly to consumers. As discussed later in this module's Industry Connection feature, Amazon and its business partners sell a wide array of products and services, including books, DVDs, prescription drugs, clothing, and household products. Amazon is also an example of a pure-play company, which means that it relies exclusively on the Web to distribute its products. In recent years, companies that used to have only physical stores—called brick-and-mortar companies—have entered the virtual marketplace by establishing comprehensive Web sites

Boumen Japet/Shutterstock.com

and virtual storefronts. Walmart, the Gap, and Staples are examples of companies that supplement their traditional commerce with e-commerce. Some experts believe that these companies may become more successful than pure-play companies because of the advantages a physical space can offer, such as customers being able to visit a store to see merchandise and make returns.

8-2b Business-to-Business E-Commerce

Business-to-business (B2B) e-commerce involves electronic transactions between businesses. These types of transactions have been around for many years in the form of electronic data interchange (EDI) and electronic funds transfer (EFT). In recent years, the Internet has increased the number of B2B transactions and made B2B the fastest-growing segment of e-commerce. As discussed in Module 7, extranets have been used effectively for B2B operations, as companies rely on other companies for supplies, utilities, and services. Companies that use B2B applications for purchase orders, invoices, inventory status, shipping logistics, business contracts, and other operations report millions of dollars in savings by increasing transaction speed, reducing errors,

Under the **subscription model**, e-commerce sites sell digital products or services to customers.

Business-to-consumer (B2C) companies sell directly to consumers.

Business-to-business (B2B) e-commerce involves electronic transactions between businesses.

Table 8.2	Major E-Commerce Categories		
	Consumer	**Business**	**Government**
Consumer	C2C	C2B	C2G
Business	B2C	B2B	B2G
Government	G2C	G2B	G2G

and eliminating manual tasks. Walmart is a major player in B2B e-commerce. Its suppliers—Procter & Gamble, Johnson & Johnson, and others—sell their products to Walmart electronically, which allows them to check the inventory status in each store and replenish products in a timely manner.

8-2c Consumer-to-Consumer E-Commerce

Consumer-to-consumer (C2C) e-commerce involves business transactions between users, such as when consumers sell to other consumers via the Internet. When people use online classified ads at Craigslist or Letgo or use online auction sites such as eBay, they are using C2C e-commerce. Facebook Marketplace is also a growing player for C2C e-commerce. As a digital marketplace, it allows users to buy, sell, and trade items with other users in their area. People can also advertise products and services on organizations' intranets (discussed in Module 7) and sell them to other employees.

8-2d Consumer-to-Business E-Commerce

Consumer-to-business (C2B) e-commerce involves people selling products or services to businesses, such as when a consumer creates online surveys for a company to use. Another example is when businesses use crowdsourcing by asking consumers to perform services—such as contributing to a Web site—for a fee.

8-2e Government and Nonbusiness E-Commerce

E-commerce applications are used by many government and other nonbusiness organizations, including the U.S. Department of Defense, the Internal Revenue Service, and the Department of the Treasury. These applications are broadly called **e-government** (or just "e-gov") applications and are divided into these categories:

- *Government-to-citizen (G2C)*—Tax filing and payments; completing, submitting, and downloading forms; requests for records; online voter registration
- *Government-to-business (G2B)*—Sales of federal assets, license applications and renewals
- *Government-to-government (G2G)*—Disaster assistance and crisis response
- *Government-to-employee (G2E)*—E-training

Local, state, and federal agencies are either developing e-gov presence or enhancing their existing e-gov Web sites. A user-focused government Web site should include the following features:[17]

Responsive design. The users of a government Web site may use smartphones, tablets, or desktops to access the Web site for needed information. The Web site should provide easy access to the requested information in the proper format, regardless of the device in use.

Interactive searchable calendars. The Web site should help visitors to stay informed with up-to-date and searchable calendars for local events, meetings, and activities. The site should remove outdated activities promptly.

Search facility. The Web site should provide a search tool that enables visitors to search by keywords and find needed information anywhere on the site and in its related documents.

Online forms with online payment tools. The Web site should provide accessible online forms that users can download and from which users can make payments. This increases convenience and reduces unnecessary paperwork. In addition, it helps the agency to achieve its green goals.

Consistent design. The Web site should be unique to the community that it serves and provide a consistent look and feel throughout the site. Such a site serves as a key tool for promoting tourism as well as economic development and marketing.

E-mail alerts. The Web site should offer e-mail alerts related to emergencies and breaking news. It is even more beneficial if the site allows users to subscribe to specific areas of interest and modify those settings online.

Intuitive navigation. The Web site should organize its content so that users can find needed information quickly by using logical searches. This will help users who are not familiar with the site to search and find information from multiple departments.

Consumer-to-consumer (C2C) e-commerce involves business transactions between users, such as consumers selling to other consumers via the Internet.

Consumer-to-business (C2B) e-commerce involves people selling products or services to businesses, such as when a consumer creates online surveys for a company to use.

E-government applications can include government-to-citizen, government-to-business, government-to-government, and government-to-employee transactions. Services include tax filing, online voter registration, disaster assistance, and e-training for government employees.

Exhibit 8.2
USA.gov home page (*https://www.usa.gov*)

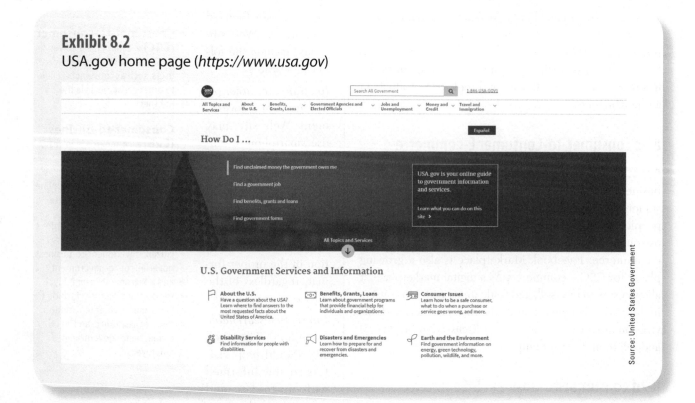

Source: United States Government

Organizational (intrabusiness) e-commerce involves e-commerce activities that take place inside an organization, typically via the organization's intranet. These activities can include the exchange of goods, services, or information among employees.

ADA compliance. The Web site must be ADA compliant as required by law.

User-friendly access. Similar to any other system, a user-focused government Web site should provide easy access to frequently requested information in the header and footer of each page and provide multiple links to address frequently asked questions.

The home page. The Web site should utilize its front page (or home page) as efficiently and effectively as possible. The front page is the most valuable real estate on any Web site and can play a major role in its success. This page is the gateway to the system and should provide a quick glance at the latest news, events, and items of community interest. It should provide upcoming calendar items and direct links to some of the site's information hotspots.

Exhibit 8.2 shows the home page of *USA.gov*, a Web site for delivering government-related information to users.

Universities are an example of nonbusiness organizations that use e-commerce applications; for example, many universities use Web technologies for online classes, registration, and grade reporting. In addition, nonprofit, political, and social organizations use e-commerce applications for activities such as fundraising, political forums, and purchasing.

8-2f Organizational or Intrabusiness E-Commerce

Organizational (intrabusiness) e-commerce involves e-commerce activities that take place inside an organization, typically via the organization's intranet (discussed in Module 7). These activities are not part of the nine major categories we just discussed. However, they do support overall e-business activities. They can include the exchange of goods, services, or information among employees (such as C2C e-commerce, as discussed previously). As an example, a department at an academic institution might make a request to the print shop for educational or marketing brochures. The transaction typically has an associated cost that is charged against the department's budget. Other examples include conducting training programs and offering human resource services. Some of these activities, though not specifically related to buying and selling, are considered supporting activities in Porter's value chain. For example, a human resources department supports the personnel involved in producing and distributing a company's products.

8-3 B2C E-Commerce Cycle

As Exhibit 8.3 shows, five major activities are involved in conducting B2C e-commerce:

1. *Information sharing*—A B2C e-commerce company can use a variety of methods to share information with its customers, such as company Web sites, online catalogs, e-mail, online advertisements, video conferencing, message boards, and newsgroups.

2. *Ordering*—Customers can use electronic forms or e-mail to order products from a B2C site.

3. *Payment*—Customers have a variety of payment options, such as credit cards, e-checks, and digital wallets. Electronic payment systems are discussed in the section titled "E-Commerce Supporting Technologies."

4. *Fulfillment*—The process of delivering products or services to customers varies depending on whether physical products (books, videos, CDs) or digital products (software, music, electronic documents) are being delivered. For example, delivery of physical products can take place via air, sea, or ground at varying costs and with different options. Delivery of digital products is more straightforward and usually involves a simple download, although products are typically verified with digital signatures (see Module 5). Fulfillment also varies depending on whether the company handles its own fulfillment operations or outsources them. Fulfillment often includes delivery address verification and digital warehousing, which maintains digital products on storage media until they are delivered. Several third-party companies are available to handle fulfillment functions for e-commerce sites.

5. *Service and support*—Service and support are even more important in e-commerce than in traditional commerce, given that e-commerce companies do not have a physical location to help maintain current customers. Because maintaining current customers is less expensive than attracting new customers, e-commerce companies should make an effort to improve customer service and support by using methods such as e-mail confirmations and product updates, chatbots, online surveys, help desks, and guaranteed secure transactions.

The activities listed in Exhibit 8.3 are the same in traditional commerce and probably occur in the same sequence, too. However, each stage has been transformed by Web technologies and the Internet.

Exhibit 8.3
Major activities in B2C e-commerce

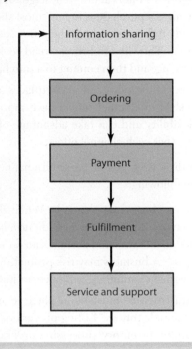

8-3a B2C E-Commerce Evolution: Multichannel, Cross-Channel, and Omnichannel

Because of the increasing competition among traditional and e-commerce businesses, both groups are deploying multiple sales channels to attract more customers and provide them additional convenience. These channels include multichannel, cross-channel, and omnichannel. Let's look at each strategy.[18]

Multichannel. A customer purchases an item using one of a business's channels, including in-store purchases, cell phones, the company's Web site, social media channels, comparison shopping engines, third-party marketplaces, and other companies' Web sites. These various channels are not connected to one another, and different departments and channels do not share data with each other. If a customer orders online and goes to the business's physical location, salespeople will not have access to the customer's purchase history. In this scenario, channels are in competition with one another, so for multichannel brands, consumers have to choose one channel and

> With the **multichannel** strategy, a customer purchases an item using one of a business's channels, including in-store purchases, cell phones, the company's Web site, social media channels, comparison shopping engines, third-party marketplaces, and other companies' Web sites.

stick to it. Multichannel retailing has some distinct advantages, as follows:[19]

1. It targets consumers at different stages of their activities. Unless a purchase is urgent, most shoppers are not ready to buy a product when they see it for the first time. They like to browse, read reviews, compare pricing, and then commit to a purchase.

2. It leverages the power of marketplaces and search engines. Multichannel sellers have more freedom and flexibility and can take advantage of different features that each channel offers.

Some disadvantages of the multichannel strategy include the following:

1. Selling on the wrong channels. While diversification is key to reaching a larger audience, launching a product on an unrelated channel can do more harm than good. A business may risk promoting products to the wrong community, audience, or industry.

2. An infrastructure must be in place to maintain a multichannel strategy. Listing on various channels, maintaining inventory, processing orders, and providing customer service can be very challenging if the business does not have an infrastructure in place.

Cross-channel. A customer uses several channels to buy an item. This strategy offers freedom and convenience to the customer. For example, a "click & collect" approach allows customers to order online and pick up an item in a store or at some agreed-upon location. This strategy is being adopted by all sorts of businesses. Alternatively, a customer might try on some items of clothing in a store, think about it later at home, and eventually order those clothes online. Or, a customer might receive a coupon in the mail and then go online and purchase the item using the coupon. As another example, a customer might pick out a product in a catalog and then buy it by phone. Using a cross-channel strategy, channels are not in competition and can complement each other. There are several advantages of the cross-channel strategy:[20]

- It makes buyers' purchase activities more enjoyable by catering to their habits.

- It makes customer service more personal.
- It attracts new customers faster.
- It improves the company's brand image.
- It affords a unique view of a business's customers.
- It increases sales opportunities.
- It allows a business to know its customers better.

A couple of disadvantages of this strategy include limited resources and the challenges involved in integrating various channels.

Omnichannel. This strategy seeks to integrate physical stores, the Internet, and mobile technologies. Using this strategy, sales associates who cannot find a product at their particular store can quickly find it somewhere in the company's operations and have it sent to the customer free of charge. The strategy is designed to create seamless communication among all sales channels. Similarly, the company's Web site can draw products from any of the company's physical stores. Some of the advantages of omnichannel include the following:[21]

- It improves customer satisfaction and retention.
- It meets customers where they are.
- It retains more customers.
- It increases revenue.
- It improves brand recognition.

The main disadvantage of this strategy is its complexity. It requires a large number of people in many different places to be on the same page. Also, it requires seamless integration between people, software, and processes in order to be successful.

To improve the efficiency and effectiveness of an omnichannel strategy, businesses should integrate conversational commerce into their operations. **Conversational commerce** enables a business and its customers to communicate throughout the entire buying process using various tools. Popular communication tools include live chats, chatbots, messaging apps, and voice assistants.[22]

Many of the information technology tools discussed in this book could help to successfully implement the three B2C strategies we just discussed. They also could bridge the gap between the various channels. Let's now explore four examples of IT tools deployment.

1. Many companies, including eBay, provide image search capabilities on their apps so that shoppers can find a product by sharing a photo with the app and then have it identify similar products in the company's digital catalog. The customer then decides whether to buy the product.[23]

With the **cross-channel** strategy, a customer uses several channels to buy an item.

The **omnichannel** strategy seeks to integrate physical stores, the Internet, and mobile technologies.

Conversational commerce enables a business and its customers to communicate throughout the entire buying process using various tools.

2. As you will learn in Module 14, many companies are using augmented reality (AR) and virtual reality (VR) to improve the customer experience and offer more ways to purchase products. One such company is IKEA, a leading home furnishing retailer based in Sweden. The IKEA catalog introduced an augmented reality feature that provides a virtual preview of how furniture will look in a particular room. Using a mobile device with the help of an AR app, customers can see how furniture looks in their living space before buying it.[24]

3. Ray-Ban is using AR that allows customers to virtually try on glasses and see how they look before purchase. This application offers a good opportunity for online businesses to sell the exact product a customer wants in terms of its size, color, and appearance.[25]

4. Microsoft Dynamics 365 for Sales and Dynamics 365 AI for Sales are being deployed in multichannel applications that use AI, mixed reality, and social and mobile capabilities for seamless implementation. The platform allows customers to shop using any method they like, and it generates real-time analytics, enabling the business to measure the effectiveness of the channel.[26]

8-4 B2B E-Commerce: A Second Look

B2B e-commerce may include the activities shown in Exhibit 8.3. However, other technologies are used extensively, including intranets, extranets, virtual private networks, EDI, and EFT. B2B e-commerce reduces delivery time, inventory requirements, and prices and helps business partners share relevant, accurate, and timely information. The end result is improved supply chain management among business partners.

B2B e-commerce also lowers production costs and improves accuracy by eliminating many labor-intensive tasks, such as creating invoices and tracking payments manually. In addition, the information flow among business partners is improved by creating a direct online connection in the supply chain network, which reduces delivery time. In other words, raw materials are received faster, and information related to customers' requests is transferred faster. Improved electronic communication between business partners improves overall communication, which results in better inventory management and control.

8-4a Major Models of B2B E-Commerce

There are three major models of B2B e-commerce, based on who controls the marketplace—the seller, the buyer, or an intermediary (third party). This results in three marketplace models: the seller-side marketplace, the buyer-side marketplace, and the third-party exchange marketplace. A fourth marketplace model, trading partner agreements, which facilitate contracts and negotiations among business partners, is also gaining popularity. The following sections discuss these models.

Seller-Side Marketplace

The **seller-side marketplace** model occurs most often. In this model, sellers who cater to specialized markets, such as chemicals, electronics, and auto components, come together to create a common marketplace for buyers—sort of a one-stop shopping model. Sellers can pool their market power, and buyers' searches for alternative sources are simplified.

A popular application of the seller-side model is **e-procurement**, which enables employees in an organization to order and receive supplies and services directly from suppliers. Typically, a company negotiates reduced prices with suppliers ahead of time. E-procurement streamlines the traditional procurement process, which reduces costs, saves time, and improves relationships between suppliers and participating organizations.

E-procurement applications often have purchase-approval procedures that allow users to connect only to company-approved e-catalogs that give employees pre-negotiated prices. The main objectives of e-procurement are to prevent purchases from suppliers that are not on the approved list of sellers and eliminate the processing costs of purchases. Not following this process can be costly for the receiving partner because it can result in paying higher prices for supplies. E-procurement can also qualify customers for volume discounts or special offers.

E-procurement applications can automate some buying and selling activities, which reduces costs and improves processing speeds. Companies that use these applications expect to control inventory more effectively, reduce purchasing overhead, and improve the manufacturing production

The **seller-side marketplace** model occurs most often. In this model, sellers who cater to specialized markets, such as chemicals, electronics, and auto components, come together to create a common marketplace for buyers—sort of a one-stop shopping model.

E-procurement enables employees in an organization to order and receive supplies and services directly from suppliers.

In a **buyer-side marketplace** model, a buyer or group of buyers opens an electronic marketplace and invites sellers to bid on announced products or make a request for quotation (RFQ). Using this model, buyers can manage the procurement process more efficiently, lower administrative costs, and implement uniform pricing.

The **third-party exchange marketplace** model is not controlled by sellers or buyers. Instead, it is controlled by a third party, and the marketplace generates revenue from the fees charged for matching buyers and sellers.

A **vertical market** concentrates on a specific industry or market. The utilities industry, the beef and dairy industries, and the sale of medical products are examples of vertical markets.

A **horizontal market** concentrates on a specific function or business process and automates it for different industries.

cycle. E-procurement will likely be integrated into standard business systems with the trend toward computerized supply chain management (discussed in Module 11).

Major vendors of e-commerce and B2B solutions include I2 Technologies, IBM, Oracle, and SAP. The "E-Procurement at Schlumberger" box highlights e-procurement applications at Schlumberger.

Buyer-Side Marketplace

Large corporations (such as General Electric or Boeing) as well as consortiums of large companies use the **buyer-side marketplace** model. In this model, a buyer or group of buyers opens an electronic marketplace and invites sellers to bid on announced products or make a request for quotation (RFQ). Buyers can manage the procurement process more efficiently, lower administrative costs, and implement uniform pricing. Companies invest in buyer-side marketplaces with the goal of establishing new sales channels that increase their market presence and lower the cost of each sale. By participating in buyer-side marketplaces, sellers can do the following:

- Conduct sales transactions.
- Automate the order management process.
- Conduct postsales analysis.
- Automate the fulfillment function.
- Improve understanding of buying behaviors.
- Provide an alternative sales channel.
- Reduce order placement and delivery time.

Third-Party Exchange Marketplace

The **third-party exchange marketplace** model is not controlled by sellers or buyers. Instead, it is controlled by a third party, and the marketplace generates revenue from the fees charged for matching buyers and sellers. A **vertical market** concentrates on a specific industry or market, such as the utilities industry, the beef and dairy industries, or the sale of medical products. A **horizontal market** concentrates on a specific function or business process and automates it for different industries. Employee benefits administration and media buying are examples of horizontal markets.

This model offers suppliers a direct channel of communication to buyers through online storefronts. The interactive procedures in the marketplace have features such as product catalogs, requests for information (RFI), rebates and promotions, broker contacts, and product sample requests.

E-Procurement at Schlumberger

⟫ Finance | Application | Reflective Thinking

Schlumberger, an oil field-services provider, developed an e-procurement system for order processing that has reduced its cost per order. The system reduces costs by streamlining the paperwork that was required to route purchase orders for approval and for other administrative tasks. The old centralized electronic data interchange (EDI) procurement system was replaced with a Web-based system that enables employees to contact any approved supplier directly from their workstations. The system has an easy-to-use, flexible interface that has allowed Schlumberger to conduct business with a more diverse group of suppliers. The Internet connection for the system is inexpensive and fast, and the system's open platform has been an advantage.[27]

Questions and Discussions

1. How is the e-procurement system able to reduce costs at Schlumberger?
2. What are two advantages of the e-procurement system?

Trading Partner Agreements

The main objectives of **trading partner agreements** are to automate negotiating processes and enforce contracts between participating businesses. Using this model, business partners can send and receive bids, contracts, and other information needed when offering and purchasing products and services. This model will become more common with the development of electronic business eXtensible Markup Language (ebXML), a worldwide project to use XML to standardize the exchange of e-commerce data, including electronic contracts and trading partner agreements.

Using this model enables customers to submit electronic documents via the Internet; previously, contracts and agreements required hard copies with signatures. The Digital Signature Act of 1999 gives digital signatures the same legal validity as handwritten signatures. Accepting an electronic trading agreement binds the parties to all its terms and conditions.

With ebXML, contracts can be transmitted electronically, and many processes between trading partners can be performed electronically, including inventory status, shipping logistics, purchase orders, reservation systems, and electronic payments. The main advantage of ebXML or XML over HTML is that you can assign data-type definitions to information on a Web page so browsers select only the data requested in a search. This feature makes data transfer easier because not all data is transferred—just the data needed in a particular situation. The feature is particularly useful in m-commerce (mobile commerce) because loading only the necessary data in a browser makes searches more efficient. This process reduces traffic on the Internet and helps prevent delays during peak usage hours.

The "B2B E-Commerce Growth and Best Practices" box highlights B2B growth and some recommendations for successful implementation of a B2B strategy.

Trading partner agreements automate negotiating processes and enforce contracts between participating businesses.

B2B E-Commerce Growth and Best Practices

➤➤ Finance | Technology in Society | Application | Reflective Thinking

The expansion of B2B e-commerce shows no sign of slowing down; according to Forrester, it will reach $1.8 trillion in the United States by 2023.[28] B2B e-commerce is estimated to be nearly 2.5 times larger than B2C online retail and is growing rapidly, which presents a great opportunity for many businesses.[29] "Channel shifting" is the main factor behind this forecast, as more businesses are replacing phone sales and other offline channels with online shopping. Interestingly enough, the entire supply chain network is participating in this trend, including manufacturers, wholesalers, and distributors. Cost-cutting and improving customer service are the major incentives for this growth.[30]

To be successful and maintain their growth rates, B2B e-commerce companies should consider the following strategies.[31]

- Implement smart product offerings: specific promotions and pricing for different customers.
- Improve the user experience and ease of online shopping.
- Offer mobile tools for anytime/anywhere shopping.
- Offer tools for specific B2B transactions, including bulk ordering, repeat ordering, and scheduled ordering.
- Offer customer self-service and administration.
- Implement real-time inventory and pricing.
- Allow key customers to order directly from suppliers through standard procurement channels.
- Integrate ordering systems with all back-office technologies.

Questions and Discussions

1. What is "channel shifting" in B2B e-commerce?
2. What are three recommendations for implementing successful B2B e-commerce?

Mobile Commerce in Action: Fast-Food Restaurants

➤➤ **Finance | Technology in Society | Application | Reflective Thinking**

Mobile commerce is making fast food faster by combining ordering, payment, and pickup into one simple task. Chipotle Mexican Grill uses an app for all of its locations that enables customers to order their favorite food and then pick it up at the restaurant. The app also allows customers to save their favorite foods for reordering in the future. Domino's, Papa John's, Pizza Hut, and Starbucks have been using mobile apps for several years. Starbucks is one of the leaders in using mobile payment. According to Starbucks, mobile orders and mobile payments accounted for more than 25 percent of its U.S. transactions in 2021.[32]

James R. Martin/Shutterstock.com

Taco Bell offers a mobile-ordering app that enables customers to order and pay for food and then pick it up in the restaurant or the drive-through window. The app shows all the items that customers see when they go to the restaurant, with all options for each item. The app also allows customers to individualize orders—for example, no pickle or tomato on an order. The GPS on the smartphone alerts the restaurant to a customer's location so the restaurant knows when to prepare an order.

The automated machines that prepare most fast food, along with the mobile apps, enable these restaurants to operate with fewer employees. As a result, operating costs are going down. McDonald's, Chick-fil-A, and KFC are also using mobile ordering apps.[33]

Questions and Discussions

1. What are two advantages of mobile payment systems compared to traditional payment systems? How might mobile payment systems give a company a competitive advantage?
2. What are the two most important features of the Taco Bell mobile ordering app? Discuss.

8-5 Mobile and Voice-Based E-Commerce

Mobile commerce (m-commerce), based on the Wireless Application Protocol (WAP), has been around for several years, particularly in European countries. M-commerce is the use of handheld devices such as smartphones or wireless devices to conduct business transactions, such as making stock trades with an online brokerage firm. Supporting technologies for m-commerce applications include wireless wide area networks (WWANs), 4G and 5G networks (discussed in Module 6), and short-range wireless communication technologies, such as Wi-Fi, WiMAX, Bluetooth (discussed in Module 6), and RFID (discussed in Module 11).

Many telecommunication companies offer smartphones. In addition, a wide variety of popular m-commerce applications are available for iOS and Android devices, including apps for games, entertainment, news, shopping, and travel information. Some apps are free, others must be purchased, and some offer in-app purchases that allow customers to obtain enhanced features.

Mobile user-to-user applications, such as those for sharing games and pictures, are also popular. The box titled "Mobile Commerce in Action: Fast-Food Restaurants" highlights the applications of m-commerce in fast-food restaurants.

Mobile commerce (m-commerce) is the use of handheld devices such as smartphones or wireless devices to conduct business transactions.

The next step in e-commerce is **voice-based e-commerce**, which relies on voice recognition and text-to-speech technologies that have improved dramatically in the past decade.[34,35,36] For example, you can simply speak the name of the Web site or service you want to access, use voice commands to search a database by product name, and then find the merchant with the most competitive prices. Voice assistant platforms such as Amazon's Alexa, Apple's Siri, and Google Assistant are moving voice commerce to the next level. Using Alexa, customers can order all sorts of items from Amazon using their voices.[37] Companies such as Walmart and Target have teamed up with Google to allow customers to use Google Assistant for voice-based shopping.[38,39]

Siri lets users send messages, make calls, set reminders, and perform other tasks using their voices. (Android devices use Google Voice for this purpose.) Cortana from Microsoft and Alexa from Amazon also offer voice interfaces, as you will learn in Module 13. One method of conducting voice-based e-commerce is by using a digital wallet, which is discussed in the next section. In addition to storing financial information, a digital wallet can store information such as a customer's address and driver's license number. Security features for voice-based e-commerce should include the following:

- Call recognition, so that calls have to be placed from specific mobile devices

- Voice recognition, so that authorizations have to match a specific voice pattern

- Shipping to a set address that cannot be changed by voice commands

Georgejmclittle/Shutterstock.com

8-6 E-Commerce Supporting Technologies

A number of technologies and applications support e-commerce activities, including electronic payment systems, digital marketing, mobile marketing, and search engine optimization. They are discussed in the following sections.

8-6a Electronic Payment Systems

An **electronic payment** is a transaction in which money is exchanged electronically. This type of payment usually involves the use of the Internet, other computer networks, and digitally stored value systems. Payment cards—including credit cards, debit cards, charge cards, and smart cards—are the most popular instruments for electronic payment transactions. **Smart cards** have been used in Europe, Asia, and Australia for many years and are slowly gaining acceptance in the United States because of their multiple functions. A smart card is about the size of a credit card and contains an embedded microprocessor chip for storing important financial and personal information. The chip can be loaded with information and updated periodically.

E-cash, a secure and convenient alternative to bills and coins, complements credit, debit, and charge cards and adds convenience and control to everyday cash transactions. E-cash usually works with a smart card; the amount of cash stored on the chip can be "recharged" electronically.

An **e-check**, the electronic version of a paper check, offers security, speed, and convenience for online transactions. Many utility companies offer

Voice-based e-commerce relies on voice recognition and text-to-speech technologies.

Electronic payment refers to money that is exchanged electronically. It usually involves use of the Internet, other computer networks, and digitally stored value systems. It includes credit cards, debit cards, charge cards, and smart cards.

A **smart card** is about the size of a credit card and contains an embedded microprocessor chip for storing important financial and personal information. The chip can be loaded with information and updated periodically.

An **e-check**, the electronic version of a paper check, offers security, speed, and convenience for online transactions.

E-cash, a secure and convenient alternative to bills and coins, complements credit, debit, and charge cards and adds convenience and control to everyday cash transactions.

A **digital wallet**, which is available for most handheld devices, offers a secure, convenient, and portable tool for online shopping. A digital wallet stores personal and financial information, such as credit card numbers, passwords, and PINs.

PayPal is a popular online payment system used for many online transactions. Users with valid e-mail addresses can set up accounts and make secure payments using their credit cards or bank accounts.

Venmo users can transfer funds to others via a mobile app; both the sender and receiver have to live in the United States.

customers the opportunity to use e-checks to make payments, and most banks accept e-checks for online bill paying. E-checks are a good solution when other electronic payment systems are too risky or otherwise not appropriate.

A **digital wallet**, which is available for most handheld devices, offers a secure, convenient, and portable tool for online shopping. A digital wallet stores personal and financial information, such as credit card numbers, passwords, and PINs. Digital wallets can be used for micropayments

> **Payment cards—including credit cards, debit cards, charge cards, and smart cards—are the most popular instrument for electronic payment transactions.**

(as discussed later in this section); online shoppers find them useful because personal and financial information does not have to be reentered each time shoppers place an order.

You are probably familiar with **PayPal**, a popular online payment system used on many auction sites. Users with valid e-mail addresses can set up PayPal accounts and make secure payments for online transactions using their credit cards or bank accounts.

Another mobile payment service is Venmo by PayPal. **Venmo** users can transfer funds to others via a mobile app; both the sender and receiver have to live in the United States.

Challenges in Using Mobile Payment Systems

➤ Finance | Technology in Society | Application | Reflective Thinking

Credit and debit cards have some serious shortcomings. They can be lost, hacked, and easily copied. They are difficult to replace. Also, each bank account has its own credit card. Thus, if you have 12 accounts, you might have 12 separate credit cards. Despite these shortcomings, credit cards remain very popular and are used in both e-commerce and traditional commerce. That's because everyone in the credit card industry—banks, stores, and users—agrees on the standards and the interface.

There are many players in the mobile payment environment, and their numbers are increasing. Major players include PayPal, Venmo, Google, Apple, Square, Facebook, Groupon, Dwolla, and LevelUp. Mobile carriers and credit card companies are also involved in mobile payments.

The following are among the main challenges that must be overcome to make mobile payment a mainstream payment system:[40,41]

- Overcoming security concerns
- Offering special incentives, similar to those offered by credit cards
- Resolving issues related to international transactions
- Resolving issues related to multicurrency and payment methods
- Improving user adoption of mobile payment methods

Questions and Discussions

1. Who are the top four players in mobile payment systems?
2. What are the top three challenges that must be overcome to make mobile payment a mainstream payment system? Discuss.

Apple Pay is a mobile payment service that works based on NFC (near field communication) technology. Customers can use their iPhones, Apple Watches, or iPads to pay for products and services in online or brick-and-mortar businesses that accept Apple Pay.

Google Pay is another popular payment system that enables users to purchase products and services using Android-compatible devices with an NFC chip. Some of its features include the following:[42]

- Supports major banks in the United States and many other countries
- Integrates with major mobile banking apps
- Allows in-store as well as in-app online payments
- Allows users to save mobile tickets, passes for shows, and boarding passes
- Provides multiple layers of security
- Allows users to request cash in the app or to send money to others
- Allows users to transfer money to their bank accounts instantly

Micropayments are transactions on the Web that involve very small amounts of money. They began as a way for advertisers to pay for costs per view or costs per click; a typical cost is one-tenth of a cent. Such fractional amounts are difficult to handle with traditional currency methods, and electronic micropayments reduce handling costs for financial institutions. Payment amounts are accumulated for customers until they are large enough to offset the transaction fee, and then the account deduction or charge is submitted to the bank. Of course, micropayment systems charge a fee for tracking and processing transactions. PayPal is an example of a payment system that offers services for micropayment transactions.

The information box titled "Challenges in Using Mobile Payment Systems" highlights some of the challenges of using mobile payment systems.

8-6b Digital Marketing

Digital marketing is any form of marketing deployed on digital channels, devices, or platforms to promote a product or service. This may include the Internet, social media, search engines, SMS, text ads, digital billboards, e-mail, and video marketing. A large portion of digital marketing is Web marketing.

Web marketing uses the Web and its supporting technologies to promote goods and services. Web marketing is the same as Internet marketing or online marketing.

Although traditional media such as radio and TV are still used for marketing, the Web offers many unique capabilities. To better understand Web marketing, review the following list of terms:

- *Ad impression*—This refers to one user viewing one ad.
- *Banner ads*—Usually placed on frequently visited Web sites, these ads are rather small (around 468 × 60 pixels) and employ simple animation. Clicking a banner ad displays a short marketing message or transfers the user to another Web site.
- *Click*—When users click URLs or banner ads, they are transferred to other Web sites or shown marketing messages, and this is recorded by the Web server. For example, each time a certain keyword used for a search takes a user to a particular Web page, the advertiser who owns that site pays the search engine a cost per click (discussed later in this list). A consortium of Yahoo!, Microsoft, Google, and the Interactive Advertising Bureau has formed the Click Measurement Working Group, which is trying to define what a "legal and valid" click should be.
- *Click-through rate (CTR)*—This is computed by dividing the number of clicks an ad gets by the total impressions bought. For example, if an advertiser buys 100,000 impressions and gets 20,000 clicks, the CTR is 20 percent (20,000/100,000).
- *Cookie*—This is information a Web site stores on the user's hard drive so it can be used for a later visit. For example, a cookie can help a Web site greet a returning visitor by name. This information is also used to record user preferences and browsing habits.
- *Cost per click (CPC)*—This refers to the cost of each click on an ad. For example, $1.25 CPC means that for every click an advertiser gets, the advertiser pays $1.25 to the sponsoring Web site. MIVA (*www.miva.com*) is an example of a cost-per-click network.
- *Cost per thousand (CPM)*—Most Web and e-mail advertising is priced based on the cost per

> **Micropayments** are transactions on the Web involving very small amounts of money. They began as a method for advertisers to pay for costs per view or costs per click.
>
> **Digital marketing** is any form of marketing deployed on digital channels, devices, or platforms to promote a product or service.
>
> **Web marketing** uses the Web and its supporting technologies to promote goods and services.

thousand ad impressions. (*M* stands for *mille*, which means "thousand.") For example, a $125 CPM means it costs $125 for 1,000 ad impressions.

- *Hit*—Any element of a Web page (including text, graphics, and interactive items) that is clicked counts as a hit to a server. Hits are not the preferred unit of measurement for site traffic because the number of hits per page can vary widely, depending on the number of graphics, type of browser used, and page size.

- *Meta tag*—This HTML tag does not affect how a Web page is displayed; it simply provides information about a Web page, such as keywords that represent the page content, the Web designer, and frequency of page updates. Search engines use this information (particularly keywords) to create indexes.

- *Page view (PV)*—This refers to one user viewing one Web page.

- *Pop-up ads*—These display ads appear on top of a browser window, blocking the user's view.

- *Pop-under ads*—These display ads appear underneath a browser window. They are less intrusive than pop-up ads.

- *Splash screen*—A Web page displayed when the user first visits the site; it is designed to capture the user's attention and motivate the user to browse the site. The splash screen may display the company's logo as well as a message about any requirements for viewing the site, such as the need to install plug-ins.

- *Spot leasing*—Search engines and directories offer space that companies can purchase for advertising purposes. Spots have an advantage over banner ads because their placement is permanent; banner ad placement can change from visit to visit. However, spots can be more expensive than banner ads, especially on high-traffic sites such as Yahoo!.

Intelligent agents (discussed in Module 13) and push technology (discussed in Module 14) are also used as Web-marketing tools. Intelligent agents are artificial intelligence applications that can be used for Web marketing. For example, product-brokering agents can alert customers about a new product. Push technology is the opposite of pull technology, in which users search the

iStock.com/solidcolours

Web to find (pull) information. With push technology, information is sent to users based on their previous inquiries, interests, or specifications. This technology can be used to send and update marketing information, product and price lists, and product updates. The "Challenges in Using Digital Ads" box discusses some of the challenges of using digital ads.

8-6c Mobile Marketing

According to a recent survey, approximately 60 percent of Internet access is through mobile devices,[43] such as smartphones and tablets. Online businesses should have a mobile marketing strategy in order to stay competitive. Popular mobile marketing strategies include the following:[44]

1. App-based marketing: This strategy uses mobile apps, but an online business does not necessarily need to develop its own app. Services such as Google AdMob assist advertisers in creating mobile ads that appear within third-party mobile apps. Facebook helps advertisers create mobile ads that can be integrated with Facebook's mobile apps. Facebook's mobile Promoted Post ads integrate with Facebook's news feeds, which is a powerful method to get the word out.

2. In-game mobile marketing: This strategy uses mobile ads that appear within popular mobile games and can take several forms—such as banner pop-ups, full-page image ads, or video ads—that appear between loading screens.

3. Location-based marketing: This strategy uses ads that appear on mobile devices based on the location of a user relative to a specific business location (such as within a two-mile radius of a business).

4. QR codes (quick response codes, discussed in Module 11): This strategy allows a user to scan a QR code; the user is then transferred to a Web site that displays a marketing message for a product or service.

5. Mobile search ads: This strategy uses basic search engine ads, such as those from Google or Bing, that are designed for mobile devices. These ads usually include additional features such as "click-to-call" or "click for maps."

6. Mobile image ads: This strategy uses image-based ads, such as banners, that appear on mobile devices. Because of screen size limitations, these images must be specifically designed for mobile devices.

7. SMS (Short Message Service) and MMS (Multimedia Messaging Service): Use this strategy to send short messages with offers to mobile device users.

SMS only uses text, while MMS uses multimedia that combines text, sound, and video.

8-6d Search Engine Optimization

Search engine optimization (SEO) is a method for improving the volume or quality of traffic to a Web site. It helps a Web site receive a high ranking in search results, which tends to generate more revenue for the Web site. For the average keyword used in a search, a search engine might list hundreds or thousands of Web sites, but most people visit only the top 5 or 10 sites and ignore the rest. Therefore, it is important to be among the top sites.

A comprehensive Web marketing campaign should use a variety of methods, and SEO is another method that can help improve business. Some companies offer SEO services. Unlike Web-marketing methods that involve

> **Search engine optimization (SEO)** is a method for improving the volume or quality of traffic to a Web site. A higher ranking in search results should generate more revenue for a Web site.

Mobile Marketing at Starbucks

➤➤ Finance | Technology in Society | Application | Reflective Thinking

Starbucks has been using mobile technology since 2007, from mobile payment to mobile ordering. According to Adam Brotman, the chief digital officer who oversees digital strategy for over 29,000 retail locations in 76 countries, mobile technology is a part of the company's overall digital strategy. Starbucks integrates mobile technology, the Internet, and social media to engage with its customers and improve customer relationships. Digital technology is used to reach out to customers through targeted communications.[45,46]

Mobile messaging marketing (SMS and MMS) allows Starbucks to communicate with customers and generate sales. One of Starbucks' most popular marketing applications is its commerce app, which allows customers to earn rewards and pay for items purchased through their mobile devices.

Kritchanut/Shutterstock.com

Questions and Discussions

1. What is the function of the mobile app at Starbucks?
2. How does Starbucks use mobile messaging marketing?

Challenges in Using Digital Ads

➤➤➤ Finance | Technology in Society | Social and Ethical Issues | Social Responsibility

Advertisers lose billions of dollars every year as a result of phony traffic to Web sites. Phony traffic is created by bots that are controlled by hijacked PCs around the world. As of 2022, approximately 38 percent of Web traffic was automated and driven by bots.[47]

As an example, one study indicates that as many as 48 million Twitter accounts may not be run by humans! Many of the "likes," "retweets," and "followers" in your Twitter account may be generated by bots.[48]

Songsrpeople.com is an example of a Web site that generates most of its traffic by bots, according to the security firm White Ops. Interestingly enough, major corporations such as Target, Amazon, and State Farm have display ads on the site. However, most of the visitors to the Web site are not human; they are computer-generated. Bots mislead advertisers, creating the impression that a Web site receives lots of traffic, which allows the site to charge advertisers more for putting ads there. Some bots are so sophisticated that they can mimic a human shopper by clicking from one site to another, "watching" videos, or even adding items to shopping carts. There are thousands of these sites on the Internet, according to government authorities and Internet security experts, who are trying to identify the sites and put them on a blacklist. In the meantime, advertisers need to distinguish legitimate traffic from phony traffic before investing in digital ads.[49]

Questions and Discussions

1. What are two challenges in using digital ads?
2. How do bots mislead advertisers?

---

paying for listings on search engines, SEO aims at increasing a Web site's performance on search engines in a natural (and free) fashion. As you learned in Module 7, a typical search engine such as Google or Bing uses a crawler or spider to find a Web site and then, based on the site's contents and relevance, indexes it and gives it a ranking. Optimizing a Web site involves editing a site's contents and HTML code to increase its relevance to specific keywords. SEO includes techniques that make it easier for search engines to find and index a site for certain keywords. The following are some common ways to optimize a Web site's traffic:

- *Keywords*—Decide on a few keywords that best describe the Web site and use them consistently throughout the site's contents.

- *Page title*—Make sure the page title reflects the site and its contents accurately.

- *Inbound links*—Get people to comment on your Web site, using one of your top keywords.

- *Content*—Update your Web content regularly.

- *Links to others*—Develop relationships with other Web sites.

8-7 E-Commerce and Beyond: Social Commerce

As of October 2021, more than 4.5 billion consumers were using social networks such as TikTok, Facebook, Instagram, Twitter, Pinterest, and Tumblr, and this number increases daily.[50] Users of these social networks influence the purchasing decisions of many customers by recommending certain products or services to their friends. Some social networks also provide links that enable users to buy products and services directly. According to Gartner, 74 percent of consumers rely on social networks to guide their purchasing decisions.[51] Peer-to-peer Web sites such as eBay have enabled people to communicate with each other and conduct e-commerce operations.

Social media, by providing a community of people with similar interests, is all about insight and product discovery. Web sites like Pinterest and Wanelo are similar to virtual malls and digital catalogs; customers are able to browse and connect with others who have similar interests.[52]

What is social commerce (s-commerce)? Several definitions are offered by different online sites and e-commerce experts.[53,54] For the purposes of this book, we define **social commerce** as a subset of e-commerce that is influenced by social networks and other online media and enhanced by the ever-increasing power of smartphones.

Several categories of social networks and online media collectively constitute social commerce.[55]

1. Social networking sites: Users of these sites recommend a product or service to a friend, or the site offers a direct link for shopping, such as the Shop tab on Facebook or the Buy button on Twitter.[56] In 2015, Google announced "Purchases On Google," the equivalent of Buy buttons that enabled consumers to buy products directly from mobile search ads.[57,58] In 2015, Pinterest announced Buyable Pins. When users see a Pin with a blue price, they can buy the product directly within Pinterest using a mobile device.[59] Pinterest's image-search capability makes it easier to find a product for purchase. In 2016, Pinterest introduced two new features that further enhanced its s-commerce capabilities. First, users can search for products with their smartphone cameras. They can use the Pinterest search feature and tap the visual search button on any item they like, and Pinterest will automatically do a visual search for it.[60] Second, a user can click on an image inside a Pinterest page to have Pinterest search its archives for matches. Users can even filter their visual search results by topic to find exactly what they are looking for.[61] Selling on Instagram is now possible with checkout; this feature allows shoppers to pay for items directly in posts.[62]

2. Group buying platforms: These Web sites offer a product or service at a huge discount if a certain number of customers agree to buy the product or service in a given time period, such as within 24 hours. Popular examples include Groupon and LivingSocial.

3. Peer-to-peer e-commerce platforms: These Web sites are community-based marketplaces that enable customers to communicate directly with each other and conduct e-commerce operations. Popular examples include Amazon Marketplace and Etsy.

4. Recommendation Web sites: These Web sites aggregate customers' opinions related to products or services they have purchased and then recommend them to other customers with the same interests. Some also offer incentives to customers for sharing details about their purchases with friends through social media. Popular examples include TripAdvisor and Yelp.

5. Participatory e-commerce: These Web sites allow users to participate in the production process and bring a product or service to the sites in a collaborative fashion. Popular examples include CutOnYour-Bias and Kickstarter.

6. Social advice: These Web sites provide shopping advice and opinions through chats and forums. Popular examples include GoTryItOn and eBags.

7. User-curated shopping: These Web sites provide a platform for users to create products and generate listings of products that others can choose from. Popular examples include Lyst, Farfetch, and Shopstyle.

> **Social commerce** is a subset of e-commerce that is influenced by social networks and other online media.

Social Commerce at Coca-Cola Company

▶▶ Finance | Technology in Society | Application | Reflective Thinking | Global

While Coke already has one of the most recognizable names in the business world, the company still aims to enhance its position in the marketplace. A recent campaign focused on product personalization. For the first time in its history, Coke printed 250 of the most popular first names in each country on its Coke bottle labels, instead of the actual Coke logo. Coke then used mass media such as television, radio, and social media to communicate to customers that their favorite drink might have their name on it. Each bottle also included the hashtag #ShareACoke to remind consumers to post pictures of their personalized Coke bottles on social media using the hashtag. The experience of seeing one's own name on a Coke bottle was so different and unique that consumers actually paid higher prices to get one of their "own"

(Continued)

bottles of Coke and then shared their experience on social media. Images of Coke bottles were shared on Instagram, Twitter, and Facebook with the #ShareACoke hashtag and then displayed across digital billboards throughout each country. To enhance its campaign, Coca-Cola created a Web site where consumers could create virtual Coke bottles with the names of their friends and family to be shared on social media. The result of this campaign was millions of posted pictures, thousands of virtual Coke bottles made, and three times more bottles of Coke sold than Pepsi in the United Kingdom during the s-commerce campaign period.[63]

Questions and Discussions

1. How did Coca-Cola Company use social media to promote its Coke campaign?
2. Why was the campaign a success? Discuss.

This module's Industry Connection focuses on Amazon, one of the leaders in e-commerce.

The information box "Social Commerce at Coca-Cola Company" shows how the company is using s-commerce.

8-8 Hypersocial Organizations

Hypersocial organizations are companies that leverage social media to turn their businesses into social processes and better connect with their customers to sell more products and services. Hypersocial organizations share information through many different avenues. The most popular is direct social media interaction, such as Facebook posts, Twitter pages, and Instagram. Hypersocial organizations may also use blogs, podcasts, videos on YouTube, and their own company Web sites.

Social media are perceived by many people around the world as authentic sources of information. The complaints that many customers post on social media are viewed as accurate, even though some of them may have been fabricated. (Consider the customer reviews of restaurants on Yelp, and Amazon's lawsuit against "fake reviewers" in 2015.)[64]

Problem-solving platforms such as YouTube's "how-to" videos are seen as reliable. This reliability factor is proven because if one video does not solve a problem or answer a question, hundreds more

may be able to help. There are many interesting statistics and findings on the role of social media in influencing consumers' purchasing decisions and attracting potential buyers to a business. Below are some statistics and findings published in 2020:[65]

- Social media influences 71 percent of consumer buying decisions.
- Consumers who are influenced by social media are four times more likely to spend more on purchases.
- Marketing by social media influencers is one of the most effective ways to reach your audience.
- The top five social media for social referrals in 2020 were Facebook, Instagram, TikTok, Twitter, and YouTube.
- Social media influence consumer buying decisions in four ways: They shorten a customer's journey, provide social proof, amplify the power of influencers, and provide the influence of "stories."

To stay competitive, organizations need to rethink how they interact with this new interconnected world. Companies must understand the power of social media and use it to their advantage.

Hypersocial organizations leverage the power of online communities. There are four key elements for a successful community: members, content, member profiles, and transactions.[66]

The importance of members is probably the most vital element. The more members a community has, the better it is. Facebook and Twitter are frequently compared to one another, but Facebook is viewed as a more powerful community because of its huge membership. The content in these communities is important as

> **Social media should be integrated into all operations from sales to marketing and for ongoing sustainability.**

Hypersocial organizations are companies that leverage social media to better connect with customers and increase sales through the social process.

well. Organizations need high-quality content to help their communities grow. The member profiles capture key information used to attract new members or increase knowledge about the community.

Finally, there is the transaction element: The more easily a community helps its members engage in a transaction, buy something, or discover information, the more likely it is that they will tell others, which will increase membership. If these four elements are managed properly, organizations can gain a competitive advantage.

Social media have created a huge platform that consumers can use to express opinions about a business, positive or negative. The days in which only companies had a voice regarding their products and services are long gone. Now consumers engage with one another and exchange information. Social media allow hypersociality to scale to the point where it has an impact on organizations. Consumers can get direct recommendations from other consumers instead of getting biased information from companies.

The four pillars of hypersociality describe a return to natural human interactions for businesses and consumers. The four pillars are briefly explained here.

1. Tribe versus market segment: Tribes have their own language and protocols, and their members identify with each other in some way, such as people from different economic and social classes that share the same interest. Companies should forget market segments and focus on tribes, which are based on group behavioral characteristics. (Market segments are based on individual consumer traits.) Companies need to reach tribes with members who influence each other.

2. Human-centric versus company-centric: Human centricity directs all company activities and decisions toward providing value to the people who are a company's customers, employees, or business partners. A hypersocial organization should engage with customers and satisfy their needs directly using social media. Personalization technologies used on Web sites such as Amazon demonstrate this.

3. Information channels versus knowledge channels: Hypersocial organizations should forget information channels and concentrate on knowledge networks. As noted, the majority of customers follow peers on social media. Customers already have some basic knowledge about a company and its products and services and have heard comments from peers in their tribes. Companies should share knowledge and

work to gain trust using social media. Gaining trust in an online world is more challenging than in the traditional world, and social media can play a major role here.

4. Social messiness versus process hierarchy: Hypersocial organizations should forget about process and hierarchies and embrace social messiness. This new paradigm will be less rigid and predefined but will allow people in an organization to interact at a human level. People can make mistakes, but over time, they will correct themselves. This pillar realizes that the benefits of leveraging social media are much greater than its negatives.

A growing number of organizations have adopted the hypersocial organization model. Huffington Post,[67] Airbnb,[68] Martell Home Builders,[69] and *Glamour* magazine[70] are a few examples. The "Hypersocial Organization in Action: Spotify" box describes how Spotify has become a successful hypersocial organization.

8-9 Social Media Information Systems

A **social media information system (SMIS)** includes all the components found in other information systems (discussed in Module 1), such as hardware, software, people, and procedures that support content sharing among its members or users. Three additional components of an SMIS include the following:

Application (app) providers: Social media sites such as Facebook, Twitter, LinkedIn, and Snapchat that create features and functions for the app and make them available for free to their users.

User communities: All the people who use any of the social media apps.

Sponsors: Organizations and businesses that pay money to social media sites to advertise their products and services, such as Walmart, Macy's, and Intel. Organizations and businesses can also use social media sites

> A **social media information system (SMIS)** includes all the components found in other information systems, such as hardware, software, people, and procedures that support content sharing among its members or users.

Hypersocial Organization in Action: Spotify

▶▶ Finance | Technology in Society | Application | Reflective Thinking

Spotify, the world's largest on-demand music service provider, is a Swedish commercial music streaming, podcast, and video service. As of the second quarter of 2021, Spotify had 365 million users, including 165 million paid subscribers worldwide.[71]

In an already crowded and established market, it's rare to see a company with such success and such a fast growth rate. Spotify's hypersocial integration changes the way users listen to music, making for a compelling listening experience that is completely personalized and social.

Spotify uses social media to distribute its content, products, and brands. The main reason this approach has been so successful is that it makes discovering music and sharing with friends very easy. New members can simply sign up using their Facebook user names, which gives them the ability to access their account and save listening preferences from any location. Spotify uses a graph search (discussed in Module 7) to show which friends or family members are already on Spotify and allows users to share a playlist, follow friends' activities, and subscribe to playlists. Additionally, Spotify makes it easy for users to seamlessly share any track or playlist on Facebook or Twitter.

Spotify has successfully established a clear boundary between sharing and privacy. Users can opt in or opt out. Those who want to share music both actively and passively can do so, and those who would rather not share do not have to.[72]

Questions and Discussions

1. For which purpose does Spotify use social media?
2. What are two reasons for Spotify's success?

---

free of charge to promote their products and services and connect with their customers by creating fan pages and publishing FAQs, blogs, and podcasts. Businesses also publish how-to videos and enable certain customers to help each other solve problems. Sponsors usually generate revenue through advertising.

SMISs play a major role in fostering hypersocial organizations (as discussed earlier in the module) by creating communities to transform interactions with users, customers, employees, and business partners into a mutually productive relationship. They also enable communities, tribes, or hives that are related by a common interest. They facilitate business activities such as sales and marketing for sponsors and help sponsors establish bonds and loyalties with their customers.

As of January 2021, there were approximately 4.66 billion worldwide Internet users.[73] At the same time, there were over 4.48 billion active users of social media worldwide.[74] An SMIS could generate the following key information for a business that is properly designing and using such a strategic tool:[75]

- Valuable insights about customers—who they are, where they live, what they like, and how they feel about a brand

- Increased brand awareness and loyalty by connecting with customers and responding to their concerns in real time

- Targeted ads based on location, demographics, and gender with real-time results

- Increased Web site traffic and search ranking—the more social media activities there are, the higher the business's search ranking will be

- Finding out what competitors are doing and making strategic decisions in real time to combat them

- Sharing new and dynamic content with customers in real time
- Building relationships with customers before, during, and after a transaction

Before designing an SMIS, an organization should clearly define its social media policy, and the policy should be clearly explained to all affected employees. Many companies' social media policies are available online; they should be consulted before an organization designs its own policy, which will enable it to implement best practices. In its basic form, an organization's social media policy should do the following:[76]

- Protect the company's reputation.
- Eliminate legal issues.
- Protect the privacy of all impacted individuals.
- Raise brand awareness.

Industry Connection: Amazon[77]

Amazon, a leader in B2C e-commerce, offers a variety of products and services, including books, CDs, videos, games, free e-cards, online auctions, and other shopping services and partnership opportunities. Rarely is there an item that Amazon does not carry! By using customer accounts, shopping carts, and its 1-Click feature, Amazon makes shopping fast and convenient and uses e-mail for order confirmation and customer notifications of new products tailored to customers' shopping habits. In 2019, Amazon introduced one-day delivery to its Prime customers to keep competitors such as Walmart at bay. In addition, Amazon has created an open forum with customers by posting their book and product reviews and allowing them to rate products on a scale of one to five stars. Amazon is also one of the major players in the cloud computing environment. Here are some of the options that customers have on Amazon:

- Search for books, music, and many other products and services.
- Browse in hundreds of product categories, from audio books, jazz, and video documentaries to coins and stamps available for auction.
- Get personalized recommendations based on previous purchases.
- Sign up for an e-mail subscription service to get the latest reviews of new titles in categories of interest.
- Create wish lists that can be saved for later viewing.

- Search the contents of books on specific keywords and view selected pages of some books.

Amazon is known for its personalization system, which is used to recommend goods, and its collaborative filtering, which is used to improve customer service. (Both features are discussed in Module 11.) Amazon also collaborates with business partners via Amazon Marketplace, where other merchants can sell their products. Customers can also use Amazon's Alexa to order products directly through their devices in addition to signing up for a subscription service for certain products.

Module Summary

8-1 Define e-commerce and its advantages, disadvantages, and business models. E-commerce is buying and selling goods and services over the Internet. E-business encompasses all the activities a company performs in selling and buying products and services using computers and communication technologies. Some of the advantages of e-commerce include creating better relationships with suppliers, customers, and business partners and creating "price transparency."

8-2 Explain the major categories of e-commerce. They include C2C, C2B, C2G, B2C, B2B, B2G, G2C, G2B, and G2G.

8-3 Describe the five major activities of the business-to-consumer e-commerce cycle. They include information sharing, ordering, payment, fulfillment, and service and support.

8-4 Summarize the four major models of business-to-business e-commerce. They include seller-side marketplace, buyer-side marketplace, third-party exchange marketplace, and trading partner agreements.

8-5 Describe mobile-based and voice-based e-commerce. Mobile commerce (m-commerce) is the use of handheld devices, such as smartphones or wireless devices, to conduct business transactions. Voice-based e-commerce relies on voice recognition and text-to-speech technologies.

8-6 Explain four supporting technologies for e-commerce. They include electronic payment systems, digital marketing, mobile marketing, and search engine optimization.

8-7 Explain social commerce and the reasons for its popularity. Social commerce is a subset of e-commerce that is influenced by social networks and other online media. More than four billion consumers use social networks such as Facebook, Instagram, Twitter, Pinterest, and Tumblr, and this number increases daily.

8-8 Explain hypersocial organizations and their growing popularity. Hypersocial organizations are companies that leverage social media to turn their businesses into social processes and better connect with their customers to sell more products and services. Hypersocial organizations share information through many different avenues. The most popular is direct social media interaction, such as Facebook posts, Twitter pages, and Instagram.

8-9 Explain social media information systems. A social media information system (SMIS) includes all the components found in other information systems, such as hardware, software, people, and procedures that support content sharing among its members or users. Three additional components of an SMIS include applications (apps), user communities, and sponsors.

Key Terms

- Advertising model
- Brokerage model
- Business-to-business (B2B)
- Business-to-consumer (B2C)
- Buyer-side marketplace
- Click-and-brick e-commerce
- Consumer-to-business (C2B)
- Consumer-to-consumer (C2C)
- Conversational commerce
- Cross-channel
- Digital marketing
- Digital wallet
- E-business
- E-cash
- E-check
- E-commerce
- E-government (or just "e-gov")
- Electronic payment
- E-procurement
- Horizontal market
- Hypersocial organizations
- Infomediary model

- Merchant model
- Micropayments
- Mixed model
- Mobile commerce (m-commerce)
- Multichannel
- Omnichannel
- Organizational (intrabusiness) e-commerce
- PayPal
- Search engine optimization (SEO)
- Seller-side marketplace
- Smart cards
- Social commerce
- Social media information system (SMIS)
- Subscription model
- Third-party exchange marketplace
- Trading partner agreements
- Value chain
- Venmo
- Vertical market
- Voice-based e-commerce
- Web marketing

Reviews and Discussions

1. List two advantages and two disadvantages of e-commerce.
2. What are the nine categories of e-commerce?
3. Provide an example of five activities of the business-to-consumer e-commerce cycle.
4. Explain four major models of business-to-business e-commerce.
5. What are two advantages of mobile-based and voice-based e-commerce?
6. What is search engine optimization (SEO)? How can an e-commerce business benefit from SEO?
7. What is social commerce? What are two reasons for its growing popularity?
8. What are the four pillars of hypersociality? Discuss.

Projects

1. Local, state, and federal government agencies are establishing e-gov sites to improve the efficiency and effectiveness of their operations. After reading the information presented in this module and other sources, write a one-page paper that summarizes six advantages of using e-gov applications for running a city. What are some of the challenges?

2. Yelp is a successful social networking site. After reading the information presented in this module and other sources, write a one-page paper that describes the business model used by Yelp. How does Yelp generate revenue? How can businesses benefit from this social networking site? Who are the top two competitors of Yelp? What are a couple of challenges for running a social media site such as Yelp?

3. Twitter is a very popular social networking site both for personal and business use. After reading the information presented in this module and other sources, write a one-page paper that summarizes five ways a business can use Twitter to increase its revenue. What does "trending" mean on Twitter? What are promoted tweets?

4. A Mediterranean restaurant chain with more than 25 locations in Southern California is trying to expand its operations. After reading the information presented in this module and other sources, write a two-page paper that outlines a mobile marketing program for this company. What are three mobile marketing strategies that you recommend? What are the bases of your recommendations for reaching the largest number of potential customers at a moderate cost?

5. Multichannel, cross-channel, and omnichannel are being used increasingly by all types of businesses. After reading the information presented in this module and other sources, write a two-page paper that compares and contrasts these three strategies. Provide one advantage and one disadvantage of each strategy. Also provide examples of three companies that are using each strategy. Why is omnichannel being adopted by a growing number of companies? Discuss. What is the role of conversational commerce in this strategy?

6. The hypersocial model is gaining popularity. After reading the information in this module and other sources, write a two-page paper that lists four organizations you consider to be hypersocial. What are the bases of your classification? What are two factors that make an organization hypersocial? What are two advantages of a hypersocial organization compared to a traditional model?

Module Quiz

1. Webrooming occurs when consumers physically inspect a product in a store to get a look and feel for it—and then buy it from an online store because it is cheaper to do so. True or False?

2. The merchant model transfers the old retail model to the e-commerce world by using the medium of the Internet. True or False?

3. Access through mobile devices is a feature of a successful government Web site. True or False?

4. All of the following are components of a social media information system except:
   a. Application (app) providers
   b. Sponsors
   c. User communities
   d. All of these options

5. All of the following could further expand voice-based e-commerce except:
   a. Alexa (Amazon)
   b. Cortana (Microsoft)
   c. Firefox (Mozilla)
   d. Assistant (Google)

6. All of the following are popular mobile marketing strategies except:
   a. App-based marketing
   b. In-game mobile marketing
   c. Location-based marketing
   d. Customer-based marketing

Case Study 8-1
Widespread Applications of Mobile Ads
⟫ **Finance | Technology in Society | Application | Reflective Thinking | Global**

In 2017, mobile advertising expenditures in the United States were $60.7 billion. They are expected to reach over $138 billion by 2025. The United States is expected to remain the largest regional ad market, closely followed by China, the United Kingdom, Japan, and Germany.[78,79,80]

Businesses are increasingly using mobile ads. Location data from mobile devices is the key element for a successful mobile ad campaign. Facebook and Google are the two biggest players that generate the highest revenue from mobile ads. PlaceIQ, a technology firm headquartered in New York City (*https://www.placeiq.com/who-we-are/*), collects billions of data points from mobile devices and other sources and can track potential customers as they move from one retail location to another—such as between car dealerships. PlaceIQ can also help businesses find out if mobile ads can translate to an actual visit by a customer. In addition to its huge data set for business, PlaceIQ offers location data and analytics tools to businesses and allows them to do their own advertising.

Audi is using PlaceIQ data to measure how many potential customers will visit its dealerships before and after they have seen ads. Audi also wants to target potential customers who are visiting their competitors' showrooms. Starcom Media Group is using PlaceIQ to find out how mobile location data can be helpful and eventually attract more customers to a business.[81]

Julius Kielaitis/Shutterstock.com

Answer the following questions:
1. What does PlaceIQ do for businesses?
2. How can PlaceIQ data be used for omnichannel e-commerce? Explain.
3. What privacy concerns might consumers have about PlaceIQ's business model?
4. How is Audi using PlaceIQ services to inform its e-commerce strategy?

Case Study 8-2
Bridging the Gap between E-Commerce and Traditional Commerce

▶ Finance | Technology in Society | Application | Reflective Thinking

Tools and technologies such as mobile devices and social media are helping to bridge the gap between e-commerce and traditional commerce. Potential buyers often see what their social networking friends have to say about products before making a purchase. Transparency is the key, given that buyers can now compare prices from nearly anywhere—including from a physical store.

Ken Wolter/Shutterstock.com

New sets of technologies are being introduced that track customers when they are inside a store. Apple's iBeacon, which competes with near field communication (NFC), is one such technology. It is a small wireless device that uses Bluetooth to detect and communicate with iPhones and iPads that run iOS7 and beyond.[82] A GPS guides a customer to a store; iBeacon then tracks the customer inside the store. (Qualcomm has developed its own version of iBeacon, Gimbal proximity beacons, which work with either iOS or Android.)

There are many potential applications of this technology. For example, a retailer can send a coupon as soon as it detects that a customer has walked to a particular aisle and is looking at a particular product. In Apple stores, as soon as a customer walks by the iPhone table, the customer gets a notification about upgrades. Major League Baseball has announced that it will use iBeacon to customize fans' experiences at ballparks through its "At the Ballpark" app. Some businesses are using iPads as cash registers; these customers can potentially be tracked by Apple. Given Apple's huge user base, this technology has potential for tremendous growth.[83,84]

Privacy issues may be a concern as these tools roll out, given that customers will be tracked in stores that are equipped with this technology. However, customers may not mind this tracking as long as there is something in it for them.

Neiman Marcus is one of the latest retailers to test Bluetooth beacons to guide customers to in-store sales. Additionally, it wants to merge the online and in-store shopping experience—"clicks to bricks" or "bricks to clicks," as it is called in the industry. The app knows if a customer who has browsed the retailer Web site will be guided to the right item in the store.[85]

Amazon Go, a cashier-less grocery store, has completely automated the grocery shopping experience. By doing so, it has taken customer tracking to a new level, among other things!

Answer the following questions:

1. What is the function of Apple's iBeacon?
2. What are the differences between iBeacon and GPS?
3. How might a retail business benefit from iBeacon?
4. What are some concerns that customers may have about this technology?

Module

9

Global Information Systems

Learning Objectives

After studying this module, you should be able to…

9.1 Discuss the reasons for globalization and for using global information systems, including e-business and Internet growth.

9.2 Describe global information systems and their requirements and components.

9.3 Explain the four types of organizational structures used with global information systems.

9.4 Examine five obstacles to using global information systems.

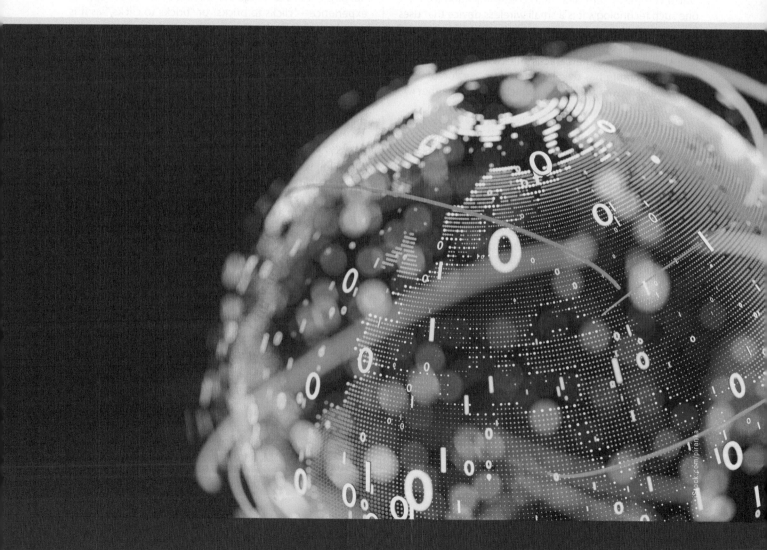

In this module, you review the reasons that organizations should go global and adopt global information systems. These reasons include the rise in e-business and the growth of the Internet. Global information systems are a growing application of telecommunications and networking; you learn the requirements and components of these systems as well as the types of organizational structures used with global information systems. Offshore outsourcing, as one beneficiary of global information systems, is also discussed. Finally, you explore some obstacles to using global information systems.

9-1 Why Go Global?

The global economy is creating customers who demand integrated worldwide services, and the expansion of global markets is a major factor in developing global information systems to handle these integrated services. To understand the need for integrated worldwide services, consider the example of a U.S.-based shoe company that procures leather in Italy and has the upper parts of its shoes produced there because of the high quality of leather and the expertise in shoe stitching available. The uppers are then shipped to China, where they are attached to soles; the company thereby takes advantage of the inexpensive manufacturing labor available in that country. The shoes are then shipped to Ireland for testing because of Ireland's high concentration of high-tech facilities. Finally, the shoes are shipped to a variety of retail outlets in the United States, where they are sold. The entire supply-chain logistics—from Italy to China to Ireland—must be managed and coordinated from the company's U.S. headquarters. This example shows why companies choose other countries for different manufacturing processes and how important integration is in making sure all these processes are coordinated.[1]

Many companies have become international. For example, in 2021, McDonald's reported revenues of approximately $8.71 billion in the United States. In the same period, its international revenue was $12.09 billion. In other words, more than 58 percent of its total revenue came from outside the United States.[2] According

> The growing trend toward global customers and products means globalization has also become an important factor in purchasing and the supply chain.

to Bespoke Investment Group in 2017, U.S. stocks that got 50 percent of their revenues from overseas were up by more than 19 percent versus U.S. companies that got 90 percent of their revenues within the United States. The stocks of the companies in the latter group were up only by 4.5 percent.[3]

Major corporations, such as Procter & Gamble, IBM, HP, McDonald's, Unilever, Nestlé, and Motorola, have been prime users of global information systems. Because today's multinational corporations operate in a variety of markets and cultures, a clear understanding of factors such as customs, laws, technological issues, and local business needs and practices is a prerequisite to the success of a global information system.

Airline reservation systems are considered the first large-scale interactive global system; hotels, rental car companies, and credit card services also now require worldwide databases to serve their customers more efficiently and effectively.[4] Global products, which are products or services that have been standardized for all markets, are becoming increasingly important in international marketing efforts. In addition, a manufacturer might "regionalize" operations—that is, move them to another country—because of advantages available in certain regions. For example, raw materials might be less expensive in Indonesia than in Singapore, and specialized skills needed for production might be available in India but not in Brazil.

The growing trend toward global customers and products means globalization has also become an important factor in purchasing and the supply chain. Worldwide purchasing gives suppliers the incentive to consider foreign competition as well as domestic competition. Furthermore, large global organizations can reduce costs in purchasing, manufacturing, and distribution because they have access to cheaper labor and can sell products and services locally as well as internationally.[5,6] The "Global Information Systems at Rohm & Haas" box highlights the use of global information systems at Rohm & Haas.

9-1a E-Business: A Driving Force

E-business is a major factor in the widespread use of global information systems. As discussed in Module 8, e-business includes transactions that support revenue generation as well as those that focus on buying and selling goods and services. These revenue-generating transactions include creating demand for goods and services, offering sales support and customer service, and facilitating communication between business partners. An effective global information system can support all these activities.

E-business builds on the advantages and structures of traditional business by adding the flexibility that networks offer. By generating and delivering timely and relevant information supported by networks, e-business creates new opportunities for conducting commercial activities. For example, by using online information for commercial activities, e-business makes it easier for different groups to cooperate. Branches of a multinational company can share information to plan a new marketing campaign, different companies can work together to design new products or

offer new services, and businesses can share information with customers to improve customer relations.

The Internet can simplify communication, improve business relationships, and offer new opportunities to both consumers and businesses. As e-business matures and more companies conduct business online, consumers can engage in comparison shopping more easily, for example. Even though direct buyer–seller communication has increased, there are still new opportunities for intermediaries. For example, some businesses can become intermediaries or brokers to track special markets, notify clients of bargains or changes in market conditions, locate hard-to-find items, and even conduct searches for special products on clients' behalf.

Of course, it is the Internet that makes e-business possible. Small companies have discovered they can not only conduct business online just as large companies do, but they can also lower costs by using the Internet to replace internal networks. The following section discusses the Internet's growth, which has contributed to the increase in e-business.

9-1b Growth of the Internet

Today, the Internet is a part of daily life in most parts of the world. According to the Miniwatts Marketing Group, which tracked the worldwide growth of the Internet from 2000 to 2021, the highest growth has occurred in Africa and the lowest has been in North America. As of March 2021, there were approximately 5.17 billion

Global Information Systems at Rohm & Haas

▶▶ Finance | Technology in Society | Application | Reflective Thinking | Global

Rohm & Haas, part of Dow Chemical, has production units in many countries. In the past, the sites in each country operated independently and had their own inventory systems. A major problem with this setup was that a particular site might not be able to supply customers with the products they wanted. For example, if the site in France reported to customers that it was out of a certain product, it did not have an easy way to check whether the site in Germany, only 20 miles away, had a supply of the same product. To solve these problems, Rohm & Haas overhauled its global information system by upgrading the order entry system and installing a company-wide materials management system. These systems were tied in with a global demand planning system. Rohm & Haas can now provide better service to its customers and ship products from other sites as quickly as needed. These improvements have given Rohm & Haas more of a competitive advantage in the global marketplace.[7]

Questions and Discussions

1. How did Rohm & Haas solve the problems with its order entry system?
2. What is the main advantage of the new system at Rohm & Haas?

worldwide Internet users: Asia with 2.76 billion, Europe with 738 million, Latin America and the Caribbean with 498 million, Africa with 594 million, North America with 348 million, the Middle East with 199 million, and Oceania/Australia with 30 million.[8]

With the explosive growth of the Internet and e-commerce, businesses that are active in the global market should make their Web sites more appealing to global customers. Some companies create separate Web sites for each country in which they do business.

This is called "localization of a Web site." When using localization, the company's main Web site needs to make a clear and specific reference to its additional Web sites, preferably through drop-down menus. Still, some global customers may only use the main Web site. The information box "Making a Company Web Site Global" offers some practical suggestions. The "Global Internet: Presents a Huge Payoff for Global E-commerce" box highlights the potential of global e-commerce.

Making a Company Web Site Global

➤➤ Finance | Technology in Society | Application | Reflective Thinking | Global

Here are some suggestions for making a company Web site global:[9]

Rawpixel.com/Shutterstock.com

- *Language*—Present your Web site in one of the seven most-used languages: English, French, Italian, German, Spanish, Japanese, or Chinese.

- *Font*—Make sure the Web site's main features are readable in different languages, depending on which font is selected.

- *Cultural differences*—Keep cultural variation in mind. For example, although white is the color of purity in the United States, it is the color of mourning in Eastern cultures. Also, a woman smiling without covering her mouth would be considered sexually suggestive in Japan.

- *Currency*—Make sure the Web site includes a currency conversion feature.

- *Date format*—This varies around the world. Many countries use the day/month/year format instead of month/day/year.

- *Spare use of graphics and flash features*—Because of bandwidth limitations in many parts of the world, you may want to keep the Web site rather simple.

- *E-mail*—Be prepared to send and receive e-mails in foreign languages.

- *Payments*—Not everybody uses credit cards. In Germany, for example, bank transfers are popular, whereas in Japan, both cash on delivery (COD) and bank transfers are popular.

- *International logistics*—To ship internationally, you must address the various regulations that pertain to each country.

- *International listing*—List your Web site with international search engines and indexes.

- *Local involvement*—Invite local people to review the Web site before you launch it to the global market.

- *International marketing*—Promote your Web site in specific languages.

Questions and Discussions

1. What are three recommendations for making a company's Web site global? What challenges might a company face when transitioning to a global Web site?

2. What are two benefits that a company may receive from its global Web site?

Global Internet: Presents a Huge Payoff for Global E-commerce

⫸ Finance | Technology in Society | Reflective Thinking | Global

As of 2021, nearly 5.17 billion people throughout the world have access to the Internet. Connecting all these people to the Web presents significant business opportunities, among other things. Amazon's Project Kuiper is planning to put 3,236 satellites into orbit to provide high-speed Internet to any point on the globe. Four other companies are building and launching high-speed Internet satellites in addition to Amazon, including Elon Musk's SpaceX, OneWeb (backed by SoftBank), Telesat, and Boeing. According to ARK Invest analyst Sam Korus, if everyone gets connected to the Internet, the total addressable market for e-commerce nearly doubles and companies such as Amazon will gain significant benefits. Among all the key players, Amazon has a clear competitive advantage because of its initial satellite foundation for Amazon Web Services and its ability to bundle Internet access with other offerings over a standalone Internet broadband network.[10]

The total cost of the Amazon project is not yet known, but it is estimated to be over $3 billion, or $1 million per satellite. There are also technical challenges for connecting remote African or Alaskan villages. Ground infrastructure is needed for a real-time connection. Amazon will build 12 satellite facilities around the world to provide the vital link needed to transmit data to and from satellites in orbit.[11]

Questions and Discussions

1. What is the potential for global e-commerce if Amazon's Project Kuiper gets implemented?
2. What other companies are building and launching high-speed Internet satellites? What is driving these companies to make such a massive investment?

9-1c The Rise of Non-English Speakers on the Internet

The number of non-English speakers on the Internet is on the rise. As of January 2021, the top 10 languages on the Internet were English, Chinese, Spanish, Arabic, Portuguese, Indonesian/Malaysian, Japanese, Russian, French, and German. These languages represent about 77 percent of the world's Internet users.[12]

More content is also being developed in other languages. As of September 2021, about 61 percent of the Internet's content was in English, but this number will likely change as other languages gain in popularity online.[13]

As of 2021, India, the second most populated country in the world with nearly 1.39 billion people, had about 624 million Internet users, 448 million social media users, and 1.10 billion mobile connections.[14]

This growing diversity of language on the Internet, both for developing content and a greater number of users, offers great opportunities and some challenges for global companies. Global companies must respond by offering content in multiple languages and making Web sites accessible in multiple languages. See the "Making a Company Web Site Global" box.

cybrain/Shutterstock.com

9-1d Mobile Computing and Globalization

Mobile computing and mobile apps play a major role in further globalization and in bringing more people online. Because many economically developing nations do not have an established communication network in place, mobile networks are an attractive alternative for these countries.

In Vietnam, with a population of 98 million people, Internet penetration was 73 percent in 2022 and there were 156 million cellular mobile connections.[15] In Indonesia, with a population of 277 million people, Internet penetration was 73 percent in 2022 and there were 370 million cellular mobile connections.[16]

Mobile apps play a major role in globalization by offering basic social services and commerce such as banking, payment, and agricultural information for economically developing nations.

Below are some examples of apps that are bringing more people online throughout the world:[17]

- M-Pesa: A mobile-payment service in Africa started in 2007 by Safaricom, a Kenyan subsidiary of Vodafone Group PLC, this app offers basic banking functions to more than 28.3 million users as of 2021.[18]

- SoukTel: Based in the Middle East, this app offers information about jobs and social services. Its job-matching feature uses text messages to communicate with job seekers in Jordan, Rwanda, Tunisia, and other countries.

- Esoko: Based in Ghana, Esoko is a type of social networking site for farmers. Using text messaging, it sends weather alerts, product price information, and ads.

- Frogtek: Based in Latin America, this app helps small retailers in economically developing nations to track inventory and sales using mobile devices such as smartphones and tablets.

- Ver Se' Innovation: Based in Bengaluru (formerly Bangalore), India, this app offers classified ads related to jobs and properties and uses iPay as an electronic payment system.

9-2 Global Information Systems: An Overview

A **global information system (GIS)** works across national borders, facilitates communication between headquarters and subsidiaries in other countries, and incorporates all the technologies and applications found in a typical information system to gather, store, manipulate, and transmit data across cultural and geographic boundaries.[19] In other words, a GIS is an information system for managing global operations, supporting an international company's decision-making processes, and dealing with complex variables in global operations and decision making.

> A **global information system (GIS)** works across national borders, facilitates communication between headquarters and subsidiaries in other countries, and incorporates all the technologies and applications found in a typical information system to gather, store, manipulate, and transmit data across cultural and geographic boundaries.

With a GIS in place, an international company can increase control over its subsidiaries and better coordinate their activities, thereby gaining access to new global markets.[20] Strategic planning is also a core function of a GIS. By being able to efficiently share information among subsidiaries, international companies can track performance, production schedules, shipping alternatives, and accounting items.

A GIS can be defined along two dimensions: control and coordination. Control consists of using managerial power to ensure adherence to the organization's goals. Coordination is the process of managing interaction among activities in different, specialized parts of an organization. Control requires a centralized architecture for data, standardized definitions used across the organization, standard formats for reports, defined behaviors for different processes (such as how to respond when a customer has a complaint), and performance-tracking systems. Coordination requires a decentralized architecture for data, standardization within departments, the ability to communicate these standards to other departments, collaboration systems, and technologies that support informal communication and socialization. The trade-off between the amount of control needed and the amount of coordination needed defines the organization's globalization strategy. Global organizations may use a combination of high control and high coordination, high control and low coordination, low control and high coordination, or low control and low coordination.[21]

> With a GIS in place, an international company can increase control over its subsidiaries and better coordinate their activities, thereby gaining access to new global markets.

High coordination has the following advantages:[22]

- Flexibility in responding to competitors in different countries and markets
- The ability to respond in one country to a change in another country
- The ability to maintain control of market needs around the world
- The ability to share and transfer knowledge between departments and international branches
- Increased efficiency and effectiveness in meeting customers' needs
- Reduced operational costs

9-2a Components of a Global Information System

Although a GIS can vary quite a bit depending on a company's size and business needs, most GISs have two basic components: (1) a global database and (2) information-sharing technologies.

Global Database

Designing and implementing a global database is a technical challenge, mainly because of the different character sets required for the names of people and places and the different formats required for phone numbers and postal codes. Currency conversion is also a challenge in database development, although some software is available for this task. For example, the software corporation SAP offers valuable features and capabilities for GISs.

Information-Sharing Technologies

International companies can use a variety of technologies for an integrated GIS. Small companies might outsource to take advantage of expertise that is not available inside their organizations. On the other hand, large companies with the resources and technical expertise might develop custom applications to be shared across borders. Depending on the system's use, a GIS might consist of a network for e-mail, remote data entry, audio, video, computer conferencing, and distributed databases. However, small companies might take advantage of existing public network providers, such as the Internet or value-added networks, for international communication.[23] Value-added networks are private, multipoint networks managed by a third party and used by organizations on a subscription basis. They offer electronic data interchange standards, encryption, secure e-mail, data synchronization, and other services.

However, with the popularity of the Internet, they are not used as much anymore; today, businesses of all sizes typically use the Internet to conduct international business. No matter what the organization's size or scope, an integrated network for global control over the organization's resources is the foundation of any GIS. (See the information box titled "The Internet and Globalization in Action.")

An information system manager faces design and implementation issues when developing a global network. In addition to the usual components of a domestic network, a global network requires bridges, routers, and gateways that allow several networks to connect worldwide. In addition, a global network must have switching nodes to guide packets to their destinations.[24] (These components were discussed in Module 6.)

An information system manager must determine which communication media are best to meet global performance and traffic needs; such media include fiber optics, satellite, microwave, or conventional phone lines. Factors to consider include bandwidth, range, noise, and cost. You learned about bandwidth and range in Module 6. Global providers such as T-Mobile, AT&T, and Verizon can supply information on range specifications for companies. The noise factor involves a medium's degree of immunity to outside electronic interference. As always, component, installation, and leasing costs must be balanced with these other factors.

In addition, an information system manager must choose the best transmission technology for the global network's needs. Without reliable transmission, a network has no value. Current transmission technologies include synchronous, asynchronous, multiplexing, digital (baseband), and analog (broadband). With synchronous transmission, both parties are connected at the same time, as in a phone call. With asynchronous transmission, parties do not have to be connected at the same time, as with e-mail. However, an international company is restricted to the transmission technologies supported by the telecommunication infrastructures of the countries where its subsidiaries are located. Information system managers must select the right network and protocol to manage connections and minimize error rates.

Information system managers must also consider the company's objectives when determining the network architecture. For example, if the company's international communication requirements only entail simple file sharing and if response time is not a critical factor, half-duplex transmission (one direction at a time) used with a value-added network is probably adequate. However, if the company uses multimedia applications (such as video conferencing and electronic meeting systems) in addition

The Internet and Globalization in Action

▶▶ Finance | Technology in Society | Application | Global

The Internet allows entrepreneurs in economically developing nations to start and expand businesses without making large investments. For example, Muhammad Hassaan Khan, a young entrepreneur, was able to establish Zuha Innovation, a design and consulting business based in Faisalabad, Pakistan. The Internet has lowered the barriers for small businesses all over the world, and entrepreneurs have responded, including people from India, China, Mexico, and Brazil. Online businesses can be launched regardless of where the creator is located; all that is needed is Internet access. These businesses vary widely, from e-commerce sites selling local products to bloggers making incomes from advertising revenue. As Adam Toren, president of *YoungEntrepreneur.com*, put it, "The Internet brings all continents, races, cities, and villages together into a global network of trade and communications."[25]

Questions and Discussions

1. How has Zuha Innovation benefited from the Internet?
2. Do you agree with the statement "The Internet brings all continents, races, cities, and villages together into a global network of trade and communications"? Discuss.

---

to normal file and database sharing, full-duplex transmission (both directions simultaneously) is more efficient. Furthermore, a private network or a dedicated leased line provides stability in transmission protocols when there is inadequate telecommunication infrastructure.

A network's main function is to allow users to share information. After a global network is in place, therefore, an international company must decide which types of information-sharing technology it will use, such as electronic meeting systems, video conferencing, group support systems, FTP, data synchronization, and application sharing. (See the "Video-Conferencing Systems Support Globalization" box on video conferencing.)

While making these decisions, information system managers should keep in mind that standardized software and hardware are the ideal but are not always feasible. For example, using the same hardware in another country might be desirable, but it is not as simple as shipping the system to the other country and plugging it in. Vendors might not offer technical support in that country, or the other country's electrical standards may differ. As for using the same software in other countries, that becomes more complicated because of differences in language, business methods, and **transborder data flow (TDF)**, which is subject to restrictions on how data can be captured and transmitted. TDF requires knowledge of national laws and international agreements on privacy protection and data security. However, thanks to cooperation and coordination among countries, these problems are becoming more manageable.[26]

9-2b Requirements of Global Information Systems

What makes an information system global? A GIS must be capable of supporting complex global decisions. This complexity stems from the global environment in which **multinational corporations (MNCs)** operate. MNCs are organizations with assets and operations in at least one country other than their home country. They deliver products and services across national borders and are usually centrally managed from their headquarters. A global environment includes six kinds of factors:[27]

- Legal—Intellectual property laws, patent and trademark laws, TDF regulations, and so forth
- Cultural—Languages, ethical issues, and religious beliefs
- Economic—Currency, tax structure, interest rates, monetary and fiscal policies
- Political—Government type and stability, policies toward MNCs, and so on

> **Transborder data flow (TDF)** restricts what type of data can be captured and transmitted in foreign countries.
>
> A **multinational corporation (MNC)** is an organization with assets and operations in at least one country other than its home country. An MNC delivers products and services across national borders and is usually centrally managed from its headquarters.

Video-Conferencing Systems Support Globalization

> **Finance | Technology in Society | Application | Reflective Thinking | Global**

Video-conferencing applications have been growing rapidly in recent years. Undoubtedly, the COVID-19 pandemic has expedited the adoption of these applications. Organizations usually have two choices for the deployment of this technology: on-premises or cloud based. The driving force behind this growth is the increase in globalization and workforce mobility. Video conferencing is the next best alternative to conducting face-to-face business meetings, for a fraction of the cost, and it can be used in different time zones and locations around the world.

Video-conferencing systems provide a more effective environment for business meetings than e-mail and telephone conversations. Therefore, they are used increasingly by international companies to maintain business relationships between headquarters and regional offices spread across the globe. In recent years, the capabilities of desktop video conferencing have significantly improved, and it's available at a much lower cost than traditional video conferencing systems. With desktop video conferencing, participants can have multiple video windows open at one time. They also have interfaces to a conference installed on their workstations, so the systems are easier for employees to use. The reduced cost has made the technology more affordable for smaller companies.[28]

Key players in the video-conferencing market include ZTE Corporation, Microsoft, Adobe Systems, Blue Jeans Network, Cisco Systems, Poly, Avaya, Sprint, and Zoom.[29]

Questions and Discussions

1. What are two applications of video conferencing in a business setting?
2. What are two reasons for the growth of video-conferencing applications?

- Technological (availability and access)—The Internet, mobile technology, smartphones, artificial intelligence, and so forth

- Environmental—Factors such as climate change, natural disasters, and pollution

In international business planning, it is critical to understand the global risks of operating an MNC—specifically, the political, foreign exchange, and market risks. Political risks include the problems caused by an unstable government, which is an important consideration given the many political uprisings of recent years. An unstable government can result in currency rates fluctuating, power changing hands rapidly and unpredictably, and other issues that affect company operations. A company might decide not to set up offices in many parts of the Middle East or Africa, for example, despite the low costs available in those countries, because of their unstable political situations.

In addition, managing global operations requires considering potential conflicts between the governments of the country where the company is based and the country where the subsidiary is located.

A GIS, like any information system, can be classified according to the different kinds of managerial support it provides: operational, tactical, and/or strategic. Strategic support involves broad and long-term goals; tactical support concentrates on medium-range activities that move the organization toward achieving long-term goals; and operational support involves day-to-day activities.

Based on these classifications, a GIS should collect, process, and generate different types of information in formats that are suitable for each type of support.

The complexities of global decision making mean that a GIS has some functional requirements that differ from a domestic information system's requirements. In addition, the line between operational and tactical management has blurred.

> **A GIS, like any information system, can be classified according to the different kinds of managerial support it provides: operational, tactical, and/or strategic.**

Globalization in Action: Alibaba

▶▶▶ Finance | Technology in Society | Application | Reflective Thinking | Global

One of the major beneficiaries of globalization and the Internet is Alibaba (*www.alibaba.com*), based in China. Alibaba, founded in 1999 as a part of Alibaba Group, is a global platform for wholesale trade with over 117,000 employees; it serves millions of buyers and suppliers around the world.

Alibaba accounts for 80 percent of all online retail sales in China. Most of its revenue comes from advertising on its various sites; more than 14.5 billion transactions are handled by the Web site per year.

Using this platform, small businesses can sell their products to more than 200 countries. Sellers on Alibaba are usually manufacturers and distributors based in China and other manufacturing countries around the world, such as the United States, India, and Pakistan. As an example, the platform allows a business in Germany to find a manufacturer in China and have its merchandise produced and shipped. Alibaba manages this entire process. Using AliExpress, Tmall Global, and Lazada, Alibaba has created marketplaces for doing e-business around the world.

The platform is supported by other Web sites in the Alibaba Group such as *Taobao.com* (China's largest shopping Web site), *Tmall.com* (a branded goods Web site), *Alipay.com* (electronic payment similar to PayPal), and others.[30,31]

Questions and Discussions

1. What are two companies in the United States that compete with Alibaba? What advantages does each company have?
2. What Web sites support Alibaba's operations? How?

The first four of the following requirements are classified as operational, and the remaining ones are strategic:

- *Global data access*—Online access to information from locations around the world allows management to monitor global operations from the company's headquarters. Ideally, global networks provide a real-time communication link with global subsidiaries by integrating voice, data, and video. Several MNCs, such as Hewlett-Packard, General Electric, Texas Instruments, and IBM, have corporate databases linked worldwide.

- *Consolidated global reporting*—This is a crucial tool for managing overseas subsidiaries. These reports should include accounting and financial data, manufacturing updates, and inventory. The reports enable management to compare financial information in all the subsidiaries. Because of differences in accounting procedures and regulatory standards, these comparisons can be difficult. However, consolidated global reporting can help lessen these difficulties.

- *Communication between headquarters and subsidiaries*—To facilitate decision making and planning, a GIS should provide an effective means of communication between the MNC's headquarters and its subsidiaries.

- *Management of short-term foreign exchange risks*—A mix of free-floating (no government intervention), managed-floating, and fixed-exchange rates characterizes today's international monetary system. Currency rates can change daily, so management must minimize the impact of currency fluctuations in countries where the parent company and the subsidiaries are located. To manage foreign exchange risks, many companies have developed expert systems and decision support systems (as discussed in Modules 12 and 13). An interesting observation in recent years is the rise of the U.S. dollar compared to other currencies, which has had a negative impact on some MNCs' income and profit.

- *Strategic planning support*—This is the core of any GIS: a focus on regionalizing resources more effectively and responding to rapid environmental changes, such as increased political and foreign exchange risks and global competition.

- *Management of global tax risks*—Designing tax-risk management systems requires detailed knowledge of international finance, international monetary systems, and international tax law.

9-2c Implementation of Global Information Systems

Implementing a GIS can be difficult because countries have different cultures, politics, social and economic infrastructures, and business methods. International policies can vary, too, which affects communication and standardization. Furthermore, some have argued that a truly global corporation does not exist, much less a GIS to support its operations. Several issues must be addressed before a company implements a GIS, including the following:[32,33]

- An organization must identify its business opportunities in the global marketplace.

- Decision makers must justify the organization's investment in a GIS, given the substantial commitment of resources that must be made, usually years in advance.

- The organization's personnel need to be screened for technical and business expertise, because implementing a GIS is more challenging than implementing a domestic information system.

- Migration to the GIS needs to be coordinated carefully to help personnel move from the old familiar system to the new one.

Using information systems on a global scale is more challenging than doing so on a local scale. The challenges, which are discussed in more detail later in this module, involve such factors as infrastructure, languages, time zones, and cultures. To design a successful GIS, management must first determine the kind of information that global companies need to share. In addition, management cannot assume that the company's products or services will continue selling the same way; global competition

In a **multinational structure**, production, sales, and marketing are decentralized, and financial management remains the parent's responsibility.

A **global structure** uses highly centralized information systems. Subsidiaries have little autonomy and rely on headquarters for all process and control decisions as well as system design and implementation.

and possible changes in customers' needs and preferences must be considered.[34] Evaluating the entire organization's operational efficiency is critical in coordinating international business activities, so global companies need to change their production and marketing strategies in an effort to respond to the global market. The "Globalization in Action: Alibaba" box highlights Alibaba as a global company.

9-3 Organizational Structures and Global Information Systems

The following four types of organizations do business across national borders:

- Multinational organizations
- Global organizations
- International organizations
- Transnational organizations

The organization's structure usually determines the architecture of its GIS, as you will see in the following sections, which discuss each of these structural types.

9-3a Multinational Structure

In a **multinational structure** (see Exhibit 9.1), production, sales, and marketing are decentralized, and financial management remains the parent company's responsibility. Tyco Corporation is an example of a company with a multinational structure.[35] Tyco's focus is local—responding to customers' needs in a subsidiary's location. So, the company's subsidiaries operate autonomously but regularly report to the parent company. Another company that has a multinational structure is Nestlé, which uses scores of different financial systems at its subsidiaries around the world. The company's multinational structure is an advantage because it reduces the need for communication between subsidiaries and headquarters, allowing subsidiaries to make many decisions on their own.[36]

Local hardware and software vendors influence which applications a multinational company chooses. Inevitably, each subsidiary operates on a different platform, and uniform connections are economically impractical.

9-3b Global Structure

An organization with a **global structure**, sometimes called a "franchiser," uses highly centralized information systems.[37] Subsidiaries have little autonomy and rely on headquarters for all process and control decisions as well as system

Exhibit 9.1
Multinational structure

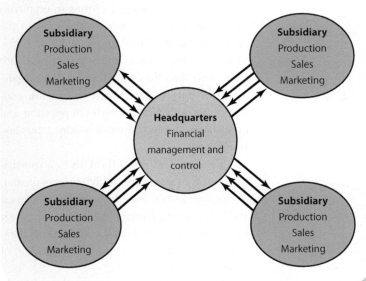

Subsidiary
Production
Sales
Marketing

Subsidiary
Production
Sales
Marketing

Headquarters
Financial management and control

Subsidiary
Production
Sales
Marketing

Subsidiary
Production
Sales
Marketing

design and implementation. Consequently, an extensive communication network is necessary to manage this type of organization, and a GIS fits well into this structure.

Unfortunately, the integration needed to manage production, marketing, and human resources is difficult to achieve with a global structure because of the heavy reliance on headquarters. To achieve organizational efficiency, duplicate information systems have to be developed.[38] Products are usually created, financed, and produced in the headquarters' country, and subsidiaries have the responsibility of selling, marketing, and tailoring the products to their countries' requirements and tastes. For example, McDonald's, in order to appeal to local tastes, changed the burgers it serves in India to a 100 percent vegetarian product consisting of potatoes, peas, carrots, and some Indian spices.

In addition to McDonald's, Mrs. Fields' Cookies and Kentucky Fried Chicken are companies that have a global structure.[39,40] Yet another example is General Motors, which uses a GIS to integrate inventory information from all over the world. General Motors also uses electronic meeting systems to coordinate its research and development efforts throughout the world.[41,42]

> **McDonald's, in order to appeal to local tastes, changed the burgers it serves in India to a 100 percent vegetarian product consisting of potatoes, peas, carrots, and some Indian spices.**

Exhibit 9.2 shows the global structure, with a one-way flow of services, goods, information, and other resources.

9-3c International Structure

An organization with an **international structure** operates much like a multinational corporation, but subsidiaries depend on headquarters more for process and production decisions. Information systems personnel are regularly exchanged among locations to encourage joint development of applications for marketing, finance, and production. This exchange encourages a

An organization with an **international structure** operates much like a multinational corporation, but subsidiaries depend on headquarters more for process and production decisions.

Exhibit 9.2
Global structure

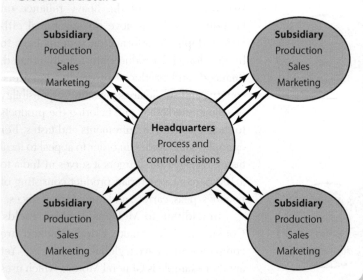

usually focuses on optimizing supply sources and using advantages available in subsidiary locations. Many companies do this when they look for manufacturing facilities in countries where labor is less expensive than it is in the parent country. For example, China, India, Vietnam, and other countries have cheaper labor costs than the United States does. Again, a GIS fits into this structure well by integrating global activities through cooperation and information sharing between headquarters and subsidiaries.

The architecture of the GIS in a transnational structure requires a higher level of standardization and uniformity for global efficiency, and yet it must maintain local responsiveness. Universal data dictionaries and standard databases, for example, enhance the integration of GISs.

The level of cooperation and worldwide coordination needed for a transnational structure does not fully exist in today's global environment. However, with increasing cooperation between nations, this structure is becoming more feasible. Citigroup, Sony, and Ford, to name a few, have been striving to adopt a transnational structure. In fact, the globalizing trend is forcing many organizations to gravitate toward this structure because of competition with companies that already share innovations across borders and maintain responsiveness to local needs. These companies have increased efficiency in production costs because production can

cooperative culture in geographically dispersed personnel, and using a GIS to support an international structure is more feasible because of this cooperative nature. Subsidiaries' GISs can be centralized or decentralized, depending on the extent to which they cooperate.

Exhibit 9.3 shows an international structure that uses two-way communication. For example, expertise information flows from headquarters to subsidiaries, and financial information flows from subsidiaries to headquarters. Heavy-equipment manufacturers such as Caterpillar Corporation usually have this structure.

9-3d Transnational Structure

In an organization with a **transnational structure**, the parent company and all the subsidiaries work together in designing policies, procedures, and logistics for delivering products and services to the right market. This type of organization might have several regional divisions that share authority and responsibility, but in general it does not have its headquarters in a particular country. A transnational organization

> In an organization with a **transnational structure**, the parent and all the subsidiaries work together in designing policies, procedures, and logistics for delivering products and services to the right market.

Exhibit 9.3
International structure

Subsidiary — Financial information

Subsidiary — Financial information

Headquarters — Expertise for process and production decisions

Subsidiary — Financial information

Subsidiary — Financial information

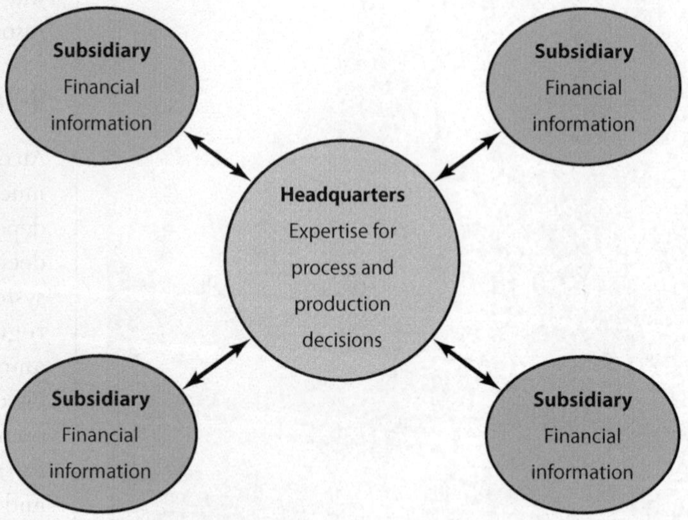

Exhibit 9.4
Transnational structure

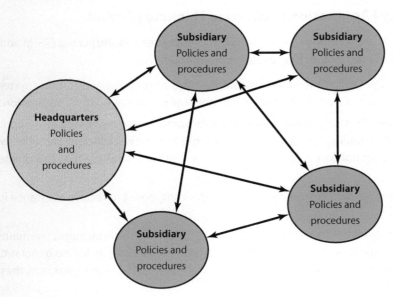

be spread across more locations. Exhibit 9.4 shows the transnational structure, with cooperation between headquarters and subsidiaries as well as between subsidiaries. Foreign exchange systems that allow traders and brokers from around the world to interact are an example of information systems that support this structure. The information box titled "Global Information System at FedEx" highlights the applications of GISs at Federal Express.

9-3e Global Information Systems Supporting Offshore Outsourcing

Offshore outsourcing is an alternative for developing information systems. With this approach, an organization chooses an outsourcing firm in another country that can provide needed services and products. Initially, offshore outsourcing was used mostly in manufacturing to find cheap labor, but now it is used for many information technology tasks, including the following:

- Medical diagnosis
- Tax preparation
- Programming
- Application development
- Web site development
- Help desk/user support
- Quality assurance/software testing

With **offshore outsourcing**, an organization chooses an outsourcing firm in another country that can provide needed services and products.

The widespread availability of the Internet, improved telecommunication systems, the reduced cost of communication, and increased bandwidth have made offshore outsourcing more attractive for all types of organizations. A GIS plays an important role in supporting offshore outsourcing by providing a global network that all participants can use for coordinating development activities, such as product design and global marketing campaigns. Table 9.1 lists the top 10 countries for outsourcing software development in 2021.[43] Some of the criteria used to rate the countries include language proficiency, local government's support of offshore business, the potential labor pool, existing infrastructure (roads, rail service, and airports), and quality of the educational system.

9-4 Obstacles to Using Global Information Systems

A GIS helps an organization improve its global coordination, manage the factors that promote globalization, and maintain a competitive edge by supporting

Table 9.1	Top 10 Countries for Outsourcing Software Development in 2021
China	
Hungary	
India	
Philippines	
Poland	
Russia	
South Korea	
Taiwan	
Ukraine	
Vietnam	

Global Information System at FedEx

▶▶ Finance | Technology in Society | Application | Reflective Thinking | Global

To support its operations in over 220 countries and territories around the world, FedEx uses a sophisticated GIS. In addition to the Internet and mobile networks, the FedEx system has several more components:

- *COSMOS (Customer Operations Service Master Online System)*—This component is a computerized tracking system that monitors every package from the time it is picked up from the customer until it is delivered to its destination.[44]

- *Command & Control: Delivery in Any Weather*—This is a satellite-to-ground-level operations system based in Memphis, Tennessee. It serves as a weather assistant, enabling FedEx to deliver packages in the most efficient and effective way regardless of weather conditions. The central part of this component is a relational database that coordinates FedEx logistics throughout the world.[45]

- *FedEx Global Trade Manager*—Using *www.fedex.com*, customers can access this component to receive assistance for international shipping.[46]

- *FedEx INTrade, Traders Information Exchange System*—This component connects FedEx and the brokerage community. By doing so, it eliminates a number of tasks and functions that used to be performed manually, including generating summary sheets, broker release notification reports, and electronic commercial invoices. The system makes all these documents available electronically.[47]

Questions and Discussions

1. What are three examples of IT tools being used by FedEx?
2. What is the function of COSMOS (Customer Operations Service Master Online System) at FedEx?

---

strategic planning. However, like any information system project, there are potential problems in implementing and maintaining a GIS. Companies that are planning to use GISs should analyze these problems and try to address them. Taking a proactive approach can increase the chances of success in using this technology. The following factors, some of which are discussed in more detail in later sections, can hinder the success of a GIS:[48,49]

- Lack of standardization (including differences in time zones, taxes, language, and work habits)
- Cultural differences
- Diverse regulatory practices
- Poor telecommunication infrastructures
- Lack of skilled analysts and programmers

A more subtle obstacle to GIS development is an organization's unwillingness to delegate control of information systems to host countries. To achieve true integration on an international scale, organizations must empower key personnel in other countries and rely on feedback and information-sharing technologies.

9-4a Lack of Standardization

Lack of standardization can impede the development of a cohesive GIS that is capable of sharing information resources across borders. Electronic data interchange, e-mail, and telecommunication standards vary throughout the world, and trying to work with all the various standards is impractical. Also, although open-source systems are increasing in popularity and the technology to link diverse systems is available, few organizations can meet the costs of integrating different platforms.

Too much standardization can be a problem as well, decreasing an organization's flexibility in responding to local preferences—even time differences. For example, an organization should not insist that all its subsidiaries use the metric system. It should allow subsidiaries to use the measuring systems they are familiar with, converting from one system to the other when necessary.

Time zones can also pose difficulties in managing a GIS. For example, information systems personnel who are managing a centralized GIS under international standards and sharing information resources across time zones might have difficulties finding the right time to take the system offline for backup and maintenance.[50] A balance of international system development standards—allowing ease of integration, modularization, custom tailoring of systems, and applications for local responsiveness—is needed.

Sharing software is difficult and impractical when these factors are considered. Only 5 to 15 percent of a company's applications are truly global in nature. Most applications are local in nature and cannot be integrated into a GIS infrastructure. Even if the software can be integrated globally, support and maintenance problems might result. If the network goes down, who is responsible for bringing the system back online? Moreover, employees calling the help desk might not speak the same language as the help desk personnel. Therefore, coordination and planning for variations in local needs are critical for using a GIS.[51]

9-4b Cultural Differences

Cultural differences in values, attitudes, and behaviors play an important role in using GISs. For example, in some cultures, using technology is considered a boring, low-level task; in others, being technologically knowledgeable is seen as a sign of social importance. For example, a travel-oriented Web site aimed at customers who make last-minute reservations at lower prices may work well in certain cultures but not as well in other countries where advance planning is expected, and last-minute reservations are not "rewarded" with lower prices.[52]

Organizations might also need to consider cultural differences when examining content and images on their Web sites. Photos of women dressed in a certain way might be acceptable in the Western world but unacceptable in the Middle East, for instance. Cultural issues are best addressed with education and training.

> In some cultures, using technology is considered a boring, low-level task; in others, being technologically knowledgeable is seen as a sign of social importance.

9-4c Diverse Regulatory Practices

Diverse regulatory practices also impede the integration process. This obstacle does not necessarily apply to transborder data flow (TDF) regulations; it applies to policies on business practices and technological use. Many countries also restrict the type of hardware and software that can be imported or used, and the vendors that an organization normally deals with might not service certain countries.[53]

For example, the Chinese police, in a sharp increase of the country's online censorship efforts in 2019, questioned and detained a number of Twitter users, even though the social media platform is blocked in China and most people in the country cannot see it.[54]

In addition to China, several other countries have blocked social media, including Pakistan, North Korea, Cuba, Iran, Bangladesh, Vietnam, Mauritius, Egypt, and Syria.[55] Adopting open-source systems could eliminate part of this problem. However, as mentioned, few organizations are capable of adopting these systems.

Jurisdiction issues regarding the contents of a GIS can also be challenging. ISPs, content providers, servers, and organizations that own these entities might be scattered throughout the world and operate under different rules and regulations. For example, Yahoo! was sued in French courts because Nazi memorabilia was being sold on its auction site, which is an illegal activity in France. To date, French and U.S. courts have not agreed on the resolution or even on which court has jurisdiction.[56] Determining jurisdiction in cases involving cyberspace is difficult.

The nature of intellectual property laws and how they are enforced in different countries also varies. Software piracy is a problem in all countries, but several have piracy rates higher than 90 percent. This problem has resulted in an estimated loss of $40 billion worldwide.[57] Other legal issues include privacy and cybercrime laws as well as censorship and government control, which vary widely from country to country. The "General Data Protection Regulation (GDPR)" section in Module 4 provides examples of some of the privacy law differences between the United States and the European Union (EU). The GDPR covers a series of laws that protect EU citizens' personal data, including genetic information, health records, racial or ethnic origin, and religious beliefs. The goal is to create more consistent protection of consumer and personal data across the member states of the EU. Any company that sells products or services to EU residents must be aware of this law and its consequences, regardless of the company's location. In this respect, there is no difference between EU-based companies and international companies. If any organization's Web site collects regulated data from EU users, it is liable to comply to the GDPR. A violator could be fined up to 4 percent of the company's global annual revenue, depending on the nature of the violation. Under the GDPR, individuals can easily transfer their personal data between service providers; this practice is called "right to portability."

Interestingly enough, the GDPR is playing a role in privacy issues within U.S.-based MNCs. For example, the GDPR is probably part of the reason that companies such as Facebook began asking its users to review their privacy settings. It is up to users to decide what to share and what not to share. Although Facebook is a U.S.-based company, the GDPR rules affect how it operates in other countries because its users are connected globally.[58]

9-4d Poor Telecommunication Infrastructures

Before adding a GIS, international companies must take into consideration the telecommunication infrastructures of the countries where subsidiaries are located. An organization might have the resources and skills to implement a worldwide integrated system but not be able to change an existing telecommunication infrastructure. Furthermore, differences in telecommunication systems make it difficult to consolidate them. Implementing a GIS that encompasses 25 countries, for instance, is expensive and cumbersome when each country has different service offerings, price schedules, and policies.

In countries where Internet access is slower or more costly, Web pages should not have content with lots of graphics and animation that require more bandwidth. However, people in countries such as South Korea, where high-speed access is common, expect sophisticated Web sites with many graphic features.

Even when the telecommunication infrastructure in two countries is comparable, differences in standards can cause problems. For example, a company with branches in the United States and Egypt might face problems of different Internet protocols, higher costs, slower speeds, and less reliability in Egypt.

9-4e Lack of Skilled Analysts and Programmers

Having skilled analysts and consultants with the knowledge to implement a GIS is critical, particularly with the severe shortage of qualified information systems professionals in the United States and Western Europe. When forming integrated teams, companies must consider the nature of each culture and differences in skills in other countries.[59] Ideally, an organization would link the skills of people from different countries to form a "dream team." However, cultural and political differences can affect the cooperative environment needed for global integration. Training and certification programs, many of which are offered through the Internet, are one possible solution for narrowing this skills gap in economically developing nations.

The Industry Connection feature highlights the SAP Corporation as a leader in enterprise computing and global information systems.

Industry Connection: SAP Corporation[60]

SAP, founded by five former IBM employees in 1972, is one of the leading providers of business software. Its applications can be used to manage finances, assets, production operations, and human resources. The latest version of its enterprise resource planning software, SAP ERP 7.0, includes comprehensive Web-enabled products. SAP offers a Web interface for customers called *www.mySAP.com* and provides e-business applications, including customer relationship management (CRM) and supply chain management (SCM) systems. From the beginning, SAP products have been designed for use with multiple languages and currencies, which is particularly useful for companies that need to support global operations. In addition, SAP includes upgrades for global aspects of information systems. In addition to products for enterprise resource planning and SCM (both discussed in Module 11), SAP offers the following software:

SAP Supplier Relationship Management: Helps manage a company's relationships with its suppliers by automating procurement processes, managing the supply chain, and creating a collaborative environment between the company and its suppliers.

SAP Product Lifecycle Management (PLM): Includes services for coordinating manufacturing processes, from developing product prototypes to producing the final product to ensuring compliance with industry standards and regulations.

SAP-HANA: Used for in-memory business analytics, streamlining of applications, and predictive analysis in real time. Because it does its calculations in memory, the software delivers extremely fast response times. It can be used on-premises or in the cloud.

Module Summary

9-1 Discuss the reasons for globalization and for using global information systems, including e-business and Internet growth. The global economy is creating customers who demand integrated worldwide services, and the expansion of global markets is a major factor in developing global information systems to handle these integrated services. The Internet can simplify communication, improve business relationships, and offer new opportunities to both consumers and businesses.

9-2 Describe global information systems and their requirements and components. A global information system (GIS) works across national borders, facilitates communication between headquarters and subsidiaries in other countries, and incorporates all the technologies and applications found in a typical information system to gather, store, manipulate, and transmit data across cultural and geographic boundaries. Their requirements include global data access, consolidated global reporting, and communication between headquarters and subsidiaries. Most GISs have two basic components: a global database and information-sharing technologies.

9-3 Explain the four types of organizational structures used with global information systems. They include multinational organizations, global organizations, international organizations, and transnational organizations.

9-4 Examine five obstacles to using global information systems. They include lack of standardization (including differences in time zones, taxes, language, and work habits), cultural differences, diverse regulatory practices, poor telecommunication infrastructures, and lack of skilled analysts and programmers.

Key Terms

- Global information system (GIS)
- Global structure
- International structure
- Multinational corporations (MNCs)
- Multinational structure
- Offshore outsourcing
- Transborder data flow (TDF)
- Transnational structure

Reviews and Discussions

1. Provide three reasons for globalization.
2. As of March 2021, how many people worldwide were using the Internet?
3. Define *global information system*.
4. What are two key components of a global information system?
5. Define the four types of organizational structures used with global information systems.
6. What are five obstacles to using global information systems?
7. Define *transborder data flow (TDF)*.
8. Why is designing a global database more challenging than designing a domestic database?

Projects

1. Like FedEx, UPS is a major player in global logistics. After reading the information presented in this module and other sources, write a one-page paper that describes three IT tools that UPS uses in its global logistics. What are two differences between global logistics and domestic logistics?

2. The availability and speed of Internet connections play a major role in the success of a GIS. After reading the information presented in this module and other sources, write a one-page paper that lists the 10 countries with the fastest Internet connections. Is the United States among the top 10?

3. Offshore outsourcing increases with the use of GISs. After reading the information presented in this module and other sources, write a one-page paper that describes four factors a company should consider when looking for a country to provide it with IT services. What are two reasons that India has become one of the top IT outsourcing countries in the world?

4. Information-sharing technologies are among the major components of a successful GIS. After reading the information presented in this module and other sources, write a one-page paper that lists three such technologies; also mention the specific task support and decision-making support that each technology provides.

5. Understanding cultural differences can play a major role in the success of a GIS. After reading the information presented in this module and other sources, write a two-page paper that identifies five such differences between the United States and Saudi Arabia. How would you resolve such differences?

6. There are major differences between U.S. privacy laws and those in the EU. After reading the information presented in this module, Module 4, and other sources, write a two-page paper that identifies five such differences. List three U.S. companies that have been sued by the EU for not following their privacy laws. For each company, list one violation.

Module Quiz

1. Globalization has become an important factor in purchasing and the supply chain. True or False?

2. From 2000 through 2021, the highest Internet growth has occurred in North America. True or False?

3. Transborder data flow restricts what type of data can be captured and transmitted in foreign countries. True or False?

4. All of the following organizations do business across national borders except:
   a. Multinational organizations
   b. Global organizations
   c. International organizations
   d. Domestic organizations

5. All of the following are among the obstacles to using global information systems except:
   a. Well-established telecommunication infrastructures
   b. Cultural differences
   c. Diverse regulatory practices
   d. Lack of standardization

6. All of the following companies are among the key players for building and launching high-speed Internet satellites except:
   a. Amazon
   b. SpaceX
   c. OneWeb
   d. Cisco Systems

Case Study 9-1
Global Information Systems at Toyota Motor Company

▶▶ **Finance | Technology in Society | Application | Reflective Thinking | Global**

The Toyota Motor Company is a global automobile manufacturer that operates on five different continents. In the United States, it runs five major assembly plants. To manage its operations efficiently and effectively around the globe, Toyota uses several types of information systems. It uses the Internet and global networks to communicate with its offices, plants, and dealerships around the world.[61]

Toyota is one of the founders of the Toyota Production System, an early version of the Just In Time (JIT) inventory system.[62] This system allows Toyota to have on hand the exact number of components needed at any time to continue its operations, given that waste often occurs when components are inventoried and stored. To use a JIT inventory system, Toyota's GIS must be capable of managing real-time inventory, not only within its own manufacturing facilities but in all of its suppliers' facilities. Because of this, Toyota requires all of its suppliers to have a system capable of interfacing with the one Toyota uses for its own operations.

Toyota worked with Dell, Microsoft, and WorldCom (a part of Verizon Communications) to develop a "Dealer Daily" system that offers a centralized data center for the more than 1,100 Toyota and Lexus dealers in the United States. This system allows dealers to spend more time focusing on selling cars and less time on paperwork. For example, the system is capable of providing a response to a financing application in 15 seconds.[63]

Using Oracle E-Business Suite 12.1, Toyota Motor Europe (TME) implemented Toyota's Vehicle Order Management (VOM) system. This system, which encompasses 13 countries, enables TME to improve its European operations by reducing delivery time to customers and managing inventory more efficiently. As a result, the system reduces operating costs.[64]

Answer the following questions:

1. What role do global networks play in the effective implementation of JIT?
2. What role does the Dealer Daily system play in Toyota's implementation of a GIS?
3. What is the function of Vehicle Order Management (VOM)?
4. How many countries will be impacted by VOM and in which part of the world?

Case Study 9-2
Information Technologies Support Global Supply Chain
▶ Finance | Technology in Society | Social and Ethical Issues | Reflective Thinking | Global

An efficient and effective supply chain plays a major role in the success of a multinational corporation (MNC). MNCs deal with a myriad of issues, including quality of raw materials, scarcity of materials, the locations where the materials' ingredients or components are grown or manufactured, and the counterfeiting of materials (especially in the pharmaceutical industry). MNCs also face environmental challenges, such as tsunamis in the Philippines, monsoons in Thailand, and volcanos in Indonesia. Piracy and theft of intellectual property are yet another set of issues that MNCs must deal with.[65]

Because supply chains are often outsourced and subcontracted, controlling each point of the supply chain becomes a challenge. Although IT cannot solve all these problems, it can provide timely information that executives in MNCs can use to quickly respond to them. MNCs use data warehouses and analytics to analyze, pinpoint, and quickly deliver key information related to parts of the supply chain. RFIDs, GPSs, and QR codes have significantly improved the efficiency of these supply chains.

3d Brained/Shutterstock.com

Ports America, for example, uses optical character recognition cameras to scan each container, RFID tags to match trucks to their contents, and GPS sensors to identify equipment locations and cargo movements. Computer networks and the Internet have created unparalleled connections throughout the world. Major logistics companies such as UPS and FedEx are using state-of-the-art information technologies to efficiently deliver products and services around the globe.[66]

Answer the following questions:

1. What are some of the challenges that MNCs face with intellectual property?
2. What are some of the environmental challenges that MNCs face?
3. How can information technology assist with the problem of counterfeiting?
4. How can information technology assist with logistics?

Part 3

IS Development, Enterprise Systems, MSS, AI, and Emerging Trends

ESB Professional/Shutterstock.com

Module

10 Building Successful Information Systems

Learning Objectives

After studying this module, you should be able to…

10.1 Apply the systems development life cycle as a method for developing information systems.

10.2 Explain the tasks involved in the planning phase.

10.3 Explain the tasks involved in the requirements-gathering and analysis phase.

10.4 Explain the tasks involved in the design phase.

10.5 Explain the tasks involved in the implementation phase.

10.6 Explain the tasks involved in the maintenance phase.

10.7 Describe new trends in systems analysis and design, including service-oriented architecture, rapid application development, extreme programming, and agile methodology.

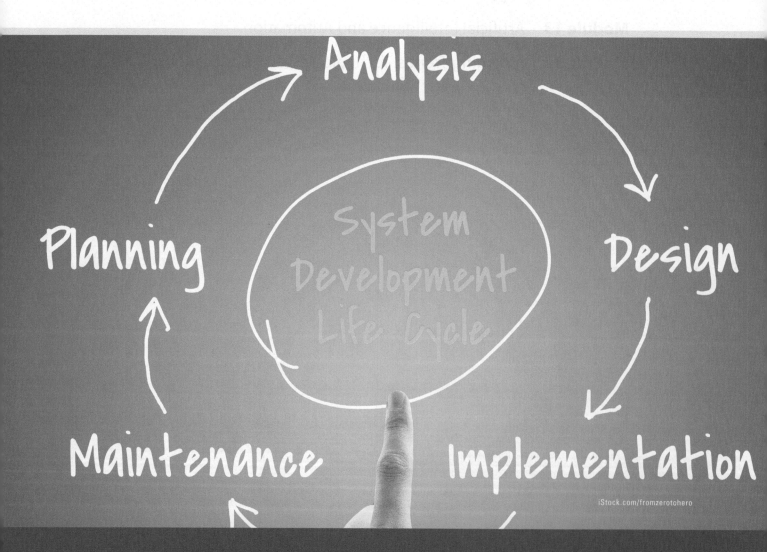

iStock.com/fromzerotohero

This module explains the systems development life cycle (SDLC), a model for developing a system or project. The cycle is usually divided into five phases, and you learn about the tasks involved in each phase. For example, in the first phase—planning—a feasibility study is typically conducted, and the SDLC task force is formed. You also learn about two alternatives to the SDLC model: self-sourcing and outsourcing. Finally, you review new trends in systems analysis and design, such as service-oriented architecture, rapid application development, extreme programming, the agile methodology, low-code, and no-code.

10-1 Systems Development Life Cycle: An Overview

In the information systems field, system failure can happen for several reasons, including missed deadlines, users' needs that are not met, dissatisfied customers, lack of support from top management, and exceeding the budget. Old equipment that cannot handle a system's capacity requirements and peak times can also cause system failure. Using a system development method can help prevent these failures. Designing a successful information system requires integrating people, software, and hardware. To achieve this integration, designers often follow the **systems development life cycle (SDLC)**, also known as the "waterfall model." It is a series of well-defined phases performed in sequence that serves as a framework for developing a system or project. Exhibit 10.1 shows the phases of the SDLC, which are explained throughout this module. In this model, each phase's output (results) becomes the input for the next phase. When following this model, keep in mind that the main goal of an information system is delivering useful information in a timely manner to the right decision maker.

Systems planning today is about evaluating all potential systems that need to be implemented. A preliminary analysis of requirements is done, and a feasibility study is conducted for each system. Then the organization decides which ones are a "go" and proceeds to the next phase.

Information system projects are often an extension of existing systems or involve replacing an old technology with a new one. However, sometimes an information system needs to be designed from scratch, and the SDLC model is particularly suitable in these situations. For existing information systems, some SDLC phases might not be applicable, although the SDLC model can still be used. In addition, when designing information systems, projecting the organization's growth rate is important; otherwise, the system could become inefficient shortly after it is designed.

10-2 Phase 1: Planning

During the **planning phase**, which is one of the most crucial phases of the SDLC model, the systems designer must define the problem the organization faces, taking care not to define symptoms rather than the underlying problem. The problem can be identified internally or externally. An example of an internally identified problem would be management voicing concern about the organization's lack of a competitive edge in the marketplace. An example of an externally identified problem would be suppliers noting inefficiency in the inventory control procedure.

After identifying the problem, an analyst or team of analysts assesses the current and future needs of the organization or a specific group of users by answering the following questions:

- Why is this information system being developed?

- Who are the system's current and future users?

> The **systems development life cycle (SDLC)**, also known as the "waterfall model," is a series of well-defined phases performed in sequence that serves as a framework for developing a system or project.
>
> During the **planning phase**, which is one of the most crucial phases of the SDLC model, the systems designer must define the problem the organization faces, taking care not to define symptoms rather than the underlying problem.

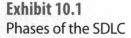

Exhibit 10.1
Phases of the SDLC

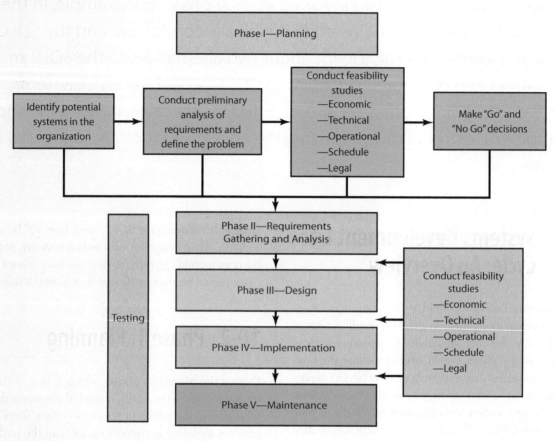

- Is the system new, or is it an upgrade or extension of an existing system?
- Which functional areas (departments) will be using the system?

As part of this assessment, analysts must examine the organization's strategic goals, how the proposed system can support these goals, which factors are critical to the proposed system's success, and the criteria for evaluating the proposed system's performance. Establishing evaluation criteria ensures objectivity throughout the SDLC process.

In addition, analysts must get feedback from users on the problem and the need for an information system. During this phase, they need to make sure users understand the four Ws:

- *Why*—Why is the system being designed? Which decisions will be affected?
- *Who*—Who is going to use the system? Is it going to be used by one decision maker or a group of decision makers? This question is also about types of users. For example, will the Marketing

Department be using the system? Will the Manufacturing Department be using the system as suppliers or as consumers of information?
- *When*—When will the system be operational? When in the business process (in what stages) will the system be used?
- *What*—What kind of capabilities will the system provide? How will these capabilities be used?

The end result of this phase should give users and top management a clear view of what the problem is and how the information system will solve the problem. As an example, here is a look at how ABC Furniture is planning for an information system to solve the problem of inaccurate inventory forecasts. Currently, ABC Furniture buys wood from New England Wood (NEW).

- *Why*—ABC Furniture needs an information system to track inventory, generate a more accurate forecast of product demand, and track requirements for wood to be ordered from NEW.

Clearly, a more accurate inventory will help reduce inventory costs, improve ABC Furniture's relationship with NEW and with distributors, ensure that the company's products are available for retailers, and improve ABC's image in the marketplace.

- *Who*—The main users of the information system will be the procurement group responsible for placing orders with NEW, the manufacturing division responsible for tracking inventory and ensuring that demand for finished goods is met, the sales personnel who take orders from distributors, and possibly distributors who take orders from retailers.

- *When*—The system must become operational within the next four months because the company's main competitor is planning to open a new store in six months. Furthermore, the system must support the materials-ordering stage, the production-planning stage, and the shipping stage of the manufacturing process. It must also supply information for the marketing campaign that ABC Furniture is planning to run in five months and support ABC's expansion into a new region.

- *What*—On the inbound side, the system must track pending and received deliveries, quantities of raw materials, orders placed for raw materials, and raw material levels from all of ABC's suppliers, including NEW. On the operations side, the system must provide information on inventory levels of all products, raw materials, work in progress at each stage of manufacturing, quality of raw materials received, quality of finished goods inspected, and rejects. On the outbound side, the system must track placed orders, unfulfilled orders, and fulfilled orders for each finished product as well as the order history for each distributor and retailer.

10-2a Formation of the Task Force

To ensure an information system's success, users must have input in the phases of the SDLC. For this reason, a task force is formed from representatives of different departments (including IT), systems analysts, technical advisors, and top management. This team collects user feedback and works to get users involved from the beginning.

The system designers and analysts should explain the goals and benefits of the new system so the task force knows what to look for in user input. Generally, an information system has two groups of users from whom the task force should gather feedback: internal and external. **Internal users** are employees who will use the system regularly; they can offer important feedback on the system's strengths and weaknesses. **External users** are not employees, but they do use the system; they include customers, contractors, suppliers, and other business partners. Although external users are not normally part of the task force, their input is essential.

Using a task force for designing an information system is similar to using the joint application design approach. **Joint application design (JAD)** is a collective activity involving users, top management, and IT professionals. It centers on a structured workshop (called a JAD session) in which users and system professionals come together to develop an application. It involves a detailed agenda, visual aids, a leader who moderates the session, and a scribe who records the specifications. It results in a final document containing definitions for data elements, workflows, screens, reports, and general system specifications. An advantage of the JAD approach is that it incorporates varying viewpoints from different functional areas of an organization to help ensure that collected requirements for the application are not too narrow and one-dimensional in focus.[1]

10-2b Feasibility Study

Feasibility is the measure of how beneficial or practical an information system will be to an organization; it should be measured continually throughout the SDLC process. (See the information box titled "A Feasible Project Becomes Unfeasible.") Upper management is often frustrated by information systems that are unrelated to the organization's strategic goals or have an inadequate payoff, by poor communication between system users and designers, and by designers' lack of

Internal users are employees who will use the system regularly; they can offer important feedback on the system's strengths and weaknesses.

External users are not employees, but they do use the system; they include customers, contractors, suppliers, and other business partners. Although they are not normally part of the task force, their input is essential.

Joint application design (JAD) is a collective activity involving users, top management, and IT professionals. It centers on a structured workshop (called a JAD session) where users and system professionals come together to develop an application.

consideration for users' preferences and work habits. A detailed feasibility study that focuses on these factors can help ease management's frustration with investing in information systems.[2]

During the planning phase, analysts investigate a proposed solution's feasibility and determine how to present the solution to management in order to obtain funding. The tool used for this purpose is a **feasibility study**, and it usually has five major dimensions, as discussed in the following sections: economic, technical, operational, scheduling, and legal.

Economic Feasibility

Economic feasibility assesses a system's costs and benefits. Simply put, if implementing the system results in a net gain of $250,000 but the system costs $500,000, the system is not economically feasible. To conduct an economic feasibility study, a team of systems analysts must identify all costs and benefits—tangible and intangible—of the

> Feasibility is the measure of how beneficial or practical an information system will be to an organization; it should be measured continually throughout the SDLC process.

A **feasibility study** analyzes a proposed solution's feasibility and determines how to present the solution to management. It usually has five major dimensions: economic, technical, operational, scheduling, and legal.

Economic feasibility assesses a system's costs and benefits.

proposed system. The team must also be aware of opportunity costs associated with the information system. Opportunity costs measure what you would miss by not having a system or feature. For example, if your competitor has a Web site and you do not, what is the cost of not having a site, even if you do not really need one? What market share are you likely to lose if you do not have a Web site?

To assess economic feasibility, the team tallies tangible development and operating costs for the system and compares them with expected financial benefits of the system. Development costs include the following:

- Hardware and software
- Software leases or licenses
- Computer time for programming, testing, and prototyping
- Maintenance costs for monitoring equipment and software
- Personnel costs—salaries for consultants, systems analysts, network specialists, programmers, data entry clerks, computer operators, secretaries, and technicians
- Supplies and other equipment
- Training employees who will be using the system

A Feasible Project Becomes Unfeasible

▶▶ Finance | Technology in Society | Application

WestJet Airlines, a Canadian discount airline in Calgary, announced that it was stopping development on a new reservation system called AIRES, even though it had invested $30 million in the project. The problem was not with Travelport, the company developing the system. WestJet simply grew faster than anticipated, and the original specifications for the reservation system did not address this fast growth. Management wanted to add features, such as the capability to partner with international carriers, but the system had been planned to fit a small discount airline, not a large international airline. WestJet suspended the work of 150 internal IT specialists and about 50 outside consultants. This example illustrates the need for conducting feasibility studies through a project's life cycle. If WestJet had continued the project, the potential losses could have exceeded $30 million.[3]

Questions and Discussions

1. Why did the reservation system at WestJet Airlines become unfeasible?
2. Did WestJet make the right decision to stop the project after spending $30 million? Discuss.

Operating costs for running the system are typically estimated, although some vendors and suppliers can supply costs. These costs can be fixed or variable, depending on rate of use. After itemizing these costs, the team creates a budget. Many budgets do not allow enough for development costs, especially technical expertise (programmers, designers, and managers), and for this reason, many information system projects go over budget.

An information system's scope and complexity can change after the analysis or design phases, so the team should keep in mind that an information system project that is feasible at the outset could become unfeasible later. Integrating feasibility checkpoints into the SDLC process is a good idea to ensure the system's success. Projects can always be canceled or revised at a feasibility checkpoint, if needed.

To complete the economic feasibility study, the team must identify benefits of the information system, both tangible and intangible. Tangible benefits can be quantified in terms of monthly or annual savings; for example, implementing the new system might result in increased profits or it might allow an organization to operate with three employees rather than five. The real challenge is assessing intangible costs and benefits accurately; attaching a realistic monetary value to these factors can be difficult.

Intangible benefits are difficult to quantify in terms of dollar amounts, but if they are not at least identified, many information system projects cannot be justified. Examples of intangible benefits include improved employee morale, better customer service and satisfaction, more efficient use of human resources, increased flexibility in business operations, and improved communication. For example, you could quantify customer service as maintaining current total sales and increasing them by 10 percent to improve net profit. Other measures have been developed to assess intangibles, such as quantifying employee morale with rates of on-time arrival to work or working overtime. Customer satisfaction, though intangible, can be measured by using satisfaction surveys, and the Internet has made this method easier.

After collecting information on costs and benefits, the team can do a cost-effectiveness analysis. This analysis is based on the concept that a dollar today is worth more than a dollar one year from now. If the system does not produce enough return on the investment, the money can be better spent elsewhere. The most common analysis methods are payback, net present value (NPV), return on investment (ROI), and internal rate of return (IRR). The final result of this task is the cost–benefit analysis (CBA) report, which is used to sell the system to top management. This report can vary in format but should include the following sections: an executive summary, introduction, scope and purpose, analysis method, recommendations, justifications, implementation plans, summary, and appendix items, which can include supporting documentation. Some examples of useful supporting documentation are organizational charts, workflow plans, floor plans, statistical information, project sequence diagrams, and timelines or milestone charts.

Technical Feasibility

Technical feasibility is an assessment of the technology that will be used in the system. The team needs to assess whether the technology to support the new system is available or feasible to implement. For example, full-featured, autonomous delivery trucks for the supply chain system are not technically feasible at this point. However, given the pace of technological development, many of these problems will eventually have solutions. Lack of technical feasibility can also stem from an organization lacking the expertise, time, or personnel to implement the new system. This problem is also called "a lack of organizational readiness." In this case, the organization can take steps to address its shortcomings and then consider the new system. Extensive training is one solution to this problem.

> The major question to answer when conducting operational feasibility is whether the information system is worth implementing.

Operational Feasibility

Operational feasibility is the measure of how well the proposed solution will work in the organization and how internal and external customers will react to it. The major question to answer is whether the information system is worth implementing. To assess operational

Technical feasibility is an assessment of the technology to be used in the system. The team needs to assess whether the technology to support the new system is available or feasible to implement.

Operational feasibility is the measure of how well the proposed solution will work in the organization and how internal and external customers will react to it.

feasibility, the team should address the following questions:

- Is the system doing what it is supposed to do? For example, will the information system for ABC Furniture reduce orders for raw materials by tracking inventory more accurately?
- Will the information system be used?
- Will there be resistance from users?
- Will top management support the information system?
- Will the proposed information system benefit the organization?
- Will the proposed information system affect customers (both internal and external) in a positive way?

Scheduling Feasibility

Scheduling feasibility assesses whether the new system can be completed on time. For example, an organization might need a wireless network immediately because of a disaster that destroyed the existing network. If the new system cannot be delivered in time, the loss of customers could force the organization out of business. In this case, the proposed system might not be feasible from a scheduling standpoint. The problem of missing deadlines is common in the information systems field, but designers can often minimize this problem by using project management tools, as discussed later in the module.

Legal Feasibility

Legal feasibility is an assessment of legal issues; it typically addresses questions such as the following:

- Will the system create any legal issues in the country where it will be used?
- Are there any political repercussions of using the system?
- Is there any conflict between the proposed system and legal requirements? For example, does the system take the Information Privacy Act into account?

10-3 Phase 2: Requirements Gathering and Analysis

In the **requirements-gathering and analysis phase**, analysts define the problem and generate alternatives for solving it. During this phase, the team attempts to understand the requirements for the system, analyzes these requirements to determine the main problem with the current system or processes, and looks for ways to solve problems by designing the new system.

The first step in this phase is gathering requirements. Several techniques are available for this step, including interviews, surveys, observations, and the JAD approach described earlier. The intent is to find out the following:

- What users do
- How they do it
- What problems they face in performing their jobs
- How the new system would address these problems
- What users expect from the system
- What decisions are made
- What data is needed to make decisions
- Where data comes from
- How data should be presented
- What tools are needed to examine data for the decisions that users make

All this information can be recorded. The team uses the information to determine what the new system should do (process analysis) and what data is needed for this process to be performed (data analysis).

The team uses the information collected during the requirements-gathering phase to understand the main problems, define the project's scope—including what it should and should not do—and create a document called the *system specifications*. This document is then sent to all key users and task-force members for approval. The creation of this document indicates the end of the analysis phase and the start of the design phase.

There are two major approaches to the analysis and design of information systems: the structured systems analysis and design (SSAD) approach and the object-oriented approach. (The object-oriented approach was introduced in Module 3 with the discussion of object-oriented databases.) The onset of the Web plus the release of Java, an object-oriented language, created the push for a different approach than SSAD. To understand the difference between the two approaches, first realize that any system has three parts: process, data, and user interface. Analyzing requirements in the analysis phase is done from the perspective of the process and data. The SSAD approach treats process and data independently and is a sequential approach that requires completing the analysis before beginning the design. The object-oriented approach combines process and data analysis; the line between analysis and design is so thin that they seem to be a single phase instead of the two distinct phases shown in Exhibit 10.1.

These two approaches use different tools for creating analysis models. Table 10.1 shows some examples of tools used in the SSAD approach.

Exhibit 10.2 shows an example of a data flow diagram for ABC Furniture's inventory management system and Exhibit 10.3 shows a context diagram.

Table 10.1 Examples of Tools Used in SSAD Analysis Models

Modeling Tool	What Is Analyzed	What It Is Used For
Data flow diagram (DFD)	Process analysis and design	Helps break down a complex process into simpler, more manageable, and more understandable subprocesses; shows how data needed by each process flows between processes and what data is stored in the system; also helps define the system's scope
Flowchart	Process analysis	Illustrates the logical steps in a process but does not show data elements and associations; can supplement a DFD and help analysts understand and document how a process works
Context diagram	Process analysis and design	Shows a process at a more general level and is helpful for showing top management and the task force how a process works
Conceptual data model (such as an entity relationship model)	Data analysis	Helps analysts understand the data requirements a system must meet by defining data elements and showing the associations between them

Exhibit 10.2
Data flow diagram for ABC Furniture's inventory management system

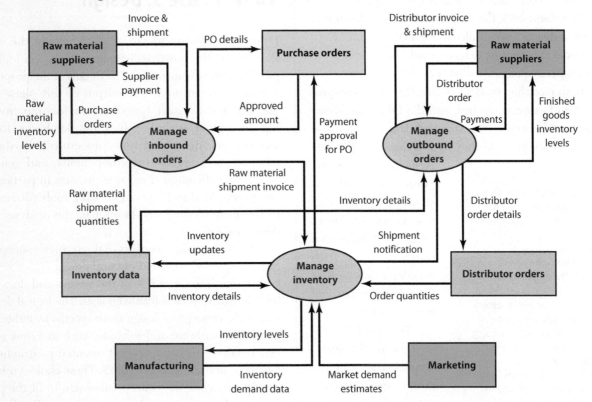

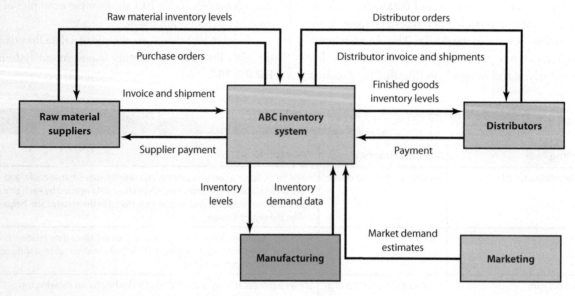

Exhibit 10.3
Context diagram for ABC Furniture's inventory management system

Notice in Exhibit 10.2 that processes are indicated with ovals. Anything that interacts with the system but is not part of it is considered an external entity and is shown as a blue rectangle. Data stores (databases, file systems, even file cabinets) are shown as gray rectangles.

In Exhibit 10.3, the DFD has been simplified into a context diagram, also called a "Level 0 diagram." Each process in this context diagram could be broken down into a separate diagram called "Level 1."

Both modeling tools show data flows between processes and external entities, and the DFD also shows data flows between processes and data stores. These data flows are general; they do not show specific data elements. For example, "Purchase orders" is shown in Exhibit 10.2 instead of all the pieces of data that make up a purchase order, such as order number, order date, item number, and item quantity.

The models created during the analysis phase constitute the design specifications. After confirming these specifications with users, analysts start designing the system.

10-4 Phase 3: Design

During the **design phase**, analysts choose the solution that is the most realistic and offers the highest payoff for the organization. The details of the proposed solution are outlined. The output of this phase is a document with exact specifications for implementing the system, including files and databases, forms and reports, documentation, procedures, hardware and software, networking components, and general system specifications. For large projects in particular, computer-aided systems engineering tools (discussed in the next section) are helpful in the analysis and design phases.

The design phase consists of three parts: conceptual design, logical design, and physical design. The conceptual design is an overview of the system and does not include hardware or software choices. The logical design makes the conceptual design more specific by indicating particular hardware and software, such as Linux servers, Windows clients, an object-oriented programming language, and a relational DBMS. These choices usually require changing the conceptual design to fit the platforms and programming languages chosen. Finally, the

> During the **design phase**, analysts choose the solution that is the most realistic and offers the highest payoff for the organization. Details of the proposed solution are outlined. The output of this phase is a document with exact specifications for implementing the system, including files and databases, forms and reports, documentation, procedures, hardware and software, networking components, and general system specifications.

physical design is created for a specific platform, such as choosing Dell servers running Ubuntu Linux, Dell laptops running Windows 11 and Internet Explorer, Java for the programming language, and SQL Server 2021 for the relational DBMS.

> **During the design phase, analysts choose the solution that is the most realistic and offers the highest payoff for the organization.**

10-4a Computer-Aided Systems Engineering

Systems analysts use **computer-aided systems engineering (CASE)** tools to automate parts of the application development process. These tools are particularly helpful for investigation and analysis in large-scale projects because they automate parts of the design phase. Analysts can use the tools to modify and update several design versions in an effort to choose the best version. CASE tools support the design phase by helping analysts do the following:

- Keep models consistent with each other.
- Document models with explanations and annotations.
- Ensure that models are created according to specific rules.
- Create a single repository of all models related to a single system, which ensures consistency in analysis and design specifications.
- Track and manage changes to the design.
- Create multiple versions of the design.

CASE tools are similar to computer-aided design (CAD) tools used by architects and engineers. Their capabilities vary depending on the product but generally include the following:

- Graphics tools, such as data flow diagrams, to illustrate a system's operation
- Dictionary tools designed to record the system's operation in detail
- Prototyping tools for designing input and output formats, forms, and screens

- Code generators to minimize or eliminate programming efforts
- Project management tools to help control the system's schedule and budget

Several CASE tools are available, including the CA ERwin Process Modeler (*http://erwin.com*), Oracle Designer (*www.oracle.com/technetwork/developer-tools/designer/overview/index-082236.html*), and Visible System's Visible Analyst (*https://www.visiblesystemscorp.com/Products/Analyst/*). CASE tools usually include the following output:

- Specifications documents
- Documentation of the analysis, including models and explanations
- Design specifications with related documentation
- Logical and physical design documents based on the conceptual design
- Code modules that can be incorporated into the system

10-4b Prototyping

Prototyping has been around for many years in physical science.

Computer-aided systems engineering (CASE) tools automate parts of the application development process. These tools are particularly helpful for investigation and analysis in large-scale projects because they automate parts of the design phase.

In **prototyping**, a small-scale version of the system is developed, but one that is large enough to illustrate the system's benefits and allow users to offer feedback.

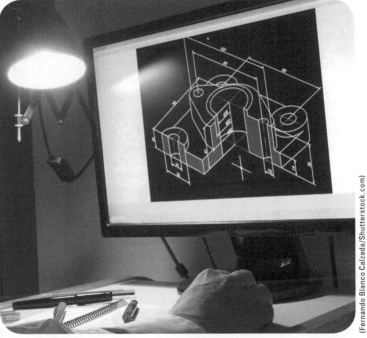

(Fernando Blanco Calzada/Shutterstock.com)

Building a small working model first is easier and less expensive than building the entire system. Prototypes can also be tested to detect potential problems and devise solutions.

Prototyping has gained popularity in designing information systems because needs can change quickly and lack of specifications for the system can be a problem. Typically, a small-scale version of the system is developed, but one that is large enough to illustrate the system's benefits and allow users to offer feedback. Prototyping is also the fastest way to put an information system into operation. Prototypes are usually used for the following purposes:

- *Gathering system requirements*—During the planning phase, designing a prototype and showing it to users is a good way to gather additional information and refine requirements for the proposed system.

- *Helping to determine system requirements*—If users are not sure about the type of information system they want, a prototype can serve as a valuable tool for demonstrating the system's functional capabilities, after which users can be asked for their reactions.

- *Determining a system's technical feasibility*—If a system appears to be technically unfeasible, a prototype can show users that a particular task can be done. This type of prototype is called a **proof-of-concept prototype**.

- *Selling the proposed system to users and management*—Prototypes are sometimes used to sell a proposed system to users and management by showing some of its features and demonstrating how beneficial it could be to the organization. This type of prototype is called a **selling prototype**.

Prototyping is usually done in four steps:[4]

1. Define the initial requirements.
2. Develop the prototype.
3. Review and evaluate the prototype.
4. Revise the prototype.

Defining the initial requirements involves agreement between users and designers that prototyping is the most suitable approach for solving a problem. After agreeing on the approach, users and designers work together to gather information about the prototype's components and how these components relate to one another. The team might decide on one of the following approaches for constructing the prototype: using an external vendor, using software packages or fourth-generation programming languages, or using high-level programming languages and developing the prototype from scratch.

Including users and top management in the construction phase is essential because some problems that crop up during construction can be solved only by users or top management. For example, top management typically must solve problems of financing a system, and lack of specifications is a problem better suited for users to solve. In addition, during this phase, users and top management can learn more about the problems the information system will solve, and the team of users and designers can learn a lot about decision making in the organization.

After the prototype is complete, users begin using it and evaluating its performance. Depending on the outcome, one of the following decisions is made: revise the prototype, cancel the information system project, develop a new prototype, or build a complete system based on the prototype. Regardless of the decision, the prototype has provided useful information to the team of users and designers. At this point, the problem is better defined and the system's operations are understood more clearly.

Prototyping Development Tools

Numerous tools can be used for constructing a system prototype. Widely used tools include spreadsheet packages, such as Microsoft Excel, and database management packages, such as Microsoft Access. Visual Basic is commonly used to code the logic required for processes. CASE tools and third- and fourth-generation programming languages can be used to quickly develop prototypes. Prototyping tools for user interface design include Figma, InVision Studio, Adobe XD, and Webflow (*https://webflow.com/blog/prototyping-tools*).

If a system appears to be technically unfeasible, a **proof-of-concept prototype** can show users that a particular task can be done.

A **selling prototype** is used to sell a proposed system to users or management by showing some of its features.

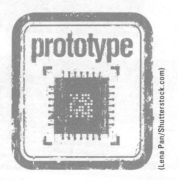

(Lena Pan/Shutterstock.com)

Advantages and Disadvantages of Prototyping

As mentioned, prototyping offers several advantages:

- It provides a method for investigating an environment in which the problem is poorly defined and information is difficult to gather.

- It reduces the need to train information system users because the users are involved in developing the system.

- It reduces costs because building a model is less expensive than building the complete system. If users and top management decide the system should not be developed, the organization will not lose all the money that would have been spent on building a complete system.

- It increases the system's chance of success by encouraging users' involvement.

- It is easier to modify a prototype than a complete system.

- It improves documentation because users and designers can walk through several versions of the system.

- It improves communication among users, top management, and information systems personnel because seeing a concrete model often prompts potential users of the system to ask questions, express opinions, and point out shortcomings and strengths.

Even with all these advantages, prototyping has some disadvantages:

- It might require more support and assistance from users and top management than they are willing to offer.

- The prototype might not reflect the final system's actual operation and could therefore be misleading.

- Developing a prototype might lead analysts and designers to forego comprehensive testing and documentation. If the prototype works, the team might be convinced that the final system will work, too, and this assumption can be misleading.

10-5 Phase 4: Implementation

During the **implementation phase**, the solution is transferred from paper to action, and the team configures the system and procures components for it. A variety of tasks take place in the implementation phase, including the following:

- Acquiring new equipment
- Hiring new employees
- Training employees
- Planning and designing the system's physical layout
- Coding
- Testing
- Designing security measures and safeguards
- Creating a disaster recovery plan

When an information system is ready to be converted, designers have several options:

- *Parallel conversion*—In **parallel conversion**, the old and new systems run simultaneously for a short time to ensure that the new system works correctly. However, this approach is costly and can be used only if an operational system is already in place.

- *Phased-in–phased-out conversion*—In **phased-in–phased-out conversion**, as each module of the new system is converted, the corresponding part of the old system is retired. This process continues until the entire system is operational. Although this approach is not suitable in all situations, it can be effective in accounting and finance.

- *Plunge (direct-cutover) conversion*—In **plunge (direct-cutover) conversion**, the old system is stopped and the new system is implemented. This approach is risky if there are problems with the new system, but the organization can save on costs by not running the old and new systems concurrently.

During the **implementation phase**, the solution is transferred from paper to action, and the team configures the system and procures components for it.

In **parallel conversion**, the old and new systems run simultaneously for a short time to ensure that the new system works correctly.

In **phased-in–phased-out conversion**, as each module of the new system is converted, the corresponding part of the old system is retired. This process continues until the entire system is operational.

In **plunge (direct-cutover) conversion**, the old system is stopped and the new system is implemented.

- *Pilot conversion*—In **pilot conversion**, an analyst introduces the system in only a limited area of the organization, such as a division or department. If the system works correctly, it is implemented in the rest of the organization in stages or all at once.

10-5a IT Project Management

According to a report published in 2022, 70 percent of all projects fail to deliver what was promised to customers.[5] Another study published in 2022 reveals some interesting facts about the importance of project management:[6]

- Companies without project management are more likely to miss deadlines and go over budget.
- Sixty-seven percent of projects fail due to lack of project management.
- Only 23 percent of companies use project management software and tools.

Poor project management and improper use of project management tools and techniques have a lot to do with such a high failure rate.[7] **IT project management** includes activities required to plan, manage, and control the creation and delivery of an information system. Activities include everything that takes place during the SDLC process. As mentioned earlier, IT projects fail for several different reasons, including:

- Missed deadlines
- Users' needs that are not met
- Dissatisfied customers
- Lack of support from top management
- Exceeding the budget
- Inadequate planning
- Insufficient communication among team members

- Inadequate project management tools and techniques

The implementation of an information system can be a complex task. To manage this complexity and keep the implementation plan under budget and on schedule, systems analysts employ project management tools and techniques. These tools help systems analysts solve scheduling problems, plan and set goals, and highlight potential bottlenecks. Project management software such as Wrike, Smartsheet, and Clarizen enables systems analysts to study the cost, time, and resource impacts of schedule changes. Additional project management software is available at *http://infogoal.com/pmc/pmcswr.htm*. Project management techniques are also used, including PERT (program evaluation review technique), CPM (critical path method), and Gantt charts.

PERT and CPM techniques work by determining the "critical path" for the completion of a series of interrelated activities. This includes all activities that are crucial for the completion of the project, with zero slack time. If any activities are delayed, the entire project is delayed. Activities that are not on the critical path are more flexible and can be delayed without delaying the project.

To establish a PERT or CPM network, the analyst identifies all the activities needed for the completion of the project, identifies and establishes a prerequisite list (the activities that have to be accomplished first), and calculates the critical path duration.

Exhibit 10.4 shows several paths that lead from the beginning to the end of a project. The duration of each path is determined by the durations of the activities that make up that path. Here are some examples:

$1 \rightarrow 2 \rightarrow 4 \rightarrow 6 \rightarrow 7 = 5 + 15 + 6 + 11 = 37$

$1 \rightarrow 4 \rightarrow 6 \rightarrow 7 = 13 + 6 + 11 = 30$

Exhibit 10.4
PERT network

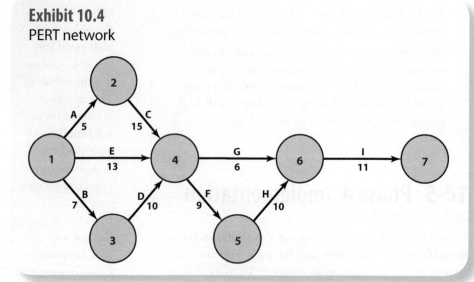

$$1 \rightarrow 4 \rightarrow 5 \rightarrow 6 \rightarrow 7 = 13 + 9 + 10 + 11 = 43$$
$$1 \rightarrow 3 \rightarrow 4 \rightarrow 5 \rightarrow 6 \rightarrow 7 = 7 + 10 + 9 + 10 + 11 = 47$$
$$1 \rightarrow 3 \rightarrow 4 \rightarrow 6 \rightarrow 7 = 7 + 10 + 6 + 11 = 34$$
$$1 \rightarrow 2 \rightarrow 4 \rightarrow 5 \rightarrow 6 \rightarrow 7 = 5 + 15 + 9 + 10 + 11 = 50$$

In these examples, the last path is the critical path because it takes the longest to be completed. While this path is being completed, the other paths will be completed as well. The activities on the other paths can be delayed for some time, and the project will still be completed on time. However, all the activities on the last path must be completed on time if the project is to be finished on time.

Using the critical path, the systems analyst can establish a Gantt chart. A Gantt chart lists completion times (sometimes called "milestones") on the x-axis and all the activities on the y-axis. This allows the systems analyst to monitor the progress of the project and detect any delay in the daily operation of the project. If a delay is spotted, the systems analyst must consider additional resources to enable the entire project to be completed on schedule. Exhibit 10.5 illustrates a Gantt chart.

The following are seven guidelines for successful IT project management:[8]

- Assign a project manager to the information systems being developed.
- Identify a goal for every project meeting.
- Document each project meeting with an e-mail, memo, wiki entry, or (if applicable) internal social media.
- Conduct regular face-to-face meetings with project technical staff.
- A new person should take over as a project manager for team members who are falling behind.
- Build in slack time for a project without disclosing it to the team members.
- Assign the best available technical people to the project.

10-5b Request for Proposal

A **request for proposal (RFP)** is a written document with detailed specifications that is

> A **request for proposal (RFP)** is a written document with detailed specifications that is used to request bids for equipment, supplies, or services from vendors.

Exhibit 10.5
Gantt chart

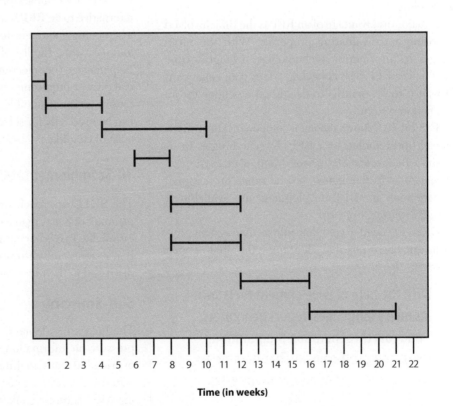

A **request for information (RFI)** is a screening document for gathering vendor information and narrowing the list of potential vendors. It can help manage the selection of vendors by focusing on crucial project requirements.

Insourcing happens when an organization's team develops the system internally.

used to request bids for equipment, supplies, or services from vendors. It is usually prepared during the implementation phase and contains detailed information about the functional, technical, and business requirements of the proposed information system. Drafting an RFP can take 6 to 12 months, but with the proper software, the Internet, and other online technologies, time and costs can be reduced.

A crucial part of this process is comparing bids from single and multiple vendors. Using a single vendor to provide all the information system's components is convenient, but the vendor might not have expertise in all areas of the information system's operations.

The main advantage of an RFP is that all vendors get the same information and requirements, so bids can be evaluated more fairly. Furthermore, all vendors have the same deadline for submitting bids, so no vendor has the advantage of having more time to prepare an offer. RFPs are also useful in narrowing down a long list of prospective vendors.

A major disadvantage of an RFP is the time involved in writing and evaluating proposals. With the rapid changes in information technologies, a lengthy time frame makes RFPs less appealing. Many companies cannot wait 6 to 12 months to decide on a vendor for an information system.

Exhibit 10.6 shows the main components of an RFP. You can find templates for RFPs by searching at Business-in-a-Box (*www.biztree.com*) and at *https://offers.hubspot.com/rfp-templates*. Several other professional software tools for RFP development are available at *www.g2.com/categories/rfp*.

Given the need to complete information system projects as quickly as possible, shortening the time needed to write and evaluate proposals is often necessary. One alternative to an RFP is a **request for information (RFI)**, a screening document for gathering vendor information and narrowing the list of potential vendors. An RFI can help manage the selection of vendors by focusing on crucial project requirements. However, an RFI has its limitations. It is not suitable for complex projects because it can be used only for selecting three or four finalists from a list of candidates.

Exhibit 10.6

Main components of an RFP for ABC Furniture's inventory system

1. Introduction
    a. Background and organizational goals of ABC
2. System Requirements
    a. Problems to be solved
    b. Details of preliminary analyses
    c. Key insights gained
3. Additional Information
    a. Hardware available
    b. Software preferences
    c. Other existing systems and integration requirements
    d. Understanding of benefits to be gained
    e. Business understanding necessary (for the bidder to work with ABC)
    f. Technology and technical know-how necessary
4. Project Time Frame
5. Contact Information and Submission Procedures

10-5c Implementation Alternatives

The SDLC approach is sometimes called **insourcing**, meaning that an organization's team develops the system internally. Two other approaches for developing information systems are self-sourcing and outsourcing, which are discussed in the following sections.

Self-Sourcing

The increasing demand for timely information has put pressure on information systems teams, who are already overloaded with maintaining and modifying existing systems. In many organizations, the task of keeping existing systems running takes up much of the available computing resources and personnel, leaving few resources

With the help of development tools such as query languages, report generators, and fourth-generation programming languages, self-sourcing has become an important part of information system resources.

for developing new systems. The resulting inability to respond to users' needs has increased employee dissatisfaction and caused a backlog in systems development both in well-managed and poorly managed organizations. In recent years, therefore, more end users have been developing their own information systems with little or no formal assistance from the information systems team. These users might not know how to write programming code, but they are typically skilled enough to use off-the-shelf software, such as spreadsheet and database packages, to produce custom-built applications.[9,10] This trend, called **self-sourcing** (or end-user development), has resulted from long backlogs in developing information systems, the availability of affordable hardware and software, and organizations' increasing dependence on timely information.

With the help of development tools such as query languages, report generators, and fourth-generation programming languages, self-sourcing has become an important part of information system resources. It is also useful in creating one-of-a-kind applications and reports. Self-sourcing can help reduce the backlog in producing information systems and improve flexibility in responding to users' information needs. Backlogs, however, are just the tip of the iceberg. When the backlog list is long, end users often stop making new requests for many of the applications they need because they believe these requests would just make the list longer. The list of applications that are not requested is often longer than the backlog, and is called the "invisible" backlog.

Although self-sourcing can solve many current problems, managers are concerned about end users' inadequate systems analysis and design background and the loosening of system development standards. Other disadvantages of self-sourcing include the following:

- Possible misuse of computing resources
- Lack of access to crucial data
- Lack of documentation for the applications and systems that end users develop
- Inadequate security for the applications and systems that end users develop
- Applications developed by end users that are not up to information system standards
- Lack of support from top management
- Lack of training for prospective users

Self-sourcing gives end users the power to build their own applications in a short time and create, access, and modify data. This power can be destructive, however, if the organization does not apply control and security measures. For example, end users' access to computing resources must be controlled to prevent interfering with the efficiency of the organization's information-processing functions.

To prevent the proliferation of information systems and applications that are not based on adequate systems development principles, organizations should develop guidelines for end users and establish criteria for evaluating, approving or rejecting, and prioritizing projects. Criteria could include asking questions such as "Can any existing application generate the proposed report?" or "Can the requirements of multiple users be met by developing a single application?"

Classifying and cataloging existing applications is necessary to prevent end users from developing applications that basically handle the same functions as an existing application; this redundancy can be costly. In addition, data administration should be enforced to ensure the integrity and reliability of information. Creating private data should be minimized, if not eliminated. Sometimes, for the sake of efficient data processing, redundant data can exist; however, it should be monitored closely. This task is becoming more difficult, however, because the number of end users using diverse data is growing. The best approach to

With **self-sourcing**, end users develop their own information systems with little or no formal assistance from the information systems team. These users might not know how to write programming code, but they are typically skilled enough to use off-the-shelf software, such as spreadsheet and database packages, to produce custom-built applications.

control the proliferation of invalid and inconsistent data in corporate databases is controlling the flow of data, such as with rigorous data-entry procedures that the database administrator establishes.

Outsourcing

With the **outsourcing** approach, an organization hires an external vendor or consultant who specializes in providing development services. This approach can save the cost of hiring additional staff while meeting the demand for more timely development of information systems projects. Companies offering outsourcing services include IBM Global Services, Accenture, Infosys Technologies, and the Hewlett Packard Enterprise (HPE) and DXC alliance.

With the development of Web 2.0, another form of outsourcing has become popular: **crowdsourcing**. This refers to the process of outsourcing tasks that are traditionally performed by employees or contractors to a large group of people (a crowd) through an open call. Say your town's city hall is developing a Web site to better serve the community. Using crowdsourcing, it would invite everybody to participate in the design process. Crowdsourcing has become popular with publishers, journalists, editors, and businesses that want to take advantage of the collaborative capabilities offered by Web 2.0. InnoCentive (*www.innocentive.com*) is a company that is very active in crowdsourcing. It works with organizations to solve their problems, taking advantage of the power of diverse thinking inside and outside the organization.

An outsourcing company that employs the SDLC approach has the following options:

- *Onshore outsourcing*—The organization chooses an outsourcing company in the same country.

- *Nearshore outsourcing*—The organization chooses an outsourcing company in a neighboring country, such as when a U.S. organization chooses a company in Canada or Mexico.

- *Offshore outsourcing*—The organization chooses an outsourcing company in any part of the world (usually not in a neighboring country), as long as it can provide the needed services.

Although outsourcing has the advantages of being less expensive, delivering information systems more quickly, and giving an organization the flexibility to concentrate on its core functions as well as other projects, it does have some disadvantages. They include the following:

- *Loss of control*—Relying on the outsourcing company to control information system functions can result in the system not fully meeting the organization's information requirements.

- *Dependency*—If the organization becomes too dependent on the outsourcing company, changes in the outsourcing company's financial status or managerial structure can have a major impact on the organization's information system.

- *Vulnerability of strategic information*—Because third parties are involved in outsourcing, the risk of leaking confidential information to competitors increases.

10-6 Phase 5: Maintenance

During the **maintenance phase**, the information system is operating, enhancements and modifications to the system have been developed and tested, and hardware and software components have been added or replaced. The maintenance team assesses how the system is working and takes steps to keep the system up and running. As part of this phase, the team collects performance data and gathers information on whether the system is meeting its objectives by talking with users, customers, and other people affected by the new system. If the system's objectives are not being met, the team must take corrective action. Creating a help desk to support users is another important task in this phase. With the ongoing nature of the SDLC approach, maintenance can lead to starting the cycle over at the planning phase if the team discovers the system is not working correctly.

10-7 New Trends in Systems Analysis and Design

The SDLC model might not be appropriate in the following situations:

- There is a lack of specifications—that is, the problem under investigation is not well defined.

- The input–output process cannot be identified completely.
- The problem is "ad hoc," meaning it is a one-time problem that is not likely to reoccur.
- Users' needs keep changing, which means the system undergoes several changes. The SDLC model might work in the short term, but in the long term it is not suitable.

For these situations, other approaches are more suitable, as described in the following sections.

10-7a Service-Oriented Architecture

Service-oriented architecture (SOA) is a philosophy and a software and system development methodology that focuses on the development, use, and reuse of small, self-contained blocks of code (called services) to meet the software needs of an organization. SOA attempts to solve software development issues by recognizing, accepting, and leveraging the existing services. Checking inventory status, customer credit, and shipping status are a few examples of such services. More specifically, a service could be a database table, a set of related database tables, one or more data files in any format, or data obtained from another service.

The fundamental principle behind SOA is that blocks of code can be reused in a variety of applications, allowing new business processes to be created from a pool of existing services. These services should be organized so they can be accessed when needed via a network. SOA offers many potential benefits to organizations, including reduced application development time, greater flexibility, and an improved return on investment.

In any business organization, some things do not change very often, such as an order processing system. These elements often represent a major part of a business and are therefore called core business functions. At the same time, some functions and activities change on a regular basis, such as taxes and the contents of a marketing campaign. SOA advocates that core business functions and the dynamic functions that change all the time should be decoupled. SOA allows an organization to pick and choose services that respond most effectively to the customer's needs and market demands. Services or blocks of code can be replaced, changed, or even combined.

Many organizations use SOA as a philosophy and methodology. For example, Starwood Hotels and Resorts Worldwide is replacing its legacy room-reservation system with an SOA-based system. By using SOA, they can offer as many as 150 service-based applications built on Web standards. T-Mobile uses SOA for internal integration and reuse and for external, revenue-generating services. This enables T-Mobile to work effectively with third-party content providers, such as Time Warner and the Bertelsmann Group, to deliver services to customers.[11]

10-7b Rapid Application Development

Rapid application development (RAD) concentrates on user involvement and continual interaction between users and designers. It combines the planning and analysis phases of the SDLC into one phase and develops a prototype of the system. RAD uses an iterative process (also called "incremental development") that repeats the design, development, and testing steps as needed, based on feedback from users. RAD is also known as a low-code or no-code systems development approach (as explained later in the module), although the RAD environment might require some coding, particularly for user interface design.

It uses visual interfaces to allow IS personnel to drag various components from the software library, connect them in specific ways, and create an application with little or no coding required.[12] After the initial prototype, the software library is reviewed, reusable components are selected from the library and integrated with the prototype, and testing is conducted. After these steps, the remaining phases are similar to the SDLC approach. One shortcoming of RAD is a narrow focus, which might limit future development. In addition, because these applications are built quickly, the quality might be lower.

10-7c Extreme Programming

Extreme programming (XP) is a method for developing software

Service-oriented architecture (SOA) is a philosophy and a software and system development methodology that focuses on the development, use, and reuse of small, self-contained blocks of code (called services) to meet the software needs of an organization.

Rapid application development (RAD) concentrates on user involvement and continual interaction between users and designers. It combines the planning and analysis phases of the SDLC into one phase and develops a prototype of the system. It uses an iterative process (also called "incremental development") that repeats the design, development, and testing steps as needed, based on feedback from users.

Extreme programming (XP) is a method for developing software applications and information system projects in which the project is divided into smaller functions and developers cannot go on to the next phase until the current phase is finished. Each function of the overall project is developed in a step-by-step fashion.

In **pair programming**, two programmers participate in one development effort at one workstation. Each programmer performs the action that the other is not currently doing.

Agile methodology is similar to XP in focusing on an incremental development process and timely delivery of working software. However, there is less emphasis on team coding and more emphasis on limiting the project's scope.

applications and information system projects. Kent Beck, during his work on the Chrysler Comprehensive Compensation System, created this method as a way of establishing specific goals and meeting them in a timely manner. XP divides a project into smaller functions, and developers cannot go on to the next phase until the current phase is finished. Analysts write down features the proposed system should have—called the "story"—on index cards. The cards include the time and effort needed to develop these features, and then the organization decides which features should be implemented and in what order, based on current needs.[13] Each function of the overall project is developed in a step-by-step fashion. At the beginning, it is similar to a jigsaw puzzle; individually, the pieces make no sense, but when they are combined, a complete picture can be seen. The XP method delivers the system to users as early as possible and then facilitates changes that the users suggest. In the XP environment, programmers are usually organized into teams of two, sharing a workstation and working on the same code. This is called **pair programming** (also referred to as "sharing a keyboard"); each programmer performs the actions that the other programmer is not currently performing. In this way, they can detect and correct programming mistakes

as they go, which is faster than correcting mistakes after the entire program has been written. There is also better communication between programmers during code development.

XP is a major departure from traditional software development, such as the SDLC model, which looks at the project as a whole. XP uses incremental steps to improve a system's quality, addressing major issues that have not been examined before. The SDLC develops the entire system at once. Like RAD, XP uses a software library for reusable pieces that can be integrated into the new system. IBM, Chrysler, and Microsoft, among others, have used this method successfully. Its key features are as follows:

- Simplicity
- An incremental process
- Responsiveness to changing requirements and changing technology
- Teamwork
- Continual communication among key players
- Immediate feedback from users

The "Extreme Programming in Action" box highlights the use of XP at Sabre Holdings Corp. and other companies.

10-7d Agile Methodology

Agile methodology is similar to XP in focusing on an incremental development process and timely delivery of working software. However, there is less emphasis on team coding and more emphasis on limiting the project's scope. Agile methodology focuses on setting a minimum

Extreme Programming in Action

▶ Finance | Technology in Society | Application | Reflective Thinking

Sabre Holdings Corp. has adopted many XP principles, including having programmers share a keyboard. Using the XP method has improved the quality of software at Sabre and reduced the number of errors. According to the Sustainable Computing Consortium, defective software costs U.S. companies more than $100 billion annually and accounts for 45 percent of computer downtime. XP has also been used by IBM, which has introduced smaller releases and involved customers in the testing process for many years.[14]

Questions and Discussions

1. What has Sabre Holdings Corp. achieved by using the XP methodology?
2. What percentage of computer downtime is associated with defective software?

number of requirements and turning them into a working product. The Agile Alliance organization (*www.agilealliance.org*) has developed guidelines for this method, which emphasizes collaboration between programmers and business experts, preferably with face-to-face communication, and working in teams. Goals of this step-by-step approach include responding to changing needs instead of sticking to a set plan and developing working, high-quality software. The agile methodology also strives to deliver software quickly to better meet customers' needs.

There are two popular agile frameworks: Scrum and Kanban.[15] Scrum focuses on a delivery cadence called a sprint and meeting structures that include planning, commitment, and daily standup meetings, which allow teams to communicate updates on their development status and strategies. A sprint ends with a demo meeting where the key features of the system are shown to the users. A follow-up meeting completes the process; the team discusses what went well and what needs improvement in the next round.

Kanban is a visual system for managing a project as it moves through various processes. Using this framework, the design team pulls user requests from an intake board and funnels them through a staged development process until they are completed. Although Scrum is more popular than Kanban, both are focused on delivering finished products fast within a transparent culture. They both help with improving processes and break a project into smaller, more manageable pieces.

The Agile Alliance has written a manifesto that includes the following principles:[16]

- Satisfy the customer through early and consistent delivery of valuable software.

- Welcome changing requirements, even late in development.

- Have businesspeople and developers work together daily throughout the project.

- Build projects around motivated individuals. Give them the environment and support they need and trust them to get the job done.

- Always attend to technical excellence. Good design enhances agility.

- At regular intervals, the team should reflect on how to become more effective, then tune and adjust its behavior accordingly.

The information box titled "Agile Methodology at HomeAway, Inc." discusses how agile methods are used at HomeAway.

10-7e Low-Code and No-Code Development

As you learned earlier, self-sourcing or end-user development requires the end user to understand the off-the-shelf software to be used for application development. In the relatively new platforms known as *low-code* and *no-code*, there is no such requirement. Users need minimal or no knowledge of coding or the tools deployed for applications development.

No-code, sometimes called *point-and-click development* or simply *click development*, does not require any previous knowledge of coding. The user (sometimes called the citizen developer) can drag and drop application components, connect them together, and create an application. No-code platforms have prebuilt drag-and-drop elements that have been coded for reuse; the user defines what the application does rather than how the application does it. Some popular no-code development platforms include Airtable, AppGyver (SAP SE), AppSheet (Google), Appy Pie, and AWS Honeycode (Amazon).

In a **low-code** environment, some coding knowledge is needed by developers. Popular low-code platforms include Appian, Claris FileMaker (Apple), DWkit, AppSheet (Google), and Looker (Google). Some low-code platforms offer no-code functionality as well; examples include Appian, Mendix, Microsoft PowerApps, OutSystems, and Salesforce Lightning. The low-code market is expected to grow from $13.8 billion in 2021 to $30 billion by 2025.[17]

Some of the advantages of low-code and no-code development include the following:[18]

- Ease of use

- Fast application development

- Reduced costs

- Increased productivity

- Availability of easy change and modification

Some of the disadvantages of low-code and no-code development include the following:[19]

- Users must have a clear understanding of what they need.

- The platform may not support all the users' requirements.

No-code, sometimes called *point-and-click development* or simply *click development*, does not require any previous knowledge of coding. The user can drag and drop application components, connect them together, and create an application.

In a **low-code** environment, some coding knowledge is needed by developers.

- Security issues are possible due to lack of control.
- The user does not own the source code.

A growing number of companies are using low-code and no-code platforms to speed up the application development process and reduce costs. HealthBridge, a healthcare and financial services company, hired the software company Boomi to create a low-code platform for processing medical claims. The platform helped Health-Bridge speed up claim processing and create a self-service portal for its customers to reduce call center volume one year ahead of schedule.[20]

NOAA Fisheries, a U.S. government agency with over 4,000 employees, is responsible for the nation's ocean resources and their habitats. To increase its efficacy in dealing with a growing number of projects, the agency deployed no-code as an alternative to traditional application development tools. The agency used Smartsheet's no-code platform to establish a PMO (project management office) so that professionals who are not trained project managers could build tools, templates, and processes. The platform has assisted the agency in keeping pace with demand and keeping its community satisfied; the agency has seen a 40 percent increase in employee engagement.[21]

The public health department of Tarrant County, Texas, deployed Quickbase, a cloud-based, Web-facing, low-code database platform, for vaccine registrations. The system was up and running within a couple of days, enabling thousands of people to register daily.[22]

The Industry Connection highlights CA Technologies, which offers several systems development tools.

Agile Methodology at HomeAway, Inc.

▶ Finance | Technology in Society | Application | Reflective Thinking

Based in Austin, Texas, HomeAway, Inc. (a part of Expedia, Inc.) is one of the world's leading online marketplaces for vacation rentals. Its sites represent approximately 1 million vacation rental-home listings throughout 190 countries and territories around the world.[23]

At HomeAway, 250 software developers use agile as the methodology for software and systems development. In the past, individual developers and system designers used different systems development methodologies, but for the past six years, agile has been the company-wide methodology. According to Jack Yang, HomeAway's vice president of engineering, no one was forced to move to agile methods, but over time the systems designers found that it was the best methodology for keeping up with change, especially unexpected change that needs to be addressed quickly. If HomeAway's experience is any indication, agile methodology continues to become a mainstream tool for software and systems development. Companies and system developers choose it for its team-driven, collaborative, and modular aspects over the nonflexible, sequence-driven SDLC approach.[24]

Questions and Discussions

1. Why did HomeAway switch to agile methodology from other systems development methodologies?
2. What are two advantages of agile methodology compared with other methodologies?

Industry Connection: CA Technologies[25]

CA Technologies (a part of Broadcom) offers several products and services for use in enterprise IT management, including managing information systems, networks, security platforms, storage, applications, and databases. The company offers a variety of hardware, software, and services for business use as well as home use in the following categories: application development and databases; application performance management; database management; infrastructure and operations management; mainframe applications; project, portfolio, and financial management; security management; service management; and storage and recovery management. It is also involved in the cloud computing environment.

(Continued)

One product from CA Technologies is the ERwin Process Modeler, a CASE tool used for a variety of systems analysis and design activities. It is a modeling tool that can help systems analysts visualize complex systems with many inputs, processes, and outputs as well as create workflow and data flow modeling, such as DFDs. ERwin can also be used to create databases and design, share, and reuse physical and logical models.

Module Summary

10-1 Apply the systems development life cycle as a method for developing information systems. The systems development life cycle (SDLC), also known as the "waterfall model," is a series of well-defined phases performed in sequence that serves as a framework for developing a system or project. In this model, each phase's output (results) becomes the input for the next phase.

10-2 Explain the tasks involved in the planning phase. During the planning phase, which is one of the most crucial phases of the SDLC model, the systems designer must define the problem the organization faces, taking care not to define symptoms rather than the underlying problem. The problem can be identified internally or externally.

10-3 Explain the tasks involved in the requirements-gathering and analysis phase. In this phase, analysts define the problem and generate alternatives for solving it. During this phase, the team attempts to understand the requirements for the system, analyzes these requirements to determine the main problem with the current system or processes, and looks for ways to solve problems by designing the new system.

10-4 Explain the tasks involved in the design phase. During the design phase, analysts choose the solution that is the most realistic and offers the highest payoff for the organization. The details of the proposed solution are outlined, and the output of this phase is a document with exact specifications for implementing the system, including files and databases, forms and reports, documentation, procedures, hardware and software, networking components, and general system specifications.

10-5 Explain the tasks involved in the implementation phase. During the implementation phase, the solution is transferred from paper to action, and the team configures the system and procures components for it. A variety of tasks take place in the implementation phase, including acquiring new equipment, hiring new employees, training employees, planning and designing the system's physical layout, coding, testing, designing security measures and safeguards, and creating a disaster recovery plan.

10-6 Explain the tasks involved in the maintenance phase. During the maintenance phase, the information system is operating, enhancements and modifications to the system have been developed and tested, and hardware and software components have been added or replaced. The maintenance team assesses how the system is working and takes steps to keep the system up and running. As part of this phase, the team collects performance data and gathers information on whether the system is meeting its objectives by talking with users, customers, and other people affected by the new system.

10-7 Describe new trends in systems analysis and design, including service-oriented architecture, rapid application development, extreme programming, the agile methodology, low-code, and no-code. The SDLC model might not be appropriate if there is a lack of specifications—that is, the problem under investigation is not well defined or the input–output process cannot be identified completely. In these situations, the analyst should use the newer methodologies.

Key Terms

- Agile methodology
- Computer-aided systems engineering (CASE)
- Crowdsourcing
- Design phase
- Economic feasibility
- External users
- Extreme programming (XP)
- Feasibility study
- Implementation phase
- Insourcing
- Internal users
- IT project management
- Joint application design (JAD)
- Legal feasibility
- Low-code
- Maintenance phase
- No-code
- Operational feasibility
- Outsourcing

- Pair programming
- Parallel conversion
- Phased-in–phased-out conversion
- Pilot conversion
- Planning phase
- Plunge (direct-cutover) conversion
- Proof-of-concept prototype
- Prototyping
- Rapid application development (RAD)
- Request for information (RFI)
- Request for proposal (RFP)
- Requirements-gathering and analysis phase
- Scheduling feasibility
- Self-sourcing
- Selling prototype
- Service-oriented architecture (SOA)
- Systems development life cycle (SDLC)
- Technical feasibility

Reviews and Discussions

1. What are the five phases in the systems development life cycle?
2. What are the five major dimensions of a feasibility study?
3. What are three examples of activities performed during the planning phase?
4. What are examples of three tasks involved in the requirements-gathering and analysis phase?
5. What are examples of three tasks performed during the design phase?
6. What are examples of three tasks performed during the implementation phase?
7. What are examples of three tasks performed during the maintenance phase?
8. List five new trends in systems analysis and design.

Projects

1. A startup Internet company has generated the following cash balances for the first six years of its IS projects: –$250,000, –$180,000, $225,000, $340,000, $410,000, and $425,000. Using the NPV function in Excel, calculate the net present value of these projects at an 8.5 percent interest rate. What is the IRR of this project? If a bank is willing to give the company a loan at 15 percent to implement these projects, should the company accept the loan (assuming there are no other conditions)? Why or why not?

2. The CTO of the company mentioned in Project 1 has decided to acquire a CASE tool to help expedite and better document the Web site that is being designed for the company's e-commerce operations. The CTO has narrowed these choices to the CA ERwin Process Modeler and Oracle Designer. Based on the information provided in this module and other sources, which tool would you recommend? What are the three major factors behind your recommendation?

3. The CTO of the company mentioned in Project 1 also wants to invest in project management software. The choices have been narrowed to Wrike and Smartsheet. Based on the information provided in this module and other sources, which software would you recommend? What are the three major factors behind your recommendation? What are three tasks performed by typical project management software?

4. After reading the information presented in this module and other sources, write a one-page paper that identifies two companies (besides those mentioned in this book) that have been using SOA as a systems development methodology. What specific advantages has SOA offered these companies?

5. After reading the information presented in this module and other sources, write a one-page paper that identifies two companies (besides those mentioned in this book) that have been using crowdsourcing as an alternative to a traditional systems development approach. What are two advantages of using crowdsourcing to develop a system or application? What are two disadvantages?

6. After reading the information presented in this module and other sources, write a one-page paper describing three countries that are prime candidates for offshore IT outsourcing for systems development projects. What are the three main criteria that should be considered in choosing a suitable candidate? Why has India become a top choice for IT outsourcing?

Module Quiz

1. When there is a lack of specifications, service-oriented architecture (SOA) is preferred to SDLC for designing a system. True or False?

2. Planning is the last phase of the SDLC process. True or False?

3. PERT and CPM techniques work by determining the "critical path" for the completion of a series of interrelated activities. True or False?

4. All of the following are included in SDLC except:
   a. Planning
   b. Requirements-gathering and analysis
   c. IT project management
   d. Design

5. One of the following is not a type of conversion method during the implementation process:
   a. Parallel conversion
   b. Service-oriented architecture (SOA) conversion
   c. Phased-in–phased-out conversion
   d. Plunge (direct cutover) conversion

6. IT projects fail for all of the following reasons except:
   a. Users' needs that are not met
   b. Dissatisfied customers
   c. Missed deadlines
   d. Support from top management

Case Study 10-1
Systems Development with a No-Code Platform
➤ **Finance | Technology in Society | Application**

As discussed earlier in the module, low-code and no-code platforms enable users to design applications (particularly mobile apps) in a matter of days and weeks at a moderate cost. Large technology companies such as Microsoft, Alphabet, and Amazon AWS are increasing their market presence in low-code and no-code platforms, either through in-house development or by acquiring smaller companies. Below are some interesting statistics about low-code platforms:[26]

- By 2030, the global low-code development market is predicted to generate revenues of $187 billion.
- By 2024, low-code application development will be responsible for more than 65 percent of application development activity.
- By 2024, 75 percent of large enterprises will be using at least four low-code development tools.
- Twenty-four percent of low-code users had no development experience at all before using low-code platforms.

New York City used a no-code platform from a startup company called Unqork (*www.unqork.com/about/index*) to build and launch a coronavirus crisis-management platform in days. The platform allows New York officials to map the virus and identify hot spots as well as connect residents to critical services. This platform can be customized for other cities, counties, or states and can go live in 48 to 72 hours.[27]

Schneider Electric used OutSystems, a popular low-code platform, to launch 60 apps in 20 months, with most delivered in just 10 weeks. Ricoh USA, an information management and digital services company, used OutSystems to replace its legacy systems, achieving a 253 percent ROI and payback in just seven months. Thinkmoney, a UK-based banking services provider, used OutSystems to implement a mobile digital banking system in just 14 weeks. Vodafone, Hewlett Packard Enterprise, Honda, ExxonMobil, and Humana are other examples of companies that have successfully deployed this platform for application development.[28]

Some of the capabilities of OutSystems as a typical low-code platform include the following:[29]

- Drag-and-drop UI
- Cross-platform apps
- The ability to add your own code when needed
- The ability to deliver apps and update them with one click
- The ability to automatically check dependencies and handle all deployment processes
- Availability of flexible mobile experience

Answer the following questions:

1. What are two advantages of low-code and no-code platforms for systems development?
2. How did New York City use a no-code platform?
3. What are three capabilities of a typical low-code platform?

Case Study 10-2
Crowdsourcing Pays Off

▶▶▶ Finance | Technology in Society | Application | Reflective Thinking | Global

Crowdsourcing is not only used for relatively simple tasks such as designing a Web site or a case for a smartphone. Today, it is increasingly being used in more complex designs as well. Precyse Technologies provides supply-chain products and solutions that assist organizations in tracking their inventories using RFID technology. The company was having difficulty improving the performance and battery life of a particular RFID device; there were not adequate internal resources to tackle the problem. So, Precyse asked InnoCentive, a crowdsourcing provider, for assistance, believing that it would provide quick access to a worldwide talent pool and a higher return on investment (ROI). Ultimately, the company received more than 300 ideas from global experts for solving its problem. The company narrowed the pool of ideas down to three finalists, from which a winner was chosen. The whole process took approximately four months and saved the company an estimated $250,000.[30]

(Rawpixel.com/Shutterstock.com)

Answer the following questions:

1. What are some typical applications of crowdsourcing?
2. What are some advantages of crowdsourcing?
3. How could crowdsourcing reduce the cost of systems design?
4. Are there certain problems you would not want to use crowdsourcing to solve?

Module
11
Enterprise Systems

Learning Objectives
After studying this module, you should be able to…

11.1 Explain how supply chain management is used within an organization.

11.2 Describe customer relationship management systems.

11.3 Describe knowledge management systems.

11.4 Describe enterprise resource planning systems.

11.5 Explain advantages and disadvantages of cloud-based enterprise systems.

iStock.com/metamorworks

An **enterprise system** is an application that is used in all the functions of a business and supports decision making throughout the organization. An enterprise resource planning system is used to coordinate operations, resources, and decision making among manufacturing, production, marketing, and human resources departments. As you have learned in previous modules, intranets and Web portals are used by many organizations to improve communication among departments and increase overall efficiency. Enterprise systems are another way to make important information readily available to decision makers throughout an organization.

In this module, you learn about the following enterprise systems: supply chain management (SCM), customer relationship management (CRM), knowledge management systems (KMS), and enterprise resource planning (ERP). With each type of enterprise system, you review the system's goals, the information technologies used for it, and any relevant issues. The module also reviews cloud-based enterprise systems that are replacing traditional enterprise systems.

> An **enterprise system** is an application that is used in all the functions of a business and supports decision making throughout the organization.
>
> A **supply chain** is an integrated network consisting of an organization, its suppliers, transportation companies, and brokers used to deliver goods and services to customers.
>
> **Supply chain management (SCM)** is the process of working with suppliers and other partners in the supply chain to improve procedures for delivering products and services.

11-1 Supply Chain Management

A **supply chain** is an integrated network consisting of an organization, its suppliers, transportation companies, and brokers used to deliver goods and services to customers. As Exhibit 11.1 shows, in a manufacturing firm's supply chain, raw materials flow from suppliers to manufacturers (where they are transformed into finished goods), then to distributors, then to retailers, and finally to consumers. Supply chains exist both in service and manufacturing organizations, although the chain's complexity can vary widely in different organizations and industries. In manufacturing, the major links in the supply chain are suppliers, manufacturing facilities, distribution centers, retailers, and customers. In service organizations—such as those in real estate, the travel industry, temporary labor, and advertising—these links include suppliers (service providers), distribution centers, and customers.

Supply chain management (SCM) is the process of working with suppliers and other partners in the supply chain to improve procedures for delivering products and services. An SCM system coordinates the following functions:

- Procuring materials (in service organizations, this can include resources and information)
- Transforming materials into intermediate and finished products or services
- Distributing finished products or services to customers

Exhibit 11.1
Manufacturing firm's supply chain configuration

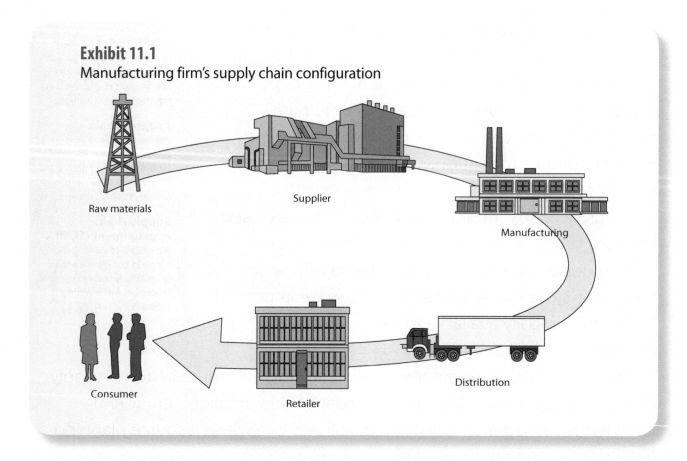

In a manufacturing firm's SCM system, communication takes place among the following areas:

- *Product flow*—Managing the movement of goods all the way from suppliers to customers; this process includes customer service and support

- *Information flow*—Overseeing order transmissions and delivery status updates throughout the order-processing cycle

- *Finances flow*—Handling credit terms, payment schedules, and consignment and title ownership arrangements

An SCM system must manage communication in all these areas as part of overseeing the manufacturing process and managing inventory and delivery. Four key decisions in SCM are related to manufacturing:

- *Location*—Where should manufacturing facilities be placed?

- *Inventory*—When should an order be placed? How much should be ordered?

- *Production*—What should be produced? How much should be produced?

- *Transportation*—Which transportation systems will reduce costs and expedite the delivery process?

For organizations that do not have in-house resources to develop an SCM system, several vendors offer comprehensive solutions: SAP (*https://www.sap.com/products/digital-supply-chain.html*), Oracle (*https://www.oracle.com/applications/supply-chain-management/*), Ariba (*www.ariba.com*), and Manhattan Associates (*www.manh.com*). In addition, hosting services are now available for SCM systems; this trend is called "software as a service" (SaaS, as discussed in Module 14). The "Supply Chain Management at Coca-Cola Company" box highlights the supply chain at Coca-Cola.

A growing trend in SCM is green logistics and green SCM, which encompasses all SCM activities, including manufacturing, packaging, transportation, and warehousing. Green logistics advocates a type of SCM that minimizes environmental impacts, including climate change, air pollution, water pollution, soil degradation, solid waste, noise, vibration, and accidents. Many of the information technology tools discussed in this book could assist organizations to achieve their green goals: green computing (discussed in Module 4); management support systems (discussed in Module 12); collaborative planning, forecasting, and replenishment (CPFR); 3D and 4D printing; and Internet of Things (IoT, as discussed later in this module). The "Green SCM in Action: Walmart" box highlights green SCM at Walmart.

Supply Chain Management at Coca-Cola Company

➤➤ Finance | Application | Reflective Thinking

The Coca-Cola Company is the world's largest beverage company. Its 500 brands are sold in more than 200 countries.[1] The company needed a more modern SCM system that would work well with its other systems. The new SCM system would also need to provide processes and information to assist with acquisitions of other companies, and it would need to integrate information from manufacturing with its retail operations. To achieve these goals, Coca-Cola decided to implement a new supply chain management system at its 17 European plants, replacing several of the existing systems.

(Vytautas Kielaitis/Shutterstock.com)

SAP ERP was adopted as the main system, with certain applications outsourced to DXC (*https://dxc.com/us/en?merger=true*). The new SCM implementation has succeeded by providing more automation and by streamlining various SCM processes. It also assists in bringing newly acquired companies online in a timely manner. More important, the new SCM system links supply-and-demand data into a single system. Overall, the new system provides key decision makers with timely and relevant information that improves the overall efficiency and effectiveness of the entire supply chain operation.[2]

Questions and Discussions

1. Why did the Coca-Cola Company implement an SCM system?
2. How does the SCM system impact the efficiency of the entire supply chain operation?

11-1a SCM Technologies

Information technologies and the Internet play a major role in implementing a successful SCM system. These tools are explained in the following sections.

Electronic Data Interchange

Electronic data interchange (EDI) enables business partners to send and receive information about business transactions. Many companies substitute EDI for printing, mailing, and faxing paper documents, such as purchase orders, invoices, and shipping notices. By using the Internet and established Web protocols for the electronic exchange of information, companies can improve the efficiency and effectiveness of the supply chain process. EDI expedites the delivery of accurate information in the following processes, among others:

- Transaction acknowledgments
- Financial reporting
- Invoice and payment processing
- Order status
- Purchasing

- Shipping and receiving
- Inventory management and sales forecasting

In addition, using the Internet and Web protocols for EDI lowers the cost of transmitting documents. This method is called Web-based EDI or Open EDI. It also has the advantage of being platform independent and easy to use.

Nevertheless, transmitting across the Internet does involve more security risks than traditional EDI, which uses proprietary protocols and networks. Using EDI does have some drawbacks. For instance, EDI uses proprietary standards. An EDI provider sets up an EDI network (as a virtual private network, or VPN), and organizations enroll in the network. EDI is more beneficial when there are more companies in the EDI network because the cost per partner is higher when the number of partners is small. For this reason, large companies tend to insist that their suppliers and distributors become part of the same EDI network, which many

> **Electronic data interchange (EDI)** enables business partners to send and receive information about business transactions.

Green SCM in Action: Walmart

▶▶▶ Finance | Social Responsibility | Reflective Thinking | Global

Walmart says its best practices for sustainability are part of its supply chain DNA and are achieved through collaboration among all key players both inside and outside the company.[3]

Walmart's sustainability initiatives are designed to achieve a number of goals. To achieve these goals, several policies have to be implemented within the company and with its key partners in the supply chain network. Some of Walmart's sustainability goals are as follows:[4]

- Target zero emissions in its own operations by 2040.
- Achieve 100 percent renewable energy by 2035.
- With coordination among its suppliers and other business partners, avoid or eliminate 1 gigaton of greenhouse gas emissions from the global SCM by 2030. In April 2022, Walmart announced that it had surpassed the midway point in accomplishing this goal.
- Restore at least 50 million acres of land and 1 million square miles of ocean by 2030.
- Achieve zero waste in Walmart's operations in the United States and Canada by 2025.

At its sustainability milestone summit in April 2019, Walmart announced that for the first time, its U.S. stores would carry reusable bags that are available to customers for purchase. The goal of this campaign was to help reduce plastic waste and increase customer convenience by placing reusable bags in easy-to-find and highly visible places in stores. As part of the launch, Walmart rolled out an assortment of reusable bags made with postconsumer recycled content.[5,6,7]

Questions and Discussions

1. How has Walmart made its supply chain more sustainable?
2. What was the goal of Walmart's rollout of reusable bags?

---

small suppliers and distributors cannot afford. With the advent of eXtensible Markup Language (XML), organizations can use the Internet and Open EDI to perform the same function that EDI performs, so traditional EDI has declined in popularity.

Internet-Enabled SCM

Internet-enabled SCM improves information sharing throughout the supply chain, which helps reduce costs for information transmission and improves customer service. For instance, many companies use point-of-sale (POS) systems that scan what is being sold and collect this data in real time. This information helps organizations decide what to reorder to replenish stock; the information is sent via the Internet to suppliers so they can synchronize production with actual sales. Internet-enabled SCM can improve the following SCM activities:

- *Purchasing/procurement*—Purchasing and paying for goods and services online, bargaining and

renegotiating prices and term agreements, using global procurement strategies
- *Inventory management*—Providing real-time stock information, replenishing stock quickly and efficiently, tracking out-of-stock items
- *Transportation*—Allowing customers to use the Internet for shipping and delivery information
- *Order processing*—Checking order placement and order status, improving the speed and quality of order processing, handling returned goods and out-of-stock notifications to customers
- *Customer service*—Responding to customers' complaints, issuing notifications (such as product recalls), providing around-the-clock customer service
- *Production scheduling*—Coordinating just-in-time (JIT) inventory programs with vendors and suppliers, coordinating production schedules between companies and their vendors and suppliers, conducting customer demand analysis

E-Marketplaces

An **e-marketplace** is a third-party exchange (a business-to-business or B2B business model) that provides a platform for buyers and sellers to interact with each other and trade more efficiently online. E-marketplaces help businesses maintain a competitive edge in the supply chain in the following ways:

- Providing opportunities for sellers and buyers to establish new trading partnerships

- Providing a single platform for prices, availability, and stock levels that is accessible to all participants

- Solving time-constraint problems for international trade and making it possible to conduct business around the clock

- Making it easy to compare prices and products from a single source instead of spending time contacting each seller

- Reducing marketing costs more than traditional sales channels can

E-distributors are common examples of e-marketplaces. An e-distributor is a marketplace owned and operated by a third party that provides an electronic catalog of products. For example, an e-distributor might offer a catalog containing a variety of hardware and software products so that a network administrator can order all the equipment and applications needed for an organization's network instead of purchasing components from several different vendors. Another common offering from e-distributors is maintenance, repair, and operations (MRO) services; a company can purchase an MRO package that might include services from different vendors, but the e-distributor coordinates them into one package for customers. This packaging is an example of a horizontal market, which concentrates on coordinating a business process or function involving multiple vendors. E-distributors offer fast delivery of a wide selection of products and services, usually at lower prices, and they help companies reduce the time and expense of searching for goods.

As you learned in Module 8, third-party exchanges bring together buyers and sellers in vertical and horizontal markets. Buyers can gather information on products and sellers, and sellers have access to more potential buyers. Examples of third-party exchanges include PowerSource

(littleny/Shutterstock.com)

Online (*www.powersourceonline.com*) and *Farms.com* (*www.farms.com*).

Online Auctions

Auctions help determine the price of goods and services when there is no set price in the marketplace. An **online auction** is a straightforward yet revolutionary business concept. By using the Internet, it brings traditional auctions to customers around the globe and makes it possible to sell far more goods and services than at a traditional auction. It is based on the brokerage business model discussed in Module 8, which brings buyers and sellers together in a virtual marketplace. Typically, the organization hosting the auction collects transaction fees for the service. Online auctions are particularly cost-effective for selling excessive inventory. Some companies use **reverse auctions**, which invite sellers to submit bids for products and services. In other words, there is one buyer and many sellers: a one-to-many relationship. The buyer can choose the seller that offers the service or product at the lowest price.

An **e-marketplace** is a third-party exchange (B2B model) that provides a platform for buyers and sellers to interact with each other and trade more efficiently online.

By using the Internet, an **online auction** brings traditional auctions to customers around the globe and makes it possible to sell far more goods and services than at a traditional auction.

A **reverse auction** invites sellers to submit bids for products and services. In other words, there is one buyer and many sellers: a one-to-many relationship. The buyer can choose the seller that offers the service or product at the lowest price.

Collaborative Planning, Forecasting, and Replenishment

Collaborative planning, forecasting, and replenishment (CPFR) is used to coordinate supply chain members through point-of-sale (POS) data sharing and joint planning (see Exhibit 11.2). In other words, any data collected with POS systems is shared with all members of the supply chain, which is useful in coordinating production and planning for inventory needs. The goal is to improve operational efficiency and manage inventory. With a structured process of sharing information among supply chain members, retailers can compare customer demands or sales forecasts with a manufacturer's order forecast, for example. If there is a discrepancy between forecasts, members can get together and decide on the correct quantity to order.

One main obstacle to improving supply chain performance is companies that don't have enough information about what customers want, which can lead to lost sales and unsold inventory for retailers and manufacturers. CPFR has the advantage of decreasing merchandising, inventory, and logistics costs for all supply chain members.

Coordinating the supply chain can be difficult. To understand these problems, recall the example of ABC Furniture Company, which was used in Module 10. ABC Furniture buys wood from New England Wood and buys hardware (nuts, bolts, and so forth) from Vermont Hardware. ABC Furniture also uses a distributor, Furniture Distribution Company (FDC), to send the final products to retailers. Therefore, ABC Furniture's supply chain includes New England Wood and Vermont Hardware on what's called the "upstream" side of the supply chain and includes FDC, retailers, and customers on the "downstream" side of the supply chain.

The retailer is the only partner in this supply chain that knows exactly how many pieces of furniture have been sold

Exhibit 11.2
CPFR process

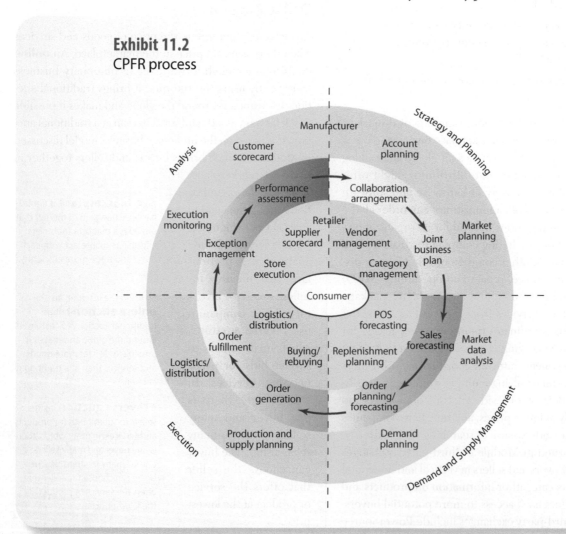

and how many are available in inventory; without agreements in place, most retailers do not share this information. The distributor, FDC, knows only how many pieces retailers order to replenish their stock, which does not indicate exact numbers sold. So, FDC places an order with ABC Furniture based on its forecasts of orders from retailers. ABC Furniture does not know exactly how much inventory FDC has on hand, but only the quantity of orders FDC has placed. So, ABC Furniture orders supplies from New England Wood and Vermont Hardware based on the distributor's forecasts.

If a retailer gets more products than it can sell or stock, it returns the products to FDC, which absorbs part of the cost. FDC, in turn, sends some products back to ABC Furniture, which absorbs this cost. ABC Furniture now has too many products in its inventory and must slow down manufacturing. However, it cannot return lumber to New England Wood, so it ends up paying for carrying extra raw materials in inventory. As a result, ABC Furniture might suffer from having the highest costs in the supply chain, and retailers suffer the least.

CPFR ensures that inventory and sales data are shared across the supply chain, so everyone knows the exact sales and inventory levels. The collaborative part of this process is the agreement between all supply chain partners that establishes how data is shared, how problems with overstock are solved, and how to ensure that costs for each partner are shared or minimized. The agreement also encourages retailers to share important data with the distributor and manufacturer, often by offering them better discounts. Retailers are also motivated to sell more to give themselves more leverage with ABC Furniture, which in turn helps ABC Furniture because added sales improve its bottom line.

Even with an agreement in place, unforeseen problems can crop up, so planning for these "exceptions" is important. Handling unforeseen problems is called *exception management*, and lessons learned during this process can be used in future planning.

3D Printing

3D printing or additive manufacturing is a process for making a physical object from a three-dimensional digital model. The process is accomplished through the application of many successive thin layers of material.

The global 3D printing market is expected to grow from $12.6 billion in 2021 to $34.8 billion by 2026, a 22 percent yearly increase. Simplification in the development of customized products, reductions in manufacturing costs and process downtime, government investments in 3D printing projects, and development of new, industrial-grade 3D printing materials are major factors accelerating market growth. This growth includes applications in developing prototypes for end-user products as well as deployment in manufacturing to improve efficiency.[8]

3D printers have been around for more than three decades, but their high cost and complexity made them affordable only to large companies for much of that time. Advances in digital scanners and software technologies have made them accessible and more affordable for smaller organizations.

3D printing offers some of the same advantages of prototyping, as discussed in Module 10, such as cost reduction, decreasing risk, improving communication among decision makers, increasing feedback, and personalization of products and services. 3D printing impacts almost all industries, including food, the military, electronics, toys, medicine, healthcare, and automobiles.

These printers can make products that traditional factories are unable to make—including human tissue.

3D printing could also have a positive impact on environmental and sustainability issues by reducing waste, generating longer lifespans for products, reducing transportation, and creating fewer unsold products.[9]

3D printing plays a major role in SCM:[10]

- Manufacturing lead times are significantly reduced.
- Customer demand is met more quickly and more specifically.
- Manufacturers print on demand, eliminating the need to carry inventory.
- New designs come to market much quicker.
- Materials are used more efficiently, as leftovers can be used for other projects.

The "3D Printing in Action: The Medical Field" box highlights the applications of 3D printing technology in the medical field.

4D Printing

4D printing is based on 3D printing technology with one significant difference. **4D printing** uses special materials and sophisticated designs that are "programmed" to prompt 3D printed objects to change their shape and structure by the influence of external factors. These

> **3D printing** or additive manufacturing is a process for making a physical object from a three-dimensional digital model. The process is accomplished through the application of many successive thin layers of material.
>
> **4D printing** uses special materials and sophisticated designs that are "programmed" to prompt 3D printed objects to change their shape and structure by the influence of external factors.

external factors may include temperature, light, or other environmental stimuli. This technology enables companies to manufacture products that can self-assemble, reshape themselves, or otherwise react to changing conditions.[11] Popular applications of 4D printing include the following:[12]

- *Aerospace*—To make self-deploying structures for air ventilation, engine cooling, and other similar uses
- *Defense*—To make military uniforms that can alter their camouflage or better protect against poisonous gases or shrapnel on contact
- *Medical*—For tissue engineering and smart biomedical devices and the fabrication of nanoparticles and nanorobots for chemotherapy
- *Automotive*—To produce car components that can adapt to changing environmental

conditions. Examples include improved airbags and car seats that provide adaptive support and comfort.

- *Consumer goods*—Could be used to make flat-pack furniture pieces such as chairs and tables, which would self-assemble when triggered

Drones

A drone is a specialized robot that is designed to fly and perform certain automated tasks. Drones come in various shapes and sizes, and they vary in sophistication—many drones are used for recreation, but this is changing. Several companies are using drones in SCM; Walmart uses drones to count inventory in warehouses and is testing drones for indoor operations.

3D Printing in Action: The Medical Field

⏩ Finance | Social Responsibility | Reflective Thinking | Technology in Society

3D printing technology is increasingly being used in the medical field to improve patient care and reduce medical costs. These printers are also used for presentations, media events, and other medical PR activities.

3D printing lowers the risks and costs of complex surgeries. Boston Children's Hospital has used the technology to assist surgeons, doctors, and medical students; it helped a neurosurgeon save the life of a 4-month-old. To do this, hospital technicians used standard imaging to print a high-resolution copy of a child's brain a few days before the surgery. The surgeon examined the model, slowly developed a tactile feel for the challenge, and then rehearsed the surgery. Cincinnati Children's Hospital and a children's hospital in New York have used 3D printing technology to print organs, such as hearts made from their patients' CT or MRI scans, to practice complex surgical procedures ahead of time.

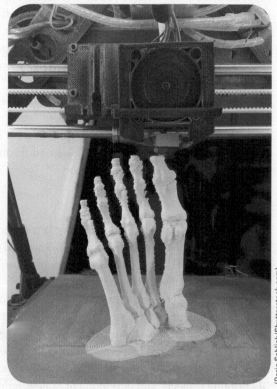

(Dario Sabljak/Shutterstock.com)

A 3D-printed model of a five-year-old child at Nicklaus Children's Hospital in Miami helped surgeons know exactly how to operate before the first incision.[13] The technology also helped save the life of a 56-year-old mother of three with a brain aneurysm at Kaleida Health's Gates Vascular Institute in Buffalo, New York.

3D printing could assist the medical field by helping to create the following:[14,15] tissue with blood vessels; low-cost prosthetic parts; prescription drugs; tailor-made medical sensors; medical models, such as cancerous tumors; bone that promotes the growth of bone in any shape; heart valves; ear cartilage; medical equipment; cranium replacements; synthetic skin; and organs such as the liver, heart, and kidney.

Questions and Discussions

1. What are three applications of 3D printing technology in the medical field?
2. How has Boston Children's Hospital used 3D printing technology?

Drones can carry inventory and deliver it to specified locations. They are particularly useful for last-mile deliveries in urban areas with heavy traffic congestion. They also work well for delivering medicine and relief packs to remote and rural areas.

Amazon is opening hundreds of physical stores that could be used as airports for drone delivery fleets.

In agriculture, drones are used to supervise animals, and in a dangerous environment, such as oil fields, they can perform maintenance tasks.[16] Domino's is testing pizza delivery by drones in New Zealand. Customers who request a drone delivery will receive a notification when their delivery is getting close to the destination. After the customer steps outside their house or apartment and presses a button on their smartphone, the drone will lower the food via a tether. Once the package is released, the drone pulls the tether back up and flies back to the Domino's location.[17]

Experts believe drones will play a major role in last-mile logistics and complement traditional logistics systems.

With further advancements in autonomous piloting, "sense and aware" technologies, and increased battery life, drones should become an integral part of a modern SCM.[18]

The Federal Aviation Administration (FAA) has not fully finalized safety regulations for commercial applications of drones. As the applications for drones increase, tougher regulations will evolve to improve their safety.[19] Five popular applications of drones in the supply chain are summarized here:[20]

- *Warehousing*—Drones can fly around large warehouses, distribution centers, and yards reading inventory RFID tags for continuous monitoring of inventory, preventing inventory mismatches, and determining item locations.

- *Last-mile delivery*—After regulatory approval, drones can be used to deliver groceries, clothing, medications, and other items to certain areas. On May 3, 2019, a drone in Baltimore became the first to deliver an organ. Experts believe that the practice will become more common because drones

can provide a cheaper and more efficient transport option. Transplant organs need to be delivered quickly after being removed from donors' bodies, making drones an attractive transport option.[21]

- *Farming and agriculture*—Equipped with sensors, cameras, and GPS, drones can spot areas of insect infestation, areas needing watering, sections needing fertilizer, failing plants, and other problem areas. Farmers can then specifically target those areas for treatment, improving crop yields at moderate costs.

- *Construction*—Drones can be used for surveying, progress tracking, inspections, security, safety, risk mitigation, and bid processing for bridges, tunnels, towers, factories, power plants, power lines, pipelines, and windfarms.

- *Global infrastructure*—Drones can be used for inspections, monitoring, providing estimates, and handling insurance claims.

Internet of Things (IoT)

We discussed the Internet of Things (IoT), Internet of Everything (IoE), and Industrial Internet of Things (IIoT) in Module 7. In this section, we briefly explain their role in improving the efficiency and effectiveness of SCM. The number of IoT devices is projected to reach 75 billion worldwide by 2025, a fivefold increase in 10 years.[22]

This growth will impact SCM in many ways, from automation of the manufacturing process to improved visibility of products in transit and in the warehouse. When products are transferred from manufacturers, suppliers, distribution centers, retailers, and finally to customers, IoT devices can provide timely information that decision makers can use to improve the effectiveness of their decisions.

> Marketing strategies in a CRM system focus on long-term relationships with customers instead of transactions.

With the help of IoT, the timely arrival of products, temperature controls, and even potential traffic jams can be anticipated by decision makers ahead of time. In other words, a reactive process is converted to a proactive process—a truck driver will be able to avoid a congested route before getting stuck.[23] By allowing devices to communicate with each other in a timely

(Valentin Valkov/Shutterstock.com)

A **radio frequency identification (RFID)** tag is a small electronic device consisting of a small chip and an antenna. This device provides a unique identification for a card or an object carrying the tag.

Exhibit 11.3
RFID tags

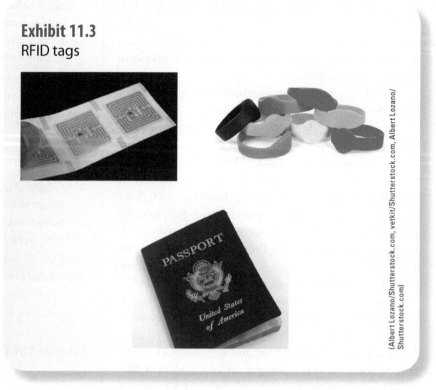

(Albert Lozano/Shutterstock.com, vetkit/Shutterstock.com, Albert Lozano/Shutterstock.com)

manner, IoT will assist SCM to achieve the following goals:[24]

- Reduce loss of inventory in warehouses or products in transit.
- Reduce fuel costs by choosing the best routes and avoiding traffic jams.
- Ensure temperature stability during product transit, particularly for perishable products.
- Manage warehouse inventory for out-of-stock items.
- Improve customer service by fast and efficient delivery of products and quick notification of order status.
- Gather business intelligence regarding product usage by customers after a product is sold.

Radio Frequency Identification: An Overview

A **radio frequency identification (RFID)** tag is a small electronic device consisting of a microchip and an antenna (see Exhibit 11.3). This device performs the same task as barcodes, universal product codes (UPCs), and magnetic strips on credit and debit cards: It provides a unique identification for the card or the object carrying the tag.

Unlike barcodes and other systems, RFID devices do not have to be in contact with the scanner to be read. Exhibit 11.4 shows an RFID reader. Because of its embedded antenna, it can be read from a distance of about 20 feet. The RFID tag's advantages, along with its decreasing price (less than 10 cents per tag), have made this device more popular with the retail industry and other industries.

There are two types of RFID tags: passive and active. Passive RFID tags have no internal power supply, so they can be very small. Typically, they absorb the signal from the receiver device, convert this signal into energy, and use this energy to respond to the receiver. Passive tags usually last longer than active tags; the best ones last about

Exhibit 11.4
An RFID reader

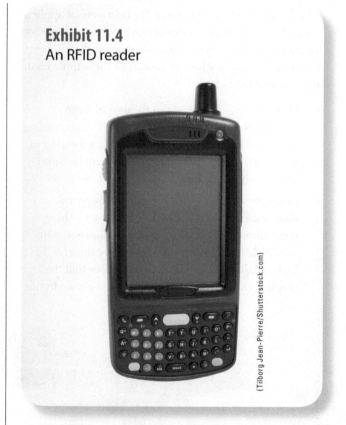

(Tilborg Jean-Pierre/Shutterstock.com)

10 years. Active RFID tags have an internal power source, are usually more reliable than passive tags, and can broadcast signals over a much wider range. These tags can also be embedded in a sticker or under the skin (human or animal).

Coca-Cola Company Uses RFID-Based Dispensers for Generating Business Intelligence

▶▶ Finance | Application | Reflective Thinking | Technology in Society

Coca-Cola's "Freestyle" dispensing system offers more than 100 varieties of soda, juice, tea, and flavored water to customers. The dispensers not only give customers many choices of soft drinks by allowing them to mix their own flavor combinations, they collect valuable business intelligence that Coca-Cola uses to improve the efficiency and effectiveness of its soft drink production and distribution. The dispensers contain cartridges that are tagged with RFID chips, and each dispenser contains an RFID reader. The system collects data on which drinks customers buy and how much they purchase. This information is then transmitted through a wireless network to a data warehouse system in Atlanta, Georgia. Coca-Cola analyzes the data and generates reports on how new drinks are performing in the marketplace.[25]

Questions and Discussions

1. How do Coca-Cola's RFID-based dispensers generate business intelligence?
2. How might Coca-Cola use this data for decision making?

Despite RFID's advantages, there are some technical problems and some privacy and security issues. On a technical level, signals from multiple readers can overlap, signals can be jammed or disrupted, and the tags are difficult to remove. Privacy and security issues include a person's ability to read a tag's contents after an item has left the store, tags being read without the customer's knowledge, and tags with unique serial numbers being linked to credit card numbers.

RFID Applications

RFID devices have been used by many organizations in the public and private sectors, including Walmart, the U.S. Department of Defense, Toyota, and the Gap. Table 11.1 lists some common applications of RFID, divided into five major categories.[26]

The "Coca-Cola Company Uses RFID-Based Dispensers for Generating Business Intelligence" box describes how Coca-Cola uses RFID.

Quick Response Codes

A **QR (quick response) code** is a matrix barcode consisting of black modules arranged in a square pattern on a white background. It offers a larger storage capacity than standard UPC barcodes (see Exhibit 11.5). Although they have been around for many years, QR codes have recently grown in popularity, particularly as a marketing tool.

Compared to conventional barcodes, QR codes have the following features:[27]

- High storage capacity
- Small printout size

Table 11.1	**RFID Applications**
Category	**Examples**
Tracking and identification	Railway cars and shipping containers, livestock and pets, supply chain management (tracking merchandise from manufacturers to retailers to customers), inventory control, retail checkout and point-of-sale systems, recycling, and waste disposal
Payment and stored-value systems	Electronic toll systems, contactless credit cards (require no swiping), subway and bus passes, casino tokens, concert tickets
Access control	Building access cards, ski lift passes, car ignition systems
Anticounterfeiting	Casino tokens, high-denomination currency notes, luxury goods, prescription drugs, and passports; since 2007, all U.S. passports have embedded RFID chips to deter fraud and improve security
Healthcare	Tracking medical tools and patients (particularly newborns and patients with Alzheimer's), process control, monitoring patient data

- Dirt and dust resistance
- Readable from any direction
- Compatible with the Japanese character set

QR codes can be read by smartphones that are equipped with cameras. The scanner app must first be downloaded to the

> A **QR (quick response) code** is a matrix barcode consisting of black modules arranged in a square pattern on a white background.

Exhibit 11.5
A QR code

(rangizzz/Shutterstock.com)

smartphone to enable the camera to read the QR code. This eliminates the need for bulky handheld scanners, which is one reason for the QR code's growing popularity over barcodes and RFID tags.

You can see QR codes in magazine advertisements and on billboards, restaurant menus, Web pages, blogs, and social networking sites—even on T-shirts and sporting gear. In fact, a major reason for their popularity is that they can store (and digitally present) much more data, including URL links, geographic coordinates, and text. Businesses, too, may start using more QR codes— on their business cards, coffee mugs, Web sites, pop-up banners, and so forth—to convey information to their business partners. In other words, business employees will no longer need to carry paper documents around with them. QR codes could also be used in trade shows to attract customers to a business's Web site.[28]

During the COVID-19 pandemic, the popularity of contactless operations and QR code downloads soared. Nearly all large restaurants replaced physical menus with QR codes. Experts believe this change is probably permanent. There may be more future opportunities for QR codes, such as placing digital orders on-premises and keeping track of customer data and past orders for various marketing purposes.[29]

QR codes could offer some challenges, however. Some users do not scan them for important information, such as nutritional facts. According to a recent study conducted at the University of Delaware, only 1 percent of consumers used their smartphones to scan a QR code to access extra information. Another 20 percent clicked a link, and about 50 percent used the QR code when a separate scanning device was offered to them.[30]

You can create a QR code online for free. One way is to use the Google URL shortener (*http://goo.gl*), which automatically creates a QR code for a Web page each time a URL is shortened.[31] You can find several other free Web sites that generate QR codes at *https://mashtips. com/websites-create-qr-code/*.

The information box "QR Codes in Action" highlights several companies that are using QR codes as a marketing tool.

QR Codes in Action

➤➤ Finance | Application | Reflective Thinking | Technology in Society

Sacre Bleu Wine, headquartered in Prior Lake, Minnesota, employs social media— including Facebook, Twitter, and YouTube—for its advertising campaigns. The company also added a QR code to the labels on its two types of wines: Cabernet Sauvignon and Sauvignon Blanc. The QR code enables the company to deliver important information to its consumers when they purchase its wines. Customers who scan the QR code with their smartphones are transferred to a Web site that includes information on promotions, special offers, and recommendations from top chefs for mixing and matching the wine with various foods. This is an inexpensive way for the company to promote its products and create customer loyalty.[32,33]

Here are other examples of companies that are using QR codes in an effective way:

• Best Buy uses QR codes to keep a record of what its customers are scanning in its stores.[34]

(Luckylight/shutterstock.com)

- Calvin Klein has used QR codes for billboards since 2010.[35]
- Dell Computer has used QR codes for an online contest in which entrants could win a new laptop.[36]
- McDonald's uses QR codes to display nutritional information.[37]
- Pepsi uses QR codes to push video content.[38]
- Ralph Lauren uses QR codes to draw consumers into its store locations.[39]
- Starbucks uses QR codes as a payment method.[40]

Questions and Discussions

1. What are two examples of companies that are using QR codes? For what purpose are they using QR codes?
2. What are two advantages of using QR codes as a marketing tool? What are some potential challenges of this approach?

11-1b Global Supply Chain Management

Global supply chain management incorporates management processes around the globe that integrate the network of suppliers, manufacturers, warehouses, and retail outlets in order to source high-quality raw materials, efficiently convert them to finished goods, and ship them in the right quantities to the right locations in a timely manner with the highest possible quality. For successful integration of a global supply chain, communication must take place among the following three areas:[41]

- Flows of information: Purchase orders, shipping notices, and invoices
- Flows of materials: Raw and finished products
- Flows of finances: Payments and refunds

For a successful implementation of a global supply chain management system, three key factors should be properly integrated: people (with skills and knowledge of the supply chain), processes (sourcing, distribution, transportation, warehousing, sales, and customer service), and SCM technologies, including EDI, the Internet, e-marketplaces, online auctions, CPFR, 3D and 4D printing, IoT, RFID, and QR codes.

Most of the benefits and drawbacks of global information systems discussed in Module 9 apply to global supply chain management. Specific benefits and drawbacks of global supply chain management are listed below:[42]

Benefits

- It will expand sourcing opportunities. Organizations will have a broad selection of workers, materials, and products. This could lead to higher-quality products with lower costs.
- It will enhance and increase access to new customers in new markets and possibly customers with new needs. This will improve the organization's top line as well as its bottom line.
- It will extend growth opportunities as a result of accessing new markets.

> **Global supply chain management** incorporates management processes around the globe that integrate the network of suppliers, manufacturers, warehouses, and retail outlets in order to source high-quality raw materials, efficiently convert them to finished goods, and ship them in the right quantities to the right locations in a timely manner with the highest possible quality.

Drawbacks

- It will create large-scale and challenging management issues, including inventory management and distribution issues.
- It could involve high risks, such as natural disasters, port closures, and political uprisings.
- It will involve global competition with other players that are competing for the same resources.
- It will face challenges for information collection because the key elements of the supply chain network are scattered throughout the world.
- It will face legal issues related to business practices, privacy, and transborder data flow.

11-2 Customer Relationship Management

Customer relationship management (CRM) consists of the processes a company uses to track and organize its contacts with customers. The main goal of a CRM system is to improve services offered to customers and use customer contact information for targeted marketing. Businesses know that keeping and maintaining current customers is less expensive than attracting new customers, and an effective CRM system is useful in meeting this goal.

Marketing strategies in a CRM system focus on long-term relationships with customers instead of transactions. These strategies include identifying customer segments, improving products and services to meet customers' needs, improving customer retention, and identifying a company's most profitable (and loyal) customers. To get the most out of these strategies, a CRM system helps organizations make better use of data, information, and knowledge to understand their customers.[43] A CRM system captures information about customer interactions for sales personnel and customer service representatives so they can perform their jobs more effectively and efficiently. This information can include customers' preferences, backgrounds, income, gender, and education.

CRM is more than just tracking and organizing contacts with customers. It gives organizations more complete pictures of their customers. CRM systems include tools for conducting complex analyses on customer data, such as a data warehouse and data-mining tools, as discussed in Module 3. With these systems, organizations can integrate demographic and other external data with customers' transaction data to better understand customer behavior. Based on this analysis, organizations can better target products and services to customers and manage customer issues, which increases customer satisfaction and retention. In addition, organizations can classify customers based on how valuable they are to the organization and manage them accordingly.

A grocery store offering loyalty cards with discounts to its customers is an example of how transaction data can be used in a CRM system. Knowing that a customer bought four gallons of milk the previous week does not give a grocery store much information, but with loyalty cards, the store can track all sorts of information on specific customers. When customers apply for loyalty cards, for example, they can be asked to give demographic information, such as name, age, marital status, and address. So, instead of knowing that "Customer 49 bought four gallons of milk last week," a store can learn that "Matias Ayala, 35 years old, married, and residing in zip code 11223, bought four gallons of milk last week." With this information, the store can assume that Ayala has young children (or clearly is not lactose intolerant!). In addition, if Ayala purchases no cereal that same week, the store can assume that Ayala is buying cereal from another store, because the purchase of a large amount of milk along with the assumption that Ayala has young children means that the children are probably eating cereal. Therefore, the store decides to send coupons for discounted cereal to Ayala. This is referred to as "cross-selling"—getting the customer to buy additional products. The store might also send Ayala coupons for a more expensive brand of milk in the hope that the family will decide it prefers that brand. This practice is called "upselling."

Organizations can also pay external agencies for additional data about their potential customers. This data might be public or semiprivate and might include details such as whether customers own their homes, the value of their homes, and their estimated mortgage or rent payments. This gives organizations more information to analyze.

With a CRM system, an organization can do the following:[44]

- Provide services and products that meet customers' needs.

- Offer better customer service through multiple channels (traditional as well as the Internet).

- Increase cross-selling and upselling of products to increase revenue from existing customers.

- Help sales personnel close deals faster by offering data on customers' backgrounds.

- Retain existing customers and attract new ones.

Several IT tools discussed throughout this book are used to improve customer service. For example, e-mail, the Internet, Web portals, and automated call centers have played a major role in CRM systems. E-commerce sites use e-mail to confirm items purchased, confirm shipping arrangements, and send notifications about new products and services. Web portals and extranets such as *FedEx.com* allow customers to perform useful tasks, such as checking the status of shipments and arranging a

Customer relationship management (CRM) consists of the processes a company uses to track and organize its contacts with customers. It improves services offered to customers and uses customer contact information for targeted marketing.

package pickup. Database systems, data warehouses, and data-mining tools are effective in tracking and analyzing customers' buying patterns, which help businesses meet customers' needs. This information can also be used to generate predictive analytics that an organization can use for future planning in offering new products and services. The emergence of big data analytics and the Internet of Everything may open up additional channels for reaching customers, increasing revenue, and improving customer service. A CRM system includes the following activities:

- Sales automation
- Order processing
- Marketing automation
- Customer support
- Knowledge management
- Personalization technology

These activities are discussed in more detail in the following sections. The "CRM at Delta Air Lines" box highlights CRM applications at Delta.

11-2a CRM Applications

Typically, CRM applications are implemented with one of two approaches: on-premises CRM or Web-based CRM. Organizations with an established IT infrastructure often choose on-premises CRM, which is implemented much like any other IT system. With Web-based CRM, the company accesses the application via a Web interface instead of running the application on its own computers and pays to use CRM software as a service (SaaS), which is similar to Web-hosting services. The SaaS vendor also handles technical issues. (SaaS is covered in more detail in Module 14.) Several software packages are available for setting up a CRM system, including Optima Technologies ExSellence (*www.optima-tech.com*), Infor CRM (*www.infor.com/solutions/crm*), and SAP CRM (*http://help.sap.com/CRM*). Although these packages vary in capabilities, they share the following features:

- *Salesforce automation*—Assists with such tasks as controlling inventory, processing orders, tracking customer interactions, and analyzing sales forecasts

CRM at Delta Air Lines

➤➤ Finance | Application | Reflective Thinking

(Sorbis/Shutterstock.com)

Delta Air Lines serves more than 200 million customers each year. It offers service to 275 destinations on six continents.[45]

Using applications from Salesforce, a leader in CRM services, Delta implemented a CRM to assist and improve communication and collaboration among its sales teams. One of the major reasons the company needed this program was to enable global sales representatives to share account information and address customers' needs.

Delta used Sales Cloud for account, activity, and contact information. The system provides essential information when sales representatives call on existing accounts or offer services to new customers. An app automates corporate and agency programs and assists sales representatives to track any request.

According to Kristen Shovlin, vice president of Sales Operations, the system gives Delta complete visibility into opportunities and programs across the globe. Sales teams are able to access the system using their mobile devices and offer customer service anytime and from anywhere. Delta also implemented a Chatter social network for further improving collaboration among team members. This platform helps employees share files and find needed information in a timely manner. Chatter has made real-time collaboration a reality at Delta.[46]

Questions and Discussions

1. What are the applications of CRM at Delta Air Lines?
2. How does Chatter help improve customer service?

and performance. It also assists with collecting, storing, and managing sales contacts and leads.

- *eCRM or Web-based CRM*—Allows Web-based customer interaction and is used to automate e-mail, call logs, Web site analytics, and campaign management. Companies use campaign management to customize marketing campaigns; for example, a marketing campaign could be tailored to customers in Southern California or customers in the 18 to 35 age bracket.

- *Survey management*—Automates electronic surveys, polls, and questionnaires, which is useful for gathering information on customers' preferences.

- *Automated customer service*—Used to manage call centers and help desks and sometimes to answer customers' queries automatically.

The integration of CRM, IoT, social media, and analytics has created an environment for CRM to do the following to attract new customers and better serve existing customers:[47]

- *Social CRM*—Interaction with customers through the Internet and social media.

- *Individualized messaging*—Specially tailored messages to customers through analytics using their social media information.

- *Hypertargeting*—Delivery of highly customized content to highly specific customer subgroups of the total customer population. This creates personal communication that makes the customer feel special.

11-2b
Personalization Technology

Personalization is the process of satisfying customers' needs, building customer relationships, and increasing profits by designing goods and services that meet customers' preferences better. It involves not only customers' requests but also the interaction between customers and

the company. You are probably familiar with Web sites that tailor content based on interests and preferences. Amazon, for example, suggests products users might enjoy based on past browsing and purchasing habits.

Customization, which is somewhat different from personalization, allows customers to modify the standard offering of a product, such as selecting a different home page to be displayed each time a browser is opened. As another example, after registering with Yahoo!, a user can customize the start page by choosing a preferred layout, content, and colors. There are many examples of customization in retail, too, such as Build-A-Bear Workshops, where children can design their own teddy bears, or Nike, which allows customers to create their own shoes by selecting styles and colors.[48]

Because personalization and customization help companies meet customers' preferences and needs, customers often have a more efficient shopping experience and, as a result, are less likely to switch to competitors to get similar products or services. However, using personalization requires gathering a lot of information about customers' preferences and shopping patterns, and some customers get impatient with answering long surveys about their preferences. In addition, collecting this information might affect customers' sense of privacy. For example, drug-store customers might be concerned that the drug store has their prescription histories, and that the information might be misused and even affect their insurance coverage. To ease these concerns, companies should include clear privacy policies on their Web sites stating how personal information is collected and used.

Amazon is known for using personalization to recommend products to customers with the message "Customers who bought this item also bought" followed by a list of suggestions. Amazon's recommendation system is made up of a huge database containing customers' previous purchases and a recommendation algorithm. When a customer logs on to Amazon, the recommendation system first checks the customer's purchase history and that of similar customers. Using this information, a list of recommended products is displayed, based on the customer's shopping history and choices by other customers who have similar purchase histories. In addition, Amazon gives customers an opportunity to rate the recommendations. The more items the customer purchases and the more recommendations the customer rates, the better the recommendations are tailored to the customer.[49]

Many other companies use personalization technology to improve customer service. For example, if you buy a suit from *Nordstrom.com*, the site might suggest shoes or a tie that goes with the suit or a similar suit in the same category. If you buy a song from Apple iTunes, other songs purchased by listeners like you are suggested. Google also provides personalized services for Google account holders. Users can get personalized search results that are reordered based on their searching histories. Avni Shah, Google's product manager, has explained that if a user has "fly fishing" in their search history and then searches on "bass," more weight is given to search results that point to Web pages about fish rather than pages about musical instruments. Google also has a bookmark feature so users can save useful search results for later use. Unlike Yahoo!'s MyWeb feature, which saves the text of Web pages, this feature simply saves the link to the page.[50]

(10 FACE/Shutterstock.com)

> **Customization, which is somewhat different from personalization, allows customers to modify the standard offering of a product, such as selecting a different home page to be displayed each time a browser is opened.**

To implement a personalization system, several IT tools are needed, including the Internet, databases, data warehouse/data marts, data-mining tools, mobile networks, and collaborative filtering. **Collaborative filtering (CF)** is a search for specific information or patterns using input from multiple business partners and data sources. It identifies groups of people based on common interests and recommends products or services based on what members of the group purchased or did not purchase. It works well for a single product category, such as books, computers, and so forth. One drawback of CF is that it needs a large sample of users and content to work well. In addition, it is not useful for making recommendations across unrelated categories, such as predicting that customers who liked a particular song would also like a particular computer.[51]

One application of collaborative filtering is making automatic predictions about customers' preferences and interests based on those of similar users. For example, if a user rates several movies and is then added to a database that contains other users' ratings, a CF system can predict the user's ratings for movies that the user has not evaluated. You may have seen this feature used on *Netflix.com*, where lists of other movies you might like are displayed. Recently, Netflix paid $1 million to the team that won a contest to come up with the best algorithm for improving the accuracy of the Netflix recommendation system. Other Web sites that use CF systems to improve customer service are Amazon, Barnes and Noble, LinkedIn, YouTube, and Pandora Radio.

The information box "Amazon's Personalization Assists Sellers on Its Marketplace" explains how Amazon uses personalization technologies to increase the efficiency and effectiveness of its marketplace.

> **Collaborative filtering (CF)** is a search for specific information or patterns using input from multiple business partners and data sources. It identifies groups of people based on common interests and recommends products or services based on what members of the group purchased or did not purchase.

Amazon's Personalization Assists Sellers on Its Marketplace

▶▶▶ Finance | Application | Reflective Thinking

Amazon was one of the first companies to use data-mining tools and personalization technologies to tailor goods and services to its customers' purchasing habits. Since 2009, the company has also used its personalization technologies to assist the third-party sellers that provide goods and services in Amazon's various marketplaces around the world.

Amazon Marketplace was launched in November 2000. It allows sellers to offer new and used products right next to Amazon's own offerings using Amazon's infrastructure. As of 2021, Amazon has over 2.5 million sellers in Amazon marketplaces based in 10 countries, serving more than 200 million customers worldwide. More than 2,000 new sellers join Amazon every day.[52]

Amazon uses its personalization technologies to offer predictive, data-driven recommendations to all of its sellers. Personalization technologies help these sellers manage all aspects of their inventories, including how much to carry, what to carry, and how to expand into new markets and geographical locations. Managing inventory during seasonal changes and managing product offerings during the holidays are challenging tasks. Amazon makes recommendations by using customer data on its site and the data available on social media. Recently, Amazon began recommending products to its sellers that they can sell outside their home countries.[53]

Questions and Discussions

1. How is Amazon's personalization technology helping its sellers?
2. Why does Amazon invest in personalization for its sellers?

11-3 Knowledge Management

Knowledge management (KM) is a technique used to improve CRM systems (and many other systems) by identifying, storing, and disseminating "know-how"—facts about how to perform tasks. Know-how can be explicit knowledge (formal, written procedures) or tacit knowledge (personal or informal knowledge). Knowledge is an asset that should be shared throughout an organization to generate business intelligence and maintain a competitive advantage in the marketplace. Knowledge management, therefore, draws on concepts of organizational learning, organizational culture, and best practices to convert tacit knowledge into explicit knowledge, create a knowledge-sharing culture in an organization, and eliminate obstacles to sharing knowledge. In this respect, knowledge management shares many of the goals of information management but is broader in scope because information management tends to focus on just explicit knowledge.

Knowledge is more than information and data. It is also contextual. Explicit knowledge, such as how to close a sale, can be captured in data repositories and shared. Expert salespeople can document how they close sales successfully, and this documentation can be used to train new salespeople or those who are struggling to close sales. Tacit knowledge, however, cannot be captured as easily. Knowledge that someone has gained through experience might vary depending on the context in which it was gained. Typically, the best way to gather such information is interactively—for example, by asking employees specific questions about how they would handle an issue. Because interaction is a key part of managing tacit knowledge, a knowledge management system (KMS) must encourage open communication and the exchange of ideas, typically via e-mails, instant messaging, internal company wikis, video conferencing, and tools such as Zoom, WebEx, and GoToMeeting, which create virtual instructional environments.

By storing knowledge captured from experts, a knowledge repository can be created for employees to refer to when needed. The most common example is creating a knowledge base of typical customer complaints and solutions. Dell Computer uses this type of knowledge base so when customers call about problems their computers are having, the steps for solving the problem are documented and readily accessible, which shortens response times.

> **A knowledge management system can track how often an employee participates in knowledge-sharing interactions with other employees and track any resulting improvements in performance.**

Knowledge management (KM) draws on concepts of organizational learning, organizational culture, and best practices to convert tacit knowledge into explicit knowledge, creates a knowledge-sharing culture in an organization, and eliminates obstacles to sharing knowledge.

Knowledge bases can also be used when new products are being designed. A company can store past experiences with similar designs, mistakes made in testing, and other experiences to help speed up the delivery timetable and avoid making the same mistakes. This use of knowledge bases is particularly helpful in designing software products and services.

Employees might be reluctant to share their expertise because, once everybody knows what they know, they might think their value to the organization would be diminished. To motivate them to share knowledge, rewards must be offered. A knowledge management system can track how often an employee participates in knowledge-sharing interactions with other employees and track any resulting improvements in performance. This information can be used to reward employees for sharing tacit knowledge. Reward systems can be set up for sharing explicit knowledge, too—by tracking how often an employee contributes to a company's internal wiki, for example.

A simple knowledge management system might consist of using collaboration software (discussed in Module 12), such as Google Apps for Work or Microsoft SharePoint Server, to create, manage, and distribute documents in an organization. These documents include the kind of information discussed previously, such as outlines of procedures for customer service representatives or reports of past design efforts. Other tools and technologies might include database management systems, data-mining tools, and decision support systems (discussed in Module 12). Knowledge management plays a key role in the success of a CRM system because it helps businesses use their knowledge assets to improve customer service and productivity, reduce costs, and generate more revenue. A knowledge management system should help an organization do one or more of the following:[54]

- Promote innovation by encouraging the free exchange of ideas.

- Improve customer service by reducing response time.

- Increase revenue by reducing the delivery time for products and services.

- Improve employee retention rates by rewarding employees for their knowledge.

Because of the importance of knowledge, knowledge management, and knowledge management systems, some organizations have created an executive position called chief knowledge officer (CKO). This individual is responsible for overseeing knowledge management within an organization. The CKO also makes sure that key knowledge resources are properly collected, stored, and disseminated among key decision makers and ensures that the organization profits from knowledge resources, including its employees, its processes, and its intellectual property. Finally, the CKO tries to maximize the return on investment (ROI) related to knowledge management, knowledge management systems, and processes.

The information box "Knowledge Management in Action" highlights the applications of knowledge management at BMW.

The following four companies successfully use KM and KMS in their operations.[55,56]

- Ford, the global automaker, has applied knowledge management principles in its operations for decades. The company's product development processes have been major users of KM and KMS. Ford uses KM to maintain quality standards across its product lines, which enabled the company to raise quality by 18 percent and reduce its warranty costs by $1 billion. Long-time adoption of KM at Ford has enabled the company to make system improvements as it gathers more information and experiences.

- GE uses principles of KM and KMS through its corporate executive council. The council meets for two days to share information and experience. This knowledge is shared throughout the company, allowing management to understand the reasons for successes and failures and learn from best practices.

- Amazon, one of the most successful e-commerce businesses in the world, has used the principles of KM and KMS since its inception. This adoption has enabled Amazon to implement a simple interface that allows customers to easily find products on its Web site. The site has a consistent presentation throughout and is supported by a powerful personalization technology.

- Pratt & Whitney is an international aerospace manufacturer based in Connecticut. Using KM and KMS, the company focuses on how to centralize knowledge in the company for universal access. This practice has helped the company preserve the knowledge and expertise of some of its retiring engineers, saving Pratt & Whitney over $25 million in the process.

11-4 Enterprise Resource Planning

Enterprise resource planning (ERP) is an integrated system that collects and processes data and manages and coordinates resources, information, and functions throughout an organization. A typical ERP system has many components, including hardware, software, procedures, and input from all functional areas. To integrate information for the entire organization, most ERP systems use a unified database to store data for various functions (see Exhibit 11.6). Table 11.2 summarizes the functions of these components.

A well-designed ERP system offers the following benefits:

- Increased availability and timeliness of integrated information
- Increased data accuracy and improved response time
- Improved customer satisfaction
- Improved employee satisfaction
- Improved planning and scheduling
- Improved supplier relationships
- Improved reliability of information
- Reductions in inventory costs
- Reductions in labor costs
- Reductions in order-to-fulfillment time

Enterprise resource planning (ERP) is an integrated system that collects and processes data and manages and coordinates resources, information, and functions throughout an organization.

Exhibit 11.6
ERP configuration

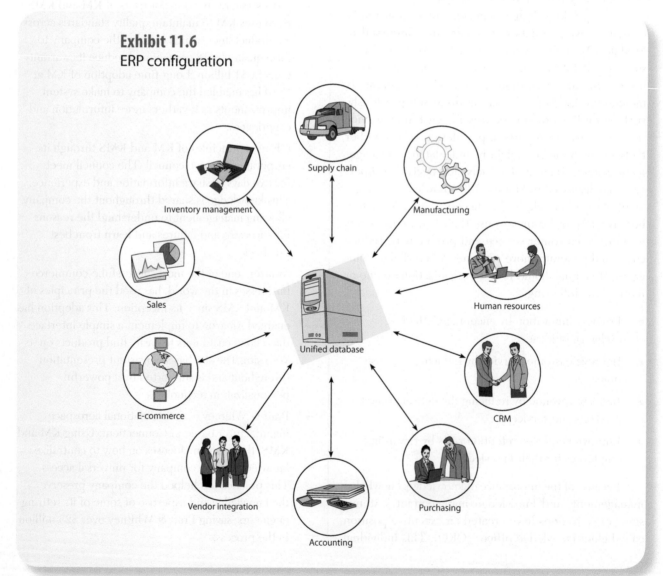

Table 11.2 ERP Components

Components	Functions
Unified database	Collects and analyzes relevant internal and external data and information needed by other functions
Inventory management	Provides inventory status and inventory forecasts
Supply chain	Provides information on supply chain members, including suppliers, manufacturing, distribution, and customers
Manufacturing	Provides information on production costs and pricing
Human resources	Provides information on assessing job candidates, scheduling and assigning employees, and predicting future personnel needs
CRM	Provides information on customers and their needs and preferences
Purchasing	Provides information related to the purchasing function, including e-procurement
Accounting	Tracks financial information, such as budget allocations, debits, and credits
Vendor integration	Integrates information for vendors, such as offering automated downloads of data on product pricing, specifications, and availability
E-commerce	Provides B2C information related to order status and B2B information related to suppliers and business partners
Sales	Provides information on sales and marketing

Along with all its advantages, an ERP system also has drawbacks, such as high costs, difficulties in installation, a need for extensive training, and compatibility problems with legacy systems.

The "ERP Streamlines Operations at Naghi Group" box summarizes some of the benefits in operational efficiency that Naghi Group gained from an ERP system.

Knowledge Management in Action

➤➤ Finance | Application | Reflective Thinking | Global

Multinational corporations deliver products and services across international borders. Within this environment, connecting customers with fast, current, and accurate information can be a challenging task. Organizations resolve the often-decentralized nature of their operations with responsive customer service, and a comprehensive KMS can play a major role. A KMS can distribute knowledge and experiences digitally across any organizational structure, providing quick and reliable answers both to customers and agents.

BMW, which includes the Mini and Rolls-Royce brands, is one of the world's leading automakers. It operates in more than 140 countries, and its contact center receives four million inquiries every year. Responding to these queries in an efficient and effective manner is a major goal at BMW.

Verint (*https://www.verint.com/our-company/*), a customer engagement software company based in Huntington, New York, developed a KMS to capture and disseminate knowledge and experiences throughout the organization. The system uses a central knowledge base to support three key customer touchpoints at BMW: customer self-service, the contact centers, and the car dealerships. The system was initially offered to the 250 agents in BMW's contact centers and then extended to cover customer-facing touchpoints for the company's brands. The system was designed to provide "customer-centric" instead of "document-centric" information—in other words, information needed by customers is delivered at multiple touchpoints regardless of time, place, or the device used.[57]

Questions and Discussions

1. What benefits does knowledge management offer to BMW?
2. What are the three key customer touchpoints that receive needed information from the KMS?

ERP Streamlines Operations at Naghi Group

➤➤ Finance | Application | Reflective Thinking

Naghi Group, based in Jeddah, Saudi Arabia, operates several companies that together offer a wide range of products and services throughout the Middle East. Unfortunately, the legacy software that the firm was using was not able to communicate and integrate with the distribution and manufacturing software it was using. This lack of integration cost Naghi Group many hours each month as it tried to reconcile the data from various sources and generate critical financial-management reports. It needed an ERP system to integrate its major functional areas, including finance, sales, and supply chain management. It also needed to monitor inventory status and purchasing activity. The solution was ERP software—specifically, Vormittag Associates' S2K Distribution Suite. Now, the firm's managers are able to view financial data, keep track of inventory status, and analyze its customers' purchasing activities in real time. The ERP system has streamlined operations and improved customer service; it has also contributed to more timely business decisions.[58]

Questions and Discussions

1. What was achieved by the ERP system at Naghi Group?
2. Why did Naghi Group invest in an ERP system?

Most ERP systems are available as modules, so an organization can purchase only the components it needs and add others later, if needed. Having modular components is a major factor in the success of ERP systems because it keeps costs down. More than 40 vendors, such as SAP, Oracle, Sage Group, and Microsoft, offer ERP software with varying capabilities. If an organization decides to use a full-featured ERP system, the systems development life cycle (SDLC) method introduced in Module 10 can be useful.

11-5 Cloud-Based Enterprise Systems

Organizations have two options for choosing an enterprise system such as SCM, CRM, or ERP. They can either choose the on-premises option or the cloud version. The on-premises option is similar to any IS implementation, and the steps outlined in Module 10 will apply. Cloud computing is discussed in detail in Module 14. Briefly, cloud computing is accessed through remote servers and customers use it like a utility service. Cloud providers are responsible for providing hardware, software, and other needed utility programs. The advantages and disadvantages of cloud-based enterprise systems are listed below. For the most part, these advantages and disadvantages apply to traditional enterprise systems as

well, with minor differences. The specific advantages are as follows:[59,60]

- Cost savings: Cloud computing costs are paid incrementally, saving organizations money. Also, because the software development cost is divided among many participants, it is generally cheaper than traditional computing methods.

- Increased storage: Organizations can store more data than they can on private computer systems, and storage can grow as the organization grows.

- Highly automated: No longer do IT personnel need to worry about keeping software up to date. The "what version of the software do I need" dilemma is eliminated.

- Flexibility and scale: Cloud computing offers much more flexibility and scale than traditional computing methods. It can offer vertical and horizontal flexibility and scale.

- Increased mobility: Employees can access information wherever they are, rather than having to remain at their desks. Cloud computing offers true portability for both data and application.

- Allows IT to shift focus: No longer having to worry about constant server updates and other computing issues, the adopting organization is free to concentrate on innovation and growing the business. Mission-critical applications become the main focus.

- Improved security: Although some people think that cloud computing may be less secure than traditional computing, you should remember that most providers of cloud services will have multiple copies of your data for redundancy, often in different geographic locations. Therefore, it is highly unlikely that they will lose your data.

With all these advantages, there are also a few disadvantages that organizations should consider:[61,62]

- Lack of customization: The adopting organization has to accept the standard offering of the cloud provider, which may not meet the organization's specific needs. For this reason, some manufacturing operations still use on-premises ERP systems that are best suited for those specific operations.

- Possible downtime: Cloud platforms sometimes go down, and this is a major disadvantage. Service outages are always a possibility and can occur for many reasons, although cloud platforms are increasingly becoming more reliable.

- Vendor lock-in: When an organization signs a contract with a particular vendor, switching to another vendor may become difficult. In addition to increased costs, the migration to another provider might temporarily expose the organization's data, which could cause additional security and privacy risks.

The Industry Connection highlights Salesforce as a leader in enterprise systems.

Industry Connection: Salesforce[63]

Salesforce, a leader in CRM services, offers enterprise applications that can be customized to meet companies' needs. Its products and services include the following:

CRM applications: Products such as Cloud Platform for CRM and Cloud Infrastructure for CRM are used for salesforce automation, sales management, and contact management.

Sales analytics: Sales Cloud enables management to discover which salespeople are closing the most deals and how long tasks take. Customizable dashboards offer instant access to real-time information, allow monitoring of critical factors for sales, marketing, service, and other departments, and produce consolidated analyses from a variety of data sources.

Chatter: This is a social networking and collaborative application that works with Sales Cloud. All users of Salesforce can access Chatter for no additional cost. Similar to Facebook pages, Chatter enables groups to collaborate on projects, share information and documents, and control privacy so information is only shown to appropriate team members.

Service and support: Service Cloud offers a customer portal, call center, and knowledge base. With information from these features, users can analyze who is asking for support and how long responses take, examine employee performance, and determine which reps handle most of the customer inquiries.

Commerce cloud (formerly called Demandware): This tool brings together e-commerce, m-commerce, and store operations and provides a platform that businesses use to engage with their customers over any channel (mobile, Web, store, call center, and others) or device.

Marketing automation: This includes Google Adwords, campaign management, marketing analytics, and marketing dashboards. Users can track multichannel campaigns, from generating sales leads to closing sales.

Force.com Builder: This tool allows developers to create add-on applications that can be integrated into Salesforce applications and hosted by Salesforce.

Salesforce1: This platform provides the customer with interfaces for mobile, cloud, and social networking sites.

Wave: This analytics tool makes it easier for decision makers to explore data, gain new insights, and take quick action from multiple devices.

Einstein: This set of artificial intelligence capabilities, including machine learning, predictive analytics, and natural language processing, helps users of Salesforce to better serve customers.

Tableau (*www.tableau.com*) and Slack (*https://slack.com*) are also a part of Salesforce now. Tableau is a data visualization tool used for data analysis and generating business intelligence; Slack is a communication and collaboration platform.

Module Summary

11-1 Explain how supply chain management is used within an organization. Supply chains exist both in service and manufacturing organizations, although the chain's complexity can vary widely in different organizations and industries. Organizations use supply chain management to create the most efficient link between their suppliers and consumers. A proper integration of people, processes, and technology makes this possible.

11-2 Describe customer relationship management systems. Customer relationship management (CRM) consists of the processes a company uses to track and organize its contacts with customers. The main goal of a CRM system is to improve services offered to customers and use customer contact information for targeted marketing. Businesses know that keeping and maintaining current customers is less expensive than attracting new customers, and an effective CRM system is useful in meeting this goal.

11-3 Describe knowledge management systems. Knowledge management (KM) is a technique used to improve CRM systems (and many other systems) by identifying, storing, and disseminating "know-how"—facts about how to perform tasks. A knowledge management system can track how often an employee participates in knowledge-sharing interactions with other employees and track any resulting improvements in performance.

11-4 Describe enterprise resource planning systems. Enterprise resource planning (ERP) is an integrated system that collects and processes data and manages and coordinates resources, information, and functions throughout an organization. A typical ERP system has many components, including hardware, software, procedures, and input from all functional areas.

11-5 Explain advantages and disadvantages of cloud-based enterprise systems. Cost savings, increased storage, high automation, flexibility and scale, and increased mobility are among their advantages. Lack of customization, possible downtime, and vendor lock-in are some disadvantages.

Key Terms

- 3D printing
- 4D printing
- Collaborative filtering (CF)
- Collaborative planning, forecasting, and replenishment (CPFR)
- Customer relationship management (CRM)
- Customization
- Electronic data interchange (EDI)
- E-marketplace
- Enterprise resource planning (ERP)
- Enterprise system
- Global supply chain management
- Knowledge management (KM)
- Online auction
- Personalization
- QR (quick response) code
- Radio frequency identification (RFID)
- Reverse auctions
- Supply chain
- Supply chain management (SCM)

Reviews and Discussions

1. Define *supply chain management*.
2. What are four examples of SCM technologies?
3. What are two applications of 3D and 4D printing?
4. What are two applications of RFID?
5. What are three applications of CRM?
6. Define *knowledge management* and *knowledge management systems*.
7. What are three advantages of enterprise resource planning systems?
8. What are two advantages and two disadvantages of cloud-based enterprise systems?

Projects

1. SenseAware by FedEx provides key information for improving the logistics of a supply chain network. After reading the information presented in this module and other sources, write a one-page paper that explains the key features of SenseAware. Which information technologies are being used?

2. After reading the information presented in this module and other sources, write a one-page paper that identifies two companies (besides those mentioned in this module) that have implemented a green supply chain network. What has been achieved by these systems? Why is green SCM gaining popularity? What are two obstacles for implementing these systems? Discuss.

3. 3D and 4D printing technologies play a major role in improving the efficiency and effectiveness of SCM. After reading the information presented in this module and other sources, write a two-page paper that identifies three ways SCM benefits from these technologies. Identify two companies that are using 3D printing and two companies that are using 4D printing in their SCM, and then list two advantages of using these technologies in each company.

4. After reading the information presented in this module and other sources, write a two-page paper that describes the differences between a domestic supply chain and an international supply chain. Why is the international supply chain more challenging to manage?

5. RFID is playing a major role in increasing the efficiency and effectiveness of supply chain management. After reading the information presented in this module and other sources, write a one-page paper that describes the experience of a company that uses RFID in supply chain management. What are two advantages and two disadvantages of using RFID for this purpose? What is the relationship between RFID and IoT? What role does RFID play in an IoT environment?

6. Most experts believe that an ERP system, even with all the advantages it offers, also has drawbacks, such as high costs, difficulties in installation, a need for extensive training, and compatibility problems with legacy systems. After reading the information presented in this module and other sources, write a two-page paper that recommends some ways to minimize these drawbacks.

Module Quiz

1. Most ERP systems use a unified database to store data for various functions. True or False?

2. Personalization allows customers to modify the standard offering of a product, such as selecting a different home page to be displayed each time you open your Web browser. True or False?

3. A reverse auction invites sellers to submit bids for products and services. True or False?

4. An SCM system coordinates all of the following functions except:
   a. Procuring materials
   b. Transforming materials into intermediate and finished products or services
   c. Distributing finished products or services to customers
   d. Advertising finished products to customers

5. IoT assists SCM to achieve all of the following goals except:
   a. Enhancing the production process by finding the best workers
   b. Reducing loss of inventory in warehouses or products in transit
   c. Reducing fuel costs by choosing the best routes and avoiding traffic jams
   d. Managing warehouse inventory for out-of-stock items

6. A CRM system includes all of the following activities except:
   a. Sales automation
   b. Production operations
   c. Order processing
   d. Marketing automation

Case Study 11-1
ERP at Amazon
➤ Finance | Application | Reflective Thinking | Global

Worldwide, more than 2.5 million active sellers in the Amazon marketplace offer products and make significant earnings. Nearly 30,000 of these sellers can earn as much as $1 million annually. They must ensure consistent operations ranging from product offerings to accounting and logistics. An ERP system is an ideal platform to support such dynamic and growing business operations.

A typical high-volume seller in the Amazon marketplace deals with millions of products that require rigorous management for product listings. There may be thousands of informational requirements for each SKU (stock keeping unit) or ASIN (Amazon standard identification number) that the sellers must list in the marketplace. With the Amazon

iStock.com/TeamJackson

ERP system, sellers get access to an automated and vigorous product management function that helps them increase their product listing efficiency and avoid errors during listing. As a result, sellers can sell their products to millions of Amazon Prime members and other buyers from around the world. The ERP system also helps Amazon sellers to quantify their profitability in the marketplace. For example, they can calculate their gross and net profit per product as well as manage other costs, such as wages and overhead.

The ERP system also collects all relevant data about sellers' stores in the Amazon marketplace. Sellers can use this data to analyze their sales and then market the right products in the future in terms of timing and quantity. The ERP system also includes advanced analytics tools that can help sellers analyze market trends and plan a winning strategy for their stores. The automation tools offered by the ERP system can be used to increase the efficiency and effectiveness of store operations, such as issuing purchase orders to vendors, projecting cash requirements, and developing shipping plans.[64]

Answer the following questions:

1. How many sellers are active in the Amazon marketplace throughout the world?
2. What are two tasks that the ERP system performs for a typical Amazon seller?
3. What types of analytics does Amazon ERP perform for a typical seller in the marketplace?

Case Study 11-2
CRM at Starbucks
➤ Finance | Application | Reflective Thinking

With more than 33,000 retail stores in 80 countries, Starbucks uses a CRM system called My Starbucks Idea, which is powered by Salesforce.[65] The system, which includes an interactive forum, gives the Starbucks community an online presence and allows the company to collect feedback from its customers. It also integrates the company's physical stores with social media sites such as Facebook, Twitter, and Google. On the system's Web site (*https://ideawake.com/*

my-starbucks-idea-creates-mobile-drive-thru-cake-pops-and-more/), customers offer ideas, make comments, and cast votes on issues arranged into three major categories: product ideas, experience ideas, and involvement ideas. The system enables Starbucks to receive a steady stream of feedback and ideas from customers, which helps the bottom line and strengthens the bond with those customers. Since its inception, the Web site has collected over 190,000 ideas, with over 2 million votes and 277 ideas implemented, leading to several successful innovations for the company. My Starbucks Idea is a crowdsourcing success story.[66]

Answer the following questions:

1. What is My Starbucks Idea?
2. What has the Starbucks CRM achieved? How does it help the bottom line?
3. Which software platform is behind the Starbucks CRM system?
4. Is My Starbucks Idea a typical crowdsourcing project? Discuss.

Module 12

Supporting Decisions and Processes

Learning Objectives

After studying this module, you should be able to...

12.1 Examine the three types of decisions made in each phase of the decision-making process.

12.2 Describe a decision support system.

12.3 Explain an executive information system's importance in decision making.

12.4 Summarize the uses for a geographic information system.

12.5 Describe collaboration systems or collaboration software, including their types and the criteria for their selection.

12.6 Apply the eight guidelines for designing a management support system.

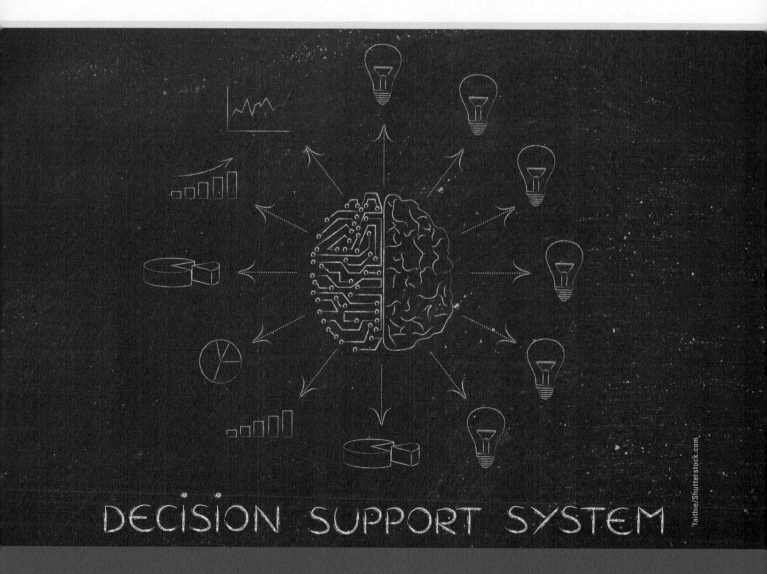

DECISION SUPPORT SYSTEM

This module begins by summarizing the phases of the decision-making process and the types of decisions that are made. Next, you learn about a decision support system (DSS), its components, and its capabilities, and see how it can benefit an organization. In addition, you learn about other management support systems used in decision making: executive information systems (EISs), geographic information systems (GISs), and collaboration systems. This module concludes with an overview of guidelines for designing a management support system.

12-1 Types of Decisions in an Organization

In a typical organization, decisions fall into one of these categories:

- *Structured decisions*—**Structured decisions**, or programmable tasks, can be automated because a well-defined standard operating procedure exists for these types of decisions. Record keeping, payroll, and simple inventory problems are examples of structured tasks. Information technologies are a major support tool for making structured decisions. Transaction-processing systems, discussed in Module 1, are ideal for these types of decisions.

- *Semistructured decisions*—**Semistructured decisions** are not quite as well defined by standard operating procedures, but they include a structured aspect that benefits from information retrieval, analytical models, and information systems technology. For example, preparing budgets has a structured aspect in calculating percentages of available funds for each department. Semistructured decisions are often used in sales forecasting, budget preparation, capital acquisition analysis, and computer configuration. Decision support systems, discussed later in the module, are suitable for these types of decisions.

- *Unstructured decisions*—**Unstructured decisions** are typically one-time decisions, with no standard operating procedure pertaining to them. The decision maker's intuition plays the most important role, as information technology offers little support for these decisions. Areas involving unstructured decisions include research and development, hiring and firing, and introducing a new product. These decisions are mostly long term, and they require external data sources for their implementation. Executive information systems, which are discussed later in the module, are suitable for these types of decisions.

Semistructured and unstructured decisions are challenging because they involve multiple criteria, and often users have to choose between conflicting objectives. For example, a manager might want to give raises to employees to boost morale and increase employee retention but has been asked to reduce the total cost of production. These two objectives conflict, at least in the short run. Exhibit 12.1 shows organizational levels (operational, tactical, and strategic) and the types of decisions made at each level.

Different types of information systems have been developed to support certain aspects and types of decisions. Collectively, these systems are called **management support systems (MSSs)**, and each type is designed with its own goals and objectives, as discussed in this module.

Structured decisions, or programmable tasks, can be automated because a well-defined standard operating procedure exists for these types of decisions.

Semistructured decisions include a structured aspect that benefits from information retrieval, analytical models, and information systems technology.

Unstructured decisions are typically one-time decisions, with no standard operating procedure pertaining to them.

Management support systems (MSSs) are the different types of information systems that have been developed to support certain aspects and types of decisions. Each type of MSS is designed with unique goals and objectives.

Exhibit 12.1
Organizational levels and types of decisions

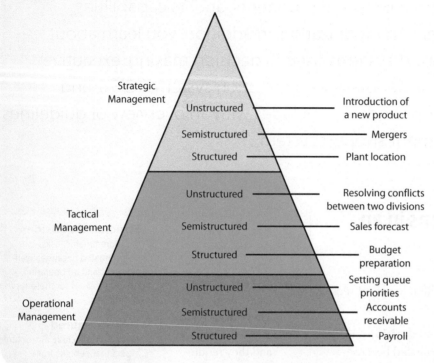

Strategic Management
- Unstructured — Introduction of a new product
- Semistructured — Mergers
- Structured — Plant location

Tactical Management
- Unstructured — Resolving conflicts between two divisions
- Semistructured — Sales forecast
- Structured — Budget preparation

Operational Management
- Unstructured — Setting queue priorities
- Semistructured — Accounts receivable
- Structured — Payroll

12-1a Phases of the Decision-Making Process

Herbert Simon, winner of the 1978 Nobel Prize in Economics, defines three phases in the decision-making process: intelligence, design, and choice.[1] A fourth phase, implementation, can be added. The following sections explain these phases.

In the **intelligence phase**, a decision maker examines the organization's environment for conditions that need decisions. Data is collected from a variety of sources (internal and external) and processed. From this information, the decision maker can discover ways to approach the problem.

In the **design phase**, the objective is to define criteria for the decision, generate alternatives for meeting the criteria, and define associations between the criteria and the alternatives.

Intelligence Phase

In the **intelligence phase**, a decision maker (e.g., a marketing manager) examines the organization's environment for conditions that need decisions. Data is collected from a variety of sources (internal and external) and processed. From this information, the decision maker can discover ways to approach the problem. This phase has three parts. First, you determine what the reality is—identify what is really going on so you can define the problem. Second, you get a better understanding of the problem by collecting data and information about it. Third, you gather data and information needed to define alternatives for solving the problem.

As an example, say an organization has noticed a decrease in total sales over the past six months. To pinpoint the cause of the problem, the organization can collect data from customers, the marketplace, and the competition. After the data has been processed, analysis can suggest possible remedies. Information technologies, particularly database management systems, can help in this analysis. In addition, many third-party vendors, such as Nielsen and Dow Jones, specialize in collecting data about the marketplace, the competition, and the general status of the economy. The information they collect can support the intelligence phase of decision making.

Design Phase

In the **design phase**, the objective is to define criteria for the decision, generate alternatives for meeting the criteria, and define associations between the criteria and the alternatives. Criteria are goals and objectives that decision makers establish in order to achieve certain performance levels. For example, the criterion in the previous example of decreased sales might simply be to increase sales. To make this criterion more specific, you can state it as "Increase sales by 3 percent each month for the next three months." Next, the following alternatives could be generated:

- Assign more salespeople to the target market.
- Retrain and motivate current salespeople.
- Reassign current salespeople.
- Revamp the product to adjust to consumers' changing tastes and needs.
- Develop a new advertising campaign.
- Reallocate existing advertising to other media.

Defining associations between alternatives and criteria involves understanding how each alternative affects the criteria. For example, how would increasing the sales force increase sales? By how much does the sales force need to be increased to achieve a 3 percent increase in sales? Generally, information technology does not support this phase of decision making very much, but collaboration systems and video-conferencing systems, discussed later in this module, can be useful.

> Semistructured and unstructured decisions are challenging because they involve multiple criteria, and often users have to choose between conflicting objectives.

Choice Phase

The **choice phase** is usually straightforward. From the practical alternatives, the best and most effective course of action is chosen. It starts with analyzing each alternative and its relationship to the criteria to determine whether it is feasible. For instance, for each salesperson added, how are sales expected to increase? Will this result be economically beneficial? After a thorough analysis, the choice phase ends with decision makers recommending the best alternative. For the problem of decreased sales, the organization might decide to use the first alternative, assigning more salespeople to the target market. A DSS can be particularly useful in this phase. DSSs are discussed later in the module; these systems help sort through possible solutions to choose the best one for the organization. Typically, they include tools for calculating cost–benefit ratios, among other things. For example, say an organization is deciding which of three transportation systems to use for shipping its products to retail outlets. A DSS can assess cost factors and determine which transportation system minimizes costs and maximizes profits. Generally, information technologies are more useful in the intelligence and choice phases than in the design phase.

Implementation Phase

In the **implementation phase**, the organization devises a plan for carrying out the alternative selected in the choice phase and obtains the resources to implement the plan. In other words, ideas are converted into actions. Information technologies, particularly DSSs, can also be

useful in this phase. A DSS can help an organization do a follow-up assessment on how well a solution is performing. In the previous example of selecting a transportation system, a DSS might reveal that the system the organization chose is not performing as well as expected and suggest an alternative.

12-2 Decision Support Systems

For the purposes of this book, a **decision support system (DSS)** is an interactive information system consisting of hardware, software, data, and models (mathematical and statistical) designed to assist decision makers in an organization. The emphasis is on semistructured and unstructured tasks. A DSS should meet the following requirements:

- Be interactive.
- Incorporate the human element as well as hardware and software.
- Use both internal and external data.
- Include mathematical and statistical models.
- Support decision makers at all organizational levels.
- Emphasize semistructured and unstructured tasks.

During the **choice phase**, the best and most effective course of action is chosen.

In the **implementation phase**, the organization devises a plan for carrying out the alternative selected in the choice phase and obtains the resources to implement the plan.

A **decision support system (DSS)** is an interactive information system consisting of hardware, software, data, and models (mathematical and statistical) designed to assist decision makers in an organization. Its three major components are a database, a model base, and a user interface.

12-2a Components of a Decision Support System

A DSS, shown in Exhibit 12.2, includes three major components: a database, a model base, and a user interface. In addition, a fourth component, the DSS engine, manages and coordinates these major components. The database component includes both internal and external data; a database management system (DBMS) is used for creating, modifying, and maintaining the database. This component enables a DSS to perform data analysis operations.

The **model base** component includes mathematical and statistical models that, along with the database, enable a DSS to analyze information. A model is a representation of a real-life situation. For example, Microsoft Excel includes hundreds of financial, mathematical, and statistical models. Excel calls them functions. Decision makers can also build their own models from scratch. As an example, consider the PMT function in Excel. To calculate the payment of a loan, the function needs three input variables: interest rate, number of payments, and present value. A decision maker can manipulate any of these variables to reach a certain outcome. As another example, consider the break-even point, which can also be programmed in Excel. If the fixed cost is $500,

> The **model base** component includes mathematical and statistical models that, along with the database, enable a DSS to analyze information.

the variable cost is $10 per unit, and the selling price is $15 per unit, the break-even point would be 100 units. Below this number, the organization would lose money; above this number, the organization makes money. A model base management system (MBMS) performs tasks similar to a DBMS in accessing, maintaining, and updating models in the model base. For example, an MBMS might include tools for conducting a what-if analysis so that a forecasting model can generate reports showing how forecasts vary, depending on certain factors.

Finally, the user interface is how users access the DSS, such as when querying the database or model base, for help in making decisions. From the end user's point of view, the interface is the most important part of a DSS and must be as flexible and user friendly as possible. Because most DSS users are senior executives with little computer training, user friendliness is essential in these systems.[2]

12-2b DSS Capabilities

DSSs include the following types of features to support decision making:

- *What-if analysis*—Shows the effect of a change in one variable, answering questions such as "If labor costs increase by 4 percent, how is the final cost of a product affected?" and "If the advertising budget increases by 2 percent, what is the effect on total sales?"

Exhibit 12.2
Components of a DSS

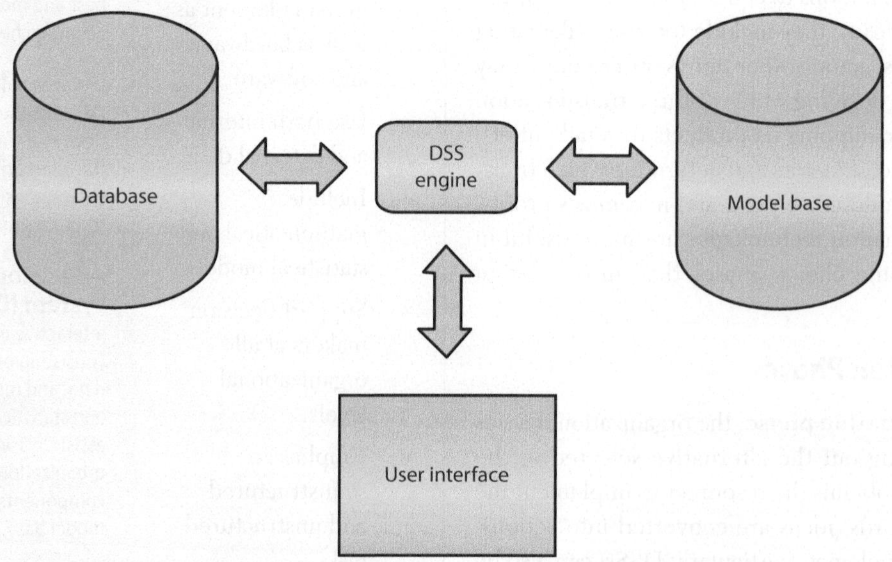

- *Goal seeking*—The reverse of what-if analysis. It asks what has to be done to achieve a particular goal—for example, how much to charge for a product to generate a $200,000 profit or how much to advertise a product to increase total sales to $10 million.

- *Sensitivity analysis*—Enables you to apply different variables, such as determining the maximum price you could pay for raw materials and still make a profit or determining how much the interest rate has to go down for you to be able to afford a $200,000 house with a monthly payment of $1,400.

- *Exception reporting analysis*—Monitors the performance of variables that are outside a defined range, such as pinpointing the region that generated the highest total sales or the production center that went over budget.

- *Optimization analysis*—Enables a decision maker to manipulate a series of key variables in order to maximize profit or minimize costs. In these situations, the decision maker is given a series of constraints. For example, you have 100 units of labor and 200 units of leather. How many pairs of shoes and bags do you have to make to maximize profit? Naturally, each pair of shoes and each bag uses different amounts of resources and each one contributes to total profit with different margins.

Rawpixel/Shutterstock.com

> **Because most DSS users are senior executives with little computer training, user friendliness is essential in these systems.**

A typical DSS has many more capabilities, such as graphical analysis, forecasting, simulation, statistical analysis, and modeling analysis.

12-2c Roles in the DSS Environment

To design, implement, and use a DSS, several roles are involved. These roles include the user, managerial designer, technical designer, and model builder.[3]

Users comprise the most important role because they are the ones using the DSS. Therefore, the system's success depends on how well it meets their needs. Users can include department or organizational units in addition to people.

A **managerial designer** defines the management issues in designing and using a DSS. These issues do not involve the technological aspects of the system; they are related to management's goals and needs. This person specifies data requirements, what models are needed, how these models might be used, and how users want to view the results (graphics, text, and so forth). This role addresses questions such as the following:

- What type of data should be collected, and from what sources?
- How recent should the collected data be?
- How should the data be organized?
- How should the data be updated?
- What should be the balance between aggregated (lump sum) and disaggregated (itemized) data?

The **technical designer** focuses on how the DSS is implemented and usually addresses the following questions:

- How should the data be stored (centralized, decentralized, or distributed)?
- What type of file structure should be used (sequential, random, or indexed sequential)?
- What type of user access should be used? Should it be menu driven, such as in Query by Example? Or,

> A **managerial designer** defines the management issues in designing and using a DSS. These issues do not involve the technological aspects of the system; they are related to management's goals and needs.
>
> The **technical designer** focuses on how the DSS is implemented and usually addresses questions about data storage, file structure, user access, response time, and security measures.

should access be via the command line, such as in Structured Query Language?

- What type of response time is required?
- What types of security measures should be installed?

The technical designer might be a computer specialist or a consultant from outside the company and may use a commercial DSS package or write the system's code from scratch.

> **You can quantify the benefit of saving time, for instance, by measuring the two hours a manager wasted looking for information that a DSS could have made available immediately.**

A **model builder** is the liaison between users and designers. For example, during the design phase, the model builder might explain users' needs to the managerial designer or technical designer. Later, during the implementation phase, this person might explain the output of a regression analysis to users, describing the assumptions underlying the model, its limitations, and its strengths. The model builder is responsible for supplying information on what the model does, what data inputs it accepts, how the model's output should be interpreted, and what assumptions go into creating and using the model. Typically, requirements for what the model should do come from the managerial designer, implementation of the model is carried out by the technical designer, and specifications for the model come from the model builder. The model builder can also suggest new or different applications of a DSS.

12-2d Costs and Benefits of Decision Support Systems

Some DSSs can be developed from resources already available in the organization, which can reduce costs, but many require new hardware and software. Before making this investment, organizations should weigh the costs and benefits of using a DSS. Costs and benefits can be difficult to assess, however, because these systems are focused on effectiveness rather than efficiency. In addition, a DSS facilitates improvements but does not necessarily cause them. For example, how do you assign a monetary value to facilitating communication or expediting problem solving?

Peter G. Keen, a former MIT professor, conducted a study on how organizations use DSSs and concluded that the decision to build a DSS seems to be based on value rather than cost. He outlined the benefits of a DSS as follows:[4]

- An increased number of alternatives examined
- Fast response to unexpected situations
- The ability to make one-of-a-kind decisions
- New insights and learning
- Improved communication—for example, between management and employees
- Improved control over operations, such as controlling the cost of production
- Cost savings from being able to make better decisions and analyze several scenarios (what-ifs) in a short period
- Better decisions
- More effective teamwork
- Time savings
- Better use of data resources

As this study indicates, most of the benefits are intangible and difficult to assess. They can be quantified to a degree, although the quantification might vary depending on the person doing the calculations. You can quantify the benefit of saving time, for instance, by measuring the two hours a manager wasted looking for information that a DSS could have made available immediately. Of course, you would probably also notice that a manager who did not have to waste this much time is less frustrated and more productive, but quantifying these results is harder or at least requires more work, such as conducting interviews or surveys.

The benefit of improving communication and interactions between management and employees is perhaps the most difficult to quantify, but it is one of the most important.[5] DSSs can improve how decision makers view themselves, their jobs, and the way they spend time. Therefore, improving communication and expediting learning are among the main objectives of a DSS.[6,7]

A DSS is said to have achieved its goals if employees find it useful in doing their jobs. For example, a portfolio manager who uses a financial DSS to analyze different scenarios would certainly find the ease of analyzing a variety of variables, such as the interest rate and economic

A **model builder** is the liaison between users and designers. This person is responsible for supplying information on what the model does, what data inputs it accepts, how the model's output should be interpreted, and what assumptions go into creating and using the model.

forecasts, to be useful. The manager can quickly try different values for these variables to determine which variable has the greatest effect and decide which portfolio will be the most profitable. In addition, some DSSs result in savings on clerical costs and others improve the decision-making process. The "Decision Support Systems at Nestlé" box describes DSS applications at Nestlé, an international food and beverage company.

12-3 Executive Information Systems

Executive information systems (EISs), a branch of DSSs, are interactive information systems that give executives easy access to internal and external data.

They typically include "drill-down" features (explained in Module 3) and a digital dashboard for examining and analyzing information. (Some experts consider executive support systems and executive management systems to be variations of EISs; this book considers them EISs.)

Ease of use plays an important role in the success of an EIS. Because most EIS users are not computer experts, simplicity of the system is crucial; EIS designers should focus on simplicity when developing a user interface. Typically, graphical user interfaces (GUIs) are used, but adding

> **Executive information systems (EISs)**, which are branches of DSSs, are interactive information systems that give executives easy access to internal and external data. They typically include "drill-down" features and a digital dashboard for examining and analyzing information.

Decision Support Systems at Nestlé

➤➤ Finance | Reflective Thinking | Global

Nestlé, the world's largest food and beverage company, has its headquarters in Vevey, Switzerland. It offers more than 2,000 brands ranging from global icons to local favorites. The company does business in more than 186 countries worldwide (*www.nestle.com/aboutus*).

Accurate forecasting, which is the basis for precise planning, optimizes customer service, minimizes inventory overstocks, and establishes the groundwork for effective marketing at Nestlé. To deliver on its promise of "Good Food, Good Life," Nestlé has introduced over 10,000 products aimed at improving consumers' lives with better and healthier foods and beverages.

To offer the right amounts of these products to customers, Nestlé relies on forecasting customers'

iStock.com/Michael Derrer Fuchs

demand. A successful retailer must have its shelves full when customers show up for their favorite foods. Forecasting demand in the food business is a multifaceted and complex task. It is influenced by factors such as seasonality, weather conditions, fluctuation in demand, other retail trends, and the perishable nature of many products. These factors collectively make it difficult to plan production and organize logistics. Marcel Baumgartner, head of global demand planning at Nestlé, said, "To have the right quantity of the right products at the right place and time, we rely heavily on being able to predict the orders our customers will place as precisely as possible."

Nestlé uses statistical models and various internal and external data sources to generate accurate forecasts that meet customers' demands. Before using SAS Forecast Server, Nestlé was using SAP APO's underlying forecasting techniques, accompanied by models from the open-source statistical software R, integrated into APO. The forecasts then were revised by Nestlé's demand planners.

The new SAS system enhances and complements previous systems. It enables key decision makers to drill down through customer hierarchies and execute tasks such as integrating the impact of promotions and special offers into the statistical models. This process collectively improves efficiency and effectiveness of operations and makes Nestlé more competitive in the marketplace.[8]

Questions and Discussions

1. Why is forecasting demand in the food business a multifaceted and complex task?
2. Which platform from SAS is used by Nestlé?

features such as multimedia, virtual reality, and voice input and output can increase ease of use.

Another important factor in an effective EIS is access to both internal and external data so executives can spot trends, make forecasts, and conduct different types of analyses. For an EIS to be useful, it should also collect data related to an organization's "critical success factors"—issues that make or break a business. In banks and financial institutions, interest rates are considered a critical success factor; for car manufacturers, location of dealerships might be a critical success factor.

Most EISs include a **digital dashboard**, which integrates information from multiple sources and presents it in a unified, understandable format, often as charts and graphs. Digital dashboards and scorecards offer up-to-the minute snapshots of information and assist decision makers in identifying trends and potential problems. A typical digital dashboard offers four capabilities, including consolidation, drill-down, slice-and-dice, and pivot analysis. Consolidation usually aggregates data. For example, sales for northern, central, and southern California are added to generate the total sales for the state of California. Drill-down analysis is the reverse of consolidation. For example, the total sales in California will be broken down into three regions: northern, central, and southern. You can further break it down to go into a specific city or a part of a city. As discussed in Module 3, slice-and-dice analyzes different pieces of information and provides granularity or specificity—for example, the performance

of a product in a given period and in a given sales region. Pivot analysis rotates data to get a different perspective of the same data. As an example, rows and columns of a table will be swapped. Many digital dashboards are Web based, such as the sales dashboards available on HubSpot. Exhibit 12.3 shows an example of a digital dashboard.

The following are some important characteristics of an EIS:[9,10]

- Tailored to meet management's information needs
- Can extract, compress, filter, and track critical data
- Provides online status access, trend analysis, and exception reporting
- Offers information in graphical, tabular, and text formats
- Includes statistical analysis techniques for summarizing and structuring data
- Retrieves data in a wide range of platforms and data formats
- Contains customized application-development tools
- Supports electronic communication, such as e-mail and video conferencing

Graphs and charts play an important role in an EIS environment for delivering information to its users. Listed next are popular types of charts used by an EIS.

- **Line charts (or time-series charts)** show data changes over time. Line charts are suitable for time-series analysis. In this type of analysis, one variable is time, and the other variable could be total sales, total production cost, total advertising budget, or something else. By using line charts, you can easily depict advertising budget trends, total sales trends, or administrative cost trends.

A **digital dashboard** integrates information from multiple sources and presents it in a unified, understandable format, often as charts and graphs. It offers up-to-the minute snapshots of information and assists decision makers in identifying trends and potential problems.

Line charts (or time-series charts) show data changes over time.

Exhibit 12.3
Digital dashboard

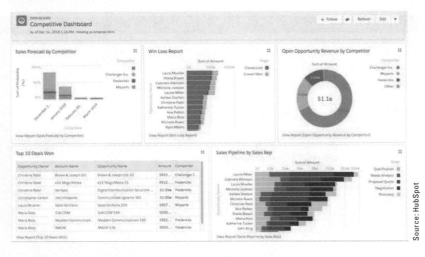

Source: HubSpot

- **Pie charts** are used to show the proportions of different data items. For example, you can split the total costs of production by breaking them down into utility costs, rental costs, and supply costs.

- **Bar charts** emphasize the differences among data items. As examples, you can use bar charts to compare the total sales figures for five products from a particular company, to compare the oil production levels for five oil wells, to compare the student populations of six state universities, or to compare sales data in three different regions.

- **XY (scatter) charts** show relationships between two sets of data—for example, total sales and advertising budgets or years of education and yearly income.

- **Column charts** are useful for showing data changes over a period of time or for illustrating comparisons among items. For example, you can compare the performances of three salespersons over three periods of time or compare the sales performances of three products in three different regions.

Generally, executives perform six tasks for which an EIS is useful: tracking performance, flagging exceptions, ranking, comparing, spotting trends, and investigating/exploring. Exception or variance reporting is another useful technique that managers use to flag data that is unusual or out of normal boundaries. Both unusual and periodic events can be defined to trigger visual cues or activate intelligent agents to perform a specific task. Intelligent agents, covered in Module 13, are "smart"

programs that carry out repetitive tasks and can be programmed to make decisions based on specified conditions. Exhibit 12.4 shows a screen from one EIS platform, Tableau.

12-3a Reasons for Using EISs

An EIS can put a wealth of analytical and decision-making tools at managers' fingertips and includes graphical representations of data that help executives make critical decisions. In addition, executives can use EISs to share information with others more quickly and easily. Managers can use these tools to improve the efficiency and effectiveness of decision making in the following ways:

- Increase managers' productivity by providing fast and easy access to relevant information.

- Convert information into other formats, such as bar charts or graphs, to help managers analyze different business scenarios and see the effect of certain decisions on the organization.

Pie charts are used to show the proportions of different data items.

Bar charts emphasize the differences among data items.

XY (scatter) charts show relationships between two sets of data—for example, total sales and advertising budgets or years of education and yearly income.

Column charts are useful for showing data changes over a period of time or for illustrating comparisons among items.

Exhibit 12.4
Salesforce starter system

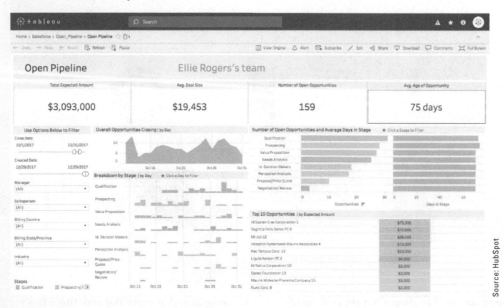

Source: HubSpot

- Spot trends and report exceptions, such as gathering data on profitability and production costs at a manufacturing plant to determine whether closing the plant is more beneficial than keeping it open.

12-3b Avoiding Failure in Design and Use of EISs

As with other management support systems, effective design and implementation of an EIS requires top-management support, user involvement, and the right technologies. The following factors can lead to a failed EIS:[11, 12]

- The corporate culture is not ready, there is organizational resistance to the project, or the project is viewed as unimportant.
- Management loses interest or is not committed to the project.
- Objectives and information requirements cannot be defined clearly or the system does not meet its objectives.
- The system's objectives are not linked to factors critical to the organization's success.
- The project's costs cannot be justified.
- Developing applications takes too much time or the system is too complicated.

- Vendor support has been discontinued.
- It does not contain the information that senior executives need because there is a lack of understanding about what the executives' work involves. Designers must determine what types of information executives need before designing a system.

The information box "Executive Information Systems at Hyundai Motor Company" describes the EIS applications at Hyundai.

12-4 Geographic Information Systems

Executives often need to answer questions such as the following:

- Where should a new store be located to attract the most customers?
- Where should a new airport be located to keep environmental impacts to a minimum?
- What route should delivery trucks use to reduce driving time?
- How should law enforcement resources be allocated?

Executive Information Systems at Hyundai Motor Company

➤ Finance | Reflective Thinking | Global

Hyundai Motor Company (HMC) is one of the world's largest automotive manufacturers. It employs more than 121,000 people and has several subsidiaries around the world, as well as manufacturing plants in Seoul, Tokyo, Peking, Detroit, and Frankfurt.

HMC's executive information system, designed with SAS software, supports and facilitates executive decision making throughout the corporation. The company's Enterprise Information and Management System (EIMS) has three main components: a warning system, a goal-oriented system, and a DSS. The warning system alerts executives to any problems with current sales and production volume figures, compares the figures with past performance, and reports any deviations. The goal-oriented system keeps executives informed about progress the corporation is making toward its long-term goals. The DSS provides executives with timely and accurate information related to decision-making activities. To deliver the needed information, the system gathers data from human resources, domestic and international sales, and production. The EIMS enables executives to make decisions proactively rather than reactively.[13]

JuliusKielaitis/Shutterstock.com

Questions and Discussions

1. What are the three main components of the Enterprise Information and Management System at Hyundai?
2. What are the sources of data for EIMS? How might they be used to inform decision making?

A well-designed **geographic information system (GIS)** can answer these questions and more. This system captures, stores, processes, and displays geographic information or information in a geographic context. For example, a GIS can show the locations of all city streetlights on a map. A GIS uses spatial and nonspatial data and specialized techniques for storing coordinates of complex geographic objects, including networks of lines (roads, rivers, streets) and reporting zones (zip codes, cities, counties, states). Most GISs can superimpose the results of an analysis on a map, too. Typically, a GIS uses three geographic objects:

- *Points*—The intersections of lines on a map, such as the location of an airport or a restaurant
- *Lines*—Usually a series of points on a map (e.g., a street or a river)
- *Areas*—Usually a section of a map, such as a particular zip code or a large tourist attraction

Digitized maps and spatially oriented databases are two major components of a GIS. For example, say you want to open a new store in southwest Portland, Oregon, and would like to find out how many people live within walking distance of the planned location. With a GIS, you can start with the map of the United States and zoom in repeatedly until you get to the street map level. You can mark the planned store location on the map and draw a circle around it to represent a reasonable walking distance. Next, you can request a summary of U.S. Census data on everyone living inside the circle who meets certain conditions, such as a particular income level, age, or marital status. A GIS can provide all kinds of information that enables you to zero in on specific customers. A GIS can perform the following tasks:

- Associate spatial attributes, such as a manufacturing plant's square footage, with points, lines, and polygons on maps.

> A **geographic information system (GIS)** captures, stores, processes, and displays geographic information or information in a geographic context. For example, a GIS can show the locations of all city streetlights on a map.

- Integrate maps and database data with queries, such as finding zip codes with a high population of senior citizens with relatively high income.

A GIS can support some sophisticated data management operations, such as the following:

- Show the customers who live within a 5-mile radius of the Super Grocery at the corner of 34th and Lexington. A database cannot answer this question because it cannot determine the latitude/longitude coordinates of the store, compute distances using the specified location as the center, identify all zip codes within this circle, and pull out the customers living in these zip codes.

- Show the customers whose driving route from work to home and back takes them through the intersection of 34th and Lexington. A database cannot address this query, either. In this case, the GIS maps customers' home and work locations and determines all possible routes. It can then narrow down the customer list by picking only those whose shortest route takes them through the specified intersection.

A GIS with analytical capabilities evaluates the impact of decisions by interpreting spatial data. Modeling tools and statistical functions are used for forecasting purposes, including trend analysis and simulations. Many GISs offer multiple windows so you can view a mapped area and related nonspatial data simultaneously; points, lines, and polygons can be color-coded to represent nonspatial attributes. A zoom feature is common for viewing geographic areas in varying levels of detail, and map overlays can be useful for viewing such things as gas lines, public schools, or fast-food restaurants in a specified region. A buffering feature creates pin maps that highlight locations meeting certain criteria, such as finding a new store location based on population density. Exhibit 12.5 shows an example of output from Microsoft Power BI, which uses visuals from the Environmental Systems Research Institute (ESRI), a major vendor of GIS software. To see examples of different types of maps, visit *www.esri.com*.

A common example of a GIS—and one you have probably used often—is Google Maps, which provides driving directions. Google Maps is an interactive GIS that identifies routes from start to destination, overlays routes on a map, shows locations of nearby landmarks, and estimates distances and driving times. It is also considered a DSS because you can change routes by dragging different points and have a what-if analysis performed on alternative routes (such as taking back roads instead of the highway), including estimates of driving time to help you decide which route is best. Google Maps has a user-friendly interface that helps you visualize the route; after you make a decision, you can print driving directions and a map.

12-4a GIS Applications

GISs integrate and analyze spatial and nonspatial data from a variety of sources. Although they are used mainly in government and utility companies, more businesses are using them, particularly in marketing, manufacturing, insurance, and real estate. No matter what category a GIS falls into, most applications require a GIS to handle converting data to information, integrating data with maps, and conducting different types of

Exhibit 12.5
Sales leads by location: an example of a pin map

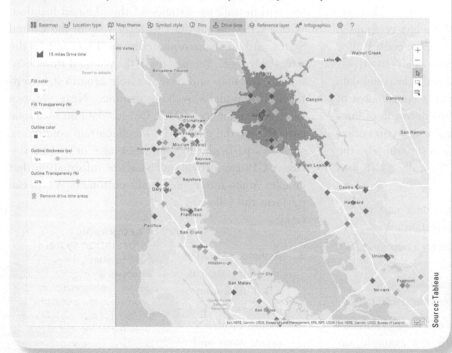

Source: Tableau

analysis. GIS applications can be classified in the following categories, among several others:

- *Education planning*—Analyzing demographic data to change school district boundaries or to decide where to build new schools.

- *Urban planning*—Tracking changes in ridership on mass-transit systems and analyzing demographic data to determine new voting districts, among many other uses.

- *Government*—Making the best use of personnel and equipment while dealing with tight budgets, dispatching personnel and equipment to crime and fire locations, and maintaining crime statistics.

- *Insurance*—Combining data on community boundaries, street addresses, and zip codes with search capabilities to find information (some from federal and state agencies) on potential hazards, such as natural disasters, auto-rating variables, and crime rate indexes.[14,15]

- *Marketing*—Pinpointing areas with the greatest concentration of potential customers, displaying sales statistics in a geographic context, evaluating demographic and lifestyle data to identify new markets, targeting new products to specific populations, analyzing market share and population growth in relation to new store locations, and evaluating a company's market position based on geographic location.[16,17] For example, Pepsico uses a GIS to find the best locations for new Pizza Hut and Taco Bell outlets.

- *Real estate*—Finding properties that meet buyers' preferences and price ranges, using a combination of census data, multiple listing files, mortgage information, and buyer profiles. GISs help establish selling prices for homes by surveying an entire city to identify comparable neighborhoods and average sales prices. GISs can also be used for appraisal purposes to determine relationships between national, regional, and local economic trends and the demand for local real estate.[18]

- *Transportation and logistics*—Managing vehicle fleets, coding delivery addresses, creating street networks for predicting driving times, and developing maps for scheduling routing and deliveries.[19] Uber, with its app that allows a customer to set a pickup location on a smartphone, uses GIS applications. The app allows a customer to see a photo of the driver, track where the vehicle is, and rate the driver's performance at the end

of the ride. The credit card on file allows the customer to finalize the transaction seamlessly, with accuracy and speed.[20]

GM is using GIS to determine locations where customers buy certain GM models and then target its ads specifically to those areas. In the past, their ads targeted the general public using a "shotgun approach." Bruce Wong, manager of advanced network analytics at GM, said, "GIS allows us to spend less money to generate higher sales."[21]

Walgreens, one of the largest drugstore chains in the United States, uses GIS applications for all sorts of activities. They use GIS to visualize local community trends, to order vaccines and prevent shortages, and to map the best locations for their stores.[22]

The Web site *gisgeography.com/gis-applications-uses/* lists more than 1,000 GIS applications broken down into 56 categories. It is updated on a regular basis. Glance through this Web site and find areas that are close to your personal and professional interests.[23]

The information box "GISs for Fighting Disease" discusses how GISs can be used to monitor and reduce the spread of disease.

> **A GIS can provide all kinds of information that enables you to zero in on specific customers.**

12-5 Collaboration Systems

In today's business environment, decision makers often work in groups, so you hear the terms *group computing* or *collaborative computing* used often. All major software vendors are competing to enter this market or increase their market share in this fast-growing field. The popularity and adoption of collaboration software increased significantly during the COVID pandemic.

A **collaboration system or collaboration software** assists teams in communicating, collaborating, and coordinating their activities. The system is a collection of applications that supports decision makers by providing access to a shared environment and information. A shared environment could be a database, an

> A **collaboration system or collaboration software** assists teams in communicating, collaborating, and coordinating their activities.

GISs for Fighting Disease

▶ Finance | Application | Technology in Society | Reflective Thinking | Global

Public health officials and government agencies around the globe use GISs, demographic information, remote-sensing data, and even Google Maps to help fight diseases such as avian flu, malaria, H1N1 (swine flu), and SARS. With a GIS, health officials can map the spread of an epidemic and identify high-risk population areas before the epidemic reaches them, which can help decrease the death rate and reduce the spread of the infectious disease by tracking its origins. During the COVID-19 pandemic, GISs were used for mapping different parts of the United States to track the spread of the virus. This data provided key decision makers with valuable information for disease forecasting, predicting outbreaks, and identifying disease clusters or hotspots.[24]

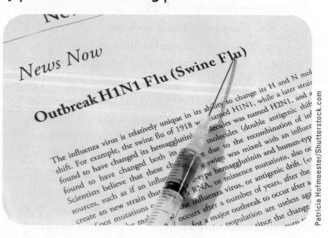

Patricia Hofmeester/Shutterstock.com

GISs can also be useful in the following tasks:[25,26]

- Locating contaminated water sources for water-borne diseases
- Plotting confirmed and suspected cases of a disease on a map
- Identifying existing medical infrastructures
- Determining how far people have to travel to reach a healthcare center and whether public transportation is available
- Monitoring virus mutations and their locations during an outbreak and assisting in early identification of infected people or animals
- Determining the geographic distribution of diseases
- Planning and targeting interventions
- Routing healthcare workers, equipment, and supplies to remote locations
- Locating the nearest healthcare facility

Questions and Discussions

1. What are three examples of diseases that can be tracked using GIS?
2. Mention three applications of GIS that you are familiar with.

e-mail from the chief executive, or a video clip promoting a new product or service. There are literally hundreds of collaboration software applications on the market with diverse capabilities and price tags. Table 12.1 lists general capabilities of collaboration software. Of course, not all applications offer all the capabilities listed.

Advantages of collaboration software include the following:

- It enables a decision maker to communicate more easily with other team members.

- It increases productivity.
- It enables a decision maker to coordinate and collaborate with team members scattered throughout the world.
- It facilitates teamwork.
- It saves time by providing timely information to all team members.
- Because decision makers do not have to travel as much (which includes paying for planes, hotels, and meals), costs as well as stress levels are reduced.

Table 12.1 General Capabilities of Collaboration Software

Analytics	Guest access
Audio and video conferencing	Messaging
Automated appointment books	Multipresenter function
Boards to create and manage tasks	Notifications
Brainstorming	Personal dashboard
Calendar	Presentation streaming
Chat	Reporting
Contact management	Scheduling
Customizable chatbots	Screen sharing
Dashboards	Search within message threads
Database access	Shared calendar
Diagrams	Synchronous editing
Discussion boards	Task management
Document management	Time tracking
E-mail	Timeline
File management to upload and share files	To-do lists
File sharing	Video calling
Filters and sorting	Video conferencing
General search	Whiteboarding
Group calendars	Workflow automation

- Because decision makers are not traveling long distances, they have more time to talk with one another and solve problems.

- Shyness is not as much of an issue when using collaboration software as it is in face-to-face meetings.

Disadvantages of collaboration software include the following:

- Lack of the human touch—Gestures, handshakes, eye contact, and other nonverbal cues can be lost, which can hinder the effectiveness of meetings. New developments in virtual reality technologies (discussed in Module 14) could solve this problem, however.

- Unnecessary meetings—Because arranging a collaboration session is easy, there is a tendency to schedule more meetings than are necessary, which wastes time and energy.

- Security problems—Collaboration software has the same security problems as other data communication systems, so there is the possibility that an organization's private information could fall into the hands of unauthorized people. Tight security measures for accessing collaboration sessions and transferring data are essential.

12-5a Types of Collaboration Software

Collaboration software can be used in two modes: synchronous and asynchronous. Using synchronous or real-time software allows team members to work together at the same time. For example, they can edit a document or conduct a brainstorming session simultaneously. Asynchronous software enables team members to work together at different times. E-mail is an example of an asynchronous tool. For example, a team member may leave a message or send a document to another team member. The recipient can respond at a later time and date. Based on their features and capabilities, collaboration software is broadly divided into three groups: communication software, task management software, and document and content management software.[27]

Communication software, which also includes audio and video conferencing, provides chat, messaging, or video features that enable real-time communication. It could include text conversations using direct messages or group chats or video communication in private or public channels. Video-conferencing features enable team members to see and talk to each other regardless of their locations. Team members are able to reply to a particular message in a group chat or a private channel without distracting other teammates. Communication software also provides a file-sharing feature that makes it easy to upload and share files. The top three collaboration software programs for communication include Slack, Zoho Cliq, and join.me. In addition to using video-conferencing features available in the software, team members can also use third-party tools. The "New Generations of Video-Conferencing Systems" box highlights popular video-conferencing applications.

Task management software enables team members to prioritize and track tasks, which helps to keep track of deadlines. To make this process more efficient, the software provides boards,

Communication software, which also includes audio and video conferencing, provides chat, messaging, or video features that enable real-time communication.

Task management software enables team members to prioritize and track tasks, which helps to keep track of deadlines.

New Generations of Video-Conferencing Systems

➤➤➤ Finance | Application | Technology in Society | Reflective Thinking

Increasingly, consumers and businesspersons use computers and mobile devices for one-to-one video calls. Group video calls are also on the rise. Several options are available; they are either free or very inexpensive. Here are some popular examples:

- Microsoft's Skype—Offers individual video calls for free; group video calling requires a plan with different subscription fees. The maximum number of group participants is 50.[28]

- Apple's FaceTime—Offers service free of charge on Apple iPhone, iMac, iPad, and iPod Touch devices.[29]

- Tango Video Calls—Allows video chats among different devices, including Windows phones, Android phones, iPhones, tablets, and PCs.[30]

- Google's Hangouts—Allows video chats for up to nine people.[31]

- ooVoo from ooVoo LLC—Allows up to eight participants in group video chats. The free service is available on the Internet with PCs, Macs, iPhones, and other smartphones and tablets.[32]

- *Zoom.us* from Zoom Video Communications—Allows high-definition video conferencing with several features. It works over wired and Wi-Fi Internet connections or cellular 3G, 4G, and 5G.[33,34]

Questions and Discussions

1. What are two reasons that businesspersons use computers and mobile devices for one-to-one video calls?
2. What features would be important in a video-conferencing system for a company considering the many options? Discuss.

---

timelines, and calendars. Any IT project, such as designing an order entry system or designing an e-commerce Web site, involves a number of tasks that must be accomplished before a project is up and running. Task management software helps a team member keep to-do lists and other notes in one place. The software helps team members to move one task along before starting another, and to monitor work progress effectively. Most of the time, tasks aren't related or dependent on one another. Task management software is relatively easy to learn, and it is accessible on nearly all platforms. On the other hand, project management software (discussed in Modules 2 and 10) is all about collaboration and coordination in order to finish a project. There are some overlaps between project management tools and task management apps. The latter emphasizes improving the productivity of each member of the team. A recent Project Management Institute study revealed some interesting facts about projects, their performance, and completion time:

9.9 percent of every dollar is wasted by organizations due to poor project performance, 43 percent of projects are not completed within budget, and 48 percent of projects are not completed on time.[35]

Key features of task management software include the following:

- Boards to create and manage tasks
- Task assignment tools to appoint team members to various tasks
- Task prioritization tools to move tasks and set the project schedule
- Planning and scheduling tools to create plans and meet deadlines using timelines and calendars
- File management tools for uploading and sharing files

The top three software programs for task management include Asana, Zoho Connect, and Wrike.

Document and content management software enables team members to store and share information and work together on different files. Most of these tools track the history of changes that different team members make. Key features of document and content management software include the following:

- Document and content management tools that enable team members to store and track documents and files.

- Business writing tools that enable team members to write content together and create consistent, professional business documents.

- Synchronous editing tools that allow several team members to edit the same document at the same time and see changes in real time.

- A variety of templates that enable team members to create documents faster.

The top three software programs in this area include Google Apps for Work, Confluence, and Samepage. Microsoft Office SharePoint Server is also a popular collaboration software application for creating, managing, and sharing documents and Web services. (See the nearby box on SharePoint Server.) Also, the "Remote Collaboration with Google Apps for Work" box highlights the major components of Google Apps for Work as a comprehensive tool for remote collaboration.

12-5b Which Collaboration Software Is Right for You?

As mentioned earlier, many collaboration software packages are on the market, with varying price tags and capabilities. Before you choose one, consider the following factors.[36,37]

1. Define your needs. For what purpose do you need collaboration software? As you can see from Table 12.1, collaboration software offers many capabilities, although not all packages offer all the features listed. You should compare your needs against the offerings of a particular software package. For example, if a digital dashboard is one of your requirements, you must make sure that the software package you choose offers this feature.

2. Collaboration software comes with different price tags. The most expensive software may not necessarily be right for you. You may be able to choose less expensive software that offers all the features you need.

3. Not all vendors offer the same quality of support and service. You should evaluate vendor support,

> **Document and content management software** enables team members to store and share information and work together on different files.

Microsoft Office SharePoint Server: A Popular Collaboration Platform

➤➤ Finance | Application | Technology in Society | Reflective Thinking

Microsoft Office SharePoint Server 2019, part of the Microsoft Office suite, is used to improve collaboration, provide content management features, carry out business processes, and provide access to information that is essential to organizational goals (*https://docs.microsoft.com/en-us/sharepoint/what-s-new/new-and-improved-features-in-sharepoint-server-2019*). You can create SharePoint sites that support content publishing, content management, records management, and business intelligence needs. You can also conduct searches for people, documents, and data as well as access and analyze large amounts of business data. SharePoint Server 2019 provides a single, integrated location where employees can collaborate with team members, find organizational resources, search for experts and information, manage content and workflow, and use the information they find to make better decisions.[38]

Questions and Discussions

1. What are two business applications of Microsoft Office SharePoint Server?
2. What are two features or capabilities of Microsoft Office SharePoint Server? How might they be used in an organization?

Remote Collaboration with Google Apps for Work

➤➤ Finance | Application | Technology in Society | Reflective Thinking

As you have learned, a number of tools are available for remote collaboration. Google Apps for Work offers one of the most complete options to enable users to collaborate remotely in an effective way. Its four major components include tools for communication, storage, collaboration, and management of a collaboration process.

For communication, it offers Gmail, Hangouts (for voice and video calls), and Calendar. For storing, sharing, and synchronizing documents and collaboration contents, Drive can be used. For collaboration, Google Apps for Work offers Docs (for word processing), Sheets (spreadsheets), Forms (surveys and questionnaires), Slides (presentations), and Sites (Web sites).

For management, Admin and Vault are available. Admin enables the addition and deletion of users, device management, and configuration of security and privacy settings. Admin and Vault offer tools to maintain the privacy and integrity of data and the collaboration process. Vault is also used to manage, store, search, and export the contents of collaboration sessions.

Yeamake/Shutterstock.com

Google Drawings can be used for creating flowcharts, organizational charts, maps, concept maps, data flow diagrams, and other charts. All of these tools are cloud based, meaning team participants can use them from anywhere and at any time.[39,40]

Questions and Discussions

1. What are two business applications of Google Apps for Work?
2. What are two features or capabilities of Google Apps for Work? How might they be used in an organization?

---

frequency of updates and patches, availability of newsletters, and user groups. These important factors must be considered before making a final decision.

12-6 Guidelines for Designing a Management Support System

Before designing any management support system, the system's objectives should be defined clearly, and then the system development methods discussed in Module 10 can be followed. Because MSSs have a somewhat different purpose than other information systems, the

important factors in designing one are summarized in the following list:

- *Support from the top*—Without a full commitment from top management, the system's chances of success are low.

- *Clearly defined objectives and benefits*—Costs are always in dollars, but benefits are qualitative. The design team should spend time identifying all costs and benefits in order to present a convincing case to top management. When benefits are intangible, such as improving customer service, the design team should associate the benefit with a measurable factor, such as increased sales.

- *Identifying executives' information needs*—Examine the decision-making process that executives use to find out what kinds of decisions they are making—structured, semistructured, or unstructured—and what kind of information they need to make these decisions.

- *Keeping lines of communication open*—This is important to ensure that key decision makers are involved in designing the MSS.

- *Keeping the system's complexity hidden and the interface simple*—Avoid using technical jargon when explaining the system to executives, because they might lose interest if they think the system is too technical. Executives are not interested in the choice of platform or software, for example. Their main concern is getting the information they need in the simplest way possible. In addition, the system must be easy for executives to learn, with little or no training. To most executives, the interface is the system, so its ease of use is a crucial factor in the system's success.

- *Keeping the "look and feel" consistent*—Designers should use standard layouts, formats, and colors in windows, menus, and dialog boxes for consistency and ease of use. That way, a user who has learned the database portion of the system, for example,

should be able to switch to the report-generating portion with little trouble because the interface is familiar. You can see this in Microsoft Office, which uses similar features, such as formatting toolbars, in all its applications. Users accustomed to Word, for example, can learn how to use Excel quickly because the interface is familiar.

- *Designing a flexible system*—Almost all aspects of an MSS, including the user interface, change over time because of rapid developments in technology and the dynamic business environment. A flexible system can incorporate changes quickly.

- *Making sure response time is fast*—MSS designers must monitor the system's response time at regular intervals, as executives rarely tolerate slow response times. In addition, when a system function takes more than a few seconds, make sure a message is displayed to state that the system is processing the request. Using a progress bar can help reduce frustration, too.

The Industry Connection highlights the software and services available from SAS Incorporated, one of the leaders in decision support systems.

Industry Connection: SAS, Inc.[41]

SAS was founded in the early 1970s to analyze agricultural research data. Eventually, it developed into a vendor of software for conducting comprehensive analysis and generating business intelligence information for a variety of decision-making needs. Products and services offered by SAS include the following:

SAS Business Intelligence: Analyzes past data to predict the future; it includes features for reporting, queries, analysis, online analytical processing, and integrated analytics.

Data Integration: Gives organizations a flexible, reliable way to respond quickly to data integration requirements at a reduced cost.

SAS Analytics: Provides an integrated environment for modeling analyses, including data mining, text mining, forecasting, optimization, and simulation; provides several techniques and processes for collecting, classifying, analyzing, and interpreting data to reveal patterns and relationships that can help with decision making.

Module Summary

12-1 Examine the three types of decisions made in each phase of the decision-making process. Structured decisions, or programmable tasks, can be automated because a well-defined standard

operating procedure exists for these types of decisions. Semistructured decisions are not quite as well defined by standard operating procedures, but they include a structured aspect that benefits from information retrieval, analytical models, and information systems technology. Unstructured decisions are typically one-time decisions, with no standard operating procedure pertaining to them. Executive information systems offer some support for these types of decisions.

12-2 Describe a decision support system (DSS). A DSS is an interactive information system consisting of hardware, software, data, and models (mathematical and statistical) designed to assist decision makers in an organization. Its three major components are a database, a model base, and a user interface.

12-3 Explain an executive information system's importance in decision making. Executive information systems (EISs), which are branches of DSSs, are interactive information systems that give executives easy access to internal and external data. They typically include "drill-down" features and a digital dashboard for examining and analyzing information.

12-4 Summarize the uses for a geographic information system (GIS). A GIS captures, stores, processes, and displays geographic information or information in a geographic context. For example, a GIS can show the locations of all city streetlights on a map.

12-5 Describe collaboration systems or collaboration software, including their types and the criteria for their selection. A collaboration system assists teams in communicating, collaborating, and coordinating their activities. The system is a collection of applications that supports decision makers by providing access to a shared environment and information. The three types of collaboration systems are communication software, task management software, and document and content management software.

12-6 Apply the eight guidelines for designing a management support system. They include (1) support from the top, (2) clearly defined objectives and benefits, (3) identifying executives' information needs, (4) keeping lines of communication open, (5) keeping the system's complexity hidden and the interface simple, (6) keeping the "look and feel" consistent, (7) designing a flexible system, and (8) making sure response time is fast.

Key Terms

- Bar charts
- Choice phase
- Collaboration system or collaboration software
- Column charts
- Communication software
- Decision support system (DSS)
- Design phase
- Digital dashboard
- Document and content management software
- Executive information systems (EISs)
- Geographic information system (GIS)
- Implementation phase
- Intelligence phase

- Line charts (or time-series charts)
- Management support systems (MSSs)
- Managerial designer
- Model base
- Model builder
- Pie charts
- Semistructured decisions
- Structured decisions
- Task management software
- Technical designer
- Unstructured decisions
- XY (scatter) charts

Reviews and Discussions

1. What are examples of structured, semistructured, and unstructured decisions in a business organization? Provide one example for each.

2. What are three main components of a decision support system?

3. What are two unique features of an executive information system?

4. What are three applications of a geographic information system?

5. What is a collaboration system or collaboration software?

6. What are three types of collaboration software?

7. What are four examples of graphs and charts used by an EIS?

8. Provide three business examples of what-if analysis.

Projects

1. After reading the information presented in this module and other sources, write a two-page paper that compares and contrasts Slack and Zoho Cliq as two leading e-collaboration software applications. Which one would you recommend to a company with over 200 employees scattered throughout four offices in California? What are the bases of your recommendation? Mention one more product that competes with these two.

2. After reading the information presented in this module and other sources, write a two-page paper that compares and contrasts Samepage and Confluence. Which one would you recommend to the company mentioned in Project 1? What are the bases of your recommendation? Mention one more product that competes with these two.

3. After reading the information presented in this module and other sources, write a one-page paper that describes five key applications of GISs in the insurance industry. How can these applications help the bottom line? What are three applications of GISs in the city where you live?

4. ESRI (*www.esri.com/products*) is one of the major providers of GIS software. What are two examples of location analytics software? What types of businesses benefit the most from this type of GIS? What are some of the features of ESRI Maps for Office?

5. Google Apps for Work is a leading platform for remote collaboration. After reading the information presented in this module and other sources, write a two-page paper that identifies five key features of this platform. What are two other platforms that closely compete with this platform? Which platform would you recommend to the company mentioned in Project 1? What is the basis of your recommendation?

6. SAS Business Intelligence & Analytics (*www.sas.com/en_us/solutions/business-intelligence.html*) and Tableau (*https://www.tableau.com/*) are popular packages used to design an EIS. After reading the information presented in this module and other sources, write a two-page paper that identifies four key features of each package. What types of businesses will benefit the most from these packages?

Module Quiz

1. Government agencies are the only users of GISs. True or False?

2. Slack is an example of collaboration software. True or False?

3. A digital dashboard integrates information from multiple sources and presents it in a unified, understandable format, often as charts and graphs. True or False?

4. All of the following are important factors in designing a management support system except:
   a. Support from the top
   b. Clearly defined objectives and benefits
   c. Making sure response time is slow
   d. Keeping lines of communication open

5. All of the following are examples of video-conferencing systems except:
   a. Microsoft's SharePoint
   b. Microsoft's Skype
   c. Apple's FaceTime
   d. Google's Hangouts

6. All of the following are components of a DSS except:
   a. A database
   b. An intermediary base
   c. A model base
   d. A user interface

Case Study 12-1
UPS Deploys Routing Optimization with a Big Payoff
➤ **Finance | Application | Technology in Society | Reflective Thinking**

The UPS ORION (On-Road Integrated Optimization and Navigation) system reduces delivery miles and fuel usage of the company's trucks and sets the stage for enhanced customer service. The system not only reduces overall delivery costs, it is also a great move toward sustainability. ORION saves UPS about 1.5 million gallons of fuel per year, which has reduced emissions of carbon dioxide by 14,000 metric tons per year.

Victor Maschek/Shutterstock.com

To challenge the system and further improve the algorithm, UPS invited its most experienced drivers to try to "beat the system." UPS driver Tim Ahn said, "I get options that I would have actually never thought of before. It's a new way of thinking to make me more efficient."[42]

According to Chuck Holland, vice president of industrial engineering at UPS, it takes about six days to train a driver to work with ORION. Typically, ORION can save six to eight miles per day for each driver, although some drivers still outperform the system. ORION is currently deployed throughout the United States for route planning. Another algorithm used by UPS provides predictive maintenance that has helped the company reduce its vehicle maintenance expenses by approximately 15 percent.[43]

In 2018, UPS introduced UPSNav, which was a major upgrade to ORION. UPSNav optimizes entire routes, providing turn-by-turn directions to loading docks and other delivery and pickup locations that are sometimes hard to find. UPSNav is loaded to a DIAD (Delivery Information Acquisition Device), which is in its fifth generation now. DIAD is mounted to the driver's dashboard for hands-free operation, and it displays a map showing drivers where to turn. UPSNav reduces miles driven, fuel consumed, and carbon emissions, and at the same time allows UPS to offer better service to its customers. The system includes 250 million locations from ORION's map and allows drivers and other UPS staff to quickly update maps if a delivery or pickup point changes. UPSNav can dynamically adjust and update throughout the day to recalculate routes, considering factors like changing traffic conditions, weather conditions, and the remaining deliveries and pick-up requests. The new tool has been particularly useful for drivers who are new to their routes, but every driver has seen improvements. According to Jack Levis, senior program director at UPS, "Our drivers now have the best suite of route optimization and navigation technologies in the industry."[44]

Answer the following questions:
1. What are three advantages of using ORION at UPS?
2. How is this system helping UPS to be more sustainable?
3. What are two improvements as a result of the UPSNav upgrade?
4. How might UPS continue to improve this system? What next steps might the company take?

Case Study 12-2
GPS Technology and Analytics Combat Crime
➤ **Finance | Application | Technology in Society | Reflective Thinking**

Due to budget cuts, the city of Camden, New Jersey, lost half of the police force that served its 75,000 residents. According to the Federal Bureau of Investigation (FBI), Camden was one of the most dangerous cities in the United States in 2011.

A type of MSS called Real Time Tactical Information Center, a $4.5 million project, changed the crime rate in Camden significantly. The system combines gunshot-spotting cameras, in-cruiser GPS technology, and analytics to provide real-time information for the police force. Violent and nonviolent crimes have been reduced by 30 and 38 percent, respectively, and aggravated assaults with firearms are down 61 percent.

Camden County Police Chief Scott J. Thomson said the system reduced 911 response time from the 9-minute national average to 90 seconds in Camden. The system eliminated police dispatchers by automatically sending the two nearest police officers to a crime scene; their police cars are GPS-tracked.

The system also includes 120 cameras positioned around the city that send updated information every 1.5 seconds to patrol car computer screens. This information enables officers to see where emergencies are happening at any given time. Squad cars are also equipped with cameras that can take pictures of license plates, which are run instantly through the FBI's National Crime Information Center. Additionally, the system keeps track of officers' movements throughout the city and alerts them when they are not spending adequate time in each location.[45]

Answer the following questions:

1. What are the three main components of Camden's Real Time Tactical Information Center?
2. How was the system able to reduce the average 911 response time to 90 seconds in Camden?
3. What is the role of the 120 cameras located around the city?
4. How might this technology be used for other purposes?

Module 13

Artificial Intelligence and Automation

Learning Objectives

After studying this module, you should be able to…

13.1 Define *artificial intelligence* and explain how AI technologies support decision making.

13.2 Describe an expert system, its applications, and its components.

13.3 Describe case-based reasoning, including the four Rs involved in its design and implementation.

13.4 Summarize each of the four types of intelligent agents and how they are used.

13.5 Describe fuzzy logic and its uses.

13.6 Explain machine learning and artificial neural networks.

13.7 Describe how genetic algorithms are used.

13.8 Explain natural-language processing and its major categories.

13.9 Describe the five benefits of integrating AI technologies into decision support systems.

13.10 Explain contextual computing.

13.11 Explain AI impacts on automation.

13.12 Describe the ethical issues of AI.

This module covers the use of intelligent information systems, beginning with artificial intelligence (AI). It discusses the ways in which AI technologies are used in decision making, with an overview of robotics as one of the earliest AI applications. Next, the module discusses expert systems—their components and the ways these systems are used. Case-based reasoning and intelligent agents are also discussed as applications of AI. Next, the module discusses fuzzy logic, machine learning, artificial neural networks, genetic algorithms, and natural-language processing systems as well as the advantages of integrating AI technologies into decision support systems. The module then provides an overview of contextual computing and explains AI impacts on automation. Finally, it provides an overview of the ethical issues of AI.

13-1 What Is Artificial Intelligence?

According to a report by the consulting firm Accenture, artificial intelligence could double the annual economic growth rate by 2035. The study was modeled on 12 developed economies, including the United States.[1] So what is artificial intelligence?

Artificial intelligence (AI) consists of related technologies that try to simulate and reproduce human thought and behavior, including thinking, speaking, feeling, and reasoning. AI technologies apply computers to areas that require knowledge, perception, reasoning, understanding, and cognitive abilities.[2] To achieve these capabilities, computers must be able to do the following:

- Understand common sense (see the "Computers Understanding Common Sense" box).
- Understand facts and manipulate qualitative data.
- Deal with exceptions and discontinuity.
- Understand relationships between facts.
- Interact with humans in their own language.
- Deal with new situations based on previous learning.

Information systems are concerned with capturing, storing, retrieving, and working with data, but AI technologies are concerned with generating and displaying knowledge and facts. In the information systems field, as you have learned, programmers and systems analysts design systems that help decision makers by providing timely, relevant, accurate, and integrated information. In the AI field, knowledge engineers try to discover "rules of thumb" that enable computers to perform tasks usually handled by humans. Rules used in the AI field come from a diverse group of experts in areas such as mathematics, psychology, economics, anthropology, medicine, engineering, and physics. AI encompasses several related technologies discussed in this module, including robotics, expert systems, fuzzy logic systems, intelligent agents, machine learning, artificial neural networks, genetic algorithms, and natural-language processing.

> **Artificial intelligence (AI)** consists of related technologies that try to simulate and reproduce human thought and behavior, including thinking, speaking, feeling, and reasoning. AI technologies apply computers to areas that require knowledge, perception, reasoning, understanding, and cognitive abilities.

Although these applications and technologies may not offer true human intelligence, they are certainly more intelligent than traditional information systems. Over the years, the capabilities of these systems have improved in an attempt to close the gap between artificial intelligence and human intelligence. The following section discusses possibilities for using AI technologies in decision-making processes.

13-1a AI Technologies Supporting Decision Making

As you know, information technologies are used to support many phases of decision making. The most recent developments in AI technologies promise new areas of decision-making support. Table 13.1 lists some applications of AI-related technologies in various organizations.[3,4,5]

Table 13.1　Applications of AI Technologies

Field	Organization	Application
Energy	Arco and Tenneco Oil Company	Neural networks used to help pinpoint oil and gas deposits
Government	Internal Revenue Service	Software used to read tax returns and spot fraud
Human services	Merced County, California	Expert systems used to decide if applicants should receive welfare benefits
Marketing	Spiegel	Neural networks used to determine most likely buyers from a long list
Telecommunications	BT Group	Heuristic searches used for a scheduling application that provides work schedules for more than 20,000 engineers
Transportation	American Airlines	Expert systems used to schedule the routine maintenance of airplanes
Inventory/forecasting	Hyundai Motors	Neural networks and expert systems used to reduce delivery time by 20 percent and increase inventory turnover
Inventory/forecasting	SCI Systems	Neural networks and expert systems used to reduce on-hand inventory by 15 percent, resulting in $180 million in annual savings
Inventory/forecasting	Reynolds Aluminum	Neural networks and expert systems used to reduce forecasting errors by 2 percent, resulting in an inventory reduction of 1 million pounds
Inventory/forecasting	Unilever	Neural networks and expert systems used to reduce forecasting errors from 40 to 25 percent, resulting in multimillion-dollar savings

Decision makers use information technologies in the following types of decision-making analyses:[6]

- *What-is*—This analysis is commonly used in transaction-processing systems and management information systems. For example, if you enter a customer account number, the system displays the customer's current balance. However, these systems lack the capability to report real-time information or predict what could happen in the future. For example, reports generated by accounting information systems that show performance over the preceding fiscal quarter consist of past events, so decision makers cannot do much with this information.

- *What-if*—This analysis is used in decision support systems. Decision makers use it to monitor the effect of a change in one or more variables. This type of analysis is available in spreadsheet programs, such as Microsoft Excel.

Computers Understanding Common Sense

➤➤ Finance | Reflective Thinking

Humans take common sense for granted. For example, we know that fish are found in the ocean, trees and bushes are found in the woods, and people eat food. We know that when you drop a ball, it will fall. To computers, understanding such simple things is a challenge, but this is changing.

At Carnegie Mellon University, a computer called Never Ending Image Learner runs 24 hours a day and goes through the Web finding and analyzing images in order to build a visual database that can recognize associations among these images. There are billions of images on the Web; Facebook alone contains more than 200 billion images.[7]

Since it was begun in July 2013, Never Ending Image Learner has analyzed more than 3 million images and identified 1,500 types of objects and 1,200 types of scenes. As a result, the computer has learned 2,500 associations; for example, it knows that buildings are vertical instead of lying on their sides and that most automobiles have four wheels. As the number of analyzed images grows, the computer learns more and increases the number of associations. The interesting aspect of this project is that researchers are enabling a computer to teach itself common sense without any human intervention.[8]

Questions and Discussions

1. What is the computer called Never Ending Image Learner at Carnegie Mellon University trying to achieve?
2. Why is it important that computers understand common sense? Discuss.

> **Information systems are concerned with capturing, storing, retrieving, and working with data, but AI technologies are concerned with generating and displaying knowledge and facts.**

In addition to what-is and what-if analyses, decision makers often need to answer the following questions about information: Why? What does it mean? What should be done? When should it be done? AI technologies have the potential to help decision makers address these questions.

Artificial Intelligence versus Augmented Intelligence

The so-called next generation of AI is called *augmented intelligence*, *intelligence augmentation*, or *cognitive augmentation*. **Augmented intelligence**'s goal is to complement decision makers, not to replace them. Just imagine if every one of us was given a super-intelligent assistant that is always with us and helping us to do our jobs smarter and faster. Rather than taking jobs, intelligent augmentation enables humans and machines to complement one another.[9] Recent innovations in AI chips will equip more devices with AI capabilities, potentially leading to what Deloitte calls "pervasive intelligence." Smart devices from robots to cameras to medical devices could offer much greater efficiency and effectiveness to organizations that deploy them. A diverse group of industries will benefit from pervasive intelligence, including manufacturing, healthcare, construction, logistics and distribution, automobiles and transportation, agriculture, energy, and security.[10]

To learn what AI is doing in our everyday lives and see how far AI has come, read the "AI in Action: Retail Industry" box.

> The goal of **augmented intelligence** is to complement decision makers, not replace them.

AI in Action: Retail Industry

➤ Finance | Application | Technology in Society | Reflective Thinking

AI technology has assisted many retailers to improve their top and bottom lines by increasing foot traffic, enhancing customer service, and offering personalized products and services. Below are 10 successful examples.[11]

Sephora, a retailer of personal care and beauty products, uses an AI-powered product called Color IQ that scans customers' skin to provide customized shade recommendations for foundation and concealer. This has increased foot traffic and helped Sephora to provide personalized, creative, and unique shopping experiences for its customers.

Olay Skin Advisor uses machine learning to provide beauty product recommendations from its antiaging skincare line. The AI tool analyzes customers' selfies to diagnose their "skin age" and problem areas.

Stitch Fix, an online clothing subscription service, uses an AI tool to tailor apparel recommendations to its customers. The AI tool uses customers' measurements and feedback, current styles and trends, and the expertise of clothing experts to provide a personalized experience.

North Face uses IBM Watson to help its customers find the best jacket for themselves. Watson asks customers a series of questions about the type of jacket they want and its purpose, such as for commuting, snowboarding, hiking, or skiing. Based on this information, the site offers recommendations.

ASOS, an online fashion retailer, uses an AI tool to recommend clothing sizes to shoppers based on what they have purchased and kept in the past. The AI tool also analyzes items that customers have returned so it can make better recommendations next time.

Best Buy, REI, 1-800-Flowers, Domino's, Uber, and Wingstop allow their customers to use Amazon's Alexa to buy a product or service using voice commands, which makes the process much faster.

Pinterest's Lens feature uses an AI tool and the camera of the Pinterest app to allow visitors to take photos and then search for visually similar pins. Target uses the same technology licensed from Pinterest to allow customers to explore, discover, and buy products at Target's Web site.

(Continued)

Amazon Go is a cashier-less grocery store that has completely automated the grocery shopping experience. Using an app, shoppers check in, and then sensors throughout the store track which items they put in their baskets. Amazon automatically charges shoppers when they leave the store.

eBay uses an AI tool to help its sellers manage their inventory based on demand and assist them with competitive pricing.

Tommy Hilfiger uses the Facebook Messenger chatbot to provide a more personalized and interactive shopping experience. The AI tool replies to customer queries and offers style advice and product recommendations.

Questions and Discussions

1. What is AI doing for Sephora? How might it help the company's bottom line?
2. How is AI helping Stitch Fix? Discuss.

13-1b Robotics

Robots are one of the most successful applications of AI. You are probably familiar with robots used in factories from watching news reports. They are far from being intelligent, but progress has been steady. They perform well at simple, repetitive tasks and can be used to free workers from tedious or hazardous jobs. Currently, robots are used mainly on assembly lines in Japan and the United States as part of computer-integrated manufacturing, but they are also used in the military, aerospace, and medical industries as well as for performing such services as delivering interoffice mail to employees.

OliverSved/Shutterstock.com

The cost of industrial robots ranges from $100,000 to $150,000 or more. Typically, their mobility is limited. For example, they might have only a fixed arm that moves objects from one point to another. Some robots have limited vision that is useful for locating and picking up objects, as long as the objects are isolated from other objects. A robot's operation is controlled by a computer program that includes commands such as when and how far to reach, which direction to go or turn, when to grasp an object, and how much pressure to apply. Programming languages for controlling robots include Variable Assembly Language (VAL), Functional Robotics (FROB), and A Manufacturing Language (AML). These languages are usually proprietary, meaning they are specific to individual robot manufacturers.

One of the most advanced and most popular robots is Honda's Advanced Step in Innovative Mobility, or ASIMO (*https://asimo.honda.com*). Honda's intelligence technologies enable ASIMO to coordinate with other robots. It recognizes moving objects, sounds, gestures, multiple environments, faces, and postures. ASIMO is also able to choose between stepping back and yielding the right-of-way or continuing to move forward based on the predicted movement of oncoming people. It can automatically recharge its battery when the charge falls below a certain level.

Personal robots have attracted a lot of attention. These robots have limited mobility, limited vision, and some speech capabilities. Currently, they are used mostly as prototypes to test services such as helping the elderly, bringing breakfast to the table, cooking, opening doors, and carrying trays and drinks. Examples include Twendy-One, Motoman, ApriAttenda Robot, and PR2. One of the most successful and advanced personal robots on the market today, PR2 performs many ordinary tasks around the home and office.

> **Robots** are one of the most successful applications of AI. They perform well at simple, repetitive tasks and can be used to free workers from tedious or hazardous jobs.

Robots offer the following advantages over humans in the workplace:

- They do not fall in love with coworkers, get insulted, or call in sick.
- They are consistent.
- They can be used in environments that are hazardous to humans, such as working with radioactive materials.
- They do not spy for competitors, ask for a raise, or lobby for longer breaks.

Another type of robot that is gaining in popularity is a **soft robot**. Soft robots are not made of hard physical materials like conventional robots; they are made of elastomer, a material similar to rubber. They are simpler to make and less expensive than conventional robots.[12] They are used for a number of applications, such as the following:[13]

- High-speed food handling
- Precise pick and place
- Adaptive grasping
- Warehouse logistics
- Advanced assembly
- Medicine

Recently, some interesting robots have been introduced that go beyond the capabilities of traditional robots. Here are three examples:

- A palm-sized toy robot named Cozmo recognizes faces, plays games, and expresses a range of emotions. When it recognizes a new person, Cozmo is social and polite. When it is ignored, it becomes unhappy or plays on its own. It gets frustrated when it loses a game and celebrates when it wins one.[14]
- DoNotPay, designed by Stanford University student Joshua Browder, serves as a lawyer and has already successfully contested over 160,000 parking tickets in London and New York. Just like a human lawyer, it asks questions and provides answers. It is free to use and has saved its users millions of dollars.[15]
- Scientists at the University of Warsaw in Poland have designed a tiny robot that moves like a caterpillar and is powered by light. This soft robot can walk, climb, and push objects that are 10 times its own mass.[16]

Robots can also work in a cloud environment where they can tap into additional resources that they do not have in their own capabilities, such as greater memory, computational power, and collective learning.

Developments in AI-related fields, such as expert systems and natural-language processing, will affect the future development of the robotics industry. For example, natural-language processing will make it easier to communicate with robots in human languages.

As robots become more sophisticated and more organizations integrate them into daily operations, human-robot teams create a new challenge for management. If the integration is done properly, productivity can improve significantly. Management must make sure to educate their employees that robots will not replace everyone, and in many cases will complement and assist employees. Today's sophisticated collaborative robots, such as autonomous mobile robots, are specifically designed to work with people. Trust building between human and robot teammates includes cognitive, affective, and emotional components. Managers must convey these ideas to employees before integrating robots into human-robot teams.[17]

The "Medical Robotics in Action" box highlights an application of robotics in the medical field.

> A **soft robot** is made of elastomer, is simpler to make and less expensive than conventional robots, and is used for an increasing number of applications.
>
> **Expert systems** mimic human expertise in a particular field to solve a problem in a well-defined area.

catwalker/Shutterstock.com

13-2 Expert Systems

Expert systems have been one of the most successful AI-related technologies and have been around since the 1960s. They mimic human expertise in a particular field to solve a problem in a well-defined area. For the purposes of this book, an expert system consists of programs that mimic human thought and behavior in a specific area that human experts have addressed successfully. The first expert system, called DENDRAL, was developed in the mid-1960s at Stanford University to determine the chemical structure of molecules. For expert systems to be successful, they must be applied to an activity that human experts have already handled, such as tasks in medicine, geology, education, and oil exploration. For example, COGITO (by Italy-based Expert System) is used for monitoring what consumers are saying in blogs, comment sections, message boards, and Web-based articles. It is also used in search engines to better understand users' queries.[18]

Decision support systems generate information by using data, models, and well-defined algorithms, but expert systems work with heuristic data. Heuristics consist of common sense, rules of thumb, educated guesses, and instinctive judgments, and using heuristic data encourages the application of knowledge based on experience to solve or describe a problem. In other words, heuristic data is not formal knowledge, but it helps in finding a solution to a problem without following a rigorous algorithm.

Medical Robotics in Action

▶▶ Finance | Application | Technology in Society | Social and Ethical Issues | Reflective Thinking

Robots have been used in the medical field for two decades. They have been used to train medical personnel, they have assisted elderly patients during rehabilitation, and they have allowed surgeons to make smaller incisions for certain types of surgery. In addition, they have been used during training processes as dummies to mimic a live patient's feelings of pain.[19]

At 5 feet, 4 inches and 140 pounds, the RP-VITA (Remote Presence Virtual Independent Telemedicine Assistant) by iRobot Corporation is the first robot to receive clearance by the U.S. Food and Drug Administration for use in hospitals.[20]

To make the robot resemble humans as closely as possible, it has a video screen for a head, a microphone and speaker for a mouth, and two high-definition cameras for eyes. One of its functions is to assist doctors in making hospital rounds remotely. Controllable by a tablet computer using a wired or wireless network, it is able to move around and is intelligent enough to avoid obstacles.

RP-VITA does not offer medical advice, nor does it treat patients. Instead, it is used by doctors and nurses to communicate with their patients. It can also be used with InTouch Health's cloud service to provide doctors and nurses with real-time electronic medical records. The robot can connect with diagnostic devices such as otoscopes for examining the inside of patients' ears; it can also perform an ultrasound.[21]

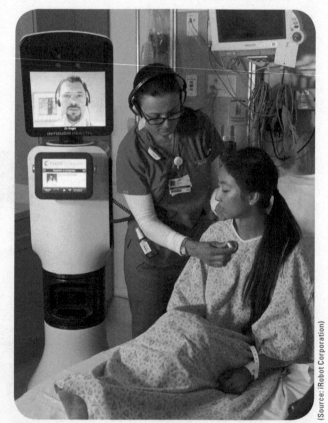

(Source: iRobot Corporation)

Questions and Discussions

1. What does the RP-VITA robot do?
2. What are three applications of robots in the medical field?

13-2a Components of an Expert System

A typical expert system includes the components described in the following list and shown in Exhibit 13.1:

- *Knowledge acquisition facility*—A **knowledge acquisition facility** is a software package with manual or automated methods for acquiring and incorporating new rules and facts so that the expert system is capable of growth. This component works with the knowledge base management system (described later in this list) to ensure that the knowledge base is as up to date as possible.

- *Knowledge base*—A **knowledge base** is similar to a database, but in addition to storing facts and figures, it keeps track of rules and explanations associated with facts. For example, a financial expert system's knowledge base might keep track of all figures constituting current assets, including cash, deposits, and accounts receivable. It might also keep track of the fact that current assets can be converted to cash within one year. An expert system in an academic environment might include facts about all graduate students, such as GMAT (Graduate Management Admission Test) scores and grade point averages (GPAs), as well as a rule specifying that classified graduate students must have a GMAT of 650 or better and a GPA of 3.4 or better. To be considered part of a true expert system, the knowledge base component must include the following types of knowledge:

- *Factual knowledge*—Facts related to a specific discipline, subject, or problem. For example, facts related to kidney problems might include kidney size, blood levels of certain enzymes, and duration and location of pain.

> A **knowledge acquisition facility** is a software package with manual or automated methods for acquiring and incorporating new rules and facts, making the expert system capable of growth.
>
> A **knowledge base** is similar to a database, but in addition to storing facts and figures, it keeps track of rules and explanations associated with facts.

Exhibit 13.1
An expert system configuration

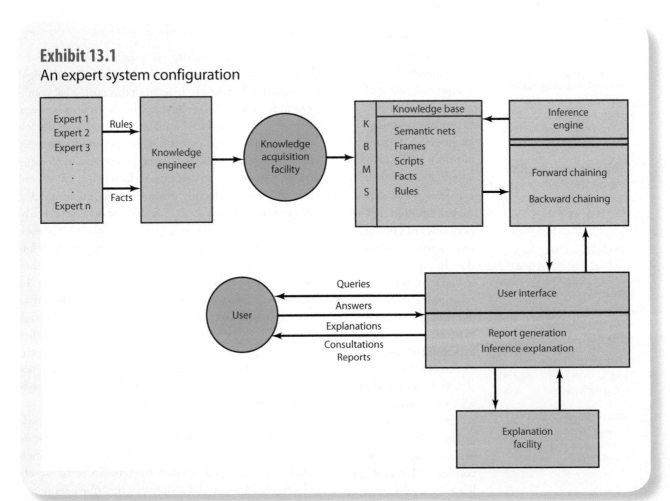

- *Heuristic knowledge*—Rules related to a problem or discipline. For example, the general rules indicating that a patient has a kidney problem could include severe pain in the lower back and high levels of creatinine and blood urea nitrogen.

- *Meta-knowledge*—Meta-knowledge is knowledge about knowledge. It enables an expert system to learn from experience and examine and extract relevant facts to determine the path to a solution. It also guides future planning or execution phases of an expert system. For example, knowing how an expert system makes decisions is considered meta-knowledge. Although this type of knowledge is not currently available in expert systems, integrating neural networks into expert systems is one possibility for acquiring meta-knowledge.

- *Knowledge base management system*—A **knowledge base management system (KBMS)**, similar to a DBMS, is used to keep the knowledge base updated with changes to facts, figures, and rules.

- *User interface*—This is the same as the user interface component of a decision support system. It provides user-friendly access to the expert system. Although graphical user interfaces (GUIs) have improved this component, one goal of AI technology is to provide a natural language for the user interface, as discussed later in the module.

- *Explanation facility*—An **explanation facility** performs tasks similar to what a human expert does by explaining to end users how recommendations are derived. For example, in a loan evaluation expert system, the explanation facility states why an applicant was approved or rejected. In a medical expert system, it explains why the system concluded that a patient has a kidney stone, for instance. This component is important because it helps give users confidence in the system's results.

- *Inference engine*—An **inference engine** is similar to the model base component of a decision support system (discussed in Module 12). By using different techniques such as forward and backward chaining, an inference engine manipulates a series of rules. Some inference engines work from a matrix of facts that includes several rows of conditions and rules, similar to a decision table. In this case, rules are evaluated one at a time, and then advice is provided. Some inference engines also learn from doing.

In **forward chaining**, a series of "if–then–else" condition pairs is performed. The "if" condition is evaluated first, and then the corresponding "then–else" action is carried out. For example, "if" the temperature is less than 80°F and the grass is 3 inches long, "then" cut the grass or "else" wait. A medical diagnostic expert system could evaluate a problem as follows:

- If the patient's temperature is over 101°F and

- If the patient has a headache, then

- It's very likely (a 95 percent chance) that the patient has the flu, or else search for other diseases.

In **backward chaining**, the expert system starts with the goal—the "then" part—and backtracks to find the right solution. In other words, to achieve this goal, what conditions must be met? To understand the differences between forward chaining and backward chaining, consider the following example. In an expert system that provides financial advice for investors, the system might use forward chaining and ask 50 questions to determine which of five investment categories—oil-gas, bonds, common stocks, public utilities, or transportation—is more suitable for an investor.[22] In addition, each investor is in a specific tax bracket, and each investment solution provides a different tax shelter. In forward chaining, the system evaluates all the "if–then–else" conditions before making the final recommendation. In backward chaining, the system might start with the public utilities category specified by the investor and go through all the "if" conditions to see whether the investor qualifies for this investment category. The backward-chaining technique can be faster in some situations because it does not have to consider irrelevant rules, but the solution the system recommends might not be the best one.

Other techniques are used for representing knowledge in the expert system's knowledge base, such as semantic (associative) networks that represent information as links and nodes, frames that store conditions or objects in hierarchical order, and scripts that describe a sequence

A **knowledge base management system (KBMS)**, similar to a DBMS, is used to keep the knowledge base updated with changes to facts, figures, and rules.

An **explanation facility** performs tasks similar to what a human expert does by explaining to end users how recommendations are derived.

An **inference engine** is similar to the model base component of a decision support system. By using different techniques such as forward and backward chaining, it manipulates a series of rules.

In **forward chaining**, a series of "if–then–else" condition pairs is performed.

In **backward chaining**, the expert system starts with the goal—the "then" part—and backtracks to find the right solution.

DNA Fingerprinting

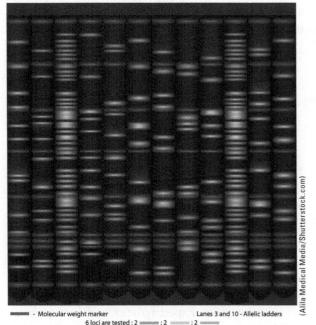

- Molecular weight marker   Lanes 3 and 10 - Allelic ladders
6 loci are tested : 2 ▬▬▬ ; 2 ▬▬▬ ; 2 ▬▬▬

(Alila Medical Media/Shutterstock.com)

of events. For a child's birthday party, for example, events might include buying a cake, inviting friends, lighting the candles, and serving the cake. A script for generating a purchase order might include events such as identifying the quantity to order, identifying the supplier and gathering data, generating the purchase order and sending it to the supplier, updating accounts payable, and informing the receiving department that an order has been placed.

13-2b Uses of Expert Systems

Many companies are engaged in research and development of expert systems. These systems are now used in areas such as the following:

- *Airline industry*—American Airlines developed an expert system to manage frequent-flier transactions.

- *Forensics lab work*—Expert systems are used to review DNA samples from crime scenes and generate results quickly and accurately, helping reduce the backlog in labs and get data entered in national crime databases faster.[23]

- *Banking and finance*—JPMorgan Chase developed a foreign currency trade expert system to assess historical trends, new events, and buying and selling factors.

- *Education*—Arizona State University developed an expert system to teach math and evaluate students' math skills.

- *Food industry*—Campbell's Soup Company developed an expert system to capture expertise that a long-time employee had about plant operations and sterilizing techniques.

- *Personnel management*—IBM developed an expert system to assist in training technicians; it has reduced training time.

- *Security*—Canada Trust Bank (now part of TD Canada Trust) developed an expert system to track credit card holders' purchasing trends and to report deviations, such as unusual activity on a card.

- *U.S. government*—Expert systems have been developed to monitor nuclear power plants and to assist the Internal Revenue Service, Immigration and Naturalization Service, U.S. Postal Service, Department of Transportation, Department of Energy, and Department of Defense in decision-making processes.

- *Agriculture*—The National Institute of Agricultural Extension Management has designed an expert system to diagnose pests and diseases in rice crops and suggest preventative measures.[24]

The information box "Expert Systems in the Baltimore County Police Department" highlights a real-life

Expert Systems in the Baltimore County Police Department

➤➤ **Finance | Application | Technology in Society | Social and Ethical Issues | Reflective Thinking**

In Baltimore County, Maryland, an expert system was developed so detectives could analyze information about burglary sites and identify possible suspects. Data entered in the system included information about known burglars, records of 300 solved burglary cases, and records of 3,000 unsolved cases. Then, 18 detectives were interviewed to gather their

(Continued)

knowledge about local burglaries. Detectives can enter additional information about burglaries, such as neighborhood characteristics, the type of property stolen, and the type of entry used; they can also get information on possible suspects. The system is now used in other police departments in the United States.[25]

Questions and Discussions

1. Why does Baltimore County use an expert system?
2. What are two advantages of using an expert system in this organization? Discuss.

Case-based reasoning (CBR) is a problem-solving technique that matches a new case (problem) with a previously solved case and its solution, the details of which have been stored in a database. After finding a match, the CBR system offers a solution; if no match is found, even after more information is supplied, the human expert must solve the problem.

application of an expert system, this one in burglary and crime detection. The system reduced the time and expenses needed for police operations.

13-2c Criteria for Using Expert Systems

An expert system should be used if one or more of the following conditions exists:

- Extensive human expertise is needed but a single expert cannot tackle the problem alone. (An expert system can integrate the experience and knowledge of several experts more easily.)
- The knowledge needed can be represented as rules or heuristics; a well-defined algorithm is not available.
- The decision or task has already been handled successfully by human experts, allowing the expert system to mimic human expertise.
- The decision or task requires consistency and standardization. (Because computers are more accurate at following standard procedures, an expert system can be preferable to humans in this situation.)
- The subject domain is limited. (Expert systems work better if the problem under investigation is narrow.)
- The decision or task involves many rules (typically between 100 and 10,000) and complex logic.
- There is a scarcity of experts in the organization or key experts are retiring. (An expert system can be used to capture the knowledge and expertise of a long-time employee who is retiring.)

13-2d Criteria for Not Using Expert Systems

The following situations are unsuitable to expert systems:

- There are very few rules (less than 10). Human experts are more effective at solving these problems.

- There are too many rules (usually more than 10,000). Processing slows to unacceptable levels.
- There are well-structured numerical problems (such as those for payroll processing), which means that standard transaction-processing methods can handle the situation more quickly and economically.
- A broad range of topics is involved, but there are not many rules. Expert systems work better when there are deep and narrow problem areas.
- There is a lot of disagreement among experts.
- The problems require human expertise—for example, a combination of the five senses, such as taste and smell. Selecting a perfume is a problem better solved by human experts.

13-2e Advantages of Expert Systems

An expert system can have the following advantages over humans:

- It never becomes distracted, forgetful, or tired. Therefore, it is particularly suitable for monotonous tasks that human workers might object to.
- It duplicates and preserves the expertise of scarce experts and can incorporate the expertise of many experts.
- It preserves the expertise of employees who are retiring or leaving an organization.
- It creates consistency in decision making and improves the decision-making skills of nonexperts.

13-3 Case-Based Reasoning

Expert systems solve a problem by going through a series of if–then–else rules, but **case-based reasoning (CBR)** is a problem-solving technique that matches a new case (problem) with a previously solved case and its solution, the details of which have been stored in a database. Each case in the database is stored with a description and keywords that identify it. If there is no exact match between the new case and cases stored in the database, the system can query the user for clarification or more information. After finding a match, the CBR system offers a solution; if no match is found, even after more information is supplied, the human expert must solve the problem. The new case and its solution are then added to the database.

In the design and implementation of any case-based reasoning application, there are four Rs involved: retrieve, reuse, revise, and retain.

1. To solve the current case (problem), the system compares it with past cases stored in the database and retrieves the most similar case.

2. The retrieved case is reused to solve the current problem.

3. The retrieved case is revised, if necessary, for further enhancement.

4. The solution is retained as a part of the library for future use.

Hewlett-Packard uses CBR to assist users of its printers; this system performs the role of a help desk operator. Users' past complaints and difficulties are stored in a database as cases and solutions. This information is used in dealing with new users, who likely have the same problems as users in the past. In the long term, these systems can improve customer service and save money by reducing the number of help desk employees.

As another example, some banks use a CBR system to qualify customers for loans, using parameters from past customers stored in a database. These parameters include gross income, number of dependents, total assets, net worth, and loan amount requested. The database also stores the final decision on each application (acceptance or rejection). When a new customer applies for a loan, the CBR system can compare the application with past applications and provide a response. The new application and its outcome then become part of the database for future use.

13-4 Intelligent Agents

Intelligent agents, also known as *bots* (short for robots), are software capable of reasoning and following rule-based processes; they are becoming more popular, especially in e-commerce. They are also called *virtual agents*

(VAs) or *intelligent virtual agents (IVAs)*. A sophisticated intelligent agent has the following characteristics:[26]

> **Intelligent agents** are software capable of reasoning and following rule-based processes; they are becoming more popular, especially in e-commerce.

- *Adaptability*— Able to learn from previous knowledge and go beyond information given previously. In other words, the system can make adjustments.

- *Autonomy*—Able to operate with minimal input. The system can respond to environmental stimuli, make a decision without users telling it to do so, and take preemptive action, if needed.

- *Collaborative behavior*—Able to work and cooperate with other agents to achieve a common objective.

- *Humanlike interface*—Able to interact with users in a more natural language.

- *Mobility*—Able to migrate from one platform to another with a minimum of human intervention.

- *Reactivity*—Able to select problems or situations that need attention and act on them. An agent with this capability typically responds to environmental stimuli.

> **Intelligent agents can collect information about customers, such as items purchased, demographic information, and expressed and implied preferences.**

Most intelligent agents today fall short of these capabilities, but improvement is expected in the near future. One important application of intelligent agents that is already available is Web marketing. Intelligent agents can collect information about customers, such as items purchased, demographic information, and expressed and implied preferences. E-commerce sites then use this information to better market their products and services to customers. Other agents, called *product-brokering agents*, can alert customers to new products and services. Amazon has used these agents successfully.

Shopping and information agents help users navigate through the vast resources available on the Web and provide better results in finding information. These agents can navigate the Web much faster than humans and gather more consistent, detailed information. They can serve as search engines, site reminders, or personal surfing assistants.

Personal agents perform specific tasks for a user, such as remembering information for filling out Web forms or completing e-mail addresses after the first few characters are typed.

Data-mining agents work with a data warehouse, detecting trends and discovering new information and relationships among data items that were not readily apparent.

Intelligent agents are also used for smart or interactive catalogs, called "virtual catalogs." A virtual catalog displays product descriptions based on customers' previous experiences and preferences.

Intelligent agents that are currently available fall into these categories:

- Shopping and information agents
- Personal agents
- Data-mining agents
- Monitoring and surveillance agents

These are discussed in the following sections.

13-4a Shopping and Information Agents

Shopping and information agents help users navigate through the vast resources available on the Web and provide better results in finding information. These agents can navigate the Web much faster than humans and gather more consistent, detailed information. They can serve as search engines, site reminders, or personal surfing assistants. Pricewatch.online (*https://www.pricewatch.online/*) is a commercial shopping agent that finds the lowest price for many items and displays all competitive prices. Honey (*https://www.joinhoney.com*) is another popular price-checking site for online shopping. Another comparison-shopping agent is available at *www.bookfinder.com/textbooks*. This agent searches over 150 million books for sale, including new editions, used and out-of-print books, and textbooks. It also recommends booksellers that offer the best prices and selection.

Usenet and newsgroup agents have sorting and filtering features for finding information. For example, DogPile (*www.dogpile.com*) searches the Web by using several search engines, including Google, Yahoo!, and Yandex, to find information for users. DogPile can remove duplicate results and analyze the results to sort them, with the most relevant results at the top.

13-4b Personal Agents

Personal agents perform specific tasks for a user, such as remembering information for filling out Web forms or completing e-mail addresses after the first few characters are typed. An e-mail personal agent can usually perform the following tasks:

- Generate auto-response messages.
- Forward incoming messages.
- Create e-mail replies based on the content of incoming messages.

13-4c Data-Mining Agents

Data-mining agents work with a data warehouse, detecting trends and discovering new information and relationships among data items that were not readily apparent. Volkswagen Group uses a data-mining agent that acts as an early-warning system about market conditions. For example, the data-mining agent might detect a problem that could cause economic conditions to worsen, resulting in delayed payments from customers. Having this information early enables decision makers to come up with a solution that minimizes the negative effects of the problem.

Intelligent Agents in Action

> **Finance | Application | Technology in Society | Social and Ethical Issues | Reflective Thinking**

Intelligent agents cost approximately 2 percent of what a live human assistant costs. Here are some examples of intelligent agents in real-life practice:

- SFR, which is a division of Vodafone, a mobile communications company, uses a virtual agent to facilitate 750,000 conversations a month. The intelligent agent answers customers' questions about their accounts and about the company's services and offerings.[27]

- The French division of eBay uses an intelligent agent named Louise to assist in over 200,000 customer conversations a day in six countries. According to eBay, Louise performs assigned tasks with an 88 percent problem-solving rate. Currently, it handles 30 percent of client contacts for *eBay.fr*.[28]

- Apple uses its intelligent agent, Siri, on its iPhone, iPad, and iPod Touch devices. Siri enables a user's voice commands to send messages, make calls, set reminders, and much more.[29] It is also used in the HomePod, a Siri-based speaker.

- IBM Watson is being marketed as an intelligent agent. For a fee, it can be used at call centers, in the medical field, in insurance companies, and much more.[30,31]

- IntelliResponse offers an intelligent agent that is used by banks, airlines, and telecommunications companies to answer customers' questions and provide other relevant information about products and services directly from the company's Web site.[32]

- Microsoft's Cortana, a voice-enabled assistant, is able to set reminders, recognize natural voices, and answer questions about current weather and traffic conditions, sports scores, and other topics.[33]

- Viv (Viv Labs) is an intelligent assistant with AI capabilities that is able to answer a number of queries for its users and becomes smarter as it is being used. It is expected to work with a diverse group of Internet-connected devices, helping to power a million different apps.[34]

- Amazon's Alexa-controlled Echo is a wireless speaker that serves as an intelligent assistant and helps you put items in a shopping cart to eventually order a product. Using this software, Amazon's 1 Click becomes "no click."[35] Alexa's voice commands can be spoken into Amazon's smaller Echo Dot.[36]

- Google's Home is an intelligent assistant powered by Google Assistant that allows conversation and answers questions. A user can ask it to play a song or get directions to a restaurant, among other things.[37]

Questions and Discussions

1. What are two applications of IBM Watson as an intelligent agent?
2. What are three applications of Amazon's Alexa as an intelligent agent?

Monitoring and surveillance agents usually track and report on computer equipment and network systems to predict when a system crash or failure might occur.

13-4d Monitoring and Surveillance Agents

Monitoring and surveillance agents usually track and report on computer equipment and network systems to predict when a system crash or failure might occur. NASA's Jet Propulsion Laboratory has an agent that monitors inventory, planning, and the scheduling of equipment to keep costs down.[38]

The "Intelligent Agents in Action" box highlights real-life applications of several commercial intelligent agents.

13-5 Fuzzy Logic

Have you ever been given a questionnaire that asks ambiguous questions but expects yes or no responses? Although you might be tempted to use words such as *usually*, *sometimes*, and *only if*, you know the software used to analyze responses simply cannot deal with anything

Fuzzy logic allows a smooth, gradual transition between human and computer vocabularies and deals with variations in linguistic terms by using a degree of membership.

but clear-cut yes and no responses. However, with the development of fuzzy logic, a wide variety of responses is possible in questionnaires and other survey tools. **Fuzzy logic** allows a smooth, gradual transition between human and computer vocabularies and deals with variations in linguistic terms by using a degree of membership. A degree of membership shows how relevant an item or object is to a set. A higher number indicates more relevance and a lower number indicates less relevance. For example, when heating water, you might say it is warm as the temperature increases from 50°C to 75°C. What about when the water's temperature reaches 85°C, though? You can describe it as warmer, but at what point do you describe the water as hot? Describing varying degrees of warmness and assigning them membership in certain categories of warmness involves a lot of vagueness.

Fuzzy logic is designed to help computers simulate vagueness and uncertainty in common situations. Lotfi A. Zadeh developed the fuzzy logic theory in the mid-1960s by using a mathematical method called "fuzzy sets" for handling imprecise or subjective information.[39] Fuzzy logic allows computers to reason in a fashion similar to humans and makes it possible to use approximations and vague data yet produce clear and definable answers.

Fuzzy logic works based on the degree of membership in a set (a collection of objects). For example, 4 feet, 5 feet, and 6 feet could constitute a set of heights for a population. Fuzzy sets have values between 0 and 1, indicating the degree to which an element has membership in the set. At 0, the element has no membership; at 1, it has full membership.

In a conventional set (sometimes called a "crisp" set), membership is defined in a black-or-white fashion; there's no room for gray. For instance, if 90 percent or higher means a "Pass" grade in a course, getting 89.99 percent does not give you membership in the "Pass" area of this crisp set. Therefore, despite getting 89.99 percent, you have failed the course. In this example, there is a very small difference between the two grades (0.01), but it means the difference

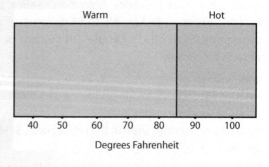

Exhibit 13.2
Example of a conventional set

between passing and failing. In other words, a small difference has a huge impact. This does not happen in a fuzzy logic environment. To help you understand the membership function better, Exhibit 13.2 shows an example of a conventional set. In this example, 84.9°F is considered warm and 85.1°F is considered hot. This small change in temperature can cause a large response in the system.

Exhibit 13.3 shows the same set but with fuzzy logic conventions. For example, 80°F has a membership of 30 percent in the fuzzy set "Warm" and 40 percent in the fuzzy set "Hot." All temperatures from 40° to 100°F make up the membership set.

13-5a Uses of Fuzzy Logic

Fuzzy logic has been used in search engines, chip design, database management systems, software development, and other areas.[40] You might be more familiar with its uses in appliances, as shown in the following examples:

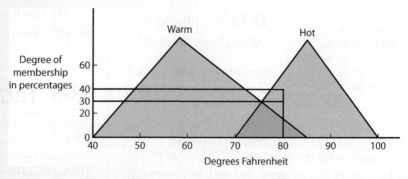

Exhibit 13.3
Degree of membership in a fuzzy system

- Dryers that convert information on load size, fabric type, and flow of hot air into drying times and conditions
- Refrigerators that set defrosting and cooling times based on usage patterns
- Shower systems that suppress variations in water temperature
- TVs that adjust screen color and texture for each frame and stabilize the volume based on the viewer's location in the room[41,42]

> Fuzzy logic has been used in search engines, chip design, database management systems, software development, and other areas.

The box "Fuzzy Logic in Action" highlights how the U.S. Department of Defense uses fuzzy logic.

13-6 Machine Learning

Machine learning is a process and procedure by which knowledge is gained through experience. In other words, computers learn without being explicitly programmed. Facebook has been successfully using machine learning in its news feed. If you read a friend's posts frequently or if you "Like" a friend's posts, Facebook includes more of this friend's posts in your news feed. If you stop reading or liking this friend's posts, Facebook adjusts your news feed accordingly.

A well-publicized achievement in machine learning is AlphaGo from Google, which defeated Korean grandmaster Lee Sedol in four of five matches in the 2,500-year-old Chinese game Go. This is not the first time that a computer program has won a game against a human player: checkers, chess, *Othello*, and *Jeopardy* are other examples. Go is more complex than these other games, however, requiring instinct and some degree of perception.

Machine learning is being applied to identifying faces in photos, recognizing commands spoken into smartphones, designing more intelligent robots, and much more. Table 13.2 highlights the applications of machine learning (ML) in selected companies.[43] One of the best-known applications of machine learning is artificial neural networks.[44]

Artificial neural networks (ANNs) are networks that learn and are capable of performing tasks that are difficult with conventional computers, such as playing

> **Machine learning** is a process and procedure by which knowledge is gained through experience. In other words, computers learn without being explicitly programmed.
>
> **Artificial neural networks (ANNs)** are networks that learn and are capable of performing tasks that are difficult with conventional computers, such as playing chess, recognizing patterns in faces and objects, and filtering spam e-mail.

Fuzzy Logic in Action

⏩ Finance | Technology in Society | Reflective Thinking

In addition to its increasing use in household appliances, fuzzy logic is being applied to multicriteria decision making in which no exact data is available. Today, most new cars let you know when it is time to change the oil based on engine speed and the particular distance traveled, not on the traditional notion of doing it every 3,000 miles. Likewise, the U.S. Department of Defense uses fuzzy logic to solve complex problems in such areas as assessing the cost and benefit of individual weapon systems and evaluating alternative weapons development strategies (e.g., spending more money on ground weapons than on air defense). Using qualitative and quantitative data, a panel of subject-matter experts combines linguistics, rule-based decision support, and maps.[45]

Questions and Discussions

1. How is fuzzy logic being used in the automobile industry? Discuss.
2. How is the Department of Defense using fuzzy logic? Discuss.

chess, recognizing patterns in faces and objects, and filtering spam e-mail. Like expert systems, ANNs are used for poorly structured problems—when data is fuzzy and uncertainty is involved. Unlike an expert system, an ANN cannot supply an explanation for the solution it finds because an ANN uses patterns instead of the if–then–else rules that expert systems use.

An ANN creates a model based on input and output. For example, in a loan application problem, input data consists of income, assets, number of dependents, job history, and residential status. The output data is acceptance or rejection of the loan application. After processing many loan applications, an ANN can establish a pattern that determines whether an application should be approved or rejected.

As shown in Exhibit 13.4, an ANN has an output layer, an input layer, and a middle (hidden) layer where learning takes place. If you are using an ANN for approving loans in a bank, the middle layer is trained by using past data (from old loan applications, in which the decisions are known) that includes both accepted and rejected applications. Based on the pattern of data entered in the input layer—applicant information, loan amount, credit

rating, and so on—and the results in the output layer (the accept or reject decision), nodes in the middle layer are assigned different weights. These weights determine how the nodes react to a new set of input data and mimic decisions based on what they have learned. Every ANN has to be trained, and when organizational policies change, the network needs to be retrained so it can mimic the new policies. Deep learning is also a type of ANN that includes many layers to deal with complex problems that may have very large data sets.

ANNs are used for many tasks, including the following:

- Bankruptcy prediction
- Credit ratings
- Investment analysis
- Oil and gas exploration
- Target marketing
- Computer and network security

The "Neural Networks in Microsoft and the Chicago Police Department" box discusses real-life applications of neural networks.

Table 13.2 Applications of Machine Learning in Selected Companies

Company	Application Area	Specific Applications
Yelp	Large-scale image processing	ML improves users' experiences. ML assists the company to compile, categorize, and label millions of images more efficiently.
Pinterest	Enhanced content discovery	ML is used for recommendation algorithms in advertising monetization and to reduce churn for e-mail newsletter subscribers.
Facebook	Chatbots and user experience	ML is used to improve customer service and retention and filter out spam and poor-quality content; ML can also be used to read images to visually impaired users.
Twitter	Timeline creation and management	ML evaluates each tweet in real time and "scores" it according to various metrics based on individual preferences, then displays tweets that are likely to drive the most engagement.
Alphabet (parent company of Google)	Artificial neural networks	ML is used for natural-language processing, speech translation, and search ranking and predictive systems.
Edgecase (originally Compare Metrics)	Enhancing e-commerce conversion rates	ML improves customers' experiences by helping them find items they want to buy and bringing online browsing closer to the traditional retail experience.
Baidu	Voice search	ML is used for natural-language processing, voice search, and voice pattern recognition systems, real-time translation, and biometric security.
HubSpot	More intelligent sales	ML more effectively identifies prospective customers and better serves existing customers.
Salesforce	Intelligent customer relationship management (CRM)	Salesforce uses ML called Einstein to improve all aspects of CRM by creating more comprehensive lead scoring and more effective customer service and by creating more sales opportunities.

Exhibit 13.4
Artificial neural network configuration

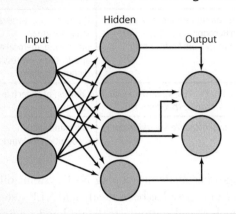

13-7 Genetic Algorithms

Genetic algorithms (GAs) are a type of artificial intelligence used mostly to find solutions to optimization and search problems. John Holland developed genetic algorithms in the 1940s at the Massachusetts Institute of Technology; the term applies to adaptive procedures in a computer system that are based on Darwin's ideas about natural selection and survival of the fittest.[46]

Genetic algorithms are used for optimization problems that deal with many input variables, such as issues in jet engine design, portfolio development, and network design. The algorithms find the combination of inputs that generates the most desirable outputs, such as the stock portfolio with the highest return or the network configuration with the lowest cost. Genetic algorithms can examine complex problems without any assumptions of what the correct solution should be. In a GA system, the following techniques are used:

- *Selection or survival of the fittest*—Gives preference or a higher weight to better outcomes.

> **Genetic algorithms (GAs)** are search algorithms that mimic the process of natural evolution. They are used to generate solutions to optimization and search problems using such techniques as mutation, selection, crossover, and chromosome.

Neural Networks in Microsoft and the Chicago Police Department

▶▶ Finance | Technology in Society | Reflective Thinking

Microsoft is using neural network software to maximize its returns on direct mail. Each year, Microsoft sends out approximately 40 million pieces of direct mail to 8.5 million registered customers. The goal of these mailings is to encourage customers to upgrade their software or buy other Microsoft products. The first mailing goes out to all the customers in the company's database. The second mailing goes out only to customers who are most likely to respond; neural network software is used to cull the latter from the former. According to Microsoft spokesman Jim Minervino, the neural network software BrainMaker has increased the rate of response from 4.9 to 8.2 percent. This has resulted in a significant savings for the company—the same revenue at 35 percent less cost.[47]

(FeyginFoto/Shutterstock.com)

The Chicago Police Department used neural network software to predict which of their police officers were likely to engage in misconduct. BrainMaker compared the conduct of current officers with the conduct of those who had previously been terminated for disciplinary reasons. This comparison produced a list of officers that might be "at risk."[48]

To see a list of popular applications for artificial neural network software, go to *www.g2.com/categories/artificial-neural-network*.

Questions and Discussions

1. What was achieved by neural networks at Microsoft?
2. How is the Chicago Police Department using neural networks?

• *Crossover*—Combines good portions of different outcomes to achieve a better outcome.

• *Mutation*—Tries combinations of different inputs randomly and evaluates the results.

• *Chromosome*—Presents a set of parameters that defines a proposed solution to the problem the GA is trying to address. It is usually represented as a simple string (a sequence of characters).

Genetic algorithms are already used with neural networks and fuzzy logic systems to solve scheduling, engineering design, and marketing problems, among others. For example, a docking algorithm uses a neural network and fuzzy functions with a GA to find the best and shortest route for a robot to take to a docking bay.[49,50] Researchers at General Electric and Rensselaer Polytechnic Institute used a GA to design a jet engine turbine in one-fourth the time it took to develop a model manually. It improved the design by 50 percent and kept better pace with the many variables involved than an expert system did.[51]

You can find more information on the uses of GAs in robotics, telecommunications, computer games, and other fields at *www.brainz. org/15-real-world-applications-genetic-algorithms*.

13-8 Natural-Language Processing

Despite constant efforts to make information systems user friendly, they still require a certain degree of computer literacy and skills. As mentioned in Module 2, **natural-language processing (NLP)** was developed so users could communicate with computers in human language. Although GUI elements such as menus and icons have helped with communication problems between humans and computers, GUIs still involve some training, can be cumbersome to use, and often differ depending on the operating system or application. An NLP system provides a question-and-answer setting that is more natural and easier for people to use. It is particularly useful with databases. Table 13.3 lists some currently available NLP systems.

At the time of this writing, NLP products are not capable of a dialogue that compares with conversations between humans. The size and complexity of human

Table 13.3 | NLP Systems

NLP System	Use
Nuance Communications Dragon Speech Recognition Software (*https://www.nuance.com/index.html*)	Business data retrieval, legal document processing, medical and ER applications, professional dictation systems
AT&T Natural Voices Wizzard Speech (*https://wizzardsoftware.com/*)	Creation of speech from computer-readable text
e-Speaking (*https://e-speaking.com*)	Voice and speech recognition for Windows

languages has made developing NLP systems difficult. However, progress has been steady, and NLP systems for tasks such as call routing, stock and bond trading, and banking by phone are already available.

NLP systems are generally divided into the following categories:[52]

• Interfaces to databases

• Machine translation, such as translating from French to English

• Text scanning and intelligent indexing programs for summarizing large amounts of text

• Generating text for automated production of standard documents

• Speech systems for voice interaction with computers

NLP systems usually perform two types of activities. The first is interfacing: accepting human language as input, carrying out the corresponding command, and generating the necessary output. The second is knowledge acquisition: using the computer to read large amounts of text and understand the information well enough to summarize important points and store information so the system can respond to inquiries about the content. The "NLP in Action: The Healthcare Industry" box highlights several real-life applications of NLP systems in healthcare.

13-9 Integrating AI Technologies Into Decision Support Systems

AI-related technologies, such as expert systems, natural-language processing, and artificial neural networks, can improve the quality of decision support systems (DSSs).

They can add explanation capabilities (by integrating expert systems) and learning capabilities (by integrating ANNs) and create an interface that is easier to use (by integrating an NLP system). These systems are sometimes called integrated or intelligent DSSs (IDSSs); the result is a more efficient, powerful DSS.[53,54] AI technologies, particularly expert systems and natural-language processing, can be integrated into the database, model base, and user interface components of a DSS.

The benefits of integrating an expert system into the database component of a DSS are as follows:[55]

- Adding deductive reasoning to traditional DBMS functions
- Improving access speed
- Improving the creation and maintenance of databases
- Adding the capability to handle uncertainty and fuzzy data
- Simplifying query operations with heuristic search algorithms

Similarly, you can add AI technologies to a DSS's model base component. For example, expert systems can be added to provide reasons and explanations for output from the model base, to include heuristics in the model base's analysis capabilities, to incorporate fuzzy sets in the model-building process, to reduce the time and cost of calculating data for models, and to select the best model for the problem.[56]

In addition, integrating expert system capabilities into the user interface can improve the quality and user friendliness of a DSS. This integration can add features such as an explanation capability (explaining responses in more nontechnical terms). Integrating NLP can improve the effectiveness of an interface by making it more interactive and easier to use, particularly for decision makers who are not computer savvy. Virtual assistants such as Siri, Cortana, Alexa, and Facebook's M have made interfaces with mobile devices easier and more conversational. Google Assistant carried these capabilities one step forward by making the mobile interface more adaptive; it can learn, and the user can personalize it. It remembers facts and can be trained.[57] The box "AI Technologies for Decision Making" shows how some companies are using AI technologies to make decisions.

NLP in Action: The Healthcare Industry

▶▶ Finance | Technology in Society | Reflective Thinking

The healthcare industry could significantly benefit from various NLP applications. NLP systems could reduce administrative healthcare costs and improve the accuracy of data. Listed next are a few examples:

- NLP-based clinical decision support: As an example, the system can be used to set up colonoscopy follow-up appointments for patients. The system can extract relevant text from various files and then set a follow-up for a patient.
- Automated dictation system: Doctors record diagnostic information about a patient or an X-ray, and the NLP system generates a Microsoft Word document to be sent to the patient or other doctors.
- Text summarization: An NLP-based system can extract clinical information from multiple reports and generate a single document for a doctor's review.
- Clinical data and virtual administrative assistants: An NLP-based system could accommodate such requests as scheduling an office visit or paying any outstanding medical bills.
- Real-time translation services: An NLP-based system can provide real-time translation with a high degree of accuracy for patients and clinicians, similar to services offered by companies such as Google and Microsoft.

Questions and Discussions

1. What are two applications of NLP in the healthcare industry?
2. How can real-time translation services offered by an NLP system help the bottom line?

13-10 Contextual Computing: Making Mobile Devices Smarter

We have been using GPSs on our smartphones for years. A GPS delivers location-based services—for example, telling you which street to take when you're traveling across town. GPS is a great service for a traveler who is not familiar with a city. Applications such as Apple's Siri and Google Now carry this idea a bit further. For example, Google Now uses information it has about a particular user to offer weather forecasts, street directions, or sports scores for games the user is interested in. It provides such information based on a user's previous behavior and current location.

Another example of context-aware software is Microsoft's MoodScope, which is able to sense a user's mood by analyzing phone calls, text messages, Internet access, and other smartphone activities. Although this application is in the development stages, it showed 93 percent accuracy in a small sample size of 32 users in China and the United States. These kinds of applications could have significant commercial value. For example, a user's mood could be shared with Spotify, the commercial music streaming service, to play a special song. The user's mood could be shared on the user's Facebook timeline to encourage or discourage other types of communication. It could also be shared with a Web site that might target the user with comfort food. However, such applications must be used carefully to avoid invading a user's privacy.[58,59]

Contextual computing is expected to make AI technologies even smarter. For example, your smartphone may soon be able to predict with 80 percent probability that you will receive a job offer if you go to a particular job fair, based on information you have included on your social media sites. What if you wanted to know the chances that you and your girlfriend will get married? Qualcomm, the chip maker for smartphones and other computing devices, has launched a line of "brain-inspired" Zeroth processors to expedite contextual computing. According to the company, this line of software tools and technologies enables handheld

AI Technologies for Decision Making

▶▶ Finance | Technology in Society | Reflective Thinking

A growing number of companies are using AI applications to improve decision making and gain a competitive advantage. Google,[60] Facebook,[61] Amazon, Alibaba, and American Express are just a few examples. AI has generated some well-known products, such as Apple's Siri and Google's self-driving cars. American Express uses AI technology to help protect over $1 trillion in purchase charges annually. (Using the technology, the decision to accept a charge is made in less than 2 milliseconds.)[62]

Amazon uses AI to predict events—which Web site a customer will read next or which ad someone is likely to click on. Sales predictions and predicting fraud are other AI applications at Amazon.

AI technologies use algorithms to make predictions from large sets of data without having to be reprogrammed on each new data set. These algorithms become smarter as more data becomes available. Other decision-making areas include demand forecasting, predicting the likelihood that a customer will select a product revealed in a search query, and predicting the likelihood that a customer will click a related link or finally purchase a product.[63]

Customer reviews and ratings play a major role in any online business. Amazon uses AI technologies to make customer reviews and rankings more useful. The system gives more weight to newer reviews from customers. The system uses several criteria for its ratings, such as purchase date (newer reviews are weighted more heavily than older ones), whether other customers found them useful, and confirmed purchases of a product.[64]

Sony uses AI technology to assess the prices of real estate. The program is able to estimate the latest market prices and automatically learn when prices fluctuate.[65]

Questions and Discussions

1. How is Amazon using AI to help its bottom line?
2. How is Sony using AI technology?

Contextual Computing in Action

▶▶▶ Finance | Technology in Society | Reflective Thinking

In addition to Google Assistant and Microsoft Cortana, the following devices and applications fall within the contextual computing domain:

Smartphones are increasingly smarter and are becoming context-aware devices. They take advantage of GPS sensors, Wi-Fi, Bluetooth, accelerometers, thermometers, and social media data. By using all of these features, smartphones can provide users with information on what is happening in their surroundings.[66]

The Nest thermostat is another example of a context-aware device. It programs itself according to the user's schedule and can even tell whether someone is in a room. According to Nest Labs, the thermostat programs itself and then pays for itself by saving on energy costs.[67]

Aether Cone is the first music player that thinks. It listens to the user's requests, analyzes the habits and listening patterns of the user, and learns the user's tastes to play the right music at the right time of day or week.[68,69]

EasilyDo, available for iOS and Android devices, handles calendar appointments, travel times, and birthdays. It can grab travel plans and boarding passes from the user's e-mail and manage contacts.[70]

EverythingMe, available for Android devices, is a context-aware launcher that delivers everything users need from their phones in just one tap. The launcher gathers and delivers requests based on such criteria as the user's location, time of day, and individual preferences.[71]

Questions and Discussions

1. Why and how has a smartphone become a context-aware device? Discuss.
2. Mention three context-aware devices that you have personal experience with. How have the devices made improvements in your life? Discuss.

---

devices to learn as they receive feedback from their environment.[72]

Humans make decisions based on what they know and how they feel about something, drawing on experiences they have accumulated throughout their lives. For example, when you hear a noise in a dark alley, you may quickly change directions. If you see a friend who looks sad, you ask if something is wrong. These scenarios seem difficult for computers to understand and react to properly, but it is what contextual computing is designed to achieve.

Sometimes referred to as our sixth, seventh, and eighth senses, **contextual computing** refers to a computing environment that is always present, can feel our surroundings, and—based on who we are, where we are, and whom we are with—offer recommendations.[73]

The principle behind contextual computing is that computers can both sense and react to their environments, similar to how human brains understand and interpret stimuli.[74,75] In essence, contextual computing allows for tailoring a course of action to a user in a particular situation and environment, based on what the computer knows about the user. To achieve this, many of the information technologies discussed in this textbook can be used, including computer networks, software, hardware, database systems, and AI technologies.

In recent years, a technology called ambient computing has gained popularity. Ambient computing is similar to context-aware computing in that it uses a variety of technologies, including motion tracking, speech recognition, gestures, wearables, and artificial intelligence, to interact with users in their surrounding environment.

The "Contextual Computing in Action" box highlights several context-aware applications and devices.

> **Contextual computing**
> refers to a computing environment that is always present, can feel our surroundings, and—based on who we are, where we are, and whom we are with—offer recommendations.

13-11 AI and Automation

Machine learning and AI are spreading rapidly with the advent of self-driving cars, software that can respond to customer service inquiries, and robots that can manage assembly lines, flip hamburgers, cook pizza, and check store inventory. Robotic process automation (RPA) offers a number of advantages for organizations that deploy robots strategically for the right applications:[76]

- Cost effectiveness: RPA could reduce operational costs by as much as 25 to 50 percent.

- Improved accuracy and quality: By reducing human errors and eliminating cases of rework, RPA increases accuracy and quality.

- Consistency: RPA provides consistency in performing activities across the board.

- Improved analytics: Providing access to accurate data from various sources improves the quality of analytics.

- Increased employee productivity: RPA frees employees from mundane tasks so they can focus more on mission-critical activities such as customer service.

- Increased customer satisfaction: RPA helps to deliver high-quality products and services, which enhances customer satisfaction.

- Speed: RPA speeds up the execution and delivery of products and services.

- Reconciliation from multiple systems: RPA enhances the tallying of data and information from multiple systems without human intervention.

- Versatility: RPA is applicable across industries and has the ability to perform a wide range of tasks.

Potential job losses, initial investment costs, and a shortage of skilled labor are among the disadvantages of RPA. Potential job losses have received the most attention in recent years, as robots could partially or completely take over the following nine jobs, in addition to those already taken over in manufacturing and other fields: telemarketer, loan officer, credit analyst, cashier, line cook, paralegal, accountant, roofer, and bus driver.[77] Jobs considered the safest from the effects of automation are those that require managing people, high-level expertise, and dealing with unpredictable environments. These jobs include engineers, scientists, healthcare providers, educators, and IT professionals, as well as gardeners, plumbers, and elder care providers.

Different studies and experts offer different opinions on the impact of AI on employment. According to Kai Fu Lee, an AI expert and venture capitalist, automation will cause major changes in the workforce. He predicts that 40 percent of the world's jobs will be replaced by robots capable of automating tasks by 2034. This will impact both blue-collar and white-collar professions.[78]

According to a study by the McKinsey Global Institute, automation could eliminate as many as 73 million U.S. jobs by 2030, but economic growth and rising productivity could offset most of the losses. Worldwide, up to 800 million workers could be displaced and as many as 375 million may need to learn new skills for new occupational categories. Countries providing high wages, such as the United States, are more vulnerable to job losses due to automation.[79] To minimize the impacts of automation, businesses should constantly educate and retrain their employees to prepare them for new technology. As UCLA professor Bhagwan Chowdhry said, businesses might best serve their employees and themselves by offering constant education. He suggests that 40 percent of employees' time should be spent on training and re-training.[80]

13-12 Ethical Issues of AI

According to a Gallup poll, 85 percent of Americans used at least one AI-powered device, program, or service in 2018.[81] The adoption of this technology will increase in the future as prices go down and capabilities improve. To increase the chances of success and reduce risks in AI adoption, organizations should establish sound governance and an ethical framework for the technology and examine the following five issues before the AI system is deployed:[82,83]

1. Defining the AI goals. If the AI system is being used to classify pictures in an online photo album, it involves a much lower risk than a system used to detect objects in front of a self-driving car.

2. Defining the complexity of the problem. As the problem gets more complex, the chances of an AI system's failure increases. For example, extracting meaning from a full-motion video is more complex than doing the same from still images.

3. Defining the environment as stable or variable. When financial data is used to approve or reject the creditworthiness of a customer, the environment is considered stable; in contrast, when a self-driving car is operating on an open road, the environment is considered highly variable and unpredictable.

4. Defining and guarding against bias. When the AI system is designed to make predictions about people, it often contains a risk of bias. AI designers should consider the diversity of the world's population and establish measures to monitor how the AI system responds.

5. Defining the level of human involvement. As the autonomy of the AI system increases, its monitoring should increase as well. An autonomous AI system involves more risks than an augmented AI system, which allows a human to be the final decision maker.

The widespread adoption of AI technology by individuals and businesses will bring about a number of ethical issues that have to be carefully examined. The following five issues are important:

1. AI bias. AI algorithms and programs are developed by programmers and software engineers who are mostly men, and it is possible that their biases influence these programs. According to Gartner research, 85 percent of AI projects will deliver erroneous results due to bias in data, algorithms, or the teams responsible for managing the projects. As an example, an Amazon recruiting system that looked for patterns in résumés to pick the best candidates taught itself that male candidates were preferable. The algorithm put a lower weight on résumés that included the word *women* or *women's* or that mentioned women's colleges. Another example revealed how women are prevented from learning about good jobs in the first place—a Carnegie Mellon University study found that Google ads showed high-income jobs to men at a much higher rate than it did to women.[84] In another case, software used to predict future criminals showed bias against black people. If AI tools are used correctly, they can become a powerful platform for implementation of ethical decisions.[85]

2. AI mistakes. AI mistakes, or so-called "artificial stupidity," can happen when AI programs are deployed before they are fully developed. Users and decision makers must guard against AI mistakes and use AI with careful consideration. Below are a few recent examples of AI errors:[86,87]

   - Google Translate showed gender bias in Turkish–English translations.
   - Apple Face ID was beaten by a 3D-printed mask that cost only $150.
   - An Amazon Echo device randomly blasted music when the resident was out.
   - Amazon's Alexa assistant told a child to take on a potentially lethal challenge.[88]

   - A Tesla driver was killed in a crash while the autopilot feature was active.
   - An Uber self-driving car killed a pedestrian in 2018.
   - AI predictions for the 2018 World Cup were almost all wrong.

3. Wealth inequality. Experts believe that AI will increase inequality between the rich and poor. This issue could be analyzed in two ways: (1) Consider traditional manufacturing companies such as Ford or General Motors and the number of people they employed, as opposed to AI-based companies such as Alphabet or Facebook. The wealth generated by traditional companies was distributed among a much greater number of workers than in AI-based companies. (2) Wealthier people can afford to deploy AI tools in their economic activities, which could help them gain economic advantages. In other words, those who have access to better technology will be able to get further ahead economically.[89]

4. Humanity. Widespread deployment of AI technology could impact humanity and human behavior. As you may recall from Module 2, IBM's Watson answered *Jeopardy* questions without exactly understanding them, but with a high degree of confidence and speed. A robot may be able to offer better customer service or do a better job in marketing a product or service. Humans in a work environment are often limited in the amount of attention and patience they can expend on another person. AI tools can access and deploy unlimited resources in building relationships and offering services. These superior features of AI tools may impact human behavior in a negative way.

5. Unemployment. Undoubtedly, AI will have an impact on employment. For example, jobs such as welding and soldering on assembly lines, food preparation, and packaging could become mostly automated. Self-driving cars could replace millions of truck drivers in the United States alone. Although AI has created many new jobs, they require a high level of expertise and education, whereas jobs displaced by AI mostly involve blue-collar workers who frequently have less economic means.

Industry Connection: Alyuda Research[90]

Alyuda Research is a major developer of neural networks and trading software for businesses and individuals. Its products and services include the following:

Tradecision: Provides tools to help investors and brokers make better decisions, such as advanced charting and automated trading. Includes modules for model building, strategies, alerts, simulations, and data analysis.

Scorto Credit Decision: Offers several methods for developing models for credit scoring—such as decision trees, neural networks, and fuzzy logic—and includes software for loan portfolio analysis.

NeuroIntelligence: Used to analyze and process data sets; find the best neural network architecture; train, test, and optimize a neural network; and apply the network to new data sets.

Module Summary

13-1 Define *artificial intelligence* and explain how AI technologies support decision making. Artificial intelligence (AI) consists of related technologies that try to simulate and reproduce human thought and behavior, including thinking, speaking, feeling, and reasoning. AI technologies apply computers to areas that require knowledge, perception, reasoning, understanding, and cognitive abilities. They can be used in diverse industries such as manufacturing, healthcare, and banking.

13-2 Describe an expert system, its applications, and its components. Expert systems mimic human expertise in a particular field to solve a problem in a well-defined area. Components of an expert system include a knowledge acquisition facility, a knowledge base, a knowledge base management system (KBMS), a user interface, an explanation facility, and an inference engine.

13-3 Describe case-based reasoning, including the four Rs involved in its design and implementation. Case-based reasoning (CBR) is a problem-solving technique that matches a new case (problem) with a previously solved case and its solution, the details of which have been stored in a database. After finding a match, the CBR system offers a solution; if no match is found, even after more information is supplied, the human expert must solve the

problem. The four Rs involved are retrieve, reuse, revise, and retain.

13-4 Summarize each of the four types of intelligent agents and how they are used. Shopping and information agents help users navigate through the vast resources available on the Web and provide better results in finding information. Personal agents perform specific tasks for a user, such as remembering information for filling out Web forms or completing e-mail addresses after the first few characters are typed. Data-mining agents work with a data warehouse, detecting trends and discovering new information and relationships among data items that were not readily apparent. Monitoring and surveillance agents usually track and report on computer equipment and network systems to predict when a system crash or failure might occur.

13-5 Describe fuzzy logic and its uses. Fuzzy logic allows a smooth, gradual transition between human and computer vocabularies and deals with variations in linguistic terms by using a degree of membership. It is used in appliances, search engines, automobiles, and much more.

13-6 Explain machine learning and artificial neural networks. Machine learning is a process and procedure by which knowledge is gained through experience. In other words, computers learn without being explicitly programmed. Artificial neural networks (ANNs) are networks that learn and are capable of performing tasks that are difficult with conventional computers, such as playing chess, recognizing patterns in faces and objects, and filtering spam e-mail.

13-7 Describe how genetic algorithms are used. Genetic algorithms (GAs) are search algorithms that mimic the process of natural evolution. They are used to generate solutions to optimization and search problems using such techniques as mutation, selection, crossover, and chromosome.

13-8 Explain natural-language processing and its major categories. Natural-language processing (NLP) was developed so users could communicate with computers in human language. Its major categories include interfaces to databases, machine translation, text scanning and intelligent indexing programs for summarizing large amounts of text, generating text for automated production of standard documents, and speech systems for voice interaction with computers.

13-9 Describe the five benefits of integrating AI technologies into decision support systems:

(1) Adding deductive reasoning to traditional DBMS functions, (2) improving access speed, (3) improving the creation and maintenance of databases, (4) adding the capability to handle uncertainty and fuzzy data, and (5) simplifying query operations with heuristic search algorithms.

13-10 Explain contextual computing. Contextual computing refers to a computing environment that is always present, can feel our surroundings, and—based on who we are, where we are, and whom we are with—offer recommendations.

13-11 Explain AI impacts on automation. Machine learning and AI are spreading rapidly with the advent of self-driving cars, software that can respond to customer service inquiries, and robots that can manage assembly lines, flip hamburgers, cook pizza, and check store inventory. Robotic process automation (RPA) offers a number of advantages, such as cost effectiveness and improved accuracy and quality, for organizations that deploy robots strategically for the right applications.

13-12 Describe the ethical issues of AI. They include AI bias, AI mistakes, wealth inequality, humanity, and unemployment.

Key Terms

- Artificial intelligence (AI)
- Artificial neural networks (ANNs)
- Augmented intelligence
- Backward chaining
- Case-based reasoning (CBR)
- Contextual computing
- Data-mining agents
- Expert systems
- Explanation facility
- Forward chaining
- Fuzzy logic
- Genetic algorithms (GAs)

- Inference engine
- Intelligent agents
- Knowledge acquisition facility
- Knowledge base
- Knowledge base management system (KBMS)
- Machine learning
- Monitoring and surveillance agents
- Natural-language processing (NLP)
- Personal agents
- Robots
- Shopping and information agents
- Soft robot

Reviews and Discussions

1. Define *artificial intelligence* and *augmented intelligence*.
2. What are five major components of an expert system?
3. Define *case-based reasoning*. What are the four Rs?
4. What are two advantages of integrating AI technologies into decision support systems?
5. What are two applications of contextual computing in your daily life? Could this technology make you a more productive knowledge worker?
6. What are three impacts of AI in the workplace?
7. What are three ethical issues of AI? Discuss.
8. What are three advantages of natural-language processing?

Projects

1. After reading the information presented in this module and other sources, write a one-page paper that discusses the advantages and disadvantages of robotic surgery. When it comes to cost, which one is cheaper: a human doctor or a robot? The da Vinci Surgical System is an example of a robot used in surgery. What are two positive and two negative aspects of this system?

2. Contextual computing has generated a lot of excitement in the computing community. After reading the information presented in this module and other sources, write a one-page paper that discusses the advantages and disadvantages of this platform. In addition to Google Now, what other software applications currently offer this capability?

3. Nina, from *Nuance.com*, is being marketed as an intelligent agent. After reading the information presented in this module and other sources, write a one-page paper that explains the applications of this software. What types of businesses will benefit the most from it?

4. Case-based reasoning systems have been used in a variety of disciplines. In the future, they may also be used in the medical field. After reading the information presented in this module and other sources, write a one-page paper that explains how case-based reasoning systems will be used in the medical field. How might it bring healthcare costs down?

5. Intelligent agents are being used in a variety of applications. After reading the information presented in this module and other sources, write a one-page paper that discusses the applications of these agents in the e-commerce environment. Identify three such agents and their specific applications in e-commerce.

6. Nuance Communication's Dragon Speech Recognition Software and AT&T's Natural Voices Wizzard Speech are two popular commercial NLPs currently on the market. After reading the information presented in this module and other sources, write a two-page paper that explains key features of each NLP. What are some of the business applications of each software program? What types of businesses will benefit the most from these types of software?

Module Quiz

1. Contextual computing refers to a computing environment that is always present, can feel our surroundings, and—based on who we are, where we are, and whom we are with—offer recommendations. True or False?

2. Intelligent agents are also known as bots (short for robots). True or False?

3. In backward chaining, a series of "if–then–else" condition pairs are performed. True or False?

4. All of the following are benefits of integrating AI into DSS except:
   a. Adding deductive reasoning to traditional DBMS functions
   b. Improving access speed
   c. Simplifying query operations with heuristic search algorithms
   d. All of these choices

5. Robotic process automation offers all of the following advantages except:
   a. Increased costs
   b. Improved accuracy and quality
   c. Increased employee productivity
   d. Increased customer satisfaction

6. All of the following are ethical issues of AI except:
   a. AI bias
   b. AI mistakes
   c. Wealth inequality
   d. All of these choices

Case Study 13-1
AI-Based Software Helps Businesses Better Understand Customers
➤➤ Finance | Reflective Thinking

AI-based software is getting smarter at analyzing qualitative data, words, and phrases, and in understanding the relationships among these things. These programs can analyze data generated through focus groups, surveys, online forums, call centers, help desks, and social media, and then use the data to generate new insights. Such new insights could help businesses offer better customer service as well as products and services that are more appealing to their customers.

For example, Scotts Miracle-Gro, a major provider of lawn, garden, and outdoor-living products and services, noticed that a large number of customers were canceling their lawn-fertilizer service. Not knowing what was causing the problem, the company conducted a survey and asked customers to rank their satisfaction with Scotts' offerings and other feedback.

Using AI-based software called Luminoso (*www.luminoso.com*), Scotts analyzed the data, which indicated customers were canceling the service because they expected better customer service from the company. Although the words *customer service* were not cited specifically in the survey, the software was able to associate words such as "listen" or "not responsive" to come up with the finding. According to David Erdman, a senior analyst at Scotts, the company examined its customer service to make improvements.

Luminoso performs its analyses by accessing a large database that stores common-sense knowledge and relationships (such as "if you drop a ball, it will fall") to help explain how words and phrases relate to each other.[91]

Answer the following questions:

1. What problems was Scotts Miracle-Gro facing?
2. Which software was used to analyze data collected by Scotts?
3. How does a software tool such as Luminoso analyze data?
4. What are some strategic applications of software tools such as Luminoso?

Case Study 13-2
NLP: Making a Smartphone Smarter
➤➤ **Finance | Technology in Society | Reflective Thinking**

Natural-language processing makes more sense in a mobile environment than in a desktop environment because mobile device users are on the go and want to use their hands as little as possible. NLP adds a user-friendly environment and enhances data entry and data input for mobile users. Also, the increased memory and speed of mobile devices (as well as the increased speed of mobile and wireless networks) make them good candidates for NLP. As a result, voice-activated functions, speech-to-text dictation, and voice-activated dialing are now available for most smartphones, and voice-driven apps are getting smarter. For example, instead of saying "Call 551-535-1922" to dial a phone number, users can now say "Dial Dad" or "Phone my father."

Nuance's Dragon Dictation, available as an iPhone app, allows users to dictate everything from memos and e-mails to Twitter updates. Dragon for E-mail offers similar capabilities for Microsoft Outlook. Also, for the iPhone, Jibbigo (*https://jibbigo-translator-2-0.soft112.com/*) translates words, phrases, and simple sentences. Voice-driven apps such as Google Voice Search, Bing Voice Search, and Microsoft Tellme are among the more popular smartphone applications. Vlingo (*https://vlingo.en.softonic.com/android*), a multiplatform app, serves as a "virtual assistant" and is used for such services as making restaurant reservations (OpenTable, *https://www.opentable.com*) and booking movie tickets (Fandango, *www.fandango.com*).

Apple's Siri, available on iPhone 4S and beyond, and Google Assistant, available on Google's Pixel and other Android phones, are other entrants in the fast-growing, voice-activated mobile-device market. One of the challenges with voice-activated mobile devices is to get them to understand what you mean, not just what you say. Other challenges include the use of foreign names, accents, and maintaining accuracy in noisy environments.[92,93]

Answer the following questions:

1. How can NLP make a smartphone smarter?
2. What are some examples of voice-based software used by iPhones?
3. What are some of the challenges to be overcome before achieving a full-featured voice-activated mobile device?
4. Compare and contrast Apple's Siri and Pixel's Google Assistant. Which one do you prefer and why?

Module
14
Emerging Trends, Technologies, and Applications

Learning Objectives

After studying this module, you should be able to…

14.1 Summarize new trends in software and service distribution.

14.2 Describe virtual reality components and applications.

14.3 Explain non-fungible tokens (NFTs) and their business applications.

14.4 Discuss the metaverse, its foundation, and its applications.

14.5 Describe the foundation, models, and applications of cloud computing.

14.6 Discuss uses of nanotechnology.

14.7 Describe blockchain technology and cryptocurrency.

14.8 Explain quantum computing and its applications.

This module discusses new trends in software and service distribution, including pull technology, push technology, and software as a service (SaaS). You also learn about virtual reality components and applications, including the cave automatic virtual environment (CAVE) and augmented reality, and you learn how virtual worlds are becoming a new platform for communication and collaboration. You learn about non-fungible tokens and metaverse applications. Next, you learn about cloud computing and its models and applications. The module then provides an overview of how nanotechnology is being used and its future applications. You learn about blockchain technology and cryptocurrency. Finally, quantum computing and its current and future applications are discussed.

14-1 Trends in Software and Service Distribution

Recent trends in software and service distribution include pull technology, push technology, and application service providers, although pull technology has been around since the Web began. All these trends are discussed in the following sections.

14-1a Pull and Push Technologies

With **pull technology**, a user states a need before getting information, as when a URL is entered in a Web browser so the user can go to a certain Web site. However, this technology is not adequate for marketing certain products and services or for providing customized information. People rarely request marketing information, for example. With **push technology**, also known as *webcasting*, a Web server delivers information to users (who have signed up for the service) instead of waiting for them to request the information be sent to them. Webcasting is supported by many Web browsers and is also available from vendors (as described later in this section). With push technology, your favorite Web content can be updated in real time and sent to your desktop or your mobile device. Push technology can be effective for business-to-consumer (B2C) and business-to-business (B2B) marketing as well. For example, a car manufacturer can send the latest information on new models, prices, and features to all its dealers in real time. Network administrators also use push technology when

they need antivirus updates to be automatically downloaded on employees' workstations.

Push technology delivers content to users automatically at set intervals or when a new event occurs. For example, you often see notices such as "A newer version of Adobe Flash is available. Would you like to install it?" In this case, the vendor (Adobe) is pushing the updated product to you as soon as it is available, which is the event triggering the push. Of course, this assumes you have already downloaded a previous version of Adobe Flash; by doing so, you have signed up for pushed updates. The same process applies to content updates, such as news and movie releases. When users sign up, they specify what content they want (sports, stock prices, political news, etc.) and consent to the "push." They can also specify how often the content should be pushed. For example, if you have subscribed to an online news service and have indicated that you are interested in the latest economic news on China, the service will send you such news as soon as it becomes available and will do so in the future as well. You do not need to make any further requests.

Push technology streamlines the process of users getting software updates and updated content. It benefits vendors, too, because by keeping in constant

With **pull technology**, a user states a need before getting information, as when a URL is entered in a Web browser so the user can go to a certain Web site.

With **push technology**, also known as *webcasting*, a Web server delivers information to users (who have signed up for the service) instead of waiting for them to request the information be sent to them.

touch with users, they build customer loyalty. This benefit often outweighs the costs of adding servers and other technology resources needed to use push technology. Push technology also improves business relations and customer service because users get the information they need in a more timely fashion.

Here are three examples of push technology:

> **Push technology streamlines the process of users getting software updates and updated content.**

- *Microsoft Azure Notification Hubs*—Provides a push engine that enables a user to send notifications to any platform (Windows, iOS, Android, etc.) It is useful for consumers as well as businesses. Listed next are a few applications:[1]

  - Sending breaking news notifications

  - Sending location-based coupons to users who have signed up for the service

  - Sending event-related notifications to users or groups

  - Sending promotional contents to consumers

  - Notifying users of enterprise events

  - Sending codes for multifactor authentication

- *Apple Push Notification*—Sends alerts, such as news updates or social networking status changes, to Apple devices.

- *Facebook Push Notification*—Facebook uses push technology to alert its users to important activities in their accounts, such as comments on the user's status updates.

14-1b Application Service Providers

Internet service providers (ISPs) provide access to the Internet. Under a more recent business model called **application service providers (ASPs)**, access to software or services is provided for a fee. **Software as a service (SaaS)**, also known as *on-demand software*, is a model in which ASPs deliver software to users for a fee; the software is for temporary or long-term

Application service providers (ASPs) provide access to software or services for a fee.

Software as a service (SaaS), also known as *on-demand software*, is a model in which ASPs deliver software to users for a fee; the software is for temporary or long-term use.

use. With this delivery model, users do not need to be concerned with new software versions and compatibility problems because the ASP offers the most recent version of the software. Users can also save all application data on the ASP's server, so the software and data are portable. This flexibility is convenient for those who travel or work in different locations, but it can also create privacy and security issues. Saving data on the ASP's servers instead of on users' own workstations might leave the data more exposed to theft or corruption by attackers.

Here is a simple example of how SaaS might work: Say you want to edit a Microsoft Word document, Module14.doc, and you need word-processing software for this task. With SaaS, you do not need the software to be installed on your computer. You simply access it from the SaaS provider site. You can then run the software from the provider's server or on your computer without taking up your own computing resources. The location of the Module14.doc file does not matter. You make use of the provider's SaaS service to edit the document, which stays on your hard drive (or wherever you had it stored—a flash drive, for example). The word-processing application is not stored on your computer, so the next time you access the software from the provider's SaaS site, you might get a newer version. SaaS deals only with software, not with data and document storage or with hardware resources, such as processing power and memory.

The SaaS model can take several forms, such as the following:

- Software services for general use, such as office suite packages

- A specific service, such as credit card processing

- A service in a vertical market, such as software solutions for doctors, accountants, and attorneys

Generally, the advantages of outsourcing—less expensive, information delivered more quickly—apply to the ASP model, too. However, ASPs have some specific advantages, including the following:

- The customer does not need to be concerned about whether software is current.

- Information systems (IS) personnel are free to focus on applications, such as customer relationship management (CRM) and financial information systems, that are more strategically important to the organization.

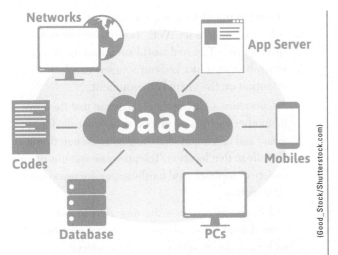

Networks
App Server
Codes
Mobiles
Database
PCs

(Good_Stock/Shutterstock.com)

- Software development costs are spread over several customers, so vendors can absorb some expenses of software development and develop more improved software.

- Software is kept up to date, based on users' requests.

- The ASP contract guarantees a certain level of technical support.

- An organization's software costs can be reduced to a predictable monthly fee.

Here are some of the disadvantages of ASPs:

- Generally, users must accept applications as provided by ASPs; software customized to users' needs is not offered.

- Because an organization has less control over how applications are developed, there is the risk that they might not fully meet the organization's needs.

- Integration with the customer's other applications and systems might be challenging.

Google, Microsoft, Salesforce, NetSuite, Basecamp, and Mint are all companies that offer SaaS. Google offers Google Apps for Work, which includes several Google products similar to traditional office suites—Gmail for Business, Google Calendar, Google Talk, Google Docs, and Google Sites, among others. (The Standard Edition is free.) Microsoft Office 365 competes with Google by offering cloud-based office services called Microsoft Office Suite. Salesforce offers a variety of enterprise applications using the SaaS model, including CRM. NetSuite offers ERP and Financial Software Suite. Basecamp is a Web-based project collaboration tool that allows users to share files, set deadlines, assign tasks, and receive feedback. Mint is a Web-based personal financial management service. SaaS is also common with human resources applications and has been used in ERP systems with vendors such as Workday.

Popular variations of the SaaS model include DaaS, BaaS, and SECaaS, which are briefly explained next. Most of the advantages and disadvantages of the SaaS model are also applicable to these three variations.

The **data as a service (DaaS)** model delivers data storage, integration, processing, and analytics services over the cloud. For example, DMD Marketing Corporation, based in Rosemont, Illinois, has adopted the DaaS model. According to the company, DaaS provides its users with faster access to their data, which reduces data processing times. The company can also quickly refresh data, giving it an edge over competitors.[2]

The **backup as a service (BaaS)** model provides off-site data storage for files, folders, or the entire contents of a hard drive. These contents are regularly backed up by the service provider and are available at any time to users through their network connection. Convenience, safety, ease of recovery, and affordability are among the key advantages of this model.[3]

The **security as a service (SECaaS)** model provides cybersecurity services on a subscription basis. This alternative eases the responsibilities of the in-house security staff, scales security needs as the organization grows, and avoids the costs and maintenance of on-premises alternatives. Some examples of services that a typical provider offers include continuous monitoring, data loss prevention, business continuity, e-mail security,

> The **data as a service (DaaS)** model delivers data storage, integration, processing, and analytics services over the cloud.

> The **backup as a service (BaaS)** model provides offsite data storage for files, folders, or the entire contents of a hard drive.

> The **security as a service (SECaaS)** model provides cybersecurity services on a subscription basis.

> "The distinction between immersion in a VR world and analyzing the same information using blueprints, numbers, or text is the difference between looking at fish in an aquarium and putting on your scuba gear and diving in."

antivirus management, spam filtering, identity and access management, intrusion protection and detection, network security, Web security, and vulnerability scanning.[4]

14-2 Virtual Reality

According to Allied Market Research, the augmented and virtual reality market will reach $571.4 billion globally by 2025. This is a 63.3 percent CAGR (compound annual growth rate).[5] Facebook, Microsoft, Google, Snapchat, Canon, GoPro, Sony, Samsung, and HTC are among the front-runners in this field. So, what is virtual reality?

Virtual reality (VR) uses computer-generated, three-dimensional images to create the illusion of interaction in a real-world environment. Stereo sound and tactile sensations enhance the feeling of being immersed in a three-dimensional real world. In VR terminology, the everyday physical world is referred to as an *information environment*.

Before VR technology, even the best graphics programs used a two-dimensional environment to illustrate a three-dimensional object. VR technology has added the third dimension so users can interact with objects in a way that has not been possible before. Thomas Furness, a notable VR pioneer, said, "The distinction between immersion in a VR world and analyzing the same information using blueprints, numbers, or text is the difference between looking at fish in an aquarium and putting on your scuba gear and diving in."[6]

Virtual reality began with military flight simulations in the 1960s, but these VR systems were rudimentary compared with today's systems. In the 1990s, Japan's Matsushita built a virtual kitchen that enabled its customers to change fixtures and appliances and then alter their design on a computer and virtually walk around the kitchen space. A customer's preferences could become the blueprint for the kitchen's final design. This was the first VR system designed not for games but for general public use.[7]

As you read through the following sections, you need to be familiar with these terms:

- *Simulation*—Giving objects in a VR environment texture and shading for a 3D appearance.
- *Interaction*—Enabling users to act on objects in a VR environment, as by using a data glove to pick up and move objects.
- *Immersion*—Giving users the feeling of being part of an environment by using special hardware and software (such as a CAVE, as discussed later in this section). The real world surrounding the VR environment is blocked out so users can focus their attention on the virtual environment.
- *Telepresence*—Giving users the sense that they are in another location (even one geographically far away) and can manipulate objects as though they are actually in that location. Telepresence systems use a variety of sophisticated hardware, as discussed in a later section.
- *Full-body immersion*—Allowing users to move around freely by combining interactive environments with cameras, monitors, and other devices.
- *Networked communication*—Allowing users in different locations to interact with and manipulate the same world at the same time by connecting two or more virtual worlds.

14-2a Types of Virtual Environments

There are two major types of user environments in VR: egocentric and exocentric. In an **egocentric environment**, the user is totally immersed in the VR world. The most common technology used with this environment is a head-mounted display (HMD). Another technology, a virtual retinal display (VRD), uses lasers. Exhibit 14.1 shows an example of a head-mounted display.

Exhibit 14.1
Egocentric VR technology

franz12/Shutterstock.com

Virtual reality (VR) uses computer-generated, three-dimensional images to create the illusion of interaction in a real-world environment.

In an **egocentric environment**, the user is totally immersed in the VR world.

In an **exocentric environment**, the user is given a "window view" of VR. Data is still rendered in 3D, but users can only view it on a screen. They cannot interact with objects, as in an egocentric environment. The main technology used in this environment is 3D graphics.

14-2b Components of a Virtual Reality System

The following are the major components of a VR system:

- *Visual and aural systems*—These components allow users to see and hear the virtual world. HMDs, mentioned earlier, contain two small TV screens, one in front of each eye, along with a magnifying lens to generate the view. Sensing devices on top of the helmet determine the orientation and position of the user's head. The information is then transmitted to the computer, which generates two pictures, so each eye has a slightly different view, just as humans' eyes do. HMDs can also incorporate stereo sound into a VR environment to make it more convincingly real. With VRDs, a very low-power laser beam carrying an image is projected onto the back of the user's eyes. As with an HMD, users can move their heads in any direction without losing sight of the image. The top five VR headsets on the market include Oculus Rift, Sony PlayStation VR, HTC Vive, Samsung Gear VR, and Microsoft HoloLens.[8]

- *Manual control for navigation*—This component allows the user to navigate in the VR environment and control various objects. The most commonly used device is the data glove (see Exhibit 14.2). With it, users can point to, "grab," and manipulate objects and experience limited tactile sensations, such as determining an object's shape, size, and hardness or softness. A data glove can also be used as an input device, much like a mouse. Users can use a data glove with software to open a dialog box or pull down a menu, for example. A data glove is covered with optical sensors that send information to a computer that reconstructs the user's movements graphically. The agent representing the user's hand in the virtual world duplicates the user's hand movements.

- *Central coordinating processor and software system*—This component generates and manipulates high-quality graphics in real time, so it needs a very fast processor. To display images in real time, 3D image graphics must be rendered rapidly, and the screen's refresh rate has to be extremely fast.

- *Walker*—This input device captures and records movements of the user's feet as the user walks or turns in different directions.

14-2c CAVE

A **cave automatic virtual environment (CAVE)** consists of a cube-shaped room in which the walls are rear-projection screens. A CAVE uses holographic devices that create, capture, and display images in true 3D form (see Exhibit 14.3). People can enter other CAVEs in other locations as well, no matter how far away they are geographically, and interact with other users. High-speed digital cameras capture one user's presence and movements and then re-create and send these images to users in other CAVEs. In this way, people can carry on a conversation as though they are all in the same room.

CAVEs are used for research in many fields, including archaeology, architecture, engineering, geology, and physics. Some engineering companies use CAVEs to improve product design and development. With a CAVE, they can create and test prototypes, develop interfaces, and simulate factory layouts and assembly lines, for example, without investing in physical

Exhibit 14.2
VR components

Floris Leeuwenberg/Corbis NX/Getty Images

In an **exocentric environment**, the user is given a "window view" of VR. Data is still rendered in 3D, but users can only view it on a screen. They cannot interact with objects, as in an egocentric environment.

A **cave automatic virtual environment (CAVE)** consists of a cube-shaped room in which the walls are rear-projection screens. A CAVE uses holographic devices that create, capture, and display images in true 3D form.

Exhibit 14.3
Example of a CAVE

equipment and layouts. Many universities, including Brown, the University of Illinois at Urbana–Champaign, and Duke, use CAVEs for geological research, architectural studies, and anatomy studies.

14-2d Virtual Reality Applications

The U.S. military uses VR systems for flight simulations. In medicine, they are used for "bloodless" surgery. In the entertainment industry, they are used in games and theaters. Eventually, they will be used for user interfaces in information systems. Some newspapers, such as the *New York Times*, allow subscribers to read and view news events in a VR environment. The *New York Times* sent subscribers Google VR viewers for this purpose; readers can use them to view news stories in a 360-degree immersive fashion. You might have seen an example of this technology in the movie *Minority Report*, in which actor Tom Cruise's character uses a 3D user interface to examine documents, graphics, and video files in crime reports. This technology has been used in many real-life applications.

VR systems can be used for many other business applications, too. For example, a VR system can be used for site selection when a company wants to open a new plant. A simulation model combined with VR capabilities allows a virtual walk-through of the potential site, which is a more realistic view than is possible with maps and blueprints. The following are some current business applications of VR systems:

- *Assistance for the disabled*—Virtual reality helps extend the capabilities of the disabled. For example, quadriplegics can use an HMD to get a 360-degree view of their surroundings, and people with cerebral palsy can learn how to operate a motorized wheelchair in a VR environment.[9]

- *Architectural design*—Architects and engineers use VR systems to create blueprints and build prototypes to show to clients. With a VR system, several versions of a design can be created to demonstrate to clients the outcome of modifying different factors. Architects and engineers can also use VR systems to safely test different conditions (such as wind shear) without the expense of using physical materials.

- *Education*—VR systems are used in educational games and simulations, such as VR "flashcards" for teaching math skills. Incorporating visuals, sound, and touch into a game can help improve the learning process. For example, in a world geography class, a VR globe could be used with touch technology that displays different facts about a country—language, population, political system, and so forth—when a student touches it.

- *Flight simulation*—Commercial airlines and the military have been using flight simulators for many years. Flight simulators are used for training pilots to handle new equipment or unusual operating conditions. Training in a VR environment is safer and less expensive than training on actual equipment.

Google Cardboard is a VR platform developed by Google for use with an HMD and a smartphone app. The user places the smartphone inside Cardboard and views objects through the HMD. The platform is intended as a low-cost system to encourage interest and development in VR applications. This $20 device saved the life of a baby who was missing a lung and half a heart by providing images in 3D virtual reality that could not be seen in a 2D environment. Doctors at Nicklaus Children's Hospital in Miami used the device to map out an operation that they couldn't have envisioned otherwise. Using the device made it possible to move around and see the heart from different angles—similar to being inside the heart and examining its structure.[10]

VR systems can also be used in videoconferencing and collaboration systems. Current technologies using TV screens cannot fully capture the sense of other people being physically present, and people cannot shake hands or engage in direct eye contact effectively. VR systems could help overcome these obstacles by giving participants the impression of being in the same room, which makes achieving true interaction more possible. With data gloves, participants can even shake hands, even though they may be thousands of miles apart. This scenario

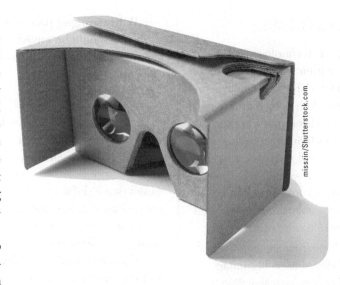

misszin/Shutterstock.com

might sound like science fiction, but the technology already exists. It gives new meaning to the old AT&T slogan "Reach out and touch someone."

Relatively recent applications of VR are used in therapy for sexual assault victims, victims of motor-vehicle accidents, people who are fearful of heights, flying, or public speaking, and people who suffer from eating disorders and alcoholism. The difference between a human therapist and VR-based therapy is that a virtual-reality exposure is created in the latter environment. By putting on the headset, the patient is immersed in the environment and sees things happen as they do in a real-life situation. In one study, participants reported often significant reductions in symptoms of posttraumatic stress disorder.[11]

The "Virtual Reality at Lockheed Martin" box highlights the applications of VR at Lockheed Martin.

Virtual Reality at Lockheed Martin

▶▶ Finance | Technology in Society | Application

Lockheed Martin Aeronautics Company, with headquarters in Bethesda, Maryland, builds some of the most sophisticated military aircraft in the world. A virtual reality and simulation laboratory that the company built in Littleton, Colorado, is used to simulate and test new products and processes before introducing them into the market. The lab can be used for testing space systems, satellites, launch vehicles, and missile defense systems. According to Lockheed Martin, the virtual reality technology brings production costs down by making models of products and testing them before physically manufacturing them. Naturally, modifications of a model are a lot simpler and cheaper than modifying an actual product. One of the lab's first products in which VR was used was the Air Force's GPS III system (a $1.46-billion project), also referred to as *next-generation GPS*. According to the company, the lab may also be used for NASA's Orion project, which will develop a space vehicle to take astronauts to the International Space Station and beyond. Lockheed Martin spokesman Michael Friedman said the principle behind using virtual reality technology is that "it is easier to move electrons than it is to move molecules."[12]

Questions and Discussions

1. How did virtual reality reduce production costs at Lockheed Martin?
2. What are additional applications of VR technology?

14-2e Obstacles in Using VR Systems

One major obstacle to using VR technology is that not enough fiber-optic cables are currently available to carry the data transmissions needed for a VR environment capable of re-creating a conference. With people in different geographical locations, high-speed transmission capabilities are necessary for participants to interact in real time. Without them, having to wait several seconds every time you want to act in a VR environment would be frustrating.

VR systems have generated a lot of excitement in recent years, but the following problems must be solved before this technology's potential can be realized:

- *Confusion between the VR environment and the real environment*—The possibility of users becoming unable to distinguish reality from virtual reality is a potential danger, particularly if people come to believe that anything they do in the virtual environment is acceptable in the real world. This risk is especially a concern in computer games that allow users to torture or kill others.

- *Mobility and other problems with HMDs*—With current technology, users are "tethered" to a limited area while wearing an HMD and cannot switch to performing tasks outside the virtual world without removing the gear. In addition, refresh rates in HMDs still are not quite fast enough, so a degree of visual distortion can happen while wearing an HMD.

- *Difficulty representing sound*—Representing sound in a 3D environment is difficult if the sound needs to move, such as a plane passing overhead. Creating stationary sound is easy, but re-creating the effect of sound fading or getting louder as an object moves away or closer is much harder with current technology.

- *Need for additional computing power*—VR systems require a lot of memory and speed to manipulate large graphics files and provide the instantaneous response needed to give the impression of a real world. Drawing and refreshing frames continuously and rapidly requires extremely fast computers with a lot of memory.

A **virtual world** is a simulated environment designed for users to interact with one another via avatars.

An **avatar** is a 2D or 3D graphical representation of a person in the virtual world; avatars are used in chat rooms and online games.

Augmented reality (AR) is a branch of virtual reality that generates a virtual scene that is overlaid on the real object.

With the rapid pace of technology, however, these problems should be solved in the near future so that VR systems can be used more widely.

14-2f Virtual Worlds

A **virtual world** is a simulated environment designed for users to interact with each other via avatars. An **avatar** is a 2D or 3D graphical representation of a person in the virtual world; avatars are used in chat rooms and online games (see Exhibit 14.4). According to researchers, there are new applications for avatars, such as role-playing for corporate diversity training, teaching, and for diverse business conferences.[13]

Users can manipulate objects in the simulated world and experience a limited telepresence that gives them the feeling of being in another location. Communication between users can take the form of text, graphical icons, and sound. You can shop while you are at Second Life, a virtual world platform developed by Linden Lab; there are also fan sites, blogs, forums, news sites, and classified ads. Currently, virtual worlds are used most often for gaming, social networking, and entertainment. However, they are beginning to be used in business and education. For example, IBM is using virtual worlds for client training. Other organizations use virtual worlds to conduct a variety of business activities, such as marketing and sales, product development, recruiting, and team meetings. Northrop Grumman Corporation uses Second Life for displaying prototypes, performing simulations, and training employees in situations that would be dangerous, expensive, or unfeasible in the physical world. The National Oceanic and Atmospheric Administration (NOAA) also uses Second Life as a marketing channel to reach new customers.[14] Widely used virtual worlds include the following:

- *Second Life (https://secondlife.com/)*
- *ActiveWorlds (https://www.activeworlds.com/)*
- *Entropia Universe (https://www.entropiauniverse.com/)*
- *Habbo (https://www.habbo.com/)*
- *RuneScape (https://play.runescape.com/)*

14-2g Augmented Reality

Augmented reality (AR) is a branch of virtual reality that generates a virtual scene that is overlaid on the real object. The goal is to enhance the user's perception of the real-world objects that the user is seeing or interacting with. Augmented reality was first used in the 1960s for

Exhibit 14.4

Avatars in Second Life

This is how you will initially appear in Second Life. You can customize your appearance later.

military applications, including combat awareness, training, and communication between aircraft and pilots. It is currently used as a marketing tool in fields such as education, entertainment, and medicine.

Augmented reality is similar to virtual reality, with one distinction between the two: Augmented reality users stay in the real-world environment while interacting with objects, whereas virtual reality users are immersed in the virtual world. AR users are aware that they are still in the real world, while VR users are tricked into thinking they are in a new virtual world.

In such an environment, it is difficult for a user to distinguish between real and digital objects. Imagine digital cats and dogs placed among several real cats and dogs; the virtual ones are so real that users may not see a difference between the two. Microsoft's HoloLens and Magic Leap offer a type of augmented reality environment in which virtual objects appear to be part of the real world.[15]

Google Glass and Yelp's Monocle are two popular examples of an AR platform. Monocle is a feature that allows users to view businesses around them by using the camera on their device and pointing it at their surroundings. As introduced in Module 2, Google Glass displays information in a hands-free format, and it can communicate with users and the Web in a natural language.

There are hundreds of AR apps for both iOS and Android devices. A diverse group of companies and organizations are using these apps in creative ways. A study conducted by Hidden Ltd. showed that 74 percent of customers buy a product after seeing it through AR, versus 45 percent after seeing a product in 2D or print.[16] A few examples of companies and organizations that are using AR include the following:

1. BMW is using AR that projects a map of the road with such clarity on the car's windshield that the driver can see buildings, traffic signs, and hazards. According to

BMW, this technology not only improves the safety of drivers, it also makes the traveling experience more enjoyable.[17]

2. The U.S. Postal Service (USPS) uses AR that allows customers to compare the size of an item to the size of shipping boxes available from USPS. This gives customers a good idea about which box to purchase before shipping an item.[18] Another popular example is Wayfair's Android app, which allows customers to shop for furniture using augmented reality. Using the app, customers can visualize furniture in their own home just by holding up their smartphones and pointing at the furniture they want.[19]

3. The IBM In-Store AR shopping app enables shoppers to have a pleasant and informed experience when shopping for products, including food items. When a consumer points a smartphone at an item, the app displays all sorts of information, including nutritional facts for food. A customer can also specify certain factors such as the amount of sugar in a product or the rating of a product by other customers. For example, when the customer points at the cereal shelf in a grocery store, the app displays cereals that meet the consumer's specifications. The app can also display incentives and even loyalty points. In addition, the app helps stores to manage their inventory and carry the products that customers want.[20]

4. The Lufthansa AR app promotes its premium economy seats. When passengers open the app, they are asked to draw anything that can fly. Then, passengers scan the image with the app to view a 3D model of the premium economy seat. At that point, passengers can see all the features of the seat, including additional leg space compared to other airlines' economy seats. This interactive app is used as a marketing tool.[21]

Mixed reality (MR) overlays virtual objects on real objects and anchors virtual objects to real-world objects so they can interact with one another.

5. Siemens is a German multinational conglomerate headquartered in Berlin and Munich and the largest industrial manufacturing company in Europe, with branch offices overseas. Because of the technical nature of its products, marketing staff had a difficult time conveying to potential customers the capabilities of the products, particularly at trade shows. The AR app solved this problem in a major way. Now the AR app serves as a strong marketing tool that walks potential customers through the various features of each product in an interactive manner.[22]

14-2h Mixed Reality

There is yet another type of virtual reality that falls between AR and VR called *mixed reality*, or *hybrid reality*. Mixed reality merges real and virtual objects to produce new visualizations where real and digital objects interact in real time. Mixed reality brings together the best of both worlds and attempts to combine virtual and augmented reality. **Mixed reality (MR)** overlays virtual objects on real objects and anchors virtual objects to real-world objects so they can interact with one another. In mixed reality, a user remains in the real-world environment while digital contents are added that are trackable. In addition, a user can interact with virtual objects. This form of mixed reality can be considered an advanced version of AR. As an example, Magic Leap is an MR platform that enables content extraction and spatial browsing, enabling 3D exploration.[23]

Microsoft's HoloLens is a popular MR platform that maps out the user's environment using spatial mapping, which allows holograms to interact with the surfaces of the environment. Users can interact with their surroundings using their gaze, voice, and air tap gestures, which provides a natural experience. HoloLens users can also connect with each other to share the same MR experiences. This brings a high degree of interactivity and allows MR to become a natural platform for interaction.[24] The "Mixed Reality in Action" box illustrates three real-life applications of mixed reality.

Mixed Reality in Action

⏩ Finance | Technology in Society | Application | Reflective Thinking

Microsoft's HoloLens MR platform is used by a diverse group of businesses as a collaboration tool, modeling tool, and prototyping tool. Three such applications are presented in this feature box.

(Continued)

Diverse teams of designers, engineers, marketers, and manufacturers at the toy manufacturer Mattel are spread all over the world. They use HoloLens as a collaboration tool for their popular brands like Barbie and Hot Wheels. HoloLens enables them to come together in a spatial project room, reducing the need to travel. One of Mattel's designers demonstrated how manipulating a 3D model of a toy truck allowed design flaws to be identified earlier in the production cycle, which saved the company a lot of money.

Trimble Plumbing and Heating Company uses HoloLens as a modeling tool. It allows Trimble's workers to see a project schematic before the project is completed. In one case, using HoloLens' 3D modeling capabilities, workers found that planned plumbing schematics were incompatible with other fixtures. Because the problem was identified before any work had been done on-site, Trimble saved money.[25]

Volvo allows its customers to use HoloLens to customize their cars before purchase. HoloLens enables consumers to accomplish everything that was once done in a showroom simply by wearing a HoloLens device and using natural hand movements. As a result, Volvo saves money by not having actual cars in its showrooms and improves customer service at the same time.[26]

Questions and Discussions

1. Why does Mattel use HoloLens?
2. How is Volvo using HoloLens? How can HoloLens be used as a modeling tool? Discuss.

14-3 Non-Fungible Tokens

A **non-fungible token (NFT)** is a one-of-a-kind crypto asset in which each token is unique and backed by a blockchain. As you will learn later in this module, a *blockchain* is a decentralized and distributed network used to record transactions across connected devices as blocks of data that cannot be altered after being recorded. The word *non-fungible* means that a token is not mutually interchangeable, as opposed to fungible tokens that are interchangeable. NFTs are digital representations of virtual and real-world assets, and they can be applied to any asset, including online-only assets like digital artwork as well as real assets such as real estate. NFTs give individuals and businesses an opportunity to make money by digitizing assets, monetizing intellectual properties, and verifying the authenticity of physical assets on the Internet. Like cryptocurrencies, NFTs are based on decentralized finance (DeFi), in which assets and market players act on a P2P (peer-to-peer) basis and in a decentralized network. DeFi eliminates the involvement of intermediaries such as banks or government agencies. Because every NFT is unique, it can be used to authenticate ownership of digital assets like artworks, recordings, and virtual real estate. Because NFTs are backed by blockchain, the tokens cannot be copied, removed, or destroyed. Blockchain technology enables NFTs to be traced back to their real owners and eliminates the need for third-party verification. The following are some popular examples of NFTs:

- Twitter co-founder Jack Dorsey's first-ever tweet, "just setting up my twtrr," was sold for $2.9 million.[27]

- "Charlie Bit my Finger" was originally a YouTube video of Charlie Davies-Carr, an infant in England, biting the finger of his big brother, Harry Davies-Carr, and then laughing after Harry yells "OWWWW." That video got over 880 million views and became an NFT that sold for over $760,000.[28]

- Mike Winkelmann, an artist who goes by the name Beeple, created artwork of a screen-covered rotating metal box that shows an astronaut walking through changing landscapes. Winkelmann sold the work as an NFT for $69 million through a first-of-its-kind auction at Christie's.[29]

To better understand non-fungible tokens, you should also know about fungible and semi-fungible tokens. **Fungible tokens** are representations of assets on a blockchain that are interchangeable. A bitcoin is a good example; every coin has the same value as any other coin and there is no uniqueness involved.

> A **non-fungible token (NFT)** is a one-of-a-kind crypto asset in which each token is unique and backed by a blockchain.
>
> **Fungible tokens** are representations of assets on a blockchain that are interchangeable.

Semi-fungible tokens (SFTs) can be traded as both fungible and non-fungible. As an example, consider two concert tickets for a famous musician that can be exchanged as SFTs. After the exchange and when the concert ends, the tickets lose their face value and become collectible or NFTs. There are many applications of NFTs, and the number of applications is growing on a daily basis. Listed next are a few popular examples:[30]

- *Identification, certification, and documentation*—Because NFTs contain code with a unique set of information, they can be used to tokenize documentation such as birth certificates, medical records, and licenses.
- *Real estate*—NFTs enable sales of digital real estate in both the virtual and real world.
- *Unique memorabilia*—NFTs enable authentication and transactions involving artwork, luxury brands, sports collectibles, and other collectibles.
- *Supply chain and logistics*—NFTs on blockchain provide immutability and transparency, which keeps supply chain data authentic and reliable.
- *Gaming*—NFTs provide an opportunity for gamers to take ownership of digital properties that they buy or win within a game. Players can then take the assets outside the games and exchange them for real money or something else.

A growing number of companies are getting involved with NFTs. For example, Taco Bell, Pizza Hut, Nike, and Pringles are creating their own NFTs. Visa bought an NFT for $150,000 in 2021, and Adidas spent $156,000 for a digital piece of art.[31] Several Web sites allow users to make, buy, and sell NFTs.[32] Their drawbacks include excessive hype, exaggeration in pricing, uncertainty, and environmental issues of blockchain technology.[33]

14-4 The Metaverse: Definition, Foundation, and Applications

There is no universal definition for the *metaverse*; the term may mean different things to different people and companies. However, most experts agree that the metaverse is more than just virtual reality. It is the intersection of blockchain, Web 3.0, and virtual reality. VR, AR, and MR provide a foundation for the metaverse. For the purposes of this book, we define the **metaverse** as a 3D virtual world that provides a seamless digital environment where users can do almost everything they do in the real world, such as playing games, shopping, buying real estate, and attending conferences.

A fully functional metaverse platform should include the entire universe of shared virtual spaces linked together. A user should be able to teleport among these shared virtual spaces.[34] The metaverse is a digital reality where people work, play, and socialize. Other names for the metaverse include the next Internet, the mirror world, the AR Cloud, the Magicverse, the Spatial Internet, and Live Maps.[35] The metaverse offers several advantages and opportunities as follows:[36]

- Enables consumers to test products before purchasing them
- Gives medical professionals powerful insights about patients regardless of their physical locations
- Makes gaming more realistic
- Allows consumers to visit other countries and places without leaving their rooms
- Provides enhanced communication for work and education
- Offers new openings for businesses and marketers

The metaverse also includes some drawbacks:

- Confusion between what is real and what is virtual
- Security and privacy concerns
- The digital divide, because the metaverse needs high-speed communication with sophisticated I/O devices to achieve its full potential

Several major players in the metaverse environment are involved in its applications, development, and implementation. In addition to Meta (formerly Facebook), Microsoft, Alphabet, and Snapchat, key players include the following:[37]

- Nvidia (*www.nvidia.com/en-us/*), the chipmaker giant, provides tools for other companies to create their own metaverses. Most notable among these tools is its recently launched Omniverse platform, which provides an extensible, open platform for virtual collaboration and real-time simulation. According to Nvidia, creators, designers, researchers, and engineers can connect major design tools, assets, and projects to collaborate in a shared virtual space.

- Unity Software (*https://unity.com/*) provides the architecture and technology necessary to create the metaverse, including AR, VR, and RT3D (Real-Time 3D).

- OpenSea (*https://opensea.io/*) provides the world's first and largest NFT marketplace for buying and selling.

- Active Theory (*https://activetheory.net/home*) builds metaverses for brands.

- Amazon Web Services (AWS), Microsoft Azure, and Google Cloud Platform provide infrastructure for reliable and high-speed Internet connections for metaverses.

- Decentraland (*https://decentraland.org/*) enables users to create, interact with, and monetize content and apps. Users can purchase virtual pieces of land in the metaverse, which they can travel to, build virtual properties on, and monetize. This 3D virtual world is owned by its users, allowing them to create virtual properties from theme parks to galleries and then charge users to visit them. Decentraland is powered by Ethereum blockchain technology. Sotheby's has recently established its own metaverse gallery for curated virtual art in Decentraland.

- Epic Games (*www.epicgames.com/site/en-US/home*) is a leading interactive entertainment company and provider of 3D engine technology. It operates Fortnite, one of the world's most popular games, and provides an end-to-end digital ecosystem for developers and creators to build, distribute, and operate games and other content.

- Roblox (*www.roblox.com/*) provides a global platform where millions of users interact every day to imagine, create, and share experiences in immersive, user-generated 3D worlds. The Roblox Suite allows gamers to create their own games or create another world with friends or other users.

14-5 Cloud Computing: Foundation, Applications, and Models

The following sections discuss recent trends in networking, including cloud computing and its various applications and models. Some forms of cloud computing, such as software as a service, grid computing, and utility computing, have been around for some time. Other models have emerged as applications whose popularity has exploded in recent years. According to Oracle, 80 percent of all enterprise and mission-critical workloads will move to the cloud by 2025.[38] Listed next are 10 of the most popular applications of cloud computing.[39]

1. Scalable usage: Cloud computing offers scalable resources through various subscription models. Examples include Netflix, Amazon Prime Video, and Hulu.

2. Chatbots: Chatbots leverage the computing capabilities of the cloud to provide personalized, context-relevant customer experiences. Examples include Siri, Alexa, Google Assistant, and Microsoft Cortana.

3. Worldwide communication: Cloud infrastructure provides communication tools on a global scale. Examples include E-mail, Zoom, Skype, and WhatsApp.

4. Global productivity tools: Cloud infrastructure provides essential productivity tools that enable knowledge workers to communicate and collaborate on a global scale. Examples include Microsoft Office 365 and Google Apps for Work.

5. Business process and enterprise systems: Cloud infrastructure provides an environment for effective utilization of enterprise systems such as CRM, ERP, and SCM. Examples include Salesforce, SAP, and Adobe Systems.

6. Backup and recovery: Cloud infrastructure provides flexibility and scale for backup and recovery. Examples include Box, Dropbox, Google Drive, and Amazon S3.

7. Application development: Cloud infrastructure provides a scalable cross-platform for application development, including game development. Examples include Amazon Lumberyard, Unity, Blender, and Unreal Engine.

8. Testing and development: Cloud infrastructure provides flexibility and scale for testing and development with moderate costs. Examples include WebLOAD, LoadStorm, and BlazeMeter.

9. Big data analytics: Cloud infrastructure provides a flexible environment for many open-source big data tools. Examples include Hadoop, Cassandra, and HPCC.

10. Social networking: Social media are among the most popular and widespread applications of cloud computing. Examples include Facebook, LinkedIn, and Twitter.

> Cost savings are a major advantage of grid computing because companies do not have to purchase additional equipment.

14-5a Grid Computing

Generally, **grid computing** involves combining the processing powers of various computers (see Exhibit 14.5). With this configuration, users can make use of other computers' resources to solve problems involving large-scale, complex calculations, such as circuit analysis or mechanical design—problems that a single computer is not capable of solving in a timely manner. Each participant in a grid is referred to as a "node." Cost savings is a major advantage of grid computing because companies do not have to purchase additional equipment. In addition, processing on overused nodes can be switched to idle servers and even desktop systems. Grid computing has already been used in bioinformatics, oil and gas drilling, and financial applications.

Other advantages of grid computing include the following:

- *Improved reliability*—If one node in the grid fails, another node can take over.

- *Parallel processing*—Complex tasks can be performed in parallel, which improves performance. In other words, a complex task can be split into smaller tasks that run simultaneously on several nodes.

- *Scalability*—If needed, more nodes can be added for additional computing power without affecting the network's operation. Upgrades can also be managed by segmenting the grid and performing the upgrade in stages without any major effect on the grid's performance.

Grid computing involves combining the processing powers of various computers. With this configuration, users can make use of other computers' resources to solve problems involving large-scale, complex calculations, such as circuit analysis or mechanical design—problems that a single computer is not capable of solving in a timely manner.

Utility (on-demand) computing is the provision of IT services on demand. Users pay for computing or storage resources on an as-needed basis, similar to the way one pays for utilities such as heat and water.

Exhibit 14.5
A grid computing configuration

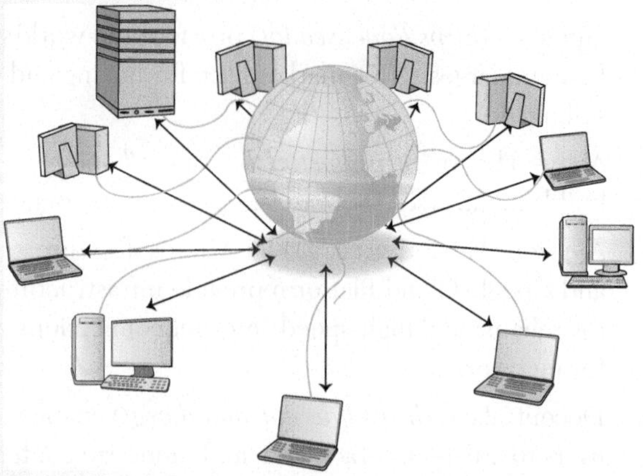

Grid computing does have some drawbacks. Some applications cannot be spread among nodes, so they are not suitable for grid computing, and applications requiring extensive memory that a single node cannot provide cannot be used on a grid. In addition, licensing agreements can be challenging, and synchronizing operations in several network domains can be difficult and require sophisticated network management tools. Finally, some organizations are resistant to sharing resources, even if doing so benefits them.

14-5b Utility (On-Demand) Computing

Utility (on-demand) computing is the provision of IT services on demand. Users pay for computing or storage resources on an as-needed basis, similar to the way one pays for utilities such as heat and water. Convenience and cost savings are two main advantages of utility computing, but this service does have drawbacks in the areas of privacy and security. Because the service is outside the company's location, theft or corruption of data is a concern.

Utility computing can work with the SaaS model you learned about earlier. Returning to the example of editing a Word document, suppose the Module14.doc file is very large because it contains a lot of images. You notice that your computer is running slowly because it has an older CPU and does not have enough RAM to handle the file size adequately. With utility computing, you can request computing power and memory from the provider. It is like leasing a more powerful computer just for the time you need it. Although SaaS deals only with software, utility computing handles hardware resources such as CPU processing and memory.

Universities and research centers take advantage of utility computing to run complex programs for which they do not have the necessary resources. Sun Microsystems (now a part of Oracle) and IBM offer this service in the form of storage and virtual servers. Other companies offer virtual data centers that allow users to combine memory, storage, and computing capabilities—Liquid Computing's LiquidIQ, for example. Other vendors include ENKI, Joyent, and Layered Tech. Even NASA leases its supercomputer for a fee, which both brings in income and ensures that the supercomputer is used.

> Universities and research centers take advantage of utility computing to run complex programs for which they do not have the necessary resources.

14-5c Cloud Computing

Cloud computing uses one platform to incorporate many technologies, including the SaaS model, Web 2.0, grid computing, and utility computing; hence, a variety of resources can be provided to users over the Internet. Business applications are accessed via a Web browser, and data is stored on the providers' servers.[40] In addition, cloud providers such as Amazon set up an environment that enables you to subscribe to SaaS, utility computing, grid computing, and other services you need, and then coordinate all these services for you.

Nearly all tech vendors are involved in cloud computing. BTC Logic, an IT consulting firm, has classified cloud computing into seven areas and identified some of the top players in each category (see Table 14.1).[41]

Going back to the example of editing the Module14.doc file, say you are using your iPhone instead of your computer. Clearly, your iPhone does not have the storage space to save such a large file, and it does not have the necessary computing power or Word software installed. With cloud computing, you can subscribe to Word at the provider's SaaS site, store the document on an external storage unit provided by the vendor, and run Word on a multiprocessor system the vendor provides. You might even get extra RAM from another computer available in the cloud. The cloud provider coordinates all these tasks for you. Your iPhone is simply the device for viewing the document while you are editing it, and because it is a mobile device, you can do your work anywhere. In other words, the document, the software, and the computing resources are like a cloud that surrounds you wherever you go and are available whenever you need them.

14-5d Cloud Computing Components

Generally, cloud computing includes components in the form of infrastructure as a service (IaaS), platform as a service (PaaS), and software as a service (SaaS). See Exhibit 14.6.

Infrastructure as a service (IaaS), also called *hardware as a service (HaaS)*, is a type of cloud computing whereby computer infrastructure (such as storage,

Cloud computing uses one platform to incorporate many technologies, including the SaaS model, Web 2.0, grid computing, and utility computing; hence, a variety of resources can be provided to users over the Internet. Business applications are accessed via a Web browser, and data is stored on the providers' servers.

Infrastructure as a service (IaaS), also called *hardware as a service (HaaS)*, is a type of cloud computing whereby computer infrastructure (such as storage, hardware, servers, and networking components) is delivered as a service.

Table 14.1	Cloud Computing Categories and Top Players
Category	**Top Players**
Foundations (tools and software that make it possible to build cloud infrastructure)	VMware, Microsoft, Red Hat
Infrastructure	Amazon, IBM
Network services (the communication components that combine with cloud foundation and infrastructure to form cloud architecture)	Level 3 Computing Services, Amazon, Cisco, Citrix
Platforms	Amazon, IBM
Applications	Google, Salesforce, Oracle, Dropbox
Security	EMC/RSA, Symantec, IBM
Management	IBM, Amazon

Exhibit 14.6
Cloud computing

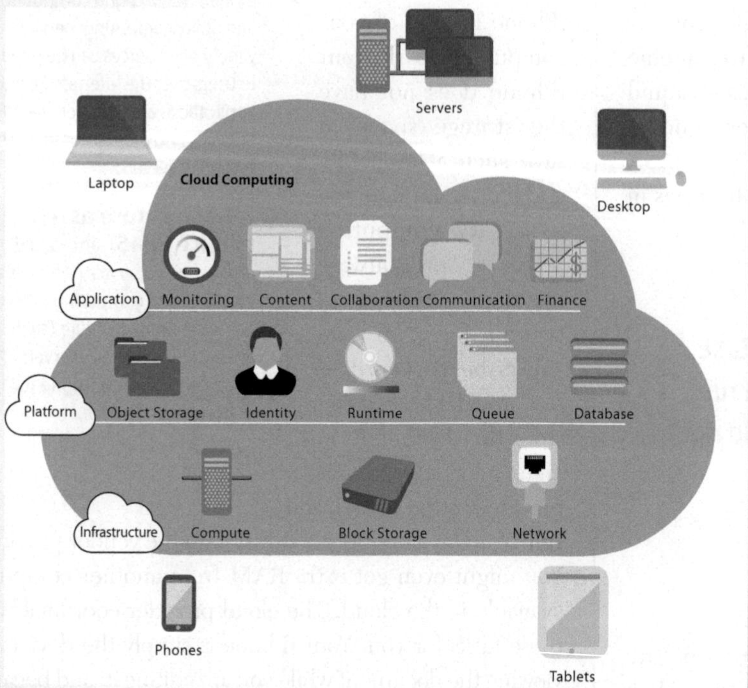

Platform as a service (PaaS) provides a computing platform and a computing solution as a service. Clients use the platform and environment to build applications and services over the Internet. PaaS services are hosted in the cloud and accessed by clients through their Web browsers. PaaS automates the configuration, deployment, and ongoing management of applications in the cloud. Popular examples include AWS Elastic Beanstalk, Windows Azure, *Heroku.com*, *Force.com*, Google App Engine, Apache Stratos, and Red Hat's OpenShift.

Cloud computing has many of the advantages and disadvantages of distributed computing. With this platform, users can request services, applications, and storage. For small and medium-sized businesses, it means they do not have to invest in expensive equipment to compete effectively with large companies and can concentrate on the services and products they provide. Cloud computing services typically require a fee, although some are free. Google Apps for Work, which includes Gmail, Google Talk, and Google Docs, provides commonly used applications accessed via a Web browser; software and data are stored on Google's servers, not on the user's computer. The standard edition for personal use is free.[42] The "Cloud Computing in Support of Small Businesses" box highlights several applications of cloud computing for small businesses.

> **Platform as a service (PaaS)** provides a computing platform and a computing solution as a service. Clients use the platform and environment to build applications and services over the Internet.

hardware, servers, and networking components) is delivered as a service. The service provider owns the equipment and is responsible for housing, running, and maintaining it. This model is particularly popular in data centers where the infrastructure is used as an outsourced service and the center is billed only by usage.

Cloud Computing in Support of Small Businesses

➤ Finance | Technology in Society | Application

Cloud computing could put small businesses on the same footing as large corporations by offering flexibility and scale to grow. In a way, cloud computing gives small businesses a competitive advantage by not forcing them to incur significant expenses upfront for IT services and infrastructure—businesses can get what they need from cloud providers and pay as they go. However, security and downtime are concerns that small businesses have about cloud deployment.

Cloud computing gives small businesses cheaper, faster, and easier access to tools and applications they need. Twitter for marketing and Google's Gmail are among the early applications used by small businesses. According to a survey conducted by Emergent Research, 74 percent of small businesses (companies with fewer than 50 employees) use cloud-based applications for online banking and social media.

(Continued)

Julia Suriano, co-owner of Kebroak BBQ Company, a seven-person operation based in Hialeah, Florida, was expecting a baby. The company imports and distributes charcoal to retailers and restaurants across the country. She needed access to company data at any time and from anywhere. Cloud computing was the answer. In addition to using Gmail and social media, the company switched from Intuit QuickBooks' desktop software to its cloud-based accounting software. Kebroak BBQ also adopted Dropbox for storage. Now Suriano has access to critical data from anywhere.[43]

Questions and Discussions

1. What are two advantages of using cloud computing in small businesses? Discuss.
2. What cloud computing tools benefit small businesses?

14-5e Cloud Computing Alternatives

There are six options when using cloud computing: public, private, hybrid, multicloud, community cloud, and distributed clouds. Organizations usually choose which option to use based on their security needs and the level of involvement their IT managers require.

With a **public cloud**, users connect with an off-site infrastructure over the Internet. Because the public cloud services and the infrastructure are shared by a large number of users, this option offers the greatest cost savings and is the most popular of the six. However, it also carries higher security and privacy risks. Therefore, it is more suitable for organizations that need scalability (the ability to add or drop resources), have collaborative projects over the Web, and offer standard applications over the Web, such as e-mail. Public cloud computing requires the least amount of involvement by IT managers. Overall, security and reliability are the main concerns with this option. Examples of public cloud services are Amazon Elastic Compute Cloud (EC2), IBM Blue Cloud, Google AppEngine, and Windows Azure Services Platform.

In a **private cloud**, the services and the infrastructure are run on a private network. Naturally, this option offers better security and privacy than a public cloud. Because a participating organization purchases and maintains the software and infrastructure itself, this option offers less cost savings than a public cloud. It is recommended for organizations that operate on highly secure data.

It is important to mention that some providers of public cloud services offer private versions of their public clouds. Also, some providers of private cloud services offer public versions of their private cloud. A private cloud achieves cost savings by integrating fragmented infrastructures, automating common data center tasks, and providing financial accuracy and responsibility. In addition, an organization gains a greater degree of automation through the standardization of previously custom-configured services into predefined infrastructure products offered in a controlled self-service manner. Major private cloud services are Eucalyptus, Elastra Enterprise Cloud Server, VMware Private-Cloud Architecture, and Microsoft Azure.

Organizations that operate on both private and public data may choose a hybrid cloud. A **hybrid cloud** is a collection of at least one private cloud and at least one public cloud. In a hybrid cloud environment, there are a variety of public and private options, with multiple providers. An organization may run its sensitive data on a private cloud and its public information on the public cloud with less security and privacy. A hybrid cloud allows an organization to take advantage of the scalability and cost-effectiveness that a public cloud computing environment offers without exposing mission-critical applications and data to the outside world. However, this option may require multiple security platforms, and making sure that all systems communicate with each other efficiently might be a challenge.

Multicloud refers to using more than a single public cloud in an organization. An organization may decide to use a specific service from each cloud provider in order to create the best possible platform. For example, different services may come from different public cloud providers such as Amazon, Google, Microsoft, IBM, HP Enterprise, or Oracle. This option reduces the dependency of an organization on one specific provider. This mix-and-match feature of multicloud increases business agility and operational cost efficiency. However, this

> With a **public cloud**, users connect with an off-site infrastructure over the Internet.
>
> In a **private cloud**, services and the infrastructure are run on a private network.
>
> A **hybrid cloud** is a collection of at least one private cloud and at least one public cloud. In a hybrid cloud environment, there are a variety of public and private options, with multiple providers.
>
> **Multicloud** refers to using more than a single public cloud in an organization.

platform may be more complex than a public cloud environment to manage and presents a greater security risk.[44]

With the **community cloud**, the cloud infrastructure is designed for exclusive use by a specific community of users from organizations that share common concerns (e.g., security requirements as well as policy, mission, and compliance considerations). This infrastructure may be owned, managed, and operated by one or more of the organizations in the community, a third party, or some combination. However, the infrastructure may exist on or off premises.

With this alternative, the costs are spread over fewer users than with a public cloud (but more than with a private cloud) to realize its full cost-savings potential.[45,46] Allocation of costs and responsibilities, governance, and the implementation of a tight security system are among the challenges that must be overcome when choosing this option.

Distributed cloud computing reduces latency and improves performance by distributing cloud services such as data sets, storage, and processing to different physical locations that are closer to the users. A specific location may be shared by several users in the same geographical area. This alternative reduces some of the challenges involved in using a hybrid cloud.[47]

14-5f Edge Computing

In the distributed world of Internet of Things (IoT), edge computing is playing a major role. **Edge computing** pushes processing and data to the near edge of the network, which enables timely collection, processing, and analysis of data. In other words, edge computing provides on-device processing and analytics in real time. On the other hand, cloud computing processes data in centralized cloud and data centers that may not be as fast and efficient for time-sensitive information. Edge computing will not replace cloud computing; rather, they complement one another. The following 10 trends are accelerating the growth and applications of edge computing:[48]

1. Widespread adoption and applications of IoT

2. Widespread adoption of remote work and telecommuting, particularly after the COVID-19 pandemic

3. Digital transformation, including IIoT, smart factories, e-commerce, and m-commerce

4. 5G adoption and an increase in the number of connected devices

5. Analytics and AI in smart factories, retail outlets, remote offices, and other locations

6. Increases in the numbers of digital twins, which are computerized representations of objects in the real world

7. Increasing adoption and applications of AR, VR, and MR

8. Privacy regulations, including GDPR (discussed in Module 4)—edge computing enables organizations to store and process data at the edge of a network and follow relevant laws while still doing business globally

9. Smart cities and autonomous technology

10. An increasing number of natural disasters, such as fires, floods, and hurricanes. Storing data on the edge and in the cloud could speed up response time for rescue workers.

The "Edge Computing in Action" box highlights four real-life applications of edge computing.[49]

Edge computing is different from fog computing. In fog computing, a single centralized computing device processes data from multiple edge devices in a network; in edge computing, each device in a network processes its own data. The following are some of the advantages of edge computing:[50,51]

- Real-time data analysis at the edge (any device connected to the network) that is not in a remote data center or cloud.

- Lower operating costs due to the smaller operational and data management expenses of local devices.

- Reduced network traffic because less data is transmitted from local devices via a network to a data center or cloud.

- Improved application performance due to lower delay levels on the edge of the network.

- Increased network performance by eliminating or reducing latency, due to local processing of data.

- Conventional cloud computing is vulnerable to DDoS attacks and power outages due to having centralized servers. Edge computing distributes processing, storage, and applications across a wide range of devices and data centers, which makes it difficult for any single disruption to take down the network.

With the **community cloud**, the cloud infrastructure is designed for exclusive use by a specific community of users from organizations that share common concerns.

Distributed cloud computing reduces latency and improves performance by distributing cloud services such as data sets, storage, and processing to different physical locations that are closer to the users.

Edge computing pushes processing and data to the near edge of the network, which enables timely collection, processing, and analysis of data.

Edge Computing in Action

⫸ Finance | Technology in Society | Application | Reflective Thinking

Envision, a power producer, manages a network of 20,000 wind turbines. Three million sensors are installed on these turbines, producing over 20 terabytes of data at a time. Envision has reduced its data-analysis time from 10 minutes to just seconds using edge computing. As a result, the wind turbines' production has increased by 15 percent.

Edge computing has helped Coca-Cola boost overall sales from its Freestyle vending machines by analyzing and reporting the popularity of over 100 combinations of carbonated and noncarbonated drinks on an hourly basis. This technology enabled the company to increase its offering of Caffeine-Free Diet Coke in vending machines and make it a top five brand during the afternoon.

Edge computing helped General Electric's digital locomotives to perform at or near peak performance levels, which resulted in increased revenue. Behind this top performance level are more than 200 embedded sensors that collect gigabytes of operational data and process more than 1 billion instructions per second to apply algorithms in real time.

Edge computing has helped the city of Palo Alto, California, in several ways. Its parking space sensor program notifies drivers about available parking spaces, which helps reduce traffic congestion and air pollution. Its smart traffic signal project enables traffic lights to work in sync with connected vehicles, resulting in reduced wait times for traffic lights to turn green.

Questions and Discussions

1. How does edge computing impact the world of data analytics and business information?
2. What are some additional applications of edge computing? Discuss.

- Enhanced scalability by allowing companies to expand their computing capacity through a combination of IoT devices and edge data centers at a moderate cost.

- Data centers can easily target desirable markets without having to invest in expensive infrastructure expansion. Edge computing also empowers IoT devices to gather exceptional amounts of actionable data because they are always on and connected.

- With IoT edge computing devices and edge data centers positioned closer to end users, there is less chance of a network problem in a distant location affecting local customers. Even in the event of a nearby data center outage, IoT edge computing devices will continue to operate effectively on their own because they have built-in capability and can handle vital processing functions.

14-5g Cloud Computing Security

Most experts believe that security is a concern when using a cloud computing platform, and users play an important role in its success. An organization that uses cloud computing should provide end-user education, force software updates, and work with the cloud computing provider to spot unusual activities.

In a cloud computing environment, there are two types of security issues: client (the user) side and server (the provider) side. The organization using the cloud services does not have much control over the server-side security issues; the provider is responsible for that. However, the client-side security is the responsibility of the organization using the cloud services. Many of the security measures discussed in Modules 5 and 6 can be used to improve client-side security.

Cloud computing could be more secure than an on-premises data center for the following reasons.[52,53]

1. Greater technical expertise: Top cloud providers may employ hundreds of security professionals, as their profitability and reputation depend on ensuring that customers' data remains secure within the cloud. Such a team of security experts is out of reach and not affordable for many smaller organizations.

2. Physical separation: Data in the cloud may be stored on a server physically located anywhere in the world, making a physical attack much less likely. On the other hand, a physical threat to data security and integrity is quite possible in an on-premises data center.

3. Fewer vulnerabilities: Top cloud providers have more resources to find and fix vulnerabilities before hackers can exploit them. Such vulnerabilities include unpatched security holes and phishing e-mails. Some cloud providers hire ethical hackers to perform penetration testing in order to find and fix security holes.

4. Better resiliency: Natural disasters such as floods, hurricanes, tornadoes, and wildfires show just how fragile data can be when backed up on-premises. Using public cloud providers to back up your information makes it much more likely that you can recover from unexpected disasters.

5. Newer technology: Major cloud providers use the latest technology to give their customers more state-of-the-art computing resources. These resources also make cloud data centers easier to support, maintain, and patch. On the other hand, on-premises data centers deal with many legacy systems that are difficult to manage.

6. Using AI: Major cloud providers use AI in their security programs, which makes it easier to find and eliminate vulnerabilities and get automatically smarter while doing it.

However, there are several security risks when using cloud computing and they must be analyzed carefully. Gartner, an analyst firm, has identified seven cloud-computing security risks:[54]

- *Privileged user access*—Who has access to your data

- *Regulatory compliance*—Availability of external audits and security certifications

- *Data location*—Specific jurisdictions and commitment to local privacy

- *Data segregation*—How your data is kept separate from other data in the cloud

- *Recovery*—What will happen to your data in case of a disaster

- *Investigative support*—Contractual commitment to support specific forms of investigation

- *Long-term viability*—What will happen to your data if the provider goes out of business

Before choosing one, an organization must make sure a cloud provider has a clear policy regarding these

Nanotechnology incorporates techniques that involve the structure and composition of materials on a nanoscale.

> An organization must make sure a cloud provider has a clear policy regarding security risks and has indicated in writing how it will deal with each of them.

security risks and has indicated in writing how it will deal with each of them. Additionally, some level of trust between the provider and the user is needed. Without it, using cloud computing becomes a risky venture.

14-6 Nanotechnology

Nanotechnology incorporates techniques that involve the structure and composition of materials on a nanoscale. Based on the nanometer, which is one-billionth of a meter, nanotechnology has become an exciting development in many fields. For example, scientists are working on miniature devices that can unclog arteries, detect and eradicate cancer cells, filter water pollution, and more. Their use in treating heart attack and stroke victims has been garnering close attention in recent years. Researchers are developing nanocapsules for a "clot-busting" drug. The nanocapsule can target a specific clot and break open and release medication exactly when it is needed. This is far more accurate than traditional methods, such as when a drug is administered through an IV.[55]

A report published in 2022 predicts substantial applications of nanotechnology in future medical devices used for diagnostics, therapeutics, and research. Some of the products include applications for bone restorative material, dental filling material, hearing aids, cardio rhythm management devices, biochips, medical textiles, and wound dressing.[56]

In January 2021, Exogenesis Corporation announced the release of its nanoMesh hernia repair product with surface nano-modification—the first of its kind.[57]

Nanotechnology is also being developed to make computers much faster and smaller, with more memory. However, nanotechnology is currently too expensive to justify its use in many applications. Further research and development should reduce its cost in the future.

In the field of information systems, the current technology for miniaturizing transistors and other microprocessor components might reach its limit in the next decade, so new technologies, including nanotechnology, will be necessary.[58] Nanotechnology might also play a role in the following areas:

- Energy (reduction of energy consumption, increase in the efficiency of energy production, more environmentally friendly energy systems)
- Information and communication (larger and faster storage devices, faster and cheaper computers, display monitors with low energy consumption)
- Heavy industry (aerospace, construction, refineries, vehicle manufacturing)

Some consumer goods that incorporate nanotechnology are already on the market. They use what are called *nanomaterials*. Nanomaterials have been added to sports gear, such as tennis and golf balls and tennis rackets, to make them more durable and improve their responsiveness; tennis balls that incorporate nanomaterials bounce better. Nanomaterials have also been applied as coatings on eyewear for increased comfort and durability, and they are used in clothing and footwear to cut down bacteria growth and improve stain resistance.[59] In addition, IBM has developed the scanning tunneling microscope (STM), which is capable of imaging atoms and incorporating nanomaterial layers into hard disk recording heads and magnetic disk coatings. This technology might also improve electronic circuits and data storage devices. As mentioned in Module 2, IBM is replacing silicon with carbon nanotubes (CNTs) in its computer chips.

14-7 Blockchain Technology and Cryptocurrency

Blockchain technology is a relatively recent application of computer networks, the Internet, and encryption technology. A **blockchain** is a decentralized and distributed network that is used to record transactions across connected devices as blocks of data that cannot be altered after being recorded (see Exhibit 14.7). When they are recorded, the transactions are grouped together into blocks, which are then linked together to create chains—hence the name *blockchain*.[60] With the growing applications of IoT, blockchain's role and applications are increasing on a daily basis in business and society. Some experts call it a distributed ledger that records every transaction with a high degree of accuracy. According to Forrester Research, blockchain's "potential is undeniable: Blockchain technology, if implemented appropriately, supports new business and trust models."

Exhibit 14.7
A blockchain

a-image/Shutterstock.com

In a blockchain environment, the network is directly shared without a central administrator and transactions can be verified and processed independently. The distributed network is protected through encryption technology that makes the network accessible only to authorized users. Due to its high security, the data quality is better in a blockchain environment and transactions are processed faster at a lower cost. An uncertain regulatory environment and lack of widespread adoption of the technology are among its disadvantages. In addition to cryptocurrency applications, which are discussed later in this section, there are numerous current and future applications of blockchain technology. Nine such applications are:[61]

> A **blockchain** is a decentralized and distributed network that is used to record transactions across connected devices as blocks of data that cannot be altered after being recorded.

- *Tracking food and other goods*—Blockchain technology can securely track the entire supply chain of ingredients from the point where they were harvested to their final purchase by consumers. It can even record the price that was paid to farmers and indicate the fairness of the price.
- *Secure software development*—A blockchain-based tracking system ensures the security of the code, tracks every step of the development process, and speeds up the process of finding any problems in the code.

- *Digital content management*—Blockchain-based tools help manage copyrights and other intellectual properties by proving authorship of content and tracking who has accessed the content, therefore reducing piracy.

- *Improving healthcare records' integrity*—Blockchain technology provides tools for storing complete medical records of patients and making them available securely to authorized users, such as doctors and other medical personnel.

- *Mortgage approval process*—Blockchain-based tools could give borrowers the option of storing their financial information in a secure blockchain network and then sharing it with potential lenders, which can significantly speed up the mortgage approval process.

- *Improving and speeding up insurance claims processing*—Blockchain-based tools could help cut down on fraudulent payments and double payments for the same claim and can streamline the process when multiple firms are involved in an incident.

- *Audit trails*—A blockchain database could provide unaltered data in various forms to companies such as law firms or accounting firms so they can audit a particular case all in one place.

- *Electronic voting*—A blockchain network could guarantee the authenticity and reliability of the electronic voting process and allow voters to use any device of their choice to vote securely.

- *Smart contracts*—A blockchain network could automatically transfer money when certain conditions are met. Ethereum, which is also the name of a popular cryptocurrency, is one of the most popular smart contract platforms. This technology could scientifically enhance e-commerce and m-commerce transactions.

Due to the popularity of blockchain technology, a new type of cloud service is gaining in popularity. **Blockchain as a service (BaaS)** is third-party, cloud-based infrastructure that organizations can use to develop their own blockchain and smart contract applications. This service has advantages

> **Blockchain as a service (BaaS)** is third-party cloud-based infrastructure that organizations can use to develop their own blockchain and smart contract applications.

Blockchain Technology in Action: Walmart and Alibaba

➤➤➤ Finance | Technology in Society | Application | Reflective Thinking

Many companies such as Walmart, Alibaba, and American Express are using distributed ledger technologies in blockchain to run their businesses more efficiently and improve customer trust and safety. Managing the supply chain in a multinational company such as Walmart can be a complex task, and traceability of products from the factory, farm, or supplier to the customer can be challenging. In these situations, supply chain transparency becomes very important, especially if something goes wrong—for example, when food items are contaminated. In such a case, a company must have accurate, real-time information so it can notify customers and pull contaminated items off shelves. This is where blockchain can play a major role. IBM is working with Walmart, Kroger, and Nestlé to allow participants in their supply chain networks to share information. If all goes according to plan, the benefits will be increased safety, faster crisis management, and improved customer trust.

Alibaba uses blockchain to fight *food fraud*—substitution or misrepresentation of food for economic gain. Food fraud occurred in the Tesco horsemeat scandal, where some packaged beef meals were found to contain up to 60 percent horsemeat. Alibaba, in collaboration with four companies from New Zealand and Australia, are combining a blockchain ledger with QR-coded product tags. Any product movement is recorded on an open ledger. Every concerned person will have access to the ledger and know exactly what a product contains, as well as its origin and destination. This system should significantly improve food safety and should boost consumer confidence.[62]

Questions and Discussions

1. Why did Walmart deploy blockchain technology? Discuss.
2. What are two applications of blockchain technology at Alibaba?

and disadvantages that are similar to the SaaS model. The following are three examples of companies that offer BaaS:[63]

- Dragonchain (*https://dragonchain.com*) is an enterprise and start-up platform that offers flexible and scalable blockchain applications.

- Bloq (*www.bloq.com*) is a managed infrastructure for building on blockchain networks.

- Chain (*https://chain.com/*) is cloud blockchain infrastructure that enables organizations to build financial services from scratch.

Amazon AWS, Microsoft, Oracle, SAP, HPE, and IBM also offer BaaS.

The nearby box highlights how Walmart and Alibaba are using blockchain technology.

Cryptocurrency is probably the most popular application of blockchain technology. **Cryptocurrency** is digital money created from computer codes. It is monitored by a peer-to-peer Internet protocol. With cryptocurrency, an individual owns the private key and the corresponding public key that make up the cryptocurrency address. Several types of cryptocurrencies are available on the market. Some of the most popular, based on their market capitalization, include Bitcoin (BTC), Ethereum (ETH), Binance Coin (BNB), Tether (USDT), Solana (SOL), and Cardano (ADA).

Each coin is designed for a specific purpose and has some unique applications. For example, Bitcoin is known for its scarcity and durability and is used for a "store of value." A store of value is an asset class that can maintain its worth or increase in value over time.[64]

Ethereum is mostly used for smart contracts. Binance Coin (BNB) is used for trading, payment processing, entertainment, investment, loans, and funds transfer.

Tether (USDT) is a Stablecoin, a type of cryptocurrency intended to keep its valuation stable. It may be pegged to a currency like the U.S. dollar. This type of cryptocurrency is suitable for investors who want to avoid the high volatility of other cryptocurrencies while keeping value within the crypto market.

Solana (SOL) is known for its fast transaction speeds and low transaction processing fees. As an open source blockchain platform, Solana is used by developers of NFTs, decentralized finance (DeFi), and other software projects.

Cardano (ADA) is used for smart contracts and decentralized applications and protocols. It is also used for funds transfer with low fees.

The main difference between an electronic payment system (such as PayPal or credit cards) and cryptocurrency is not having a third party such as a bank or financial institution between the sender and receiver. Cryptocurrency is a peer-to-peer operation that can take place between two parties anywhere in the world. Some advantages of a cryptocurrency include the following:[65]

- Cannot be counterfeited or reversed by the sender

- Immediate settlement—can be sent from person to person, similar to an e-mail

- Lower transaction fees

- No risk for credit theft

- Available to anyone with a smartphone and Internet access

- Global access without linkage to any particular currency or monetary system

Some disadvantages of a cryptocurrency include the following:[66]

- Not widely accepted

- No way to reverse the payment

- Uncertainty with respect to regulations

- Potential for financial loss because of data loss

- Potential for high price volatility and manipulation

- Impact on the environment because of heavy energy consumption caused by cryptocurrency mining

- Often not exchangeable for fiat currency (currency that a government has declared to be legal tender, but is not backed by a physical commodity, such as gold—the U.S. dollar is an example of fiat currency)

> **Cryptocurrency** is digital money created from computer codes. It is monitored by a peer-to-peer Internet protocol.
>
> **Quantum computing** uses quantum mechanics to generate and manipulate quantum bits, or *qubits*. A quantum computer solves problems considered impossible for traditional computers.

14-8 Quantum Computing

Quantum computing uses quantum mechanics to generate and manipulate quantum bits, or *qubits*. A quantum computer solves problems considered impossible for traditional computers. Traditional computers use bits, which is a stream of electrical or optical pulses representing 1s or 0s (discussed in Module 2). A qubit is the basic unit of quantum information and represents numerous possible

Table 14.2 Traditional Computers Versus Quantum Computers

Traditional Computer	Quantum Computer
It is a large-scale, integrated multipurpose computer.	It is a high-speed parallel computer based on quantum mechanics.
Information storage is by bit, based on voltage or charge.	Information storage is by quantum bit based on the direction of an electron's spin.
Information processing is performed by logic gates such as NOT, AND, OR.	Information processing is performed by quantum logic gates.
Circuit operation is administered by classical physics.	Circuit operation is administered by quantum mechanics.
It uses the binary codes 0 or 1 to represent information.	It uses the qubits codes 0 or 1, and both of them simultaneously to run computers faster.
Operations are defined by Boolean algebra.	Operations are defined by linear algebra.

combinations of 1 and 0 at the same time. This capability of being simultaneously in multiple states is called *superposition*. By deploying the quantum properties of superposition and entanglement, qubits offer exponentially greater computing power than binary bits. *Entanglement* means that the two members of a pair exist in a single quantum state.[67]

Quantum computers will not replace traditional computers because they are not suitable for all applications. They are fast for specific calculations in which a user can use the superposition capability to perform a kind of computational parallelism. Some companies are already using quantum computing to develop lighter and more powerful batteries for electric cars and to help create new and effective drugs. Some businesses are buying quantum computers, while others are using quantum computers made available through cloud computing services. Table 14.2 illustrates some of the differences between traditional computers and quantum computers.[68]

14-8a Popular Applications of Quantum Computing

Quantum computing is being applied to a diverse group of applications both in business and in the scientific world. The following are among the most popular applications.[69,70]

Computer and Network Security

Quantum computing is able to offer very strong encryption technology to protect digital assets and make it nearly impossible to break encrypted documents or networks. Encryption technology is the greatest defense against hackers and for protecting information assets, particularly those that deal with financial and medical information.

Despite the advantages of quantum computers, however, they can also be used to pose a serious security threat to current technology. According to security experts, it could take at least 20 years to get quantum-proof encryption developed and deployed on a mass scale. In the meantime, a powerful quantum computer could crack a sophisticated encryption algorithm in a fraction of the time that it takes a traditional computer. Security professionals should deploy multiple security measures to protect information assets in their organizations.[71]

Aviation Industry

Quantum computing allows complex computer modeling and simulation of diverse aeronautical scenarios. This will help with routing and scheduling of aircrafts and keeping the sky safer. Major aerospace companies such as Lockheed Martin and Airbus are actively researching and investing in this area and want to take advantage of the immense power of quantum computing.

Data Analytics

Quantum computing can assist in solving problems on a large scale with multiple variables. For example, NASA is using quantum computing for analyzing the vast amount of data it collects about the universe and for researching better and safer methods for space missions.

Forecasting

Quantum computing could significantly improve forecasting complex scenarios such as the weather or economic cycles. These situations involve numerous input variables that traditional computing has difficulty dealing with. Quantum computing can handle these situations with ease and accuracy.

Pattern Matching

Finding patterns among similar or dissimilar objects and predicting future events based on the behavior and pattern of these objects have many real-life applications. However, for real-time processing of such applications, immense computing power is needed that quantum computing can handle. As an example, Volkswagen is using this technology to inform drivers of traffic conditions 45 minutes in advance.

Medical and Pharmaceutical Research

There are countless possibilities for how different drugs impact different patients and how patients may respond to various treatments. Currently, it takes more than 10 years to bring the average new drug to market and get FDA approval. Quantum computing could significantly expedite this process with its immense processing power. Improving cancer treatment is among the top priorities using this technology. In 2015, researchers at the Roswell Park Cancer Institute came up with a new technique that uses quantum computing to optimize radiotherapy in a manner that is three to four times faster than that of a traditional computer.[72]

A report published in 2022 discussed the applications of quantum computing to fight neurological problems caused by the effects of COVID-19. Real-time neuron tracking enabled by quantum computers can be beneficial for neurologists because it could help determine if a patient's brain activity is slowing down as the patient ages. Quantum sensors offer new tools to determine how these health problems progress in patients, which in turn can contribute to a treatment plan. Additionally, this technology could reduce medical costs and expedite treatment and recovery.[73]

Self-Driving Cars

Most major car manufacturers and several tech companies, including Apple and Alphabet, are developing self-driving car technologies. Alphabet and Volkswagen are using quantum computers to develop batteries, transportation technology, and self-driving technology. Using quantum computing, Volkswagen has already optimized traffic flow for 10,000 taxis in Beijing and is constantly making improvements.

The Industry Connection highlights Mechdyne Corporation and its virtual reality products.

Industry Connection: Mechdyne Corporation[74]

Mechdyne developed the first commercial CAVE system with rear-projection screens and offers a wide variety of VR hardware, software, and services, including the following:

CAVELib: An application programming interface (API) with tools for creating interactive three-dimensional applications

Trackd: Enhanced VR software for the immersive-displays industry; capable of incorporating input from a variety of devices

Conduit for Google Earth Pro: Includes features such as stereoscopic viewing for true depth perception to emulate real-life settings and real-time changes in viewing perspectives as users navigate through the environment to simulate a real-world experience

Module Summary

14-1 Summarize new trends in software and service distribution, including pull/push technology and software as a service (SaaS). With pull technology, a user states a need before getting information. With push technology, also known as webcasting, a Web server delivers information to users. SaaS, also known as on-demand software, is a model in which ASPs deliver software to users for a fee; the software is for temporary or long-term use.

14-2 Describe virtual reality components and applications. Virtual reality (VR) uses computer-generated, three-dimensional images to create the illusion of interaction in a real-world environment. There are two major types of user environments in VR: egocentric and exocentric. Applications of VR include areas such as assistance for the disabled, architectural design, and education.

14-3 Explain non-fungible tokens (NFTs) and their business applications. An NFT is a one-of-a-kind crypto asset in which each token is unique and backed by a blockchain. Applications of NFTs include identification, certification, and documentation; real estate transactions; transactions of unique memorabilia; the supply chain and logistics; and gaming.

14-4 Discuss the metaverse, its foundation, and its applications. The metaverse is a 3D virtual world that provides a seamless digital environment in which users can do almost everything they do in the real world, such as playing games, shopping, buying real estate, and attending conferences. The metaverse enables consumers to test products before purchasing them, gives medical professionals powerful insights about patients regardless of their physical locations, makes gaming more realistic, and much more.

14-5 Describe the foundation, models, and applications of cloud computing. Cloud computing uses one platform to incorporate many recent technologies, including the SaaS model, Web 2.0, grid computing, and utility computing; hence, a variety of resources can be provided to users over the Internet. Business applications are accessed via a Web browser, and data is stored on the providers' servers.

14-6 Discuss uses of nanotechnology. Nanotechnology incorporates techniques that involve the structure and composition of materials on a nanoscale. It is used in areas such as energy, information and communication, and heavy industry.

14-7 Describe blockchain technology and cryptocurrency. A blockchain is a decentralized and distributed network that is used to record transactions across connected devices as blocks of data that cannot be altered after being recorded. Cryptocurrency is digital money created from computer codes. It is monitored by a peer-to-peer Internet protocol.

14-8 Explain quantum computing and its applications. Quantum computing uses quantum mechanics to generate and manipulate quantum bits or qubits. Its applications include computer and network security, the aviation industry, data analytics, and forecasting.

Key Terms

- Application service providers (ASPs)
- Augmented reality (AR)
- Avatar
- Backup as a service (BaaS)
- Blockchain
- Blockchain as a service (BaaS)
- Cave automatic virtual environment (CAVE)
- Cloud computing
- Community cloud
- Cryptocurrency
- Data as a service (DaaS)
- Distributed cloud computing
- Edge computing
- Egocentric environment

- Exocentric environment
- Fungible tokens
- Grid computing
- Hybrid cloud
- Infrastructure as a service (IaaS)
- Metaverse
- Mixed reality (MR)
- Multicloud
- Nanotechnology
- Non-fungible token (NFT)
- Platform as a service (PaaS)
- Private cloud
- Public cloud
- Pull technology

- Push technology
- Quantum computing
- Security as a service (SECaaS)
- Semi-fungible tokens (SFTs)

- Software as a service (SaaS)
- Utility (on-demand) computing
- Virtual reality (VR)
- Virtual world

Reviews and Discussions

1. Define *virtual reality*. What are three main components of a VR system?
2. What are two applications of NFTs?
3. What are three business applications of virtual reality?
4. What are two applications of the metaverse?

5. What are three applications of nanotechnology?
6. What are two advantages of blockchain technology?
7. List three popular types of cryptocurrencies.
8. List two differences between a traditional computer and a quantum computer.

Projects

1. After reading the information presented in this module and other sources, write a one-page paper that describes two companies (besides those mentioned in this module) that have been using VR. What are two advantages and two disadvantages of using VR? What is the main difference between a VR system and a human being when they are used for therapy? What are two examples of companies that are using AR? For which purposes are AR systems being used?

2. Virtual worlds are being used for communication and collaboration. After reading the information presented in this module and other sources, write a one-page paper that describes two companies (besides those mentioned in this module) that have been using virtual worlds. What are two advantages and two disadvantages of using virtual worlds? What are two examples of companies that provide virtual-world platforms?

3. Quantum computing has generated a lot of excitement in both business and industry. After reading the information presented in this module and other sources, write a two-page paper that describes the experience of three companies that have been using quantum computing. Explain two advantages and two disadvantages of quantum computing. List three areas or applications that are most suitable for quantum computing implementation.

4. Most experts believe that security and privacy risks are two concerns of the cloud computing environment. After reading the information presented in this module and other sources, write a two-page paper that outlines five recommendations for improving the security and privacy of information in cloud computing. List five reasons that cloud computing could offer better security than traditional on-premises data centers.

5. After reading the information presented in this module and other sources, write a two-page paper that describes two companies (besides those mentioned in this module) that have been using NFTs. Explain how these companies might generate revenue from their NFTs. How might NFTs be used in the metaverse environment?

6. After reading the information presented in this module and other sources, write a two-page paper that identifies two companies (besides those mentioned in this module) that have been using blockchain technology. Explain the advantages of using blockchain in these companies and their major reasons for adopting the technology. What is the main difference between security protection when using blockchain versus other security measures? Why is BaaS (blockchain as a service) gaining popularity?

Module Quiz

1. A blockchain is a decentralized and distributed network used to record transactions across connected devices as blocks of data that can be altered after being recorded. True or False?

2. Augmented reality (AR) is a branch of virtual reality that generates a virtual scene that is overlaid on a real object. True or False?

3. Quantum computing uses quantum mechanics that generates and manipulates quantum bits or qubits. True or False?

4. All of the following are among the advantages of edge computing except:
   a. Real-time data analysis
   b. Lower operating costs
   c. Reduced network traffic
   d. All of these choices

5. All of the following are among the current business applications of VR systems except:
   a. Deep learning
   b. Assistance for the disabled
   c. Architectural design
   d. Flight simulation

6. All of the following are alternatives when using cloud computing except:
   a. Multicloud
   b. Edge cloud
   c. Hybrid cloud
   d. Distributed cloud

Case Study 14-1
Cloud Computing at InterContinental Hotels Group (IHG)
➤➤ Finance | Technology in Society | Application | Reflective Thinking

InterContinental Hotels Group (IHG) operates over 4,000 hotels in 100 countries under seven brands, including Holiday Inn and InterContinental. It is also the largest Western supplier of hotel rooms in China.[75]

IHG uses several types of cloud computing platforms to improve the efficiency and effectiveness of its operations. In addition to cost savings, the company said it moved into cloud computing because it wanted a faster and more flexible way of getting a new system up and running, and because of the cloud's ease of integrating various applications under a single platform. According to Bryson Koehler, IHG's senior vice president of revenue and guest information, savings also come in other ways, "such as improved flexibility and the ability to deliver a more tailored experience to end users." IHG is building a private cloud for its CRM applications using Salesforce.com's CRM. It is also building a private cloud called Camelot for its loyalty program. Camelot performs several major tasks. First, it analyzes current guest

(iStock.com/stevegeer)

activity and maintains historical records for future use. Second, it is used for promotions tailored to individual guests. Third, it runs revenue management and room-yield operations, from which room rates are calculated.

The public cloud at IHG is used for application development and testing. This includes steps similar to the systems development life cycle (SDLC) discussed in Module 10. The platform chosen for this operation was Amazon Web Services' Elastic Compute Cloud infrastructure. At least three cloud delivery models are in use at IHG, including SaaS, IaaS, and a private cloud.[76]

Answer the following questions:

1. What are some of the reasons that IHG moved into cloud computing?
2. What are the three cloud delivery models used at IHG?
3. How does IHG use different cloud delivery models?
4. Why are business functions separated into different cloud models?

Case Study 14-2
Virtual Reality Enhances "Try Before You Buy" Concept
⬤➤ Finance | Technology in Society | Application | Reflective Thinking

A growing number of businesses are using VR, AR, and MR in creative ways to sell more products and services, improve customer service, and reduce operational costs. These technologies enable businesses to promote their products in an entirely new way. Here are a few examples: Audi, the German car maker, uses VR at its dealerships, which allows customers to configure their new Audi and experience their dream car virtually in real time.[77] Manufacturers such as Boeing and Airbus use virtual technology to eliminate the need for expensive, full-scale prototypes of their designs.[78] Marriott International uses VR for event planning. Event organizers and customers can get a realistic idea of how their event will look with a VR-powered headset. Users can get 360-degree, 3D views of custom-designed room set-ups and all the fixtures, making event planning easier than ever.[79]

As another example, Lowe's operates more than 2,370 home improvement and hardware stores in the United States and Canada. In select U.S. markets, Lowe's gives its customers the opportunity to design their perfect bathroom or kitchen and then, using VR, walk through the finished space to get the look and feel of the final product. The VR/AR platform used by Lowe's is called Holoroom and is powered by Marxent's Visual Commerce application. Lowe's Holoroom customers work with a trained sales associate to choose from thousands of SKUs (stock keeping units), from paint and flooring to plumbing fixtures and appliances. According to Marxent, the items chosen by customers are added to the design as virtual 3D objects. After all the items are added and the customer is satisfied, the customer puts on an Oculus Rift headset (by Meta) to view the design space, get the look and feel, and make any adjustments. Customers can share the designed space with others by sending it to YouTube 360 and can view it at home with a Lowe's-supplied Google Cardboard. To bring their virtual design to life in the real world, customers order the products and services they selected.[80]

Answer the following questions:

1. How is VR changing sales?
2. What are some additional applications for VR and sales? Discuss.
3. How does Holoroom work at Lowe's?
4. What are two advantages of using Holoroom at Lowe's?

Endnotes

1

1. Pisani, J. "Small Business On-the-Go? Smartphones Can Help." *USA Today*. 25 May 2014. Accessed 20 October 2014 @ http://www.usatoday.com/story/money/business/2014/05/25/small-business-smartphone-apps/9445917/.

2. Dhvanesh. "Best Business Apps for iPhone and iPad in 2021." Igeeksblog.Com. 19 April 2021. Accessed 20 October 2021 @ https://www.igeeksblog.com/best-iphone-business-apps/.

3. Karmin, C. "Smartphones to Open Doors at Some Hotels." *Wall Street Journal*. 26 January 2014. Accessed 20 October 2021 @ https://www.wsj.com/articles/SB10001424052702304856504579339130820876304.

4. Reinhard, C-G. "YouTube Brands: 5 Outstanding Leaders in YouTube Marketing." Mashable. Accessed 5 July 2010 @ http://mashable.com/2009/06/01/youtube-brands/.

5. Evans, M. "34 Ways to Use YouTube for Business." GigaOm. 28 July 2009. Accessed 20 October 2021 @ https://gigaom.com/2009/07/28/34-ways-to-use-youtube-for-business/.

6. Liedtke, M. "Starbucks, Pepsi, Wal-Mart Pull YouTube Ads after They Were Placed on Racist Videos." *Chicago Tribune*. 24 March 2017. Accessed 6 November 2017 @ http://www.chicagotribune.com/bluesky/technology/ct-google-youtube-ad-boycott-20170324-story.html.

7. Rash, W. "Google, YouTube Face Obstacles in Effort to Rein in Fraudulent Content." eWeek. 14 March 2018. Accessed 8 March 2019 @ https://www.eweek.com/cloud/google-youtube-face-obstacles-in-effort-to-rein-in-fraudulent-content.

8. Salinas, S. "Nestlé and Others Have Suspended YouTube Ads Over News of a Pedophile Network on the Site." CNBC. 20 February 2019. Accessed 8 March 2019 @ https://www.cnbc.com/2019/02/20/disney-pulls-youtube-ads-over-pedophile-network-report.html.

9. Unknown. Number of monthly active Facebook users worldwide as of 2nd quarter 2021. Statista.com. 10 September 2021. Accessed 10 September 2021 @ https://www.statista.com/statistics/264810/number-of-monthly-active-facebook-users-worldwide/.

10. Gaudin, S. "Half of Social Networkers Post Risky Information, Study Finds." *InfoWorld*. 4 May 2010. Accessed 5 July 2010 @ www.infoworld.com/d/security-central/half-social-networkers-post-risky-information-study-finds-623?source=IFWNLE_nlt_wrapup_2010-05-04.

11. "First ATM Opens for Business." A&E Television Networks. Accessed 20 November 2016 @ http://www.history.com/this-day-in-history/first-atm-opens-for-business.

12. DeCambre, M. "This Is What the ATM of the Future Looks Like." Quartz. 13 June 2014. Accessed 20 November 2016 @ http://qz.com/219950/behold-the-atm-of-the-future-jpmorgan-is-now-rolling-out/.

13. Lee, J. "More Banks Turn to Biometrics to Keep an Eye on Security." NerdWallet. 20 May 2016. Accessed 20 November 2016 @ https://www.nerdwallet.com/blog/banking/biometrics-when-your-bank-scans-your-voice-face-or-eyes/.

14. Fernandes, D. "Banks Use ATM Apps to Entice Millennials." *Boston Globe*. 3 September 2015. Accessed 20 November 2016 @ http://www.betaboston.com/news/2015/09/03/banks-use-atm-apps-to-entice-millennials/.

15. Trichur, R. "Withdraw Cash Without a Card? There's an App for That." *Wall Street Journal*. 15 March 2015. Accessed 20 November 2016 @ http://www.wsj.com/articles/withdraw-cash-without-a-card-theres-an-app-for-that-1426459107.

16. Whitehouse, K. "Chase ATMs to Give Cash Via Smartphones." *USA Today*. 26 January 2016. Accessed 20 November 2016 @ http://www.usatoday.com/story/money/business/2016/01/26/chase-rolling-out-atms-give-cash-via-phone/79374222/.

17. "Making Pizza Since 1960." biz.dominos.com. Accessed 21 January 2013 @ https://biz.dominos.com/web/public/about-dominos/history.

18. "Domino's Pizza Hits Unprecedented $1 Billion in U.S. Digital Sales in One Year, Thanking Customers with Weeklong 50% Off Pizza Online Offer." biz.dominos.com. Accessed 21 January 2013 @ http://www.prnewswire.com/news-releases/dominos-pizza-hits-unprecedented-1-billion-in-us-digital-sales-in-one-year-thanking-customers-with-weeklong-50-off-pizza-online-offer-158409165.html.

19. Horowitz, B. "Domino's App Lets You Voice-Order Pizza." *USA Today*. 17 June 2014. Accessed 20 October 2014 @ http://www.usatoday.com/story/money/business/2014/06/16/dominos-voice-ordering-app-nuance-fast-food-restaurants/10626419/.

20. "Domino's to Roll Out Tweet-a-Pizza." 14 May 2015. *USA Today*. Accessed 1 December 2015 @ http://www.usatoday.com/story/money/2015/05/12/dominos-pizza-tweet-a-pizza-twitter-tweet-to-order-fast-food-restaurants/27175005/.

21. Bell, K. "You Can Now Order Domino's Pizza from a Facebook Messenger Bot." Mashable. 15 September 2016. Accessed 20 November 2016 @ http://mashable.com/2016/09/15/dominos-pizza-facebook-bot/#SNqwYdYmIOqG.

22. Bayly, L. "Domino's Debuts Pizza Delivery by Robot." CNBC. 18 March 2016. Accessed 20 November 2016 @ http://www.cnbc.com/2016/03/18/dominos-debuts-pizza-delivery-by-robot.html.

23. Zillman, C. "Domino's Is One Step Closer to Delivering Pizzas by Drone." *Fortune*. 25 August 2016. Accessed 20 November 2016 @ http://fortune.com/2016/08/25/dominos-pizza-drone-delivery.

24. "Domino's Testing Self-Driving Pizza Delivery." CNN. 29 August 2017. Accessed 6 November 2017 @ http://money.cnn.com/2017/08/29/technology/ford-dominos-self-driving-car/index.html.

25. Peters, B. "Domino's Pizza Just Began Delivery to Parks, Beaches, Thousands of Hot Spots." *Investor's Business Daily*. 16 April 2018. Accessed 8 March 2019 @ https://www.investors.com/news/dominos-pizza-hotspots-delivery/.

26. Smith, C. "Domino's Developing In-Car Pizza Ordering App Because Why Not?" Motor1.com. 26 March 2019. Accessed 27 March 2019 @ https://www.motor1.com/news/315498/dominos-creating-app-in-car-pizza/.

27. Benveniste, A. "Domino's Is Launching a Pizza Delivery Robot Car." CNN.com. 13 April 2021. Accessed 10 September 2021 @ https://edition.cnn.com/2021/04/12/tech/dominos-pizza-delivery-robot/index.html.

28. Schlesinger, J., and Day, A. "Card Sharks: ATM Skimming Grows More Sophisticated." CNBC. 16 September 2017. Accessed 6 November 2017 @ https://www.cnbc.com/2017/09/15/card-sharks-atm-skimming-grows-more-sophisticated.html.

29. Finkle, J. "ATM Makers Warn of 'Jackpotting' Hacks on U.S. Machines." Reuters. 27 January 2018. Accessed 8 March 2019 @ https://www.reuters.com/article/us-cyber-atms-usa/atm-makers-warn-of-jackpotting-hacks-on-u-s-machines-idUSKBN1FG0WU.

30. Bidgoli, H. *Handbook of Management Information Systems: A Managerial Perspective*. San Diego, CA: Academic Press, 1999.

31. Admin/Project Management. "Strategic Information System | Competitive Advantage & Market Research." Planningtank.com. 08 December 2020. Accessed 10 October 2021 @ https://planningtank.com/project-management/strategic-information-system.

32. Unknown. "Characteristics of Strategic Information Management." Includehelp.com. Accessed 10 October 2021 @ https://www.includehelp.com/MIS/characteristics-of-strategic-information-management.aspx.

33. Unknown. "The Home Depot: Helping Doers Get More Done through a Data-Driven Approach." Accessed 20 October 2021 @ https://cloud.google.com/customers/the-home-depot.

34. Unknown. "The Home Depot's Data-Driven Focus on Customer Success." Accessed 20 October 2021 @ https://cloud.google.com/customers/featured/the-home-depot.

35. "The Home Depot Transitions to Fujitsu U-Scan Retail Self-Checkout Software." Fujitsu.com. 13 January 2010. Accessed 20 October 2010 @ https://www.fujitsu.com/us/about/resources/news/press-releases/2010/fai-20100113.html.

36. "5 Technologies That Will Change the Way You Shop." Corporate.homedepot.com. 30 January 2017. Accessed 10 November 2017 @ https://corporate.homedepot.com/newsroom/nrf-2017-technologies-change-how-you-shop.

37. Cain, Á. "Home Depot Plans to Foil Shoplifters with Power Tools That Won't Work If They're Stolen." Insider. 22 July 2021. Accessed 10 September 2021 @ https://www.businessinsider.com/home-depot-fights-shoplifters-special-power-tools-2021-7.

38. Sarah, F. G. "Small Companies Can Benefit from an HRIS." 26 September 2012. Accessed 2 January 2014 @ https://workforce.com/news/small-companies-can-benefit-from-an-hris.

39. Osterhaus, E. "Compare Web-Based Human Resources (HR) Software." 17 December 2013. Accessed 2 January 2014 @ www.softwareadvice.com/hr/web-based-hr-software-comparison.

40. "UPS Uses Technology and Operational Efficiencies to Reduce Fuel Consumption and Emissions." UPS Pressroom. Accessed 20 January 2012 @ www.pressroom.ups.com/Fact+Sheets/ci.UPS+Uses+Technology+and+Operational+Efficiencies+to+Reduce+Fuel+Consumption+and+Emissions.print.

41. "Why UPS Trucks Never Turn Left." YouTube. Accessed 20 January 2012 @ www.youtube.com/watch?v=HV_bJxkdNDE&feature=relmfu.

42. Terdiman, D. "UPS Turns Data Analysis into Big Savings." CNET. 2 April 2010. Accessed 20 January 2012 @ https://www.cnet.com/news/ups-turns-data-analysis-into-big-savings/.

43. "UPS Changes the Delivery Game with New Intercept Service." UPS Pressroom. 26 March 2007. Accessed 20 January 2012 @ https://postandparcel.info/17040/news/ups-changes-the-delivery-game-with-new-intercept-service/.

44. Gudema, L. "7 Marketing Technologies Every Company Must Use." *Harvard Business Review*. 3 November 2014. Accessed 20 November 2016 @ https://hbr.org/2014/11/7-marketing-technologies-every-company-must-use.

45. Porter, M. "How Competitive Forces Shape Strategy." *Harvard Business Review* (March–April 1979).

46. Hays, C. "What Walmart Knows About Customers' Habits." *New York Times*. 14 November 2004. Accessed 28 January 2013 @ www.nytimes.com/2004/11/14/business/yourmoney/14wal.html?_r=1&.

47. Matney, L. "Walmart Is Bringing VR Instruction to All of Its U.S. Training Centers." Oath Tech Network. 31 May 2017. Accessed 6 November 2017 @ https://techcrunch.com/2017/05/31/walmart-is-bringing-vr-instruction-to-all-of-its-u-s-training-centers/.

48. Wehner, M. "Walmart Is Deploying In-Store Autonomous Robots in over 50 Locations." BGR Media, LLC. 28 October 2017. Accessed 6 November 2017 @ http://bgr.com/2017/10/28/walmart-robots-store-locations-50-states/.

49. Schuman, E. "Walmart's Mobile Checkout Trial Is a Major Advance." *Computerworld*. 23 April 2018. Accessed 8 March 2019 @ https://www.computerworld.com/article/3269226/walmart-s-mobile-checkout-trial-is-a-major-advance.html.

50. "Shop as Fast as you Text." Accessed 12 October 2021 @ https://texttoshop.walmart.com/what-it-can-do.

51. Porter, M. "How Competitive Forces Shape Strategy." *Harvard Business Review* (March–April 1979).

52. Dean, B. "Netflix Subscriber and Growth Statistics: How Many People Watch Netflix in 2021?" backlinko.com. 7 October 2021. Accessed 10 October 2021 @ https://backlinko.com/netflix-users.

53. McEntee, K. "Cloud Connect Keynote: Complexity and Freedom." Netflix Tech Blog. 8 March 2011. Accessed 9 August 2011 @ http://techblog.netflix.com/2011/03/cloud-connect-eynote-complexity-and.html.

54. Thompson, C. "If You Liked This, You're Sure to Love That." *New York Times Magazine*. 21 November 2008. Accessed 9 August 2011 @ www.nytimes.com/2008/11/23/magazine/23Netflix-t.html?pagewanted=all.

55. Sadeh, G. "How Netflix Uses Big Data to Create Content and Enhance User Experience." ClickZ. 20 March 2019. Accessed 10 September 2021 @ https://www.clickz.com/how-netflix-uses-big-data-content/228201/.

56. Yu, A. "How Netflix Uses AI, Data Science, and Machine Learning — From a Product Perspective." Medium. 27 February 2019. Accessed 10 September 2021 @ https://becominghuman.ai/how-netflix-uses-ai-and-machine-learning-a087614630fe.

57. Unknown. "Retail Technology: 5 Trends That Are Changing Retail as We Know It." Plug and Play Tech Center. 5 January 2021. Accessed 20 October 2021 @ https://www.plugandplaytechcenter.com/resources/retail-technology-5-trends-are-changing-retail-we-know-it/.

58. Quirk, M. B. "Neiman Marcus, Nordstrom & Other Retailers Trying Out Smart Fitting Room Mirrors." Consumerist.com. 11 May 2015. Accessed 1 December 2015 @ http://consumerist.com/2015/05/11/neiman-marcus-nordstrom-other-retailers-trying-out-smart-fitting-room-mirrors/.

59. Charlton, G. "11 Great Ways to Use Digital Technology in Retail Stores." eConsultancy.com. 18 July 2013. Accessed 1 December 2015 @ https://econsultancy.com/blog/63087-11-great-ways-to-use-digital-technology-in-retail-stores/.

60. Linthicum, D. "The Cloud Job Market: A Golden Opportunity for IT Pros." *InfoWorld*. 1 July 2010. Accessed 3 July 2010 @ http://www.infoworld.com/d/cloud-computing/the-cloud-job-market-golden-opportunity-it-pros-817.

61. Kawamoto, D. "CISOs' Salaries Expected to Edge Above $240,000 in 2018." *InformationWeek*. 1 September 2017. Accessed 6 November 2017 @ https://www.darkreading.com/application-security/cisos-salaries-expected-to-edge-above-$240000-in-2018/d/d-id/1329787.

62. "10 Jobs That Didn't Exist 10 Years Ago." *Kiplinger*. 15 February 2011. Accessed 20 January 2012 @ https://digitalmarketinginstitute.com/blog/10-jobs-didnt-exist-10-years-ago.

63. Strohmeyer, R. "The 6 Hottest New Jobs in IT." *InfoWorld*. 14 June 2011. Accessed 20 January 2012 @ www.infoworld.com/t/information-technology-careers/the-6-hottest-new-jobs-in-it-052?page=0,0&source=IFWNLE_nlt_daily_2011-06-18.

64. Granville, V. "6000 Companies Hiring Data Scientists." Data Science Central. 29 December 2013. Accessed 20 November 2016 @ http://www.datasciencecentral.com/profiles/blogs/6000-companies-hiring-data-scientists.

65. Chang, R. "What Is a Data Scientist?" Quora. 4 September 2015. Accessed 20 November 2016 @ https://www.quora.com/What-is-a-data-scientist-3.

66. "What Do Data Scientists Do?" University of Wisconsin. Accessed 20 November 2016 @ http://datasciencedegree.wisconsin.edu/data-science/what-do-data-scientists-do/.

67. Zhang, V., and Neimeth, C. "Top 5 Traits of Highly Effective Data Scientists." *InfoWorld*. 15 August 2017. Accessed 6 November 2017 @ http://www.infoworld.com/article/3215868/data-science/top-5-traits-of-highly-effective-data-scientists.html.

68. Davis, J. "Microsoft Launches Online Data Science Degree Program." *InformationWeek*. 15 July 2016. Accessed 20 November 2016 @ http://www.informationweek.com/big-data/big-data-analytics/microsoft-launches-online-data-science-degree-program/d/d-id/1326276.

69. Thibodeau, Patrick. "Gartner's Crystal Ball Foresees an Emerging 'Super Class' of Technologies." *ComputerWorld*. 6 October 2014. Accessed 10 September 2019 @ http://www.computerworld.com/article/2691607/one-in-three-jobs-will-be-taken-by-software-or-robots-by-2025.html.

70. Thibodeau, P. "Gartner Lays Out Its Top 10 Tech Trends for 2015." *InfoWorld*. 8 October 2014. Accessed 20 October 2014 @ http://www.infoworld.com/article/2692501/internet-of-things/gartner-lays-out-its-top-10-tech-trends-for-2015.html?source=IFWNLE_nlt_cloud_2014-10-09#tk.rss_cloudcomputing.

71. Franklin Jr., C. "Gartner's 10 Tech Predictions That Will Change IT." *InformationWeek*. 28 October 2016. Accessed 20 November 2016 @ http://www.informationweek.com/devops/gartners-10-tech-predictions-that-will-change-it/d/d-id/1327316?_mc=NL_IWK_EDT_IWK_mobile_20161101&elq=cf87b4524ae74a69a06446f66cf9fc64&cid=NL_IWK_EDT_IWK_mobile_20161101&elqTrackId=f7beab6016e84b7ba7e916766fd1c2b4&elqaid=74368&elqat=1&elqCampaignId=24079&image_number=1.

72. This information has been gathered from the Microsoft Web site and other promotional materials. For detailed information and updates, visit www.microsoft.com.

73. Babcock, C. "FedEx Locks in Customers by Tying Shipping Data to Back-Office Apps." *InformationWeek*. 12 September 2006. Accessed 3 July 2010 @ https://www.informationweek.com/software/fedex-locks-in-customers-by-tying-shipping-data-to-back-office-apps.

74. Gage, D. "FedEx: Personal Touch." *Baseline*. 13 January 2005. Accessed 3 July 2010 @ www.baselinemag.com/c/a/Projects-Supply-Chain/FedEx-Personal-Touch.

75. Zimmerman, A. "Check Out the Future of Shopping." *Wall Street Journal Online*. 18 May 2011. Accessed 20 January 2012 @ http://online.wsj.com/article/SB10001424052748703421204576329253050637400.html?mod=djem_jiewr_IT_domainid.

2

1. Alabaster, J. "IBM Moving to Replace Silicon with Carbon Nanotubes in Computer Chips." *Computerworld*. 29 October 2012. Accessed 21 January 2013 @ www.computerworld.com/s/article/9232997/IBM_moving_to_replace_silicon_with_carbon_nanotubes_in_computer_chips.

2. Marquardt, M. "The Rise of Carbon Nanotube Electronics." Embedded Computing Design. 8 February 2022. Accessed 22 February 2022 @ https://www.embeddedcomputing.com/technology/security/hardware-security/the-rise-of-carbon-nanotube-electronics.

3. Neuman, S. "IBM Announces Breakthrough in Chip Technology." NPR. 9 July 2015. Accessed 1 December 2015 @ http://www.npr.org/sections/thetwo-way/2015/07/09/421477061/ibm-announces-breakthrough-in-chip-technology.

4. "IBM 2nm Chip Breakthrough Claims More Power with Less Energy." BBC. 2 May 2021. Accessed 20 October 2021 @ https://www.bbc.com/news/technology-57009930.

5. Paul, I. "IBM Watson Wins Jeopardy, Humans Rally Back." *PCWorld*. 17 February 2011. Accessed 9 August 2011 @ www.pcworld.com/article/219900/ibm_watson_wins_jeopardy_humans_rally_back.html.

6. Hamm, S. "Watson on Jeopardy! Day Two: The Confusion over an Airport Clue." Building a Smarter Planet. 15 February 2011. Accessed 20 October 2021 @ https://asmarterplanet.com/blog/2011/02/watson-on-jeopardy-day-two-the-confusion-over-an-airport-clue.html.

7. IBM. "This Is Watson." Accessed 8 February 2012 @ https://www.ibm.com/blogs/think/category/this-is-watson/.

8. Sareen, H. "IBM Watson-Powered Mobile Apps Can Reinvigorate Brick-and-Mortar Retailers." *Wired*. 19 March 2014. Accessed 10 September 2019 @ https://www.wired.com/insights/2014/03/ibm-watson-powered-mobile-apps-can-reinvigorate-brick-mortar-retailers/.

9. Gaudin, S. "App as Fitness Instructor? Watson-Based App Aims to Keep You Healthier." *Computerworld*. 12 November 2014. Accessed 10 September 2019 @ http://www.computerworld.com/article/2846757/app-as-fitness-instructor-watson-based-app-aims-to-keep-you-healthier.html.

10. O'Neil, S. "Startup Pitch: IBM's Watson Powers New Travel Advice Tool Wayblazer." Tnooz. 7 October 2014. Accessed 10 September 2019 @ http://www.tnooz.com/article/startup-pitch-wayblazer-aims-travel-insights-service/.

11. "H&R Block with IBM Watson Reinventing Tax Preparation." HRB Digital LLC. 2 February 2017. Accessed 12 November 2017 @ https://www.hrblock.com/tax-center/newsroom/around-block/partnership-with-ibm-watson-reinventing-tax-prep.

12. "Watson to Gain Ability to 'See' with Planned $1B Acquisition of Merge Healthcare." Clinical Leader. 6 August 2015. Accessed 1 December 2015 @ http://www.clinicalleader.com/doc/watson-to-gain-ability-planned-acquisition-merge-healthcare-0001.

13. "IBM's Supercomputer Watson to Help Fight Brain Cancer." BBC. 3 March 2014. Accessed 20 October 2021 @ https://www.bbc.com/news/technology-26662230.

14. Martin, A. "Softbank's Supercomputer Solution for Call Centers Is Elementary: Watson." *Wall Street Journal*. 14 April 2015. Accessed 1 December 2015 @ http://blogs.wsj.com/digits/2015/04/14/softbanks-supercomputer-solution-for-call-centers-is-elementary-watson/?mod=ST1.

15. Nick, T. "A Modern Smartphone or a Vintage Supercomputer: Which Is More Powerful?" Phonearena. 14 June 2014. Accessed 1 December 2015 @ http://www.phonearena.com/news/A-modern-smartphone-or-a-vintage-supercomputer-which-is-more-powerful_id57149.

16. Desjardins, J. "The Supercomputer in Your Pocket." Visual Capitalist. 19 August 2015. Accessed 20 October 2021 @ https://www.visualcapitalist.com/the-supercomputer-in-your-pocket/.

17. "Number of Available Applications in the Google Play Store from December 2009 to July 2021." Statista. 23 September 2021. Accessed 20 October 2021 @ https://www.statista.com/statistics/266210/number-of-available-applications-in-the-google-play-store/.

18. "Number of Available Apps in the Apple App Store from 2008 to 2021." Statista. 31 August 2021. Accessed 20 October 2021 @ https://www.statista.com/statistics/268251/number-of-apps-in-the-itunes-app-store-since-2008/.

19. "The Disruptors: Touchless Computing." CNBC. Accessed 2 January 2014 @ http://video.cnbc.com/gallery/?play=1&video=3000178509.

20. Ibid.

21. Welch, C. "Reading News Through Gestures: The *New York Times* to Release Leap Motion App." *The Verge*. 18 July 2013. Accessed 2 January 2014 @ www.theverge.com/2013/7/18/4535284/new-york-times-to-release-leap-motion-gesture-app.

22. Shah, A. "Screens That Fold and Roll Will Arrive as Early as Next Year." *Computerworld*. 8 July 2016. Accessed 20 November 2016 @ http://www.computerworld.com/article/3093450/computer-hardware/screens-that-fold-and-roll-will-arrive-as-early-as-next-year.html.

23. Haselton, T. "Samsung Just Announced the First Foldable Phone You Can Buy and It Will Cost $1,980." CNBC. 20 February 2019. Accessed 11 March 2019 @ https://www.cnbc.com/2019/02/20/samsung-galaxy-fold-release-date-price-specs.html.

24. Papazoglou, G. "Foldable Phones: The Case For and Against this Latest Trend." fieldscale.com. 14 November 2018. Accessed 11 March 2019 @ https://fieldscale.com/blog/foldable-phones-for-against-2/.

25. Elgan, M. "The Dark Side of Folding-Screen and Dual-Screen Smartphones." *Computerworld*. 3 November 2018. Accessed 11 March 2019 @ https://www.computerworld.com/article/3317520/the-dark-side-of-folding-screen-and-dual-screen-smartphones.html.

26. Haselton, T. "Microsoft's New $1,500 Folding Phone Is a Huge Improvement from Last Year." CNBC. 21 October 2021. Accessed 10 November 2021 @ https://www.cnbc.com/2021/10/21/microsoft-surface-duo-2-review-a-huge-improvement-from-last-year.html.

27. Fu, A. "What Is Cloud Printing? How Cloud Printing Works." Uniprint. 7 February 2018. Accessed 11 March 2019 @ https://www.uniprint.net/en/what-cloud-printing/.

28. Associated Press. "Hear Google's Virtual Assistant Mimic a Human Voice to Book an Appointment by Phone – Video." *The Guardian*. 8 May 2018. Accessed 21 April 2019 @ https://www.theguardian.com/technology/video/2018/may/09/new-google-assistant-mimics-human-voice-video.

29. Saleem, U. "5 Most Reliable High Capacity SSDs to Buy in 2022." Appuals. 27 December 2021. Accessed 22 February 2022 @ https://appuals.com/best-reliable-ssds/.

30. Prigge, M. "Cloud Storage: The Final Nail in Tape's Coffin." *InfoWorld*. 24 September 2012. Accessed 21 January 2013 @ www.infoworld.com/d/data-explosion/cloud-storage-the-final-nail-in-tapes-coffin-202891?source=IFWNLE_nlt_daily_2012-09-24.

31. Associated Press. "5 Reasons Your Business Will Love Cloud Storage." EZ Computer Solutions. Accessed 21 April 2019 @ https://www.ezcomputersolutions.com/blog/5-reasons-for-business-cloud-storage/.

32. Rathnam, L. "Why Is Cloud Storage a Good Idea?" Cloudwards. 8 March 2018. Accessed 21 April 2019 @ https://www.cloudwards.net/cloud-storage-good-idea/.

33. "TOP 500 LIST - JUNE 2021." TOP500.org. Accessed 20 October 2021 @ https://www.top500.org/lists/top500/list/2021/06/.

34. "Apple Sells Three Million iPads in 80 Days." Apple Press Info. 22 June 2010. Accessed 5 July 2010 @ https://www.apple.com/se/newsroom/2010/06/22Apple-Sells-Three-Million-iPads-in-80-Days/.

35. Cox, A. "Best Business iPad Apps of 2021." 26 July 2021. Accessed 20 October 2021 @ https://www.techradar.com/best/best-business-ipad-apps.

36. Ferguson, S. "Smart Wearables Hold Productivity Potential in Enterprises." *InformationWeek*. 9 September 2016. Accessed 20 November 2016 @ http://www.informationweek.com/mobile/mobile-devices/smart-wearables-hold-productivity-potential-in-enterprises/d/d-id/1326829?.

37. Kelsky, A. "Wearable Technology's Impact on the Manufacturing Industry." Exclusive. 3 August 2015. Accessed 20 October 2021 @ https://exclusive.multibriefs.com/content/wearable-technologys-impact-on-the-manufacturing-industry/science-technology.

38. Thompson, C. "Wearable Tech Is Getting a Lot More Intimate." Entrepreneur. 26 December 2013. Accessed 18 July 2019 @ www.entrepreneur.com/article/230555.

39. "Computex Offers a Look at Our Tech Hardware Future." *Computerworld*. 7 June 2014. http://www.computerworld.com/s/article/9248945/Computex_offers_a_look_at_our_tech_hardware_future.

40. Greene, J. "Google, Nike, Jawbone and the Fight to Win Wearable Computing." CNET. 2 May 2013. Accessed 2 January 2014 @ http://news.cnet.com/8301-11386_3-57582475-76/google-nike-jawbone-and-the-fight-to-win-wearable-computing/.

41. Savage, M. "Thousands of Swedes Are Inserting Microchips Under Their Skin." NPR.

22 October 2018. Accessed 21 April 2019 @ https://www.npr.org/2018/10/22/658808705/thousands-of-swedes-are-inserting-microchips-under-their-skin.

42. Farr, C. "A Giant Insurer Is Offering Free Apple Watches to Customers Who Meet Walking Goals." CNBC. 15 November 2018. Accessed 21 April 2019 @ https://www.cnbc.com/2018/11/14/unitedhealthcare-gives-free-apple-watches-if-walking-goals-met.html.

43. "What's the Difference between Office 365 and Office 2016?" Microsoft. Accessed 20 November 2016 @ https://support.office.com/en-us/article/What-s-the-difference-between-Office-365-and-Office-2016-ed447ebf-6060-46f9-9e90-a239bd27eb96.

44. Devine, R. "What Is Microsoft Office 365?" Windows Central. 22 September 2015. Accessed 20 November 2016 @ http://www.windowscentral.com/what-microsoft-office-365.

45. Moran, M. "Top 10 Benefits of Microsoft Office 365." LinkedIn. 22 September 2015. Accessed 20 November 2016 @ https://www.linkedin.com/pulse/top-10-benefits-microsoft-office-365-michael-j-moran.

46. Berrios, F. "Office 365 Pros and Cons." Credera. 9 June 2014. Accessed 20 November 2016 @ https://www.credera.com/blog/technology-insights/microsoft-solutions/office-365-pros-cons/.

47. Mills, A. "5 Things to Know About the iOS 11.1 Update." GottaBeMobile. 31 October 2017. Accessed 12 November 2017 @ https://www.gottabemobile.com/5-things-to-know-about-the-ios-11-1-update/.

48. "Most Popular Programming Languages in 2021." Stackscale.com. 13 September 2021. Accessed 20 October 2021 @ https://www.stackscale.com/blog/popular-programming-languages-2021/.

49. This information has been gathered from the IBM Web site and other promotional materials. For detailed information and updates, visit www.ibm.com.

50. Sherr, I. "Manage Your Money." *Wall Street Journal.* 27 August 2012. Accessed 21 January 2013 @ http://online.wsj.com/article/SB10000872396390444405804577559160257519518.html?mod=djem_jiewr_IT_domainid.

51. Ludwig, L. "The Rise of the Robo Advisors – Should You Use One?" Investor Junkie. 2 April 2019. Accessed 21 April 2019 @ https://investorjunkie.com/35919/robo-advisors/.

52. Gruman, G. "Why Field Service Workers Love Their iPads." *InfoWorld.* 16 May 2014. Accessed 10 September 2019 @ http://www.infoworld.com/d/mobile-technology/why-field-service-workers-love-their-ipads-241135?source=IFWNLE_nlt_daily_pm_2014-05-16.

3

1. Smalltree, H. "Business Intelligence Case Study: Gartner Lauds Police for Crime-Fighting BI." TechTarget. 5 April 2007. Accessed 5 July 2010 @ http://searchbusinessanalytics.techtarget.com/news/1507220/Business-intelligence-case-study-Gartner-lauds-police-for-crime-fighting-BI.

2. Kim, S. H., Yu, B., and Chang, J. "Zoned-Partitioning of Tree-Like Access Methods." *Information Systems* 33(3) (2008): 315–331.

3. Jackson, J. "Graph Databases Find Answers for the Sick and Their Healers." *Computerworld.* 6 June 2014. Accessed 20 October 2014 @ http://www.computerworld.com/s/article/9248929/Graph_databases_find_answers_for_the_sick_and_their_healers.

4. "How Graph Databases Are Transforming Online Dating." Bitnine. 28 September 2016. Accessed 1 May 2019 @ https://bitnine.net/blog-graph-database/how-graph-databases-are-transforming-online-dating/.

5. Sadowski, G., and Rathle, P. "Why Modern Fraud Detection Needs Graph Database Technology." Neo4j. 4 January 2016. Accessed 1 May 2019 @ https://neo4j.com/blog/fraud-detection-graph-database-technology/.

6. Woods, D. "50 Shades of Graph: How Graph Databases Are Transforming Online Dating." *Forbes.* 14 February 2014. Accessed 20 October 2014 @ http://www.forbes.com/sites/danwoods/2014/02/14/50-shades-of-graph-how-graph-databases-are-transforming-online-dating/.

7. Storey, V. C., and Goldstein, R. C. "Knowledge-Based Approaches to Database Design." *MIS Quarterly* (March 1993): 25–32.

8. Rauch-Hindin, W. "True Distributed DBMSs Presage Big Dividends." *Mini-Micro Systems* (May 1987): 65–73.

9. Brueggen, D., and Lee, S. "Distributed Database Systems: Accessing Data More Efficiently." *Journal of Information Systems Management* (Spring 1995): 15–20.

10. Inmon, W. H. *Building the Data Warehouse.* 4th ed. New York: Wiley, 2005.

11. "About Marriott International: A World of Opportunity." Marriott. Accessed 27 January 2013 @ www.marriott.com/marriott/aboutmarriott.mi.

12. Swanborg, R. "CRM: How Marriott Broke Down Customer Data Siloes." *CIO* (USA). 16 November 2009. Accessed 27 January 2013 @ https://www.computerworld.com/article/2764959/crm--how-marriott-broke-down-customer-data-siloes.html.

13. Tremblay, M. C., Fuller, R., Berndt, D., et al. "Doing More with More Information: Changing Healthcare Planning with OLAP Tools." *Decision Support Systems* 43(4) (2007): 1305–1320.

14. IBM Cloud Education. "Text Mining." IBM. 16 November 2020. Accessed 10 September 2021 @ https://www.ibm.com/cloud/learn/text-mining.

15. St. Jeor, C. "Text Analytics: 5 Examples to Open Your Eyes to Your Own Opportunities." Zencos. 01 October 2020. Accessed 10 September 2021 @ https://www.zencos.com/blog/text-mining-examples-advanced-analytics/.

16. "Data Lake vs. Data Warehouse." Talend. Accessed 10 September 2021 @ https://www.talend.com/resources/data-lake-vs-data-warehouse/.

17. Nicas, J. "How Airlines Mine Personal Data In-Flight." *Wall Street Journal.* 8 November 2013. Accessed 2 January 2014 @ https://www.wsj.com/articles/SB10001424052702304384104579139923818792360.

18. "How Amazon Is Solving Big-Data Challenges with Data Lakes." All Things Distributed. 20 January 2020. Accessed 10 September 2021 @ https://www.allthingsdistributed.com/2020/01/aws-datalake.html.

19. Marr, B. "What Are the Best Big Data Cloud Storage Providers? Here Are the Top 6." *Forbes.* 11 May 2020. Accessed 10 September 2021 @ https://www.forbes.com/sites/bernardmarr/2020/05/11/what-are-the-best-big-data-cloud-storage-providers-here-are-the-top-6/?sh=71a7be565cd2.

20. Bertolucci, J. "Big Data Analytics: Descriptive vs. Predictive vs. Prescriptive." *InformationWeek.* 31 December 2013. Accessed 10 September 2019 @ http://www.informationweek.com/big-data/big-data-analytics/big-data-analytics-descriptive-vs-predictive-vs-prescriptive/d/d-id/1113279.

21. "About Us." Airbnb Newsroom. Accessed 10 September 2019 @ https://www.airbnb.com/about-us.

22. Carr, J. "Why an Airbnb Data Scientist Does Actual Scientific Experiments." Accessed 20 October 2022 @ https://mixpanel.com/blog/tag/airbnb/.

23. "Airbnb Now Uses Analytics to Boost Bookings." Pymnts. 3 July 2015. Accessed 1 December 2015 @ http://www.pymnts.com/news/2015/airbnb-now-uses-analytics-to-boost-bookings/.

24. Hansen, A. "3 Major Types of Mobile Analytics." Tune. 14 May 2014. Accessed 23 November 2017 @ https://www.tune.com/blog/3-major-types-of-mobile-analytics/.

25. Farmer, D. "Getting Your Hands on Data with Mobile Analytics." *InfoWorld.* 16 July 2014. Accessed 10 September 2019 @ http://www.infoworld.com/t/business-intelligence/getting-your-hands-data-mobile-analytics-246331?source=IFWNLE_nlt_daily_pm_2014-07-16.

26. Dykes, B. "Web Analytics vs. Mobile Analytics: What's the Difference?" Analytics Hero. 24 July 2013. Accessed 10 September 2019 @ http://www.analyticshero.com/2013/07/24/web-analytics-vs-mobile-analytics-whats-the-difference/.

27. Vijayan, J. "Time Has Come for Chief Analytics Officers." *Computerworld.* 11 October 2012. Accessed 18 December 2012 @ https://www.computerworld.com/article/2492218/time-has-come-for-chief-analytics-officers.html.

28. "eBay Study: How to Build Trust and Improve the Shopping Experience." W. P. Carey News. 8 May 2012. Accessed 10 September 2019 @ https://news.wpcarey.asu.edu/20120508-ebay-study-how-build-trust-and-improve-shopping-experience.

29. Vijayan, J. "How Predictive Analytics Can Deliver Strategic Benefits." *Computerworld.* 20 September 2011. Accessed 11 November 2011 @ www.computerworld.com/s/article/9220131/How_predictive_analytics_can_deliver_strategic_benefits.

30. Laney, D. "3D Data Management: Controlling Data Volume, Velocity, and Variety." META Group. 6 February 2001. Accessed 10 September 2019 @ https://studylib.net/doc/8647594/3d-data-management-controlling-data-volume-velocity-and-variety.

31. Marr, B. "Why Only One of the 5 Vs of Big Data Really Matters." IBM Big Data & Analytics Hub. 19 March 2015. Accessed

23 November 2017 @ https://bicorner. com/2015/04/17/why-only-one-of-the-5-vs-of-big-data-really-matters/.

32. Hagen, C., et al. "Big Data and the Creative Destruction of Today's Business Models." ATKearney. January 2013. Accessed 2 January 2014 @ https://www.co.kearney.com/analytics/article?/a/big-data-and-the-creative-destruction-of-today-s-business-models.

33. "How Will Big Data Revolutionize Retail?" SAS. Accessed 2 January 2014 @ https://data-flair.training/blogs/big-data-in-retail-industry/#:~:text=Big%20data%20analytics%20helps%20retailers,that%20are%20in%20high%20demand.

34. Jennings, R. "The Future of Retail: It's All in Big Data." *Forbes.* 26 November 2013. Accessed 2 January 2014 @ www. forbes.com/sites/netapp/2013/11/26/future-of-retail-big-data.

35. "Why Big Data Matters in PR." National. 19 August 2016. Accessed 20 October 2022 @ https://www.national.ca/en/perspectives/detail/why-big-data-matters-in-pr/.

36. Brandon, A. "Why Big Data Analytics Could Spell Big Energy Savings." TIBCO Spotfire. 27 February 2013. Accessed 2 January 2021 @ https://www.tibco.com/blog/2013/02/27/why-big-data-analytics-could-spell-big-energy-savings/.

37. Kennedy, K. "Analysis of Huge Data Sets Will Reshape Health Care." *USA Today.* 24 November 2013. Accessed 2 January 2014 @ www.usatoday.com/story/news/nation/2013/11/24/big-data-health-care/3631211.

38. Armerding, T. "The 5 Worst Big Data Privacy Risks (and How to Guard Against Them)." *InfoWorld.* 8 December 2014. Accessed 10 September 2019 @ https://www. infoworld.com/article/2856262/the-5-worst-big-data-privacy-risks-and-how-to-guard-against-them.html#tk.IFWNLE__2014-12-08.

39. Herold, R. "10 Big Data Analytics Privacy Problems." SecureWorld. 1 August 2014. Accessed 10 September 2019 @ https://www.secureworldexpo. com/10-big-data-analytics-privacy-problems.

40. Ibid.

41. King, J. "Data Analytics: Eye-Popping Results from Intel, UPS and Express Scripts." *Computerworld.* 15 July 2013. Accessed 2 January 2014 @ www.computerworld.com/s/article/9240746/Data_analytics_Eye_popping_results_from_Intel_UPS_and_Express_Scripts.

42. Ibid.

43. Verma, A. "Internet of Things and Big Data – Better Together." Whizlabs. 1 August 2018. Accessed 1 May 2019 @ https://www.whizlabs. com/blog/iot-and-big-data/.

44. Patrizio, A. "IDC: Expect 175 Zettabytes of Data Worldwide by 2025." Network World. 3 December 2018. Accessed 1 May 2019 @ https://www.networkworld.com/article/3325397/idc-expect-175-zettabytes-of-data-worldwide-by-2025.html.

45. Duval, J. "What Is Database Marketing and When Can It Be Used?" CustomerThink. 21 August 2013. Accessed 1 December 2015 @ http://customerthink.com/what_is_database_marketing_and_when_can_it_be_used/.

46. Woods, L. "Strengths & Weaknesses of Database Marketing." Bizfluent. 26 September 2017. Accessed 1 December 2019

@ https://bizfluent.com/info-8154604-strengths-weaknesses-database-marketing.html.

47. Kokemuller, N. "The Advantages & Disadvantages of Database Marketing." Chron. Accessed 1 December 2015 @ http://smallbusiness.chron.com/advantages-disadvantages-database-marketing-22810.html.

48. Kirkpatrick, D. "Database Marketing: Hearst Increases Direct Mail Response 25%, Creates 200% ROI." MarketingSherpa. 11 October 2012. Accessed 20 November 2016 @ https://www.marketingsherpa.com/article/case-study/hearst-increases-mail-response.

49. "Changing the Way You Think About Data." Tableau. Accessed 25 March 2019 @ https://www.tableau.com/.

50. Hughes, M. "Building Caterpillar Market Share with a Database." Database Marketing Institute. Accessed 10 September 2019 @ http://www.dbmarketing.com/articles/Art125.htm.

51. Ibid.

52. "What Is Power BI?" Microsoft. 6 February 2019. Accessed 25 March 2019 @ https://docs.microsoft.com/en-us/power-bi/power-bi-overview.

53. This information has been gathered from the Oracle Web site and other promotional materials. For detailed information and updates, visit www.oracle.com.

54. Parry, M. "Big Data on Campus." *New York Times.* 18 July 2012. Accessed 14 December 2012 @ www.nytimes. com/2012/07/22/education/edlife/colleges-awakening-to-the-opportunities-of-data-mining. html?pagewanted=all&_r=0.

55. "Company Info." Accessed 25 October 2021 @ https://newsroom.spotify.com/company-info/.

56. "Spotify's Premium Subscribers 2015-2021." Statista. 11 August 2021. Accessed 25 October 2021 @ https://www.statista.com/statistics/244995/number-of-paying-spotify-subscribers/#:~:text=As%20of%20the%20second%20quarter,than%20doubled%20since%20early%202017.

57. Rangaiah, M. "How Spotify Is Using Big Data to Enhance Customer Experience." AnalyticsSteps. 6 January 2021. Accessed 25 October 2021 @ https://www.analyticssteps.com/blogs/how-spotify-using-big-data.

58. Exposito, S. "Some People Were Just Not Buying 'Only You,' Spotify's Attempt at Flattery through Data-mining." *Los Angeles Times.* 3 June 2021. Accessed 25 October 2021 @ https://www.latimes.com/entertainment-arts/music/story/2021-06-03/spotify-only-you-birth-chart.

4

1. Samson, T. "Want a Job? This Site Reveals If You Have a Chance." *InfoWorld.* 11 November 2011. Accessed 28 January 2013 @ www.infoworld.com/t/information-technology-careers/want-job-site-reveals-if-you-have-chance-178745.

2. Porup, J. M. "How and Why Deepfake Videos Work—and What Is at Risk." *CSO.* 8 November 2018. Accessed 25 March 2019 @ https://www.csoonline.com/article/3293002/fraud/what-are-deepfakes-how-and-why-they-work.amp.html.

3. Wallach, O. "How to Spot Fake News." Visual Capitalist. 10 February 2021. Accessed 25 October 2021 @ https://www.visualcapitalist. com/how-to-spot-fake-news/.

4. Dwyer, C. "10 Ways to Spot Fake News." *Psychology Today.* 4 October 2019. Accessed 25 October 2021 @ https://www.psychologytoday. com/us/blog/thoughts-thinking/201910/10-ways-spot-fake-news.

5. Hamblen, M. "Privacy Worries Are on the Rise, New Poll of U.S. Consumers Shows." *Computerworld.* 30 January 2017. Accessed 23 November 2017 @ http://www.computerworld. com/article/3163207/data-privacy/privacy-worries-are-on-the-rise-new-poll-of-u-s-consumers-shows.html.

6. Read, B. "A MySpace Photo Costs a Student a Teaching Certificate." Chronicle of Higher Education. 27 April 2007. Accessed 6 August 2010 @ http://chronicle.com/blogs/wiredcampus/a-myspace-photo-costs-a-student-a-teaching-certificate/2994.

7. Harper, B. "Harvard Rescinds Acceptances for Prospective Students Due to Offensive Memes." 5 June 2017. Accessed 23 November 2017 @ https://www.thecrimson.com/article/2017/6/5/2021-offers-rescinded-memes/.

8. Hoyt, E. "Social Media Guidelines for Students." Fastweb. 11 January 2017. Accessed 22 May 2019 @ https://www.fastweb.com/student-life/articles/social-media-guidelines-for-students.

9. Ante, S., and Weber, L. "Memo to Workers: The Boss Is Watching." *Wall Street Journal.* 22 October 2013. Accessed 2 January 2014 @ http://online.wsj.com/news/articles/SB10001424052702303672404579151440488919138?mod=djem_jiewr_IT_domainid.

10. Pace, J., and Dozier, K. "White House Task Force Urges Limit on NSA Snooping." *Associated Press.* 18 December 2013. Accessed 2 January 2014 @ https://apnews.com/article/cb3eedabffc14d4fa6c64365ca18c24e.

11. "NSA Spying on Americans." Electronic Frontier Foundation. Accessed 2 January 2014 @ www.eff.org/nsa-spying/timeline.

12. "Health Information Privacy." U.S. Department of Health and Human Services. Accessed 1 December 2015 @ http://www.hhs.gov/ocr/privacy/.

13. "FACTA Disposal Rule Goes into Effect June 1." Federal Trade Commission. 1 June 2005. Accessed 1 December 2015 @ https://www.ftc.gov/news-events/press-releases/2005/06/facta-disposal-rule-goes-effect-june-1.

14. "Children's Online Privacy Protection Rule (COPPA)." Federal Trade Commission. Accessed 1 December 2015 @ https://www.ftc.gov/enforcement/rules/rulemaking-regulatory-reform-proceedings/childrens-online-privacy-protection-rule.

15. De Groot, J. "A Definition of GDPR (General Data Protection Regulation)." Digital Guardian. 3 January 2019. Accessed 18 March 2019 @ https://digitalguardian.com/blog/what-gdpr-general-data-protection-regulation-understanding-and-complying-gdpr-data-protection.

16. "The Five Key Business Benefits of GDPR." Open Access Government. 16 April 2018. Accessed 18 March 2019 @

https://www.openaccessgovernment.org/the-five-key-business-benefits-of-gdpr/44554/.

17. Chee, F. Y. "European Consumer Groups Want Regulators to Act Against Google Tracking." Reuters. 26 November 2018. Accessed 18 March 2019 @ https://www.reuters.com/article/us-eu-google-privacy/european-consumer-groups-want-regulators-to-act-against-google-tracking-idUSKCN1NW0BS.

18. Porter, J. "Google Accused of GDPR Privacy Violations by Seven Countries." The Verge. 27 November 2018. Accessed 18 March 2019 @ https://www.theverge.com/2018/11/27/18114111/google-location-tracking-gdpr-challenge-european-deceptive.

19. Tschabitscher, H. "The Number of Emails Sent Per Day in 2019 (and 20+ Other Email Facts)." Lifewire. 3 January 2019. Accessed 20 March 2019 @ https://www.lifewire.com/how-many-emails-are-sent-every-day-1171210.

20. Conner, C. "Do These 8 Things Now to Reduce Email Risks." Forbes. 29 May 2017. Accessed 22 May 2019 @ https://www.forbes.com/sites/cherylsnappconner/2017/05/29/do-these-8-things-now-to-reduce-email-risks/#38b916b37bc8.

21. Wawro, A. "How to Protect Yourself from Supercookies." PCWorld. 26 August 2011. Accessed 23 November 2017 @ https://www.pcworld.com/article/238895/how_to_protect_yourself_from_supercookies.html.

22. Lauer, D. "Facebook's Ethical Failures Are Not Accidental; They Are Part of the Business Model." Springer Link. 5 June 2021. Accessed 25 October 2021 @https://link.springer.com/article/10.1007/s43681-021-00068-x.

23. "A Timeline of Trouble: Facebook's Privacy Record and Regulatory Fines." Guild.co. 4 August 2021. Accessed 8 March 2022 @ https://guild.co/blog/complete-list-timeline-of-facebook-scandals/.

24. Feiner, L. "Facebook Whistleblower Reveals Identity, Accuses the Platform of a 'Betrayal of Democracy.'" CNBC. 3 October 2021. Accessed 25 October 2021 @https://www.nbcnews.com/tech/social-media/facebook-whistleblower-reveals-identity-accuses-platform-betrayal-democracy-n1280668.

25. Liptak, A. "Cambridge Analytica's Use of Facebook Data Was a 'Grossly Unethical Experiment.'" The Verge. 18 March 2018. Accessed 25 March 2019 @ https://www.theverge.com/2018/3/18/17134270/cambridge-analyticas-facebook-data-underscores-critical-flaw-american-electorate.

26. "Identity Theft Victim Statistics." Accessed 10 September 2019 @ http://www.identitytheft.info/victims.aspx.

27. DiPietro, B. "Experiment Shows Speed at Which Stolen Data Travels." 16 April 2015. Wall Street Journal. Accessed 1 December 2015 @ http://blogs.wsj.com/digits/2015/04/16/experiment-shows-speed-at-which-stolen-data-travels/?mod=ST1.

28. "Businesses Can Have Their Identities Stolen, Too, Experts Warn." Pymnts. 14 June 2018. Accessed 22 May 2019 @ https://www.pymnts.com/news/b2b-payments/2018/ncss-business-identity-theft-cybersecurity-cybercrime/.

29. Schlesinger, J., and Day, A. "Criminals Are Using a New Form of Identity Theft: Stealing Business Data." CNBC. 23 December 2018. Accessed 18 March 2019 @ https://www.cnbc.com/2018/12/21/hackers-using-identity-theft-tactics-to-scam-businesses-out-of-data.html.

30. "General Moral Imperatives." Association for Computing Machinery. 2018. Accessed 21 July 2019 @ https://www.acm.org/binaries/content/assets/about/acm-code-of-ethics-booklet.pdf.

31. Barquin, R. "Ten Commandments of Computer Ethics." Computer Ethics Institute. Accessed 5 December 2011 @ http://www.ethicscodescollection.org/detail/411d6362-5ab5-438b-82de-7a3575412f40.

32. Cohn, C. "Social Media Ethics and Etiquette." Compukol. Accessed 1 April 2019 @ https://www.compukol.com/social-media-ethics-and-etiquette/.

33. "Internet Etiquette - 10 Rules of Netiquette." Utica Observer-Dispatch. 7 September 2012. Accessed 1 April 2019 @ https://www.uticaod.com/article/20120907/BLOGS/309079938?template=ampart.

34. "Ethics in Business Networking." Business Networking Insiders. Accessed 1 April 2019 @ https://www.bni-mn.com/ethics-in-business-networking/.

35. Cummings, J. "Six Ways to Stay Ethical." Network World. 21 July 2003. Accessed 1 April 2019 @ https://www.networkworld.com/article/2335144/six-ways-to-stay-ethical.html.

36. Kampen, M. "7 Digital Citizenship Skills Your Students Need to Know." Prodigy. 21 December 2020. Accessed 25 October 2021 @ https://www.prodigygame.com/main-en/blog/digital-citizenship/.

37. "Internet Censorship 2021 – An Analysis of 195 Countries." PureVPN. 26 May 2021. Accessed 25 October 2021 @ https://www.purevpn.com/blog/internet-censorship-2021/.

38. Kehl, D. and Morris, S. "The 2014 Open Internet Roller Coaster: The Highs and Lows of the Net Neutrality Debate." Slate. 29 December 2014. Accessed 25 October 2021 @ https://slate.com/technology/2014/12/net-neutrality-debate-2014-the-open-internet-rules-roller-coaster.html.

39. Venezia, P. "Why All Business Should Care About Net Neutrality." InfoWorld. Accessed 21 July 2014 @ http://www.infoworld.com/d/data-center/why-all-businesses-should-care-about-net-neutrality-246580?source=IFWNLE_nlt_daily_am_2014-07-21.

40. Statt, N. "Facebook Launches a Version of Messenger for Young Children." The Verge. 4 December 2017. Accessed 6 December 2017 @ https://www.theverge.com/2017/12/4/16725494/facebook-messenger-kids-app-launch-ios-iphone-preview.

41. "What Is Intellectual Property?" World Intellectual Property Organization. Accessed 6 August 2010 @ www.wipo.int/about-ip/en.

42. "What Is Copyright Protection?" WhatIsCopyright.org. 4 March 2007. Accessed 6 August 2010 @ www.whatiscopyright.org.

43. Pavento, M. "Patent Protection for E-Commerce Business Models." Jones & Askew, LLP. April 1999. Accessed 6 August 2010 @ http://www.inventorfraud.com/Benefits.aspx.

44. Tetzeli R. "Getting Your Company's Internet Strategy Right." Fortune. 18 March 1996: 72–78.

45. Fitzgerald, B. "Software Piracy: Study Claims 57 Percent of the World Pirates Software (Video)." Huffington Post. 6 December 2017. Accessed 25 March 2019 @ https://www.huffingtonpost.com/2012/06/01/software-piracy-study-bsa_n_1563006.html.

46. Marvin, R. "The Top 20 Countries for Software Piracy." SD Times. 19 November 2014. Accessed 1 December 2015 @ http://sdtimes.com/top-20-countries-software-piracy/.

47. "2018 Revulytics Software Piracy Statistics and Thoughts on the BSA Global Software Survey." Revulytics. Accessed 25 March 2019 @ https://www.revulytics.com/blog/2018-revulytics-software-piracy-statistics.

48. "2018 Software Piracy Statistics." Revulytics. Accessed 25 March 2019 @ https://www.revulytics.com/resources/stat-watch.

49. Werdmuller, B. "Why Open Source Software Isn't as Ethical as You Think It Is." words.werd.io. 29 September 2017. Accessed 22 May 2019 @ https://words.werd.io/why-open-source-software-isnt-as-ethical-as-you-think-it-is-2e34d85c3b16.

50. "Creative Commons Licenses." Accessed 22 May 2019 @ https://creativecommons.org/share-your-work/licensing-types-examples/.

51. Perrin, A. and Stake, S. "7% of Americans Don't Use the Internet. Who Are They?" Pew Research Center. 2 April 2021. Accessed 25 October 2021 @ https://www.pewresearch.org/fact-tank/2021/04/02/7-of-americans-dont-use-the-internet-who-are-they/.

52. "WIPO Cybersquatting Cases Grow by 12% to Reach New Record in 2018." World Intellectual Property Organization. 15 March 2019. Accessed 22 May 2019 @ https://www.wipo.int/pressroom/en/articles/2019/article_0003.html.

53. "Verizon Wins $33 Million in Suit Over Domain Names." New York Times. 24 December 2008. Accessed 6 August 2010 @ www.nytimes.com/2008/12/25/technology/companies/25verizon.html.

54. Shenggao, Y. "DreamWorks Wins Cybersquatting Case." China Daily. 29 March 2018. Accessed 22 May 2019 @ http://www.chinadaily.com.cn/cndy/2018-03/29/content_35937827.htm.

55. Clement, J. "Internet Usage in the United States – Statistics & Facts." Statista. 20 August 2019. Accessed 25 March 2021 @ https://www.statista.com/topics/2237/internet-usage-in-the-united-states/.

56. "Internet Users in the World by Regions – 2021 May – Updated." Internet World Stats. Accessed 25 October 2021 @ https://internetworldstats.com/stats.htm.

57. "The Digital Divide Between Rural and Urban America's Access to Internet." CBS News. 4 August 2017. Accessed 25 March 2019 @ https://www.cbsnews.com/news/rural-areas-internet-access-dawsonville-georgia/.

58. Wheeler, T. "Closing the Digital Divide in Rural America." 20 November 2014. Federal Communications Commission. Accessed 1 December 2015 @ https://www.fcc.gov/blog/closing-digital-divide-rural-america.

59. Skyrme, D. "The Virtual Organization." KM Knowledge Management. 24 March 2011. Accessed 2 February 2012 @ www.skyrme.com/kmbriefings/2virtorg.htm.

60. Hindle, T. "The Virtual Organisation." *The Economist*. 23 November 2009. Accessed 2 February 2012 @ www.economist.com/node/14301746.

61. Tessler, F. "The Hidden Danger of Touchscreens." *InfoWorld*. 11 January 2012. Accessed 2 February 2012 @ www.infoworld.com/t/laptops/the-hidden-danger-touchscreens-181774?source=IFWNLE_nlt_daily_2012-01-11.

62. Shoshany, S. "Modern Spine Ailment: Text Neck." Spine Health. 11 June 2015. Accessed 20 November 2016 @ http://www.spine-health.com/blog/modern-spine-ailment-text-neck.

63. Borkhataria, C. "Do YOU Suffer from 'Smartphone Thumb'? Doctors Warn Issue Is Becoming a Major Problem Across America." *Daily Mail*. 29 May 2017. Accessed 23 November 2017 @ http://www.dailymail.co.uk/sciencetech/article-4552760/Smartphone-thumb-major-problem-US.html.

64. "Top 10 Ways to Prevent 'Smartphone Thumb.'" VIP Plastic Surgery. Accessed 23 November 2017 @ https://vipplasticsurgery.com/Preventing-Smartphone-Thumb.

65. Wallace, K. "Half of Teens Think They're Addicted to Their Smartphones." CNN. 29 July 2016. Accessed 20 November 2016 @ http://www.cnn.com/2016/05/03/health/teens-cell-phone-addiction-parents/.

66. "7 Harmful Side Effects of Mobile Phones on Teenagers." Mom Junction. 14 March 2016. Accessed 20 November 2016 @ http://www.momjunction.com/articles/side-effects-of-mobile-phones-on-teenagers_00352682/.

67. Parker, N. "What Is Snapchat Dysmorphia? People Seeking Plastic Surgery to Look Like Snapchat Filters." *Atlanta Journal-Constitution*. 4 August 2018. Accessed 25 March 2019 @ https://www.ajc.com/news/world/what-snapchat-dysmorphia-people-seeking-plastic-surgery-look-like-snapchat-filters/rnenugYbLBW1D9K1PNA5dL/amp.html.

68. McCrum, K. "Children Reveal 'Hidden Sadness' of Parents Spending Too Much Time on Mobile Phones in Heartbreaking Video." *The Mirror*. 10 August 2015. Accessed 1 December 2015 @ http://www.mirror.co.uk/news/world-news/children-reveal-hidden-sadness-parents-6228329.

69. "Study: Kids Say Parents Spend Too Much Time on Cell Phones." 12 August 2015. CBS Minnesota. Accessed 1 December 2015 @ http://minnesota.cbslocal.com/2015/08/12/study-kids-say-parents-spend-too-much-time-on-cell-phones/.

70. "What Is Internet Addiction?" Healthy Place. Accessed 25 March 2019 @ https://www.healthyplace.com/addictions/center-for-internet-addiction-recovery/what-is-internet-addiction/.

71. Becker, D. "When Games Stop Being Fun." CNET News. 12 April 2002. Accessed 6 August 2010 @ http://news.cnet.com/2100-1040-881673.html.

72. "WHO Classifies Gaming Disorder as a Disease." *USA Today*. 18 June 2018. Accessed 25 March 2019 @ https://www.usatoday.com/videos/news/health/2018/06/18/who-classifies-gaming-disorder-disease/36140051.

73. Edwards, D. "Man Dies After Playing Computer Games for 27 Days in a Row." The Beijinger. 23 February 2011. Accessed 26 December 2011 @ www.thebeijinger.com/blog/2011/02/23/Man-Dies-After-Playing-Computer-Games-for-27-Days-in-a-Row.

74. "Xbox Addict Dies from Blood Clot." AFP. 1 August 2011. Accessed 26 December 2011 @ https://timesofmalta.com/articles/view/Xbox-addict-dies-from-blood-clot-.380776.

75. Nadu, T. "16-year-old Boy Collapses After Playing Video Game for Hours." The Hindu. 4 February 2021. Accessed 25 October 2021 @ https://www.thehindu.com/news/national/tamil-nadu/16-year-old-boy-collapses-after-playing-video-game-for-hours/article33744405.ece.

76. Geyser, W. "The Real Social Media Addiction Stats for 2022." Influencer Marketing Hub. 30 December 2021. Accessed 8 March 2022 @ https://influencermarketinghub.com/social-media-addiction-stats/.

77. Lage, A. "15 Terrifying Statistics About Cell Phone Addiction." Daily Infographic. 17 May 2017. Accessed 23 November 2017 @ http://www.dailyinfographic.com/15-terrifying-statistics-about-cell-phone-addiction.

78. Cahn, L. "This Causes 11,000 Injuries a Year—and You're Probably Doing It Every Day." *Reader's Digest*. Accessed 25 March 2019 @ https://www.rd.com/culture/texting-and-walking-injuries/.

79. "Distracted Walking a Major Pedestrian Safety Concern." Safety.com. 18 July 2018. Accessed 25 March 2019 @ https://www.safety.com/news/distracted-walking-major-safety-concern/.

80. Miles, K. "Cause of Death: Selfie." *Outside*. 16 April 2019. Accessed 22 May 2019 @ https://www.outsideonline.com/2393419/selfie-deaths.

81. Jackson, S. "10 Ways to Overcome Internet Addiction." Money Saving Pro. 5 September 2019. Accessed 10 September 2019 @ https://www.moneysavingpro.com/internet-providers/internet-addiction/.

82. "Smartphone Addiction." HelpGuide. Accessed 25 March 2019 @ https://www.helpguide.org/articles/addictions/smartphone-addiction.htm/.

83. "Explaining Green Computing." YouTube. Accessed 4 July 2010 @ www.youtube.com/watch?v=350Rb2sOc3U.

84. Murugesan, S. "Harnessing Green IT: Principles and Practices." *IT Professional* 10(1) (2006): 24–33.

85. Anam, A., and Syed, A. "Green Computing: E-waste Management through Recycling." *International Journal of Scientific & Engineering Research* 4(5) (May 2013): 1103–1106. Accessed 20 November 2016 @ http://www.academia.edu/6403222/Green_Computing_E-waste_management_through_recycling.

86. Clifford, C. "Google Is Updating Maps, Search, and Other Products to Help Consumers Save Energy and Reduce Emissions." CNBC. 6 October 2021. Accessed 25 October 2021 @ https://www.cnbc.com/2021/10/06/google-updates-maps-search-shopping-nest-for-sustainability.html#:~:text=Google%20is%20updating%20Maps%2C%20Search,save%20energy%20and%20reduce%20emissions&text=Google%20Maps%20will%20default%20to,taking%20carbon%20emissions%20into%20account.

87. "IBM Project Big Green." IBM. 10 May 2007. Accessed 4 July 2010 @ https://www.greenbiz.com/article/ibm-launches-billion-dollar-project-big-green.

88. Adams, W. M. "Power Consumption in Data Centers Is a Global Problem." DCD. 21 November 2018. Accessed 25 March 2019 @ https://www.datacenterdynamics.com/opinions/power-consumption-data-centers-global-problem/.

89. Babcock, C., and Franklin Jr., C. "Green Data Centers: 8 Companies Doing Them Right." *InformationWeek*. 8 May 2016. Accessed 20 November 2016 @ http://www.informationweek.com/data-centers/green-data-centers-8-companies-doing-them-right/d/d-id/1326498.

90. Froehlich, A. "7 Cool Data Center Innovations." *InformationWeek*. 8 February 2016. Accessed 20 November 2016 @ http://www.informationweek.com/data-centers/7-cool-data-center-innovations/d/d-id/1326436?itc=edit_in_body_cross&image_number=1.

91. This information has been gathered from the InterGuard Web site and other promotional materials. For more information and updates, visit www.interguardsoftware.com.

92. "State of Remote Work." Buffer. Accessed 18 March 2019 @ https://buffer.com/state-of-remote-work-2019.

93. Connley, C. "Salesforce, Dell and 8 Other Top Tech Companies Hiring Remote Workers Now." CNBC. 23 February 2019. Accessed 25 March 2019 @ https://www.cnbc.com/2019/02/22/salesforce-dell-and-8-other-top-tech-companies-hiring-for-remote-jobs.html.

94. "Employee Monitoring." Awareness Technologies. Accessed 28 January 2013 @ www.awarenesstechnologies.com/products_employee.html.

95. Shellenbarger, S. "Working from Home Without Slacking Off." *Wall Street Journal*. 11 July 2012. Accessed 28 January 2013 @ http://online.wsj.com/article/SB10001424052702303684004577508953483021234.html?mod=djem_jiewr_IT_domainid.

96. Newman, L. H. "How to Make Your Amazon Echo and Google Home as Private as Possible." *Wired*. 11 April 2019. Accessed 22 May 2019 @ https://www.wired.com/story/alexa-google-assistant-echo-smart-speaker-privacy-controls/.

97. Raphael, J. R. "14 Eyebrow-Raising Things Google Knows About You." *Computerworld*. 28 December 2016. Accessed 23 November 2017 @ http://www.infoworld.com/article/3150925/privacy/14-eyebrow-raising-things-google-knows-about-you.html.

98. Hautala, L. "Google Sued Over Tracking User Location Amid Privacy Concerns." CNET. 20 August 2018. Accessed 25 March 2019 @ https://www.cnet.com/news/google-sued-over-keeping-location-data-amid-privacy-concerns/.

99. Parfeni, L. "Google Street View WiFi Lawsuit to Move Ahead." Softpedia. 1 July 2011. Accessed 10 August 2011 @ http://news.softpedia.com/news/Google-Street-View-WiFi-Lawsuit-to-Move-Ahead-209339.shtml.

100. Zetter, K. "Lawsuits Pour in Over Google's Wi-Fi Data Collection." *Wired*. 26 May 2010. Accessed 10 August 2011

@ www.wired.com/threatlevel/2010/05/google-sued.

101. Axon, S. "Google Maps Lawsuit: Woman Follows Directions, Gets Run Over." Mashable. 30 May 2010. Accessed 10 August 2011 @ http://mashable.com/2010/05/30/google-maps-lawsuit.

102. Mueller, K. P. "Google Map Brings Recreation-Seeking Motorists in Droves to Clinton Township Family's Driveway." NJ.com. 11 July 2011. Accessed 10 August 2011 @ www.nj.com/business/index.ssf/2011/07/google_map_brings_recreation-s.html.

103. Brito, J. "Explaining the Google Books Case Saga." *Time*. 23 March 2011. Accessed 10 August 2011 @ http://techland.time.com/2011/03/23/explaining-the-google-books-case-saga.

104. Gross, G. "Supreme Court Declines to Hear Google's Request in Street View Lawsuit." *PCWorld*. 30 June 2014. Accessed 10 November 2014 @ http://www.pcworld.com/article/2449360/supreme-court-declines-to-hear-googles-request-in-street-view-lawsuit.html.

5

1. Morgan, S. "Cybercrime to Cost the World $10.5 Trillion Annually By 2025." Cybersecurity Ventures. 13 November 2020. Accessed 5 November 2021 @ https://cybersecurityventures.com/cybercrime-damage-costs-10-trillion-by-2025/.

2. Hamblen, M. "19% of Shoppers Would Abandon a Retailer That's Been Hacked." *Computerworld*. 23 August 2016. Accessed 20 November 2016 @ http://www.computerworld.com/article/3111447/cybercrime-hacking/19-shoppers-would-abandon-a-retailer-thats-been-hacked.html.

3. Corbin, K. "Cyber Crime Costs U.S. Economy $100 Billion and 500,000 Jobs." *InfoWorld*. 24 July 2013. Accessed 2 January 2014 @ www.infoworld.com/d/security/cyber-crime-costs-us-economy-100-billion-and-500000-jobs-223352?source=IFWNLE_nlt_sec_2013-07-25.

4. Rashid, F. Y. "Insiders Still Pose Serious Security Risks." *InfoWorld*. 29 September 2015. Accessed 10 September 2019 @ https://www.infoworld.com/article/2985459/insiders-still-pose-serious-security-risks.html.

5. Noyes, K. "IRS: Actually, That Breach Last Year Was Way Worse Than We Thought." *Computerworld*. 26 February 2016. Accessed 20 November 2016 @ http://www.computerworld.com/article/3038832/government-it/irs-actually-that-breach-last-year-was-way-worse-than-we-thought.html.

6. Ohlemacher, S. "IRS: Computer Breach Bigger Than First Thought; 334K Victims." *Business Insider*. 17 August 2015. Accessed 1 December 2015 @ https://tulsaworld.com/business/irs-computer-breach-bigger-than-first-thought-334-000-victims/article_51aba05f-b15e-5df4-acc3-387bdf675fb7.html.

7. Ledermanaugust, J. "IRS Missing Billions in ID Theft." YAHOO! Finance. 2 August 2012. Accessed 1 December 2015 @ http://finance.yahoo.com/news/irs-missing-billions-id-theft-164707999.html.

8. Constantin, L. "Ransomware Attacks Against Businesses Jumped 3X in 2016." *Computerworld*. 9 December 2016. Accessed 12 December 2016 @ http://www.computerworld.com/article/3149037/security/ransomware-attacks-against-businesses-jumped-3x-in-2016.html.

9. Winder, D. "Ransomware Reality Shock: 92% Who Pay Don't Get Their Data Back." *Forbes*. 2 May 2021. Accessed 14 March 2022 @ https://www.forbes.com/sites/daveywinder/2021/05/02/ransomware-reality-shock-92-who-pay-dont-get-their-data-back/?sh=1798e2e2e0c7.

10. Greig, J. "Ransomware: 2,300+ Local Governments, Schools, Healthcare Providers Impacted in 2021." ZDNet. 18 January 2022. Accessed 14 March 2022 @ https://www.zdnet.com/article/2300-local-governments-schools-healthcare-providers-impacted-by-ransomware-in-2021/.

11. Kochovski, A. "Ransomware Statistics, Trends and Facts for 2021 and Beyond." Cloudwards. 20 November 2021. Accessed 28 December 2021 @ https://www.cloudwards.net/ransomware-statistics/#:~:text=%205%20Key%20Ransomware%20Statistics%3A%20%201%20Ransomware,32%20percent%20pay%20the%20ransom%2C%20but...%20More%20.

12. Mixon, E. "Top 10 Ransomware Attacks of 2021." Blumira. 20 August 2021. Accessed 5 November 2021 @ https://www.blumira.com/ransomware-attacks-2021/.

13. Siwicki, B. "Tips for Protecting Hospitals from Ransomware as Cyberattacks Surge." Healthcare IT News. 3 August 2016. Accessed 20 November 2016 @ http://www.healthcareitnews.com/news/tips-protecting-hospitals-ransomware-cyber-attacks-surge.

14. Ranger, S. "Ransomware: 11 Steps You Should Take to Protect Against Disaster." ZDNet. 18 September 2019. Accessed 5 November 2021 @ https://www.zdnet.com/article/ransomware-11-steps-you-should-take-to-protect-against-disaster/.

15. Saunders, S. "Putting a Lock on Corporate Data." *Data Communications* (January 1996): 78–80.

16. McCumber, J. *Assessing and Managing Security Risk in IT Systems*. Boca Raton, FL: Auerbach, 2004.

17. Vijayan, J. "90 Percent of Companies Say They've Been Hacked." *Computerworld*. 23 June 2011. Accessed 11 August 2011 @ www.infoworld.com/d/security/90-percent-companies-say-theyve-been-hacked-118.

18. "Prevent Data Theft Using Removable Devices." Get Safe Online. 2009. Accessed 10 August 2010 @ https://www.getsafeonline.org/business/articles/data-loss-prevention/.

19. Perlroth, N. "Hackers Used New Weapons to Disrupt Major Websites Across U.S." *New York Times*. 21 October 2016. Accessed 20 November 2016 @ http://www.nytimes.com/2016/10/22/business/internet-problems-attack.html.

20. "The Most Notorious DDoS Attacks in History – 2021 Update." Cloudbric. Accessed 5 November 2021 @ https://www.cloudbric.com/blog/2021/04/most-notorious-ddos-attacks-in-history-2021-update/.

21. Newman, L. H. "What We Know About Friday's Massive East Coast Internet Outage." *Wired*. 21 October 2016. Accessed 20 November 2016 @ https://www.wired.com/2016/10/internet-outage-ddos-dns-dyn/.

22. Novo, P. "Top 10 Cybersecurity Facts & Stats in 2022." High Speed Options. 25 October 2021. Accessed 14 March 2022 @ https://www.highspeedoptions.com/resources/insights/10-cybersecurity-facts-and-stats#8.

23. Samson, T. "Cyber Criminals Tying Up Emergency Phone Lines Through TDoS Attacks." *InfoWorld*. 1 April 2013. Accessed 2 January 2014 @ www.infoworld.com/t/cyber-crime/cyber-criminals-tying-emergency-phone-lines-through-tdos-attacks-215585?source=IFWNLE_nlt_sec_2013-04-02.

24. Hulme, G. V. "Social Engineering Attacks from the Front Lines." CSO. 29 January 2015. Accessed 1 December 2015 @ http://www.csoonline.com/article/2876707/social-engineering/social-engineering-stories-from-the-front-lines.html?phint=newt%3Dinfoworld_daily&phint=idg_eid%3Da74f01173c5d192b6e17e3ba45b5c85f#tk.IFWNLE_nlt_daily_pm_2015-02-02&siteid=&phint=tpcs%3D&phint=idg_eid%3Da74f01173c5d192b6e17e3ba45b5c85f.

25. Honan, B. "Ubiquiti Networks Victim of $39 Million Social Engineering Attack." CSO. 6 August 2015. Accessed 1 December 2015 @ http://www.csoonline.com/article/2961066/supply-chain-security/ubiquiti-networks-victim-of-39-million-social-engineering-attack.html.

26. Hulsey, L. "2021 Data Compromises Increased 68 Percent Nationwide." Governing. 15 February 2022. Accessed 14 March 2022 @ https://www.governing.com/security/2021-data-compromises-increased-68-percent-nationwide.

27. Galov, N. "17+ Sinister Social Engineering Statistics for 2021." Hosting Tribunal. Accessed 14 March 2022 @ https://hostingtribunal.com/blog/social-engineering-statistics/#gref.

28. "Social Engineering Credential Compromise Jumped in 2018: Proofpoint." Dark Reading. 25 January 2019. Accessed 27 March 2019 @ https://www.darkreading.com/attacks-breaches/social-engineering-credential-compromise-jumped-in-2018-proofpoint/d/d-id/1333740.

29. Fazzini, K. "Google and Facebook Got Tricked Out of $123 Million by a Scam That Costs Small Businesses Billions Every Year — Here's How to Avoid It." CNBC. 28 March 2019. Accessed 1 April 2019 @ https://www.cnbc.com/2019/03/28/how-to-avoid-invoice-theft-scam-that-cost-google-facebook-123m.html.

30. "Combating 'Screen Snoopers.'" news4sanantonio.com. 29 June 2018. Accessed 27 March 2019 @ https://news4sanantonio.com/news/nation-world/combating-screen-snoopers.

31. Nadeau, M. "What Is Cryptojacking? How to Prevent, Detect, and Recover from It." CSO. 13 December 2018. Accessed 27 March 2019 @ https://www.csoonline.com/article/3253572/what-is-cryptojacking-how-to-prevent-detect-and-recover-from-it.html.

32. Mesenbrink, J. "Biometrics Plays Big Role with Airport Security." *Security*. 4 February 2002. Accessed 9 March 2012 @ www.securitymagazine.com/articles/biometrics-plays-big-role-with-airport-security-1.

33. Anderson, H. "Case Study: The Motivation for Biometrics." HealthCareInfoSecurity.com. 24 June 2010. Accessed 13 July 2010 @ www.healthcareinfosecurity.com/articles.php?art_id=2686.

34. Mesenbrink, J. "Biometrics Plays Big Role with Airport Security." *Security*. 4 February 2002. Accessed 9 March 2012

@ www.securitymagazine.com/articles/
biometrics-plays-big-role-with-airport-security-1.

35. Burt, C. "Telpo Reviews Success of Facial Recognition Terminals at 2022 Beijing Winter Olympics." Biometric Update. 24 February 2022. Accessed 14 March 2022 @ https://www.biometricupdate.com/202202/telpo-reviews-success-of-facial-recognition-terminals-at-2022-beijing-winter-olympics.

36. Macdonald, A. "Japan Turns to Face Biometrics for Safe and Secure Olympics Amid COVID-19." Biometric Update. 22 March 2021. Accessed 14 March 2022 @ https://www.biometricupdate.com/202103/japan-turns-to-face-biometrics-for-safe-and-secure-olympics-amid-covid-19.

37. "Facial Recognition: Is the Technology Taking Away Your Identity?" http://www.theguardian.com/technology/2014/may/04/facial-recognition-technology-identity-tesco-ethical-issues.

38. "Advertisers Start Using Facial Recognition to Tailor Pitches." *Los Angeles Times*. 21 August 2011. http://articles.latimes.com/2011/aug/21/business/la-fi-facial-recognition-20110821.

39. "Never Forgetting a Face." *New York Times*. 17 May 2014. http://www.nytimes.com/2014/05/18/technology/never-forgetting-a-face.html?_r=0.

40. "Passwords To Be Phased Out by 2025, Say InfoSec Pros." Dark Reading. 30 June 2016. Accessed 28 December 2021 @ https://www.darkreading.com/endpoint/passwords-to-be-phased-out-by-2025-say-infosec-pros.

41. Henricks, M. "Why Biometrics Is Replacing Passwords." *Forbes*. 15 April 2014. Accessed 10 November 2014 @ http://www.forbes.com/sites/sungardas/2014/04/15/why-biometrics-is-replacing-passwords/.

42. Mims, C. "The Password Is Finally Dying. Here's Mine." *Wall Street Journal*. 13 July 2014. Accessed 10 September 2019 @ https://www.wsj.com/articles/the-password-is-finally-dying-heres-mine-1405298376.

43. Sharpe, N. "7 Shocking Statistics That Prove Just How Important Laptop Security Is." Techspective. 10 September 2018. Accessed 28 March 2019 @ https://techspective.net/2018/09/10/7-shocking-statistics-that-prove-just-how-important-laptop-security-is/.

44. Yegulalp, S. "Device Loss, Not Hacking, Poses Greatest Risk to Health Care Data." *InfoWorld*. 10 November 2014. Accessed 10 September 2019 @ http://www.infoworld.com/article/2844957/data-security/device-loss-not-hacking-puts-health-care-data-most-at-risk.html#tk.IFWNLE_2014-11-10.

45. Bueb, F., and Fife, P. "Line of Defense: Simple, Complex Security Measures Help Prevent Lost and Stolen Laptops." California Society of Certified Public Accountants and Gale Group. 2006. Accessed 10 August 2010 @ www.thefreelibrary.com/Line+of+defense:+simple,+complex+security+measures+help+prevent+lost...-a0155477162.

46. Fowler, G. A. "The Best Way to Manage All Your Passwords." *Wall Street Journal*. 6 May 2014. Accessed 1 December 2015 @ http://www.wsj.com/articles/SB10001424052702303647204579545801399272852.

47. "Why You Should Use a Password Manager and How to Get Started." How-To Geek. Accessed 1 December 2015 @ http://www.howtogeek.com/141500/why-you-should-use-a-password-manager-and-how-to-get-started/.

48. "Squire, S. "Zero Login: Fixing the Flaws in Authentication." Help Net Security. 17 July 2018. Accessed 5 November 2021 @ https://www.helpnetsecurity.com/2018/07/17/zero-login/.

49. "Making a Brain Password." Aspioneer. Accessed 5 November 2021 @ https://aspioneer.com/making-a-brain-password/.

50. Piesing, M. "Researchers Can Identify You from the Way You Type and Use Your Mouse." *Business Insider*. 18 July 2014. Accessed 5 November 2021 @ https://www.businessinsider.com/electronic-dna-password-2014-7.

51. "What Is an Authentication Token?" Fortinet. Accessed 5 November 2021 @ https://www.fortinet.com/resources/cyberglossary/authentication-token.

52. "Microchipping May Be the Next-Gen Password." *Chicago Tribune*. 21 August 2017. Accessed 5 November 2021 @ https://www.govtech.com/dc/microchipping-may-be-the-next-gen-password.html.

53. "Zero Trust Security | What's a Zero Trust Network?" Cloudflare. Accessed 20 April 2019 @ https://www.cloudflare.com/learning/security/glossary/what-is-zero-trust/.

54. Kindervag, J. "Build Security Into Your Network's DNA: The Zero Trust Network Architecture for Security & Risk Professionals." Virtual Star Media. 5 November 2010. Accessed 20 April 2019 @ http://www.virtualstarmedia.com/downloads/Forrester_zero_trust_DNA.pdf.

55. "What Is a Zero Trust Architecture?" Palo Alto Network. Accessed 20 April 2019 @ https://www.paloaltonetworks.com/cyberpedia/what-is-a-zero-trust-architecture.

56. Bidgoli, H., ed. *Global Perspectives in Information Security: Legal, Social and International Issues*. Hoboken, NJ: Wiley, 2008.

57. Zurier, S. "Less Than 3% of Recycled Computing Devices Properly Wiped." Dark Reading. 20 March 2019. Accessed 27 March 2019 @ https://www.darkreading.com/vulnerabilities---threats/less-than-3--of-recycled-computing-devices-properly-wiped/d/d-id/1334208.

58. Bidgoli, H. "Integrating Real Life Cases into a Security System: Seven Checklists for Managers." *American Journal of Management*, Vol. 16(4), 2016, pp. 9–25, (ISSN: 2165-7998).

59. This information was gathered from the company Web site (www.mcafee.com) and other promotional materials. For more information and updates, visit the Web site.

60. Talbot, D. "Computer Viruses Are 'Rampant' on Medical Devices in Hospitals." *MIT Technology Review*. 17 October 2012. Accessed 2 January 2014 @ https://www.technologyreview.com/2012/10/17/183245/computer-viruses-are-rampant-on-medical-devices-in-hospitals/.

61. Morgan, S. "Patient Insecurity: Explosion of the Internet of Medical Things." Cybersecurity Ventures. 19 February 2019. Accessed 1 April 2019 @ https://cybersecurityventures.com/patient-insecurity-explosion-of-the-internet-of-medical-things/.

62. "Internet of Medical Things Market Size 2021 | Is Anticipated to Reach USD 142.45 Billion by 2026, with a CAGR of 28.9%." Fortune Business Insights. 28 April 2021. Accessed 5 November 2021 @ https://www.globenewswire.com/en/news-release/2021/04/28/2218417/0/en/Internet-of-Medical-Things-Market-Size-2021-Is-Anticipated-to-Reach-USD-142-45-Billion-by-2026-With-a-CAGR-of-28-9.html.

63. Finkle, J. "J&J Warns Diabetic Patients: Insulin Pump Vulnerable to Hacking." Reuters. 4 October 2016. Accessed 20 November 2016 @ http://www.reuters.com/article/us-johnson-johnson-cyber-insulin-pumps-e-idUSKCN12411L.

64. Niccolai, J. "Thousands of Medical Devices Are Vulnerable to Hacking, Security Researchers Say." *Computerworld*. 30 September 2015. Accessed 1 December 2015 @ http://www.computerworld.com/article/2987737/security/thousands-of-medical-devices-are-vulnerable-to-hacking-security-researchers-say.html.

65. Weaver, C. "Patients Put at Risk by Computer Viruses." *Wall Street Journal*. 13 June 2013. Accessed 2 January 2014 @ http://online.wsj.com/news/articles/SB10001424127887324188604578543162744943762?mod=djem_jiewr_IT_domainid.

66. "Company Profile." Equifax. Accessed 10 September 2019 @ https://www.equifax.com/about-equifax/company-profile/.

67. "Equifax Hack Lasted for 76 Days, Compromised 148 Million People, Government Report Says." *Fortune*. 10 December 2018. Accessed 22 May 2019 @ http://fortune.com/2018/12/10/equifax-hack-lasted-for-76-days-compromised-148-million-people-government-report-says/.

68. Cimpanu, C. "US Government Releases Post-Mortem Report on Equifax Hack." ZDNet. 7 September 2018. Accessed 22 May 2019 @ https://www.zdnet.com/article/us-government-releases-post-mortem-report-on-equifax-hack/.

6

1. "GoToMeeting." GoToMeeting. Accessed 5 February 2013 @ https://www.goto.com/offer/meeting/sem?utm_medium=cpc&gclid=EAIaIQobChMIuMvZj_KJ9AIVpzytBh2eWQUZEAAYASAAEgLjWvD_BwE&gclsrc=aw.ds.

2. Frank, B. H. "Amazon Chime Goes after WebEx, Skype for Business and Others." *Computerworld*. 14 February 2017. Accessed 26 November 2017 @ https://www.computerworld.com/article/3169607/cloud-computing/amazon-chime-goes-after-webex-skype-for-business-and-others.html.

3. Poon, L. "There Are Far More Americans Without Broadband Access than Previously Thought." Bloomberg. 19 February 2020. Accessed 10 November 2021 @ https://www.bloomberg.com/news/articles/2020-02-19/where-the-u-s-underestimates-the-digital-divide.

4. Keizer, G. "Forrester: iPad and Tablet Rivals Will Kill Netbooks." *InfoWorld*. 17 June 2010. Accessed 31 July 2010 @ www.infoworld.com/d/mobilize/forrester-ipad-and-tablet-rivals-will-kill-netbooks-633.

5. Barr, A., and Pasztor, A. "Google Invests in Satellites to Spread Internet Access." *Wall Street Journal*. 1 June 2014. Accessed 11 September 2019 @ https://www.dowjones.com/scoops/google-invests-satellites-spread-internet-access/.

6. Hellman, M. "Google Is Investing in a Superfast Fiber-Optic Cable Across the Pacific." *Time*. 23 August 2014. Accessed 11 September 2019 @ http://time.com/3106467/

google-cable-system-faster-transpacific-nec-telecom-infrastructure/.

7. Kharpal, A. "Google Plans to Build 3 New Underwater Cables to Expand Its Cloud Business." CNBC. 16 January 2018. Accessed 1 April 2019 @ https://www.cnbc.com/2018/01/16/google-plans-to-build-3-new-underwater-cables-to-expand-cloud-business.html.

8. Khan, F. "Facebook Is Building an Undersea Cable around Africa." Medium. 14 May 2020. Accessed 10 November 2021 @ https://medium.com/technicity/facebook-is-building-an-undersea-cable-around-africa-87ecb9cb21b4.

9. Handley, L. "Nearly Three Quarters of the World Will Use Just Their Smartphones to Access the Internet by 2025." CNBC. 24 January 2019. Accessed 2 May 2019 @ https://www.cnbc.com/2019/01/24/smartphones-72percent-of-people-will-use-only-mobile-for-internet-by-2025.html.

10. "Number of Available Applications in the Google Play Store from December 2009 to July 2021." Statista. 23 September 2021. Accessed 20 October 2021 @ https://www.statista.com/statistics/266210/number-of-available-applications-in-the-google-play-store/.

11. "Number of Available Apps in the Apple App Store from 2008 to 2021." Statista. 31 August 2021. Accessed 20 October 2021 @ https://www.statista.com/statistics/268251/number-of-apps-in-the-itunes-app-store-since-2008/.

12. Roberts, S. "Top 10 Most Downloaded Apps of 2021 So Far." Cyberclick. 15 March 2021. Accessed 10 November 2021 @ https://www.cyberclick.net/numericalblogen/top-10-most-downloaded-apps-of-2020-so-far.

13. Whalen, J. "Health-Care Apps That Doctors Use." Wall Street Journal. 17 November 2013. Accessed 2 January 2014 @ http://online.wsj.com/news/articles/SB10001424052702303376904579137683810827104?mod=djem_jiewr_IT_domainid.

14. Tan, K. "20 Mobile Apps for Shopping Discounts and Deals." Hongkiat. Accessed 2 January 2014 @ www.hongkiat.com/blog/mobile-shopping-apps.

15. "Americans Rank the Top 10 Best and Worst Mobile Banking Apps." The Financial Brand. 22 August 2013. Accessed 2 January 2014 @ http://thefinancialbrand.com/32967/americans-rate-the-best-and-worst-u-s-mobile-banking-apps.

16. Prindle, D. "Best Music Apps for Your Smartphone (iPhone, Android, or Windows)." Digital Trends. 19 March 2014. Accessed 2 January 2014 @ www.digitaltrends.com/mobile/best-music-apps.

17. Glasofer, D. R. "Best Apps for Anxiety." VeryWellMind. 11 August 2021. Accessed 10 November 2021 @ https://www.verywellmind.com/best-apps-for-anxiety-3575736.

18. "Forecast Number of Mobile Devices Worldwide from 2020 to 2025 (in Billions)." Statista. Accessed 1 April 2022 @ https://www.statista.com/statistics/245501/multiple-mobile-device-ownership-worldwide/.

19. "View from the Edge." Black Box Corporation. 30 April 2018. Accessed 28 December 2021 @ https://www.bboxservices.com/resources/blog/bbns/2018/04/30/802.11-wireless-standards-explained.

20. "Bluetooth 1.0 vs. 2.0 vs. 3.0 vs. 4.0 vs. 5.0 - How They Compare | Symmetry Blog." Semiconductor Store. 18 April 2018. Accessed 10 November 2021 @ https://www.semiconductorstore.com/blog/2018/Bluetooth-1-0-vs-2-0-vs-3-0-vs-4-0-vs-5-0-How-They-Differ-Symmetry-Blog/3147/.

21. Lawson, S. "Verizon to Begin Trials of 5G Wireless Next Year." Computerworld. 9 September 2015. Accessed 5 December 2015 @ http://www.computerworld.com/article/2981995/networking/verizon-to-begin-trials-of-5g-wireless-next-year.html.

22. Cha, B. "What Is 5G, and What Does It Mean for Consumers?" Recode.net. 13 March 2015. Accessed 5 December 2015 @ http://recode.net/2015/03/13/what-is-5g-and-what-does-it-mean-for-consumers/.

23. Dowling, C. "5 Industries to Gain the Most from 5G." ITProPortal. 31 July 2017. Accessed 2 April 2019 @ https://www.itproportal.com/features/5-industries-to-gain-the-most-from-5g/.

24. McLellan, C. "5G: A Transformation in Progress." ZDNet. 1 February 2019. Accessed 2 April 2019 @ https://www.zdnet.com/article/5g-a-transformation-in-progress/.

25. Fisher, T. "6G: What It Is & When to Expect It." Lifewire. 1 October 2021. Accessed 10 November 2021 @ https://www.lifewire.com/6g-wireless-4685524.

26. Apple. "iPhone in Business." Apple.com. Accessed 17 July 2010 @ http://www.apple.com/iphone/business/.

27. Gralla, P. "Smartphone Privacy: IT Caught in the Crossfire." Computerworld. 9 May 2011. Accessed 7 December 2011 @ www.computerworld.com/s/article/356168/Smartphone_Privacy_IT_Caught_in_the_Crossfire.

28. Valentino-DeVries, J. "How Your Phone Is Used to Track You, and What You Can Do About It." New York Times. 19 August 2020. Accessed @ https://www.nytimes.com/2020/08/19/technology/smartphone-location-tracking-opt-out.html.

29. Agarwal, A. "How to Secure Your Wireless (Wi-Fi) Home Network." Digital Inspiration. 7 August 2014. Accessed 5 December 2015 @ http://www.labnol.org/internet/secure-your-wireless-wifi-network/10549/.

30. Grimes, R. A. "How to Stop Wi-Fi Hackers Cold." 26 May 2015. InfoWorld. Accessed 5 December 2015 @ http://www.infoworld.com/article/2925636/security/how-to-stop-wi-fi-hackers-cold.html?phint=newt%3Dinfoworld_daily&phint=idg_eid%3Da74f01173c5d192b6e17e3ba45b5c85f#tk.IFWNLE_nlt_daily_am_2015-05-26&siteid=&phint=tpcs%3D&phint=idg_eid%3Da74f01173c5d192b6e17e3ba45b5c85f.

31. Cisco. "TelePresence." Accessed 10 November 2021 @ https://www.asktechnolink.com/productcatalog/cisco/telepresence.

32. This information has been gathered from the company Web site (www.cisco.com) and from other promotional materials. For more information and updates, visit the Web site.

33. "Data, Data Everywhere." The Economist. 25 February 2010. Accessed 16 February 2012 @ www.economist.com/node/15557443?story_id=15557443.

34. Petersen, C. "Walmart's Secret Sauce: How the Largest Survives and Thrives." 27 March 2013. Accessed 11 September 2019 @ https://www.retailcustomerexperience.com/blogs/walmarts-secret-sauce-how-the-largest-survives-and-thrives/.

35. "Walmart Takes on Industrial Vehicle Management." Food Manufacturing. 29 September 2009. Accessed 10 August 2010 @ http://www.foodmanufacturing.com/articles/2009/09/wal-mart-takes-industrial-vehicle-management.

36. Gralla, P. "Smartphone Privacy: IT Caught in the Crossfire." Computerworld. 9 May 2011. Accessed 7 December 2011 @ www.computerworld.com/s/article/356168/Smartphone_Privacy_IT_Caught_in_the_Crossfire.

37. Gahran, A. "Mobile Phone Security: What Are the Risks?" CNN. 17 June 2011. Accessed 11 August 2011 @ http://www.cnn.com/2011/TECH/mobile/06/17/mobile.security.gahran/index.html.

38. Haselton, T. "Many Apps on Your Phone Are Tracking Everywhere You Go—Here's How to Stop Them." CNBC. 12 December 2018. Accessed 1 April 2019 @ https://www.cnbc.com/2018/12/12/how-to-stop-apps-from-tracking-your-location.html.

7

1. Kemp, S. "Digital 2022: The United States of America." DataReportal. 9 February 2022. Accessed 2 April 2022 @ https://datareportal.com/reports/digital-2022-united-states-of-america.

2. Gaudin, S. "Internet Hits Major Milestone, Surpassing 1 Billion Monthly Users." Computerworld. 26 January 2009. Accessed 10 August 2010 @ https://www.computerworld.com/article/2530462/internet-hits-major-milestone--surpassing-1-billion-monthly-users.html.

3. Elgin, J. "New Generic Top-Level Domains Nearing Launch Date." Mass Media Headlines. January 2011. Accessed 16 July 2011 @ https://www.ana.net/content/show/id/21633.

4. "Get Ready for the Next Big Thing." YouTube. 2 July 2011. Accessed 16 July 2011 @ www.youtube.com/watch?v=AybZsS3NmFo.

5. "World Population Review." World Population Review. Accessed 20 November 2021 @ https://worldpopulationreview.com/country-rankings/internet-speeds-by-country.

6. Carlson, N. "This Is What Facebook Graph Search Looks Like." Business Insider. 15 January 2013. Accessed 5 February 2013 @ www.businessinsider.com/this-is-what-facebook-graph-search-looks-like-2013-1.

7. Makvana, M. "How to Enable Facebook Graph Search Right Now [Quick Tip]." Make Tech Easier. 10 August 2014. Accessed 1 July 2019 @ https://www.maketecheasier.com/enable-facebook-graph-search/.

8. Sullivan, D. "Google Launches Knowledge Graph to Provide Answers, Not Just Links." Search Engine Land. 16 May 2012. Accessed 5 February 2013 @ http://searchengineland.com/google-launches-knowledge-graph-121585.

9. Gordon, W. "Everything You Didn't Know You Could Do with Google's Voice Commands." Lifehacker. 12 June 2013. Accessed 5 December 2015 @ http://lifehacker.com/

everything-you-didnt-know-you-could-do-with-google-voi-512727229.

10. Johnson, K. "Facebook Messenger Now Has 11,000 Chatbots for You to Try." Venture Beat. 30 June 2016. Accessed 28 November 2016 @ http://venturebeat.com/2016/06/30/facebook-messenger-now-has-11000-chatbots-for-you-to-try/.

11. Magid, L. "What Is Snapchat and Why Do Kids Love It and Parents Fear It?" *Forbes.* 1 May 2013. Accessed 5 January 2014 @ www.forbes.com/sites/larrymagid/2013/05/01/what-is-snapchat-and-why-do-kids-love-it-and-parents-fear-it.

12. Tillman, M. "What Are Facebook Stories? Here's How to Use Facebook Stories and Get the Most from Them." Pocket-lint. 1 October 2021. Accessed 25 November 2021 @ https://www.pocket-lint.com/apps/news/facebook/140666-what-is-facebook-stories-and-how-does-it-work.

13. Belkin, D. "Can MOOCs and Universities Co-Exist?" *Wall Street Journal.* 11 May 2014. Accessed 20 November 2014 @ http://online.wsj.com/news/articles/SB10001424052702303825604579515521328500810?mod=djem_jiewr_IT_domainid.

14. "Market Summary: Coursera Inc." Accessed 14 November 2021 @ https://www.google.com/search?q=how+much+is+Coursera%E2%80%99s+market+value%3F&oq=how+much+is+Coursera%E2%80%99s+market+value%3F&aqs=chrome..69i57j33i10i160.7935j0j4&sourceid=chrome&ie=UTF-8.

15. Mossberg, W. "A Real-Estate App When You're Buying or Just Nosy." *Wall Street Journal.* 9 May 2012. Accessed 5 February 2013 @ http://online.wsj.com/article/SB10001424052702304451104577392112842506378.html?mod=djem_jiewr_IT_domainid.

16. Dougherty, C. "Redfin Aims to Bring E-Commerce to Home Buying." *New York Times.* 8 May 2019. Accessed 1 July 2019 @ https://www.nytimes.com/2019/05/08/business/redfin-online-real-estate.html.

17. Callow, R. "The Advantages of Buying Software Online vs. Purchasing Programs in a Box." Bright Hub. 6 May 2010. Accessed 24 February 2012 @ www.brighthub.com/environment/green-computing/articles/8187.aspx.

18. Hipshire, L. "Is Telemedicine Covered by Insurance?" GoodRX. 9 June 2020. Accessed 2 April 2022 @ https://www.goodrx.com/healthcare-access/telehealth/telemedicine-covered-health-insurance-medicare.

19. Ruiz, R. "How the Internet Is Changing Health Care." *Forbes.* 20 July 2009. Accessed 24 February 2012 @ www.forbes.com/2009/07/30/health-wellness-internet-lifestyle-health-online-facebook.html.

20. Snyder, B. "How Kaiser Bet $4 Billion on Electronic Records—and Won." *InfoWorld.* 2 May 2013. Accessed 2 January 2014 @ www.infoworld.com/d/the-industry-standard/how-kaiser-bet-4-billion-electronic-health-records-and-won-217731?source=IFWNLE_nlt_daily_am_2013-05-02.

21. Bidgoli, H. *Electronic Commerce: Principles and Practice.* San Diego, CA: Academic Press, 2002.

22. Pernice, K. and Caya, P. "10 Best Intranets of 2021: What Makes Them Great." Nngroup.

com. 11 April 2021. Accessed 20 November 2021 @ https://www.nngroup.com/articles/intranet-design/.

23. "The 2019 World's 10 Best Intranets Demonstrate That the Intranet Has Firmly Arrived as the Hub of the Digital Workplace." Business Wire. 7 January 2019. Accessed 4 April 2019 @ https://www.businesswire.com/news/home/20190107005311/en/2019-World's-10-Intranets-Demonstrate-Intranet-Firmly.

24. Mista, M. "Extranet vs. Intranet in Company Use." Chron. Accessed 24 February 2012 @ http://smallbusiness.chron.com/extranet-vs-intranet-company-use-11878.html.

25. Ling, R.R. and Yen, D.C. "Extranet: A New Wave of Internet." Go.gale. Spring 2001. Accessed 25 November 2021 @ https://go.gale.com/ps/i.do?id=GALE%7CA79630226&sid=googleScholar&v=2.1&it=r&linkaccess=abs&issn=07497075&p=AONE&sw=w&userGroupName=anon%7E805d9528. =====.

26. "Business Uses of the Internet, Intranets & Extranets." Small Business. 16 February 2021. Accessed 25 November 2021 @ https://smallbusiness.chron.com/business-uses-internet-intranets-extranets-62042.html.

27. "Web 1.0, Web 2.0 and Web 3.0 with Their Difference." Geeks For Geeks. Accessed 1 July 2019 @ https://www.geeksforgeeks.org/web-1-0-web-2-0-and-web-3-0-with-their-difference/.

28. Lin, Y. "10 LinkedIn Statistics Every Marketer Should Know in 2021 [Infographic]." Oberlo. 14 March 2021. Accessed 25 November 2021 @ https://www.oberlo.com/blog/linkedin-statistics.

29. Kawasaki, G. "Ten Ways for Small Businesses to Use LinkedIn." LinkedIn Blog. 12 April 2010. Accessed 23 February 2012 @ http://blog.linkedin.com/2010/04/12/linkedin-small-business-tips.

30. Weber, L. "LinkedIn, Lynda.com and the Skills You'll Need for Your Next Job." *Wall Street Journal.* 9 April 2015. Accessed 5 December 2015 @ http://blogs.wsj.com/digits/2015/04/09/linkedin-lynda-and-the-skills-you-need-for-your-next-job/?mod=ST1.

31. King, R. "No Rest for the Wiki." *Bloomberg BusinessWeek.* 12 March 2007. Accessed 10 August 2010 @ https://www.bloomberg.com/news/articles/2007-03-12/no-rest-for-the-wikibusinessweek-business-news-stock-market-and-financial-advice.

32. "15 Most Popular Social Media Networks That Will Rule 2021." Appy Pie. 30 September 2021. Accessed 20 November 2021 @ https://www.appypie.com/top-most-popular-social-media-sites.

33. Gaudin, S. "Americans Spend 16 Minutes of Every Hour Online on Social Nets." *Computerworld.* 17 April 2013. Accessed 5 January 2014 @ www.computerworld.com/s/article/9238469/Americans_spend_16_minutes_of_every_hour_online_on_social_nets.

34. Driver, S. "Twitter for Business: Everything You Need to Know." *Business News Daily.* 18 November 2021. Accessed 25 November 2021 @ https://www.businessnewsdaily.com/7488-twitter-for-business.html.

35. Dean, B. "Social Network Usage & Growth Statistics: How Many People Use Social Media in 2021?" Backlinko. 10 October 2021. Accessed 20 November 2021 @ https://backlinko.com/social-media-users.

36. Moth, D. "How Walmart Uses Pinterest, Facebook, Twitter and Google+." Econsultancy. 10 January 2013. Accessed 5 December 2015 @ https://econsultancy.com/how-walmart-uses-pinterest-facebook-twitter-and-google/.

37. Hanson, A. "How Walmart's PR Team Uses Twitter." *PR Daily.* 14 February 2014. Accessed 5 December 2015 @ https://arikhanson.com/case-study-walmarts-pr-team-and-how-they-use-twitter/.

38. Bursztynsky, J. "Walmart Is Bringing Livestream Shopping to TikTok on Friday." CNBC. 17 December 2020. Accessed 25 November 2021 https://www.cnbc.com/2020/12/17/walmart-is-bringing-livestream-shopping-to-tiktok-on-friday.html?__source=iosappshare%7Ccom.apple.UIKit.activity.Mail.

39. Broudie, M. "4 Ways to Use TikTok for Business." Social Media Examiner. 18 February 2020. Accessed 20 November 2021 @ https://www.socialmediaexaminer.com/4-ways-to-use-tiktok-business/.

40. Dean, B. "How Many People Use Twitter in 2022? [New Twitter Stats]." Backlinko. 5 January 2022. Accessed 5 May 2022 @ https://backlinko.com/twitter-users#twitter-statistics.

41. Newton, C. "Twitter Is Rolling Out 280-Character Tweets Around the World." The Verge. 7 November 2017. Accessed 2 December 2017 @ https://www.theverge.com/platform/amp/2017/11/7/16616076/twitter-280-characters-global-rollout.

42. Bell, K. "Twitter's New Relaxed Character Count Limits Have Finally Arrived." Mashable. 19 September 2016. Accessed 28 November 2016 @ http://mashable.com/2016/09/19/twitter-longer-tweets/#myExz9zSwqqJ.

43. "The Fastest, Simplest Way to Stay Close to Everything You Care About." Twitter. Accessed 5 February 2013 @ http://twitter.com/about.

44. "3 Powerful Twitter Case Studies Worth Reading." Scion Social. 27 March 2013. Accessed 25 November 2021 @ https://scion-social.com/blog/twitter-case-studies/.

45. "Internet of Things (IoT) Connected Devices Installed Base Worldwide from 2015 to 2025." Statista. 27 November 2016. Accessed 20 November 2021 @ https://www.statista.com/statistics/471264/iot-number-of-connected-devices-worldwide/.

46. Epps, S. "There Is No Internet of Things." *Forbes.* 17 October 2013. Accessed 2 January 2014 @ www.forbes.com/sites/forrester/2013/10/17/there-is-no-internet-of-things.

47. Manyika, J., and Chui, M. "By 2025, Internet of Things Applications Could Have $11 Trillion Impact." *Fortune.* 22 July 2015. Accessed 28 November 2016 @ http://www.mckinsey.com/mgi/overview/in-the-news/by-2025-internet-of-things-applications-could-have-11-trillion-impact.

48. Eddy, N. "6 IoT Innovations Making Cities Smarter." *InformationWeek.* 20 October 2016. Accessed 28 November 2016 @ http://www.informationweek.com/government/6-iot-innovations-making-cities-smarter/d/d-id/1326791.

49. Thibodeau, P. "All Hail the Next Big Job: Chief IoT Officer." *Computerworld.* 8 May 2015. Accessed 5 December 2015 @ http://www.infoworld.com/article/2920299/it-careers/all-hail-the-next-big-job-chief-iot-officer.

html?phint=newt%3Dinfoworld_tech_
leadership&phint=idg_eid%3D9129
4756a0e437074af2b88ac7d3cb7c#tk.
IFWNLE_tlead_2015-05-08.

50. Evans, D. "The Internet of Things:
How the Next Revolution of the Internet Is
Changing Everything." Cisco. April 2011.
Accessed 2 January 2014 @ https://www.cisco.
com/c/dam/en_us/about/ac79/docs/innov/IoT_
IBSG_0411FINAL.pdf.

51. Ibid.

52. "10 Powerful Internet of Things (IoT)
Examples of 2022 (Real-World Apps)." Software
Testing Help. 3 March 2022. Accessed 2 April
2022 @ https://www.softwaretestinghelp.com/
best-iot-examples/.

53. Hodkin, S. "The Internet of Me: Creating
a Personalized Web Experience." *Wired*.
Accessed 5 December 2015 @ http://www.
wired.com/insights/2014/11/the-internet-of-me/.

54. "The Internet of Me." Accenture. Accessed
28 November 2016 @ https://www.accenture.
com/us-en/insight-internet-of-me.

55. Claburn, T. "The 'Internet of Me' Is Getting
Real in Healthcare." *InformationWeek*. 11 May
2015. Accessed 28 November 2016 @ http://
www.informationweek.com/strategic-cio/
executive-insights-and-innovation/the-
internet-of-me-is-getting-real-in-healthcare/d/
d-id/1320348.

56. "Avoiding the Pitfalls of the Internet of
Me." 20 May 2015. g3n3ws.blogspot.com.
Accessed 5 December 2015 @ http://g3n3ws.
blogspot.com/2015/05/avoiding-pitfalls-of-
internet-of-me.html.

57. Stephenson, D. "Why Collaboration Will
Replace 'Zero Sum Game' for Internet of
Things Success." Inex Advisors. 3 September
2013. Accessed 2 January 2014 @ http://
inexadvisors.com/2013/09/03/why-zero-sum-
game-is-not-the-answer-to-internet-of-things-
success.

58. Evans, D. "The Internet of Things:
How the Next Revolution of the Internet Is
Changing Everything." Cisco. April 2011.
Accessed 2 January 2014 @ https://www.cisco.
com/c/dam/en_us/about/ac79/docs/innov/IoT_
IBSG_0411FINAL.pdf.

59. Anurag. "8 Uses, Applications, and
Benefits of Industrial IoT in Manufacturing."
NewGenApps. 15 December 2017.
Accessed 25 November 2021 @ https://www.
newgenapps.com/blogs/8-uses-applications-
and-benefits-of-industrial-iot-in-manufacturing/
amp/.

60. Transcendent. "How Connected Devices
Are Changing the Manufacturing Industry."
IoT For All. 16 October 2018. Accessed
4 April 2019 @ https://www.iotforall.com/
iiot-devices-change-manufacturing-industry/.

61. Callaham, J. "What Is a Smart
Home, and Why Should You Want
One?" Android Authority. 21 March
2021. Accessed 25 November 2021
@ https://www.androidauthority.com/
what-is-a-smart-home-806483/.

62. Midrack, R. L. "What Is a Smart
Refrigerator?" Lifewire. 18 November 2018.
Accessed 6 April 2019 @ https://www.lifewire.
com/smart-refrigerator-4158327.

63. Steers, S. "Haier Reveals World's First
'Internet of Food' Smart Fridge." Mobile
Magazine. 25 March 2021. Accessed 2 April
2022 @ https://mobile-magazine.com/5g-and-iot/

haier-reveals-worlds-first-internet-food-smart-
fridge.

64. O'Shea, D. "LG Introduces Smart
Refrigerator with Amazon Alexa-Enabled
Grocery Ordering." Retail Dive. 4 January 2017.
Accessed 6 April 2019 @ https://www.retaildive.
com/news/lg-introduces-smart-refrigerator-
with-amazon-alexa-enabled-grocery-
ordering/433366/.

65. "The 7 Most Common IoT Security
Threats in 2019." IoT For All. 5 March 2019.
Accessed 5 April 2019 @ https://www.iotforall.
com/7-most-common-iot-security-threats-2019/.

66. "9 Ways to Improve IoT Device Security."
Hewlett Packard Enterprise. 26 January 2017.
Accessed 5 April 2019 @ https://www.hpe.com/
us/en/insights/articles/9-ways-to-make-iot-
devices-more-secure-1701.html.

67. Drolet, M. "8 Tips to Secure Those IoT
Devices." *CSO*. 20 June 2016. Accessed
5 April 2019 @ https://www.csoonline.com/
article/3085607/8-tips-to-secure-those-iot-
devices.html.

68. This information has been gathered
from the company Web site (www.google.com)
and other promotional materials. For more
information and updates, visit the Web site.

69. "The Scotts Miracle-Gro Company."
Accessed 6 February 2013 @ www.
thescottsmiraclegrocompany.com.

70. "Scotts Miracle-Gro, Winner of NN/g
and IIA Intranet Awards, on Next IBF Live."
Digital Workplace Group. 30 January 2012.
Accessed 25 November 2021 @ https://
digitalworkplacegroup.com/4134-2/.

71. "Scotts Miracle-Gro's Intranet: The
Garden." Accessed 25 November 2021 @
https://www.chegg.com/homework-help/
scotts-miracle-gro-s-intranet-garden-scotts-
miracle-gro-majo-chapter-7-problem-3cs1-
solution-9781133589303-exc.

72. Balwani, S. "5 Easy Social Media
Wins for Your Small Business." Mashable
Business. 28 July 2009. Accessed 11 August
2011 @ http://mashable.com/2009/07/28/
social-media-small-business.

8

1. Porter, M. *Competitive Advantage:
Creating and Sustaining Superior
Performance*. New York: Free Press, 1985.

2. Hart, K. "33 of the Best Brands on Instagram
Right Now." Jumper Media. 24 February 2019.
Accessed 6 July 2019 @ https://jumpermedia.
co/33-of-the-best-brands-on-instagram/.

3. Mohsin, M. "10 Instagram Stats Every
Marketer Should Know in 2021 [Infographic]."
Oberlo. 16 February 2021. Accessed 28
November 2021 @ https://www.oberlo.com/blog/
instagram-stats-every-marketer-should-know.

4. Newberry, C. "44 Instagram Stats That
Matter to Marketers in 2021." Blog.hootsuite. 6
January 2021. Accessed 28 November 2021 @
https://blog.hootsuite.com/instagram-statistics/.

5. Smith, M. "How to Sell on Instagram: 8
Instagram Tips That Actually Work." Oberlo. 12
June 2019. Accessed 6 July 2019 @ https://www.
oberlo.com/blog/how-to-sell-on-instagram.

6. Khan, H. "Consumers Are Showrooming
and Webrooming Your Business, Here's
What That Means and What You Can Do
about It." Shopify. 7 June 2018. Accessed

12 September 2019 @ http://www.shopify.com/
blog/14513673-consumers-are-showrooming-
and-webrooming-your-business-heres-what-
that-means-and-what-you-can-do-about-it.

7. Banjo, S. "Home Depot Lumbers into
E-Commerce." *Wall Street Journal*. 16 April
2014. Accessed 20 November 2014 @ https://
www.wsj.com/articles/SB1000142405270230462
6304579505723441210120.

8. "Here's How Home Depot's E-Commerce
Strategy Is Driving Growth." *Forbes*.
15 February 2017. Accessed 17 December
2017 @ https://www.forbes.com/sites/
greatspeculations/2017/02/15/heres-how-
home-depots-e-commerce-strategy-is-driving-
growth/#759f65fd9b62.

9. "Home Depot's Online Sales Surge 23%
in Q1, Reflecting a Hot Home Improvement
Market." Digital Commerce. 16 May 2017.
Accessed 17 December 2017 @ https://www
.digitalcommerce360.com/2017/05/16/home-
depots-online-sales-surge-23-reflect-hot-home-
improvement-market/.

10. Risley, J. "Roundup: Home Depot
Grows Online Sales 28% in Q3." Digital
Commerce 360. 14 November 2018.
Accessed 6 April 2019 @ https://www.
digitalcommerce360.com/2018/11/14/
home-depot-grows-online-sales-28-in-q3/.

11. Schmelzer, R. "How Home Depot Is
Enhancing the Ecommerce Experience with
AI." *Forbes*. 17 October 2020. Accessed 28
November 2021 @ https://www.forbes.com/sites/
cognitiveworld/2020/10/17/how-home-depot-
is-enhancing-the-ecommerce-experience-with-
ai/?sh=25897ad62445.

12. Rappa, M. "Business Models on the Web."
Digitalenterprise.org. Accessed 22 July 2019 @
http://digitalenterprise.org/models/models.html.

13. "E-commerce Market Worth $24.3
Trillion by 2025." Globe Newswire.
24 December 2018. Accessed 10 April
2019 @ https://www.globenewswire.com/
news-release/2018/12/24/1678131/0/
en/E-commerce-Market-Worth-24-3-
Trillion-by-2025-Exclusive-Report-by-
Meticulous-Research.html.

14. "US Online Retail Sales to Reach $1 Trillion
in 2025 Astride Thriving Amazon." Consulting.
us. 14 September 2018. Accessed 10 April
2019 @ https://www.consulting.us/news/950/
us-online-retail-sales-to-reach-1-trillion-in-2025-
astride-thriving-amazon.

15. Hill, R. "Ecommerce 2020." *ECRM*.
8 January 2014. Accessed 8 January 2014 @
www.ezinepost.com/articles/article-237942.html.

16. O'Malley, G. "E-Commerce Forecast to Hit
$279B by 2015." MediaPost. 28 February 2011.
Accessed 8 January 2014 @ www.mediapost.
com/publications/article/145775/ecommerce-
forecast-to-hit-279b-by-2015.html.

17. "10 Must-Have Features of Government
Websites." MunicipalCMS. Accessed 2 July
2019 @ https://www.municipalcms.com/pview.
aspx?id=20800&catid=70.

18. "Multi-channel, Cross-channel, Omnichannel: What Difference?" GIST. 18 April
2018. Accessed 14 April 2019 @ https://
blog.markgrowth.com/multi-channel-cross-
channel-omni-channel-what-is-the-difference-
3fc9f84c84b5.

19. Ong, A. "Multi-Channel Retailing
and the Buyer's Journey: Opportunities
and Challenges." GIST. Accessed

14 April 2019 @ https://getgist.com/multi-channel-cross-channel-omni-channel/.

20. Collomb, J. "7 Advantages of Integrating a Cross-Channel Approach into Your Business." MyFeelBack. 16 May 2017. Accessed 14 April 2019 @ https://www.myfeelback.com/en/blog/advantages-cross-channel-approach.

21. "5 Benefits of Providing an Omni-Channel Retail Experience." HSO. Accessed 14 April 2019 @ https://www.hso.com/en-gb/blog/5-benefits-providing-omni-channel-retail-experience/.

22. Meyer, B. "Conversational Commerce: What It Is and How to Use It (+4 Examples)." Omnisend. 22 April 2021. Accessed 28 November 2021 @ https://www.omnisend.com/blog/conversational-commerce/.

23. O'Shea, D. "EBay Goes Live with Image Search Capabilities." Retail Dive. 27 October 2017. Accessed 14 April 2019 @ https://www.retaildive.com/news/ebay-goes-live-with-image-search-capabilities/508302/.

24. Ridden, P. "IKEA Catalog Uses Augmented Reality to Give a Virtual Preview of Furniture in a Room." Gizmag. 14 August 2013. Accessed 14 April 2019 @ http://www.gizmag.com/ikea-augmented-reality-catalog-app/28703/.

25. "10 Awesome Uses of Augmented Reality Marketing." Mashable. 26 December 2009. Accessed 14 April 2019 @ http://mashable.com/2009/12/26/augmented-reality-marketing/#53kJDRDOIPqU.

26. "The Next Generation of Business Applications." Microsoft. Accessed 14 April 2019 @ https://dynamics.microsoft.com/en-us/.

27. Ovans, A. "E-Procurement at Schlumberger." Harvard Business Review (May–June 2000): 21–22.

28. Shamorian, K. "B2B Ecommerce to Reach $1.8 Trillion by 2023." Cleverbridge. 28 February 2019. Accessed 10 April 2019 @ http://www.clvrbrdg.com/corporate/b2b-ecommerce-to-reach-1-8-trillion-by-2023/index.html.

29. "Top 5 eCommerce Trends to Take Advantage of in 2019." OroCommerce. Accessed 10 April 2019 @ https://oroinc.com/b2b-ecommerce/blog/top-5-ecommerce-trends-to-take-advantage-of-in-2019.

30. Demery, P. "B2B e-Commerce Sales Will Top $1.13 Trillion by 2020." Internet Retailer. 2 April 2015. Accessed 5 December 2015 @ https://www.digitalcommerce360.com/2015/04/02/new-report-predicts-1-trillion-market-us-b2b-e-commerce/.

31. Regan, S. "9 B2B eCommerce Best Practices That Make All the Difference." Optaros. 22 April 2014. Accessed 5 December 2015 @ https://www.the-future-of-commerce.com/2014/05/23/9-best-practices-that-make-all-the-difference-for-b2b-e-commerce/.

32. Soper, T. "More Than a Quarter of All Starbucks Orders in the U.S. Are Now Paid for with a Smartphone." Geekwire. 28 April 2021. Accessed 18 April 2022 @ https://www.geekwire.com/2021/quarter-starbucks-orders-u-s-now-paid-smartphone/.

33. Elgan, M. "How Apps Are Changing Fast Food." Computerworld. 15 February 2014. Accessed 20 November 2014 @ http://www.computerworld.com/s/article/9246346/How_apps_are_changing_fast_food.

34. Caswell, S. "Voice-Based E-Commerce Looms Large." E-Commerce Times. 28 March 2000. Accessed 14 July 2010 @ www.ecommercetimes.com/story/2838.html.

35. "Speak It, Get It: New Hound App Kicks Off Next Paradigm in User Behavior on Mobile." Business Wire. 16 May 2011. Accessed 3 March 2012 @ www.soundhound.com/index.php?action=s.press_release&pr=30.

36. Montenegro, C. "Are You Talking to Me?" The Economist. 7 June 2007. Accessed 3 March 2012 @ www.economist.com/node/9249338.

37. Kharpal, A. "Amazon's Voice Assistant Alexa Could Be a $10 Billion 'Mega-Hit' by 2020: Research." CNBC. 10 March 2017. Accessed 17 December 2017 @ https://www.cnbc.com/2017/03/10/amazon-alexa-voice-assistan-could-be-a-10-billion-mega-hit-by-2020-research.html.

38. Peltz, J. F. "Wal-Mart and Google Team Up on Voice-Activated Shopping, Challenging Amazon." Los Angeles Times. 23 August 2017. Accessed 17 December 2017 @ http://www.latimes.com/business/la-fi-walmart-voice-shopping-20170822-story.html.

39. Kumar, K. "Target Teams Up with Google for Voice-Assisted Shopping and Nationwide Delivery." Minneapolis Star Tribune. 12 October 2017. Accessed 17 December 2017 @ http://www.startribune.com/target-teams-up-with-google-for-voice-assisted-shopping-and-nationwide-delivery/450595873/.

40. Martin, J. A. "7 Reasons Mobile Payments Still Aren't Mainstream." CIO. 7 June 2016. Accessed 17 March 2018 @ https://www.cio.com/article/3080045/payment-processing/7-reasons-mobile-payments-still-arent-mainstream.html.

41. Feinstein, E. "Top 5 Challenges in Online Payments and How to Overcome Them." Direct Pay Online Digest. 2 August 2017. Accessed 17 March 2018 @ https://www.linkedin.com/pulse/top-5-challenges-online-payments-how-overcome-them-eran-feinstein/.

42. Greaves, R. "What Is Google Pay and How Does It Work? (Nov 2021)." Ecommerce-platforms. 2 November 2021. Accessed 28 November 2021 @ https://ecommerce-platforms.com/payments/what-is-google-pay#:~:text=Google%20Pay%20is%20a%20mobile%20service%20that%20enables,convenient%20solution%20for%20customers%20in%20the%20digital%20world.

43. Sterling, G. "Report: 60 Percent of Internet Access Is Mostly Mobile." Marketing Land. 19 February 2014. Accessed 12 September 2019 @ http://marketingland.com/outside-us-60-percent-internet-access-mostly-mobile-74498.

44. Marrs, M. "What Is Mobile Marketing and Why Does It Matter? (So So Much!)." Word Stream. 6 August 2019. Accessed 12 September 2019 @ http://www.wordstream.com/blog/ws/2013/08/19/what-is-mobile-marketing.

45. Overby, S. "How Starbucks Brews Its Mobile Strategy." CIO. 25 October 2012. Accessed 12 September 2019 @ http://www.cio.com/article/2390899/retail/how-starbucks-brews-its-mobile-strategy.html.

46. Johnson, L. "Starbucks Whips Up Clever SMS, MMS Campaign for Summer Drink Buzz." Retail Dive. Accessed 12 September 2019 @ https://www.retaildive.com/ex/mobilecommercedaily/starbucks-whips-up-clever-sms-mms-campaign-for-summer-drink-buzz.

47. Missulawin, I. "The Ultimate Click Fraud Statistics 2022." ClickCease. 10 March 2022. Accessed 18 April 2022 @ https://www.clickcease.com/blog/list-of-click-fraud-statistics/.

48. Newberg, M. "As Many as 48 Million Twitter Accounts Aren't People, Says Study." CNBC. 10 March 2017. Accessed 17 December 2017 @ https://www.cnbc.com/2017/03/10/nearly-48-million-twitter-accounts-could-be-bots-says-study.html.

49. Stewart, C., and Vranica, S. "Phony Web Traffic Tricks Digital Ads." Wall Street Journal. 30 September 2013. Accessed 2 January 2014 @ https://allthingsd.com/20131001/phony-web-traffic-tricks-digital-ads/.

50. "Global Social Media Stats." DataReportal. Accessed 28 November 2021 @ https://datareportal.com/social-media-users.

51. "Gartner Says Majority of Consumers Rely on Social Networks to Guide Purchase Decisions." Gartner Newsroom. Accessed 12 September 2019 @ https://www.pressebox.com/pressrelease/gartner-uk-ltd/Gartner-Says-Majority-of-Consumers-Rely-on-Social-Networks-to-Guide-Purchase-Decisions/boxid/361969.

52. Smith, C. "The Rise of Social Commerce, and How It Will Completely Transform the Way We Shop on the Internet." Business Insider. 15 October 2013. Accessed 12 September 2019 @ http://www.businessinsider.com/the-rise-of-social-commerce-2013-10.

53. Cohen, H. "What Is Social Commerce?" 2 November 2011. Accessed 12 September 2019 @ http://heidicohen.com/what-is-social-commerc/.

54. Indvik, L. "The 7 Species of Social Commerce." Mashable. 10 May 2013. Accessed 12 September 2019 @ http://mashable.com/2013/05/10/social-commerce-definition/.

55. Cavazza, F. "The Six Pillars of Social Commerce." Forbes. 1 February 2012. Accessed 12 September 2019 @ http://www.forbes.com/sites/fredcavazza/2012/02/01/the-six-pillars-of-social-commerce/.

56. "Facebook E-commerce 2.0: Instagram Shopping Launches." Yahoo News Network. 2 November 2016. Accessed 6 December 2016 @ https://ca.sports.yahoo.com/video/facebook-e-commerce-2-0-172452331.html.

57. Dholakiya, P. "4 Brands That Have Cracked the Social Commerce Code." Jeffbullas. 15 September 2014. Accessed 5 December 2015 @ http://www.jeffbullas.com/2014/09/15/4-brands-cracked-social-commerce-code/.

58. Ha, A. "Google Unveils 'Purchases on Google,' Which Are Basically Buy Buttons in Mobile Ads." Techcrunch. 15 July 2015. Accessed 5 December 2015 @ http://techcrunch.com/2015/07/15/purchases-on-google/#.rlaojc:8hoC.

59. "Buyable Pins Start Rolling Out Today!" Blog.pinterest.com. 30 June 2015. Accessed 5 December 2015 @ https://blog.pinterest.com/en/buyable-pins-rolling-out-today.

60. Lynley, M. "Pinterest Is Soon Launching a Way to Search for Products with Your Smartphone Camera." Techcrunch. 28 June 2016. Accessed 6 December 2016 @ https://techcrunch.com/2016/06/28/pinterest-is-launching-a-way-to-search-for-products-with-your-smartphone-camera/.

61. Ungerleider, N. "Pinterest Unveils New Image Search." *Fast Company*. 9 November 2015. Accessed 6 December 2016 @ http://www.fastcompany.com/3053408/fast-feed/pinterest-unveils-new-image-search.

62. Steiner, I. "Selling on Instagram Now Possible with Checkout Feature." Ecommerce Bytes. 19 March 2019. Accessed 6 April 2019 @ https://www.ecommercebytes.com/2019/03/19/selling-on-instagram-now-possible-with-checkout-feature/.

63. "Is Your Name on the Coke Bottle? Find Out Here." WBRC. 17 July 2014. Accessed April 24 2022 @ https://www.wbrc.com/story/26045391/is-your-name-on-the-coke-bottle-find-out-here/.

64. "Amazon Targets 1,114 'Fake Reviewers' in Seattle Lawsuit." BBC. 18 October 2015. Accessed 5 December 2015 @ http://www.bbc.com/news/technology-34565631.

65. Barysevich, A. "How Social Media Influence 71% Consumer Buying Decisions." SearchEngineWatch. 20 November 2020. Accessed 28 December 2021 @ https://www.searchenginewatch.com/2020/11/20/how-social-media-influence-71-consumer-buying-decisions/.

66. Gossieaux, F., and Moran, E. *The Hyper-Social Organization: Eclipse Your Competition by Leveraging Social Media.* New York: McGraw-Hill Education, 2010.

67. White, K. "Three Brands That Have Changed Their Industries with Social Infrastructure." Gigya. Accessed 5 December 2015 @ https://www.gigya.com/blog/three-brands-that-have-changed-their-industries-with-social-infrastructure/.

68. Ibid.

69. Porterfield, A. "9 Companies Doing Social Media Right and Why." Social Media Examiner. 12 April 2011. Accessed 5 December 2015 @ http://www.socialmediaexaminer.com/9-companies-doing-social-media-right-and-why/.

70. "Calling All Fashionistas." *Glamour*. Accessed 5 December 2015 @ https://www.pinterest.com/pin/388998486534903214/.

71. Dormehl, L. "Spotify Surges to 96 Million Paying Subscribers." CultofMac. 6 February 2019. Accessed @ 10 April 2018 @ https://www.cultofmac.com/605166/spotify-now-has-96-million-paying-subscribers/.

72. Salyer, P. "5 Ways Spotify Is Pioneering the Hyper-Social Business Model. Mashable. 22 March 2012. Accessed 5 December 2015 @ http://mashable.com/2012/03/22/spotify-social-media/#kcMKYaHMbOq2.

73. Johnson, J. "Worldwide Digital Population as of January 2021." Statista. 10 September 2021. Accessed November 2021 @ https://www.statista.com/statistics/617136/digital-population-worldwide/.

74. Dean, B. "Social Network Usage & Growth Statistics: How Many People Use Social Media in 2021?" Backlinko. 10 October 2021. Accessed 28 November 2021 @ https://backlinko.com/social-media-users.

75. Copp, E. "10 Benefits of Social Media for Business." HootSuite Media. 17 August 2016. Accessed 29 November 2016 @ https://blog.hootsuite.com/social-media-for-business/.

76. Fontein, D. "How to Write a Social Media Policy for Your Company." HootSuite Media. 13 January 2016. Accessed 29 November 2016 @ https://blog.hootsuite.com/social-media-policy-for-employees/.

77. This information has been gathered from the company Web site (www.amazon.com) and other promotional materials. For more information and updates, visit the Web site.

78. "Leading Mobile Advertising Markets Worldwide in 2019 and 2020, by Advertising Spending (in Billion U.S. Dollars)." Statista. Accessed 19 April 2022 @ https://www.statista.com/statistics/267112/development-of-revenue-of-mobile-advertising-worldwide/.

79. "Mobile Advertising Spending in the United States from 2017 to 2025, by Format." Statista. Accessed 28 November 2021 @ https://www.statista.com/forecasts/258488/mobile-marketing-sales-impact-in-the-us-by-type.

80. Guttmann, A. "Global Advertising Spending from 2011 to 2019." Statista. 9 August 2019. Accessed 12 September 2019 @ https://www.statista.com/statistics/236943/global-advertising-spending/.

81. Shields, M. "Audi and Starcom Turn to Data Firm PlaceIQ to Gauge Whether Mobile Ads Work." *Wall Street Journal*. 25 August 2015. Accessed 5 December 2015 @ http://blogs.wsj.com/cmo/2015/08/25/audi-and-starcom-turn-to-data-firm-placeiq-to-gauge-whether-mobile-ads-work/?mod=ST1.

82. Minyanville. "Qualcomm's Android-Capable Answer to Apple's iBeacon." Nasdaq. 11 December 2013. Accessed 2 January 2014 @ www.nasdaq.com/article/qualcomms-androidcapable-answer-to-apples-ibeacon-cm310857.

83. "With iBeacon, Apple Aims to Guide You Inside Its Stores and, Soon, Everywhere." Associated Press. 7 December 2013. Accessed 2 January 2014 @ http://gadgets.ndtv.com/mobiles/news/with-ibeacon-apple-aims-to-guide-you-inside-its-stores-and-soon-everywhere-455739.

84. Danova, T. "Apple's iBeacon Is Ready to Take Over the Retail Sector." *Business Insider*. 9 December 2013. Accessed 2 January 2014 @ https://www.businessinsider.in/apples-ibeacon-is-ready-to-take-over-the-retail-sector/articleshow/27147556.cms.

85. Gaudin, S. "Neiman Marcus Wants to Merge the Online and In-Store Shopping Experience." *Computerworld*. 19 January 2016. Accessed 6 December 2016 @ http://www.computerworld.com/article/3024226/retail-it/neiman-marcus-wants-to-merge-the-online-and-in-store-shopping-experience.html.

9

1. Bidgoli, H. "An Integrated Case-Based Approach for Deployment of Global Information Systems." *iNFORMATION—An International Interdisciplinary Journal* 19(9B) (September 2016): 4139–4156.

2. Lock, S. "Revenue of McDonald's Corporation Worldwide in 2021, by Region (in Billion U.S. Dollars)." Statista. 14 April 2022. Accessed 26 April 2022 @ https://www.statista.com/statistics/219453/revenue-of-the-mcdonalds-corporation-by-geographic-region/.

3. Shell, A. "Hottest American Stocks in 2017 Get the Bulk of Sales from Outside the U.S." *USA Today*. 26 September 2017. Accessed 25 December 2017 @ https://www.usatoday.com/story/money/2017/09/26/hottest-american-stocks-2017-get-bulk-sales-outside-u-s/681460001/.

4. Ives, B., and Jarvenpaa, S. "Application of Global Information Technology: Key Issues for Management." *Management Information Systems Quarterly* 15 (1991): 33–49.

5. Eom, S. B. "Transnational Management Systems: An Emerging Tool for Global Strategic Management." *Advanced Management Journal* 59(2) (1994): 22–27.

6. Lucas, H. *Information Systems Concepts for Managers*. San Francisco: McGraw-Hill, 1994: 137–152, 289–315.

7. Harrington, L. H. "The Information Challenge: The Dream of Global Information Visibility Becomes a Reality." *IndustryWeek* 246(7) (1997): 97–100.

8. "Internet World Stats." InternetWorldStats. Accessed 28 November 2021 @ https://www.internetworldstats.com/stats.htm.

9. "Globalizing Your Website." Schreiber Translations. Accessed 4 December 2011 @ www.schreibernet.com/site.nsf/1/globalizing-your-website-1.htm.

10. Sheetz, M. "Bezos Hired a SpaceX Vice President to Run Amazon's Satellite Internet Project after Musk Fired Him." CNBC. 7 April 2019. Accessed 15 April 2019 @ https://www.cnbc.com/2019/04/07/amazon-hired-former-spacex-management-for-bezos-satellite-internet.html.

11. Sheetz, M. "Here's Why Amazon Is Trying to Reach Every Inch of the World with Satellites Providing Internet." CNBC. 8 April 2019. Accessed 15 April 2019 @ https://www.cnbc.com/2019/04/05/jeff-bezos-amazon-internet-satellites-4-billion-new-customers.html.

12. Sitsanis, N. "Top 10 Languages Used on the Internet for 2021." Speakt. 17 January 2021. Accessed 28 November 2021 @ https://speakt.com/top-10-languages-used-internet/.

13. Arfaoui, F. "Percentage of Internet Content for Users by Language." Trustiko. 27 September 2021. Accessed 28 November 2021 @ https://trustiko.com/percentage-of-internet-content-for-users-by-language/.

14. Kemp, S. "Digital 2021: India." DataReportal. 11 February 2021. Accessed 28 November 2021 @ https://datareportal.com/reports/digital-2021-india.

15. Kemp, S. "Digital 2022: Vietnam." DataReportal. 15 February 2022. Accessed 26 April 2022 @ https://datareportal.com/reports/digital-2022-vietnam#:~:text=Internet%20use%20in%20Vietnam%20in%202022&text=Vietnam's%20internet%20penetration%20rate%20stood,percent)%20between%202021%20and%202022.

16. Kemp, S. "Digital 2022: Indonesia." DataReportal. 15 February 2022. Accessed 26 April 2022 @ https://datareportal.com/reports/digital-2022-indonesia.

17. Rusli, E. M. "Five Apps Bringing the Next Billion People Online." *Wall Street Journal*. 21 April 2015. Accessed 5 December 2015 @ http://blogs.wsj.com/digits/2015/04/21/five-apps-bringing-the-next-billion-people-online/?mod=ST1.

18. Rubinstein, M. "M-Pesa and the African Fintech Revolution." NetInterest. 10 September 2021. Accessed 26 April 2022 @ https://www.netinterest.co/p/m-pesa-and-the-african-fintech-revolution-3c1?s=r.

19. Eom, S. B. "Transnational Management Systems: An Emerging Tool for Global Strategic Management." *Advanced Management Journal* 59(2) (1994): 22–27.

20. Ives, B., and Jarvenpaa, S. "Application of Global Information Technology: Key Issues for Management." *Management Information Systems Quarterly* 15 (1991): 33–49.

21. Edwards, R., Ahmad, A., and Moss, S. "Subsidiary Autonomy: The Case of Multinational Subsidiaries in Malaysia." *Journal of International Business Studies* 33(1) (2002): 183–191.

22. Karimi, J., and Konsynski, B. R. "Globalization and Information Management Strategies." *Journal of Management Information Systems* 7(4) (1991): 7–26.

23. Bar, F., and Borrus, M. "Information Networks and Competitive Advantage: Issues for Government Policy and Corporate Strategy." *International Journal of Technology Management* 7(6–8) (1992): 398–408.

24. Yadav, V., Adya, M., Sridhar, V., and Nath, D. "Flexible Global Software Development (GSD): Antecedents of Success in Requirements Analysis." *Journal of Global Information Management* 17(1) (2009): 1–30.

25. Klein, K. "Globalization, Small Biz-Style." *Bloomberg Businessweek.* 23 January 2008. Accessed 14 July 2010 @ https://www.bloomberg.com/news/articles/2008-01-23/globalization-small-biz-stylebusinessweek-business-news-stock-market-and-financial-advice.

26. Kong, L. "Data Protection and Transborder Data Flow in the European and Global Context." *European Journal of International Law* 21(2) (2010): 441–456. Accessed 13 February 2013 @ http://ejil.oxfordjournals.org/content/21/2/441.full.

27. "General Environment: Six Factors That Influence Business." Indeed. 29 April 2021. Accessed 26 April 2022 @ https://www.indeed.com/career-advice/career-development/general-environment#:~:text=There%20are%20many%20forces%20influencing,technology%2C%20environment%20and%20legal%20factors.

28. Eastwood, G. "Video Conferencing Market to Grow to $6 Billion by 2020." UC Insight. 10 March 2015. Accessed 6 December 2016 @ https://www.fortunebusinessinsights.com/industry-reports/video-conferencing-market-100293.

29. Global Industry Analysts, Inc. "Globalization of Businesses and Workforce Mobility to Drive Global Market for Video Conferencing Systems." PRWEB. 19 February 2013. Accessed 2 January 2014 @ www.prweb.com/releases/video_conferencing_system/enterprise_ISDN_IP_system/prweb10444764.htm.

30. "Company Overview." Alibaba Group. Accessed 12 September 2019 @ http://www.alibabagroup.com/en/about/overview.

31. Broad, M. "Alibaba: What Exactly Does It Do?" *BBC.* 14 September 2014. Accessed 20 November 2014 @ http://www.bbc.com/news/business-29077495.

32. Mun, J. "Barriers for Globalization." *Yahoo! Voices.* 27 October 2008. Accessed 14 February 2013 @ https://selimdu.wordpress.com/tag/barriers-of-globalization/.

33. Haeckel, S., and Nolan, R. "Managing by Wire (Enterprise Models Driving Strategic Information Technology)." *Harvard Business Review* 71 (1993): 122–132.

34. Passino, J., and Severance, D. "Harnessing the Potential of Information Technology for Support of the New Global Organization." *Human Resource Management* 29(1) (1990): 69–76.

35. Karimi, J., and Konsynski, B. R. "Globalization and Information Management Strategies." *Journal of Management Information Systems* 7(4) (1991): 7–26.

36. Schatz, W. "Scatter-Shot Systems: There Are Lots of Ways to Buy and Manage Technology in a Decentralized Environment." *Computerworld* 30 (August 1993): 75–79.

37. Kettinger, W., Grover, V., Guha, S., and Segars, A. "Strategic Information Systems Revisited: A Study in Sustainability and Performance." *Management Information Systems Quarterly* 18(1) (1994): 31–58.

38. Ives, B., and Jarvenpaa, S. "Application of Global Information Technology: Key Issues for Management." *Management Information Systems Quarterly* 15 (1991): 33–49.

39. Fleenor, D. "The Coming and Going of the Global Corporation." *Columbia Journal of World Business* 28(4) (1993): 6–10.

40. Laudon, K., and Laudon, J. *Management Information Systems: Organization and Technology.* Upper Saddle River, NJ: Prentice Hall, 1996: 668–692.

41. Boler-Davis, A. "How GM Uses Social Media to Improve Cars and Customer Service." Hbr.org. 12 February 2016. Accessed 28 November 2021 @ https://hbr.org/2016/02/how-gm-uses-social-media-to-improve-cars-and-customer-service.

42. Kettinger, W., Grover, V., Guha, S., and Segars, A. "Strategic Information Systems Revisited: A Study in Sustainability and Performance." *Management Information Systems Quarterly* 18(1) (1994): 31–58.

43. Pham, K. "Top 10 Countries for Outsourcing Software Development 2021." Reliasoftware. 26 July 2021. Accessed 28 November 2021 @ https://reliasoftware.com/blog/top-10-countries-for-outsourcing-software-development-2021/.

44. "Technological Innovation at FedEx." FedEx. Accessed 19 February 2013 @ www.fedex.com/ma/about/overview/innovation.html.

45. Ibid.

46. "FedEx Global Trade Manager." FedEx. Accessed 19 February 2013 @ www.fedex.com/GTM?cntry_code=us.

47. "FedEx Innovation." FedEx. Accessed 19 February 2013 @ http://about.van.fedex.com/fedex-innovation.

48. Biehl, M. "Success Factors for Implementing Global Information Systems." *Communications of the ACM* 50(1) (2007).

49. Gelfand, M. J., Erez, M., and Ayean, Z. "Cross-Cultural Organizational Behavior." *Annual Review of Psychology* 58 (2007): 479–514.

50. Huff, S. "Managing Global Information Technology." *Business Quarterly* 56(2) (1991): 71–75.

51. Ambrosio, J. "Global Software: When Does It Make Sense to Share Software with Offshore Units?" *Computerworld* 2 (August 1993): 74–77.

52. Spiegler, R. "Globalization: Easier Said Than Done." *The Industry Standard* 9 (October 2000): 136–155.

53. Huff, S. "Managing Global Information Technology." *Business Quarterly* 56(2) (1991): 71–75.

54. Mozur, P. "Twitter Users in China Face Detention and Threats in New Beijing Crackdown." *New York Times.* 10 January 2019. Accessed 15 April 2019 @ https://www.nytimes.com/2019/01/10/business/china-twitter-censorship-online.html.

55. "You Won't Believe This [*sic*] Countries Banned Facebook, Twitter and YouTube." FreeBrowsingLink. Accessed 15 April 2019 @ https://www.freebrowsinglink.com/countries-banned-social-media/.

56. *Yahoo v. LICRA.* U.S. Court of Appeals (9th Cir., 2004, D.C. No. CV-00-21275-JF).

57. Business Software Alliance. "Fifth Annual BSA and IDC Global Software Piracy Study." 2007. Accessed 17 August 2010 @ https://www.bsa.org/files/reports/2007_global_piracy_study.pdf.

58. Handley, L. "US Companies Are Not Exempt from Europe's New Data Privacy Rules — And Here's What They Need to Do About It." CNBC. 25 April 2018. Accessed 4 July 2019 @ https://www.cnbc.com/2018/04/25/gdpr-data-privacy-rules-in-europe-and-how-they-apply-to-us-companies.html.

59. Huff, S. "Managing Global Information Technology." *Business Quarterly* 56(2) (1991): 71–75.

60. This information has been gathered from the company Web site (www.sap.com) and other promotional materials. For more detailed information and updates, visit the Web site.

61. Norris, R. "An Evaluation of Toyota Motor Company (TMC) Information Systems." Yahoo! Voices. 23 May 2007. Accessed 15 February 2013 @ https://www.studymode.com/essays/Toyota-Company-Marketing-Analysis-Toyota-Motor-Company-85816749.html.

62. "Toyota Production System." Toyota. Accessed 15 February 2013 @ www.toyota-global.com/company/vision_philosophy/toyota_production_system.

63. Duvall, M. "Toyota: Daily Dealings." Baseline. 5 September 2006. Accessed 15 February 2013 @ www.baselinemag.com/c/a/Infrastructure/What-Is-Driving-Toyota/2.

64. "Toyota Motor Europe Upgrades Vehicle Order Management System with Oracle E-Business Suite 12.1 to Help Improve Customer Allocation and Lead Times." Oracle. 5 October 2011. Accessed 15 February 2013 @ https://www.newswiretoday.com/news/99155/Toyota-Motor-Europe-Upgrades-Vehicle-Order-Management-System-with-Oracle-E-Business-Suite-12.1-to-Help-Improve-Customer-Allocation-and-Lead-Times/.

65. Baldwin, H. "Supply Chain 2013: Stop Playing Whack-a-Mole with Security Threats." *InfoWorld.* 30 April 2013. Accessed 2 January 2014 @ www.infoworld.com/d/security/supply-chain-2013-stop-playing-whack-mole-security-threats-217547?source=IFWNLE_nlt_sec_2013-05-02.

66. Ibid.

10

1. Wood, J., and Silver, D. *Joint Application Design*. New York: Wiley, 1989.

2. Bensaou, M., and Earl, E. "The Right Mind-Set for Managing Information Technology." *Harvard Business Review* 76(5) (1998): 109.

3. Duvall, M. "Airline Reservation System Hits Turbulence." *Baseline*. 25 July 2007. Accessed 16 July 2010 @ http://www.baselinemag.com/c/a/Business-Intelligence/Airline-Reservation-System-Hits-Turbulence/.

4. Doke, E. "An Industry Survey of Emerging Prototyping Methodologies." *Information and Management* 18(4) (1990): 169–176.

5. "Project Management Statistics: Trends and Common Mistakes in 2022." Teamstage. Accessed 5 May 2022 @ https://teamstage.io/project-management-statistics/#:~:text=9.,of%20the%20strategic%20initiatives%20fail.

6. Wise, J. "Project Management Statistics 2022: Success & Failure Rates." Earthweb. 1 May 2022. Accessed 5 May 2022 @ https://earthweb.com/project-management-statistics/.

7. Florentine, S. "More Than Half of IT Projects Still Failing." *CIO*. 11 May 2016. Accessed 16 April 2018 @ https://www.cio.com/article/3068502/project-management/more-than-half-of-it-projects-still-failing.html.

8. Grimes, R. A. "7 Indispensable Project Management Tips." *CSO*. 29 July 2014. Accessed 12 September 2019 @ https://www.csoonline.com/article/2608606/7-indispensable-project-management-tips.html.

9. Benson, D. "A Field Study of End User Computing: Findings and Issues." *MIS Quarterly* 7(4) (1983): 35–40.

10. Tayntor, C. "New Challenges or the End of EUC." *Information Systems Management* 11(3) (1994): 86–88.

11. McKendrick, J. "Ten Examples of SOA at Work, Right Now." *ZDNet*. 3 January 2006. Accessed 15 July 2010 @ www.zdnet.com/blog/service-oriented/ten-examples-of-soa-at-work-right-now/508.

12. Franklin Jr., C. "Rapid Application Development: Know the Right Tools." *InformationWeek*. 26 October 2016. Accessed 12 December 2016 @ http://www.informationweek.com/software/enterprise-applications/rapid-application-development-know-the-right-tools/a/d-id/1327294.

13. Copeland, L. "Extreme Programming." *Computerworld*. 3 December 2001. Accessed 5 May 2022 @ https://www.computerworld.com/article/2585634/extreme-programming.html.

14. Ibid.

15. Tamang, P. "Two Agile Frameworks Small Businesses Should Know About." Software Advice. 28 November 2018. Accessed 5 May 2022 @ https://www.softwareadvice.com/resources/agile-frameworks/.

16. "Principles Behind the Agile Manifesto." Accessed 16 July 2010 @ https://agilealliance.org/agile101/12-principles-behind-the-agile-manifesto/.

17. Pratt, M. K. "Low-code and No-code Development Platforms." Search Software Quality. 11 March 2021. Accessed 10 December 2021 @ https://searchsoftwarequality.techtarget.com/definition/low-code-no-code-development-platform?amp=1.

18. England, S. "What Is No Code? The Pros and Cons of No Code for Software Development." Codebots. 16 January 2020. Accessed 10 December 2021 @ https://codebots.com/low-code/what-is-no-code-the-pros-and-cons-of-no-code-for-software-development.

19. Ibid.

20. Joao-Pierre, S. R. "HealthBridge's Low-Code Strategy to Process Medical Claims." *InformationWeek*. 2 April 2021. Accessed 10 December 2021 @ https://informationweek.com/devops/project-management/healthbridges-low-code-strategy-to-process-medical-claims/a/d-id/1340573?.

21. Joao-Pierre, S. R. "NOAA Fisheries Talks Going No-Code for Project Management." *InformationWeek*. 4 August 2020. Accessed 10 December 2021 @ https://www.informationweek.com/project-management/noaa-fisheries-talks-going-no-code-for-project-management.

22. Davis, J. "Texas County Turns to Low-Code Database for Vaccine Registrations." *InformationWeek*. 23 March 2021. Accessed 10 December 2021 @ https://www.informationweek.com/software-platforms/texas-county-turns-to-low-code-database-for-vaccine-registrations.

23. "About HomeAway, Inc." Homeaway.com. Accessed 19 February 2013 @ https://www.dnb.com/business-directory/company-profiles.homeaway_inc.5539ea9434359e0ac115406fb33c378d.html.

24. Krill, P. "Agile: How It Became a Way of Life at HomeAway." *InfoWorld*. 1 May 2012. Accessed 18 February 2013 @ www.infoworld.com/d/application-development/agile-how-it-became-way-of-life-homeaway-192102?source=IFWNLE_nlt_daily_2012-05-01.

25. This information has been gathered from the company Web site (https://www.broadcom.com/) and other promotional materials. For more information and updates, visit the Web site.

26. Dilmegani, C. "32 Low Code/No Code Statistics from Reputable Sources." Research.aimultiple. 23 November 2021. Accessed 10 December 2021 @ https://research.aimultiple.com/low-code-statistics/.

27. Rosenbaum, E. "Next Frontier in Microsoft, Google, Amazon Cloud Battle Is over a World without Code." CNBC. 1 April 2020. Accessed 10 December 2021 @https://www.cnbc.com/2020/04/01/new-microsoft-google-amazon-cloud-battle-over-world-without-code.html.

28. "Low-Code Is the Future – OutSystems Named a Leader in the 2019 Gartner Magic Quadrant for Enterprise Low-Code Application." Bloomberg. 12 August 2019. Accessed 10 December 2021 @ https://www.bloomberg.com/press-releases/2019-08-12/low-code-is-the-future-outsystems-named-a-leader-in-the-2019-gartner-magic-quadrant-for-enterprise-low-code-application.

29. "OutSystems Platform." Accessed 10 December 2021 @ https://www.outsystems.com/p/modern-development/?utm_source=google&utm_medium=cpc&utm_campaign=Aquisition_G_NA_Search_Brand&utm_term=outsystems%20software&utm_content=Try-for-free&gclid=EAIaIQobChMIsem-4I3O9AIVBRDnCh1t2QC_EAAYASAAEgKzt_D_BwE.

30. York, M. "Crowdsourcing: It's Not Just for Logos and Web Design." About.com. Accessed 14 August 2011 @ http://entrepreneurs.about.com/od/casestudies/a/Crowdsourcing-Its-Not-Just-For-Logos-And-Web-Design.htm.

11

1. "Our Company." Coca-Cola Company. Accessed 20 February 2013 @ www.coca-colacompany.com/our-company.

2. "Coca-Cola Supply Chain Management Success Story." CSC. Accessed 20 February 2013 @ https://supplychainminded.com/coca-cola-supply-chain-management-success-story/.

3. O'Reilly, J. "Green Logistics the Walmart Way." Inbound Logistics. June 2013. Accessed 14 December 2016 @ http://www.inboundlogistics.com/cms/article/green-logistics-the-walmart-way/.

4. "Sustainability Goals." Accessed 28 December 2021 @ https://corporate.walmart.com/photos/sustainability-goals.

5. "Walmart to Cut 20 Million Metric Tons of Greenhouse Gas Pollution by 2015." ThinkProgress. 27 February 2010. Accessed 14 December 2016 @ https://archive.thinkprogress.org/wal-mart-to-cut-20-million-metric-tons-of-greenhouse-gas-pollution-by-2015-46a123e47cd7/.

6. "Walmart Launches New Reusable Bag Campaign; Announces 93 Million Metric Tons of Supplier Emission Reductions through Project Gigaton and Announces New Sustainable Textile Goals." Walmart. 10 April 2019. Accessed 3 May 2019 @ https://news.walmart.com/2019/04/10/walmart-launches-new-reusable-bag-campaign-announces-93-million-metric-tons-of-supplier-emission-reductions-through-project-gigaton-and-announces-new-sustainable-textile-goals.

7. McLaughlin, K. "Accelerating Climate Action: Project Gigaton™ Marks Key Milestone." Walmart. 6 April 2022. Accessed 11 May 2022 @ https://corporate.walmart.com/newsroom/2022/04/06/accelerating-climate-action-project-gigaton-marks-key-milestone.

8. "3D Printing Market." Markets and markets. Accessed 24 December 2021 @ https://www.marketsandmarkets.com/Market-Reports/3d-printing-market-1276.html?gclid=EAIaIQobChMIl57U3Pu9AIVwxXUAR0CiQsAEAAYAyAAEgLIGPD_BwE.

9. Gilpin, L. "10 Industries 3D Printing Will Disrupt or Decimate." TechRepublic. 12 February 2014. Accessed 6 December 2016 @ http://www.techrepublic.com/article/10-industries-3d-printing-will-disrupt-or-decimate/.

10. "3D Printing: Impact on Supply Chains." Scmdojo. Accessed 28 December 2021 @ https://www.scmdojo.com/3d-printing-impact-on-supply-chains/.

11. Wellers, D. and Rander, M. "4D Printing: Self-Assemble, Self-Shape, Self-Repair." *Digitalist*. 5 December 2018. Accessed 1 May 2019 @ https://www.digitalistmag.com/digital-economy/2018/12/05/4d-printing-self-assemble-self-shape-self-repair-06189497.

12. "What Is 4D Printing, Anyway?" AMFG. 5 February 2019. Accessed 1 May 2019 @ https://amfg.ai/2019/02/05/what-is-4d-printing/.

13. Zaleski, A. "How 3D Printing Saved a 5-Year-Old's Life." *Fortune*. 7 October 2015. Accessed 6 December 2016 @ http://fortune.com/2015/10/07/3d-printing-saved-a-5-year-olds-life/.

14. Lee, K. "Medical 3D Printing Lowers Risks and Cost of Complex Surgeries." SearchHealthIT. Accessed 6 December 2016 @ http://searchhealthit.techtarget.com/feature/Medical-3D-printing-lowers-risk-and-cost-of-complex-surgeries.

15. Meskó, B. "12 Things We Can 3D Print in Medicine Right Now." 3D Printing Industry. Accessed 6 December 2016 @ https://3dprintingindustry.com/news/12-things-we-can-3d-print-in-medicine-right-now-42867/.

16. Master, N. "3 Companies Successfully Using Drones in the Supply Chain." RFgen Software. 31 May 2016. Accessed 6 December 2016 @ http://www.rfgen.com/blog/3-companies-successfully-using-drones-in-the-supply-chain.

17. McFarland, M. "Domino's Delivers Pizza by Drone in New Zealand." CNN Tech. 26 August 2016. Accessed 6 December 2016 @ http://money.cnn.com/2016/08/26/technology/dominos-drone-new-zealand/.

18. Young, T. "Can Drones Be Taken Seriously in the Supply Chain?" Supply Chain Digital. 30 July 2016. Accessed 14 December 2016 @ https://www.information-age.com/can-drones-taken-seriously-supply-chain-123461906/.

19. Meola, A. "Here's What to Expect from the FAA's Upcoming Drone Regulations." *Business Insider*. 17 May 2016. Accessed 14 December 2016 @ http://www.businessinsider.com/heres-what-to-expect-from-the-faas-upcoming-drone-regulations-2016-5.

20. Craig, W. "2019 Trends: 5 Practical Uses for Drones in the Supply Chain." GSI. Accessed 3 May 2019 @ https://www.getgsi.com/2019-trends-5-practical-uses-for-drones-in-the-supply-chain/.

21. Freeman, D. "A Drone Just Flew a Kidney to a Transplant Patient for the First Time Ever — It Won't Be the Last." CNBC. 3 May 2019. Accessed 5 May 2019 @ https://www.cnbc.com/2019/05/03/drone-flies-a-kidney-to-a-transplant-patient-for-the-first-time-ever.html.

22. "Internet of Things (IoT) Connected Devices Installed Base Worldwide from 2015 to 2025." Statista. 27 November 2016. Accessed 12 September 2019 @ https://www.statista.com/statistics/471264/iot-number-of-connected-devices-worldwide/.

23. Shankar, U. "How the Internet of Things Impacts Supply Chains." Inbound Logistics. Accessed 14 December 2016 @ http://www.inboundlogistics.com/cms/article/how-the-internet-of-things-impacts-supply-chains/.

24. Smith, S. D. "Why the IoT Is the Key to Efficiency in the Supply Chain." ModusLink Global Solutions. 23 March 2016. Accessed 14 December 2016 @ https://www.moduslink.com/iot-key-efficiency-supply-chain/.

25. Weier, M. "Coke's RFID-Based Dispensers Redefine Business Intelligence." *InformationWeek*. 6 June 2009. Accessed 7 October 2010 @ www.informationweek.com/news/mobility/RFID/showArticle.jhtml?articleID=217701971.

26. Weis, S. "RFID: Technical Considerations." In *The Handbook of Technology Management*.

Edited by H. Bigdoli. Hoboken, NJ: Wiley, 2010.

27. "QR Code Features." QR Code.com. Accessed 7 December 2011 @ www.denso-wave.com/qrcode/qrfeature-e.html.

28. Campbell, A. "QR Codes, Barcodes and RFID: What's the Difference?" *Small Business Trends*. 21 February 2011. Accessed 2 December 2011 @ http://smallbiztrends.com/2011/02/qr-codes-barcodes-rfid-difference.html.

29. Lucas, A. "QR Codes Have Replaced Restaurant Menus. Industry Experts Say It Isn't a Fad." CNBC. 21 August 2021. Accessed 24 December 2021 @ https://www.cnbc.com/2021/08/21/qr-codes-have-replaced-restaurant-menus-industry-experts-say-it-isnt-a-fad.html.

30. Quinn, H. "QR Codes May Be Too Much Work for Consumers, UD Study Finds." technical.ly/Delaware. 12 June 2019. Accessed 24 July 2019 @ https://technical.ly/delaware/2019/06/12/qr-codes-may-be-too-much-work-for-consumers-university-of-delaware-study-finds/.

31. Sprague, M. "Close-Up with Google's New QR Code Generator." Search Engine Land. 7 October 2010. Accessed 2 December 2011 @ http://searchengineland.com/close-up-with-googles-new-qr-code-generator-52248.

32. Kotz, L. "Sacre Bleu Wine Adapts QR Codes to Labels." DataMart Direct. 8 August 2012. Accessed 6 March 2013 @ www.datamartdirect.com/index.php/2012/08/sacre-blue-wine-adapts-qr-codes-to-labels.

33. Ankeny, J. "How One Small Company Is Using QR Codes." Entrepreneur. 3 October 2011. Accessed 6 March 2013 @ www.entrepreneur.com/article/220359.

34. Goldberg, J. "Best Buy Deploys QR Codes to Enhance Shopping Experience." Retail Geek. Accessed 6 March 2013 @ http://retailgeek.com/best-buy-deploys-qr-codes-to-enhance-shopping-experience.

35. Tsirulnik, G. "Calvin Klein Activates Billboards with QR Codes Pushing Mobile Video Ad." Mobile Marketer. 29 July 2010. Accessed 6 March 2013 @ www.mobilemarketer.com/cms/news/advertising/6933.html.

36. Sprague, M. "QR Codes: Are You Ready for Paper-Based Hyperlinks?" Search Engine Land. 13 September 2010. Accessed 6 March 2013 @ http://searchengineland.com/qr-codes-are-you-ready-for-paper-based-hyperlinks-49684.

37. Kats, R. "McDonald's Continues Mobile Reign with QR Code Push." Mobile Marketer. 30 July 2012. Accessed 6 March 2013 @ www.mobilemarketer.com/cms/news/software-technology/13410.html.

38. Johnson, L. "PepsiCo Puts QR Codes in the Center of New Global Campaign." Marketing Dive. Accessed 28 December @ https://www.marketingdive.com/ex/mobilemarketer/cms/news/content/14090.html.

39. Lamb, R. "Ralph Lauren Steps Up Mobile Game with Customized QR Codes." *Luxury Daily*. 20 September 2011. Accessed 6 March 2013 @ www.luxurydaily.com/ralph-lauren-steps-up-mobile-game-with-customized-qr-codes.

40. Kats, R. "Starbucks Refreshes Summer Campaign with QR Codes." Marketing Dive. Accessed 28 December 2021 @ https://www.marketingdive.com/ex/mobilemarketer/cms/news/software-technology/13338.html.

41. Roy, E. "What Is Global Supply Chain Management?" Trade Ready. 16 February 2017. Accessed 1 May 2019 @ http://www.tradeready.ca/2017/topics/supply-chain-management/global-supply-chain-management/.

42. "Global Supply Chain: Advantages and Disadvantages." Studycorgi. Accessed 28 December 2021 @ https://studycorgi.com/global-supply-chain-advantages-and-disadvantages/.

43. Payne, A. *Handbook of CRM: Achieving Excellence through Customer Management*. Oxford, MA: Butterworth-Heinemann, 2005.

44. Wailgum, T. "CRM Definition and Solutions." *CIO*. Accessed 26 July 2010 @ https://www2.cio.com.au/article/617872/crm-definition-solutions/.

45. "Corporate Stats and Facts." Delta. 11 May 2022. Accessed 11 May 2022 @ http://news.delta.com/corporate-stats-and-facts.

46. "Delta Takes Off with Salesforce." Accessed 6 December 2015 @ https://www.salesforce.com/ca/customer-success-stories/delta/.

47. Wailgum, T. "CRM Definition and Solutions." *CIO*. Accessed 26 July 2010 @ https://www2.cio.com.au/article/617872/crm-definition-solutions/.

48. Clark, B. "Personalize vs. Customize: How Are They Different?" Acquire.io. 10 September 2021. Accessed 28 December 2021 @ https://acquire.io/blog/personalization-vs-customization/.

49. "Selling with Personalization: Why Amazon.Com Succeeds and You Can Too." Rich Relevance. Accessed 28 December 2021 @ https://richrelevance.com/2008/08/02/smallbiztechnology-com-selling-with-personalization-why-amazon-com-succeeds-and-you-can-too/.

50. Ibid.

51. Aaronson, J. "Personalization Technologies: A Primer." ClickZ. 24 August 2007. Accessed 26 March 2012 @ www.clickz.com/3626837.

52. "Top Ten Powerful Statistics for Amazon Sellers in 2021." Accessed 28 December 2021 @ https://channelkey.com/top-ten-powerful-statistics-for-amazon-sellers-in-2021.

53. Rao, L. "How Amazon Is Tackling Personalization and Curation for Sellers on Its Marketplace." TechCrunch. 31 August 2013. Accessed 2 January 2014 @ http://techcrunch.com/2013/08/31/how-amazon-is-tackling-personalization-and-curation-for-sellers-on-its-marketplace.

54. Koenig, M. E. D. "What Is KM? Knowledge Management Explained." Kmworld.com. 15 January 2018. Accessed 28 December 2021 @ https://www.kmworld.com/About/What_is_Knowledge_Management.

55. Scalco, D. "5 Companies Examples [sic] with A+ Knowledge Management Skills." Proprofs. 17 June 2021. Accessed 26 December 2021 @ https://www.proprofs.com/knowledgebase/blog/5-companies-knowledge-management-skills/.

56. Rosenberg, M. "The Knowledge Management Genius of Amazon.com." Learning

Solutions. 29 July 2014. Accessed 26 December 2021 @ https://learningsolutionsmag.com/articles/1480/the-knowledge-management-genius-of-amazoncom.

57. Joglekar, A. "Transform Your Business with Knowledge Management." Connect.verint. 11 September 2019. Accessed 29 December 2021 @ https://connect.verint.com/b/customer-engagement/posts/transform-your-business-with-knowledge-management.

58. Vormittag Associates. "Saudi-Based Auto and Electronics Distributor Streamlines Operations with VAI's S2K Software." VAI. Accessed 17 July 2010 @ www.vai.net/company/success-stories/naghi-group.html.

59. Bidgoli, H. "Cloud Computing Deployment: What Have We Learned from Real Life Implementations and Practices." *Journal of Strategic Innovation and Sustainability* 13(1) (2018): 36–52.

60. Brodkin, J. "Amazon and IBM Are the Cloud's Biggest Players." *InfoWorld*. 15 July 2010. Accessed 1 April 2019 @ http://www.infoworld.com/d/cloud-computing/amazon-and-ibm-are-the-clouds-biggest-players-484?page=0,0&source=IFWNLE_nlt_wrapup_2010-07-16.

61. "Advantages and Disadvantages of Cloud-Based ERP Systems." Planet Together. 6 June 2018. Accessed 1 April 2019 @ https://www.planettogether.com/blog/advantages-and-disadvantages-of-cloud-based-erp-systems.

62. Larkin, A. "Disadvantages of Cloud Computing." Cloud Academy. 26 June 2018. Accessed 1 April 2019 @ https://cloudacademy.com/blog/disadvantages-of-cloud-computing/.

63. This information has been gathered from the company Web site (www.salesforce.com) and other promotional materials. For more information and updates, visit the Web site.

64. "Amazon ERP System – What ERP System Does Amazon Go Use?" Dynamics.folio3. 6 August 2021. Accessed 30 December 2021 @https://dynamics.folio3.com/blog/amazon-erp-system/.

65. "Starbucks Company Profile." Accessed 30 December 2021 @ https://stories.starbucks.com/press/2019/company-profile/.

66. "My Starbucks Idea Creates Mobile Drive-Thru, Cake Pops, and More." Ideawake. 19 January 2021. Accessed 30 December 2021 @https://ideawake.com/my-starbucks-idea-creates-mobile-drive-thru-cake-pops-and-more/.

12

1. Simon, H. *The New Science of Management Decision*. Englewood Cliffs, NJ: Prentice-Hall, 1977.

2. Sprague, R., and Carlson, E. *Building Effective Decision Support Systems*. Englewood Cliffs, NJ: Prentice-Hall, 1982.

3. Ibid.

4. Keen, P. "Value Analysis: Justifying Decision Support Systems." *MIS Quarterly* 5(1) (1981): 1–15.

5. Alter, S. *Decision Support Systems: Current Practice and Continuing Challenges*. Reading, MA: Addison-Wesley, 1979.

6. Sauter, V. *Decision Support Systems for Business Intelligence*, 2nd Edition. Hoboken, NJ: Wiley, 2011.

7. Turban, E., Sharda, R., and Delen, D. *Decision Support and Business Intelligence Systems*, 9th Edition. Englewood Cliffs, NJ: Prentice-Hall, 2011.

8. "How to Keep Fresh Products on the Shelves." Accessed 12 January 2022 @ https://www.sas.com/content/sascom/en_nz/customers/forecasting-supply-chain-nestle.html.

9. Watson, H., and Rainer, K., Jr. "A Manager's Guide to Executive Support Systems." *Business Horizons* 34(2) (1991): 44–50.

10. Liang, L., and Miranda, R. "Dashboards and Scorecards: Executive Information Systems for the Public Sector." *Government Finance Review*. December 2001. Accessed 16 July 2012 @ https://www.thefreelibrary.com/Dashboards+and+Scorecards%3A+Executive+Information+Systems+for+the...-a081530552.

11. Glover, H., Watson, H., and Rainer, R. "20 Ways to Waste an EIS Investment." *Information Strategy: The Executive's Journal* (Winter 1992): 11–17.

12. Watson, H., and Satzinger, J. "Guidelines for Designing EIS Interfaces." *Information Systems Management* (Fall 1994): 46–52.

13. "Technology Drives Decisions at Hyundai." SAS. Accessed 2 January 2014 @ www.sas.com/success/pdf/hyundai.pdf.

14. "GIS for Insurance." eSpatial. Accessed 1 April 2012 @ http://www.esri.com/library/whitepapers/pdfs/gis-for-insurance-claims-process.pdf.

15. "GIS Software for Insurance Mapping." Caliper Corporation. Accessed 1 April 2012 @ www.caliper.com/maptitude/insurance/default.htm.

16. Romeo, J. "Target Marketing with GIS." Geospatial Solutions. May 2005. Accessed 1 April 2012 @ https://gis.smumn.edu/GradProjects/JohnsonJB.pdf.

17. "3 Simple Ways GIS Data Can Improve Marketing and Sales." ETI Software. 19 July 2016. Accessed 12 January 20221 @ https://etisoftware.com/resources/blog/3-simple-ways-gis-data-can-improve-marketing-and-sales/.

18. "GIS for Real Estate." ESRI. February 2007. Accessed 1 April 2012 @ www.esri.com/library/bestpractices/real-estate.pdf.

19. "GIS (Geographic Information System)." Accessed 12 January 2022 @ https://www.nationalgeographic.org/encyclopedia/geographic-information-system-gis/.

20. Ibid.

21. Robb, D. "Geographic Information Systems: Mapping Out Enterprise Impact." Enterprise Apps Today. 10 February 2014. Accessed 25 December 2016 @ http://www.enterpriseappstoday.com/business-intelligence/geographic-information-systems-mapping-out-enterprise-impact.html.

22. Clancy, H. "Why Walgreens Uses Interactive Maps Plus Analytics to Evaluate Store Locations." *Fortune*. 22 October 2015. Accessed 25 December 2016 @ http://fortune.com/2015/10/22/why-walgreens-uses-interactive-maps-plus-analytics-to-evaluate-store-locations/.

23. "1000 GIS Applications & Uses – How GIS Is Changing the World." GIS Geography. 25 April 2019. Accessed 13 June 2019 @ https://gisgeography.com/gis-applications-uses/.

24. Pratt, M. "GIS Systems Lead Response to COVID-19." ESRI. Spring 2020. Accessed 18 May 2022 @ https://www.esri.com/about/newsroom/arcuser/gis-systems-lead-response-to-covid-19/.

25. O'Cionnaith, F. "GIS on the Front Lines in Fighting Disease." ESRI. 19 December 2007. Accessed 1 April 2012 @ http://www.esri.com/news/arcnews/fall12articles/can-gis-help-fight-the-spread-of-malaria.html.

26. Dempsey, C. "Monitor the Swine Flu Real-time with Google Maps." GIS Lounge. 27 April 2009. Accessed 16 July 2010 @ http://gislounge.com/monitor-the-swine-flu-real-time-with-google-maps.

27. Victoria, S. "3 Types of Collaboration Software Tools to Improve Your Workflow." Ruby Garage. 19 July 2019. Accessed 13 June 2019 @ https://rubygarage.org/blog/collaboration-software-types.

28. "What Is Skype?" Support.Skype. Accessed 18 May 2022 @ https://support.skype.com/en/faq/fa6/what-is-skype#:~:text=Skype%20is%20software%20that%20enables,your%20mobile%2C%20computer%20or%20tablet.

29. "FaceTime: Be in Two Places at Once." Apple. Accessed 20 February 2013 @ www.apple.com/ios/facetime/?cid=wwa-us-kwg-features-00001&siclientid=6381&sessguid=e5147ce0-ea29-47ed-914d-e1058f57bd71&userguid=e5147ce0-ea29-47ed-914d-e1058f57bd71&permguid=e5147ce0-ea29-47ed-914d-e1058f57bd71.

30. "Tango." *Tango.me*. Accessed 20 February 2013 @ tango.me.

31. "Get Started. About Hangouts." Google. Accessed 20 February 2013 @ http://support.google.com/plus/bin/answer.py?hl=en&answer=1215273.

32. "What Is ooVoo?" OoVoo. Accessed 20 February 2013 @ https://www.oovoo.com/.

33. "One Consistent Enterprise Experience." Zoom.us. Accessed 20 February 2013 @ zoom.us.

34. Mossberg, W. S. "A Chance to Call 15 Friends to Video Chat in High Def." *Wall Street Journal*. 21 August 2012. Accessed 20 February 2013 @ http://online.wsj.com/article/SB10000872396390444443504577603383238616426.html?mod=djem_jiewr_IT_domainid.

35. Finnegan, M. "Task Management Apps: Collaborative Project Tracking Tools for the Digital Workplace." *Computerworld*. 3 April 2019. Accessed 13 June 2019 @ https://www.computerworld.com/article/3386418/task-management-apps-collaborative-project-tracking-tools-for-the-digital-workplace.html.

36. "Google Apps for Work." Google. Accessed 6 December 2015 @ https://www.google.com/work/apps/business/products/.

37. Udell, J. "For Remote Collaboration, Google Apps Still Can't Be Beat." *InfoWorld*. 18 May 2015. Accessed 6 December 2015 @ http://www.infoworld.com/article/2923216/collaboration/for-remote-collaboration-google-apps-still-cant-be-beat.html?phint=newt%3Dinfoworld_cloud_computing&phint=idg_eid%3Da74f01173c5

d192b6e17e3ba45b5c85f#tk.IFWNLE_nlt_cloud_2015-05-18&siteid=&phint=tpcs%3D&phint=idg_eid%3-Da74f01173c5d192b6e17e3ba45b5c85f.

38. "What Is SharePoint?" Microsoft. Accessed 2 January 2014 @ https://support.microsoft.com/en-us/office/what-is-sharepoint-97f5b915e6-651b-43b2-827d-fb25777f446f.

39. Victoria, S. "3 Types of Collaboration Software Tools to Improve Your Workflow." Ruby Garage. 19 July 2019. Accessed 13 June 2019 @ https://rubygarage.org/blog/collaboration-software-types.

40. "Google Apps for Work." Google. Accessed 22 September 2019 @ https://www.google.com/work/apps/business/products/.

41. This information has been gathered from the company Web site (www.sas.com) and other promotional materials. For more information and updates, visit the Web site.

42. "UPS Speeds ORION Deployment and Takes Routing Optimization to New Heights." UPS. 30 October 2013. Accessed 2 January 2014 @ www.pressroom.ups.com/Press+Releases/Archive/2013/Q4/UPS+Speeds+ORION+Deployment+And+Takes+Routing+Optimization+To+New+Heights.

43. Gilbert, E. "Predictive Analytics Route Planning Algorithm at UPS Followed a Long Path to Success." Dataversity. 19 July 2016. Accessed 30 December 2017 @ http://www.dataversity.net/predictive-analytics-route-planning-algorithm-ups-followed-long-path-success/.

44. "UPS Deploys Purpose-Built Navigation for UPS Service Personnel." UPS. 4 December 2018. Accessed 25 May 2019 @ https://www.pressroom.ups.com/pressroom/ContentDetailsViewer.page?ConceptType=PressReleases&id=1543925402585-887.

45. Miller, J. A. "How Tech Can Help Cities Reduce Crime." CIO. 9 April 2014. Accessed 22 September 2019 @ https://www.cio.com/article/291222/mobile-how-tech-can-help-cities-reduce-crime.html.

13

1. Davis, J. "AI: Economic Boom But Jobs Bust." InformationWeek. 10 July 2016. Accessed 14 December 2016 @ http://www.informationweek.com/big-data/software-platforms/ai-economic-boom-but-jobs-bust/d/d-id/1327116.

2. McCarthy, J. "What Is AI? / Basic Questions." Accessed 16 January 2022 @ http://jmc.stanford.edu/artificial-intelligence/what-is-ai/index.html#:~:text=What%20is%20artificial%20intelligence%3F,methods%20that%20are%20biologically%20observable.

3. Schwartz, E. "Smart Programs Go to Work." BusinessWeek. 2 March 1992.

4. Lesaint, D., Voudouris, C., and Azarmi, N. "Dynamic Workforce Scheduling for British Telecommunications." Interfaces 30(1) (2000): 45–56.

5. Hall, O. "Artificial Intelligence Techniques Enhance Business Forecasts." Graziadio Business Review 5(2) (2002). Accessed 15 November 2009 @ http://gbr.pepperdine.edu/022/intelligence.html.

6. Bidgoli, H. "Integration of Technologies: An Ultimate Decision-Making Aid." Industrial Management & Data Systems 93(1) (1993): 10–17.

7. Gaudin, S. "Researchers Enable Computers to Teach Themselves Common Sense." Computerworld. 27 November 2013. Accessed 2 January 2014 @ www.computerworld.com/s/article/9244403/Researchers_enable_computers_to_teach_themselves_common_sense.

8. Ibid.

9. Dickson, B. "What Is the Difference between Artificial and Augmented Intelligence?" TechTalks. 4 December 2017. Accessed 12 May 2019 @ https://bdtechtalks.com/2017/12/04/what-is-the-difference-between-ai-and-augmented-intelligence/.

10. Schatsky, D., Camhi, J., and Dongre, A. "Pervasive Intelligence." Deloitte. 7 November 2018. Accessed 12 May 2019 @ https://www2.deloitte.com/insights/us/en/focus/signals-for-strategists/pervasive-intelligence-smart-machines.html.

11. Johnson, Tara. "10 Jaw-Dropping Examples of Artificial Intelligence in Retail." Tinuiti. 29 January 2019. Accessed 13 September 2019 @ https://tinuiti.com/blog/ecommerce/examples-of-artificial-intelligence/.

12. Hicks, J. "Soft Robotics Takes Shape." Forbes. 22 April 2012. Accessed 6 December 2015 @ http://www.forbes.com/sites/jenniferhicks/2012/04/22/soft-robotics-takes-shape/.

13. "Soft Robotics." Accessed 6 December 2015 @ http://www.softroboticsinc.com/.

14. Olivarez-Giles, N. "A Robot with Personality: Anki's Cozmo Mixes Humor, Animation and AI." Wall Street Journal. 27 June 2016. Accessed 14 December 2016 @ http://www.wsj.com/articles/a-robot-with-personality-ankis-cozmo-mixes-humor-animation-and-ai-1467032404?mod=ST1.

15. Noyes, K. "Traffic Tickets Got You Down? This Robo Lawyer Has Already Saved Users $4 Million." Computerworld. 28 June 2016. Accessed 14 December 2016 @ http://www.computerworld.com/article/3089393/data-analytics/traffic-tickets-got-you-down-this-robo-lawyer-has-already-saved-users-4-million.html.

16. Gaudin, S. "Tiny Robots Move Like Caterpillars, Powered by Light." Computerworld. 23 August 2016. Accessed 14 December 2016 @ http://www.computerworld.com/article/3110631/robotics/tiny-robots-move-like-caterpillars-powered-by-light.html.

17. Edwards, J. "Human-Robot Teams: The Next IT Management Challenge." InformationWeek. 6 January 2022. Accessed 14 January 2022 @ https://www.informationweek.com/big-data/human-robot-teams-the-next-it-management-challenge.

18. "Meet Cogito, a Software that Reads for You and Really Understands." 18 May 2016. Accessed 16 January 2022 @ https://www.expert.ai/meet-cogito-software-reads-really-understands/.

19. Alison, D. "12 Advances in Medical Robotics." InformationWeek. 29 January 2011. Accessed 5 March 2013 @ www.informationweek.com/healthcare/patient/12-advances-in-medical-robotics/229100383.

20. "FDA Clears First Autonomous Telemedicine Robot for Hospitals." iRobot.com. 24 January 2013. Accessed 5 March 2013 @ https://investor.irobot.com/news-releases/news-release-details/fda-clears-first-autonomous-telemedicine-robot-hospitals.

21. Mearian, L. "Physician Robot to Begin Making Rounds." Computerworld. 25 July 2012. Accessed 5 March 2013 @ www.computerworld.com/s/article/9229616/Physician_robot_to_begin_making_rounds.

22. Kneale, D. "How Coopers & Lybrand Put Expertise into Its Computers." Wall Street Journal. 14 November 1986.

23. Roby, R. "Expert Systems Help Labs Process DNA Samples." NIJ Journal. July 2008. Accessed 16 July 2010 @ https://www.ojp.gov/pdffiles1/nij/222905.pdf.

24. Wai, K., Rahman, A., Zaiyadai, M., and Aziz, A. "Expert System in Real-World Applications." Generation5. Accessed 16 July 2010 @ https://www.semanticscholar.org/paper/Expert-System-in-Real-World-Applications-Wai-Rahman/94a7595c51fada8ecfe0b2ecc805a6d84f8517d4.

25. Adderley, R., and Musgrove, P. "Police Crime Recording and Investigation Systems—A User's View." Policing: An International Journal of Police Strategies and Management 24(1) (2001): 100–114.

26. "What Are Intelligent Agents | Features | Importance | Advantages." Accessed 15 January 2022 @ https://accountlearning.com/what-are-intelligent-agents-features-importance-advantages/.

27. "Virtual Agents Will Replace Live Customer Service Reps." Accessed 15 January 2022 @ http://www.cbpp.uaa.alaska.edu/afef/virtual%20agents.htm.

28. "Louise." Chatbots. Accessed 5 March 2013 @ www.chatbots.org/virtual_agent/louise.

29. Allen, J. "Siri vs. Google: Which Assistant Fits Your Needs?" Lifewire. 18 March 2021. Accessed 16 January 2022 @ https://www.lifewire.com/siri-vs-google-5078726.

30. Snyder, B. "Beyond 'Jeopardy': How IBM Will Make Billions from Watson." InfoWorld. 10 May 2012. Accessed 5 March 2013 @ www.infoworld.com/d/the-industry-standard/beyond-jeopardy-how-ibm-will-make-billions-watson-192814?source=IFWNLE_nlt_daily_2012-05-10.

31. Dorrier, J. "IBM's Watson Expands Commercial Applications, Aims to Go Mobile." SingularityHub. 14 October 2012. Accessed 5 March 2013 @ http://singularityhub.com/2012/10/14/ibms-watson-jeopardy-champ-expands-commercial-applications-aims-to-go-mobile.

32. "IntelliResponse." Accessed 16 January 2022 @ https://www.crunchbase.com/organization/intelliresponse.

33. Lyons, R. J. and White, A. "What Is Cortana? A Guide to Microsoft's Virtual Assistant, and How You Can Use It to Improve Your Productivity." Business Insider. 29 April 2021. Accessed 16 January 2022 @ https://www.businessinsider.com/what-is-cortana#:~:text=Microsoft's%20Cortana%20is%20a%20cloud,systems%2C%20version%202004%20and%20later.

34. Craig, C. "Smarter than Siri: Viv Promises a Truly Intelligent Assistant." InfoWorld. 15 August 2014. Accessed 13 September 2019 @ http://www.infoworld.com/t/mobile-apps/smarter-siri-viv-promises-truly-intelligent-

assistant-248405?source=IFWNLE_nlt_daily_pm_2014-08-15.

35. Kumparak, G. "Let's Call the Amazon Echo What It Is." Tech Crunch. 6 November 2014. Accessed 13 September 2019 @ http://techcrunch.com/2014/11/06/lets-call-the-amazon-echo-what-it-is/.

36. Hamblen, M. "Alexa Voice Commands Can Now Be Spoken into Amazon's Smaller Echo Dot." *Computerworld*. 3 March 2016. Accessed 14 December 2016 @ http://www.computerworld.com/article/3040610/consumerization-of-it/alexa-voice-commands-can-now-be-spoken-into-amazons-smaller-echo-dot.html.

37. "Google Home." Accessed 16 January 2022 @ https://play.google.com/store/apps/details?id=com.google.android.apps.chromecast.app&hl=en_US&gl=US.

38. Dobbs, D., Boehle, K., Goldwasser, D., and Stamps, J. "The Return of Artificial Intelligence." *Training* (November 2000).

39. Zadeh, L. "Yes, No and Relatively, Part 2." *Chemtech* (July 1987).

40. Foster, Z. "Guesstimates, Fuzzy Logic and Believe It or Not … Better Decision Making." Blogspot. 9 March 2011. Accessed 3 December 2011 @ http://talk-technology.blogspot.com/2011/03/guesstimates-fuzzy-logic-and-believe-it.html.

41. Hernández, A. B., and Hidalgo, D. B. "Fuzzy Logic in Business, Management and Accounting." Scirp.org. November 2021. Accessed 16 January 2022 @ https://www.scirp.org/journal/paperinformation.aspx?paperid=104159.

42. Kumar, N. K. S., Kumar, K. K., Rajkumar, N., and Amsavalli, K. "Search Engine Optimization by Fuzzy Classification and Prediction." Indian Journal of Science and Technology. January 2016. Accessed 16 January 2022 @ file:///C:/Users/Hossein/Downloads/Article15.pdf.

43. Shewan, D. "10 Companies Using Machine Learning in Cool Ways." WordStream. 11 December 2017. Accessed December 30, 2017 @ http://www.wordstream.com/blog/ws/2017/07/28/machine-learning-applications?amp.

44. Metz, C. "Google's AI Wins Fifth and Final Game against Go Genius Lee Sedol." *Wired*. 15 March 2016. Accessed 14 December 2016 @ https://www.wired.com/2016/03/googles-ai-wins-fifth-final-game-go-genius-lee-sedol/.

45. Feng, G. "A Survey on Analysis and Design of Model-Based Fuzzy Control Systems." *IEEE Transactions on Fuzzy Systems* 14(5) (2006): 676–697.

46. Holland, J. "Genetic Algorithms." *Scientific American* (July 1992).

47. "Maximize Returns on Direct Mail with BrainMaker Neural Network Software." California Scientific. Accessed 20 July 2010 @ www.calsci.com/DirectMail.html.

48. "Neural Network Red-Flags Police Officers with Potential for Misconduct." California Scientific. Accessed 20 July 2010 @ https://calsci.com/Police.html.

49. Wiggins, R. "Docking a Truck: A Genetic Fuzzy Approach." *AI Expert* 7(5) (1992): 28–35.

50. Marczyk, A. "Genetic Algorithms and Evolutionary Computation." *The Talk Origins Archive*. Accessed 9 May 2012 @ www.talkorigins.org/faqs/genalg/genalg.html.

51. Ibid.

52. Obermeir, K. "Natural Language Processing." *Byte* (December 1987).

53. Liu, S., Duffy, A., Whitfield, R., and Boyle, I. "Integration of Decision Support Systems to Improve Decision Support Performance." In *Knowledge and Information Systems*. London, UK: Springer, 2009.

54. Turban, E., and Watkins, P. "Integrating Expert Systems and Decision Support Systems." *MIS Quarterly* 10(2) (1986): 121–136.

55. Basu, R., Archer, N., and Mukherjee, B. "Intelligent Decision Support in Healthcare." *Analytics*. January, February 2012. Accessed 5 March 2013 @ https://pubsonline.informs.org/do/10.1287/LYTX.2012.01.05/full/.

56. Ibid.

57. Ibid.

58. Thomson, I. "Microsoft's MoodScope App Predicts Smartphones Users' Feelings." *The Register*. 28 June 2013. Accessed 13 September 2019 @ http://www.theregister.co.uk/2013/06/28/microsoft_moodscope_phone_mood_detector/.

59. Liu, Y. "MoodScope: Building a Mood Sensor from Smartphone Usage Patterns." Microsoft.com. June 2013. Accessed 16 January 2022 @ https://www.microsoft.com/en-us/research/publication/moodscope-building-mood-sensor-smartphone-usage-patterns/.

60. "Google DeepMind Teaches Artificial Intelligence Machines to Read." 17 June 2015. *MIT Technology Review*. Accessed 6 December 2015 @ https://www.technologyreview.com/2015/06/17/167617/google-deepmind-teaches-artificial-intelligence-machines-to-read/#:~:text=Artificial%20intelligence-,Google%20DeepMind%20Teaches%20Artificial%20Intelligence%20Machines%20to%20Read,Mail%20has%20unwittingly%20created%20one.&text=A%20revolution%20in%20artificial%20intelligence%20is%20currently%20sweeping%20through%20computer%20science.

61. Wilson, M. "Facebook Uses AI to Recognize Objects in Photos." BetaNews. Accessed 6 December 2015 @ http://betanews.com/2015/11/04/facebook-uses-ai-to-recognize-objects-in-photos/.

62. Anderson, G. "Amazon Uses Artificial Intelligence System to Improve Review/Rating System." RetailWire. 23 June 2015. Accessed 6 December 2015 @ http://www.retailwire.com/discussion/18364/amazon-uses-artificial-intelligence-to-improve-review-rating-system.

63. Mizroch, A. "Amazon Boosts Its Artificial Intelligence." *Wall Street Journal*. 26 August 2015. Accessed 6 December 2015 @ http://blogs.wsj.com/digits/2015/08/26/amazon-com-offers-machine-learning-platform-hires-scientists/?mod=ST1.

64. Anderson, G. "Amazon Uses Artificial Intelligence System to Improve Review/Rating System." RetailWire. 23 June 2015. Accessed 6 December 2015 @ http://www.retailwire.com/discussion/18364/amazon-uses-artificial-intelligence-to-improve-review-rating-system.

65. Mochizuki, T. "Sony Artificial Brain to Guess How Much Houses Are Worth." *Wall Street Journal*. 8 October 2015. Accessed 6 December 2015 @ http://blogs.wsj.com/digits/2015/10/08/sony-artificial-brain-to-guess-how-much-houses-are-worth/?mod=ST1.

66. "The Nest Store." Accessed 6 December 2015 @ https://store.nest.com/product/thermostat/?gclid=CPTm_I2Dh8kCFQsDaQod01cJ1Q.

67. Ibid.

68. Moon, B. "Aether Cone Gets Bluetooth Update." Geekdad. 6 March 2015. Accessed 16 January 2022 @ https://geekdad.com/2015/03/aether-cone-bluetooth/.

69. Wood, M. "The Move Toward Computing that Reads Your Mind." *New York Times*. 7 May 2014. Accessed 6 December 2015 @ http://www.nytimes.com/2014/05/08/technology/personaltech/the-app-that-knows-you.html?_r=0.

70. "EasilyDo: Your Smart Assistant." Accessed 6 December 2015 @ https://www.samsung.com/us/business/samsung-for-enterprise/solutions-exchange/assets/downloads/sse-easily-do.pdf.

71. Seifert, D. "New Android Homescreen App Says Context Is Everything." The Verge. 4 February 2014. Accessed 6 December 2015 @ http://www.theverge.com/2014/2/4/5375070/everythingme-android-contextual-app-launcher.

72. Moon, B. "Aether Cone Gets Bluetooth Update." Geekdad. 6 March 2015. Accessed 16 January 2022 @ https://geekdad.com/2015/03/aether-cone-bluetooth/.

73. Mulligan, C. "Contextual Computing Can Make Smartphones and Other Devices More Useful." *SD Times*. 22 May 2014. Accessed 6 December 2015 @ http://sdtimes.com/contextual-computing-can-make-smartphones-and-other-devices-more-useful/.

74. Cohen, R. "Contextual Computing: Our Sixth, Seventh and Eighth Senses." *Forbes*. 18 October 2013. Accessed 2 January 2014 @ www.forbes.com/sites/reuvencohen/2013/10/18/contextual-computing-our-sixth-seventh-and-eighth-senses.

75. Mortensen, P. "The Future of Technology Isn't Mobile, It's Contextual." *Fast Company*. 24 May 2013. Accessed 2 January 2014 @ https://www.fastcompany.com/1672531/the-future-of-technology-isnt-mobile-its-contextual.

76. "Advantages of Robotic Process Automation." 10xDS. 17 January 2019. Accessed 12 May 2019 @ https://www.10xds.com/blog/insights/advantages-of-robotic-process-automation/.

77. "9 Jobs Most Likely to Be Taken Over by Robots." Salary.com. 19 April 2018. Accessed 12 May 2019 @ https://www.salary.com/articles/9-jobs-taken-over-by-robots/.

78. Reisinger, D. "A.I. Expert Says Automation Could Replace 40% of Jobs in 15 Years." *Fortune*. 10 January 2019. Accessed 12 May 2019 @ http://fortune.com/2019/01/10/automation-replace-jobs/.

79. Davidson, P. "Automation Could Kill 73 Million US Jobs by 2030." Transport Topics. 1 December 2017. Accessed 12 May 2019 @ https://www.ttnews.com/articles/automation-could-kill-73-million-us-jobs-2030.

80. Makarov, I. "Automation: How Can We Reskill the Workforce?" *InformationWeek*. 25 March 2019. Accessed 12 June 2019 @ https://informationweek.com/strategic-cio/team-building-and-staffing/automation-how-can-we-reskill-the-workforce/a/d-id/1334240?.

81. Reinhart, RJ. "Most Americans Already Using Artificial Intelligence Products." Gallup. 6 March 2018. Accessed 15 June 2022 @ https://news.gallup.com/poll/228497/americans-already-using-artificial-intelligence-products.aspx.

82. Cobey, C. "How to Build Trust with Artificial Intelligence." *InformationWeek*. 29 May 2019. Accessed 6 June 2020 @ https://informationweek.com/big-data/ai-machine-learning/how-to-build-trust-with-artificial-intelligence/a/d-id/1334718?.

83. Searcy, S. "Biased AI Is Real; What Does that Mean for Women?" *InformationWeek*. 22 March 2019. Accessed 12 May 2019 @ https://informationweek.com/big-data/ai-machine-learning/biased-ai-is-real-what-does-that-mean-for-women/a/d-id/1334223.

84. Bossmann, J. "Top 9 Ethical Issues in Artificial Intelligence." World Economic Forum. 21 October 2016. Accessed 12 May 2019 @ https://www.weforum.org/agenda/2016/10/top-10-ethical-issues-in-artificial-intelligence/.

85. Krauth, O. "Artificial Ignorance: The 10 Biggest AI Failures of 2017." Tech Republic.com. 4 January 2018. Accessed 12 May 2019 @ https://www.techrepublic.com/article/the-10-biggest-ai-failures-of-2017.

86. Peng, T. "2018 in Review: 10 AI Failures." Medium. 10 December 2018. Accessed 12 May 2019 @ https://medium.com/syncedreview/2018-in-review-10-ai-failures-c18faadf5983.

87. Daws, R. "Report: AI Will Increase the Wealth Inequality Between the Rich and Poor." Artificial Intelligence News. 11 January 2018. Accessed 12 May 2019 @ https://www.artificialintelligence-news.com/2018/01/11/ai-wealth-inequality/.

88. Shead, S. "Amazon's Alexa Assistant Told a Child to Do a Potentially Lethal Challenge." CNBC. 29 December 2021. Accessed @ https://www.cnbc.com/2021/12/29/amazons-alexa-told-a-child-to-do-a-potentially-lethal-challenge.html?__source=iosappshare%7Ccom.apple.UIKit.activity.Mail.

89. Daws, R. "Report: AI Will Increase the Wealth Inequality Between the Rich and Poor." Artificial Intelligence News. 11 January 2018. Accessed 12 May 2019 @ https://www.artificialintelligence-news.com/2018/01/11/ai-wealth-inequality/.

90. This information has been gathered from the company Web site (www.alyuda.com) and other promotional materials. For more information and updates, visit the Web site.

91. Rusli, E. M. "Firms Use Artificial Intelligence to Tap Shoppers' Views." *Wall Street Journal*. 14 April 2014. Accessed 13 September 2019 @ http://online.wsj.com/news/articles/SB10001424052702303887804579501800057021822?mod=djem_jiewr_IT_domainid.

92. Yegulalp, S. "Speech Recognition: Your Smartphone Gets Smarter." *Computerworld*. 16 March 2011. Accessed 14 August 2011 @ www.computerworld.com/s/article/9213925/Speech_recognition_Your_smartphone_gets_smarter?taxonomyId=15&pageNumber=1.

93. Cringely, R. "Apple's Siri Is AI with an Attitude." *InfoWorld*. 17 October 2011. Accessed 1 December 2011 @ www.infoworld.com/t/cringely/apples-siri-ai-attitude-176323?source=IFWNLE_nlt_blogs_2011-10-18.

14

1. "What Is Azure Notification Hubs?" Microsoft. 15 December 2021. Accessed 2 June 2022 @ https://docs.microsoft.com/en-us/azure/notification-hubs/notification-hubs-push-notification-overview.

2. "What Is Data as a Service?" Accessed 26 January 2022 @ https://www.talend.com/resources/what-is-data-as-a-service/.

3. "What Is Backup as a Service (BaaS)?" Accessed 26 January 2022 @ https://www.netapp.com/cloud-services/cloud-backup/what-is-backup-as-a-services-baas/#:~:text=Online%20backup%20service%2C%20also%20known,repository%20over%20a%20network%20connection.

4. "What Is Security as a Service (SECaaS)?" Accessed 26 January 2022 @ https://www.forcepoint.com/cyber-edu/security-as-a-service-secaas.

5. "Augmented and Virtual Reality Market to Reach $571.42 Bn, Globally, by 2025 at 63.3% CAGR, Says Allied Market Research." PR Newswire. 13 December 2018. Accessed 17 May 2019 @ https://www.prnewswire.com/news-releases/augmented-and-virtual-reality-market-to-reach-571-42-bn-globally-by-2025-at-63-3-cagr-says-allied-market-research-848843301.html.

6. "Virtual Reality Pioneer: Tom Furness." Educators in VR. 31 May 2019. Accessed 26 January 2022 @ https://educatorsinvr.com/2019/05/31/virtual-reality-pioneer-tom-furness/.

7. Marquez, J. "Introduction to Virtual Reality: Humans and Automation Seminar." Spring 2002. Accessed 11 April 2012 @ http://web.mit.edu/16.459/www/VR1.pdf.

8. Lamkin, P. "The Best VR Headsets." 16 September 2015. Wareable. Accessed 6 December 2015 @ http://www.wareable.com/headgear/the-best-ar-and-vr-headsets.

9. D'Angelo, M., and Narayaran, S. "A Virtual Reality Environment to Assist Disabled Individuals." Accessed 11 April 2012 @ http://slideplayer.com/slide/6417198/.

10. Cohen, E. "Google Cardboard Saves Baby's Life." CNN. 7 January 2016. Accessed 15 December 2016 @ http://www.cnn.com/2016/01/07/health/google-cardboard-baby-saved/.

11. Thorbecke, C. "Inside the VR Therapy Designed to Help Sexual Assault Survivors Heal by Facing Attackers." ABC News. 19 April 2018. Accessed 24 June 2022 @ https://abcnews.go.com/GMA/News/inside-vr-therapy-designed-sexual-assault-survivors-heal/story?id=54485530.

12. Schneider, R. "Lockheed Starts Using Virtual Reality to Test New Products." Talking Points Memo. 26 January 2011. Accessed 2 January 2014 @ https://talkingpointsmemo.com/idealab/lockheed-starts-using-virtual-reality-to-test-new-products.

13. Hotz, R. L. "Practice Personalities: What an Avatar Can Teach You." *The Wall Street Journal*. 19 January 2015. Accessed 12 December 2015 @ http://www.wsj.com/articles/practice-personalities-what-an-avatar-can-teach-you-1421703480.

14. NOAA Virtual Lab." Accessed 26 January 2022 @ https://vlab.noaa.gov/web/mdl/noaa-virtual-lab.

15. Atanzariti, P. "What Is the Difference Between Virtual Reality, Augmented Reality and Mixed Reality?" Quora. 9 June 2015. Accessed 25 December 2016 @ https://www.quora.com/What-is-the-difference-between-virtual-reality-augmented-reality-and-mixed-reality.

16. "Pepsi and Coca-Cola Embrace New Technology." Augmented Pixels Co. Accessed 6 December 2015 @ http://augmentedpixels.com/pepsi-and-coca-cola-embrace-new-technology/.

17. "AR Technology of the Week: BMW Heads-Up Augmented Reality Display." SmartReality. 3 June 2014. Accessed 6 December 2015 @ https://next.reality.news/news/bmw-augmented-reality-windshield-concept-adds-gaze-detection-for-natural-interaction-0228950/.

18. Elliott, A. M. "10 Awesome Uses of Augmented Reality Marketing." 26 December 2009. Mashable.com. Accessed 6 December 2015 @ http://mashable.com/2009/12/26/augmented-reality-marketing/#5kJDRDOIPqU.

19. Perez, S. "Wayfair's Android App Now Lets You Shop for Furniture Using Augmented Reality." Techcrunch.com. Accessed 31 July 2019 @ https://techcrunch.com/2018/03/20/wayfairs-android-app-now-lets-you-shop-for-furniture-using-augmented-reality/.

20. Elliott, A. M. "10 Awesome Uses of Augmented Reality Marketing." 26 December 2009. Mashable.com. Accessed 6 December 2015 @ http://mashable.com/2009/12/26/augmented-reality-marketing/#53kJDRDOIPqU.

21. Ibid.

22. "10 Use Cases of Augmented Reality in Marketing." augment.com. 21 November 2016. Accessed 20 April 2019 @ http://www.augment.com/blog/10-use-cases-of-augmented-reality-marketing/.

23. "Mixed Reality vs Augmented Reality: What's the Difference?" NewGenApps. 4 May 2018. Accessed 15 May 2019 @ https://www.xrtoday.com/augmented-reality/mixed-reality-vs-augmented-reality/.

24. "5 Key Benefits of Mixed Reality for Manufacturers." Accessed 26 January 2022 @ https://www.themanufacturer.com/articles/5-key-benefits-mixed-reality-manufacturers/.

25. Pilkington, I. "Microsoft HoloLens 2 Brings AR to Industry." arm.com. 14 March 2019. Accessed 15 May 2019 @ https://www.arm.com/blogs/blueprint/microsofts-hololens-2-brings-augmented-reality-to-industry.

26. Danova, I. "The Industrial Applications of HoloLens." PegusApps. 29 September 2017. Accessed 15 May 2019 @ https://www.pegusapps.com/en/insights/the-industrial-applications-of-hololens.

27. Harper, J. "Jack Dorsey's First Ever Tweet Sells for $2.9m." BBC. 23 March 2021. Accessed 25 January 2022 @ https://www.bbc.com/news/business-56492358#:~:text=Twitter%20founder%20Jack%20Dorsey's%20first,by%20Mr%20Dorsey%20for%20charity.

28. Clark, M. "The 'Charlie Bit My Finger' Video is Being Auctioned as an NFT — Then Deleted 'Forever'." The Verge. 17 May 2021. Accessed 25 January 2022 @ https://www.theverge.com/2021/5/17/22437088/charlie-bit-my-finger-video-nft-deletion-youtube-auction.

29. Kastrenakes, J. "Beeple Sold an NFT for $69 Million." The Verge. 11 May 2021. Accessed 25 January 2022 @ https://www.theverge.com/2021/3/11/22325054/beeple-christies-nft-sale-cost-everydays-69-million.

30. Bernstein, C. "5 Business Use Cases for NFTs." Techtarget. 27 July 2021. Accessed 25 January 2022 @ https://whatis.techtarget.com/feature/5-business-use-cases-for-NFTs.

31. Farrington, R. "Why Big Brands Are Spending Millions on NFTs." Forbes. 25 December 2021. Accessed 25 January 2022 @ https://www.forbes.com/sites/robertfarrington/2021/12/25/why-big-brands-are-spending-millions-on-nfts/?sh=19169b356117.

32. Haselton, T. "How to Make, Buy and Sell NFTs." CNBC. 23 March 2021. Accessed 25 January 2022 @ https://www.cnbc.com/2021/03/23/how-to-create-buy-sell-nfts.html.

33. Edwards, S. "NFTs Pros & Cons: The Good, the Bad, and the Ugly." The Dales Report. 15 August 2021. Accessed 25 January 2022 @ https://thedalesreport.com/crypto-nfts/nfts-pros-cons-the-good-the-bad-and-the-ugly/.

34. Hoffman, C. "What Is the Metaverse? Is It Just Virtual Reality, or Something More?" How-To Geek. 30 December 2021. Accessed 25 January 2022 @ https://www.howtogeek.com/745807/what-is-the-metaverse-is-it-just-virtual-reality-or-something-more/amp/.

35. Hackl, C. "The Metaverse Is Coming and It's a Very Big Deal." Forbes. 5 July 2020. Accessed 25 January 2022 @ https://www.forbes.com/sites/cathyhackl/2020/07/05/the-metaverse-is-coming--its-a-very-big-deal/?sh=587144c8440f.

36. Berman, M. "Advantages and Uses of Metaverse: A Small Guide by Experts." Programming Insider. 1 August 2021. Accessed 25 January 2022 @ https://programminginsider.com/advantages-and-uses-of-metaverse-a-small-guide-by-experts/.

37. Roe, D. "There's More to the Metaverse Than Facebook and Microsoft." Reworked. 17 November 2021. Accessed 25 January 2022 @ https://www.reworked.co/digital-workplace/theres-more-to-the-metaverse-than-facebook-and-microsoft/.

38. Erickson, J. "Prediction: 80% of Enterprise IT Will Move to the Cloud by 2025." Forbes. 7 February 2019. Accessed 20 April 2019 @ https://www.forbes.com/sites/oracle/2019/02/07/prediction-80-of-enterprise-it-will-move-to-the-cloud-by-2025/#548ab2502a67.

39. "Top 10 Cloud Computing Examples and Uses." NewGenApps.com. 15 November 2017. Access 20 April 2019 @ https://www.newgenapps.com/blogs/top-10-cloud-computing-examples-and-uses/.

40. Knorr, E., and Gruman, G. "What Cloud Computing Really Means." InfoWorld. 7 April 2008. Accessed 9 March 2012 @ https://archive.nytimes.com/www.nytimes.com/idg/IDG_002570DE00740E180025742400363509.html?ref=te.

41. Brodkin, J. "Amazon and IBM Are the Cloud's Biggest Players." InfoWorld. 15 July 2010. Accessed 31 July 2010 @ www.infoworld.com/d/cloud-computing/amazon-and-ibm-are-the-clouds-biggest-players-484?page=0,0&source=IFWNLE_nlt_wrapup_2010-07-16.

42. Gaudin, S. "Small Businesses Seek to Take Off with the Cloud." http://www.computerworld.com/s/article/9250550/Small_businesses_seek_to_take_off_with_the_cloud.

43. Ibid.

44. Knorr, E., and Gruman, G. "What Cloud Computing Really Means." InfoWorld. 7 April 2008. Accessed 21 August 2010 @ https://archive.nytimes.com/www.nytimes.com/idg/IDG_002570DE00740E180025742400363509.html?ref=te.

45. Linthicum, D. "What Is Multicloud? The Next Step in Cloud Computing." InfoWorld. 25 September 2017. Accessed 6 January 2018 @ https://www.infoworld.com/article/3226484/cloud-computing/what-is-multicloud-the-next-step-in-cloud-computing.html.

46. Mell, P., and Grance, M. "The NIST Definition of Cloud Computing." NIST. September 2011. Accessed 11 April 2012 @ http://csrc.nist.gov/publications/nistpubs/800-145/SP800-145.pdf.

47. Morgan, L. "Why Distributed Cloud Is in Your Future." InformationWeek. 12 November 2020. Accessed 25 January 2022 @ https://informationweek.com/cloud/why-distributed-cloud-is-in-your-future/a/d-id/1339427?.

48. Harvey, C. "10 Trends Accelerating Edge Computing." InformationWeek. 8 October 2020. Accessed 25 January 2022 @ https://informationweek.com/strategic-cio/digital-business/10-trends-accelerating-edge-computing/d/d-id/1339097?.

49. LaBrie, G. "Top 5 Benefits of Edge Computing." Blog.wei.com. 8 January 2019. Accessed 26 January 2022 @ https://blog.wei.com/top-5-benefits-of-edge-computing.

50. Ibid.

51. Pratt, M. K. "Top 5 Benefits of Edge Computing for Businesses." Internetofthingsagenda. 29 November 2021. Accessed 26 January 2022 @ https://internetofthingsagenda.techtarget.com/tip/Top-5-benefits-of-edge-computing-for-businesses.

52. "Why the Public Cloud Is More Secure than an On-Premises Data Center." Eplexity.com. 24 September 2018. Accessed 16 May 2019 @ https://eplexity.com/why-the-public-cloud-is-more-secure-than-an-on-premises-data-center/.

53. Linthicum, D. "How the Cloud has Made You More Secure." InfoWorld. 26 October 2018. Accessed 16 May 2019 @ https://www.infoworld.com/article/3316637/how-the-cloud-has-made-you-more-secure.html.

54. Brodkin, J. "Gartner: Seven Cloud-Computing Security Risks." InfoWorld. 2 July 2008. Accessed 3 December 2011 @ www.infoworld.com/d/security-central/gartner-seven-cloud-computing-security-risks-853?page=0,0.

55. Gaudin, S. "Nanotech Delivers Clot Busting Drugs to Heart Attack, Stroke Patients." Computerworld. 10 August 2015. Accessed 6 December 2015 @ http://www.computerworld.com/article/2965935/emerging-technology/nanotech-delivers-clot-busting-drugs-to-heart-attack-stroke-patients.html.

56. "Global Nanotechnology in Medical Devices – Market Size, Share, Trends & Growth Analysis Report – Segmented by Product, Application & Region – Industry Forecast (2022 to 2027)." Market Data Forecast. January 2022. Accessed 3 June 2022 @ https://www.marketdataforecast.com/market-reports/nanotechnology-in-medical-devices-market.

57. Ibid.

58. Wood, S., Jones, R., and Geldart, A. "Commercial Applications of Nano-Technology in Computing and Information Technology." Azonano.com. 29 October 2008. Accessed 21 August 2010 @ www.azonano.com/details.asp?ArticleID=1057.

59. "New Report on Nanotechnology in Consumer Goods." AZO Materials. 26 May 2009. Accessed 21 August 2010 @ www.azom.com/news.asp?NewsID=17263.

60. Harvey, C. "How to Use Blockchain: 10 Use Cases." InformationWeek. 18 December 2017. Accessed 14 January 2018 @ https://informationweek.com/strategic-cio/digital-business/how-to-use-blockchain-10-use-cases/d/d-id/1330652?.

61. Ibid.

62. Shilov, K. "How Walmart, Alibaba, and Others Are Shaking Up Retail with Blockchain." HackerNoon. 21 July 2018. Accessed 20 April 2019 @ https://hackernoon.com/how-walmart-alibaba-and-others-are-shaking-up-retail-with-blockchain-a34fee518d69.

63. Daley, S. "18 Blockchain-as-a-Service Companies Making the DLT More Accessible." Builtin. 11 April 2019. Accessed 25 January 2022 @ https://builtin.com/blockchain/blockchain-as-a-service-companies.

64. "Why Bitcoin Is an Excellent Store of Value." Oobit. 25 January 2021. Accessed 3 June 2022@https://www.oobit.com/blog/why-bitcoin-is-an-excellent-store-of-value/.

65. Rosic, A. "7 Incredible Benefits of Cryptocurrency." Huffington Post. 6 December 2017. Accessed 14 January 2018 @ https://www.huffingtonpost.com/ameer-rosic-/7-incredible-benefits-of-_1_b_13160110.html.

66. "The Basics of Cryptocurrency: Disadvantages of Cryptocurrency." TopBrokers. 7 August 2017. Accessed 14 January 2018 @ https://topbrokers.trade/guide/basics-cryptocurrency/cryptocurrency-disadvantages/.

67. Giles, M. "Explainer: What Is a Quantum Computer?" MIT Technology Review. 29 January 2019. Accessed 20 June 2019 @ https://www.technologyreview.com/s/612844/what-is-quantum-computing/.

68. "Quantum Computer vs Classical Computer – Difference Between Quantum Computer and Classical Computer." RF Wireless World. Accessed 20 June 2019 @ http://www.rfwireless-world.com/Terminology/Quantum-Computer-vs-Classical-Computer.html.

69. Klint, L. "Ways Quantum Computing Can Help Businesses." Pluralsight. Accessed 20 June 2019 @ https://www.pluralsight.com/resource-center/guides/quantum-computing-helping-business.

70. Martin, F. "Top 10 Unexpected Future Applications of Quantum Computers." Listverse. 10 January 2019. Accessed 20 June 2019 @ http://listverse.com/2019/01/10/top-10-unexpected-future-applications-of-quantum-computers/.

71. Giles, M. "Quantum Computers Pose a Security Threat that We're Still Totally Unprepared For." MIT Technology Review. 3 December 2018. Accessed 30 July 2019 @

https://www.technologyreview.com/s/612509/quantum-computers-encryption-threat/.

72. Nazareth, D. P., and Spaans, J. D. "First Application of Quantum Annealing to IMRT Beamlet Intensity Optimization." IOPscience. Accessed 20 April 2019 @ https://iopscience.iop.org/article/10.1088/0031-9155/60/10/4137/meta.

73. Hughes-Castleberry, K. "Quantum Sensing May Have a New Purpose in Neurology." The Quantum Insider. 5 January 2022. Accessed 3 June 2022 @ https://thequantuminsider.com/2022/01/05/quantum-sensing-may-have-a-new-purpose-in-neurology/#:~:text=January%205%2C%202022%20Quantum%20technology%20has%20already%20shown,healthcare%20systems%20

are%20becoming%20more%20efficient%20and%20affordable.

74. This information has been gathered from the company Web site (www.mechdyne.com) and other promotional materials. For more information and updates, visit the Web site.

75. "About IHG." InterContinental Hotels Group. Accessed 6 March 2013 @ www.ichotelsgroup.com/ihg/hotels/us/en/global/support/about_ihg.

76. Babcock, C. "4 Companies Getting Real Results from Cloud Computing." InformationWeek. 15 January 2011. Accessed 6 March 2013 @ www.informationweek.com/hardware/data-centers/4-companies-getting-real-results-from-cl/229000706.

77. "Top 5 Virtual Reality Business Use Cases." Business.com. 3 July 2018. Accessed 17 May 2019 @ https://www.business.com/articles/virtual-reality-business-use-cases/.

78. Finch, S. "5 Business Uses of Virtual Reality." Disruptionhub.com. 8 May 2018. Accessed 17 May 2019 @ https://disruptionhub.com/business-virtual-reality-5-uses/.

79. "5 Fantastic Examples of Brands That Use Virtual Reality (VR)." Samsung. 9 May 2018. Accessed 17 May 2019 @ https://insights.samsung.com/2018/05/09/5-fantastic-examples-of-brands-that-use-virtual-reality-vr/.

80. "Top 5 Virtual Reality Business Use Cases." Business.com. 3 July 2018. Accessed 17 May 2019 @ https://www.business.com/articles/virtual-reality-business-use-cases/.

Index

third-party exchange marketplace, **222**
3D printing, **295**, 296
three-tier architecture, 160, 161*exh*
throughput, **162**
TikTok, 196
time division multiple access (TDMA), **166**
top-level domain (TLD), 178–180, 180*t*
touchless computing, 38, 39
touch screen, 38
Toyota Motor Company, 258–259
trackball, 38
trading partner agreements, **223**
transaction-processing systems (TPSs), **7**
transborder data flow (TDF), **247**, 255
Transmission Control Protocol/ Internet Protocol (TCP/IP), **157**
transnational structure, **252**–253, 253*exh*
transparency, social media ethics, 97
Transport Layer Security (TLS), **134**
TransUnion, privacy issues, 89
Trojan programs, **120**
tuples, 62
Twitter, 4, 196, 198
   denial-of-service attacks, 122
Twitter Analytics, 74
two-tier architecture, **160**, 160*exh*

U

Uber, privacy issues, 88
ubiquitous computing, 44
uniform resource locators (URLs), **178**
uninterruptible power supply (UPS), 119
United Parcel Service (UPS), 15
universal product codes (UPCs), 3

universal resource locators. *See* uniform resource locators (URLs)
unstructured decisions, **317**
UPS ORION, 338
URL hijacking, 100
USA.gov home page, 218*exh*
user interface, 348
U.S. Postal Service (USPS) AR app, 380
utilitarian networking ethics, 97
utility (on-demand) computing, **384**–385

V

validation rule, 62
value chain, **209**, 210*exh*
   e-commerce and, 209–212
Variable Assembly Language (VAL), 344
vein analysis, 124
Venmo, **226**
Verizon's Cybersquatting Suit, 102
vertical market, **222**
very high-speed digital subscriber line (VDSL), 180
vidcast, 198
video adapters, 40
video-conferencing systems, 248, 332
video display terminals (VDTs), 104
video podcast, 198
virtual agents (VAs), 351
virtual organizations, **103**
virtual private networks (VPN), **133**, 133*exh*
virtual reality (VR), **374**, 399
   applications, 376–377
   augmented reality (AR), **378**–380
   cave automatic virtual environment (CAVE), **375**–376, 376*exh*
   components, 375, 375*exh*

   environments, 374–375
   full-body immersion, 374
   immersion, 374
   interaction, 374
   mixed reality, **380**–381
   networked communication, 374
   obstacles in using, 378
   simulation, 374
   telepresence, 374
   virtual world, **378**
   walker, 375
virtual world, **378**
virtuous networking ethics, 97
viruses, 119–**120**
vishing, 114
vodcast, 198
voice-based e-commerce, **225**
Voice over Internet Protocol (VoIP), **185**
voice recognition, 124
voting, biometrics, 126

W

walker, 375
Walmart, 292
   blockchain, 392
   social media applications at, 196
Web applications
   employment services, 186
   financial institutions, 187
   healthcare, 187–188
   higher education, 186
   politics, 189
   publishing, 186
   real estate, 186
   software distribution, 187
   tourism and travel, 185–186
Web-browsing features, 4
Web compulsions, 105
Web marketing, **227**
Web page security, biometrics, 126
webrooming, 212

Web servers, 44
Web trends, 193–198
Web 2.0 *vs.* web 3.0, 194*t*
WhatsApp Messenger, 184
white hats, **117**
wide area network (WAN), 42, **153**–154, 154*exh*, 155*t*
Wi-Fi Protected Access (WPA), 168
wiki, **194**–195
Windows Messenger, 184
Wired Equivalent Privacy (WEP), 168
Wireless Application Protocol (WAP), 224
Wireless Fidelity (Wi-Fi), **164**
wireless LANs (WLANs), 164, 164*t*
wireless network, **162**–165
wireless security, 167–169
wireless technologies, 164
wireless WANs (WWANs), 164, 164*t*
word-processing software, 47
worldwide communication, 383
Worldwide Interoperability for Microwave Access (WiMAX), **165**
World Wide Web (WWW), 180
worms, **120**

X

XY (scatter) charts, **325**

Y

Yahoo!, 88
Yelp, 196, 379
YouTube, 196
   for marketing, 5–6

Z

zero login, **132**
zero trust security, **136**